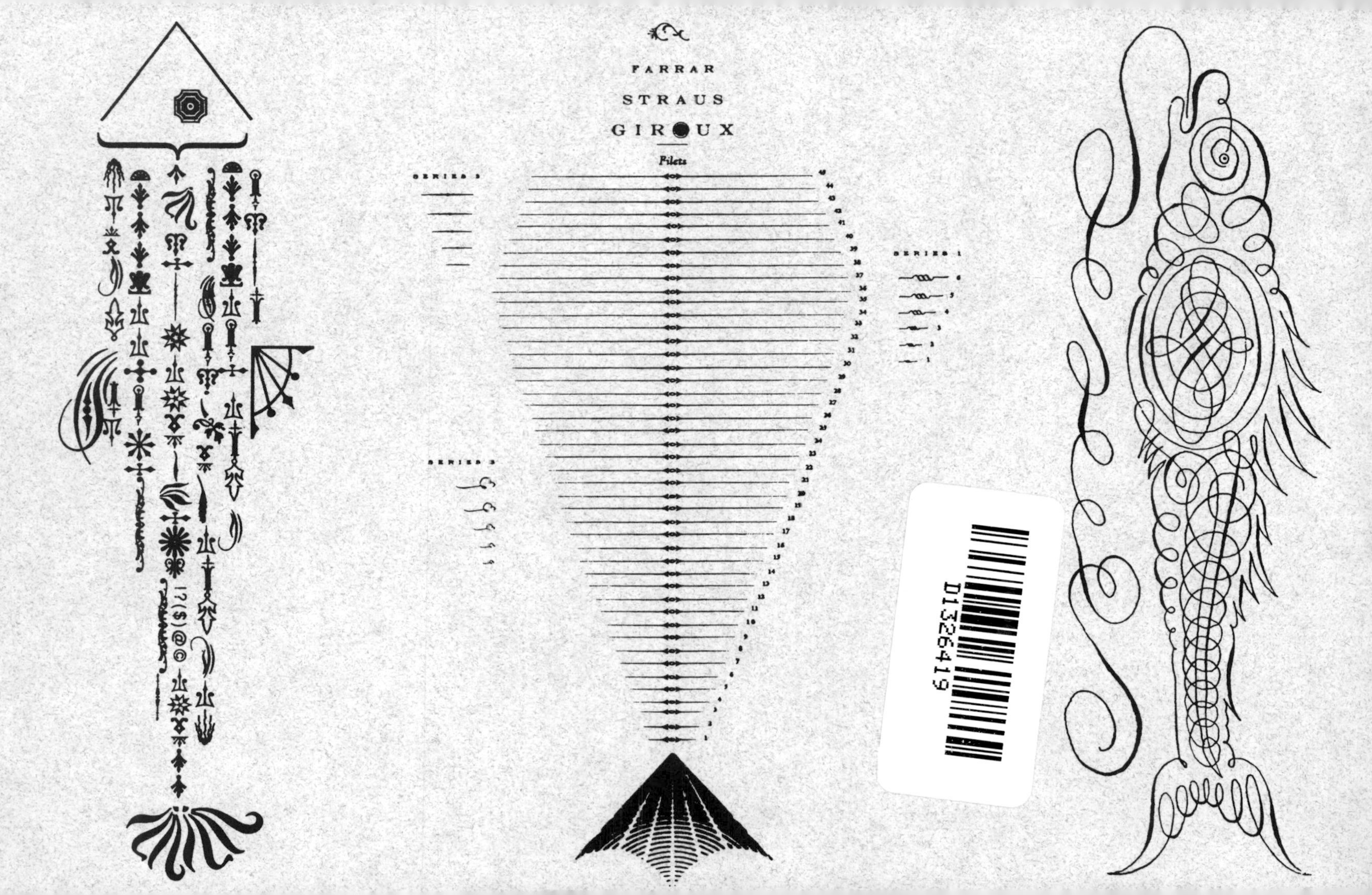
FARRAR
STRAUS
GIROUX
Filets
SERIES 2
SERIES 1
SERIES 3
!?($)@©
D1326419

50
FARRAR
STRAUS
GIROUX

FIFTY YEARS

FIFTY YEARS

A Farrar, Straus and Giroux Reader

EDITED BY ALAN D. WILLIAMS

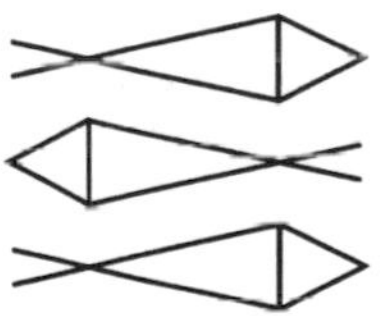

FARRAR, STRAUS AND GIROUX

NEW YORK

Printed in the United States of America

We gratefully acknowledge the generosity of the following companies who donated work and materials for the production of this book: Midland Paper for the paper on which the book is printed; Berryville Graphics for the printing and binding; and Phoenix Color Corporation for the printing of the endpapers and the case cover.

Endpaper art (from top to bottom) courtesy of Louise Fili, Barbara de Wilde, and Sara Eisenman.

The first list of a new publishing house is always an adventure. A new imprint on a book gathers character through the years, and it is our hope that readers will come to know ours and, perhaps, to feel a certain friendship for it.

Our list will be a general one, its titles selected with the wish that they will entertain, inform, stimulate. We shall shun neither the realistic nor the romantic. During these long war years there has been a sturdy increase in the number of those who enjoy reading books and want to own them, and it is therefore the publisher's fortune and privilege to meet a widened and deepened taste. Like every other individual in the world, he finds himself challenged by the confusions and distortions of the times. This is an opportunity, which excites the imagination, to interpret our own country, to survey the world, to explain science to the layman, to present the philosopher, the historian, the biographer, the storyteller, and the poet.

We are fortunate to number among our first authors some you will all know, as well as some we believe you will enjoy meeting.

John Farrar

Roger W. Straus, Jr.

The preceding page is a reproduction of the publisher's note from the Summer & Fall 1946 catalogue announcing Farrar, Straus's inaugural list.

CONTENTS

PREFACE

During the past fifty years, the landscape of book publishing in America (and elsewhere as well) has changed greatly. But this is no place to discuss those changes for good or evil.

What has not changed at Farrar, Straus and Giroux is that the company, founded in 1946, is and always has been completely editorially driven. By this I mean that all of us here feel our first and most important responsibility is toward the authors whom we present to the public. Our publishing decisions are based solely on the editors' convictions about a given novelist, poet, or essayist, and no pressure is exerted by the other wings of the firm in selecting the authors we commit to. The talented individuals who run our sales, marketing, publicity, subsidiary rights, production, design, and other departments work closely with the editors and authors to achieve the utmost possible success for the books we publish.

The success we have had at Farrar, Straus and Giroux is due first and foremost to our gifted authors, some of whom you will find represented in the pages that follow, and secondly to the dedication and good taste of men and women like John Farrar, Stanley Young, Robert Giroux, H. D. Vursell, John Peck, Sheila Cudahy, Arthur Wang, Henry Robbins, Michael di Capua, Stephen Roxburgh, Pat Strachan, and David Rieff, who have helped to choose and support these writers. Today, the editorial team working with and for our authors includes Jonathan Galassi, Elisabeth Sifton, Margaret Ferguson, Frances Foster, John Glusman, Elisabeth Dyssegaard, Beverly Reingold, Wes Adams, Elisheva Urbas, Paul Elie, and Ethan Nosowsky. All these gifted people need a gifted support system and fortunately we have—and have had—men and women who have contributed mightily in various ways. The following come to mind: Shirley Abramson, Elaine Chubb, Tom Consiglio, Carmen Gomezplata, Joy Isenberg, Dorris Janowitz, Cheryl Jenkins, Sam Kam, Judy Klein, Elaine Kramer, Cynthia Krupat, Peggy Miller, Margaret Nicholson, Terrence Smith, Anne Sullivan, Rose Wachtel, Lynn Warshow, and Robert Wohlforth.

And now, after fifty years, there is still that surge of adrenaline that flows when I get up in the morning, go to the office at Union Square to see what this author or that author has done, or what this editor or that editor has brought in. That's publishing.

Roger W. Straus

INTRODUCTION

It has been observed by an old publishing mariner that a trade-book house can be far better defined in its purposes and hopes by looking over the stern at the wake of books published than by attempting to penetrate the fogs and reefs of the future from the bow. In other words, you are what you publish rather than—in a devilishly capricious trade—what you hope to publish, however you strive to plan, as plan you must. Thus the volume at hand is at once an exercise in retrospection and, by projection, a harbinger of this remarkable house's undoubted future.

Given a seagoing metaphor, it is perhaps appropriate to note that Farrar, Straus's first office at 580 Fifth Avenue had in November 1945 been overnight transformed from being the U.S. Navy's Branch Book and Magazine's Public Information Office, headed by Lt. (jg) Roger W. Straus, Jr., into a two-and-a-half-room publishing house. This had, in turn, resulted from a recent lunch at the old Murray Hill Hotel, at which Messrs. Farrar and Straus first discussed the possibility of co-founding a new house. John Farrar, the senior partner, had, after a stint in Psychological Warfare in the Mediterranean, resigned from Farrar and Rinehart, the firm which he had co-founded with Stanley Rinehart in 1929.

The first title published by the infant company came out in August 1946, and it is from that date that the half century celebrated here is marked. The book in question, a novel by the prolific James Branch Cabell (b. 1879), had illustrations by John O'Hara Cosgrave II and was titled *There Were Two Pirates*. Roger Straus still recalls a review from the Chicago *Sun-Times* which said in effect that the $2.95 book should have been called "There Were *Three* Pirates," the author and Messrs. Farrar and Straus.

Matters soon took a steadily upward course, but perusal of the early lists does furnish some indicators of just how wide the net of a nascent publisher must be cast. In the first catalogue, Summer and Fall 1946, we find energy and ingenuity at work, but some dearth of the high distinctions which have become the house's hallmark. The titles range from *Francis* (the talking mule, that is) to a very successful United Nations handbook and a posthumous collection of Stephen Vincent Benét's poems and short stories. A burgeoning sense of commercial verities may perhaps be seen in the postponement and retitling from the second to the third list of a three-decker importation from England by Guy McCrone. Originally called *Wax Fruit: The Antimacassar Trilogy*, it reappears the following season as *Red Plush: The Story of the Moorhouse Family*, and it went on to become the company's first Book-of-the-Month Club selection.

Also on the second list, it should be swiftly noted, was *Christ Stopped at Eboli* by Carlo Levi, the searing and empathic account of the author's internal exile, under near-medieval conditions, among the peasants of southern Italy, during the Fascist regime. It is worth special mention as the first of the many enduring and treasurable books that Farrar, Straus and Giroux has published. Forty-nine years later, it is still in print, a firm bench mark of the house's style and tradition. This title signaled as well the special attention given in early years by the young house and its publisher to Italy's rising stars, including Alberto Moravia, Cesare Pavese, and Giovanni Guareschi.

The year 1949 saw the publication of Shirley Jackson's *The Lottery* and Moravia's *The Woman of Rome*, authors and titles which accelerated the house's ultimate rise to worldwide reputation as a keen searcher for, and publisher of, talent of the highest order. In somewhat different vein, 1950 brought the book that both showed how lucky and constructively eclectic the house could be and almost certainly preserved its youthful financial health: *Look Younger, Live Longer*, by Gayelord Hauser. Sources differ, but it seems to have sold, in health-food stores as well as bookstores, more than 450,000 hardcover copies over the next few years, and was a number-one best-seller. The Federal Food and Drug Administration was not entirely happy with Hauser's vatic endorsement of yogurt and blackstrap molasses as the essential staffs of life, and actually seized some copies, but the publisher fought back successfully, pointing out that the author had not recommended either of these nostrums by brand name.

From 1950 to 1955, the firm was known as Farrar, Straus and Young. Stanley Young, a playwright, teacher, and critic, had been a director since the beginning and eventually became managing director. In 1953, the eight-year-old firm of Pellegrini and Cudahy had been acquired,* and after Mr. Young returned to the theater, the company

* Roger and his colleagues have always kept a sharp eye out for the possibility of strengthening the house and its backlist through the acquisition of other firms: Creative Age Press (1951), Pellegrini & Cudahy (1953), L. C. Page & Co. (1957), McMullen Books (1958), Noonday Press (1960), Octagon Books (1968), Hill and Wang (1971), North Point Press (1992). Moreover, making arrangements with other publishers for their sales distribution has steadily increased volume from year to year.

became Farrar, Straus and Cudahy, from 1955 to 1962. Sheila Cudahy, an active partner until 1962, had brought a number of major authors as well as significant Catholic authors to add to Farrar, Straus's already solid list of religious books, and also two children's series. After two intervening years during which the company reverted to its initial name, it became Farrar, Straus and Giroux on September 21, 1964.

In Roger Straus's words from a recent interview: "The most important addition to the firm was the coming of Robert Giroux as Editor-in-Chief and later as Chairman of the Board." Bob Giroux arrived in 1955 from Harcourt, Brace, where he had been editor-in-chief of the trade department, and in his wake came what was almost certainly the greatest number of important authors to follow, on their own initiative, a single editor from house to house in the history of modern publishing. There were seventeen of them and they included T. S. Eliot, Jean Stafford, Robert Lowell, John Berryman, Bernard Malamud, Flannery O'Connor, Thomas Merton, Jack Kerouac, Peter Taylor, and Randall Jarrell. For his part, Giroux has said: "I enjoy working with Roger Straus. I admire style, and he has it, as well as great publishing flair." They are indeed very different men, having been captioned by *Time* in an admiring piece as "Giroux: Inside Man" and "Straus: Outspoken," but what they have achieved is one of the rarest and most successful synergies in publishing.

This observer believes that the main reason for the triumphs of the partnership is the fact that both men—in a publishing world increasingly canted toward marketing and accounting—regard the editorial function as the driving force of a publishing house. Straus: "The standards we maintain are the highest in terms of literary excellence, and the people who work for us truly believe in what they're doing. The authors prefer to stay with the same editors, who can give them the tender loving care that might be lacking in a company controlled by bankers or computer-heads . . . Advice to young publishers? Get yourself a damned good editor!" And of Giroux it has been written: "It is natural for certain writers to prefer to work with an editor who is himself a man of letters, who is less concerned with best-sellerdom than with the integrity of the work, and who has shown himself able, with surprising regularity, to spot books destined to become a part of the literature of our time."

It would be redundant to chronicle the high points of succeeding decades—that is the purpose of this *Reader*. Nevertheless, whenever two or three are gathered together in discussion of the company, a potpourri of subjects tends to come up repeatedly. A sampling of these might include:

—FSG has arguably the finest poetry list in town. Seamus Heaney is only the latest Nobel Prize poet. (See the honors list in the appendix.)

—Aleksandr Solzhenitsyn, Scott Turow, and Tom Wolfe sold major books for less than the highest offer, for the privilege of being published by FSG.

—John McPhee has, at this writing, twenty-five titles in print at FSG in both hard- and softcover. Susan Sontag has published all sixteen of her books, since her first in 1963, with the firm. Both are unparalleled examples of mutual publisher/author devotion.

—In 1987, FSG had the two most talked about novels of the year, both number-one *New York Times* best-sellers: Tom Wolfe's *The Bonfire of the Vanities* and Scott Turow's *Presumed Innocent*. The latter was practically the first book acquired by Jonathan Galassi after coming to FSG from Random House.

—In 1993, a book translated from the Danish, *Smilla's Sense of Snow* by Peter Høeg, sold close to 100,000 copies, confirming FSG's legendary *fin bec* when it comes to books in foreign languages.

—And then there are the offices, located on the fourth, ninth, and tenth floors of 19 Union Square West. A gingerly description (in a Columbia University magazine profile of Bob Giroux) allows that "you won't find modular furniture or glitzy excess in the offices of Farrar, Straus and Giroux." Edwin McDowell in *The New York Times* on two separate occasions referred to the quarters as "appealingly shabby" and "appealingly down at the heels." The last word should probably go to Calvin Trillin, who said of them a couple of years ago: "I suppose they'll always go on looking like they do now—like the branch office of a failing insurance company." None of this fazes President Straus. He knows he presides over the only major surviving New York publishing house founded in the aftermath of World War II, and that many if not all of the others sank on meeting the iceberg of overhead.

A note of both elegy and optimism is probably appropriate here and at the end of fifty years. For decades, the firm has been cited not only as a leading literary house (Roger has admitted only Alfred A. Knopf as "a peer" and that was some time ago) but also as virtually the only one which was a freestanding, profitable, pure trade (no textbooks) publisher. Then, in the fall of 1994, he announced that the Verlagsgruppe Georg von Holtzbrinck of Stuttgart, Germany, had bought a majority interest in the company. At the same time, Roger pointed out that it was a sale which he himself had sought. In an interview with *The American Bookseller* in January of '95, he stated: "Now, almost fifty years later, when I decided I had to put this house in order, I approached Dieter von Holtzbrinck; he didn't approach me. I chose him because he has run an enormously successful operation in Germany by letting all the houses that they control stand alone . . . I wouldn't say he was interested—he was vitally interested." He might also have pointed out that Holtzbrinck has for over a decade owned controlling shares in the United States in Henry Holt (trade books), *Scientific American*, W. H. Freeman (textbooks), and Worth Publishers, and, it is safe to say, maintained a more hands-off approach to management than any other major foreign publishing investor. (More recently, it has also acquired a controlling interest in Macmillan in the UK, which in turn owns St. Martin's Press in New York.)

As many noted at the time, the sale to Holtzbrinck took place a year after the departure from FSG of the affectionately regarded and highly admired Roger Straus III, who had (except for a ten-year stint at Harper and other houses) worked at Farrar, Straus and Giroux since 1967, rising to managing director. He and his father parted over what *Publishers Weekly* termed "philosophical differences." There have been no public statements since, but neither has anyone doubted their continuing closeness or the sincerity of the good wishes for each other's enterprises expressed by both father and son at the time of parting. (The younger Straus has pursued professionally his intense interest in photography and is now co-owner of a flourishing book-packaging business.)

"Jonathan Galassi will follow me," Roger Straus has said, to nobody's surprise. With his rare meld of commercial acumen and finely honed literary sensibilities, Galassi, hired in 1986 and editor-in-chief since 1988, is the ideal successor to lead the house. In his words: "A company needs to be profitable. We have a bottom line, of course, but it all depends on how you get there. A wonderful thing about a small house like this is that we make our own rules . . . The rules of a commodity business don't apply to us. We are a house where books are dealt with one by one, with the excitement of something new all the time. Nobody is expecting to get rich on it." Thus, Galassi will surely carry on in the same vein of enthusiasm as his predecessors and with these words of Roger Straus's ringing in his ears: "In the end it's authors and books that really matter. I read a book and I think ah, it's absolutely delicious, it's wonderful, it's marvelous. I go out and tell all my friends and relatives—the whole world. It's about being associated with authors, and having a rooting seat in the grandstand—that's what really turns me on."

Most of this celebratory volume consists of excerpts from books published by FSG over fifty years—one piece per author. The task of making the selections was given over to this outsider, a presumably objective though friendly competitor of many years, and they are his alone. The choice of authors was proposed by him and reviewed by members of the company's staff. In the case of poetry, the selections were made by Giroux, Galassi, and Elisabeth Sifton. The children's selections were made by Margaret Ferguson and Robbie Mayes.

The reader should be aware of a few guidelines.

—For reasons of space, poets are represented by poems of no longer than a page in length with the exception of T. S. Eliot's "The Death of Saint Narcissus," though several have written distinguished essays and novels as well.

—Any short stories are complete as published in book form. In the case of longer fiction and non-fiction, the excerpts are sometimes exactly as they first appeared and sometimes spliced together from different parts of the work at hand. The space breaks that indicate this—[. . .]—are differentiated from breaks specified by the author in the original text.

—The order is chronological by date of FSG publication. There are a few anomalies: Carlo Levi appears first by reason of publication year, in spite of a later retranslation of *Christ Stopped at Eboli*, but Carlos Fuentes appears much later than the original publication of *The Death of Artemio Cruz*, because of its retranslation. Mostly, the selector hopes that the impression of unbroken high achievement comes across seamlessly.

—In a very few cases, explanatory words have been added, clearly marked by brackets; e.g., [the donkey] added to identify Jiménez's muse, Platero.

Finally, a profound and genuinely heartfelt apology to the many authors of works of distinction who have had to be omitted from the body of this book. A rule of thumb was followed that each author included had to have at least two works published under the FSG imprint, but even so, this *Reader* could have been multiples longer without any diminution of quality. The list overall truly provides an embarrassment of riches, and long after this anniversary observance disappears, the honor of the imprint on the spine endures.

Alan D. Williams

[*Alan D. Williams worked for many years as an editor and executive in various publishing houses, most notably as editorial director at The Viking Press. His most recent post was as publisher at Grove Press.*]

FARRAR, STRAUS AND GIROUX

CARLO LEVI

FROM

Christ Stopped at Eboli

[Translated by Frances Frenaye]

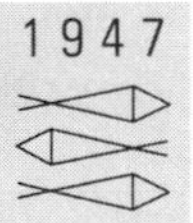

[Letter from author to Roger W. Straus]

Dear Roger,

My book Christ Stopped at Eboli *opens with the words "Many years have gone by, years of war and of what men call History." Once again, many years have gone by, years of war and history, of changes in men and things, years so crowded and dense and renewing that one cannot describe them in terms of number, for each living moment has been—as always with real things—eternal. Now you are reissuing this book fifteen years after its first American edition (your publishing house was then quite new), and it is twenty years since I wrote those first words with no idea of what would follow. A house in Florence was my refuge then from the savage death roaming the streets of a city that had reverted to a primitive jungle of shadows and wild beasts. It was there I began to unwind the thread of memory, discovering not only events of the past but the infinite, poetic contemporaneity of all time and every destiny. In this sense, the fifteen—or the twenty—years are an epoch, perhaps, or perhaps only a brief moment.*

At that time each moment could have been the last; in itself each was the last, the only moment. There was no place for embellishment, experiment—for literature—but only for the real truth that exists in and beyond things. And there was a place for love, for, even if always defenseless and truncated, it alone was able to hold together a world that without it would have been dissolved and annihilated.

The house was a refuge; the book was an act of defense that routed death. I have never reread it since in its entirety; it has remained in my memory completely objectified as a youthful image of pure energy that the melancholy, doting mind and eye cannot destroy. Who was the "I," concealed like the shoot beneath the tree bark, who was looking for the first time at those things that are elsewhere, and who wandered among those deserted fields, in the age-old stillness of that peasant world, under the unwinking eye of the she-goat?

Perhaps he was quite another person, an unknown, still unformed young man whom chance and time had caused to pass before those yellow animal eyes, before those black eyes of women and men and children

(black eyes made empty
by the tears of numberless
vigils, look
into the depth of the spirit)

so that he might find himself in that otherwhere, in that other-than-self; so that he might discover history beyond history, time out of time, and the pain that precedes all things; that he might discover himself not in the mirror of Narcissus' pool but in men and upon that arid earth? Or was he perhaps the same person as today, only then in his first concealed act of youthful faith?

Certainly all that that young man (and perhaps he was I) then experienced revealed to him the reality of a country unknown to him, and unknown languages, labor, toil, suffering, misery, and customs as well. There he came to know not only animals and magic, and ancient problems still unsolved, and the potency that withstands power, but also the pride that is ever present, a contemporaneousness that is inexhaustible, existence which is coexistence; the human being who is the locus of all contact; a motionless world of possibilities at once infinite and closed, the dark adolescence of centuries poised to stir and emerge, like butterflies from the cocoon. He learned the individual eternity of all this, the Lucania within each of us, the vital force that is ready to turn itself into form and life and institutions as it struggles with paternal, prevailing institutions which, despite their claim to an exclusive reality, are dead and gone.

It was that young man's singular good fortune (thanks to age, education, character, and an inability to accept a negative world) to be so free of his own era as to be almost exiled from time—and able, therefore, to be truly contemporary. That is, a contemporary not only of limitless contemporaneity but, in actual deeds, of the new men, the little men, the obscure men with whom he had the good luck to live, mature, and achieve self-knowledge. And so he was adolescent together with an adolescent and ineffable world, young with a young world stumbling toward dramatic liberation, and he became an adult as that world achieved adult-

hood in all the fraternal beings of all the Lucanias in every corner of the earth.

Thus Christ Stopped at Eboli *was, first, experience and painting and poetry; secondly, together with* Fear and Freedom, *theory and joy in truth; becoming finally and openly a story when, as if through a process of loving crystallization, a fresh analogous experience made that possible. The process developed in successive books, changing the author's spirit and body and words while in a period explosive with new awareness other men also changed. The process is not, and has never been, identification with a datum, a flight into objectivity, but is rather the continual discernment of love. It is—as Rocco Scotellaro, who is dear to me above all men, said in his* "Uva puttanella" *where he speaks of reading this book —an identification with (and a* love *of that identification) my eighteen cell mates in the prison of Matera.*

For this reason, Christ Stopped at Eboli *seems to me today the first moment in a long story that is continued via change and that continues to be different in me, in things, in the actions and hearts of men, in all the books I have written, and in those I am writing and will write (and that you will publish). And it will continue until I shall be capable of living the contemporaneity and coexistence and unity of all reality, and of understanding, beyond the bounds of literature, that the meaning of a gesture, a face, a word, is simple poetic freedom.*

Carlo Levi

Rome,
May, 1963

I did not go to the cemetery only to seek rest and solitude and to listen to stories. This was the one place, within bounds, that was not built up and where a few trees broke the geometrical outline of the peasants' huts. For this reason it was the first subject I chose for a picture. I went out with my canvas and brushes when the sun started to go down, set up my easel in the shade of an olive tree or behind the cemetery wall and started to paint.

The first time I did this, a few days after my arrival, my occupation appeared suspect to the sergeant, who immediately informed the mayor and meanwhile, in order to be on the safe side, sent one of his men to watch me. The *carabiniere* stood stiffly a few steps behind me and looked at my work from the first to the last stroke of the brush. It is tiresome to paint with someone looking over your shoulder, even if you're not afraid of evil influences (as they say was the case with Cézanne), but in spite of all I could do he was not to be budged; he had his orders. Gradually the expression of his stupid face shifted from inquiry to interest and finally he asked me whether I would be able to make an enlargement in oils of a photograph of his dead mother, this being to a *carabiniere* the apex of art. The hours went by, the sun set, and objects took on the enchantment of twilight, seeming to shine with a light of their own, from within rather than from without. An enormous, transparent, unreal moon hung in the rose-tinted sky over the gray olive trees and the houses lower down, like a cuttlefish bone corroded by the salt of the ocean. At this time I had a particular feeling for the moon, because for many months I had been shut up in a cell where I could not see it, and to find it again was a pleasure. As a greeting and a token of regard I painted it, round and light in the center of the sky, to the astonishment of the *carabiniere*.

At this point the twin masters of the village came to inspect my work, the decorous sergeant in his impeccable uniform with a sword at his side, and the mayor, all compliments and smiles and affected benevolence. Don Luigi, of course, was a connoisseur and wanted me to know it; he was unsparing in his praise of my technique. Besides, it was flattering to his local pride that I should find his native place worthy of painting. I took advantage of his satisfaction to suggest that if I were to do justice to its beauties I should have to go a little farther away from the village limits. The mayor and the sergeant were unwilling to commit themselves to breaking the rules, but little by little in the course of the following weeks we reached a sort of tacit agreement which enabled me, for the purpose of painting, to go two or three hundred yards out of bounds. I owed this privilege less to respect for art than to Donna Caterina's intrigues and her desire to please me and to her brother's panicky fear of falling ill. Don Luigi was perfectly well. Aside from a glandular disturbance which showed itself in his sadistic and infantile disposition but had no physical effects except a high-pitched voice and a tendency to obesity, he was bursting with health. However, to my good fortune, he was continually prey to the fear of illness: today it was tuberculosis, tomorrow heart trouble, the next day stomach ulcers; he counted his pulse, took his temperature, examined his tongue in the mirror, and every time we met I had to reassure him. At last the hypochondriac had a doctor at his beck and call. And so I could go a little afield to paint from time to time, not too often and not so far that I should be out of sight. The whole thing was to be at my own suggestion and my own risk since he had many enemies who might write anonymous letters to Matera, putting him in a bad light because he had made me this concession.

I gained very little breathing-space. The place was hemmed in by ravines, and apart from the walk leading out of the cemetery, beyond which I could not venture without going downhill and out of sight, only two paths led away from the village. One led up and down along the crest of the ravine from Gagliano to Gaglianello, and in this direction I could go as far as the Mound of the Madonna of the Angels, where the devil had appeared to the old grave-digger, not far from the last village houses. A narrower path, only a few feet wide, branched off from this to the right and went down in a series of steep zigzags to the bottom of the chasm two hundred yards below. This was the dangerous passageway that most of the peasants took every day with their donkeys and goats, when they went to their fields down by the Agri Valley, and again at night when they came back, bent over like the damned under their loads of wood or fodder. The other path was at the higher end of the village; it ran off to the right of the church, near the widow's house, to a little spring, which until a few years before was Gagliano's only supply of water. A thin stream came out of a rusty pipe and fell into a wooden trough in which the women still came at times to wash; after it spilled over from this there was nothing to drain it off and it made a marshy spot where mosquitoes bred. The path continued through fields of stubble dotted with occasional olive trees and lost itself in a labyrinth of mounds and holes in the white clay, which ended abruptly at a precipice not far from the Sauro River. Here I used to walk and paint and here one day I met a poisonous snake, but the loud barking of my dog warned me of its approach.

The strange and broken outline of this terrain made Gagliano into a sort of natural fortress, with a limited number of entrances and exits. The mayor took advantage of this lay of the land during days of what was supposed to be patriotic frenzy. He then called public meetings in order, he said, to brace up the morale of the people, herding them into the square to listen to radio broadcasts by the leaders who were then laying plans for the war with Abyssinia. When Don Luigi decided to call one of these gatherings he sent the old town crier and grave-digger through the street the evening before with his trumpet and drum, and the ancient voice was heard to shout a hundred times over, in front of every house, on one high, impersonal note: "Tomorrow morning at ten o'clock, everyone come to the square in front of the town hall to hear the radio! Nobody stay away!"

"We'll have to get up two hours before sunrise," muttered the peasants, unwilling to lose a working day, although they knew that Don Luigi would station *carabinieri* and Fascist Scouts at every exit from the village with orders not to let anyone by. Most of them managed to leave for the fields while it was still dark and the watchers had not yet arrived, but the late risers had to take their stand in the square with the women and school children, just below the balcony, from which cascaded the rapt and visceral eloquence of the mayor. They stood there with their hats on, sober and mistrustful, and his speechmaking poured over them without leaving a trace.

The gentry were all Party members, even the few like Dr. Milillo who were dissenters. The Party stood for Power, as vested in the Government and the State, and they felt entitled to a share of it. For exactly the opposite reason none of the peasants were members; indeed, it was unlikely that they should belong to any political party whatever, should, by chance, another exist. They were not Fascists, just as they would never have been Conservatives or Socialists, or anything else. Such matters had nothing to do with them; they belonged to another world and they saw no sense in them. What had the peasants to do with Power, Government, and the State? The State, whatever form it might take, meant "the fellows in Rome." "Everyone knows," they said, "that the fellows in Rome don't want us to live like human beings. There are hailstorms, landslides, droughts, malaria and . . . the State. These are inescapable evils; such there always have been and there always will be. They make us kill off our goats, they carry away our furniture, and now they're going to send us to the wars. Such is life!"

To the peasants the State is more distant than heaven and far more of a scourge, because it is always against them. Its political tags and platforms and, indeed, the whole structure of it do not matter. The peasants do not understand them because they are couched in a different language from their own, and there is no reason why they should ever care to understand them. Their only defense against the State and the propaganda of the State is resignation, the same gloomy resignation, alleviated by no hope of paradise, that bows their shoulders under the scourges of nature.

For this reason, quite naturally, they have no conception of a political struggle; they think of it as a personal quarrel among the "fellows in Rome." They were not concerned with the views of the political prisoners who were in compulsory residence among them, or with the motives for their coming. They looked at them kindly and treated them like brothers because they too, for some inexplicable reason, were victims of fate. During the first days of my stay whenever I happened to meet along one of the paths outside the village an old peasant who did not know me, he would stop his donkey to greet me and ask in dialect: "Who are you? Where are you going?" "Just for a walk; I'm a political prisoner," I would answer. "An exile? (They always said exile instead of prisoner.) Too bad! Someone in Rome must have had it in for you." And he would say no more, but smile at me in a brotherly fashion as he prodded his mount into motion.

This passive brotherliness, this sympathy in the original sense of the word, as suffering together, this fatalistic, comradely, age-old patience, is the deepest feeling the peasants have in common, a bond made by nature rather than by religion. They do not and can not have what is called political awareness, because they are literally *pagani*, "pagans," or countrymen, as distinguished from city-dwellers. The deities of the State and the city can find no worshipers here on the land, where the wolf and the ancient black boar reign supreme, where there is no wall between the world of men and the world of animals and spirits, between the leaves of the trees above and the roots below. They can not have even an awareness of themselves as individuals, here where all things are held together by acting upon one another and each one is a power unto itself, working imperceptibly, where there is no barrier that can not be broken down by magic. They live submerged in a world that rolls on independent of their will, where man is in no way separate from his sun, his beast, his malaria, where there can be neither happiness, as literary devotees of the land conceive it, nor hope, because these two are adjuncts of personality and here there is only the grim passivity of a sorrowful Nature. But they have a lively human feeling for the common fate of mankind and its common acceptance. This is strictly a feeling rather than an act of will; they do not express it in words but they carry it with them at every moment and in every motion of their lives, through all the unbroken days that pass over these wastes.

"Too bad! Someone had it in for you." You, too, are subject to fate. You, too, are here because of the power of ill will, because of an evil star; you are tossed hither and yon by the hostile workings of magic. And you, too, are a man; you are one of us. Never mind what motives impelled you, politics, legalities, or the illusion of reason. Such things as reason or cause and effect, do not exist; there is only an adverse fate, a will for evil, which is the magic power of *things*. The State is one shape of this fate, like the wind that devours the harvest and the fever that feeds on our blood. There can be no attitude toward fate except patience and silence. Of what use are words? And what can a man do? Nothing.

Armed, then, with silence and patience, taciturn and impenetrable, the few peasants who had not escaped to the fields attended the gathering in the square. They seemed not to hear the blithe trumpeting of the radio, which came from too far away, from a land of ease and progress, which had forgotten the existence of death and now called it up as a joke, with the frivolity of an unbeliever.

ALBERTO MORAVIA

FROM

The Woman of Rome

[*Translated by Lydia Holland*]

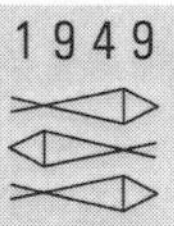

I saw Giacinti every evening during the next few days. He rang up Gisella the next morning and, as soon as she met me in the afternoon, she gave me his message. Giacinti had to leave for Milan the evening before the day I had arranged to meet Gino and this was why I agreed to see him every evening. Otherwise I would have refused, because I had vowed to myself that I did not want ever again to have a settled relationship with any one man. I thought it was better, if I was taking up this profession, to do it in earnest, with a different lover each time, rather than deceive myself into thinking I was not taking it up by letting one man keep me; with the added danger of growing fond of him or he of me, and thereby losing not only my physical liberty but my emotional liberty as well.

In any case, my ideas about normal married life had remained unchanged; and I thought that if I were to marry, it would never be to a lover who had kept me and in the end had decided to make a business relationship legal, if not moral; but rather to a young man who would love me and whom I would love in return, one out of my own class of life, with similar tastes and ideas. What I wanted, in fact, was to keep the profession I had chosen completely separate from my earlier ambitions, without any contacts or compromises, since I felt I was equally well cut out to be a good wife and a good harlot, but was quite incapable of maintaining a cautious and hypocritical middle way between the two. Also, when all was said and done, there was probably more to be made out of the scruples of many men than out of the generosity of one man alone.

Every evening Giacinti took me to have supper in the same restaurant and then came home with me, remaining with me until well on in the night. By now mother had quite given up any attempt to talk to me about my evenings, and contented herself with asking me whether

I had slept well when she brought me my coffee on a tray late next morning. Previously, I used to go and sip my coffee in the kitchen, very early, without sitting down even, in front of the stove, feeling the biting cold of the water I had washed in still on my hands and face. Now instead mother brought it to me and I drank it in bed, while she opened the shutters and began to tidy up the room. I never said anything to her that I had not already said in the past; but she had understood on her own that everything was changed in our life and she showed by her behavior that she realized perfectly well what the difference was.

She acted as if we had a tacit agreement, and seemed by her attentions to be begging me humbly to allow her to continue to serve me and make herself useful in our new way of life as she had always done before. But I must say this habit of bringing me my coffee in bed must have reassured her to some extent, because many people, and mother was one of them, endow habits with a positive worth even when they are not positive, as in the present case. With the same zeal she introduced many little changes of this kind into our daily life. For instance, she used to prepare a great bowl of boiling water for me to wash in as soon as I got up, used to put flowers in a vase in my room, and so on.

Giacinti always gave me the same amount and, without telling mother, I used to put it in a drawer in the box where she had placed her savings until now. I only kept a little small change for myself. I suppose she must have noticed the daily additions to our capital, but we never mentioned it to one another. I have noticed in the course of my life that even people who earn their livelihood by recognized means prefer not to speak about it, not only to strangers but even to friends. Probably money is linked with a sense of shame, or at least modesty, which prevents its being included in the list of ordinary topics of conversation and places it among those secret and inadmissible things which it is better not to mention; as if it were always disgracefully earned, no matter what its origin might be. But perhaps it is also true that no one likes to show the feeling money rouses in his soul, since it is a most powerful feeling and hardly ever disassociated from a sense of sin.

•

The day of my appointment with Gino came at last, and so much had happened in those ten days that I felt as if a hundred years had passed since I used to see him on my way to the studios, and used to work to save money and set up house, and considered myself an engaged girl soon to be married. He was there most punctually at the appointed time, and as I got into the car he seemed disturbed and very pale. No one likes to have a deception flung in his teeth, not even the boldest deceiver, and he must have thought a great deal and have had his suspicions during the ten days that had interrupted our usual meetings. But I showed no resentment and, as a matter of fact, I was not even pretending, because I felt perfectly serene; and when the bitterness of the first moment's disillusionment had passed, I felt a kind of indulgent and skeptical fondness for him. After all, I still liked Gino, as I knew from the first glance I gave him, and this was saying a lot.

"So your confessor's changed his mind?" he asked me after a while, as the car sped towards the villa. His tone was mocking but at the same time uncertain.

"No," I answered simply, "I've changed my mind."

"Have you finished all your work with your mother?"

"For the time being."

"Queer."

He did not know what he was saying, but he was obviously testing me to discover whether his suspicions were justified.

"Why is it queer?"

"I was only saying it for something to say."

"Don't you believe I've been busy?"

"I don't believe anything."

I had decided to show him up, but in my own way, by playing with him a little, like a cat with a mouse, without the brutal scenes Gisella had advised, which were not in harmony with my temperament.

"Are you jealous?" I asked him coquettishly.

"Me jealous? Good heavens!"

"Yes, you are—if you were sincere you'd admit it."

He took the bait I was offering. "Anyone in my place would be jealous," he said.

"Why?"

"Oh, come now! Did you think I would believe you? Such an important job of work that you can't spare five minutes to see me!"

"It's true, though," I said calmly. "I've worked very hard." And it was true—what else was it but work, and very tiring work, that I had been doing with Giacinti every evening? "And I've earned enough to pay off the rest of the installments and buy my trousseau," I added, making fun of myself. "So at last we'll be able to get married without any debts."

He said nothing; he was clearly trying to persuade himself of the truth of what I was saying, and was slowly abandoning his earlier suspicions. At that moment I made a gesture I had often made in the past. I flung my arms round his neck while he was driving and kissed him hard below the ear, whispering, "Why are you jealous? You know you're the only person in my life."

We reached the villa. Gino drove the car into the garden, shut the gate and went towards the tradesmen's entrance with me. It was twilight and the first lights were already gleaming in the windows of the houses round about, red in the bluish mist of the winter evening. It was nearly dark in the underground passage and there was a smell of slops and stuffiness. I stopped.

"I don't want to go to your room this evening," I said.

"Why not?"

"I want to make love in your mistress's room."

"You're out of your mind!" he exclaimed in scandalized horror. We had often gone into the upper rooms, but had always made love in his room in the basement.

"It's just a whim," I said. "What does it matter to you?"

"It matters a lot—something might get broken—you never know —and if they notice, what'll I do?"

"Oh, what a tragedy!" I exclaimed lightly. "You'll get fired, that's all."

"And you can speak of it in that tone!"

"How should I say it? If you really loved me you wouldn't think twice about it."

"I do love you, but I can't hear of this—don't let's even talk of it. I don't want any trouble, I don't."

"We'll be careful. They won't notice."

"No."

I felt perfectly self-possessed. "I, who am your fiancée, ask you this one favor," I exclaimed, continuing to pretend what I did not really feel, "and you refuse because you're afraid I'll put my body where your mistress puts hers and lay my head where she lays hers—but what are you thinking? That she's better than I am?"

"No, but—"

"I'm worth a thousand of her sort!" I went on. "But so much the worse for you. You can make love to your mistress's pillows and sheets—I'm going."

As I have already said, his respect and his subservience to his employers went very deep. He was nauseatingly proud of them, as if all their wealth were his, too. But seeing me speak in that way and turn away impetuously, with a determination he was not accustomed to find in me, he lost his head and ran after me.

"Wait a bit! Where are you? I was only talking! Let's go upstairs, if you like!"

I let him plead with me a little more, pretending to be offended. Then I agreed and we went to the upper floor, our arms round one another, and stopping on each step for a kiss, just like the first time, but with a change of heart—at least, speaking for myself. In his mistress's room I walked straight over to the bed and turned the covers down. He protested, once more mastered by fear. "You don't mean to get right into the bed?"

"Why not?" I replied calmly. "I don't want to get cold."

He said nothing, visibly upset. When I had prepared the bed I went into the bathroom, lit the geyser and turned on the hot-water faucet, just a trickle, so that the bath would not fill too rapidly. Gino, uneasy and dissatisfied, followed me and protested once more.

"Having a bath, too?"

"They have a bath after they've made love, don't they?"

"How should I know what they do?" he answered with a shrug. But I could see that in point of fact my boldness did not really displease him, he merely found it difficult to swallow. He was not a brave man and he liked to be on the right side of the law. But law-breaking attracted him all the more since he hardly ever allowed himself to slip. "You're right, after all," he said with a smile after a moment's pause, wavering between temptation and reluctance, as he felt the mattress with his hand. "It's comfortable here—better than in my room."

"Didn't I say so?"

We sat down together on the edge of the bed. "Gino," I said, throwing my arms round his neck, "think how lovely it will be when we have a house of our own, just for the two of us. . . . It won't be like this—but it'll be our own."

I do not know why I said this. Probably because I knew for certain by now that all those things were out of the question and I liked to worry the very spot where my conscience was most deeply pinched.

"Yes, yes," he said, and kissed me.

"I know the kind of life I want," I continued, with the cruel feeling that I was describing something lost and gone forever, "not a fine place like this—two rooms and a kitchen would be enough for me. But everything would be my own and it would be as clean as a new pin—and we'd be peaceful. We'd go out on Sunday together, eat together, sleep together. Oh, Gino, just think how lovely it'll be!"

He said nothing. As a matter of fact, I remained quite unmoved as I said all this. I felt I was playing a part, like an actor on the stage. But this made it all the more bitter, because the cold, superficial part I was playing, which awoke not the slightest echo in my conscience, was what I had really been only ten days before. Meanwhile, while I was speaking, Gino undressed me impatiently. And I noticed once more, as I had when I got into the car, that I still liked him; perhaps my body, always ready to take pleasure from him, rather than my soul which was by now estranged, made me so good-natured and quick to forgive. He caressed me and kissed me, and his caresses and kisses troubled my mind and the pleasure of my senses overcame the reluctance in my heart. "Oh Gino—you make me feel like dying!" I murmured, speaking sincerely at last as I fell back on the bed.

Later on I put my legs under the sheets and so did he, and we lay together with the embroidered sheet of that magnificent bed pulled up to our chins. Over our heads was suspended a kind of baldachin, with a cloud of white, gossamer veilings floating down over the head of the bed. The whole room was white, with long, fine curtains at the windows, beautiful low furniture against the walls, beveled mirrors, ornaments of glittering glass, marble and silver. The exquisitely fine sheets were like a caress against my body; and, if I moved ever so slightly, the mattress yielded gently to my limbs and induced a deep desire for sleep and rest. Through the open door I could hear the quietly querulous sound of the water flowing into the bath. I felt utterly content and not in the least resentful against Gino any longer. This seemed the best moment to tell him that I knew everything, because I was sure I would say it kindly, with no shadow of bitterness.

"So, Gino," I said in most caressing tones after a long silence, "your wife's called Antonietta Partini."

Perhaps he was drowsing, because he jumped violently as if someone had clapped him unexpectedly on the shoulder. "What's that you said?"

"And your little girl's called Maria, isn't that right?"

He would have liked to protest again, but he looked into my eyes and realized it was useless. Our heads lay on the same pillow, our faces side by side, and I was speaking with my mouth almost on his. "Poor Gino," I said, "why did you tell me so many lies?"

"Because I loved you," he answered violently.

"If you really loved me, you ought to have thought how unhappy I'd be when I learned the truth. But you didn't think of that, Gino, did you?"

"I loved you," he interrupted me, "and I lost my head, and—"

"That'll do," I said. "I was wretchedly unhappy for a while—I didn't think you capable of such a thing—but it's all over. Don't let's mention it again. Now I'm going to have a bath." I pushed off the sheets, slipped out of bed and went into the bathroom. Gino stayed where he was.

The bath was full of hot water, a bluish color, lovely to see among all the white tiles and shining faucets. I stood in the bath and slowly let myself down into the steaming water. Lying in it, I shut my eyes. There was no sound from the next room; Gino must be thinking over what I had said and was trying to work out some plan whereby he could avoid losing me. I smiled at the thought of him in the big double bed, with my news still like a slap in the face. But my smile was not spiteful; it was the sort of smile caused by something amusing but completely impersonal, because, as I have said, I felt no resentment towards him but rather, knowing him for what he really was, only a kind of fondness for him. Then I heard him walking about, probably dressing. After a while he peeped in at the bathroom door and looked at me like a whipped dog, as if he did not dare to enter.

"So we shan't see anything more of each other," he said humbly, after a long silence.

I realized that he really loved me in his own way, although not enough to make lying to me and deceiving me utterly repulsive. I remembered Astarita and thought that he, too, loved me in his own way. "Why shouldn't we?" I replied as I soaped one of my arms. "If I hadn't wanted to see you, I wouldn't have come today. We'll still meet, but not so often as before."

His courage seemed to return at these words. He came into the bathroom. "Shall I soap you?" he asked.

I could not help being reminded of mother, who was also so full of attention and care for me each time after she had renounced her parental authority.

"If you like," I said shortly. "Soap my back where I can't get at it." Gino picked up the soap and sponge; I stood up and he washed my back. I looked at myself in a long mirror opposite the bath and imagined I was the lady who owned all those lovely things. She, too, must stand up like that, and a maid, some poor girl like myself, had to bend over and soap her and wash her, taking care not to scratch her skin. I thought how lovely it must be to be waited on by somebody else and not do everything with your own hands: to keep still and limp while she bustles about full of respectful attention. I remembered the simple idea I had had the first time I went to the villa: without my shabby clothes, naked, I was the equal of Gino's mistress. But my fate, most unjustly, was quite different.

"That'll do," I said to Gino in irritation.

He picked up the bathrobe and I got out of the bath; he then held it out behind me and I wrapped myself in it. He wanted to embrace me, perhaps to see whether I would repel him, and I let him kiss my neck as I stood there, motionless, wrapped in the bathrobe. Then he began to dry me all over, in silence, starting with my feet, going up to my breast, eagerly and ably as if he had never done anything else in his life, and I shut my eyes and imagined once again that I was the mistress and he the maid. He took my passivity for acquiescence and I suddenly discovered that instead of drying me he was caressing me. At that I pushed him away, let the bathrobe fall and went on tiptoe barefooted into the next room. Gino stayed in the bathroom to let the water out.

I dressed quickly and then walked round the room looking at the furniture. I stopped in front of the dressing table dotted with pieces of gold and tortoise-shell. Among the hairbrushes and perfume-bottles I noticed a gold powder compact. I picked it up and looked at it closely. It was heavy, apparently made of solid gold. It was square, of rolled gold in stripes, and a large ruby was set in the catch. I had a feeling of discovery, rather than of temptation—now I could do anything, even steal. I opened my bag and put the compact into it; being heavy it slipped right down into the bottom among my loose change and keys. In taking it, I felt a kind of sensual pleasure, not unlike the sensation accepting money from my lovers caused me. As a matter of fact, I did not have any use for such a valuable compact, it did not match my clothes or the kind of life I led. I was sure I would never use it. But in stealing it, I seemed to be obeying the logic which now governed the course of my life. I thought I might as well be hanged for a sheep as a lamb.

Gino returned and, with servile attention to detail, began to tidy the bed and all the things he did not think were in their proper places. "Come on!" I said scornfully as I saw him looking around anxiously when he had finished, in order to make sure everything was in its usual place. "Come on! Your mistress won't notice a thing—you won't be fired this time!" I saw a flash of pain cross Gino's face at this and I was sorry I had said it, because it was spiteful and not even sincere.

We said nothing on the way downstairs or in the garden as we got into the car. Night had fallen some time since. And as soon as the car began to thread its way through the twisted streets of that fashionable district, I began to cry gently, as if I had been waiting only for that moment. I did not even know myself why I was crying, and yet I was filled with bitterness. I am not made to play disillusioned, angry parts, and the whole afternoon, although I had done my utmost to appear calm, disillusionment and anger had motivated many of my actions and words. Now for the first time, while I was still crying, I felt really resentful towards Gino, who, through his betrayal of me, had aroused emotions I found unpleasant and which did not suit my character. I thought how good and sweet I had always been and how perhaps I was not going to be so any more from that moment, and the thought filled me with despair. I would have liked to ask Gino heartbrokenly, "Why did you do all this? How can I ever forget it and think no more about it?" But instead I said nothing, swallowed my tears and shook my head a little to make them run down my cheeks, like one shakes a branch to rid it of its ripest fruit. I hardly noticed that meanwhile we were driving right across the city. When the car stopped, I got out and held out my hand to Gino. "I'll give you a ring," I said. He looked at me with an expression of hope that changed to amazement when he saw my face bathed in tears. But he had no time to say a word, for I ran off with a wave of the hand and a forced smile.

[. . .]

At a certain moment during the hours I spent in such seclusion a profound feeling of bewilderment always overcame me; I suddenly seemed to see the whole of my life and all of myself from all sides, with icy clear-sightedness. The things I was doing were doubled, lost the substance of their meaning, were reduced to mere incomprehensible, absurd externals. I used to say to myself, "I often bring home a man who has been waiting for me in the night, without knowing me. We struggle with one another on this bed, clutching each other like two sworn enemies. Then he gives me a piece of printed, colored paper. Next day I exchange this piece of paper for food, clothes and other articles." But these words were only the first step in a process of deeper bewilderment. They served to clear my mind of the censure, always lying in wait there, of my profession, and they showed me my profession as a series of meaningless gestures, similar in every way to the routine motions of other professions. Immediately afterwards a distant sound in the city or the creaking of some piece of furniture in the room gave me a ludicrous and almost hectic awareness of my existence. I said to myself, "Here I am and I might be elsewhere. I might exist a thousand years ago or in a thousand years' time. I might be a Negress or an old woman, fair or short." I thought how I had come out of endless night and would soon go on into another endless darkness, and that my brief passing was marked only by absurd and trivial actions. I then understood that my distress was caused, not by what I was doing, but more profoundly by the bare fact of being alive, which was neither good nor evil but only painful and without meaning.

My dismay used to make my flesh creep with fear; I used to shudder uncontrollably, feeling my hair stand on end, and suddenly the walls of my flat, the city and even the world seemed to vanish, leaving me suspended in dark, empty, endless space—suspended, what's more, in the same clothes, with the same memories, name and profession. A girl called Adriana suspended against nothingness. Nothingness seemed to me something terrible, solemn and incomprehensible, and the saddest aspect of the whole matter was my meeting this nothingness with the manners and outward appearance I bore in the evening when I used to meet Gisella in the confectionery shop where she waited for me. I found no consolation in the thought that other people also acted and moved in just as futile and inadequate a way as I did when faced with this nothingness, within this nothingness, surrounded by this nothingness. I was only amazed at their not noticing it, or not making their observations known, not referring more often to it, as usually happens when many people all at once discover the same fact.

At these times I used to throw myself onto my knees and pray, perhaps more through a habit formed in childhood than from a conscious will. But I did not use the words of the usual prayers, which seemed too long for my sudden mood. I used to throw myself onto my knees so violently that my legs hurt for some days afterwards and used to pray aloud in a voice filled with despair, saying, "Christ have mercy upon me," just these few words. It was not really a prayer but a magic formula which I thought might dispel my anguish and bring me back to reality. After having cried out impulsively in this way, with all my strength, I remained for some time with my face in my hands, utterly absorbed. At last I would become aware that my mind was a blank, that I was bored, that I was the same Adriana as ever, that I was in my own room. I touched my body half astonished at finding it whole, and getting up from my knees I slipped into bed. I felt very tired and ached all over, as if I had fallen down a rocky slope, and I went to sleep immediately.

These states of mind, however, had no influence on my daily life. I went on being the same Adriana, with the same character, who took men home for money, went about with Gisella and talked of unimportant things with my own mother and with everyone else. And I thought it was strange that I was so different alone from what I was in company, in my relationship with myself and with other people. But I did not flatter myself that I was the only one to have such violent and desperate feelings. I imagined everyone, at least once a day, must feel his own life reduced to a single point of absurd, ineffable anguish—only their knowledge apparently produced no visible effect upon them, either. They left their houses, as I did, and went about playing sincerely their insincere parts. This thought strengthened me in my belief that all men, without exception, deserve to be pitied, if only because they are alive.

FROM

The Lottery

1949

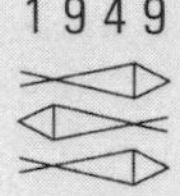

THE LOTTERY

The morning of June 27th was clear and sunny, with the fresh warmth of a full-summer day; the flowers were blossoming profusely and the grass was richly green. The people of the village began to gather in the square, between the post office and the bank, around ten o'clock; in some towns there were so many people that the lottery took two days and had to be started on June 26th, but in this village, where there were only about three hundred people, the whole lottery took less than two hours, so it could begin at ten o'clock in the morning and still be through in time to allow the villagers to get home for noon dinner.

The children assembled first, of course. School was recently over for the summer, and the feeling of liberty sat uneasily on most of them; they tended to gather together quietly for a while before they broke into boisterous play, and their talk was still of the classroom and the teacher, of books and reprimands. Bobby Martin had already stuffed his pockets full of stones, and the other boys soon followed his example, selecting the smoothest and roundest stones; Bobby and Harry Jones and Dickie Delacroix—the villagers pronounced this name "Dellacroy"—eventually made a great pile of stones in one corner of the square and guarded it against the raids of the other boys. The girls stood aside, talking among themselves, looking over their shoulders at the boys, and the very small children rolled in the dust or clung to the hands of their older brothers or sisters.

Soon the men began to gather, surveying their own children, speaking of planting and rain, tractors and taxes. They stood together, away from the pile of stones in the corner, and their jokes were quiet and they smiled rather than laughed. The women, wearing faded house dresses and sweaters, came shortly after their menfolk. They greeted one another and exchanged bits of gossip as they went to join their husbands. Soon the women, standing by their husbands, began to call to their children, and the children came reluctantly, having to be called four or five times. Bobby Martin ducked under his mother's grasping hand and ran, laughing, back to the pile of stones. His father spoke up sharply, and Bobby came quickly and took his place between his father and his oldest brother.

The lottery was conducted—as were the square dances, the teen-age club, the Halloween program—by Mr. Summers, who had time and energy to devote to civic activities. He was a round-faced, jovial man and he ran the coal business, and people were sorry for him, because he had no children and his wife was a scold. When he arrived in the square, carrying the black wooden box, there was a murmur of conversation among the villagers, and he waved and called, "Little late today, folks." The postmaster, Mr. Graves, followed him, carrying a three-legged stool, and the stool was put in the center of the square and Mr. Summers set the black box down on it. The villagers kept their distance, leaving a space between themselves and the stool, and when Mr. Summers said, "Some of you fellows want to give me a hand?" there was a hesitation before two men, Mr. Martin and his oldest son, Baxter, came forward to hold the box steady on the stool while Mr. Summers stirred up the papers inside it.

The original paraphernalia for the lottery had been lost long ago, and the black box now resting on the stool had been put into use even before Old Man Warner, the oldest man in town, was born. Mr. Summers spoke frequently to the villagers about making a new box, but no one liked to upset even as much tradition as was represented by the black box. There was a story that the present box had been made with some pieces of the box that had preceded it, the one that had been constructed when the first people settled down to make a village here. Every year, after the lottery, Mr. Summers began talking again about a new box, but every year the subject was allowed to fade off without anything's being done. The black box grew shabbier each year; by now it was no longer completely black but splintered badly along one side to show the original wood color, and in some places faded or stained.

Mr. Martin and his oldest son, Baxter, held the black box securely on the stool until Mr. Summers had stirred the papers thoroughly with his hand. Because so much of the ritual had been forgotten or discarded, Mr. Summers had been successful in having slips of paper substituted for the chips of wood that had been used for generations. Chips of wood, Mr. Summers had argued, had been all very well when the village was tiny, but now that the population was more than three hundred and likely to keep on growing, it was necessary to use something that would fit more easily into the black box. The night before the lottery, Mr. Summers and Mr. Graves made up the slips of paper and put them in the box, and it was then taken to the safe of Mr. Summers' coal company and locked up until Mr. Summers was ready to take it to the square next morning. The rest of the year, the box was put away, sometimes one place, sometimes another; it had spent one year in Mr. Graves's barn and another year underfoot in the post office, and sometimes it was set on a shelf in the Martin grocery and left there.

There was a great deal of fussing to be done before Mr. Summers declared the lottery open. There were the lists to make up—of heads of families, heads of households in each family, members of each household in each family. There was the proper swearing-in of Mr. Summers by the postmaster, as the official of the lottery; at one time, some people remembered, there had been a recital of some sort, performed by the official of the lottery, a perfunctory, tuneless chant that had been rattled off duly each year; some people believed that the official of the lottery used to stand just so when he said or sang it, others believed that he was supposed to walk among the people, but years and years ago this part of the ritual had been allowed to lapse. There had been, also, a ritual salute, which the official of the lottery had had to use in addressing each person who came up to draw from the box, but this also had changed with time, until now it was felt necessary only for the official to speak to each person approaching. Mr. Summers was very good at all this; in his clean white shirt and blue jeans, with one hand resting carelessly on the black box, he seemed very proper and important as he talked interminably to Mr. Graves and the Martins.

Just as Mr. Summers finally left off talking and turned to the assembled villagers, Mrs. Hutchinson came hurriedly along the path to the square, her sweater thrown over her shoulders, and slid into place in the back of the crowd. "Clean forgot what day it was," she said to Mrs. Delacroix, who stood next to her, and they both laughed softly. "Thought my old man was out back stacking wood," Mrs. Hutchinson went on, "and then I looked out the window and the kids was gone, and then I remembered it was the twenty-seventh and came a-running." She dried her hands on her apron, and Mrs. Delacroix said, "You're in time, though. They're still talking away up there."

Mrs. Hutchinson craned her neck to see through the crowd and found her husband and children standing near the front. She tapped Mrs. Delacroix on the arm as a farewell and began to make her way through the crowd. The people separated good-humoredly to let her through; two or three people said, in voices just loud enough to be heard across the crowd, "Here comes your Missus, Hutchinson," and "Bill, she made it after all." Mrs. Hutchinson reached her husband, and Mr. Summers, who had been waiting, said cheerfully, "Thought we were going to have to get on without you, Tessie." Mrs. Hutchinson said, grinning, "Wouldn't have me leave m'dishes in the sink, now, would you, Joe?" and soft laughter ran through the crowd as the people stirred back into position after Mrs. Hutchinson's arrival.

"Well, now," Mr. Summers said soberly, "guess we better get started, get this over with, so's we can go back to work. Anybody ain't here?"

"Dunbar," several people said. "Dunbar, Dunbar."

Mr. Summers consulted his list. "Clyde Dunbar," he said. "That's right. He's broke his leg, hasn't he? Who's drawing for him?"

"Me, I guess," a woman said, and Mr. Summers turned to look at her. "Wife draws for her husband," Mr. Summers said. "Don't you have a grown boy to do it for you, Janey?" Although Mr. Summers and everyone else in the village knew the answer perfectly well, it was the business of the official of the lottery to ask such questions formally. Mr. Summers waited with an expression of polite interest while Mrs. Dunbar answered.

"Horace's not but sixteen yet," Mrs. Dunbar said regretfully. "Guess I gotta fill in for the old man this year."

"Right," Mr. Summers said. He made a note on the list he was holding. Then he asked, "Watson boy drawing this year?"

A tall boy in the crowd raised his hand. "Here," he said. "I'm drawing for m'mother and me." He blinked his eyes nervously and ducked his head as several voices in the crowd said things like "Good fellow, Jack," and "Glad to see your mother's got a man to do it."

"Well," Mr. Summers said, "guess that's everyone. Old Man Warner make it?"

"Here," a voice said, and Mr. Summers nodded.

•

A sudden hush fell on the crowd as Mr. Summers cleared his throat and looked at the list. "All ready?" he called. "Now, I'll read the names—heads of families first—and the men come up and take a paper out of the box. Keep the paper folded in your hand without looking at it until everyone has had a turn. Everything clear?"

The people had done it so many times that they only half listened to the directions; most of them were quiet, wetting their lips, not looking around. Then Mr. Summers raised one hand high and said, "Adams." A man disengaged himself from the crowd and came forward. "Hi, Steve," Mr. Summers said, and Mr. Adams said, "Hi, Joe." They grinned at one another humorlessly and nervously. Then Mr. Adams reached into the black box and took out a folded paper. He held it firmly by one corner as he turned and went hastily back to his place in the crowd, where he stood a little apart from his family, not looking down at his hand.

"Allen," Mr. Summers said. "Anderson. . . . Bentham."

"Seems like there's no time at all between lotteries any more," Mrs. Delacroix said to Mrs. Graves in the back row. "Seems like we got through with the last one only last week."

"Time sure goes fast," Mrs. Graves said.

"Clark. . . . Delacroix."

"There goes my old man," Mrs. Delacroix said. She held her breath while her husband went forward.

"Dunbar," Mr. Summers said, and Mrs. Dunbar went steadily to the box while one of the women said, "Go on, Janey," and another said, "There she goes."

"We're next," Mrs. Graves said. She watched while Mr. Graves came around from the side of the box, greeted Mr. Summers gravely, and selected a slip of paper from the box. By now, all through the crowd there were men holding the small folded papers in their large hands, turning them over and over nervously. Mrs. Dunbar and her two sons stood together, Mrs. Dunbar holding the slip of paper.

"Harburt. . . . Hutchinson."

"Get up there, Bill," Mrs. Hutchinson said, and the people near her laughed.

"Jones."

"They do say," Mr. Adams said to Old Man Warner, who stood next to him, "that over in the north village they're talking of giving up the lottery."

Old Man Warner snorted. "Pack of crazy fools," he said. "Listening to the young folks, nothing's good enough for *them*. Next thing you know, they'll be wanting to go back to living in caves, nobody work any more, live *that* way for a while. Used to be a saying about 'Lottery in June, corn be heavy soon.' First thing you know, we'd all be eating stewed chickweed and acorns. There's *always* been a lottery," he added petulantly. "Bad enough to see young Joe Summers up there joking with everybody."

"Some places have already quit lotteries," Mrs. Adams said.

"Nothing but trouble in *that*," Old Man Warner said stoutly. "Pack of young fools."

"Martin." And Bobby Martin watched his father go forward. "Overdyke. . . . Percy."

"I wish they'd hurry," Mrs. Dunbar said to her older son. "I wish they'd hurry."

"They're almost through," her son said.

"You get ready to run tell Dad," Mrs. Dunbar said.

Mr. Summers called his own name and then stepped forward precisely and selected a slip from the box. Then he called, "Warner."

"Seventy-seventh year I been in the lottery," Old Man Warner said as he went through the crowd. "Seventy-seventh time."

"Watson." The tall boy came awkwardly through the crowd. Someone said, "Don't be nervous, Jack," and Mr. Summers said, "Take your time, son."

"Zanini."

•

After that, there was a long pause, a breathless pause, until Mr. Summers, holding his slip of paper in the air, said, "All right, fellows." For a minute, no one moved, and then all the slips of paper were opened. Suddenly, all the women began to speak at once, saying, "Who is it?," "Who's got it?," "Is it the Dunbars?," "Is it the Watsons?" Then the voices began to say, "It's Hutchinson. It's Bill," "Bill Hutchinson's got it."

"Go tell your father," Mrs. Dunbar said to her older son.

People began to look around to see the Hutchinsons. Bill Hutchinson was standing quiet, staring down at the paper in his hand. Suddenly, Tessie Hutchinson shouted to Mr. Summers, "You didn't give him time enough to take any paper he wanted. I saw you. It wasn't fair!"

"Be a good sport, Tessie," Mrs. Delacroix called, and Mrs. Graves said, "All of us took the same chance."

"Shut up, Tessie," Bill Hutchinson said.

"Well, everyone," Mr. Summers said, "that was done pretty fast, and now we've got to be hurrying a little more to get done in time." He consulted his next list. "Bill," he said, "you draw for the Hutchinson family. You got any other households in the Hutchinsons?"

"There's Don and Eva," Mrs. Hutchinson yelled. "Make *them* take their chance!"

"Daughters draw with their husbands' families, Tessie," Mr. Summers said gently. "You know that as well as anyone else."

"It wasn't *fair*," Tessie said.

"I guess not, Joe," Bill Hutchinson said regretfully. "My daughter draws with her husband's family, that's only fair. And I've got no other family except the kids."

"Then, as far as drawing for families is concerned, it's you," Mr. Summers said in explanation, "and as far as drawing for households is concerned, that's you, too. Right?"

"Right," Bill Hutchinson said.

"How many kids, Bill?" Mr. Summers asked formally.

"Three," Bill Hutchinson said. "There's Bill, Jr., and Nancy, and little Dave. And Tessie and me."

"All right, then," Mr. Summers said. "Harry, you got their tickets back?"

Mr. Graves nodded and held up the slips of paper. "Put them in the box, then," Mr. Summers directed. "Take Bill's and put it in."

"I think we ought to start over," Mrs. Hutchinson said, as quietly as she could. "I tell you it wasn't *fair*. You didn't give him time enough to choose. *Every*body saw that."

Mr. Graves had selected the five slips and put them in the box, and he dropped all the papers but those onto the ground, where the breeze caught them and lifted them off.

"Listen, everybody," Mrs. Hutchinson was saying to the people around her.

"Ready, Bill?" Mr. Summers asked, and Bill Hutchinson, with one quick glance around at his wife and children, nodded.

"Remember," Mr. Summers said, "take the slips and keep them folded until each person has taken one. Harry, you help little Dave." Mr. Graves took the hand of the little boy, who came willingly with him up to the box. "Take a paper out of the box, Davy," Mr. Summers said. Davy put his hand into the box and laughed. "Take just *one* paper," Mr. Summers said. "Harry, you hold it for him." Mr. Graves took the child's hand and removed the folded paper from the tight fist and held it while little Dave stood next to him and looked up at him wonderingly.

"Nancy next," Mr. Summers said. Nancy was twelve, and her school friends breathed heavily as she went forward, switching her skirt, and took a slip daintily from the box. "Bill, Jr.," Mr. Summers said, and Billy, his face red and his feet over-large, nearly knocked the box over as he got a paper out. "Tessie," Mr. Summers said. She hesitated for a minute, looking around defiantly, and then set her lips and went up to the box. She snatched a paper out and held it behind her.

"Bill," Mr. Summers said, and Bill Hutchinson reached into the box and felt around, bringing his hand out at last with the slip of paper in it.

The crowd was quiet. A girl whispered, "I hope it's not Nancy," and the sound of the whisper reached the edges of the crowd.

"It's not the way it used to be," Old Man Warner said clearly. "People ain't the way they used to be."

"All right," Mr. Summers said. "Open the papers. Harry, you open little Dave's."

Mr. Graves opened the slip of paper and there was a general sigh through the crowd as he held it up and everyone could see that it was blank. Nancy and Bill, Jr., opened theirs at the same time, and both beamed and laughed, turning around to the crowd and holding their slips of paper above their heads.

"Tessie," Mr. Summers said. There was a pause, and then Mr. Summers looked at Bill Hutchinson, and Bill unfolded his paper and showed it. It was blank.

"It's Tessie," Mr. Summers said, and his voice was hushed. "Show us her paper, Bill."

Bill Hutchinson went over to his wife and forced the slip of paper out of her hand. It had a black spot on it, the black spot Mr. Summers had made the night before with the heavy pencil in the coal-company office. Bill Hutchinson held it up, and there was a stir in the crowd.

"All right, folks," Mr. Summers said. "Let's finish quickly."

Although the villagers had forgotten the ritual and lost the original black box, they still remembered to use stones. The pile of stones the boys had made earlier was ready; there were stones on the ground with the blowing scraps of paper that had come out of the box. Mrs. Delacroix selected a stone so large she had to pick it up with both hands and turned to Mrs. Dunbar. "Come on," she said. "Hurry up."

Mrs. Dunbar had small stones in both hands, and she said, gasping for breath, "I can't run at all. You'll have to go ahead and I'll catch up with you."

The children had stones already, and someone gave little Davy Hutchinson a few pebbles.

Tessie Hutchinson was in the center of a cleared space by now, and she held her hands out desperately as the villagers moved in on her. "It isn't fair," she said. A stone hit her on the side of the head.

Old Man Warner was saying, "Come on, come on, everyone." Steve Adams was in the front of the crowd of villagers, with Mrs. Graves beside him.

"It isn't fair, it isn't right," Mrs. Hutchinson screamed, and then they were upon her.

FROM

The Little World of Don Camillo

[*Translated by Una Vincenzo Troubridge*]

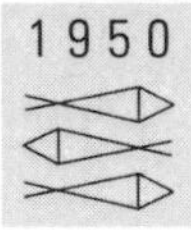

THE LITTLE WORLD

The little world of Don Camillo is to be found somewhere in the valley of the Po River. It is almost any village on that stretch of plain in Northern Italy. There, between the Po and the Apennines, the climate is always the same. The landscape never changes and, in country like this, you can stop along any road for a moment and look at a farmhouse sitting in the midst of maize and hemp—and immediately a story is born.

Why do I tell you this instead of getting on with my story? Because I want you to understand that, in the Little World between the river and the mountains, many things can happen that cannot happen anywhere else. Here, the deep, eternal breathing of the river freshens the air, for both the living and the dead, and even the dogs, have souls. If you keep this in mind, you will easily come to know the village priest, Don Camillo, and his adversary Peppone, the Communist Mayor. You will not be surprised that Christ watches the goings-on from a big cross in the village church and not infrequently talks, and that one man beats the other over the head, but fairly—that is, without hatred—and that in the end the two enemies find they agree about essentials.

And one final word of explanation before I begin my story. If there is a priest anywhere who feels offended by my treatment of Don Camillo, he is welcome to break the biggest candle available over my head. And if there is a Communist who feels offended by Peppone, he is welcome to break a hammer and sickle on my back. But if there is anyone who is offended by the conversations of Christ, I can't help it; for the one who speaks in this story is not Christ but my Christ—that is, the voice of my conscience.

A CONFESSION

Don Camillo had come into the world with a constitutional preference for calling a spade a spade. His parishioners remembered the time he found out about a local scandal involving young girls of the village with some landowners well along in years. On the Sunday following his discovery, Don Camillo had begun a simple, rather mild sermon, when he spotted one of the offenders in the front pew. Taking just enough time out to throw a cloth over the crucifix at the main altar so that Christ might not hear what was going to follow, he turned on the congregation with clenched fists and finished the sermon in a voice so loud and with words so strong that the roof of the little church trembled.

Naturally, when the time of the elections drew near, Don Camillo was very explicit in his allusions to the local leftists. What happened was not surprising, therefore: one fine evening as the priest was on his way home, a fellow muffled in a cloak sprang out of a hedge and, taking advantage of the fact that Don Camillo was handicapped by a bicycle with a basket of eggs on the handlebars, dealt the priest a mean blow with a heavy stick and then disappeared, as if the earth had swallowed him.

Don Camillo kept his own counsel. He continued to the rectory and, after putting the eggs in a safe place, went into the church to talk things over with Christ, as he always did in moments of perplexity.

"What should I do?" asked Don Camillo.

"Anoint your back with a little oil beaten up in water and hold your tongue," Christ answered from the main altar. "We must forgive those who offend us."

"Very true, Lord, but here we are discussing blows, not offenses."

"And what do you mean by that? Surely, Don Camillo, you don't mean that the injuries done to the body are more painful than those to the soul?"

"I see your point, Lord. But You should bear in mind that an attack on me, Your priest, is also an offense against You. I am really more concerned for You than for myself."

"And wasn't I a greater minister of God than you are? And didn't I forgive those who nailed me to the Cross?"

"There's no use arguing with You!" Don Camillo exclaimed. "You are always right. May Your will be done. I will forgive, but don't forget that if these ruffians, encouraged by my silence, crack my skull open, it will be Your responsibility. I could quote You several passages from the Old Testament . . ."

"Don Camillo, do you propose to teach me the Old Testament! As for this business, I assume full responsibility. And just between ourselves, that little beating this evening did you some good. It may teach you to let politics alone in My house."

Don Camillo forgave in his heart, but one thing stuck in his mind and needled him—curiosity as to the identity of his assailant.

Time passed. Then, late one evening as he was sitting in the confessional, Don Camillo recognized through the grille the face of Peppone, the leader of the extreme left.

That Peppone should come to confession at all was a sensational event, and Don Camillo was duly gratified.

"God be with you, brother; with you who, more than others, needs His Holy blessing. When did you make your last confession?"

"In 1918," replied Peppone.

"In all those years you must have committed a lot of sins with your head so crammed with crazy ideas . . ."

"Quite a few, I'm afraid," sighed Peppone.

"For example?"

"For example, two months ago I gave you a beating."

"That is very serious," replied Don Camillo, "since, by assaulting one of God's priests, you have offended God Himself."

"Oh, but I have repented," Peppone exclaimed. "And anyway it was not as God's priest that I beat you up but as my political adversary. Anyhow I did it in a moment of weakness."

"Besides this and your activities in that devilish party, have you any other sins to confess?"

Peppone spilled them out, but all in all Don Camillo found nothing very serious and let him off with twenty Our Fathers and twenty Hail Marys. While Peppone was at the altar rail saying his penance, Don Camillo went and knelt before the crucifix.

"Lord," he said, "forgive me but I'm going to beat him up for You."

"You'll do nothing of the kind," replied Christ. "I have forgiven him and you must do the same. After all, he's not such a bad soul."

"Lord, you can't trust a red! They live by lies. Just look at that face—Barabbas incarnate!"

"One face is the same as another. It's your heart, Don Camillo, that is venomous!"

"Lord, if I have been a worthy servant to You, grant me one small favor. Let me at least hit him with this candle. After all, Lord, what is a candle?"

"No," replied Christ. "Your hands were made for blessing."

Don Camillo sighed wearily. He genuflected and left the altar. As he turned to make a final sign of the cross, he found himself exactly behind Peppone, who still knelt at the altar rail and appeared absorbed in prayer.

"Lord," groaned Don Camillo, clasping his hands and looking up at the crucifix, "my hands were made for blessing, but not my feet."

"There's something in that," replied Christ, "but, I warn you, just one."

The kick landed like a thunderbolt. Peppone didn't bat an eye. After a minute he got up and sighed.

"I've been expecting that for the past ten minutes," he remarked casually. "I feel better now."

"So do I," exclaimed Don Camillo whose heart was now as light and serene as a May morning.

Christ said nothing at all, but it was easy enough to see that He too was pleased.

ABRAHAM JOSHUA HESCHEL

FROM

The Sabbath

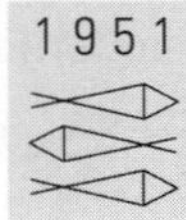

ARCHITECTURE OF TIME

Technical civilization is man's conquest of space. It is a triumph frequently achieved by sacrificing an essential ingredient of existence, namely, time. In technical civilization, we expend time to gain space. To enhance our power in the world of space is our main objective. Yet to have more does not mean to be more. The power we attain in the world of space terminates abruptly at the borderline of time. But time is the heart of existence.

To gain control of the world of space is certainly one of our tasks. The danger begins when in gaining power in the realm of space we forfeit all aspirations in the realm of time. There is a realm of time where the goal is not to have but to be, not to own but to give, not to control but to share, not to subdue but to be in accord. Life goes wrong when the control of space, the acquisition of things of space, becomes our sole concern.

Nothing is more useful than power, nothing more frightful. We have often suffered from degradation by poverty, now we are threatened with degradation through power. There is happiness in the love of labor, there is misery in the love of gain. Many hearts and pitchers are broken at the fountain of profit. Selling himself into slavery to things, man becomes a utensil that is broken at the fountain.

Technical civilization stems primarily from the desire of man to subdue and manage the forces of nature. The manufacture of tools, the art of spinning and farming, the building of houses, the craft of sailing—all this goes on in man's spatial surroundings. The mind's preoccupation with things of space affects, to this day, all activities of man. Even religions are frequently dominated by the notion that the deity resides in space, within particular localities like mountains, forests, trees or stones, which are, therefore, singled out as holy places; the deity is bound to a particular land; holiness a quality associated with things of space, and the primary question is: Where is the god? There is much enthusiasm for the idea that God is present in the universe, but that idea is taken to mean His presence in space rather than in time, in nature rather than in history; as if He were a thing, not a spirit.

Even pantheistic philosophy is a religion of space: the Supreme Being is thought to be the infinite space. *Deus sine natura* has extension, or space, as its attribute, not time; time to Spinoza is merely an accident of motion, a mode of thinking. And his desire to develop a philosophy *more geometrico*, in the manner of geometry, which is the science of space, is significant of his space-mindedness.

The primitive mind finds it hard to realize an idea without the aid of imagination, and it is the realm of space where imagination wields its sway. Of the gods it must have a visible image; where there is no image, there is no god. The reverence for the sacred image, for the sacred monument or place, is not only indigenous to most religions, it has even been retained by men of all ages, all nations, pious, superstitious or even antireligious; they all continue to pay homage to banners and flags, to national shrines, to monuments erected to kings or heroes. Everywhere the desecration of holy shrines is considered a sacrilege, and the shrine may become so important that the idea it stands for is consigned to oblivion. The memorial becomes an aid to amnesia; the means stultify the end. For things of space are at the mercy of man. Though too sacred to be polluted, they are not too sacred to be exploited. To retain the holy, to perpetuate the presence of god, his image is fashioned. Yet a god who can be fashioned, a god who can be confined, is but a shadow of man.

We are all infatuated with the splendor of space, with the grandeur of things of space. Thing is a category that lies heavy on our minds, tyrannizing all our thoughts. Our imagination tends to mold all concepts in its image. In our daily lives we attend primarily to that which the senses are spelling out for us: to what the eyes perceive, to what the fingers touch. Reality to us is thinghood, consisting of substances that occupy space; even God is conceived by most of us as a thing.

The result of our thingness is our blindness to all reality that fails to identify itself as a thing, as a matter of fact. This is obvious in our understanding of time, which, being thingless and insubstantial, appears to us as if it had no reality.

Indeed, we know what to do with space but do not know what to do about time, except to make it subservient to space. Most of us seem to labor for the sake of things of space. As a result we suffer from a deeply rooted dread of time and stand aghast when compelled to look into its face. Time to us is sarcasm, a slick treacherous monster with a jaw like a furnace incinerating every moment of our lives. Shrinking, therefore, from facing time, we escape for shelter to things of space. The intentions we are unable to carry out we deposit in space; possessions become the symbols of our repressions, jubilees of frustrations. But things of space are not fireproof; they only add fuel to the flames. Is the joy of possession an antidote to the terror of time which grows to be a dread of inevitable death? Things, when magnified, are forgeries of happiness, they are a threat to our very lives; we are more harassed than supported by the Frankensteins of spatial things.

It is impossible for man to shirk the problem of time. The more we think the more we realize: we cannot conquer time through space. We can only master time in time.

The higher goal of spiritual living is not to amass a wealth of information, but to face sacred moments. In a religious experience, for example, it is not a thing that imposes itself on man but a spiritual presence. What is retained in the soul is the moment of insight rather than the place where the act came to pass. A moment of insight is a fortune, transporting us beyond the confines of measured time. Spiritual life begins to decay when we fail to sense the grandeur of what is eternal in time.

Our intention here is not to deprecate the world of space. To disparage space, and the blessing of things of space, is to disparage the works of creation, the works which God beheld and saw "it was good." The world cannot be seen exclusively *sub specie temporis*. Time and space are interrelated. To overlook either of them is to be partially blind. What we plead against is man's unconditional surrender to space, his enslavement to things. We must not forget that it is not a thing that lends significance to a moment; it is the moment that lends significance to things.

•

The Bible is more concerned with time than with space. It sees the world in the dimension of time. It pays more attention to generations, to events, than to countries, to things; it is more concerned with history than with geography. To understand the teaching of the Bible, one must accept its premise that time has a meaning for life which is at least equal to that of space; that time has a significance and sovereignty of its own.

There is no equivalent for the word "thing" in biblical Hebrew. The word "*davar*," which in later Hebrew came to denote thing, means in biblical Hebrew: speech; word; message; report; tidings; advice; request; promise; decision; sentence; theme, story; saying, utterance; business, occupation; acts; good deeds; events; way, manner, reason, cause; but never "thing." Is this a sign of linguistic poverty, or rather an indication of an unwarped view of the world, of not equating reality (derived from the Latin word *res*, thing) with thinghood?

One of the most important facts in the history of religion was the transformation of agricultural festivals into commemorations of historical events. The festivals of ancient peoples were intimately linked with nature's seasons. They celebrated what happened in the life of nature in the respective seasons. Thus the value of the festive day was determined by the things nature did or did not bring forth. In Judaism, Passover, originally a spring festival, became a celebration of the exodus from Egypt; the Feast of Weeks, an old harvest festival at the end of the wheat harvest (*hag hakazir*, Exodus 23:16; 34:22), became the celebration of the day on which the Torah was given at Sinai; the Feast of the Booths, an old festival of vintage (*hag haasif*, Ex. 23:16), commemorates the dwelling of the Israelites in booths during their sojourn in the wilderness (Leviticus 23:42f.). To Israel the unique events of historic time were spiritually more significant than the repetitive processes in the cycle of nature, even though physical sustenance depended on the latter. While the deities of other peoples were associated with places or things, the God of Israel was the God of events: the Redeemer from slavery, the Revealer of the Torah, manifesting Himself in events of history rather than in things or places. Thus, the faith in the unembodied, in the unimaginable was born.

•

Judaism is a *religion of time* aiming at *the sanctification of time*. Unlike the space-minded man to whom time is unvaried, iterative, homogeneous, to whom all hours are alike, qualityless, empty shells, the Bible senses the diversified character of time. There are no two hours alike. Every hour is unique and the only one given at the moment, exclusive and endlessly precious.

Judaism teaches us to be attached to *holiness in time*, to be attached to sacred events, to learn how to consecrate sanctuaries that emerge from the magnificent stream of a year. The Sabbaths are our great cathedrals; and our Holy of Holies is a shrine that neither the Romans nor the Germans were able to burn; a shrine that even apostasy cannot easily obliterate: the Day of Atonement. According to the ancient rabbis, it is not the observance of the Day of Atonement, but the Day itself, the "essence of the Day," which, with man's repentance, atones for the sins of man.

Jewish ritual may be characterized as the art of significant forms in time, as *architecture of time*. Most of its observances—the Sabbath, the New Moon, the festivals, the Sabbatical and the Jubilee year—depend on a certain hour of the day or season of the year. It is, for example, the evening, morning, or afternoon that brings with it the call to prayer. The main themes of faith lie in the realm of time. We remember the day of the exodus from Egypt, the day when Israel stood at Sinai; and our Messianic hope is the expectation of a day, of the end of days.

In a well-composed work of art an idea of outstanding importance is not introduced haphazardly, but, like a king at an official ceremony, it is presented at a moment and in a way that will bring to light its authority and leadership. In the Bible, words are employed with exquisite care, particularly those which, like pillars of fire, lead the way in the far-flung system of the biblical world of meaning.

One of the most distinguished words in the Bible is the word *qadosh*, holy; a word which more than any other is representative of the mystery and majesty of the divine. Now what was the first holy object in the history of the world? Was it a mountain? Was it an altar?

It is, indeed, a unique occasion at which the distinguished word *qadosh* is used for the first time: in the Book of Genesis at the end of the story of creation. How extremely significant is the fact that it is applied to time: "And God blessed the seventh *day* and made it *holy*." There is no reference in the record of creation to any object in space that would be endowed with the quality of holiness.

This is a radical departure from accustomed religious thinking. The mythical mind would expect that, after heaven and earth have been established, God would create a holy place—a holy mountain or a holy spring—whereupon a sanctuary is to be established. Yet it seems as if to the Bible it is *holiness in time*, the Sabbath, which comes first.

When history began, there was only one holiness in the world, holiness in time. When at Sinai the word of God was about to be voiced, a call for holiness in *man* was proclaimed: "Thou shalt be unto me a holy people." It was only after the people had succumbed to the temptation of worshipping a thing, a golden calf, that the erection of a Tabernacle, of holiness in *space*, was commanded. The sanctity of time came first, the sanctity of man came second, and the sanctity of space last. Time was hallowed by God; space, the Tabernacle, was consecrated by Moses.

While the festivals celebrate events that happened in time, the date of the month assigned for each festival in the calendar is determined by the life in nature. Passover and the Feast of Booths, for example, coincide with the full moon, and the date of all festivals is a day in the month, and the month is a reflection of what goes on periodically in the realm of nature, since the Jewish month begins with the new moon, with the reappearance of the lunar crescent in the evening sky. In contrast, the Sabbath is entirely independent of the month and unrelated to the moon. Its date is not determined by any event in nature, such as the new moon, but by the act of creation. Thus the essence of the Sabbath is completely detached from the world of space.

The meaning of the Sabbath is to celebrate time rather than space. Six days a week we live under the tyranny of things of space; on the Sabbath we try to become attuned to *holiness in time*. It is a day on which we are called upon to share in what is eternal in time, to turn from the results of creation to the mystery of creation; from the world of creation to the creation of the world.

TO SANCTIFY TIME

Pagans project their consciousness of God into a visible image or associate Him with a phenomenon in nature, with a thing of space. In the Ten Commandments, the Creator of the universe identifies Himself by an event in history, by an event in time, the liberation of the people from Egypt, and proclaims: "Thou shalt not make unto thee any graven image or any likeness of any thing that is in heaven above, or that is in the earth, or that is in the water under the earth."

The most precious thing that has ever been on earth were the Two Tablets of stone which Moses received upon Mount Sinai; they were priceless beyond compare. He had gone up into the Mount to receive them; there he abode forty days and forty nights; he did neither eat bread nor drink water. And the Lord delivered unto him the Two Tablets of stone, and on them were written the Ten Commandments, the words which the Lord spoke with the people of Israel in the Mount out of the midst of fire. But when coming down the Mount at the end of forty days and forty nights—the Two Tablets in his hands—Moses saw the people dance around the Golden Calf, he cast the Tablets out of his hands and broke them before their eyes.

"Every important cult-center of Egypt asserted its primacy by the dogma that it was the *site* of creation." In contrast, the Book of Genesis speaks of the days rather than of the site of creation. In the myths there is no reference to the time of creation, whereas the Bible speaks of the creation of space in time.

Everyone will admit that the Grand Canyon is more awe-inspiring than a trench. Everyone knows the difference between a worm and an eagle. But how many of us have a similar sense of discretion for the diversity of time? The historian Ranke claimed that every age is equally near to God. Yet Jewish tradition claims that there is a hierarchy of moments within time, that all ages are not alike. Man may pray to God equally at all places, but God does not speak to man equally at all times. At a certain moment, for example, the spirit of prophecy departed from Israel.

•

Time to us is a measuring device rather than a realm in which we abide. Our consciousness of it comes about when we begin to compare two events and to notice that one event is later than the other; when listening to a tune we realize that one note follows the other. Fundamental to the consciousness of time is the distinction between earlier and later.

But is time only a relation between events in time? Is there no meaning to the present moment, regardless of its relation to the past? Moreover, do we only know what is *in* time, merely events that have an impact on things of space? If nothing happened that is related to the world of space, would there be no time?

A special consciousness is required to recognize the ultimate significance of time. We all live it and are so close to being identical with it that we fail to notice it. The world of space surrounds our existence. It is but a part of living, the rest is time. Things are the shore, the voyage is in time.

Existence is never explicable through itself but only through time. When closing our eyes in moments of intellectual concentration, we are able to have time without space, but we can never have space without time. To the spiritual eye space is frozen time, and all things are petrified events.

There are two points of view from which time can be sensed: from the point of view of space and from the point of view of spirit. Looking out of the window of a swiftly moving railroad car, we have the impression that the landscape is moving while we ourselves are sitting still. Similarly, when gazing at reality while our souls are carried away by spatial things, time appears to be in constant motion. However, when we learn to understand that it is the spatial things that are constantly running out, we realize that time is that which never expires, that it is the world of space which is rolling through the infinite expanse of time. Thus temporality may be defined as the relation of space to time.

The boundless continuous but vacuous entity which realistically is called space is not the ultimate form of reality. Our world is a world of space moving through time—from the Beginning to the End of Days.

To the common mind the essence of time is evanescence, temporality. The truth, however, is that the fact of evanescence flashes upon our minds when poring over things of space. It is the world of space that communicates to us the sense for temporality. Time, that which is beyond and independent of space, is everlasting; it is the world of space which is perishing. Things perish within time; time itself does not change. We should not speak of the flow or passage of time but of the flow or passage of space through time. It is not time that dies; it is the human body which dies in time. Temporality is an attribute of the world of space, of things of space. Time which is beyond space is beyond the division in past, present and future.

Monuments of stone are destined to disappear; days of spirit never pass away. About the arrival of the people at Sinai we read in the Book of Exodus: "In the third month after the children of Israel were gone forth out of the land of Egypt, on *this day* they came into the wilderness of Sinai" (19:1). Here was an expression that puzzled the ancient rabbis: on *this day*? It should have been said: on *that day*. This can only mean that the day of giving the Torah can never become past; that day is this day, every day. The Torah, whenever we study it, must be to us "as if it were given us today." The same applies to the day of the exodus from Egypt: "In every age man must see himself as if he himself went out of Egypt."

The worth of a great day is not measured by the space it occupies in the calendar. Exclaimed Rabbi Akiba: "All of time is not as worthy as the day on which the Song of Songs was given to Israel, for all the songs are holy, but the Song of Songs is the holiest of holies."

In the realm of spirit, there is no difference between a second and a century, between an hour and an age. Rabbi Judah the Patriarch cried: "There are those who gain eternity in a lifetime, others who gain it in one brief hour." One good hour may be worth a lifetime; an instant of returning to God may restore what has been lost in years of escaping from Him. "Better is one hour of repentance and good deeds in this world than the whole life in the world to come."

•

Technical civilization, we have said, is man's triumph over space. Yet time remains impervious. We can overcome distance but can neither recapture the past nor dig out the future. Man transcends space, and time transcends man.

Time is man's greatest challenge. We all take part in a procession through its realm which never comes to an end but are unable to gain a foothold in it. Its reality is apart and away from us. Space is exposed to our will; we may shape and change the things in space as we please. Time, however, is beyond our reach, beyond our power. It is both near and far, intrinsic to all experience and transcending all experience. It belongs exclusively to God.

Time, then, is *otherness*, a mystery that hovers above all categories.

It is as if time and the mind were a world apart. Yet, it is only within time that there is fellowship and *togetherness* of all beings.

Every one of us occupies a portion of space. He takes it up exclusively. The portion of space which my body occupies is taken up by myself in exclusion of anyone else. Yet, no one possesses time. There is no moment which I possess exclusively. This very moment belongs to all living men as it belongs to me. We share time, we own space. Through my ownership of space, I am a rival of all other beings; through my living in time, I am a contemporary of all other beings. We pass through time, we occupy space. We easily succumb to the illusion that the world of space is for our sake, for man's sake. In regard to time, we are immune to such an illusion.

Immense is the distance that lies between God and a thing. For a thing is that which has separate or individual existence as distinct from the totality of beings. To see a thing is to see something which is detached and isolated. A thing is, furthermore, something which is and can become the possession of man. Time does not permit an instant to be in and for itself. Time is either all or nothing. It cannot be divided except in our minds. It remains beyond our grasp. It is almost holy.

It is easy to pass by the great sight of eternal time. According to the Book of Exodus, Moses beheld his first vision "in a flame of fire, out of the midst of a bush: and he looked, and, behold, the bush burned with fire, and the bush was not consumed" (3:2). Time is like an eternal burning bush. Though each instant must vanish to open the way to the next one, time itself is not consumed.

Time has independent ultimate significance; it is of more majesty and more provocative of awe than even a sky studded with stars. Gliding gently in the most ancient of all splendors, it tells so much more than space can say in its broken language of things, playing symphonies upon the instruments of isolated beings, unlocking the earth and making it happen.

Time is the process of creation, and things of space are results of creation. When looking at space we see the products of creation; when intuiting time we hear the process of creation. Things of space exhibit a deceptive independence. They show off a veneer of limited permanence. Things created conceal the Creator. It is the dimension of time wherein man meets God, wherein man becomes aware that every instant is an act of creation, a Beginning, opening up new roads for ultimate realizations. Time is the presence of God in the world of space, and it is within time that we are able to sense the unity of all beings.

•

Creation, we are taught, is not an act that happened once upon a time, once and for ever. The act of bringing the world into existence is a continuous process. God called the world into being, and that call goes on. There is this present moment because God is present. Every instant is an act of creation. A moment is not a terminal but a flash, a signal of Beginning. Time is perpetual innovation, a synonym for continuous creation. Time is God's gift to the world of space.

A world without time would be a world without God, a world existing in and by itself, without renewal, without a Creator. A world without time would be a world detached from God, a thing in itself, reality without realization. A world in time is a world going on through God; realization of an infinite design; not a thing in itself but a thing for God.

To witness the perpetual marvel of the world's coming into being is to sense the presence of the Giver in the given, to realize that the source of time is eternity, that the secret of being is the eternal within time.

We cannot solve the problem of time through the conquest of space, through either pyramids or fame. We can only solve the problem of time through sanctification of time. To men alone time is elusive; to men with God time is eternity in disguise.

Creation is the language of God, Time is His song, and things of space the consonants in the song. To sanctify time is to sing the vowels in unison with Him.

This is the task of men: to conquer space and sanctify time.

We must conquer space in order to sanctify time. All week long we are called upon to sanctify life through employing things of space. On the Sabbath it is given us to share in the holiness that is in the heart of time. Even when the soul is seared, even when no prayer can come out of our tightened throats, the clean, silent rest of the Sabbath leads us to a realm of endless peace, or to the beginning of an awareness of what eternity means. There are few ideas in the world of thought which contain so much spiritual power as the idea of the Sabbath. Aeons hence, when of many of our cherished theories only shreds will remain, that cosmic tapestry will continue to shine.

Eternity utters a day.

MARGUERITE YOURCENAR

FROM

Memoirs of Hadrian

[*Translated by Grace Frick*]

1954

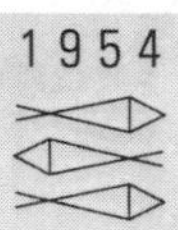

Rome is no longer confined to Rome: henceforth she must identify herself with half the globe, or must perish. Our homes and terraced roofs of tile, turned by the setting sun to rose and gold, are no longer enclosed, as in the time of our kings, within city walls. Our true ramparts now are thousands of leagues from Rome. I have constructed a good part of these defenses myself along the edges of Germanic forest and British moor. Each time that I have looked from afar, at the bend of some sunny road, toward a Greek acropolis with its perfect city fixed to the hill like a flower to its stem, I could not but feel that the incomparable plant was limited by its very perfection, achieved on one point of space and in one segment of time. Its sole chance of expansion, as for that of a plant, was in its seed; with the pollen of its ideas Greece has fertilized the world. But Rome, less light and less shapely, sprawling to the plain at her river's edge, was moving toward vaster growth: the city has become the State. I should have wished the State to expand still more, likening itself to the order of the universe, to the divine nature of things. Virtues which had sufficed for the small city of the Seven Hills would have to grow less rigid and more varied if they were to meet the needs of all the earth. Rome, which I was first to venture to call "eternal", would come to be more and more like the mother deities of the cults of Asia, bearer of youths and of harvests, sheltering at her breast both the lions and the hives of bees.

But anything made by man which aspires to eternity must adapt itself to the changing rhythm of nature's great bodies, to accord with celestial time. Our Rome is no longer the village of the days of Evander, big with a future which has already partly passed by; the plundering Rome of the time of the Republic has performed its role; the mad capital of the first Caesars inclines now to greater sobriety; other Romes will come, whose forms I see but dimly, but whom I shall have helped to mold. When I was visiting ancient cities, sacred but wholly dead, and without present value for the human race, I promised myself to save this Rome of mine from the petrification of a Thebes, a Babylon, or a Tyre. She would no longer be bound by her body of stone, but would compose for herself from the words *State, citizenry*, and *republic* a surer immortality. In the countries as yet untouched by our culture, on the banks of the Rhine and the Danube, or the shores of the Batavian Sea, each village enclosed within its wooden palisade brought to mind the reed hut and dunghill where our Roman twins had slept content, fed by the milk of the wolf; these cities-to-be would follow the pattern of Rome. Over separate nations and races, with their accidents of geography and history and the disparate demands of their ancestors or their gods, we should have superposed for ever a unity of human conduct and the empiricism of sober experience, but should have done so without destruction of what had preceded us. Rome would be perpetuating herself in the least of the towns where magistrates strive to demand just weight from the merchants, to clean and light the streets, to combat disorder, slackness, superstition and injustice, and to give broader and fairer interpretation to the laws. She would endure to the end of the last city built by man.

Humanitas, Libertas, Felicitas: those noble words which grace the coins of my reign were not of my invention. Any Greek philosopher, almost every cultured Roman, conceives of the world as I do. I have heard Trajan exclaim, when confronted by a law which was unjust because too rigorous, that to continue its enforcement was to run counter to the spirit of the times. I shall have been the first, perhaps, to subordinate all my actions to this "spirit of the times", to make of it something other than the inflated dream of a philosopher, or the slightly vague aspirings of some good prince. And I was thankful to the gods, for they had allowed me to live in a period when my allotted task consisted of prudent reorganization of a world, and not of extracting matter, still unformed, from chaos, or of lying upon a corpse in the effort to revive it. I enjoyed the thought that our past was long enough to provide us with great examples, but not so heavy as to crush us under their weight; that our technical developments had advanced to the point of facilitating hygiene in the cities and prosperity for the population, though not to the degree of encumbering man with useless acquisition; that our arts, like trees grown weary with the abundance of their bearing, were still able to produce a few choice fruits. I was glad that our venerable, almost formless religions, drained of all intransigence and purged of savage rites, linked us mysteriously to the most ancient secrets of man and of earth, not forbidding us, however, a secular explanation of facts and a rational view of human conduct. It was, in sum, pleasing to me that even these words *Humanity, Liberty, Happiness*, had not yet lost their value by too much misuse.

I see an objection to every effort toward ameliorating man's condition on earth, namely that mankind is perhaps not worthy of such exertion. But I meet the objection easily enough: so long as Caligula's dream remains impossible of fulfillment, and the entire human race is not reduced to a single head destined for the axe, we shall have to bear with humanity, keeping it within bounds but utilizing it to the utmost; our interest, in the best sense of the term, will be to serve it. My procedure was based on a series of observations made upon myself over a long period; any lucid explanation has always convinced me, all courtesy has won me over, every moment of felicity has almost always left me wise. I lent only half an ear to those well-meaning folk who say that happiness is enervating, liberty too relaxing, and that kindness is corrupting for those upon whom it is practiced. That may be; but, in the world as it is, such reasoning amounts to refusal to nourish a starving man decently for fear that in a few years he may suffer from overfeeding. When useless servitude has been alleviated as far as possible, and unnecessary misfortune avoided, there will still remain as a test of man's fortitude that long series of veritable ills, death, old age and incurable sickness, love unrequited and friendship rejected or betrayed, the mediocrity of a life less vast than our projects and duller than our dreams; in short, all the woes caused by the divine nature of things.

I should say outright that I have little faith in laws. If too severe, they are broken, and with good reason. If too complicated, human ingenuity finds means to slip easily between the meshes of this trailing but fragile net. Respect for ancient laws answers to what is deepest rooted in human piety, but it serves also to pillow the inertia of judges. The oldest codes are a part of that very savagery which they were striving to correct; even the most venerable among them are the product of force. Most of our punitive laws fail, perhaps happily, to reach the greater part of the culprits; our civil laws will never be supple enough to fit the immense and changing diversity of facts. Laws change more slowly than custom, and though dangerous when they fall behind the times are more dangerous still when they presume to anticipate custom. And nevertheless from that mass of outworn routines and perilous innovations a few useful formulas have emerged here and there, just as they have in medicine. The Greek philosophers have taught us to know something more of the nature of man; our best jurists have worked for generations along lines of common sense. I have myself effected a few of those partial reforms which are the only reforms that endure. Any law too often subject to infraction is bad; it is the duty of the legislator to repeal or to change it, lest the contempt into which that rash ruling has fallen should extend to other, more just legislation. I proposed as my aim a prudent avoidance of superfluous decrees, and the firm promulgation, instead, of a small group of well-weighed decisions. The time seemed to have come to evaluate anew all the ancient prescriptions in the interest of mankind.

One day in Spain, in the vicinity of Tarragona, when I was visiting alone a half-abandoned mine, a slave attacked me with a knife. He had passed most of his forty-three years in those subterranean corridors, and not without logic was taking revenge upon the emperor for his long servitude. I managed to disarm him easily enough; under the care of my physicians his violence subsided, and he changed into what he really was, a being not less sensible than others, and more loyal than many. Had the law been applied with savage rigor, he would have been promptly executed; as it was, he became my useful servant. Most men are like this slave: they are only too submissive; their long periods of torpor are interspersed with a few revolts as brutal as they are ineffectual. I wanted to see if well-regulated liberty would not have produced better results, and I am astonished that a similar experiment has not tempted more princes. This barbarian condemned to the mines became a symbol to me of all our slaves and all our barbarians. It seemed to me not impossible to treat them as I had treated this man, rendering them harmless simply by kindness, provided that first of all they understand that the hand which disarms them is sure. All nations who have perished up to this time have done so for lack of generosity: Sparta would have survived longer had she given her Helots some interest in that survival; there is always a day when Atlas ceases to support the weight of the heavens, and his revolt shakes the earth. I wished to postpone as long as possible, and to avoid, if it can be done, the moment when the barbarians from without and the slaves within will fall upon a world which they have been forced to respect from afar, or to serve from below, but the profits of which are not for them. I was determined that even the most wretched, from the slaves who clean the city sewers to the famished barbarians who hover along the frontiers, should have an interest in seeing Rome endure.

EDMUND WILSON

FROM

A Piece of My Mind

REFLECTIONS AT SIXTY

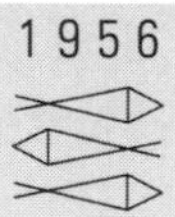

One of the most discouraging symptoms, for the American visitor in Europe, is the recent multiplication of languages. You have now the revival of Gaelic as a nationalistic gesture in Scotland as well as its installation as the official language of Ireland, and the nursing as a literary language of the local Norwegian dialect called *landsmoll* in place of Dano-Norwegian, the language in which Ibsen wrote. I learned at the Salzburg Seminar from Jugoslav students that Jugoslavia maintains four languages—Serbian, Croatian, Slovenian and Macedonian—at least three of which seemed to have literatures; and I was told that the Swiss, not content with their German, French and Italian, the second of these the language of Rousseau, the first of Burckhardt and Keller, have been cultivating as a literary medium their old Latin folk-language Romansh and even having taught in their schools the dialects of the different cantons. To an American, this seems perfect madness; to a pre-1914 internationalist, a perverse setting-back of history. As if the differences in language in Europe had not made enough trouble already! How tired we were in America of hearing how the French and the Germans could not understand one another! We could sympathize fully with the struggles of the Irish and Scottish against the English, of the Hungarians, Poles and Czechs against their Germanic oppressors; it was natural enough, to be sure, to resent the oppressor's language, especially imposed in schools to the exclusion of one's native tongue; but why cultivate tongues that are dying out or that will only be learned by the people of a relatively small nationality at the expense of those of wider currency? Surely Conrad, though his English sounds foreign, is far more important as an English writer than he could ever have been in Polish. The Irish have produced in English magnificent literature. James Joyce and Bernard Shaw are world figures, who tower above their English-born contemporaries; Yeats is one of the great English poets. But how is it possible, at this late date, to develop a folk-language like Gaelic to the point where it would be capable of anything of Joycean or Shavian complexity? It is as much, I am told, as the Irish can do, to equip it with an invented vocabulary for dealing with the phenomena of modern life. The revival of Hebrew in Israel has undoubtedly more justification. There is a need for a common language among the diversity of Jews—German, East European, Russian, British, North African and Yemenite; and Hebrew, as a literary medium, has never been entirely dead. Yet one cannot but regret this necessity. To write even in modernized Hebrew seems to lead back into a cabinned and visionary past from which the great Jewish thinkers and writers in the European and Slavic languages have succeeded in liberating themselves.

It is dismaying, then, to the non-nationalistic observer from our federated United States, to find Europe, not only not more unified, not only not in process of unification, but, on the contrary, it would appear, more lacking in coherence than ever. He may reflect, with a certain smugness, that the population of the United States includes, at the present time, large elements from all the Slavic as well as all the European nationalities, as well as many Negroes and orientals, who sometimes go on speaking their original tongues for two or three generations, and that, in spite of our recurrent anti-alien alarms and a certain amount of friction, we are not being continually torn by nationalistic feuds. We have had one bitter sectional war—between the North and the South; we have still—in the Southern states and sometimes in other places—a very bad situation between the whites and the Negroes. But the lack of cordial relations between, on the one hand, the Americans of Dutch and Anglo-Saxon blood and, on the other, the immigrants of other stocks—though it still plays a part in politics and is sometimes an impediment to social life—hardly figures today as an element that makes for disunity, just as the Dutch and the English themselves, so hostile to one another in the eighteenth century, have now become completely merged. Why on earth, the American asks, have the idiotic Europeans not organized long ago—as we and the Soviet Union have done—in a comprehensive federation? If the Soviets and the States are now powerful, and if Europe seems impotent, collapsed, as the result of suicidal wars, it is because we have this advantage. In Europe, they seem still to think only in old-fashioned terms of hegemony. Napoleon attempted this but overshot the mark in Russia and aroused the apprehensions of the English, who finally put him down. The Germans have tried the same thing, but again aroused the fears of the English, who, although they have not themselves wanted to dominate Europe—having an empire farther off and for the most part easier to handle—have prevented anyone else from doing so. The result has been a stalemate, this wreckage, both the great units stripped of their power, and the Continent, as a whole, left in fragments.

But why, the American demands, this *passion* for fragmentation? In America, we like to have our people get along as well as possible together. Our slogan is "the melting pot." There must exist some strong motivation which is hard for the American to grasp that drives even the tiniest national group both in the British Isles and on the Continent to this wrong-headed nationalism. How far this process has gone was lately brought home to me in a striking way by a discussion with a young Irishwoman who had grown up under the Eire regime. I had previously been talking about Ireland with an Irishwoman of a slightly older generation who was closer to the old intellectual Ireland, the Ireland of Yeats and Joyce, of which, through its visitors to the States and some that had settled here, I had had some attractive glimpses. She, too, had grown up in Eire, and she looked back on eleven years of Gaelic as an appalling tract of waste in her life. Since the subject was so limited, she told me, they had eventually to occupy the students by making them memorize the Gaelic vocabulary—itself a synthetic product—for the various diseases of cattle. To get away from this nationalistic education and also from the Catholic Church, she had gone to the Sorbonne to study, had mastered French and Italian, and had married an Italian, a distinguished figure in the political and literary worlds. The younger woman, however, the daughter of an Irish patriot, who had served his term in prison and who had later been an official of the Irish republic, had been brought up on the ideals of Eire and had never reacted against them. For this young woman, Gaelic was a part of her creed, as was the right—and with this I did sympathize—of Ireland to stand out of the second war. She believed, I discovered, in a world entirely made up of many small nations, each speaking its own language—the more languages, apparently, the better. Uniformity was much to be dreaded—and, besides, if you had small countries, you would have, she thought, only small wars. Though she had lived several years in the United States, any other sort of political ideal was apparently unimaginable for her.

Now, was it possible, I asked myself, for *me*, to imagine the state of mind that had gone to produce *her* ideal? I realized that it was somewhat difficult for me to put myself in the place of a member of a small nation. We had suffered from the English in the early days, but we had beaten and expelled their forces, and, besides, we had ourselves been mainly English: we had not lost the national language. If one had suffered for centuries and had lost it, one might well behave like the Irish. There was, after all, the example at home of the South. The Southerners cherished still their old rage against the northern invaders, a stout and defiant loyalty to their antiquated limitations as well as to their traditional virtues which was not unlike that of the Irish. Yet, a member myself of that power group which had subjected the South to its domination, I felt at moments the same sort of impatience with them as the British authorities felt with the Irishmen that shot their landlords. I could not help feeling annoyance that the South should keep on being silly. Yet to find oneself absorbed by a power unit can never be a pleasant experience, unless one be a born time-server or opportunist. In Europe, however, when the last war was over, both Germany and England had lost their positions, and France had already lost hers: there were no longer any big power magnets for the smaller units to cling to, and everything was flying to pieces. If one cultivated one's local language, one could try to make a cosy little world of one's own, in which everyone was everyone's friend, everyone was everyone's kinsman. They could keep one another alive and warm in the midst of the great desolation, which had looming on either side of it the threats of two terribly alien monsters: ourselves and the Soviet Union.

•

At the time when the United States was being flooded by refugees from Europe, we had to hear from them many complaints of the absence of culture in the United States—a condition which gave them pain. These complaints, to be sure, came often from persons who could themselves offer nothing but a parade of conventional opinions, who had been living in their various countries just as much unaware of contemporary creative forces—or just as supercilious about them—as they were of those in the United States, who hardly bothered to visit our galleries, our museums or our concert halls, and who sometimes did not know enough English to read American books. But some were distinguished people who simply could not rid themselves of the notion that Europe was the home of the arts and America a barbarian backwater. This attitude, for us, had its piquancy at a moment when so many of the best minds of Europe had fled to America for their souls or their lives, or had quietly, in earlier years, removed to the United States, where they found things more comfortable or freer. We had here in the States, during those years of the war, Einstein and Whitehead; Huxley, Auden and Isherwood; Thomas Mann, Vladimir Nabokov, St.-Jean Perse and the Polish poet Tuvim; Schoenberg, Stravinsky, Bartók, Hindemith, Křenek and Milhaud; Toscanini and Kusevitsky; Chelishchev, George Grosz and the Surrealists; and how many lesser figures: the Molnars, the Maughams, the Simenons; conductors, directors, actors. Some of these became American citizens and are still living in the United States. It was in Europe, though few would admit it, that the barbaric age had begun, with the results foreseen by Gibbon. At the end of Chapter

XXXVIII of the *Decline and Fall: General Observations on the Fall of The Roman Empire in the West*, he discusses the possibility of new inroads of barbarism in Europe. He is inclined to dismiss the danger of an invasion from the direction of Russia, since—writing in the reign of Catherine the Great—he believes that the improvements of "the science of war" are likely to be "accompanied with a proportionable improvement in the arts of peace and civil policy. Yet this apparent security should not tempt us to forget that new enemies and unknown dangers may *possibly* arise; and should the victorious barbarians carry slavery and desolation as far as the Atlantic ocean, ten thousand vessels would transport beyond their pursuit the remains of civilized society; and Europe would revive and flourish in the American world, which is already filled with her colonies and institutions."

•

A certain kind of European overrates the comparative importance, in the present age of the world, of a good deal of his cultural tradition, and often of his own real interest in it. For myself, as an American, I have not the least doubt that I have derived a good deal more benefit of the civilizing as well as of the inspirational kind from the admirable American bathroom than I have from the cathedrals of Europe. I do not, of course, deny the impressiveness of the many varied beauties of these monuments, nor their usefulness to the people in their time; I have enjoyed their delightful coolness and their shade from the glare of the sun on broiling days in France and Italy—though in cold weather they are likely to be unbearable. But I have had a good many more uplifting thoughts, creative and expansive visions—while soaking in comfortable baths or drying myself after bracing showers—in well-equipped American bathrooms than I have ever had in any cathedral. Here the body purges itself, and along with the body, the spirit. Here the mind becomes free to ruminate, to plan ambitious projects. The cathedrals, with their distant domes, their long aisles and their high groinings, do add stature to human strivings; their chapels do give privacy for prayer. But the bathroom, too, shelters the spirit, it tranquillizes and reassures, in surroundings of a celestial whiteness, where the pipes and the faucets gleam and the mirror makes another liquid surface, which will render you, shaved, rubbed and brushed, a nobler and more winning appearance. Here, too, you may sing, recite, refresh yourself with brief readings, just as you do in church; and the fact that you do it without a priest and not as a member of a congregation is, from my point of view, an advantage. It encourages self-dependence and prepares one to face the world, fortified, firm on one's feet, serene and with a mind like a diamond.

JUAN RAMÓN JIMÉNEZ

FROM

Selected Writings of Juan Ramón Jiménez

[*Translated by H. R. Hays*]

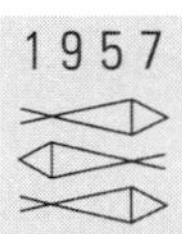

1/PLATERO

Platero [the donkey] is little, wooly, and soft, so smooth outside that you would say he was all made of cotton without any bones. Only the jet mirrors of his eyes are as hard as two black glass scarabs.

I set him free and he goes into the meadow and gently caresses the little pink, golden, and cerulean flowers with his muzzle, just touching them . . . I call gently, "Platero?" and he comes to me at a joyful little trot and it seems that he is laughing in some imaginary jingle of bells.

He eats whatever I give him. He likes tangerines, muscatel grapes, oil of amber, and dark figs with their crystalline drop of honey.

He is as gentle and finicky as a child, as a girl, but strong and dry inside as if of stone. When I ride him on Sunday through the farthest alleys of the village, the slow peasants, in clean clothes, stop to look at him:

"Steel in 'im . . ."

There is steel in him. Steel and quicksilver at the same time.

2/SPRING

In my morning doze I am annoyed by little creatures setting up a devilish shrieking. Finally, unable to sleep any longer, I desperately fling myself out of bed. Then, as I look out through the open window on the countryside, I realize that it is the birds which are making such a clamor.

I go into the garden and sing a song of thanksgiving to the god of the blue day. A free concert pours from the beaks of birds, refreshing and endless. The swallow's trill ripples from the pond, the blackbird whistles over a fallen orange, the oriole, all aflame, chatters from bush to bush, the blue titmouse bursts into long minute gusts of laughter in the tip of the eucalyptus, and in the big pine tree the sparrows argue impudently.

What a morning it is! The sun fills the earth with its silver and gold gaiety, butterflies of a hundred colors are playing everywhere, among the flowers, about the house (now inside, now outside), at the spring. The countryside everywhere bursts into explosions, into clicking, boiling with new and vigorous life.

It seems as though we were within a great honeycomb of light which is the interior of an immense, warm, flaming rose.

3/THE FLOWER BY THE ROAD

How pure, Platero, how lovely this flower by the roadside! All the herds pass alongside it (bulls, goats, colts, men) and though it is so tender and weak it still stands upright, mallow-pink and delicate on its stone wall, unstained by any impurity.

You have seen it every day when we take the shortcut at the beginning of the rise, at its green post. Now it has a little bird beside it which flies up (why?) as we approach, or it is filled like a shallow cup with clear water from a summer cloud, now it allows the bee to rob it or the fickle butterfly to adorn it.

This flower lives but a few days, Platero, even though the memory of it can be eternal. Its life will be but a day of your springtime, but a springtime of my life . . . what wouldn't I give to autumn in exchange for this divine flower, so that for our lives it might every day be a simple unending example?

4/THE THORN

As he entered the horse pasture he began to limp. I had to dismount . . .

"What's the matter, fellow?"

Platero had lifted his right forehoof a little, showing the frog, and was putting no weight on it, scarcely touching the hot sand of the road with the hoof.

With no doubt more care than old Darbon, his veterinary, I bent his leg back and looked into the red frog. A large green thorn from a sturdy orange tree was stuck in it like the round head of a little emerald dagger. While I trembled along with Platero's pain, I drew out the thorn and I took the poor thing to the stream with the yellow lilies so that the running water would lick his little wound with its long, pure tongue.

Afterwards we went on toward the white sea, I ahead, he behind, still limping and gently nudging me in the back.

5/THE THREE KINGS

How excited the children were tonight, Platero! We could not get them to bed. In the end sleep captured them, one in the armchair, one on the floor in the chimney corner, Blanca in a low chair, Pepe in the windowseat with his head on the nails studding the door, lest the kings should come by. And now behind this outward surface of life all their sleep can be felt, alive and magical, beating like a great, full, vigorous heart.

Before supper I went up with all of them. What a clamor on the staircase which on other nights frightened them so!

"I'm not afraid of the skylight, Pepe. What about you?" said Blanca, holding my hand very tightly.

And we put all their shoes on the balcony among the drying fruit. And now, Platero, Montemayor, Tita, Maria Teresa, Lolilla, Perico, you and I are going to get dressed up in blankets, quilts, and old hats. At twelve we must go by the children's windows in a masked procession with lights, beating mortars, blowing on trumpets and on the conch shell which was in the back room. You shall go along with me for I am to be Caspar and I shall wear a white cotton beard and you shall wear the Colombian flag, which I got from the house of my uncle, the consul, like a blanket . . . the children suddenly awakened, with the sleep still lingering in the corners of their amazed eyes will peep through the panes in their nightshirts, trembling and marvelling. Afterwards we shall go on in their dreams through the dawn and until tomorrow, when it is already late and the blue sky illuminates them through the shutters, they will run up, half-dressed, to the balcony to take possession of all their treasure.

Last year we laughed heartily. Platero, my little camel, now you will see what fun we are going to have tonight.

[Twelfth Night in Spain, and many Spanish-speaking countries, is equivalent to Christmas in the United States, and the Three Kings to Santa Claus.]

6/SCARLET LANDSCAPE

The summit. And yonder is the west, all purple, wounded by its own crystals which make it bleed all over. Slightly reddened, the green pine grove sharpens and the grass and little flowers, transparently aflame in the splendor of the west, make the serene moment pungent with a moist, luminous and penetrating scent.

And I linger, full of ecstasy, in the twilight. Platero, his dark eyes scarlet from the sunset, goes quietly to a pool of carmine, rose, and violet waters, dips his mouth gently into the mirrors which seem to turn liquid as he touches them and a profuse sea of darkish waters of blood pours down his huge throat.

The spot is familiar but the moment transforms it, turns it into something strange, ruined, and monumental. One would say that we are at any moment going to discover an abandoned palace . . . the evening lingers beyond itself and the hour, tinged with eternity, is infinite, peaceful, inscrutable . . .

"Come on, Platero . . ."

7/THE LITTLE GIRL

The little girl was Platero's delight. Whenever he saw her coming toward him through the lilacs, in her white dress and rice straw hat, softly calling, "Platero, little Platerooo!" the little ass wanted to break his rope and he jumped like a child and brayed madly.

Blindly confident, she crawled under him again and again, gave him little kicks, put her gleaming white hand into his pink mouth studded with large yellow teeth, or, pulling his ears which he put at her disposal, called him by all the playful variations of his name: "Platero, Plateron, Platerillo, Platerete, Platerucho!"

During those long days in which the child sailed down the river in her white cradle toward death, nobody paid any attention to Platero. She in her delirium called sadly, "Little Platerooo!" In the house, darkened now and full of sighs, the plaintive distant call of her friend could be heard. Oh melancholy summer!

With what richness God endowed you, afternoon of her funeral! September, pink and gold as it is now, was coming to an end. How the bells echoed from the cemetery, when it was over, in the clear west, pathway to glory! I came by the abandoned and moss-grown adobe walls, entered the house through the yard door, and, avoiding everyone, went to the stable and sat down to think with Platero.

8/CHILL

The moon accompanies us, large, round, and pure. In the slumbering meadows some indistinguishable black goats can be seen among the brambles . . . someone silently hides as we pass . . . Above the stone wall a huge almond tree, snowy with blossoms and moonlight, bending down its top in a white cloud, blankets the roadway, shot with March stars. A penetrating odor of oranges . . . moisture and silence . . . the Ravine of the Witches . . .

"Platero . . . how . . . cold it is!"

Platero is trotting, I don't know whether from my fear or his; he enters the brook, steps on the moon and shatters it. It is as if a swarm of clear, crystal roses, trying to stop him, gets entangled in his trot.

And Platero trots uphill, tucking in his rump as if someone were about to overtake him, now feeling the gentle warmth of the approaching village that never seems to be reached.

9/ANGELUS

Platero, look at the way the roses are falling everywhere, blue roses, pink, white ones, colorless ones. You would think that the sky was dissolving into roses. Look at the way my forehead, my shoulders, my hands are covered with roses . . . what shall I do with so many roses?

Do you know perhaps where this smooth-petaled flowering comes from (I don't know where it comes from) which softens the landscape every day and leaves it faintly pink, white, or cerulean (more roses, more roses) like a picture by Fra Angelico who painted glory on his knees?

One would think that roses were being tossed to earth from the seven tiers of Paradise. Like snow, gentle pale-tinted roses cover the tower, the roof tiles, the trees. Look, everything rough becomes delicate when they decorate it. More roses, more roses, more roses . . .

Platero, as the Angelus sounds, it seems that this quotidian life of ours loses its power and another loftier, purer, more constant force from within makes all things rise, as fountains of grace, to the stars which are set alight among the roses . . . more roses . . . your eyes which you can not see, Platero, which you raise submissively to heaven, are two lovely roses.

10/THE PARSLEY CROWN

"Let's see who gets there first!"

The prize was a book of prints I had received the day before from Vienna.

"Let's see who gets to the violets first! One . . . two . . . three!"

The children dashed off at a run, a happy tumult of pink and white in the yellow sun. For a moment, in the silence which the mute straining of their chests created in the morning, the slow hour chiming from the village clock could be heard, the minute song of a mosquito on the hill of pine trees which was filled with blue lilies, and the coming and going of the water in the brook . . . the children got to the first orange trees when Platero, who was idling nearby, became infected with the game and began to gallop along with them. They, in order not to lose, could not protest or even laugh . . .

I shouted after them, "Platero's winning, Platero's winning!"

Yes, Platero reached the violets before anyone else and paused there to roll in the sand.

The children came back panting their protests, pulling up their stockings, pushing back their hair.

"That doesn't count! That doesn't count! No! No! Oh no!"

I told them that Platero had won the race and that it was only fair to give him some kind of prize. And anyway the book which Platero couldn't read would be left for another race of theirs but Platero must get a prize.

Now sure of the book, they jumped and laughed uproariously.

"Yes, yes, yes!"

Then, thinking of myself, it seemed to me that Platero should have the first prize for his effort, I for my verses. And, taking a little parsley from the box at the door of the cottage, I made a crown and put it on his head, a fleeting first award like that won by a Lacedemonian.

11/DEATH

I found Platero stretched out on his bed of straw, his eyes soft and sad. I went to him, caressed him, talked to him and tried to get him up . . .

The poor thing moved jerkily and got up on one knee . . . He couldn't make it . . . then I stretched out his leg on the ground, caressed him again tenderly, and sent for his veterinary.

Old Darbon, when he saw him, opened his enormous toothless mouth from ear to ear and shook his red face like a pendulum above his chest.

"Not so good, eh?"

I don't know what he answered . . . that the poor animal was dying . . . that a pain . . . I don't know what poisonous root . . . the earth in the grass . . .

By midday Platero was dead. The little cottony belly was swollen like the world and his legs, rigid and discolored, were sticking upward. His curly hair looked like the motheaten tow on a doll's head which falls out in dusty sadness when you pass your hand over it.

In the silent stall, bursting into flame every time it passed through a ray of light from the little window, a beautiful tricolored butterfly circled about . . .

12/NOSTALGIA

Platero, you see us, don't you?

And you see, don't you, how the water of the well in the garden laughs peacefully, clear and cool, as now in the late afternoon light the industrious bees circle over the green and mallow-pink rosemary, turned pink and gold by the sun still lighting up the hilltop?

Platero, you see us, don't you?

You see, don't you, the little burros of the washerwomen passing over the red crest of the Old Fountain, tired, lame, sad, in the immense purity that united earth and sky in a single crystal of glory?

Platero, you see us, don't you?

You see, don't you, the children running suddenly between the rock roses whose flowers, perched on their branches, are a frivolous swarm of wandering white butterflies, spotted with carmine?

Platero, you see us, don't you?

Platero, it's true that you see us, isn't it? Yes, you see me. And I think I hear you, yes, yes, I hear your gentle, plaintive bray in the cloudless west, filling the valley of the vineyards with sweetness . . .

13/MELANCHOLY

This afternoon I have been with the children to visit the grave of Platero which is in the Pine Orchard, at the foot of a thick, paternal pine tree. Once again April had adorned the moist earth with great yellow lilies.

The blue titmice were singing high up in thc green tip, all painted with azure sky, and their mute, florid, laughing, trill pervaded the golden air of the warm afternoon like a clear dream of new love.

When we arrived the children stopped shouting. Quiet and serious, their shining eyes, fixed on mine, plied mc with anxious questions.

"Platero, friend!" (I said to the earth), "If, as I think, you are now in the meadows of the sky and are carrying the adolescent angels on your furry back, have you perhaps forgotten me? Platero, tell me, do you still remember me?"

And, as if answering my question, another fragile white butterfly, which I had not seen before, circled insistently from lily to lily, like a soul.

BERNARD MALAMUD

FROM

The Magic Barrel

1958

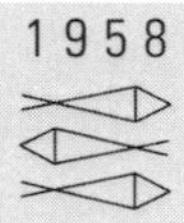

THE FIRST SEVEN YEARS

Feld, the shoemaker, was annoyed that his helper, Sobel, was so insensitive to his reverie that he wouldn't for a minute cease his fanatic pounding at the other bench. He gave him a look, but Sobel's bald head was bent over the last as he worked and he didn't notice. The shoemaker shrugged and continued to peer through the partly frosted window at the near-sighted haze of falling February snow. Neither the shifting white blur outside, nor the sudden deep remembrance of the snowy Polish village where he had wasted his youth could turn his thoughts from Max the college boy (a constant visitor in the mind since early that morning when Feld saw him trudging through the snowdrifts on his way to school) whom he so much respected because of the sacrifices he had made throughout the years—in winter or direst heat—to further his education. An old wish returned to haunt the shoemaker: that he had had a son instead of a daughter, but this blew away in the snow for Feld, if anything, was a practical man. Yet he could not help but contrast the diligence of the boy, who was a peddler's son, with Miriam's unconcern for an education. True, she was always with a book in her hand, yet when the opportunity arose for a college education, she had said no she would rather find a job. He had begged her to go, pointing out how many fathers could not afford to send their children to college, but she said she wanted to be independent. As for education, what was it, she asked, but books, which Sobel, who diligently read the classics, would as usual advise her on. Her answer greatly grieved her father.

A figure emerged from the snow and the door opened. At the counter the man withdrew from a wet paper bag a pair of battered shoes for repair. Who he was the shoemaker for a moment had no idea, then his heart trembled as he realized, before he had thoroughly discerned the face, that Max himself was standing there, embarrassedly explaining what he wanted done to his old shoes. Though Feld listened eagerly, he couldn't hear a word, for the opportunity that had burst upon him was deafening.

He couldn't exactly recall when the thought had occurred to him, because it was clear he had more than once considered suggesting to the boy that he go out with Miriam. But he had not dared speak, for if Max said no, how would he face him again? Or suppose Miriam, who harped so often on independence, blew up in anger and shouted at him for his meddling? Still, the chance was too good to let by: all it meant was an introduction. They might long ago have become friends had they happened to meet somewhere, therefore was it not his duty—an obligation—to bring them together, nothing more, a harmless connivance to replace an accidental encounter in the subway, let's say, or a mutual friend's introduction in the street? Just let him once see and talk to her and he would for sure be interested. As for Miriam, what possible harm for a working girl in an office, who met only loud-mouthed salesmen and illiterate shipping clerks, to make the acquaintance of a fine scholarly boy? Maybe he would awaken in her a desire to go to college; if not—the shoemaker's mind at last came to grips with the truth—let her marry an educated man and live a better life.

When Max finished describing what he wanted done to his shoes, Feld marked them, both with enormous holes in the soles which he pretended not to notice, with large white-chalk x's, and the rubber heels, thinned to the nails, he marked with o's, though it troubled him he might have mixed up the letters. Max inquired the price, and the shoemaker cleared his throat and asked the boy, above Sobel's insistent hammering, would he please step through the side door there into the hall. Though surprised, Max did as the shoemaker requested, and Feld went in after him. For a minute they were both silent, because Sobel had stopped banging, and it seemed they understood neither was to say anything until the noise began again. When it did, loudly, the shoemaker quickly told Max why he had asked to talk to him.

"Ever since you went to high school," he said, in the dimly-lit hallway, "I watched you in the morning go to the subway to school, and I said always to myself, this is a fine boy that he wants so much an education."

"Thanks," Max said, nervously alert. He was tall and grotesquely thin, with sharply cut features, particularly a beak-like nose. He was wearing a loose, long slushy overcoat that hung down to his ankles, looking like a rug draped over his bony shoulders, and a soggy, old brown hat, as battered as the shoes he had brought in.

"I am a business man," the shoemaker abruptly said to conceal his embarrassment, "so I will explain you right away why I talk to you. I have a girl, my daughter Miriam—she is nineteen—a very nice girl and also so pretty that everybody looks on her when she passes by in the street. She is smart, always with a book, and I thought to myself that a boy like you, an educated boy—I thought maybe you will be interested sometime to meet a girl like this." He laughed a bit when he had finished and was tempted to say more but had the good sense not to.

Max stared down like a hawk. For an uncomfortable second he was silent, then he asked, "Did you say nineteen?"

"Yes."

"Would it be all right to inquire if you have a picture of her?"

"Just a minute." The shoemaker went into the store and hastily returned with a snapshot that Max held up to the light.

"She's all right," he said.

Feld waited.

"And is she sensible—not the flighty kind?"

"She is very sensible."

After another short pause, Max said it was okay with him if he met her.

"Here is my telephone," said the shoemaker, hurriedly handing him a slip of paper. "Call her up. She comes home from work six o'clock."

Max folded the paper and tucked it away into his worn leather wallet.

"About the shoes," he said. "How much did you say they will cost me?"

"Don't worry about the price."

"I just like to have an idea."

"A dollar—dollar fifty. A dollar fifty," the shoemaker said.

At once he felt bad, for he usually charged two twenty-five for this kind of job. Either he should have asked the regular price or done the work for nothing.

Later, as he entered the store, he was startled by a violent clanging and looked up to see Sobel pounding with all his might upon the naked last. It broke, the iron striking the floor and jumping with a thump against the wall, but before the enraged shoemaker could cry out, the assistant had torn his hat and coat from the hook and rushed out into the snow.

•

So Feld, who had looked forward to anticipating how it would go with his daughter and Max, instead had a great worry on his mind. Without his temperamental helper he was a lost man, especially since it was years now that he had carried the store alone. The shoemaker had for an age suffered from a heart condition that threatened collapse if he dared exert himself. Five years ago, after an attack, it had appeared as though he would have either to sacrifice his business upon the auction block and live on a pittance thereafter, or put himself at the mercy of some unscrupulous employee who would in the end probably ruin him. But just at the moment of his darkest despair, this Polish refugee, Sobel, appeared one night from the street and begged for work. He was a stocky man, poorly dressed, with a bald head that had once been blond, a severely plain face and soft blue eyes prone to tears over the sad books he read, a young man but old—no one would have guessed thirty. Though he confessed he knew nothing of shoemaking, he said he was apt and would work for a very little if Feld taught him the trade. Thinking that with, after all, a landsman, he would have less to fear than from a complete stranger, Feld took him on and within six weeks the refugee rebuilt as good a shoe as he, and not long thereafter expertly ran the business for the thoroughly relieved shoemaker.

Feld could trust him with anything and did, frequently going home after an hour or two at the store, leaving all the money in the till, knowing Sobel would guard every cent of it. The amazing thing was that he demanded so little. His wants were few; in money he wasn't interested—in nothing but books, it seemed—which he one by one lent to Miriam, together with his profuse, queer written comments, manufactured during his lonely rooming house evenings, thick pads of commentary which the shoemaker peered at and twitched his shoulders over as his daughter, from her fourteenth year, read page by sanctified page, as if the word of God were inscribed on them. To protect Sobel, Feld himself had to see that he received more than he asked for. Yet his conscience bothered him for not insisting that the assistant accept a better wage than he was getting, though Feld had honestly told him he could earn a handsome salary if he worked elsewhere, or maybe opened a place of his own. But the assistant answered, somewhat ungraciously, that he was not interested in going elsewhere, and though Feld frequently asked himself what keeps him here? why does he stay? he finally answered it that the man, no doubt because of his terrible experiences as a refugee, was afraid of the world.

After the incident with the broken last, angered by Sobel's behavior, the shoemaker decided to let him stew for a week in the rooming house, although his own strength was taxed dangerously and the business suffered. However, after several sharp nagging warnings from both his wife and daughter, he went finally in search of Sobel, as he had once before, quite recently, when over some fancied slight—Feld had merely asked him not to give Miriam so many books to read because her eyes were strained and red—the assistant had left the place in a huff, an incident which, as usual, came to nothing for he had returned after the shoemaker had talked to him, and taken his seat at the bench. But this time, after Feld had plodded through the snow to Sobel's house—he had thought of sending Miriam but the idea became repugnant to him—the burly landlady at the door informed him in a nasal voice that Sobel was not at home, and though Feld knew this was a nasty lie, for where had the refugee to go? still for some reason he was not completely sure of—it may have been the cold and his fatigue—he decided not to insist on seeing him. Instead he went home and hired a new helper.

Having settled the matter, though not entirely to his satisfaction, for he had much more to do than before, and so, for example, could no longer lie late in bed mornings because he had to get up to open the store for the new assistant, a speechless, dark man with an irritating rasp as he worked, whom he would not trust with the key as he had Sobel. Furthermore, this one, though able to do a fair repair job, knew nothing of grades of leather or prices, so Feld had to make his own purchases; and every night at closing time it was necessary to count the money in the till and lock up. However, he was not dissatisfied, for he lived much in his thoughts of Max and Miriam. The college boy had called her, and they had arranged a meeting for this coming Friday night. The shoemaker would personally have preferred Saturday, which he felt would make it a date of the first magnitude, but he learned Friday was Miriam's choice, so he said nothing. The day of the week did not matter. What mattered was the aftermath. Would they like each other and want to be friends? He sighed at all the time that would have to go by before he knew for sure. Often he was tempted to talk to Miriam about the boy, to ask whether she thought she would like his type—he had told her only that he considered Max a nice boy and had suggested he call her—but the one time he tried she snapped at him—justly—how should she know?

At last Friday came. Feld was not feeling particularly well so he stayed in bed, and Mrs. Feld thought it better to remain in the bedroom with him when Max called. Miriam received the boy, and her parents could hear their voices, his throaty one, as they talked. Just before leaving, Miriam brought Max to the bedroom door and he stood there a minute, a tall, slightly hunched figure wearing a thick, droopy suit, and apparently at ease as he greeted the shoemaker and his wife, which was surely a good sign. And Miriam, although she had worked all day, looked fresh and pretty. She was a large-framed girl with a well-shaped body, and she had a fine open face and soft hair. They made, Feld thought, a first-class couple.

Miriam returned after 11:30. Her mother was already asleep, but the shoemaker got out of bed and after locating his bathrobe went into the kitchen, where Miriam, to his surprise, sat at the table, reading.

"So where did you go?" Feld asked pleasantly.

"For a walk," she said, not looking up.

"I advised him," Feld said, clearing his throat, "he shouldn't spend so much money."

"I didn't care."

The shoemaker boiled up some water for tea and sat down at the table with a cupful and a thick slice of lemon.

"So how," he sighed after a sip, "did you enjoy?"

"It was all right."

He was silent. She must have sensed his disappointment, for she added, "You can't really tell much the first time."

"You will see him again?"

Turning a page, she said that Max had asked for another date.

"For when?"

"Saturday."

"So what did you say?"

"What did I say?" she asked, delaying for a moment—"I said yes."

Afterwards she inquired about Sobel, and Feld, without exactly knowing why, said the assistant had got another job. Miriam said nothing more and began to read. The shoemaker's conscience did not trouble him; he was satisfied with the Saturday date.

During the week, by placing here and there a deft question, he managed to get from Miriam some information about Max. It surprised him to learn that the boy was not studying to be either a doctor or lawyer but was taking a business course leading to a degree in accountancy. Feld was a little disappointed because he thought of accountants as bookkeepers and would have preferred "a higher profession." However, it was not long before he had investigated the subject and discovered that Certified Public Accountants were highly respected people, so he was thoroughly content as Saturday approached. But because Saturday was a busy day, he was much in the store and therefore did not see Max when he came to call for Miriam. From his wife he learned there had been nothing especially revealing about their meeting. Max had rung the bell and Miriam had got her coat and left with him—nothing more. Feld did not probe, for his wife was not particularly observant. Instead, he waited up for Miriam with a newspaper on his lap, which he scarcely looked at so lost was he in thinking of the future. He awoke to find her in the room with him, tiredly removing her hat. Greeting her, he was suddenly inexplicably afraid to ask anything about the evening. But since she volunteered nothing he was at last forced to inquire how she had enjoyed herself. Miriam began something noncommittal but apparently changed her mind, for she said after a minute, "I was bored."

When Feld had sufficiently recovered from his anguished disappointment to ask why, she answered without hesitation, "Because he's nothing more than a materialist."

"What means this word?"

"He has no soul. He's only interested in things."

He considered her statement for a long time but then asked, "Will you see him again?"

"He didn't ask."

"Suppose he will ask you?"

"I won't see him."

He did not argue; however, as the days went by he hoped increasingly she would change her mind. He wished the boy would telephone, because he was sure there was more to him than Miriam, with her inexperienced eye, could discern. But Max didn't call. As a matter of fact he took a different route to school, no longer passing the shoemaker's store, and Feld was deeply hurt.

Then one afternoon Max came in and asked for his shoes. The shoemaker took them down from the shelf where he had placed them, apart from the other pairs. He had done the work himself and the soles and heels were well built and firm. The shoes had been highly polished and somehow looked better than new. Max's Adam's apple went up once when he saw them, and his eyes had little lights in them.

"How much?" he asked, without directly looking at the shoemaker.

"Like I told you before," Feld answered sadly. "One dollar fifty cents."

Max handed him two crumpled bills and received in return a newly-minted silver half dollar.

He left. Miriam had not been mentioned. That night the shoemaker discovered that his new assistant had been all the while stealing from him, and he suffered a heart attack.

•

Though the attack was very mild, he lay in bed for three weeks. Miriam spoke of going for Sobel, but sick as he was Feld rose in wrath against the idea. Yet in his heart he knew there was no other way, and the first weary day back in the shop thoroughly convinced him, so that night after supper he dragged himself to Sobel's rooming house.

He toiled up the stairs, though he knew it was bad for him, and at the top knocked at the door. Sobel opened it and the shoemaker entered. The room was a small, poor one, with a single window facing the street. It contained a narrow cot, a low table and several stacks of books piled haphazardly around on the floor along the wall, which made him think how queer Sobel was, to be uneducated and read so much. He had once asked him, Sobel, why you read so much? and the assistant could not answer him. Did you ever study in a college someplace? he had asked, but Sobel shook his head. He read, he said, to know. But to know what, the shoemaker demanded, and to know, why? Sobel never explained, which proved he read much because he was queer.

Feld sat down to recover his breath. The assistant was resting on his bed with his heavy back to the wall. His shirt and trousers were clean, and his stubby fingers, away from the shoemaker's bench, were strangely pallid. His face was thin and pale, as if he had been shut in this room since the day he had bolted from the store.

"So when you will come back to work?" Feld asked him.

To his surprise, Sobel burst out, "Never."

Jumping up, he strode over to the window that looked out upon the miserable street. "Why should I come back?" he cried.

"I will raise your wages."

"Who cares for your wages!"

The shoemaker, knowing he didn't care, was at a loss what else to say.

"What do you want from me, Sobel?"

"Nothing."

"I always treated you like you was my son."

Sobel vehemently denied it. "So why you look for strange boys in the street they should go out with Miriam? Why you don't think of me?"

The shoemaker's hands and feet turned freezing cold. His voice became so hoarse he couldn't speak. At last he cleared his throat and croaked, "So what has my daughter got to do with a shoemaker thirty-five years old who works for me?"

"Why do you think I worked so long for you?" Sobel cried out. "For the stingy wages I sacrificed five years of my life so you could have to eat and drink and where to sleep?"

"Then for what?" shouted the shoemaker.

"For Miriam," he blurted—"for her."

The shoemaker, after a time, managed to say, "I pay wages in cash, Sobel," and lapsed into silence. Though he was seething with excitement, his mind was coldly clear, and he had to admit to himself he had sensed all along that Sobel felt this way. He had never so much as thought it consciously, but he had felt it and was afraid.

"Miriam knows?" he muttered hoarsely.

"She knows."

"You told her?"

"No."

"Then how does she know?"

"How does she know?" Sobel said, "because she knows. She knows who I am and what is in my heart."

Feld had a sudden insight. In some devious way, with his books and commentary, Sobel had given Miriam to understand that he loved her. The shoemaker felt a terrible anger at him for his deceit.

"Sobel, you are crazy," he said bitterly. "She will never marry a man so old and ugly like you."

Sobel turned black with rage. He cursed the shoemaker, but then, though he trembled to hold it in, his eyes filled with tears and he broke into deep sobs. With his back to Feld, he stood at the window, fists clenched, and his shoulders shook with his choked sobbing.

Watching him, the shoemaker's anger diminished. His teeth were on edge with pity for the man, and his eyes grew moist. How strange and sad that a refugee, a grown man, bald and old with his miseries, who had by the skin of his teeth escaped Hitler's incinerators, should fall in love, when he had got to America, with a girl less than half his age. Day after day, for five years he had sat at his bench, cutting and hammering away, waiting for the girl to become a woman, unable to ease his heart with speech, knowing no protest but desperation.

"Ugly I didn't mean," he said half aloud.

Then he realized that what he had called ugly was not Sobel but Miriam's life if she married him. He felt for his daughter a strange and gripping sorrow, as if she were already Sobel's bride, the wife, after all, of a shoemaker, and had in her life no more than her mother had had. And all his dreams for her—why he had slaved and destroyed his heart with anxiety and labor—all these dreams of a better life were dead.

The room was quiet. Sobel was standing by the window reading, and it was curious that when he read he looked young.

"She is only nineteen," Feld said brokenly. "This is too young yet to get married. Don't ask her for two years more, till she is twenty-one, then you can talk to her."

Sobel didn't answer. Feld rose and left. He went slowly down the stairs but once outside, though it was an icy night and the crisp falling snow whitened the street, he walked with a stronger stride.

But the next morning, when the shoemaker arrived, heavy-hearted, to open the store, he saw he needn't have come, for his assistant was already seated at the last, pounding leather for his love.

FROM

The Selected Writings of Salvatore Quasimodo

[*Translated by Allen Mandelbaum*]

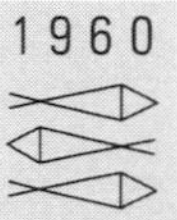

ANCIENT WINTER

Desire for your bright hands
in the penumbra of the flame:
they smelt of oak and roses;
of death. Ancient winter.

The birds were seeking grain
and suddenly were snowed under;
thus—words.
A little sun, an angel's glory,
and then the mist; and the trees
and us, made of air in the morning.

PAUL HORGAN

FROM

A Distant Trumpet

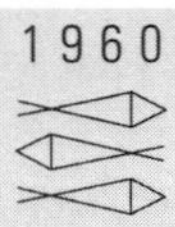

When Matthew was four years old his father went to the Army in the first months of the Civil War.

Emma Hazard kept the store open and Matthew was much with her, "helping out." Times were hard. Emma, who worked faithfully, was unable to push the family business forward in the manner of her husband. Her best qualities as a woman were not those which would bring ingenuity and shrewdness to the ideas and acts of trade. Moreover, people had less money to spend. Everyone knew certain privations. To her privation of heart at the absence of Richard in conditions of risk and danger, Emma had to add worry over the store. She concealed as much of her feeling as possible from Matthew, and made sacrifices for him so that he would have good and plentiful food, and gave him as much untroubled companionship as she could. In his own way he felt the worries of his mother, and even of the town, and without knowing just how or to what degree, he did as much as a small boy could do to sustain her, and to make her smile, and to make her show him her love in spite of her efforts not to spoil him.

Mr. Clarny received the telegram at the station when news came from the Adjutant General of the Army that Richard Hazard had been killed at the battle of Chickamauga.

He walked in person to the store bringing the apricot-colored telegram form on which he had written the message as it came from his telegraph clicker.

"Good morning, Mrs. Hazard?" he said with inquiry in his voice, for he saw Matthew playing near her before the counter.

"Yes, Mr. Clarny," she said, and her voice dropped deep into her breast, until it sounded from her very heart. She saw what the visitor held in his hands—in the left, his luxurious squashed cigar, in his right the telegram. She knew what the little paper must say.

"Matthew," she said, turning down to the child in the luminous shadow where he made his willful world of play, "just run out to the well and fetch Mother a ladle of water, we must give Mr. Clarny a drink after a walk on such a warm day."

Matthew turned his head without looking at his hero, or at his mother, and went down the store and out the back door. His breath felt dry and his insides felt squeezed. He did not know why.

Mr. Clarny put his cigar to his mouth and seemed to take speech from it. Huskily and with halved gaze, he said:

"I am obliged to hand you this message, Mrs. Hazard, from the Army at Washington."

Doing so, he raised his eyeshade and replaced it as if it were a hat, used in a gesture of respect.

"Yes," she said, "thank you," taking the telegram and not reading it, but folding it, and reaching to the counter for her black purse into which she placed the paper.

"My deepest condolences, madam," said Mr. Clarny, in an echo of many telegrams of similar occasion. He left the store by the front door which Emma shut and locked after him. She then pulled down the faded blue shade on which appeared in scrolled letters the word "Closed" carried on a ribbon supported by doves, all drawn in gold paint. She went out the back door, locked it after her, and met Matthew with his ladle of pure cold water. He walked carefully to spill as little as possible. Looking up at her with a hearty breath of accomplishment, he lifted the ladle to her. She bent over him in the wan sweet sunlight which made summery shadows of their presence in that place and that moment of hidden feeling, and took the ladle saying:

"Mr. Clarny has left, and so I will drink it, for you brought it to me."

She drank. He watched her with love making a lump in his throat, and with pleasure at being able to do for someone else something which was accepted. So she fostered his confidence in life.

"Come," she said, "we are going home."

She took his hand and led him to the well where they replaced the ladle, and then started walking homeward. To do this at such a time of day, leaving the store empty and shut, was puzzling to Matthew.

Their house was a small cottage of clapboard painted gray. The lines of the boards gave it from a little distance an engraved look. There were sycamore trees and lilac bushes about it. It had three rooms and a lean-to kitchen.

They walked home in silence, and Matthew felt his mother's hand cold and thin in his hot strenuous grasp. Her wonderful dark beauty was drained out of her. Though frightened, he skipped and whistled along by her side pretending that all was well. When, at home, in the front room darkened for cool in the heat of the day, she had to tell him that all was not well, and why, she tried to preserve her principle of dealing with him without frank emotion. But her voice at last betrayed her, and he saw her eyes fill, and he began to cry at the contagion of her anguish, and at that she gave up, took him in her hungry arms and crushed him to her heart and wept, ashamed and helpless, and without hope.

Matthew stopped crying then, and tried to pat her tears to stop in their turn. She saw his father in him, and thanked God for this, and at the same time could hardly bear to look at him, for the reminders.

She came back to herself presently, and just in time, for neighbors and friends, having heard from Mr. Clarny of the War Department telegram, began to come, to take up some of the burden of sorrow that had come to the Hazards. The War was coming home everywhere, changing lives suddenly and remorselessly.

•

Emma despite her best efforts could not maintain the store. She lost everything they put into it. She sold what she could and closed out the business, and was thinking of returning to Pittsburgh with her boy when a way was found for them to stay in Fox Creek.

Major Robert Pennypacker came one day to see her at home. His namesake, Major, the hound, greeted him with shambling suspicion and a long, wet growl, for which Matthew reproved him, but without conviction, for he did not like Major Pennypacker himself. The major was a plump man with a pale face on which an apologetic expression lingered, as though to excuse himself for the superior station he occupied in the life of the modest town of Fox Creek. His hair was sandy, and his eyes were light blue and he often blinked them both together when he smiled, to ingratiate himself. He tried too hard to seem what actually he was—a kindly man of middle age. But because of a suspicious nature he knew little happiness.

He condoled with Emma, and blinked at Matthew, and then came to his business.

"As you know, Mrs. Hazard, my wife is an invalid and is now unable to manage or even direct the affairs of my house."

Emma murmured an appropriate regret.

Yes, continued the major, it was a sad cross to bear, not only for his wife, but for him, as there was no one else to conduct a proper household. He came here today to inquire into the possibility that Mrs. Hazard might consent to become his housekeeper. He could offer her comfortable quarters for herself and boy, at a generous wage of six dollars a week, in addition to lodging, full found and keep. He was pleased to repeat to her what all agreed upon to be true—that she was known to be capable, gently mannered, honest, and diligent. There would be a cook and an upstairs maid to obey her directions, and a coachman-gardener to do heavy chores at her behest.

"And for the little fellow, here," he added, turning his doleful good will upon Matthew, "think of the ample grounds to play in, and the fine books and albums in the library to look at, and the horses to ride."

Matthew's face burned dark red. His eyes shone like coals of fire. His breath went hot over his lips. He wanted none of what was offered.

But it was for his sake entirely that Emma agreed to think the matter over, and that she decided after a few days to accept the position of housekeeper at The Fortress. She knew that nowhere else might she find for her boy such comfortable living. They went to live at The Fortress on West Hill. It was then that Matthew, as a little boy, having lost his independence along with his mother's, began to fight to recover it in any way he could imagine. The struggle remained in his imagination alone for a long time. But to be in a rich man's house, and yet not of it; to live like a rich boy and yet own nothing; to see his mother subject to other people's wishes and orders—he knew what all this meant soon enough, and he hated it all.

He was glad when he was old enough to go to school every day up on School Knob, for then he was out of The Fortress, which once he had so coveted from a distance.

•

In the late summer of '64, when school was barely begun, and bees were still above the clover in the meadows, and boys ran barefoot, and women went every day to read the Army lists on the post-office door, the town of Fox Creek, Indiana, heard some rousing news. Though he was not campaigning for re-election, it appeared that President Abraham Lincoln was obliged to make a trip by the steam cars in the second week of that September, and on a certain morning would pass through Fox Creek, westbound. Mr. Clarny had the news, and for the next few days was the most important man in town. A committee called on him to telegraph asking the President to stop in Fox Creek and say a few words from the rear car of his train. There was self-doubting anxiety until a message came back over the telegraph that said, "I will. A. Lincoln," and then followed great pride and delight.

On that September morning everything in town shook and shone in the golden sunlight. From Matt's school window up on the Knob the extra flags in town looked brand-new. Nobody worked. The firehouse band was standing loosely about the station much too early. Now and then a brass horn of the band would squeeze down the sunlight into a single blaze and send it back with a blinding glory. Nobody studied or did lessons. It was for everyone, ever since early morning, a matter of holding the breath.

The school children knew who was coming—it was Father Abraham. *Voom!* they said, firing with their mouths the cannons of the War of their fathers and older brothers and young uncles. Of all those who had never seen the War, the children were oddly nearer to knowing what it was like than their elders. But for all, the War was personified in the President. To the children he was like a grand figure in a storybook. Seven-year-old Matthew Hazard thought of him often, the Commander in Chief.

He thought of him in a great blue uniform with golden shoulder fringes and buttons, and a long cavalry saber with a gold knot, and a white horse. He saw whole meadows full of men exactly like one another following him with bayonets at the port, knees bent in arrested running, dots of light along the ranks of their black patent-leather visors. He saw the shining Army right there, crossing Fox Creek after their Commander in Chief who held out his saber to order "Forward!" It was a creek to run out of woods and through a whole lifetime. It was a heroic creek for Matthew even before he entered the first grade of school, for one frosty afternoon in early winter he saw a red fox among rusty weeds at the edge of the water; and for years he believed that the name of the creek, and of his home town, came from the very fox, that individual animal, whom he had seen: Mr. Fox of Fox Creek, Indiana, himself. And now that the Commander in Chief, President Abraham Lincoln himself, was coming here, the little creek became one of the great rivers of the world. Matthew Hazard was so excited that what meager breakfast he ate would not stay down. His mother worried until she saw him run up School Knob right afterward as muscularly wild and inventive as a large kitten.

Matthew's seat in the schoolroom was by a window that overlooked town, and the tunnels of trees on the streets that led down to the tracks, and the station, and the tracks coming to town and going. A great result of his position was that before anybody else he saw smoke at the horizon where the eastbound tracks must be. Without thinking to get permission he ran out in the school hall. From the cupola of Old School a good stout rope hung down inside the building. He seized it and swung. High above him the school bell rang out. He sang with it—*"Blanngg, mrrongg."* He danced and the rope took him up and he came down with it. He would crack the bell if he could. He told the town with his bell that the President's train was almost there. Children streamed out of their classrooms and out the main door.

He left his bell to die like the old cat, and ran with them. He came to lead them. By acting his most naturally, he had imposed himself, his will, and his effect upon others—all the children, the whole town. He was already a power in life, without knowing it. Sweetness, innocence and energy made his power. Its expressions might change in long later days, but never its source. The children following him tumbled and spilled all the way down the hill. Part of the way went over a boardwalk. The weeds in the cracks blurred green with the speed of Matt running, who believed he flew.

He was the first boy to reach the station platform. There he saw Mr. Clarny inspecting the last loops of red, white and blue bunting that were being tacked up by a firemen's committee. For the past several days Matthew had seen himself as Mr. Clarny and had acted like him. Who else was in charge of the President's visit? He rushed up to him now and asked,

"She's right on time, isn't she?"

Mr. Clarny did not even glance at him but replied with terrible civility,

"This will be a *special* train. It's not on a schedule. It'll only stay a minute."

The mid-morning breeze lifted the bunting. People hurried down the road to the station. They could all see the smoke in the eastern sky. It seemed to come and go. Now it was dense and again pale and silvery like a wave of heat. When no steam engine took form in the distance, someone said that the smoke must be a hay fire at about the old Carruthers place. Murmurs of agreement went around. Someone else asked when was the train due in, then? And Matthew answered:

"This will be a *special* train. It's not on a schedule. It'll only stay a minute."

And then it was asked why everyone had broken their necks to get down here if the train wasn't even *due in*, and if it could only stay a minute, at which Mr. Clarny scratched his brow under his green eyeshade with the thumb of his cigar hand and said inside his fat cheeks,

"Somebody rang the bell at Old School," and with that all the children, the teachers, finally everyone, turned upon Matthew and all their voices spoke over him saying, "He did it!"

It was a hard moment, full of responsibility. There was the band from the firehouse. There, the mayor's committee. Mr. Clarny and his sober preparations. Every man, woman and child. Matthew saw his mother in the crowd on the platform. She lifted her head and smiled at him as if to tell him she was proud of what he'd done, regardless. It was enough. He too felt proud, then, and his confidence became his truth, and he cried out,

"He's coming, all right!" and then threw himself down on the tracks to put his ear on a rail and listen for the faraway train. He shut his eyes and listened hard. His heart banged away on a sharp edge of a wooden sleeper. He hungered to listen to the whole United States of America, and slowly something cleared in his hearing. It was a faint thin humming, and it grew stronger, and he opened his eyes to be sure in another sense, and he shut them again, and he heard. There was a clear jarring ring of the track now. He jumped up waving his arms, vindicated.

"It's coming!" he called out, "I heard it!"

On top of his words there came on the wind like the song of a long cloud the cry of the oncoming engine's whistle out of the east. The crowd quickened, leaning out over the track to see. Other small boys fell to the tracks to listen to the rails like Matthew, and were angrily pulled to safety.

•

Then they saw it. It let out smoke and it stood far away there up the track. They could tell by the smoke that it was moving, but it seemed to be both furious and slow. Those waiting in the little town in the late summer fields felt something must crack if they had to wait much longer for the world to come down the tracks to Fox Creek. But of course the engine grew and grew, and soon the high wheels clanked by with their shining drivers, and with a golden blast of sunny steam and a ringing scream of her iron brakes the engine ground to a halt. The name of the locomotive was "Flying Dutchman," for it said so in a yellow and green sign under the engineer's window.

The rear car was four cars back, quite a way beyond the end of the station shed. The crowd broke and flowed to the rear, followed by the band. The train conductor with telegrams in his hand hurried to the office of Mr. Clarny. Matthew ran down the cindery path beside the cars. Up ahead the engine grunted and sweated and leaked. Back to the rear the crowd fanned out facing the rear platform of the train. Running low, Matthew managed to come in around the crowd by its front knees and at once began to climb up on the last car. Someone plucked him off and made him stand down properly. He was hardly where he should have been, staring upward at the canopy of the car, and the long wood-ribbed door, and the festoons of guard chains on the rear platform, before the door opened slowly, and then let itself shut again, as though someone inside had changed his mind, which made anguish for those waiting; and then again the door opened, slowly, and stooping to get out free under its top came a very tall man in a stovepipe hat and a long black rumpled coat.

The crowd let go and the band blared and drummed in general tumult. There were cries of "Old Abe!"

Matthew's mouth dropped open. There was some mistake. He had not come to see an old brown man with a scarecrow frame. He was looking for the blue and gold Commander in Chief. He wanted President Lincoln. He stared about. The grown-up faces were raised and lighted. He looked up again to the rear car.

Gazing down at him with a frown that was at the same time a smile, the man pulled off his rubbed tall hat from the back frontward across his face, and then broke at the knees like a grasshopper and gravely set the hat down on the floor and then came up again.

The crowd laughed and clapped and Matthew wildly did not know why.

The man held up one hand for silence. It fell. Fox Creek, the fields, the United States held their breath and waited. There was going to be a speech. In the stretched quiet Matthew tugged at the citizen nearest to him and asked out loud,

"Where is President Lincoln?"

"Right up there, that's him, now you hush!" was the answer, accompanied by a hard clout.

"Is *that* him?" asked Matthew and stared up at the platform, while images fell shattered for him.

The tall brown man heard him and looked down and nodded solemnly at Matthew, as if to say, yes, this was him, such as it was, and nothing could be done about it. Then the President squared his shoulders and slowly raised his right hand over the crowd again, and then scratched his neck and opened his mouth to speak.

Exactly then the engine up front let go a leak of steam with a pounding screech, and the President closed his lips and clasped his hands over his hollow middle and waited, looking blank-faced and patient. The band took the opportunity to blare and thump for a few seconds. Suddenly the engine quit screeching, and the President made several little nods, and then began again, saying,

"My—"

Blast went the engine again, and cut him off, deafening him and everyone else. He looked down at Matthew and frowned, sharing with him, now that Matthew knew who he was, an opinion about that pesky engine. He looked like a farmer making a joke, trying to be serious and scary, while all the time he really felt peart. Somebody poked Matthew and gestured, to say that the President was making up to him.

Matthew put his head down and turned hot in shame that he had not known who Mr. Lincoln was, at first. He now had to act more indifferent than ever. He scraped his foot and he knew that everybody was trying to see the boy whom the President of the United States was making up to in the midst of all the racket. The President made his thumb over his shoulder at the engine where the noise came from that shut him up, and he raised his eyebrows, and waggled his jaw making his beard go, and put apart his hands to ask what could be done about the whole scrape. He smiled. His face was so tired and marked with lines that when he smiled it was enough to turn over the hearts of those who watched.

The next thing anybody knew, the conductor was swinging up on the side of one of the cars up ahead, and the steam cut off, and the engine began to hoot out smoke, and the wheels started to turn. They went spinning, then took hold on the rails, and the President's train was moving out. Heavy soot came down over the crowd and they yelled and waved. The President bent down and took up his hat and waved it back. As the train slowly pulled out it gave several blasts with its saluting whistle.

The whistle seemed to wake Matthew up. He gazed after the last car where the President still stood looking at everyone, and Matthew thought he looked sadly at him, because—Matthew suddenly jumped with a fearful thought. The President was almost gone away, believing that Matthew Hazard did not know who he was and didn't care!

"No, there!" cried Matthew, but there was too much noise and nobody heard him.

He hit the air in a leap and began to run up the tracks after the special train under the smoky sun. He was determined to catch the train and make things right with the President. He knew he must win a race to do so, for not far to the west of the station, the tracks crossed Fox Creek on a wooden trestle with open air between the ties. If he tried to run across them he would surely put his leg through and break it. He had to catch the train on this side of the trestle. He put up his head and tried harder. He thought he was gaining, but the clackety-clack of the wheels ahead of him went faster.

Then he saw Mr. Lincoln lean out from under his rear-platform canopy into the sunlight to help him.

"Come on, come on!" said the President, though nobody could hear him.

The President clapped his hands and Matthew flew.

The President stomped his big right foot in time with running, and Matthew puffed and romped.

The engine blew and Matthew was ready to burst. The space widened between him and the last car. He was going to lose. He faltered.

"No, no!" shook the President with his head up there, and waved, "Come on, come on!"

The trestle was just ahead. Mr. Lincoln could hardly have known it was there as a trap for Matthew, but just as if he did know, he suddenly put up his long arm and took the signal cord under the roof, and yanked it hard many times. The train at once began to slow down, it rolled on to the trestle, and stopped with only the last half of the rear car on solid ground this side of Fox Creek.

•

When Matthew saw that, he knew it had stopped for him. He came up to the rear car. The door opened and some other men came out to see what had happened to jerk the train to a halt. One of them was a young officer in blue uniform. The President turned to them and nodded that things were all right, he had taken charge. They just stood there then.

The President gazed down at Matthew and said,

"Well, now."

Matthew went hollow, now that he was where he meant to be, and said nothing. The President leaned down, took Matthew by the arm, raised it, got his hand, then his other hand, and hauled him up over the guard chains and set him on the platform.

"You came to see me?" he asked seriously.

Matthew nodded.

Mr. Lincoln scraped up behind himself an unfolded chair made of fancy green and brown carpeting, and sat down. On his knees he placed Matthew.

"What about?" he asked.

Matthew knew well enough what about, but he could not speak. He hung his head. The President said,

"Just had to see the old hound dog anyhow, is that it?"

One of the men produced a watch and with barely respectful impatience, said,

"After all, Mr. President, we haven't got all day."

"Maybe you haven't, but I have, if somebody is about to break wide open unless somebody else will sit down and pay him a little mind."

"Yes, sir," said the man furiously.

The President winked at Matthew over what got grown men all het up, and asked,

"You live back there in Fox Creek?"

Matthew nodded.

"Say yes, my boy."

"Yes," said Matthew.

"That's done her. Now we can talk. What's your name?"

Matthew told him.

"All right, Matthew Carlton Hazard. What does your pappy do?"

"He was a soldier."

"He was, was he?" A long, sweet smile went over the tired old man's face. "In this war?" he asked.

"Yes, sir."

"Did you lose him?"

"Yes."

"When? Where?"

"At Chicka—"

"—mauga?" finished the President on the difficult name. "Chickamauga. Last year." He put his hands on Matthew's shoulders and gripped him hard. "God bless him," he said. "Is your mother all right?"

"Yes, sir."

"And are you?"

"Yes, sir."

"And so are we all, my boy, for we are trying to do what is right." He drew a deep, staggering breath. "Now let me tell you something, Matthew. Whatever you want to be, and do, if it is a good thing to be, and do, you can be, and do, in this land. Do you know that?"

"Yes, sir."

"If my father's child can get to be the President, your father's child can make his heart's desire. Do you hear?"

"Yes, sir."

Mr. Lincoln put his long finger like a bayonet on Matthew's breast.

"Who is your father's child, then?"

Matthew thought for a moment, and then he knew.

"Me."

"That's who he is, all right! Now then. What do you want to be?"

"Like my father."

"You mean, a soldier?"

"Yes."

The President turned to the young officer beside him and said,

"Captain, if you please."

The captain leaned down to inquire what his Commander in Chief wanted, and Mr. Lincoln reached up and took from his head his little blue cap with the squashed-in front on which were crossed rifles of brass.

"I'll make it up to you, Captain," he said, and put the cap on Matthew's head. It was somewhat too large, but it was real, and it was put there without any idea that it was funny or make-believe. "It does not fit you now," said the President, "but it will fit you some day, Matthew. And when it does, maybe you will remember kindly who put it there. Will you?"

"Yes, sir."

"When the time comes, you find your congressman and tell him you have to go to West Point. You tell him we want to get to where we won't need wars and killing, but you tell him if the Republic needs soldiers, you're aiming to be one. He'll pay attention to you, if you stick out your wishbone and dog him enough. One thing though—" The President put on a joking look. "One thing, don't tell anybody I sent you. It might do you no favor ten years from now. Who knows? Who knows?" he added with sad politeness. "Anyhow," he said, brightening, "far's I'm concerned, you're a soldier right now! It's just a case of the Army waiting a while for you!"

With that he stood Matthew off his knees, and got up and lifted him over the chains down to the ground. For the first time, he noticed that people were coming along the tracks from the station to see what had stopped the train. The President waved at them, turning away, ducking his head, as if to say that enough was enough. He nodded to a member of his party, the signal was sent to the engineer, and the train began to pull away. President Lincoln looked once more at Matthew down on the ground, waved good-by to him with an air of having finished up a good piece of business, and stooping, went inside the car through the rear door.

"What was that?" asked the nearest people, crowding about Matthew to see what he held. He pushed the officer's cap inside his shirt and ran off to the creekside. Major Pennypacker called after him, "Matt, Matt! Come right back here and tell us what the President—" but without effect. They gazed after the running figure which made a receding disturbance in the high-flowered meadow, like a small, straight wind that took its course there, bending aside the tall stalks of Queen Anne's lace and goldenrod and silver-burst long grasses, took its course as it had to do, heeding no power that sought to call it back or make it change.

He took the cap back to The Fortress and hid it with his treasures. The cap was now invested with magic, for it represented to Matthew a talisman for his whole future. It meant that one day he would be able to achieve his independence. The town had seen him receive it from the President, and thereafter, if anybody asked him about it, he lowered his head while keeping his black, brilliant gaze upon his questioner, and simply refrained from replying. It was what Emma called his "black look." It made him formidable, even as a boy, and more handsome than ever.

FROM

For the Union Dead

1964

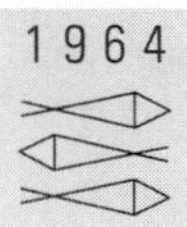

NIGHT SWEAT

Work-table, litter, books and standing lamp,
plain things, my stalled equipment, the old broom—
but I am living in a tidied room,
for ten nights now I've felt the creeping damp
float over my pajamas' wilted white . . .
Sweet salt embalms me and my head is wet,
everything streams and tells me this is right;
my life's fever is soaking in night sweat—
one life, one writing! But the downward glide
and bias of existing wrings us dry—
always inside me is the child who died,
always inside me is his will to die—
one universe, one body . . . in this urn
the animal night sweats of the spirit burn.
Behind me! You! Again I feel the light
lighten my leaded eyelids, while the gray
skulled horses whinny for the soot of night.
I dabble in the dapple of the day,
a heap of wet clothes, seamy, shivering,
I see my flesh and bedding washed with light,
my child exploding into dynamite,
my wife . . . your lightness alters everything,
and tears the black web from the spider's sack,
as your heart hops and flutters like a hare.
Poor turtle, tortoise, if I cannot clear
the surface of these troubled waters here,
absolve me, help me, Dear Heart, as you bear
this world's dead weight and cycle on your back.

FROM

77 Dream Songs

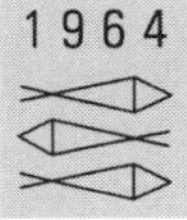

29

There sat down, once, a thing on Henry's heart
só heavy, if he had a hundred years
& more, & weeping, sleepless, in all them time
Henry could not make good.
Starts again always in Henry's ears
the little cough somewhere, an odour, a chime.

And there is another thing he has in mind
like a grave Sienese face a thousand years
would fail to blur the still profiled reproach of. Ghastly,
with open eyes, he attends, blind.
All the bells say: too late. This is not for tears;
thinking.

But never did Henry, as he thought he did,
end anyone and hacks her body up
and hide the pieces, where they may be found.
He knows: he went over everyone, & nobody's missing.
Often he reckons, in the dawn, them up.
Nobody is ever missing.

JOHN MCPHEE

FROM

A Sense of Where You Are

1965

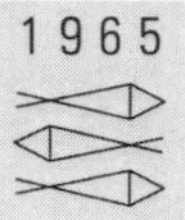

Three seasons ago, when [Bill] Bradley, as a Princeton freshman, broke a free-throw record for the sport of basketball at large, much of the outside world considered it a curious but not necessarily significant achievement. In game after game, he kept sinking foul shots without missing, until at the end of the season he had made fifty-seven straight—one more than the previous all-time high, which had been set by a member of the professional Syracuse Nationals.

The following year, as a varsity player, he averaged a little over twenty-seven points per game, and it became clear that he was the best player ever to have been seen in the Ivy League—better than Yale's Tony Lavelli, who was one of the leading scorers in the United States in 1949, or Dartmouth's Rudy LaRusso, who is now a professional with the Los Angeles Lakers. But that still wasn't saying a lot. Basketball players of the highest calibre do not gravitate to the Ivy League, and excellence within its membership has seldom been worth more, nationally, than a polite smile. However, Ivy teams play early-season games outside their league, and at the end of the season the Ivy League champion competes in the tournament of the National Collegiate Athletic Association, which brings together the outstanding teams in the country and eventually establishes the national champion. Gradually, during his sophomore and junior years, Bradley's repeatedly superior performances in these games eradicated all traces of the notion that he was merely a parochial accident and would have been just another player if he had gone to a big basketball school. He has scored as heavily against non-Ivy opponents as he has against Ivy League teams—forty points against Army, thirty-two against Villanova, thirty-three against Davidson, thirty against Wake Forest, thirty-one against Navy, thirty-four against St. Louis, thirty-six against Syracuse, and forty-six in a rout of the University of Texas. Last season, in the Kentucky Invitational Tournament, at the University of Kentucky, Princeton defeated Wisconsin largely because Bradley was busy scoring forty-seven points—a record for the tournament. The size of this feat can be understood if one remembers that Kentucky has won more national championships than any other university and regularly invites the best competition it can find to join in its holiday games.

An average of twenty points in basketball is comparable to baseball's criterion for outstanding pitchers, whose immortality seems to be predicated on their winning twenty games a year. Bradley scored more points last season than any other college basketball player, and his average was 32.3 per game. If Bradley's shooting this season comes near matching his accomplishment of last year, he will become one of the three highest-scoring players in the history of college basketball.

Those who have never seen him are likely to assume that he is seven and a half feet tall—the sort of elaborate weed that once all but choked off the game. With an average like his, it would be fair to imagine him spending his forty minutes of action merely stuffing the ball into the net. But the age of the goon is over. Bradley is six feet five inches tall—the third-tallest player on the Princeton team. He is perfectly coördinated, and he is unbelievably accurate at every kind of shot in the basketball repertory. He does much of his scoring from considerable distances, and when he sends the ball toward the basket, the odds are that it is going in, since he has made more than half the shots he has attempted as a college player. With three, or even four, opponents clawing at him, he will rise in the air, hang still for a moment, and release a high parabola jump shot that almost always seems to drop into the basket with an equal margin to the rim on all sides. Against Harvard last February, his ninth long shot from the floor nicked the rim slightly on its way into the net. The first eight had gone cleanly through the center. He had missed none at all. He missed several as the evening continued, but when his coach finally took him out, he had scored fifty-one points. In a game twenty-four hours earlier, he had begun a thirty-nine point performance by hitting his first four straight. Then he missed a couple. Then he made ten consecutive shots, totally demoralizing Dartmouth.

Bradley is one of the few basketball players who have ever been appreciatively cheered by a disinterested away-from-home crowd while warming up. This curious event occurred last March, just before Princeton eliminated the Virginia Military Institute, the year's Southern Conference champion, from the N.C.A.A. championships. The game was played in Philadelphia and was the last of a tripleheader. The people there were worn out, because most of them were emotionally committed to either Villanova or Temple—two local teams that had just been involved in enervating battles with Providence and Connecticut, respectively, scrambling for a chance at the rest of the country. A group of Princeton boys shooting basketballs miscellaneously in preparation for still another game hardly promised to be a high point of the evening, but Bradley, whose routine in the warmup time is a gradual crescendo of activity, is more interesting to watch before a game than most players are in play. In Philadelphia that night, what he did was, for him, anything but unusual. As he does before all games, he began by shooting set shots close to the basket, gradually moving back until he was shooting long sets from twenty feet out, and nearly all of them dropped into the net with an almost mechanical rhythm of accuracy. Then he began a series of expandingly difficult jump shots, and one jumper after another went cleanly through the basket with so few exceptions that the crowd began to murmur. Then he started to perform whirling reverse moves before another cadence of almost steadily accurate jump shots, and the murmur increased. Then he began to sweep hook shots into the air. He moved in a semicircle around the court. First with his right hand, then with his left, he tried seven of these long, graceful shots—the most difficult ones in the orthodoxy of basketball—and ambidextrously made them all. The game had not even begun, but the presumably unimpressible Philadelphians were applauding like an audience at an opera.

Bradley has a few unorthodox shots, too. He dislikes flamboyance, and, unlike some of basketball's greatest stars, has apparently never made a move merely to attract attention. While some players are eccentric in their shooting, his shots, with only occasional exceptions, are straightforward and unexaggerated. Nonetheless, he does make something of a spectacle of himself when he moves in rapidly parallel to the baseline, glides through the air with his back to the basket, looks for a teammate he can pass to, and, finding none, tosses the ball into the basket over one shoulder, like a pinch of salt. Only when the ball is actually dropping through the net does he look around to see what has happened, on the chance that something might have gone wrong, in which case he would have to go for the rebound. That shot has the essential characteristics of a wild accident, which is what many people stubbornly think they have witnessed until they see him do it for the third time in a row. All shots in basketball are supposed to have names—the set, the hook, the lay-up, the jump shot, and so on—and one weekend last July, while Bradley was in Princeton working on his senior thesis and putting in some time in the Princeton gymnasium to keep himself in form for the Olympics, I asked him what he called his over-the-shoulder shot. He said that he had never heard a name for it, but that he had seen Oscar Robertson, of the Cincinnati Royals, and Jerry West, of the Los Angeles Lakers, do it, and had worked it out for himself. He went on to say that it is a much simpler shot than it appears to be, and, to illustrate, he tossed a ball over his shoulder and into the basket while he was talking and looking me in the eye. I retrieved the ball and handed it back to him. "When you have played basketball for a while, you don't need to look at the basket when you are in close like this," he said, throwing it over his shoulder again and right through the hoop. "You develop a sense of where you are."

Bradley is not an innovator. Actually, basketball has had only a few innovators in its history—players like Hank Luisetti, of Stanford, whose introduction in 1936 of the running one-hander did as much to open up the game for scoring as the forward pass did for football; and Joe Fulks, of the old Philadelphia Warriors, whose twisting two-handed heaves, made while he was leaping like a salmon, were the beginnings of the jump shot, which seems to be basketball's ultimate weapon. Most basketball players appropriate fragments of other players' styles, and thus develop their own. This is what Bradley has done, but one of the things that set him apart from nearly everyone else is that the process has been conscious rather than osmotic. His jump shot, for example, has had two principal influences. One is Jerry West, who has one of the best jumpers in basketball. At a summer basketball camp in Missouri some years ago, West told Bradley that he always gives an extra hard bounce to the last dribble before a jump shot, since this seems to catapult him to added height. Bradley has been doing that ever since. Terry Dischinger, of the Detroit Pistons, has told Bradley that he always slams his foot to the floor on the last step before a jump shot, because this stops his momentum and thus prevents drift. Drifting while aloft is the mark of a sloppy jump shot.

Bradley's graceful hook shot is a masterpiece of eclecticism. It consists of the high-lifted knee of the Los Angeles Lakers' Darrall Imhoff, the arms of Bill Russell, of the Boston Celtics, who extends his idle hand far under his shooting arm and thus magically stabilizes the shot, and the general corporeal form of Kentucky's Cotton Nash, a rookie this year with the Lakers. Bradley carries his analyses of shots further than merely identifying them with pieces of other people. "There are five parts to the hook shot," he explains to anyone who asks. As he continues, he picks up a ball and stands about eighteen feet from a basket. "Crouch," he says, crouching, and goes on to demonstrate the other moves. "Turn your head to look for the basket, step, kick, follow through with your arms." Once, as he was explaining this to me, the ball curled around the rim and failed to go in.

"What happened then?" I asked him.

"I didn't kick high enough," he said.

"Do you always know exactly why you've missed a shot?"

"Yes," he said, missing another one.

"What happened that time?"

"I was talking to you. I didn't concentrate. The secret of shooting is concentration."

His set shot is borrowed from Ed Macauley, who was a St. Louis University All-American in the late forties and was later a star member of the Boston Celtics and the St. Louis Hawks. Macauley runs the basketball camp Bradley first went to when he was fifteen. In describing the set shot, Bradley is probably quoting a Macauley lecture. "Crouch like Groucho Marx," he says. "Go off your feet a few inches. You shoot with your legs. Your arms merely guide the ball." Bradley says that he has more confidence in his set shot than in any other. However, he seldom uses it, because he seldom has to. A set shot is a long shot, usually a twenty-footer, and Bradley, with his speed and footwork, can almost always take some other kind of shot, closer to the basket. He will take set shots when they are given to him, though. Two seasons ago, Davidson lost to Princeton, using a compact zone defense that ignored the remoter areas of the court. In one brief sequence, Bradley sent up seven set shots, missing only one. The missed one happened to rebound in Bradley's direction, and he leaped up, caught it with one hand, and scored.

Even his lay-up shot has an ancestral form; he is full of admiration for "the way Cliff Hagan pops up anywhere within six feet of the basket," and he tries to do the same. Hagan is a former Kentucky star who now plays for the St. Louis Hawks. Because opposing teams always do everything they can to stop Bradley, he gets an unusual number of foul shots. When he was in high school, he used to imitate Bob Pettit, of the St. Louis Hawks, and Bill Sharman of the Boston Celtics, but now his free throw is more or less his own. With his left foot back about eighteen inches—"wherever it feels comfortable," he says—he shoots with a deep-bending rhythm of knees and arms, one-handed, his left hand acting as a kind of gantry for the ball until the moment of release. What is most interesting, though, is that he concentrates his attention on one of the tiny steel eyelets that are welded under the rim of the basket to hold the net to the hoop—on the center eyelet, of course—before he lets fly. One night, he scored over twenty points on free throws alone; Cornell hacked at him so heavily that he was given twenty-one free throws, and he made all twenty-one, finishing the game with a total of thirty-seven points.

When Bradley, working out alone, practices his set shots, hook shots, and jump shots, he moves systematically from one place to another around the basket, his distance from it being appropriate to the shot, and he does not permit himself to move on until he has made at least ten shots out of thirteen from each location. He applies this standard to every kind of shot, with either hand, from any distance. Many basketball players, including reasonably good ones, could spend five years in a gym and not make ten out of thirteen left-handed hook shots, but that is part of Bradley's daily routine. He talks to himself while he is shooting, usually reminding himself to concentrate but sometimes talking to himself the way every high-school j.v. basketball player has done since the dim twenties—more or less imitating a radio announcer, and saying, as he gathers himself up for a shot, "It's pandemonium in Dillon Gymnasium. The clock is running out. He's up with a jumper. Swish!"

Last summer, the floor of the Princeton gym was being resurfaced, so Bradley had to put in several practice sessions at the Lawrenceville School. His first afternoon at Lawrenceville, he began by shooting fourteen-foot jump shots from the right side. He got off to a bad start, and he kept missing them. Six in a row hit the back rim of the basket and bounced out. He stopped, looking discomfited, and seemed to be making an adjustment in his mind. Then he went up for another jump shot from the same spot and hit it cleanly. Four more shots went in without a miss, and then he paused and said, "You want to know something? That basket is about an inch and a half low." Some weeks later, I went back to Lawrenceville with a steel tape, borrowed a stepladder, and measured the height of the basket. It was nine feet ten and seven-eighths inches above the floor, or one and one-eighth inches too low.

•

Being a deadly shot with either hand and knowing how to make the moves and fakes that clear away the defense are the primary skills of a basketball player, and any player who can do these things half as well as Bradley can has all the equipment he needs to make a college team. Many high-scoring basketball players, being able to make so obvious and glamorous a contribution to their team in the form of point totals, don't bother to develop the other skills of the game, and leave subordinate matters like defense and playmaking largely to their teammates. Hence, it is usually quite easy to parse a basketball team. Bringing the ball up the floor are playmaking backcourt men—selfless fellows who can usually dribble so adeptly that they can just about freeze the ball by themselves, and who can also throw passes through the eye of a needle and can always be counted on to feed the ball to a star at the right moment. A star is often a point-hungry gunner, whose first instinct when he gets the ball is to fire away, and whose playing creed might be condensed to "When in doubt, shoot." Another, with legs like automobile springs, is part of the group because of an unusual ability to go high for rebounds. Still another may not be especially brilliant on offense but has defensive equipment that could not be better if he were carrying a trident and a net.

The point-hungry gunner aside, Bradley is all these. He is a truly complete basketball player. He can play in any terrain; in the heavy infighting near the basket, he is master of all the gestures of the big men, and toward the edge of play he shows that he has all the fast-moving skills of the little men, too. With remarkable speed for six feet five, he can steal the ball and break into the clear with it on his own; as a dribbler, he can control the ball better with his left hand than most players can with their right; he can go down court in the middle of a fast break and fire passes to left and right, closing in on the basket, the timing of his passes too quick for the spectator's eye. He plays any position—up front, in the post, in the backcourt. And his playmaking is a basic characteristic of his style. His high-scoring totals are the result of his high percentage of accuracy, not of an impulse to shoot every time he gets the ball.

He passes as generously and as deftly as any player in the game. When he is dribbling, he can pass accurately without first catching the ball. He can also manage almost any pass without appearing to cock his arm, or even bring his hand back. He just seems to flick his fingers and the ball is gone. Other Princeton players aren't always quite expecting Bradley's passes when they arrive, for Bradley is usually thinking a little bit ahead of everyone else on the floor. When he was a freshman, he was forever hitting his teammates on the mouth, the temple, or the back of the head with passes as accurate as they were surprising. His teammates have since sharpened their own faculties, and these accidents seldom happen now. "It's rewarding to play with him," one of them says. "If you get open, you'll get the ball." And, with all the defenders in between, it sometimes seems as if the ball has passed like a ray through several walls.

Bradley's play has just one somewhat unsound aspect, and it is the result of his mania for throwing the ball to his teammates. He can't seem to resist throwing a certain number of passes that are based on nothing but theory and hope; in fact, they are referred to by the Princeton coaching staff as Bradley's hope passes. They happen, usually, when something has gone just a bit wrong. Bradley is recovering a loose ball, say, with his back turned to the other Princeton players. Before he turned it, he happened to notice a screen, or pick-off, being set by two of his teammates, its purpose being to cause one defensive man to collide with another player and thus free an offensive man to receive a pass and score. Computations whir in Bradley's head. He hasn't time to look, but the screen, as he saw it developing, seemed to be working, so a Princeton man should now be in the clear, running toward the basket with one arm up. He whips the ball over his shoulder to the spot where the man ought to be. Sometimes a hope pass goes flying into the crowd, but most of the time they hit the receiver right in the hand, and a gasp comes from several thousand people. Bradley is sensitive about such dazzling passes, because they look flashy, and an edge comes into his voice as he defends them. "When I was halfway down the court, I saw a man out of the corner of my eye who had on the same color shirt I did," he said recently, explaining how he happened to fire a scoring pass while he was falling out of bounds. "A little later, when I threw the pass, I threw it to the spot where that man should have been if he had kept going and done his job. He was there. Two points."

Since it appears that by nature Bradley is a passer first and a scorer second, he would probably have scored less at a school where he was surrounded by other outstanding players. When he went to Princeton, many coaches mourned his loss not just to themselves but to basketball, but as things have worked out, much of his national prominence has been precipitated by his playing for Princeton, where he has had to come through with points in order to keep his team from losing. He starts slowly, as a rule. During much of the game, if he has a clear shot, fourteen feet from the basket, say, and he sees a teammate with an equally clear shot ten feet from the basket, he sends the ball to the teammate. Bradley apparently does not stop to consider that even though the other fellow is closer to the basket he may be far more likely to miss the shot. This habit exasperates his coaches until they clutch their heads in despair. But Bradley is doing what few people ever have done—he is playing basketball according to the foundation pattern of the game. Therefore, the shot goes to the closer man. Nothing on earth can make him change until Princeton starts to lose. Then he will concentrate a little more on the basket.

Something like this happened in Tokyo last October, when the United States Olympic basketball team came close to being beaten by Yugoslavia. The Yugoslavian team was reasonably good—better than the Soviet team, which lost to the United States in the final—and it heated up during the second half. With two minutes to go, Yugoslavia cut the United States' lead to two points. Bradley was on the bench at the time, and Henry Iba, the Oklahoma State coach, who was coach of the Olympic team, sent him in. During much of the game, he had been threading passes to others, but at that point, he says, he felt that he had to try to do something about the score. Bang, bang, bang—he hit a running one-hander, a seventeen-foot jumper, and a lay-up on a fast break, and the United States won by eight points.

Actually, the United States basketball squad encountered no real competition at the Olympics, despite all sorts of rumbling cumulus beforehand to the effect that some of the other teams, notably Russia's, were made up of men who had been playing together for years and were now possibly good enough to defeat an American Olympic basketball team for the first time. But if the teams that the Americans faced were weaker than advertised, there were nonetheless individual performers of good calibre, and it is a further index to Bradley's completeness as a basketball player that Henry Iba, a defensive specialist as a coach, regularly assigned him to guard the stars of the other nations. "He didn't show too much tact at defense when he started, but he's a coach's basketball player, and he came along," Iba said after he had returned to Oklahoma. "And I gave him the toughest man in every game."

Yugoslavia's best man was a big forward who liked to play in the low post, under the basket. Bradley went into the middle with him, crashing shoulders under the basket, and held him to thirteen points while scoring eighteen himself. Russia's best man was Yuri Korneyev, whose specialty was driving; that is, he liked to get the ball somewhere out on the edge of the action and start for the basket with it like a fullback, blasting everything out of the way until he got close enough to ram in a point-blank shot. With six feet five inches and two hundred and forty pounds to drive, Korneyev was what Iba called "a real good driver." Bradley had lost ten pounds because of all the Olympics excitement, and Korneyev outweighed him by forty-five pounds. Korneyev kicked, pushed, shoved, bit, and scratched Bradley. "He was tough to stop," Bradley says. "After all, he was playing for his life." Korneyev got eight points.

Bradley was one of three players who had been picked unanimously for the twelve-man Olympic team. He was the youngest member of the squad and the only undergraduate. Since his trip to Tokyo kept him away from Princeton for the first six weeks of the fall term, he had to spend part of his time reading, and the course he worked on most was Russian History 323. Perhaps because of the perspective this gave him, his attitude toward the Russian basketball team was not what he had expected it to be. With the help of three Australian players who spoke Russian, Bradley got to know several members of the Russian team fairly well, and soon he was feeling terribly sorry for them. They had a leaden attitude almost from the beginning. "All we do is play basketball," one of them told him forlornly. "After we go home, we play in the Soviet championships. Then we play in the Satellite championships. Then we play in the European championships. I would give anything for five days off." Bradley says that the Russian players also told him they were paid eighty-five dollars a month, plus housing. Given the depressed approach of the Russians, Bradley recalls, it was hard to get excited before the Russian-American final. "It was tough to get chills," he says. "I had to imagine we were about to play Yale." The Russians lost, 73–59.

•

When Bradley talks about basketball, he speaks with authority, explaining himself much as a man of fifty might do in discussing a profession or business. When he talks about other things, he shows himself to be a polite, diffident, hopeful, well-brought-up, extremely amiable, and sometimes naïve but generally discerning young man just emerging from adolescence. He was twenty-one last summer, and he seems neither older nor younger than his age. He is painfully aware of his celebrity. The nature of it and the responsibility that it imposes are constantly on his mind. He remembers people's names, and greets them by name when he sees them again. He seems to want to prove that he finds other people interesting. "The main thing I have to prevent myself from becoming is disillusioned with transitory success," he said recently. "It's dangerous. It's like a heavy rainstorm. It can do damage or it can do good, permitting something to grow." He claims that the most important thing basketball gives him at Princeton is "a real period of relief from the academic load." Because he is the sort of student who does all his academic course work, he doesn't get much sleep; in fact, he has a perilous contempt for sleep, partly because he has been told that professional basketball players get along on almost none of it. He stays up until his work is done, for if he were to retire any earlier he would be betraying the discipline he has placed upon himself. When he has had to, he has set up schedules of study that have kept him reading from 6 A.M. to midnight every day for as long as eight weeks. On his senior thesis, which is due in April (and is about Harry Truman's senatorial campaign in 1940), he has already completed more research than many students will do altogether. One of his most enviable gifts is his ability to regiment his conscious mind. After a game, for example, most college players, if they try to study, see all the action over again between the lines in their books. Bradley can, and often does, go straight to the library and work for hours, postponing his mental re-play as long as he cares to. If he feels that it's necessary, he will stay up all night before a basketball game; he did that last winter when he was completing a junior paper, and Princeton barely managed to beat a fairly unspectacular Lafayette team, because Bradley seemed almost unable to lift his arms. Princeton was losing until Bradley, finally growing wakeful, scored eight points in the last two minutes.

Ivy League basketball teams play on Friday and Saturday nights, in order to avoid travelling during the week, yet on Sunday mornings Bradley gets up and teaches a nine-thirty Sunday-school class at the First Presbyterian Church. During his sophomore and junior years at the university, he met a class of seventh-grade boys every Sunday morning that he was resident in Princeton. If the basketball bus returned to Princeton at 4:30 A.M., as it sometimes did, he would still be at the church by nine-thirty. This year, having missed two months while he was in the Far East, he is working as a spot teacher whenever he is needed. Religion, he feels, is the main source of his strength, and because he realizes that not everybody shares that feeling today, he sometimes refers to "the challenge of being in the minority in the world." He belongs to the Fellowship of Christian Athletes, an organization that was set up eight years ago, by people like Otto Graham, Bob Pettit, Branch Rickey, Bob Feller, Wilma Rudolph, Doak Walker, Rafer Johnson, and Robin Roberts, for the advancement of youth by a mixture of moral and athletic guidance. Bradley has flown all over the United States to speak to F.C.A. groups. One of his topics is a theory of his that conformists and nonconformists both lack moral courage, and another is that "the only way to solve a problem is to go through it rather than around it"—which has struck some listeners as an odd view for a basketball player to have. Nevertheless, Bradley often tells his audiences, "Basketball discipline carries over into your life," continuing, "You've got to face that you're going to lose. Losses are part of every season, and part of life. The question is, can you adjust? It is important that you don't get caught up in your own little defeats." If he seems ministerial, that is because he is. He has a firm sense of what is right, and apparently feels that he has a mission to help others see things as clearly as he does. "I don't try to be overbearing in what I believe, but, given a chance, I will express my beliefs," he says. After the Olympics were over, he stayed in the Far East an extra week to make a series of speeches at universities in Taiwan and Hong Kong.

As a news story once said of Bradley—quite accurately, it seems—he is everything his parents think he is. He approximates what some undergraduates call a straight arrow—a semi-pejorative term for unfortunates who have no talent for vice. Nevertheless, considerable numbers of Princeton undergraduates have told me that Bradley is easily the most widely admired student on the campus and probably the best liked, and that his skill at basketball is not the only way in which he atones for his moral altitude. He has worked for the Campus Fund Drive, which is a sort of Collegiate Gothic community chest, and for the Orange Key Society, an organization that, among other things, helps freshmen settle down into college life. One effect that Bradley has had on Princeton has been to widen noticeably the undergraduate body's tolerance for people with high ethical standards. "He is a source of inspiration to anyone who comes in contact with him," one of his classmates says. "You look at yourself and you decide to do better."

Bradley has built his life by setting up and going after a series of goals, athletic and academic, which at the moment have culminated in his position on the Olympic basketball team and his Rhodes Scholarship. Of the future beyond Oxford, he says only that he wants to go to law school and later "set a Christian example by implementing my feelings within the structure of the society," adding, "I value my ultimate goals more than playing basketball." I have asked all sorts of people who know Bradley, or know about him, what they think he will be doing when he is forty. A really startling number of them, including teachers, coaches, college boys, and even journalists, give the same answer: "He will be the governor of Missouri." The chief dissent comes from people who look beyond the stepping stone of the Missouri State House and calmly tell you that Bradley is going to be President. Last spring, Leonard Shecter, of the New York *Post*, began a column by saying, "In twenty-five years or so our presidents are going to have to be better than ever. It's nice to know that Bill Bradley will be available." Edward Rapp, Bradley's high-school principal, once said, "With the help of his friends, Bill could very well be President of the United States. And without the help of his friends he might make it anyway."

FROM

Everything That Rises Must Converge

1965

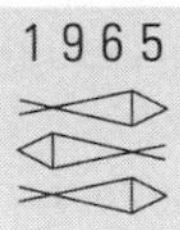

EVERYTHING THAT RISES MUST CONVERGE

Her doctor had told Julian's mother that she must lose twenty pounds on account of her blood pressure, so on Wednesday nights Julian had to take her downtown on the bus for a reducing class at the Y. The reducing class was designed for working girls over fifty, who weighed from 165 to 200 pounds. His mother was one of the slimmer ones, but she said ladies did not tell their age or weight. She would not ride the buses by herself at night since they had been integrated, and because the reducing class was one of her few pleasures, necessary for her health, and *free*, she said Julian could at least put himself out to take her, considering all she did for him. Julian did not like to consider all she did for him, but every Wednesday night he braced himself and took her.

She was almost ready to go, standing before the hall mirror, putting on her hat, while he, his hands behind him, appeared pinned to the door frame, waiting like Saint Sebastian for the arrows to begin piercing him. The hat was new and had cost her seven dollars and a half. She kept saying, "Maybe I shouldn't have paid that for it. No, I shouldn't have. I'll take it off and return it tomorrow. I shouldn't have bought it."

Julian raised his eyes to heaven. "Yes, you should have bought it," he said. "Put it on and let's go." It was a hideous hat. A purple velvet flap came down on one side of it and stood up on the other; the rest of it was green and looked like a cushion with the stuffing out. He decided it was less comical than jaunty and pathetic. Everything that gave her pleasure was small and depressed him.

She lifted the hat one more time and set it down slowly on top of her head. Two wings of gray hair protruded on either side of her florid face, but her eyes, sky-blue, were as innocent and untouched by experience as they must have been when she was ten. Were it not that she was a widow who had struggled fiercely to feed and clothe and put him through school and who was supporting him still, "until he got on his feet," she might have been a little girl that he had to take to town.

"It's all right, it's all right," he said. "Let's go." He opened the door himself and started down the walk to get her going. The sky was a dying violet and the houses stood out darkly against it, bulbous liver-colored monstrosities of a uniform ugliness though no two were alike. Since this had been a fashionable neighborhood forty years ago, his mother persisted in thinking they did well to have an apartment in it. Each house had a narrow collar of dirt around it in which sat, usually, a grubby child. Julian walked with his hands in his pockets, his head down and thrust forward and his eyes glazed with the determination to make himself completely numb during the time he would be sacrificed to her pleasure.

The door closed and he turned to find the dumpy figure, surmounted by the atrocious hat, coming toward him. "Well," she said, "you only live once and paying a little more for it, I at least won't meet myself coming and going."

"Some day I'll start making money," Julian said gloomily—he knew he never would—"and you can have one of those jokes whenever you take the fit." But first they would move. He visualized a place where the nearest neighbors would be three miles away on either side.

"I think you're doing fine," she said, drawing on her gloves. "You've only been out of school a year. Rome wasn't built in a day."

She was one of the few members of the Y reducing class who arrived in hat and gloves and who had a son who had been to college. "It takes time," she said, "and the world is in such a mess. This hat looked better on me than any of the others, though when she brought it out I said, 'Take that thing back. I wouldn't have it on my head,' and she said, 'Now wait till you see it on,' and when she put it on me, I said, 'We-ull,' and she said, 'If you ask me, that hat does something for you and you do something for the hat, and besides,' she said, 'with that hat, you won't meet yourself coming and going.' "

Julian thought he could have stood his lot better if she had been selfish, if she had been an old hag who drank and screamed at him. He walked along, saturated in depression, as if in the midst of his martyrdom he had lost his faith. Catching sight of his long, hopeless, irritated face, she stopped suddenly with a grief-stricken look, and pulled back on his arm. "Wait on me," she said. "I'm going back to the house and take this thing off and tomorrow I'm going to return it. I was out of my head. I can pay the gas bill with that seven-fifty."

He caught her arm in a vicious grip. "You are not going to take it back," he said. "I like it."

"Well," she said, "I don't think I ought . . ."

"Shut up and enjoy it," he muttered, more depressed than ever.

"With the world in the mess it's in," she said, "it's a wonder we can enjoy anything. I tell you, the bottom rail is on the top."

Julian sighed.

"Of course," she said, "if you know who you are, you can go anywhere." She said this every time he took her to the reducing class. "Most of them in it are not our kind of people," she said, "but I can be gracious to anybody. I know who I am."

"They don't give a damn for your graciousness," Julian said savagely. "Knowing who you are is good for one generation only. You haven't the foggiest idea where you stand now or who you are."

She stopped and allowed her eyes to flash at him. "I most certainly do know who I am," she said, "and if you don't know who you are, I'm ashamed of you."

"Oh hell," Julian said.

"Your great-grandfather was a former governor of this state," she said. "Your grandfather was a prosperous landowner. Your grandmother was a Godhigh."

"Will you look around you," he said tensely, "and see where you are now?" and he swept his arm jerkily out to indicate the neighborhood, which the growing darkness at least made less dingy.

"You remain what you are," she said. "Your great-grandfather had a plantation and two hundred slaves."

"There are no more slaves," he said irritably.

"They were better off when they were," she said. He groaned to see that she was off on that topic. She rolled onto it every few days like a train on an open track. He knew every stop, every junction, every swamp along the way, and knew the exact point at which her conclusion would roll majestically into the station: "It's ridiculous. It's simply not realistic. They should rise, yes, but on their own side of the fence."

"Let's skip it," Julian said.

"The ones I feel sorry for," she said, "are the ones that are half white. They're tragic."

"Will you skip it?"

"Suppose we were half white. We would certainly have mixed feelings."

"I have mixed feelings now," he groaned.

"Well let's talk about something pleasant," she said. "I remember going to Grandpa's when I was a little girl. Then the house had double stairways that went up to what was really the second floor—all the cooking was done on the first. I used to like to stay down in the kitchen on account of the way the walls smelled. I would sit with my nose pressed against the plaster and take deep breaths. Actually the place belonged to the Godhighs but your grandfather Chestny paid the mortgage and saved it for them. They were in reduced circumstances," she said, "but reduced or not, they never forgot who they were."

"Doubtless that decayed mansion reminded them," Julian muttered. He never spoke of it without contempt or thought of it without longing. He had seen it once when he was a child before it had been sold. The double stairways had rotted and been torn down. Negroes were living in it. But it remained in his mind as his mother had known it. It appeared in his dreams regularly. He would stand on the wide porch, listening to the rustle of oak leaves, then wander through the high-ceilinged hall into the parlor that opened onto it and gaze at the worn rugs and faded draperies. It occurred to him that it was he, not she, who could have appreciated it. He preferred its threadbare elegance to anything he could name and it was because of it that all the neighborhoods they had lived in had been a torment to him—whereas she had hardly known the difference. She called her insensitivity "being adjustable."

"And I remember the old darky who was my nurse, Caroline. There was no better person in the world. I've always had a great respect for my colored friends," she said. "I'd do anything in the world for them and they'd . . ."

"Will you for God's sake get off that subject?" Julian said. When he got on a bus by himself, he made it a point to sit down beside a Negro, in reparation as it were for his mother's sins.

"You're mighty touchy tonight," she said. "Do you feel all right?"

"Yes I feel all right," he said. "Now lay off."

She pursed her lips. "Well, you certainly are in a vile humor," she observed. "I just won't speak to you at all."

They had reached the bus stop. There was no bus in sight and Julian, his hands still jammed in his pockets and his head thrust forward, scowled down the empty street. The frustration of having to wait on the bus as well as ride on it began to creep up his neck like a hot hand. The presence of his mother was borne in upon him as she gave a pained sigh. He looked at her bleakly. She was holding herself very erect under the preposterous hat, wearing it like a banner of her imaginary dignity. There was in him an evil urge to break her spirit. He suddenly unloosened his tie and pulled it off and put it in his pocket.

She stiffened. "Why must you look like *that* when you take me to town?" she said. "Why must you deliberately embarrass me?"

"If you'll never learn where you are," he said, "you can at least learn where I am."

"You look like a—thug," she said.

"Then I must be one," he murmured.

"I'll just go home," she said. "I will not bother you. If you can't do a little thing like that for me . . ."

Rolling his eyes upward, he put his tie back on. "Restored to my class," he muttered. He thrust his face toward her and hissed, "True culture is in the mind, the *mind*," he said, and tapped his head, "the mind."

"It's in the heart," she said, "and in how you do things and how you do things is because of who you *are*."

"Nobody in the damn bus cares who you are."

"I care who I am," she said icily.

The lighted bus appeared on top of the next hill and as it approached, they moved out into the street to meet it. He put his hand under her elbow and hoisted her up on the creaking step. She entered with a little smile, as if she were going into a drawing room where everyone had been waiting for her. While he put in the tokens, she sat down on one of the broad front seats for three which faced the aisle. A thin woman with protruding teeth and long yellow hair was sitting on the end of it. His mother moved up beside her and left room for Julian beside herself. He sat down and looked at the floor across the aisle where a pair of thin feet in red and white canvas sandals were planted.

His mother immediately began a general conversation meant to attract anyone who felt like talking. "Can it get any hotter?" she said and removed from her purse a folding fan, black with a Japanese scene on it, which she began to flutter before her.

"I reckon it might could," the woman with the protruding teeth said, "but I know for a fact my apartment couldn't get no hotter."

"It must get the afternoon sun," his mother said. She sat forward and looked up and down the bus. It was half filled. Everybody was white. "I see we have the bus to ourselves," she said. Julian cringed.

"For a change," said the woman across the aisle, the owner of the red and white canvas sandals. "I come on one the other day and they were thick as fleas—up front and all through."

"The world is in a mess everywhere," his mother said. "I don't know how we've let it get in this fix."

"What gets my goat is all those boys from good families stealing automobile tires," the woman with the protruding teeth said. "I told my boy, I said you may not be rich but you been raised right and if I ever catch you in any such mess, they can send you on to the reformatory. Be exactly where you belong."

"Training tells," his mother said. "Is your boy in high school?"

"Ninth grade," the woman said.

"My son just finished college last year. He wants to write but he's selling typewriters until he gets started," his mother said.

The woman leaned forward and peered at Julian. He threw her such a malevolent look that she subsided against the seat. On the floor across the aisle there was an abandoned newspaper. He got up and got it and opened it out in front of him. His mother discreetly continued the conversation in a lower tone but the woman across the aisle said in a loud voice, "Well that's nice. Selling typewriters is close to writing. He can go right from one to the other."

"I tell him," his mother said, "that Rome wasn't built in a day."

Behind the newspaper Julian was withdrawing into the inner compartment of his mind where he spent most of his time. This was a kind of mental bubble in which he established himself when he could not bear to be a part of what was going on around him. From it he could see out and judge but in it he was safe from any kind of penetration from without. It was the only place where he felt free of the general idiocy of his fellows. His mother had never entered it but from it he could see her with absolute clarity.

The old lady was clever enough and he thought that if she had started from any of the right premises, more might have been expected of her. She lived according to the laws of her own fantasy world, outside of which he had never seen her set foot. The law of it was to sacrifice herself for him after she had first created the necessity to do so by making a mess of things. If he had permitted her sacrifices, it was only because her lack of foresight had made them necessary. All of her life had been a struggle to act like a Chestny without the Chestny goods, and to give him everything she thought a Chestny ought to have; but since, said she, it was fun to struggle, why complain? And when you had won, as she had won, what fun to look back on the hard times! He could not forgive her that she had enjoyed the struggle and that she thought *she* had won.

What she meant when she said she had won was that she had brought him up successfully and had sent him to college and that he had turned out so well—good looking (her teeth had gone unfilled so that his could be straightened), intelligent (he realized he was too intelligent to be a success), and with a future ahead of him (there was of course no future ahead of him). She excused his gloominess on the grounds that he was still growing up and his radical ideas on his lack of practical experience. She said he didn't yet know a thing about "life," that he hadn't even entered the real world—when already he was as disenchanted with it as a man of fifty.

The further irony of all this was that in spite of her, he had turned out so well. In spite of going to only a third-rate college, he had, on his own initiative, come out with a first-rate education; in spite of growing up dominated by a small mind, he had ended up with a large one; in spite of all her foolish views, he was free of prejudice and unafraid to face facts. Most miraculous of all, instead of being blinded by love for her as she was for him, he had cut himself emotionally free of her and could see her with complete objectivity. He was not dominated by his mother.

The bus stopped with a sudden jerk and shook him from his meditation. A woman from the back lurched forward with little steps and barely escaped falling in his newspaper as she righted herself. She got off and a large Negro got on. Julian kept his paper lowered to watch. It gave him a certain satisfaction to see injustice in daily operation. It confirmed his view that with a few exceptions there was no one worth knowing within a radius of three hundred miles. The Negro was well dressed and carried a briefcase. He looked around and then sat down on the other end of the seat where the woman with the red and white canvas sandals was sitting. He immediately unfolded a newspaper and obscured himself behind it. Julian's mother's elbow at once prodded insistently into his ribs. "Now you see why I won't ride on these buses by myself," she whispered.

The woman with the red and white canvas sandals had risen at the same time the Negro sat down and had gone further back in the bus and taken the seat of the woman who had got off. His mother leaned forward and cast her an approving look.

Julian rose, crossed the aisle, and sat down in the place of the woman with the canvas sandals. From this position, he looked serenely across at his mother. Her face had turned an angry red. He stared at her, making his eyes the eyes of a stranger. He felt his tension suddenly lift as if he had openly declared war on her.

He would have liked to get in conversation with the Negro and to talk with him about art or politics or any subject that would be above the comprehension of those around them, but the man remained entrenched behind his paper. He was either ignoring the change of seating or had never noticed it. There was no way for Julian to convey his sympathy.

His mother kept her eyes fixed reproachfully on his face. The woman with the protruding teeth was looking at him avidly as if he were a type of monster new to her.

"Do you have a light?" he asked the Negro.

Without looking away from his paper, the man reached in his pocket and handed him a packet of matches.

"Thanks," Julian said. For a moment he held the matches foolishly. A NO SMOKING sign looked down upon him from over the door. This alone would not have deterred him; he had no cigarettes. He had quit smoking some months before because he could not afford it. "Sorry," he muttered and handed back the matches. The Negro lowered the paper and gave him an annoyed look. He took the matches and raised the paper again.

His mother continued to gaze at him but she did not take advantage of his momentary discomfort. Her eyes retained their battered look. Her face seemed to be unnaturally red, as if her blood pressure had risen. Julian allowed no glimmer of sympathy to show on his face. Having got the advantage, he wanted desperately to keep it and carry it through. He would have liked to teach her a lesson that would last her a while, but there seemed no way to continue the point. The Negro refused to come out from behind his paper.

Julian folded his arms and looked stolidly before him, facing her but as if he did not see her, as if he had ceased to recognize her existence. He visualized a scene in which, the bus having reached their stop, he would remain in his seat and when she said, "Aren't you going to get off?" he would look at her as at a stranger who had rashly addressed him. The corner they got off on was usually deserted, but it was well lighted and it would not hurt her to walk by herself the four blocks to the Y. He decided to wait until the time came and then decide whether or not he would let her get off by herself. He would have to be at the Y at ten to bring her back, but he could leave her wondering if he was going to show up. There was no reason for her to think she could always depend on him.

He retired again into the high-ceilinged room sparsely settled with large pieces of antique furniture. His soul expanded momentarily but then he became aware of his mother across from him and the vision shriveled. He studied her coldly. Her feet in little pumps dangled like a child's and did not quite reach the floor. She was training on him an exaggerated look of reproach. He felt completely detached from her. At that moment he could with pleasure have slapped her as he would have slapped a particularly obnoxious child in his charge.

He began to imagine various unlikely ways by which he could teach her a lesson. He might make friends with some distinguished Negro professor or lawyer and bring him home to spend the evening. He would be entirely justified but her blood pressure would rise to 300. He could not push her to the extent of making her have a stroke, and moreover, he had never been successful at making any Negro friends. He had tried to strike up an acquaintance on the bus with some of the better types, with ones that looked like professors or ministers or lawyers. One morning he had sat down next to a distinguished-looking dark brown man who had answered his questions with a sonorous solemnity but who had turned out to be an undertaker. Another day he had sat down beside a cigar-smoking Negro with a diamond ring on his finger, but after a few stilted pleasantries, the Negro had rung the buzzer and risen, slipping two lottery tickets into Julian's hand as he climbed over him to leave.

He imagined his mother lying desperately ill and his being able to secure only a Negro doctor for her. He toyed with that idea for a few minutes and then dropped it for a momentary vision of himself participating as a sympathizer in a sit-in demonstration. This was possible but he did not linger with it. Instead, he approached the ultimate horror. He brought home a beautiful suspiciously Negroid woman. Prepare yourself, he said. There is nothing you can do about it. This is the woman I've chosen. She's intelligent, dignified, even good, and she's suffered and she hasn't thought it *fun*. Now persecute us, go ahead and persecute us. Drive her out of here, but remember, you're driving me too. His eyes were narrowed and through the indignation he had generated, he saw his mother across the aisle, purple-faced, shrunken to the dwarf-like proportions of her moral nature, sitting like a mummy beneath the ridiculous banner of her hat.

He was tilted out of his fantasy again as the bus stopped. The door opened with a sucking hiss and out of the dark a large, gaily dressed, sullen-looking colored woman got on with a little boy. The child, who might have been four, had on a short plaid suit and a Tyrolean hat with a blue feather in it. Julian hoped that he would sit down beside him and that the woman would push in beside his mother. He could think of no better arrangement.

As she waited for her tokens, the woman was surveying the seating possibilities—he hoped with the idea of sitting where she was least wanted. There was something familiar-looking about her but Julian could not place what it was. She was a giant of a woman. Her face was set not only to meet opposition but to seek it out. The downward tilt of her large lower lip was like a warning sign: DON'T TAMPER WITH ME. Her bulging figure was encased in a green crepe dress and her feet overflowed in red shoes. She had on a hideous hat. A purple velvet flap came down on one side of it and stood up on the other; the rest of it was green and looked like a cushion with the stuffing out. She carried a mammoth red pocketbook that bulged throughout as if it were stuffed with rocks.

To Julian's disappointment, the little boy climbed up on the empty seat beside his mother. His mother lumped all children, black and white, into the common category, "cute," and she thought little Negroes were on the whole cuter than little white children. She smiled at the little boy as he climbed on the seat.

Meanwhile the woman was bearing down upon the empty seat beside Julian. To his annoyance, she squeezed herself into it. He saw his mother's face change as the woman settled herself next to him and he realized with satisfaction that this was more objectionable to her than it was to him. Her face seemed almost gray and there was a look of dull recognition in her eyes, as if suddenly she had sickened at some awful confrontation. Julian saw that it was because she and the woman had, in a sense, swapped sons. Though his mother would not realize the symbolic significance of this, she would feel it. His amusement showed plainly on his face.

The woman next to him muttered something unintelligible to herself. He was conscious of a kind of bristling next to him, a muted growling like that of an angry cat. He could not see anything but the red pocketbook upright on the bulging green thighs. He visualized the woman as she had stood waiting for her tokens—the ponderous figure, rising from the red shoes upward over the solid hips, the mammoth bosom, the haughty face, to the green and purple hat.

His eyes widened.

The vision of the two hats, identical, broke upon him with the radiance of a brilliant sunrise. His face was suddenly lit with joy. He could not believe that Fate had thrust upon his mother such a lesson. He gave a loud chuckle so that she would look at him and see that he saw. She turned her eyes on him slowly. The blue in them seemed to have turned a bruised purple. For a moment he had an uncomfortable sense of her innocence, but it lasted only a second before principle rescued him. Justice entitled him to laugh. His grin hardened until it said to her as plainly as if he were saying aloud: Your punishment exactly fits your pettiness. This should teach you a permanent lesson.

Her eyes shifted to the woman. She seemed unable to bear looking at him and to find the woman preferable. He became conscious again of the bristling presence at his side. The woman was rumbling like a volcano about to become active. His mother's mouth began to twitch slightly at one corner. With a sinking heart, he saw incipient signs of recovery on her face and realized that this was going to strike her suddenly as funny and was going to be no lesson at all. She kept her eyes on the woman and an amused smile came over her face as if the woman were a monkey that had stolen her hat. The little Negro was looking up at her with large fascinated eyes. He had been trying to attract her attention for some time.

"Carver!" the woman said suddenly. "Come heah!"

When he saw that the spotlight was on him at last, Carver drew his feet up and turned himself toward Julian's mother and giggled.

"Carver!" the woman said. "You heah me? Come heah!"

Carver slid down from the seat but remained squatting with his back against the base of it, his head turned slyly around toward Julian's mother, who was smiling at him. The woman reached a hand across the aisle and snatched him to her. He righted himself and hung backwards on her knees, grinning at Julian's mother. "Isn't he cute?" Julian's mother said to the woman with the protruding teeth.

"I reckon he is," the woman said without conviction.

The Negress yanked him upright but he eased out of her grip and shot across the aisle and scrambled, giggling wildly, onto the seat beside his love.

"I think he likes me," Julian's mother said, and smiled at the woman. It was the smile she used when she was being particularly gracious to an inferior. Julian saw everything lost. The lesson had rolled off her like rain on a roof.

The woman stood up and yanked the little boy off the seat as if she were snatching him from contagion. Julian could feel the rage in her at having no weapon like his mother's smile. She gave the child a sharp slap across his leg. He howled once and then thrust his head into her stomach and kicked his feet against her shins. "Be-have," she said vehemently.

The bus stopped and the Negro who had been reading the newspaper got off. The woman moved over and set the little boy down with a thump between herself and Julian. She held him firmly by the knee. In a moment he put his hands in front of his face and peeped at Julian's mother through his fingers.

"I see yoooooooo!" she said and put her hand in front of her face and peeped at him.

The woman slapped his hand down. "Quit yo' foolishness," she said, "before I knock the living Jesus out of you!"

Julian was thankful that the next stop was theirs. He reached up and pulled the cord. The woman reached up and pulled it at the same time. Oh my God, he thought. He had the terrible intuition that when they got off the bus together, his mother would open her purse and give the little boy a nickel. The gesture would be as natural to her as breathing. The bus stopped and the woman got up and lunged to the front, dragging the child, who wished to stay on, after her. Julian and his mother got up and followed. As they neared the door, Julian tried to relieve her of her pocketbook.

"No," she murmured, "I want to give the little boy a nickel."

"No!" Julian hissed. "No!"

She smiled down at the child and opened her bag. The bus door opened and the woman picked him up by the arm and descended with him, hanging at her hip. Once in the street she set him down and shook him.

Julian's mother had to close her purse while she got down the bus step but as soon as her feet were on the ground, she opened it again and began to rummage inside. "I can't find but a penny," she whispered, "but it looks like a new one."

"Don't do it!" Julian said fiercely between his teeth. There was a streetlight on the corner and she hurried to get under it so that she could better see into her pocketbook. The woman was heading off rapidly down the street with the child still hanging backward on her hand.

"Oh little boy!" Julian's mother called and took a few quick steps and caught up with them just beyond the lamppost. "Here's a bright new penny for you," and she held out the coin, which shone bronze in the dim light.

The huge woman turned and for a moment stood, her shoulders lifted and her face frozen with frustrated rage, and stared at Julian's mother. Then all at once she seemed to explode like a piece of machinery that had been given one ounce of pressure too much. Julian saw the black fist swing out with the red pocketbook. He shut his eyes and cringed as he heard the woman shout, "He don't take nobody's pennies!" When he opened his eyes, the woman was disappearing down the street with the little boy staring wide-eyed over her shoulder. Julian's mother was sitting on the sidewalk.

"I told you not to do that," Julian said angrily. "I told you not to do that!"

He stood over her for a minute, gritting his teeth. Her legs were stretched out in front of her and her hat was on her lap. He squatted down and looked her in the face. It was totally expressionless. "You got exactly what you deserved," he said. "Now get up."

He picked up her pocketbook and put what had fallen out back in it. He picked the hat up off her lap. The penny caught his eye on the sidewalk and he picked that up and let it drop before her eyes into the purse. Then he stood up and leaned over and held his hands out to pull her up. She remained immobile. He sighed. Rising above them on either side were black apartment buildings, marked with irregular rectangles of light. At the end of the block a man came out of a door and walked off in the opposite direction. "All right," he said, "suppose somebody happens by and wants to know why you're sitting on the sidewalk?"

She took the hand and, breathing hard, pulled heavily up on it and then stood for a moment, swaying slightly as if the spots of light in the darkness were circling around her. Her eyes, shadowed and confused, finally settled on his face. He did not try to conceal his irritation. "I hope this teaches you a lesson," he said. She leaned forward and her eyes raked his face. She seemed trying to determine his identity. Then, as if she found nothing familiar about him, she started off with a headlong movement in the wrong direction.

"Aren't you going on to the Y?" he asked.

"Home," she muttered.

"Well, are we walking?"

For answer she kept going. Julian followed along, his hands behind him. He saw no reason to let the lesson she had had go without backing it up with an explanation of its meaning. She might as well be made to understand what had happened to her. "Don't think that was just an uppity Negro woman," he said. "That was the whole colored race which will no longer take your condescending pennies. That was your black double. She can wear the same hat as you, and to be sure," he added gratuitously (because he thought it was funny), "it looked better on her than it did on you. What all this means," he said, "is that the old world is gone. The old manners are obsolete and your graciousness is not worth a damn." He thought bitterly of the house that had been lost for him. "You aren't who you think you are," he said.

She continued to plow ahead, paying no attention to him. Her hair had come undone on one side. She dropped her pocketbook and took no notice. He stooped and picked it up and handed it to her but she did not take it.

"You needn't act as if the world had come to an end," he said, "because it hasn't. From now on you've got to live in a new world and face a few realities for a change. Buck up," he said, "it won't kill you."

She was breathing fast.

"Let's wait on the bus," he said.

"Home," she said thickly.

"I hate to see you behave like this," he said. "Just like a child. I should be able to expect more of you." He decided to stop where he was and make her stop and wait for a bus. "I'm not going any farther," he said, stopping. "We're going on the bus."

She continued to go on as if she had not heard him. He took a few steps and caught her arm and stopped her. He looked into her face and caught his breath. He was looking into a face he had never seen before. "Tell Grandpa to come get me," she said.

He stared, stricken.

"Tell Caroline to come get me," she said.

Stunned, he let her go and she lurched forward again, walking as if one leg were shorter than the other. A tide of darkness seemed to be sweeping her from him. "Mother!" he cried. "Darling, sweetheart, wait!" Crumpling, she fell to the pavement. He dashed forward and fell at her side, crying, "Mamma, Mamma!" He turned her over. Her face was fiercely distorted. One eye, large and staring, moved slightly to the left as if it had become unmoored. The other remained fixed on him, raked his face again, found nothing and closed.

"Wait here, wait here!" he cried and jumped up and began to run for help toward a cluster of lights he saw in the distance ahead of him. "Help, help!" he shouted, but his voice was thin, scarcely a thread of sound. The lights drifted farther away the faster he ran and his feet moved numbly as if they carried him nowhere. The tide of darkness seemed to sweep him back to her, postponing from moment to moment his entry into the world of guilt and sorrow.

FROM

The Last Gentleman

1966

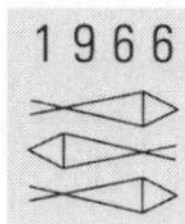

One fine day in early summer a young man lay thinking in Central Park.

His head was propped on his jacket, which had been folded twice so that the lining was outermost, and wedged into a seam of rock. The rock jutted out of the ground in a section of the park known as the Great Meadow. Beside him and canted up at mortar angle squatted a telescope of an unusual design.

In the course of the next five minutes the young man was to witness by chance an insignificant, though rather curious happening. It was the telescope which became the instrument of a bit of accidental eavesdropping. As a consequence of a chance event the rest of his life was to be changed.

He was an unusual young man. But perhaps nowadays it is not so unusual. What distinguished him anyhow was this: he had to know everything before he could do anything. For example, he had to know what other people's infirmities were before he could get on a footing with them.

Most people would have forgotten the incident in question in a week's time. But he did not. His life had come to such a pass that he attached significance to it. For until this moment he had lived in a state of pure possibility, not knowing what sort of a man he was or what he must do, and supposing therefore that he must be all men and do everything. But after this morning's incident his life took a turn in a particular direction. Thereafter he came to see that he was not destined to do everything but only one or two things. Lucky is the man who does not secretly believe that every possibility is open to him.

It was a beautiful day but only after the fashion of beautiful days in New York. The sky was no more than an ordinary Eastern sky, mild and blue and hazed over, whitened under the blue and of not much account. It was a standard sky by which all other skies are measured. As for the park, green leaves or not, it belonged to the animal kingdom rather than the vegetable. It had a zoo smell. Last summer's grass was as coarse and yellow as lion's hair and worn bare in spots, exposing the tough old hide of the earth. The tree trunks were polished. Bits of hair clung to the bark as if a large animal had been rubbing against them. Nevertheless, thought he, it is a good thing to see a park put to good hard use by millions of people, used and handled in its every square inch like a bear garden.

A 35-millimeter camera had been fitted to the telescope in place of the in-line ocular, but a lateral eyepiece allowed him to lean over from time to time and take a squint. There sprang into view a section of the cornice of a building, no doubt one of the hotels along Central Park South. But so powerful was the instrument that it was hard to say which building was being looked at. It was as if the telescope created its own world in the brilliant theater of its lenses.

He was waiting for the peregrine.

The day before, he had seen it but not photographed it. The falcon had abandoned its natural home in the northern wilderness and taken up residence on top of the hotel. From this eyrie it preyed on the fat pigeons of the park. Along the cornice it would strut, cock a yellow eye down at the great misty rectangle (the eye sunk and fierce in its socket and half eclipsed by the orbit of bone), and down it would come smoking, at two hundred miles an hour, big feet stuck out in front like a Stuka, strike the pigeons in mid-air with a thump and a blue flak-burst of feathers.

The peregrine did not return to his perch. As the young man made ready to unlimber his telescope, he loosened the thumbscrew and the barrel dropped to the horizontal. He took another look. Being of both a scientific and a superstitious turn of mind and therefore always on the lookout for chance happenings which lead to great discoveries, he had to have a last look—much as a man will open a telephone book and read the name at his thumbnail.

There in the telescope sat a woman, on a park bench, a white woman dark as a gypsy. She held a tabloid. Over her shoulder he read: ". . . parley fails."

But when he looked up he couldn't find her. The telescope was pointed toward the southeast, where a thicket of maples bordered the Great Meadow. She could only be there. Yes, now he saw: the telescope looked toward a leafy notch and through it to the summit of one of the little alps which overlook the Pond.

There she was, not twenty feet away and shimmering slightly in the pressed optic air as if she sat at the bottom of a sunlit ocean. Her coarse hair gave off rainbows. One arm was flung along the back of the bench, the hand smudged with newspaper ink. She was a neat stocky woman with a shock of hair and a handsome if somewhat meager face, like the face of an athlete, as if all strength and beauty had gone first to her body.

The woman was doing something. The soiled left hand dropped behind the bench, where by any calculation of hers it could not be seen, for the bench sat on the slope of an alp and there was nothing behind it but treetops. The blue hand felt its way down along a partition. It was an old-style bench, the sort built many years ago of a porous tufalike concrete in which pebbles had been set like raisins in a cake. A sad yellow 1901 concrete it was, enough to strike a pang to the heart. The seat was divided into thrones by scroll-shaped partitions which arched up and over to the rear, where they fastened the back into the bench. At the bottom the scroll was mortised into the bench by an ornamental tenon. Down crept the hand along the scroll. As he watched, the hand shattered into rainbows and disappeared. In another second the woman herself was gone, vanishing into the blue nimbus which rimmed the circle of light.

It did not take him long to act. Often nowadays people do not know what to do and so live out their lives as if they were waiting for some sign or other. This young man was such a person. If a total stranger had stopped him this morning on Columbus Circle and thrust into his palm a note which read: *Meet me on the NE corner of Lindell Blvd and Kings Highway in St. Louis 9* A.M. *next Thursday—have news of utmost importance,* he'd have struck out for St. Louis (the question is, how many people nowadays would not?).

The hillock was easy to find. The bench overlooked the Pond and, beyond, the Grand Army Plaza. To the north the slope fell away abruptly into a screen of privet and poplar. Below, workmen were setting out folding chairs in the plaza and draping bunting over scaffolding in preparation for a patriotic ceremony.

Setting down his case, he explored the rear of the bench. The tenon which fastened the scroll between the third and fourth thrones, counting from Fifth Avenue, was loose. It could be slid back a way in its mortise, opening a recess into the blind bottom of the scroll. The cul-de-sac so formed was the sort of place which only neighborhood boys know of (and here there were no neighborhood boys), a time-niche where one leaves a note addressed to oneself: to be opened May 20, 1995. But today there was only a scrap of tin, a disc cut from the top of an orange-juice can, folded to a semi-circle, and sealed with chewing gum. He pried it open with a fingernail. It contained a slip of paper like a supermarket receipt upon which was written in violet script:

Some say thy fault is youth,
some wantonness;
Some say thy grace is youth
and gentle sport;
Both grace and faults are lov'd
of more and less
Thou makest faults graces
that to thee resort.

It was eleven thirty. He replaced note in tin, tin in cul-de-sac, and returned to his rock in the Great Meadow where he set up his telescope, and waited.

At fifteen minutes after twelve a girl came to the bench, set down a brown paper bag, and, making no secret of it, slid back the tenon and got her note. She read the note without expression as she ate her sandwich.

His heart gave a leap. He fell in love, at first sight and at a distance of two thousand feet. It was not so much her good looks, her smooth brushed brow and firm round neck bowed so that two or three vertebrae surfaced in the soft flesh, as a certain bemused and dry-eyed expression in which he seemed to recognize—himself! She was a beautiful girl but she also slouched and was watchful and dry-eyed and musing like a thirteen-year-old boy. She was his better half. It would be possible to sit on a bench and eat a peanut-butter sandwich with her and say not a word.

But before he could think what to do, his love had finished her sandwich, wiped her mouth with Kleenex, and vanished. By the time he reached the alp, there was no sign of her.

Taking the gravel path which skirts the Pond, he crossed Central Park West, entered the Y.M.C.A., and went straight up to his room, which was furnished with a single bed and a steel desk varnished to resemble wood grain. Carefully stowing away his telescope under the Val-Pak which hung in the closet, he undressed to his shorts and lay on the bed. After gazing at the ceiling for some minutes, he fell asleep and slept soundly for five hours.

•

He was a young man of a pleasant appearance. Of medium height and exceedingly pale, he was nevertheless strongly built and quick and easy in his ways. Save for a deafness in one ear, his physical health was perfect. Handsome as he was, he was given to long silences. So girls didn't know what to make of him. But men liked him. After a while they saw that he was easy and meant no harm. He was the sort whom classmates remember fondly; they liked to grab him around the neck with an elbow and cuff him around. Good-looking and amiable as he was, however, he did not strike one as remarkable. People usually told him the same joke two or three times.

But he looked better than he was. Though he was as engaging as could be, something was missing. He had not turned out well. There is a sort who does well in school and of whom much is heard and expected and who thereafter does less and less well and of whom finally is heard nothing at all. The high tide of life comes maybe in the last year of high school or the first year of college. Then life seems as elegant as algebra. Afterwards people ask, what happened to so and so? And the answer is a shrug. He was the sort who goes away.

Even now he made the highest possible scores on psychological aptitude tests, especially in the area of problem-solving and goal-seeking. The trouble was he couldn't think what to do between tests.

New York is full of people from small towns who are quite content to live obscure lives in some out-of-the-way corner of the city. Here there is no one to keep track. Though such a person might have come from a long line of old settlers and a neighborhood rich in memories, now he chooses to live in a flat on 231st Street, pick up the paper and milk on the doorstep every morning, and speak to the elevator man. In Southern genealogies there is always mention of a cousin who went to live in New York in 1922 and not another word. One hears that people go to New York to seek their fortunes, but many go to seek just the opposite.

In his case, though, it was part of a family pattern. Over the years his family had turned ironical and lost its gift for action. It was an honorable and violent family, but gradually the violence had been deflected and turned inward. The great-grandfather knew what was what and said so and acted accordingly and did not care what anyone thought. He even wore a pistol in a holster like a Western hero and once met the Grand Wizard of the Ku Klux Klan in a barbershop and invited him then and there to shoot it out in the street. The next generation, the grandfather, seemed to know what was what but he was not really so sure. He was brave but he gave much thought to the business of being brave. He too would have shot it out with the Grand Wizard if only he could have made certain it was the thing to do. The father was a brave man too and he said he didn't care what others thought, but he did care. More than anything else, he wished to act with honor and to be thought well of by other men. So living for him was a strain. He became ironical. For him it was not a small thing to walk down the street on an ordinary September morning. In the end he was killed by his own irony and sadness and by the strain of living out an ordinary day in a perfect dance of honor.

As for the present young man, the last of the line, he did not know what to think. So he became a watcher and a listener and a wanderer. He could not get enough of watching. Once when he was a boy, a man next door had gone crazy and had sat out in his back yard pitching gravel around and hollering out to his enemies in a loud angry voice. The boy watched him all day, squatted down and watched him, his mouth open and drying. It seemed to him that if he could figure out what was wrong with the man he would learn the great secret of life.

Like many young men in the South, he became overly subtle and had trouble ruling out the possible. They are not like an immigrant's son in Passaic who decides to become a dentist and that is that. Southerners have trouble ruling out the possible. What happens to a man to whom all things seem possible and every course of action open? Nothing of course. Except war. If a man lives in the sphere of the possible and waits for something to happen, what he is waiting for is war—or the end of the world. That is why Southerners like to fight and make good soldiers. In war the possible becomes actual through no doing of one's own.

But it was worse than this in his case. It was more than being a Southerner. For some years he had had a nervous condition and as a consequence he did not know how to live his life. As a child he had had "spells," occurrences which were nameless and not to be thought of, let alone mentioned, and which he therefore thought of as lying at the secret and somehow shameful heart of childhood itself. There was a name for it, he discovered later, which gave it form and habitation. It was *déjà vu*, at least he reckoned it was. What happened anyhow was that even when he was a child and was sitting in the kitchen watching D'lo snap beans or make beaten biscuits, there came over him as it might come over a sorrowful old man the strongest sense that it had all happened before and that something else was going to happen and when it did he would know the secret of his own life. Things seemed to turn white and dense and time itself became freighted with an unspeakable emotion. Sometimes he "fell out" and would wake up hours later, in his bed, refreshed but still haunted.

When he was a youth he had lived his life in a state of the liveliest expectation, thinking to himself: what a fine thing it will be to become a man and to know what to do—like an Apache youth who at the right time goes out into the plains alone, dreams dreams, sees visions, returns and knows he is a man. But no such time had come and he still didn't know how to live.

To be specific, he had now a nervous condition and suffered spells of amnesia and even between times did not quite know what was what. Much of the time he was like a man who has just crawled out of a bombed building. Everything looked strange. Such a predicament, however, is not altogether a bad thing. Like the sole survivor of a bombed building, he had no secondhand opinions and he could see things afresh.

There were times when he was as normal as anyone. He could be as objective-minded and cool-headed as a scientist. He read well-known books on mental hygiene and for a few minutes after each reading felt very clear about things. He knew how to seek emotional gratifications in a mature way, as they say in such books. In the arts, for example. It was his custom to visit museums regularly and to attend the Philharmonic concerts at least once a week. He understood, moreover, that it is people who count, one's relations with people, one's warmth toward and understanding of people. At these times he set himself the goal and often achieved it of "cultivating rewarding interpersonal relationships with a variety of people"—to use a phrase he had come across and not forgotten. Nor should the impression be given that he turned up his nose at religion, as old-style scientists used to do, for he had read widely among modern psychologists and he knew that we have much to learn from the psychological insights of the World's Great Religions.

At his best, he was everything a psychologist could have desired him to be. Most of the time, however, it was a different story. He would lapse into an unproductive and solitary life. He took to wandering. He had a way of turning up at unlikely places such as a bakery in Cincinnati or a greenhouse in Memphis, where he might work for several weeks assaulted by the *déjà vus* of hot growing green plants.

A German physician once remarked that in the lives of people who suffer emotional illness he had noticed the presence of *Lücken* or gaps. As he studied the history of a particular patient he found whole sections missing, like a book with blank pages.

Most of this young man's life was a gap. The summer before, he had fallen into a fugue state and wandered around northern Virginia for three weeks, where he sat sunk in thought on old battlegrounds, hardly aware of his own name.

SUSAN SONTAG

FROM

Against Interpretation

1966

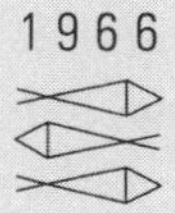

AGAINST INTERPRETATION

Content is a glimpse of something, an encounter like a flash. It's very tiny—very tiny, content.

WILLEM DE KOONING, *in an interview*

It is only shallow people who do not judge by appearances. The mystery of the world is the visible, not the invisible.

OSCAR WILDE, *in a letter*

I

The earliest experience of art must have been that it was incantatory, magical; art was an instrument of ritual. (Cf. the paintings in the caves at Lascaux, Altamira, Niaux, La Pasiega, etc.) The earliest *theory* of art, that of the Greek philosophers, proposed that art was mimesis, imitation of reality.

It is at this point that the peculiar question of the value of art arose. For the mimetic theory, by its very terms, challenges art to justify itself.

Plato, who proposed the theory, seems to have done so in order to rule that the value of art is dubious. Since he considered ordinary material things as themselves mimetic objects, imitations of transcendent forms or structures, even the best painting of a bed would be only an "imitation of an imitation." For Plato, art is neither particularly useful (the painting of a bed is no good to sleep on) nor, in the strict sense, true. And Aristotle's arguments in defense of art do not really challenge Plato's view that all art is an elaborate *trompe l'oeil*, and therefore a lie. But he does dispute Plato's idea that art is useless. Lie or no, art has a certain value according to Aristotle because it is a form of therapy. Art is useful, after all, Aristotle counters, medicinally useful in that it arouses and purges dangerous emotions.

In Plato and Aristotle, the mimetic theory of art goes hand in hand with the assumption that art is always figurative. But advocates of the mimetic theory need not close their eyes to decorative and abstract art. The fallacy that art is necessarily a "realism" can be modified or scrapped without ever moving outside the problems delimited by the mimetic theory.

The fact is, all Western consciousness of and reflection upon art have remained within the confines staked out by the Greek theory of art as mimesis or representation. It is through this theory that art as such—above and beyond given works of art—becomes problematic, in need of defense. And it is the defense of art which gives birth to the odd vision by which something we have learned to call "form" is separated off from something we have learned to call "content," and to the well-intentioned move which makes content essential and form accessory.

Even in modern times, when most artists and critics have discarded the theory of art as representation of an outer reality in favor of the theory of art as subjective expression, the main feature of the mimetic theory persists. Whether we conceive of the work of art on the model of a picture (art as a picture of reality) or on the model of a statement (art as the statement of the artist), content still comes first. The content may have changed. It may now be less figurative, less lucidly realistic. But it is still assumed that a work of art *is* its content. Or, as it's usually put today, that a work of art by definition says something. ("What X is saying is . . ." "What X is trying to say is . . ." "What X said is . . ." etc., etc.)

II

None of us can ever retrieve that innocence before all theory when art knew no need to justify itself, when one did not ask of a work of art what it said because one knew (or thought one knew) what it did. From now to the end of consciousness, we are stuck with the task of defending art. We can only quarrel with one or another means of defense. Indeed, we have an obligation to overthrow any means of defending and justifying art which becomes particularly obtuse or onerous or insensitive to contemporary needs and practice.

This is the case, today, with the very idea of content itself. Whatever it may have been in the past, the idea of content is today mainly a hindrance, a nuisance, a subtle or not so subtle philistinism.

Though the actual developments in many arts may seem to be leading us away from the idea that a work of art is primarily its content, the idea still exerts an extraordinary hegemony. I want to suggest that this is because the idea is now perpetuated in the guise of a certain way of encountering works of art thoroughly ingrained among most people who take any of the arts seriously. What the overemphasis on the idea of content entails is the perennial, never-consummated project of *interpretation.* And, conversely, it is the habit of approaching works of art in order to *interpret* them that sustains the fancy that there really is such a thing as the content of a work of art.

III

Of course, I don't mean interpretation in the broadest sense, the sense in which Nietzsche (rightly) says, "There are no facts, only interpretations." By interpretation, I mean here a conscious act of the mind which illustrates a certain code, certain "rules" of interpretation.

Directed to art, interpretation means plucking a set of elements (the X, the Y, the Z, and so forth) from the whole work. The task of interpretation is virtually one of translation. The interpreter says, Look, don't you see that X is really—or, really means—A? That Y is really B? That Z is really C?

What situation could prompt this curious project for transforming a text? History gives us the materials for an answer. Interpretation first appears in the culture of late classical antiquity, when the power and credibility of myth had been broken by the "realistic" view of the world introduced by scientific enlightenment. Once the question that haunts post-mythic consciousness—that of the *seemliness* of religious symbols—had been asked, the ancient texts were, in their pristine form, no longer acceptable. Then interpretation was summoned, to reconcile the ancient texts to "modern" demands. Thus, the Stoics, to accord with their view that the gods had to be moral, allegorized away the rude features of Zeus and his boisterous clan in Homer's epics. What Homer really designated by the adultery of Zeus with Leto, they explained, was the union between power and wisdom. In the same vein, Philo of Alexandria interpreted the literal historical narratives of the Hebrew Bible as spiritual paradigms. The story of the exodus from Egypt, the wandering in the desert for forty years, and the entry into the promised land, said Philo, was really an allegory of the individual soul's emancipation, tribulations, and final deliverance. Interpretation thus presupposes a discrepancy between the clear meaning of the text and the demands of (later) readers. It seeks to resolve that discrepancy. The situation is that for some reason a text has become unacceptable; yet it cannot be discarded. Interpretation is a radical strategy for conserving an old text, which is thought too precious to repudiate, by revamping it. The interpreter, without actually erasing or rewriting the text, *is* altering it. But he can't admit to doing this. He claims to be only making it intelligible, by disclosing its true meaning. However far the interpreters alter the text (another notorious example is the rabbinic and Christian "spiritual" interpretations of the clearly erotic Song of Songs), they must claim to be reading off a sense that is already there.

Interpretation in our own time, however, is even more complex. For the contemporary zeal for the project of interpretation is often prompted not by piety toward the troublesome text (which may conceal an aggression) but by an open aggressiveness, an overt contempt for appearances. The old style of interpretation was insistent, but respectful; it erected another meaning on top of the literal one. The modern style of interpretation excavates, and as it excavates, destroys; it digs "behind" the text, to find a sub-text which is the true one. The most celebrated and influential modern doctrines, those of Marx and Freud, actually amount to elaborate systems of hermeneutics, aggressive and impious theories of interpretation. All observable phenomena are bracketed, in Freud's phrase, as *manifest content*. This manifest content must be probed and pushed aside to find the true meaning—the *latent content*—beneath. For Marx, social events like revolutions and wars; for Freud, the events of individual lives (like neurotic symptoms and slips of the tongue) as well as texts (like a dream or a work of art)—all are treated as occasions for interpretation. According to Marx and Freud, these events only *seem* to be intelligible. Actually, they have no meaning without interpretation. To understand *is* to interpret. And to interpret is to restate the phenomenon, in effect to find an equivalent for it.

Thus, interpretation is not (as most people assume) an absolute value, a gesture of mind situated in some timeless realm of capabilities. Interpretation must itself be evaluated, within a historical view of human consciousness. In some cultural contexts, interpretation is a liberating act. It is a means of revising, of transvaluing, of escaping the dead past. In other cultural contexts, it is reactionary, impertinent, cowardly, stifling.

IV

Today is such a time, when the project of interpretation is largely reactionary, stifling. Like the fumes of the automobile and of heavy industry which befoul the urban atmosphere, the effusion of interpretations of art today poisons our sensibilities. In a culture whose already classical dilemma is the hypertrophy of the intellect at the expense of energy and sensual capability, interpretation is the revenge of the intellect upon art.

Even more. It is the revenge of the intellect upon the world. To interpret is to impoverish, to deplete the world—in order to set up a shadow world of "meanings." It is to turn *the* world into *this* world. ("This world"! As if there were any other.)

The world, our world, is depleted, impoverished enough. Away with all duplicates of it, until we again experience more immediately what we have.

V

In most modern instances, interpretation amounts to the philistine refusal to leave the work of art alone. Real art has the capacity to make us nervous. By reducing the work of art to its content and then interpreting *that*, one tames the work of art. Interpretation makes art manageable, comfortable.

This philistinism of interpretation is more rife in literature than in any other art. For decades now, literary critics have understood it to be their task to translate the elements of the poem or play or novel or story into something else. Sometimes a writer will be so uneasy before the naked power of his art that he will install within the work itself—albeit with a little shyness, a touch of the good taste of irony—the clear and explicit interpretation of it. Thomas Mann is an example of such an overcooperative author. In the case of more stubborn authors, the critic is only too happy to perform the job.

The work of Kafka, for example, has been subjected to a mass ravishment by no less than three armies of interpreters. Those who read Kafka as a social allegory see case studies of the frustrations and insanity of modern bureaucracy and its ultimate issuance in the totalitarian state. Those who read Kafka as a psychoanalytic allegory see desperate revelations of Kafka's fear of his father, his castration anxieties, his sense of his own impotence, his thralldom to his dreams. Those who read Kafka as a religious allegory explain that K. in *The Castle* is trying to gain access to heaven, that Joseph K. in *The Trial* is being judged by the inexorable and mysterious justice of God . . . Another body of work that has attracted interpreters like leeches is that of Samuel Beckett. Beckett's delicate dramas of the withdrawn consciousness —pared down to essentials, cut off, often represented as physically immobilized—are read as a statement about modern man's alienation from meaning or from God, or as an allegory of psychopathology.

Proust, Joyce, Faulkner, Rilke, Lawrence, Gide . . . one could go on citing author after author; the list is endless of those around whom thick encrustations of interpretation have taken hold. But it should be noted that interpretation is not simply the compliment that mediocrity pays to genius. It is, indeed, the modern way of understanding something, and is applied to works of every quality. Thus, in the notes that Elia Kazan published on his production of *A Streetcar Named Desire*, it becomes clear that, in order to direct the play, Kazan had to discover that Stanley Kowalski represented the sensual and vengeful barbarism that was engulfing our culture, while Blanche DuBois was Western civilization, poetry, delicate apparel, dim lighting, refined feelings and all, though a little the worse for wear, to be sure. Tennessee Williams's forceful psychological melodrama now became intelligible: it was about something, about the decline of Western civilization. Apparently, were it to go on being a play about a handsome brute named Stanley Kowalski and a faded mangy belle named Blanche DuBois, it would not be manageable.

VI

It doesn't matter whether artists intend, or don't intend, for their works to be interpreted. Perhaps Tennessee Williams thinks *Streetcar* is about what Kazan thinks it to be about. It may be that Cocteau in *The Blood of a Poet* and in *Orpheus* wanted the elaborate readings which have been given these films, in terms of Freudian symbolism and social critique. But the merit of these works certainly lies elsewhere than in their "meanings." Indeed, it is precisely to the extent that Williams's plays and Cocteau's films do suggest these portentous meanings that they are defective, false, contrived, lacking in conviction.

From interviews, it appears that Resnais and Robbe-Grillet consciously designed *Last Year at Marienbad* to accommodate a multiplicity of equally plausible interpretations. But the temptation to interpret *Marienbad* should be resisted. What matters in *Marienbad* is the pure, untranslatable, sensuous immediacy of some of its images, and its rigorous if narrow solutions to certain problems of cinematic form.

Again, Ingmar Bergman may have meant the tank rumbling down the empty night street in *The Silence* as a phallic symbol. But if he did, it was a foolish thought. ("Never trust the teller, trust the tale," said Lawrence.) Taken as a brute object, as an immediate sensory equivalent for the mysterious abrupt armored happenings going on inside the hotel, that sequence with the tank is the most striking moment in the film. Those who reach for a Freudian interpretation of the tank are only expressing their lack of response to what is there on the screen.

It is always the case that interpretation of this type indicates a dissatisfaction (conscious or unconscious) with the work, a wish to replace it by something else.

Interpretation, based on the highly dubious theory that a work of art is composed of items of content, violates art. It makes art into an article for use, for arrangement into a mental scheme of categories.

VII

Interpretation does not, of course, always prevail. In fact, a great deal of today's art may be understood as motivated by a flight from interpretation. To avoid interpretation, art may become parody. Or it may become abstract. Or it may become ("merely") decorative. Or it may become non-art.

The flight from interpretation seems particularly a feature of modern painting. Abstract painting is the attempt to have, in the ordinary sense, no content; since there is no content, there can be no interpretation. Pop Art works by the opposite means to the same result; using a content so blatant, so "what it is," it, too, ends by being uninterpretable.

A great deal of modern poetry as well, starting from the great experiments of French poetry (including the movement that is misleadingly called Symbolism) to put silence into poems and to reinstate the *magic* of the word, has escaped from the rough grip of interpretation. The most recent revolution in contemporary taste in poetry—the revolution that has deposed Eliot and elevated Pound—represents a turning away from content in poetry in the old sense, an impatience with what made modern poetry prey to the zeal of interpreters.

I am speaking mainly of the situation in America, of course. Interpretation runs rampant here in those arts with a feeble and negligible avant-garde: fiction and the drama. Most American novelists and playwrights are really either journalists or gentlemen sociologists and psychologists. They are writing the literary equivalent of program music. And so rudimentary, uninspired, and stagnant has been the sense of what might be done with form in fiction and drama that even when the content isn't simply information, news, it is still peculiarly visible, handier, more exposed. To the extent that novels and plays (in America), unlike poetry and painting and music, don't reflect any interesting concern with changes in their form, these arts remain prone to assault by interpretation.

But programmatic avant-gardism—which has meant, mostly, experiments with form at the expense of content—is not the only defense against the infestation of art by interpretations. At least, I hope not. For this would be to commit art to being perpetually on the run. (It also perpetuates the very distinction between form and content which is, ultimately, an illusion.) Ideally, it is possible to elude the interpreters in another way, by making works of art whose surface is so unified and clean, whose momentum is so rapid, whose address is so direct that the work can be . . . just what it is. Is this possible now? It does happen in films, I believe. This is why cinema is the most alive, the most exciting, the most important of all art forms right now. Perhaps the way one tells how alive a particular art form is is by the latitude it gives for making mistakes in it and still being good. For example, a few of the films of Bergman—though crammed with lame messages about the modern spirit, thereby inviting interpretations—still triumph over the pretentious intentions of their director. In *Winter Light* and *The Silence*, the beauty and visual sophistication of the images subvert before our eyes the callow pseudo-intellectuality of the story and some of the dialogue. (The most remarkable instance of this sort of discrepancy is the work of D. W. Griffith.) In good films, there is always a directness that entirely frees us from the itch to interpret. Many old Hollywood films, like those of Cukor, Walsh, Hawks, and countless other directors, have this liberating anti-symbolic quality, no less than the best work of the new European directors, like Truffaut's *Shoot the Piano Player* and *Jules and Jim*, Godard's *Breathless* and *Vivre sa Vie*, Antonioni's *L'Avventura*, and Olmi's *The Fiancés*.

The fact that films have not been overrun by interpreters is in part due simply to the newness of cinema as an art. It also owes to the happy accident that films for such a long time were just movies; in other words, that they were understood to be part of mass, as opposed to high, culture, and were left alone by most people with minds. Then, too, there is always something other than content in the cinema to grab hold of, for those who want to analyze. For the cinema, unlike the novel, possesses a vocabulary of forms—the explicit, complex, and discussable technology of camera movements, cutting, and composition of the frame that goes into the making of a film.

VIII

What kind of criticism, of commentary on the arts, is desirable today? For I am not saying that works of art are ineffable, that they cannot be described or paraphrased. They can be. The question is how. What would criticism look like that would serve the work of art, not usurp its place?

What is needed, first, is more attention to form in art. If excessive stress on *content* provokes the arrogance of interpretation, more extended and more thorough descriptions of *form* would silence. What is needed is a vocabulary—a descriptive, rather than prescriptive, vocabulary—for forms.* The best criticism, and it is uncommon, is of this sort that dissolves considerations of content into those of form. On film, drama, and painting respectively, I can think of Erwin Panofsky's essay "Style and Medium in the Motion Pictures," Northrop Frye's essay "A Conspectus of Dramatic Genres," Pierre Francastel's essay "The Destruction of a Plastic Space." Roland Barthes's book *On Racine* and his two essays on Robbe-Grillet are examples of formal analysis applied to the work of a single author. (The best essays in Erich Auerbach's *Mimesis*, like "The Scar of Odysseus," are also of this type.) An example of formal analysis applied simultaneously to genre and author is Walter Benjamin's essay "The Storyteller: Reflections on the Works of Nicolai Leskov."

Equally valuable would be acts of criticism which would supply a really accurate, sharp, loving description of the appearance of a work of art. This seems even harder to do than formal analysis. Some of Manny Farber's film criticism, Dorothy Van Ghent's essay "The Dickens World: A View from Todgers'," Randall Jarrell's essay on Walt Whitman are among the rare examples of what I mean. These are essays which reveal the sensuous surface of art without mucking about in it.

IX

Transparence is the highest, most liberating value in art—and in criticism—today. Transparence means experiencing the luminousness of the thing in itself, of things being what they are. This is the greatness of, for example, the films of Bresson and Ozu and Renoir's *The Rules of the Game*.

Once upon a time (say, for Dante), it must have been a revolutionary and creative move to design works of art so that they might be experienced on several levels. Now it is not. It reinforces the principle of redundancy that is the principal affliction of modern life.

Once upon a time (a time when high art was scarce), it must have been a revolutionary and creative move to interpret works of art. Now it is not. What we decidedly do not need now is further to assimilate Art into Thought, or (worse yet) Art into Culture.

Interpretation takes the sensory experience of the work of art for

* One of the difficulties is that our idea of form is spatial (the Greek metaphors for form are all derived from notions of space). This is why we have a more ready vocabulary of forms for the spatial than for the temporal arts. The exception among the temporal arts, of course, is the drama; perhaps this is because the drama is a narrative (i.e., temporal) form that extends itself visually and pictorially, upon a stage. What we don't have yet is a poetics of the novel, any clear notion of the forms of narration. Perhaps film criticism will be the occasion of a breakthrough here, since films are primarily a visual form, yet they are also a subdivision of literature.

granted, and proceeds from there. This cannot be taken for granted now. Think of the sheer multiplication of works of art available to every one of us, super-added to the conflicting tastes and odors and sights of the urban environment that bombard our senses. Ours is a culture based on excess, on overproduction; the result is a steady loss of sharpness in our sensory experience. All the conditions of modern life—its material plenitude, its sheer crowdedness—conjoin to dull our sensory faculties. And it is in the light of the condition of our senses, our capacities (rather than those of another age), that the task of the critic must be assessed.

What is important now is to recover our senses. We must learn to *see* more, to *hear* more, to *feel* more.

Our task is not to find the maximum amount of content in a work of art, much less to squeeze more content out of the work than is already there. Our task is to cut back content so that we can see the thing at all.

The aim of all commentary on art now should be to make works of art—and, by analogy, our own experience—more, rather than less, real to us. The function of criticism should be to show *how it is what it is*, even *that it is what it is*, rather than to show *what it means*.

X

In place of a hermeneutics we need an erotics of art.

(1964)

JANE BOWLES

FROM

The Collected Works of Jane Bowles

1966

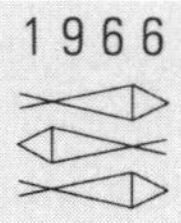

EVERYTHING IS NICE

The highest street in the blue Moslem town skirted the edge of a cliff. She walked over to the thick protecting wall and looked down. The tide was out, and the flat dirty rocks below were swarming with skinny boys. A Moslem woman came up to the blue wall and stood next to her, grazing her hip with the basket she was carrying. She pretended not to notice her, and kept her eyes fixed on a white dog that had just slipped down the side of a rock and plunged into a crater of sea water. The sound of its bark was earsplitting. Then the woman jabbed the basket firmly into her ribs, and she looked up.

"That one is a porcupine," said the woman, pointing a henna-stained finger into the basket.

This was true. A large dead porcupine lay there, with a pair of new yellow socks folded on top of it.

She looked again at the woman. She was dressed in a haik, and the white cloth covering the lower half of her face was loose, about to fall down.

"I am Zodelia," she announced in a high voice. "And you are Betsoul's friend." The loose cloth slipped below her chin and hung there like a bib. She did not pull it up.

"You sit in her house and you sleep in her house and you eat in her house," the woman went on, and she nodded in agreement. "Your name is Jeanie and you live in a hotel with other Nazarenes. How much does the hotel cost you?"

A loaf of bread shaped like a disc flopped on to the ground from inside the folds of the woman's haik, and she did not have to answer her question. With some difficulty the woman picked the loaf up and stuffed it in between the quills of the porcupine and the basket handle. Then she set the basket down on the top of the blue wall and turned to her with bright eyes.

"I am the people in the hotel," she said. "Watch me."

She was pleased because she knew that the woman who called herself Zodelia was about to present her with a little skit. It would be delightful to watch, since all the people of the town spoke and gesticulated as though they had studied at the *Comédie Française*.

"The people in the hotel," Zodelia announced, formally beginning her skit. "I am the people in the hotel."

" 'Good-bye, Jeanie, good-bye. Where are you going?'

" 'I am going to a Moslem house to visit my Moslem friends, Betsoul and her family. I will sit in a Moslem room and eat Moslem food and sleep on a Moslem bed.'

" 'Jeanie, Jeanie, when will you come back to us in the hotel and sleep in your own room?'

" 'I will come back to you in three days. I will come back and sit in a Nazarene room and eat Nazarene food and sleep on a Nazarene bed. I will spend half the week with Moslem friends and half with Nazarenes.' "

The woman's voice had a triumphant ring as she finished her sentence; then, without announcing the end of the sketch, she walked over to the wall and put one arm around her basket.

Down below, just at the edge of the cliff's shadow, a Moslem woman was seated on a rock, washing her legs in one of the holes filled with sea water. Her haik was piled on her lap and she was huddled over it, examining her feet.

"She is looking at the ocean," said Zodelia.

She was not looking at the ocean; with her head down and the mass of cloth in her lap she could not possibly have seen it; she would have had to straighten up and turn around.

"She is *not* looking at the ocean," she said.

"She is looking at the ocean," Zodelia repeated, as if she had not spoken.

She decided to change the subject. "Why do you have a porcupine with you?" she asked her, although she knew that some of the Moslems, particularly the country people, enjoyed eating them.

"It is a present for my aunt. Do you like it?"

"Yes," she said. "I like porcupines. I like big porcupines and little ones, too."

Zodelia seemed bewildered, and then bored, and she decided she had somehow ruined the conversation by mentioning small porcupines.

"Where is your mother?" Zodelia said at length.

"My mother is in her country in her own house," she said automatically; she had answered the question a hundred times.

"Why don't you write her a letter and tell her to come here? You can take her on a promenade and show her the ocean. After that she can go back to her own country and sit in her house." She picked up her basket and adjusted the strip of cloth over her mouth. "Would you like to go to a wedding?" she asked her.

She said she would love to go to a wedding, and they started off down the crooked blue street, heading into the wind. As they passed a small shop Zodelia stopped. "Stand here," she said. "I want to buy something."

After studying the display for a minute or two Zodelia poked her and pointed to some cakes inside a square box with glass sides. "Nice?" she asked her. "Or not nice?"

The cakes were dusty and coated with a thin, ugly-colored icing. They were called *Galletas Ortiz*.

"They are very nice," she replied, and bought her a dozen of them. Zodelia thanked her briefly and they walked on. Presently they turned off the street into a narrow alley and started downhill. Soon Zodelia stopped at a door on the right, and lifted the heavy brass knocker in the form of a fist.

"The wedding is here?" she said to her.

Zodelia shook her head and looked grave. "There is no wedding here," she said.

A child opened the door and quickly hid behind it, covering her face. She followed Zodelia across the black and white tile floor of the closed patio. The walls were washed in blue, and a cold light shone through the broken panes of glass far above their heads. There was a door on each side of the patio. Outside one of them, barring the threshold, was a row of pointed slippers. Zodelia stepped out of her own shoes and set them down near the others.

She stood behind Zodelia and began to take off her own shoes. It took her a long time because there was a knot in one of her laces. When she was ready, Zodelia took her hand and pulled her along with her into a dimly lit room, where she led her over to a mattress which lay against the wall.

"Sit," she told her, and she obeyed. Then, without further comment she walked off, heading for the far end of the room. Because her eyes had not grown used to the dimness, she had the impression of a figure disappearing down a long corridor. Then she began to see the brass bars of a bed, glowing weakly in the darkness.

Only a few feet away, in the middle of the carpet, sat an old lady in a dress made of green and purple curtain fabric. Through the many rents in the material she could see the printed cotton dress and the tan sweater underneath. Across the room several women sat along another mattress, and further along the mattress three babies were sleeping in a row, each one close against the wall with its head resting on a fancy cushion.

"Is it nice here?" It was Zodelia, who had returned without her haik. Her black crepe European dress hung unbelted down to her ankles, almost grazing her bare feet. The hem was lopsided. "Is it nice here?" she asked again, crouching on her haunches in front of her and pointing at the old woman. "That one is Tetum," she said. The old lady plunged both hands into a bowl of raw chopped meat and began shaping the stuff into little balls.

"Tetum," echoed the ladies on the mattress.

"This Nazarene," said Zodelia, gesturing in her direction, "spends half her time in a Moslem house with Moslem friends and the other half in a Nazarene hotel with other Nazarenes."

"That's nice," said the women opposite. "Half with Moslem friends and half with Nazarenes."

The old lady looked very stern. She noticed that her bony cheeks were tattooed with tiny blue crosses.

"Why?" asked the old lady abruptly in a deep voice. "*Why* does she spend half her time with Moslem friends and half with Nazarenes?" She fixed her eye on Zodelia, never ceasing to shape the meat with her swift fingers. Now she saw that her knuckles were also tattooed with blue crosses.

Zodelia stared back at her stupidly. "I don't know why," she said, shrugging one fat shoulder. It was clear that the picture she had been painting for them had suddenly lost all its charm for her.

"Is she crazy?" the old lady asked.

"No," Zodelia answered listlessly. "She is not crazy." There were shrieks of laughter from the mattress.

The old lady fastened her sharp eyes on the visitor, and she saw that they were heavily outlined in black. "Where is your husband?" she demanded.

"He's traveling in the desert."

"Selling things," Zodelia put in. This was the popular explanation for her husband's trips; she did not try to contradict it.

"Where is your mother?" the old lady asked.

"My mother is in our country in her own house."

"Why don't you go and sit with your mother in her own house?" she scolded. "The hotel costs a lot of money."

"In the city where I was born," she began, "there are many, many automobiles and many, many trucks."

The women on the mattress were smiling pleasantly. "Is that true?" remarked the one in the center in a tone of polite interest.

"I hate trucks," she told the woman with feeling.

The old lady lifted the bowl of meat off her lap and set it down on the carpet. "Trucks are nice," she said severely.

"That's true," the women agreed, after only a moment's hesitation. "Trucks are very nice."

"Do *you* like trucks?" she asked Zodelia, thinking that because of their relatively greater intimacy she might perhaps agree with her.

"Yes," she said. "They are nice. Trucks are very nice." She seemed lost in meditation, but only for an instant. "Everything is nice," she announced, with a look of triumph.

"It's the truth," the women said from their mattress. "Everything is nice."

They all looked happy, but the old lady was still frowning. "Aicha!" she yelled, twisting her neck so that her voice could be heard in the patio. "Bring the tea!"

Several little girls came into the room carrying the tea things and a low round table.

"Pass the cakes to the Nazarene," she told the smallest child, who was carrying a cut-glass dish piled with cakes. She saw that they were the ones she had bought for Zodelia; she did not want any of them. She wanted to go home.

"Eat!" the women called out from their mattress. "Eat the cakes."

The child pushed the glass dish forward.

"The dinner at the hotel is ready," she said, standing up.

"Drink tea," said the old woman scornfully. "Later you will sit with the other Nazarenes and eat their food."

"The Nazarenes will be angry if I'm late." She realized that she was lying stupidly, but she could not stop. "They will hit me!" She tried to look wild and frightened.

"Drink tea. They will not hit you," the old woman told her. "Sit down and drink tea."

The child was still offering her the glass dish as she backed away toward the door. Outside she sat down on the black and white tiles to lace her shoes. Only Zodelia followed her into the patio.

"Come back," the others were calling. "Come back into the room."

Then she noticed the porcupine basket standing nearby against the wall. "Is that old lady in the room your aunt? Is she the one you were bringing the porcupine to?" she asked her.

"No. She is not my aunt."

"Where *is* your aunt?"

"My aunt is in her own house."

"When will you take the porcupine to her?" She wanted to keep talking, so that Zodelia would be distracted and forget to fuss about her departure.

"The porcupine sits here," she said firmly. "In my own house."

She decided not to ask her again about the wedding.

When they reached the door Zodelia opened it just enough to let her through. "Good-bye," she said behind her. "I shall see you tomorrow, if Allah wills it."

"When?"

"Four o'clock." It was obvious that she had chosen the first figure that had come into her head. Before closing the door she reached out and pressed two of the dry Spanish cakes into her hand. "Eat them," she said graciously. "Eat them at the hotel with the other Nazarenes."

She started up the steep alley, headed once again for the walk along the cliff. The houses on either side of her were so close that she could smell the dampness of the walls and feel it on her cheeks like a thicker air.

When she reached the place where she had met Zodelia she went over to the wall and leaned on it. Although the sun had sunk behind the houses, the sky was still luminous and the blue of the wall had deepened. She rubbed her fingers along it: the wash was fresh and a little of the powdery stuff came off. And she remembered how once she had reached out to touch the face of a clown because it had awakened some longing. It had happened at a little circus, but not when she was a child.

FROM

The Heights of Macchu Picchu

[*Translated by Nathaniel Tarn*]

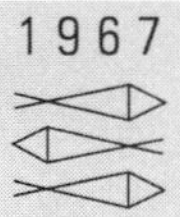

From air to air, like an empty net,
dredging through streets and ambient atmosphere, I came
lavish, at autumn's coronation, with the leaves'
proffer of currency and—between spring and wheat ears—
that which a boundless love, caught in a gauntlet fall,
grants us like a long-fingered moon.

(Days of live radiance in discordant
bodies: steels converted
to the silence of acid:
nights disentangled to the ultimate flour,
assaulted stamens of the nuptial land.)

Someone waiting for me among the violins
met with a world like a buried tower
sinking its spiral below the layered leaves
color of raucous sulphur:
and lower yet, in a vein of gold,
like a sword in a scabbard of meteors,
I plunged a turbulent and tender hand
to the most secret organs of the earth.

Leaning my forehead through unfathomed waves
I sank, a single drop, within a sleep of sulphur
where, like a blind man, I retraced the jasmine
of our exhausted human spring.

T. S. ELIOT

FROM

Poems

WRITTEN IN EARLY YOUTH

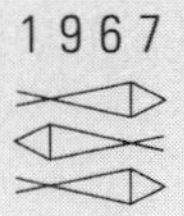

THE DEATH OF SAINT NARCISSUS

Come under the shadow of this gray rock—
Come in under the shadow of this gray rock,
And I will show you something different from either
Your shadow sprawling over the sand at daybreak, or
Your shadow leaping behind the fire against the red rock:
I will show you his bloody cloth and limbs
And the gray shadow on his lips.

He walked once between the sea and the high cliffs
When the wind made him aware of his limbs smoothly passing each
other
And of his arms crossed over his breast.
When he walked over the meadows
He was stifled and soothed by his own rhythm.
By the river
His eyes were aware of the pointed corners of his eyes
And his hands aware of the pointed tips of his fingers.

Struck down by such knowledge
He could not live men's ways, but became a dancer before God
If he walked in city streets
He seemed to tread on faces, convulsive thighs and knees.
So he came out under the rock.

First he was sure that he had been a tree,
Twisting its branches among each other
And tangling its roots among each other.

Then he knew that he had been a fish
With slippery white belly held tight in his own fingers,
Writhing in his own clutch, his ancient beauty
Caught fast in the pink tips of his new beauty.

Then he had been a young girl
Caught in the woods by a drunken old man
Knowing at the end the taste of his own whiteness
The horror of his own smoothness,
And he felt drunken and old.

So he became a dancer to God.
Because his flesh was in love with the burning arrows
He danced on the hot sand
Until the arrows came.
As he embraced them his white skin surrendered itself to the redness
of blood, and satisfied him.
Now he is green, dry and stained
With the shadow in his mouth.

THOMAS MERTON

FROM

Mystics and Zen Masters

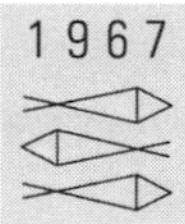

LOVE AND TAO

A hundred years ago America began to discover the Orient and its philosophical tradition. The discovery was valid, it reached toward the inner truth of Oriental thought. The intuitions of Emerson and Thoreau were rich in promises that were not afterward fulfilled by successors. America did not have the patience to continue what was so happily begun. The door that had opened for an instant, closed again for a century. Now that the door seems to be opening again (and sometimes one wonders if it is the door of the same house), we have another chance. It is imperative for us to find out what is inside this fabulous edifice. From where we stand, we can descry the residents dressed in our kind of clothing and engaged in our kind of frantic gesturing. They are tearing the place apart and rebuilding it in the likeness of our own utilitarian dwellings, department stores, and factories. Not that there is anything wrong with industrial production, with its higher standard of living. Yet we know, or should know, by this time, that our material riches unfortunately imply a spiritual, cultural, and moral poverty that are perhaps far greater than we see.

[. . .]

Everyone knows in a vague way that the *Tao Te Ching* is poetic, and indeed that it is great poetry. Most people know that it usually impresses Westerners as more than a little quietistic. Hence they treat it with condescension as a quaint impractical document of an ancient day when no one bothered much about progress. Perhaps they do not realize that some of the wisdom of the *Tao Te Ching*, which so often reminds one of the Sermon on the Mount, is absolutely necessary for us not only to progress but even to survive.

As for the *Hsiao Ching*: this is less well known in the West than the *Tao* classic. But it is no less characteristic of China. Here in this "Classic of Filial Love" we find not so much a Confucianism that is arbitrarily opposed to Taoism, as what I would venture to call a *Confucian kind of Taoism.* We must not imagine that the classic Confucianism of the third century B.C. was something purely formalistic and external, without respect for the interior, the hidden mystery in which all life has its invisible roots. On the contrary, we shall see that filial love was, for these Confucians, the taproot which was sunk most deeply in the mystery of the ethical *Tao* and which, unless it was cut by selfishness, kept both the individual and society in living contact with the mysterious will of heaven.

CLASSICS AND MASTERS

The word "Ching" which is found in the titles of these and other celebrated Chinese texts, is roughly translated as "classic." It means something more than just "book" and yet it does not have the connotations that "classic" has come to have for us. In the West, a classical work is one of the "highest class" because it embodies the peculiar literary and stylistic excellence we find in the great writers of Greece and Rome. The classical writers of Greece and Rome are those whose style is most pure and admirable. But a "Ching" is not a classic in this sense. It might be more helpful to consider the word "Ching" as corresponding to "Bible." Remember that our word "Bible" comes from the Greek *ta biblia*, or "the books." And not simply "the books," but precisely the books as contrasted with some other vehicle of tradition; that is to say, with the oral tradition. Words like "Ching" and "Bible" then, far from referring to what we would now call "Great Books" as distinct from books of a lesser literary value, mean simply the ancient traditions as contained in books rather than as orally transmitted. Such books then are not so much the ornaments and jewels of a culture as its mind and its memory, though that is not accurate if we remember that oral transmission of wisdom is more important than transmission in writing.

Hence a "Ching" is an *authoritative* book. Not that it has been written by an authoritative man (a "classical scholar" or even a "philosopher"), but that it goes back to an authority higher than man. One hesitates to use the word supernatural in connection with Chinese thought, yet the fact that the *Tao Te Ching* distinguishes a *Tao* that can be known and spoken of from the *Tao* which is unknown and unable to be named authorizes us to find here something that corresponds with our notion of God above and beyond the cosmos.

[. . .]

If we want to understand the position of writers like these ancient Chinese philosophers, we must compare them not only with

Plato or Parmenides but also with the Hebrew scribes, the transmitters of the wisdom tradition in the so-called sapiential books of the Old Testament. The ideogram which represents Tzu, in Lao Tzu (Master Lao), means both "master" and "child." Indeed, we find this ideogram combined with another in the word *hsiao*, meaning filial love. There the "son" is seen bearing the "father" on his shoulders. A master is therefore a child of the ancient Fathers, who bears their tradition with him and transmits it to future generations. Or rather, to be much more accurate, a master is a child who, like Lao Tzu, knows how to draw secret nourishment in silence from his "mother" the Tao.

Hence, we see that a master is not merely one who learns and repeats authoritative forms of words passed on from the time of the ancients; he is one who has been born to his wisdom by the mysterious all-embracing and merciful love which is the mother of all being. He is one who knows the unknown not by intellectual penetration, or by a science that wrests for itself the secrets of heaven, but by the wisdom of "littleness" and silence which knows how to receive in secret a word that cannot be uttered except in an enigma. This enigma is not a verbal riddle but the existential mystery of life itself. The wisdom of the *Tao Te Ching* leads therefore to Zen, which is at least ideally a transmission without any "Ching," passed on unaccountably from master to disciple not by means of written words but by seemingly absurd *koans*, accompanied, on occasion, by kicks and clouts on the head.

THE CLASSIC OF TAO

The literal translation of the title *Tao Te Ching* is the "Book of the Way and Its (Hidden) Power." If there is a correct answer to the question: "What is the *Tao*?" it is: "I don't know."

> Tao *can be talked about but not the eternal* Tao,
> *Names can be named, but not the Eternal Name.*
> *As the origin of heaven and earth it is nameless:*
> *As "the Mother" of all things it is namable.*

It is like an "empty bowl that can never be filled." It is like the hole in the center of the hub of a wheel, upon which all the spokes converge.

> *We make doors and windows for a room;*
> *But it is these empty spaces that make the room livable. . . .*

Look at it, but you cannot see it!
Its name is Formless.

Listen to it, but you cannot hear it!
Its name is Soundless.

Grasp at it, but you cannot get it!
Its name is Incorporeal.

It is the formless form, the imageless image. It is a "fountain spirit" of inexhaustible life and yet never draws attention to itself. It does its work without remark and without recognition. It is utterly elusive: if you think you have seen it, what you have seen is not the *Tao*. Yet it is the source of all, and all things return to it "as to their home."

The whole secret of life lies in the discovery of this *Tao* which can never be discovered. This does not involve an intellectual quest, but rather a spiritual change of one's whole being. One "reaches" the *Tao* by "becoming like" the *Tao*, by acting, in some sense, according to the "way" *(Tao)*. For the *Tao* is at once perfect activity and perfect rest. It is supreme act, *actus purissimus*. Hence human activity, even virtuous activity, is not enough to bring one into line with the *Tao*. Virtuous activity tends to be busy and showy, and even with the best intentions in the world it cannot avoid sounding the trumpet before itself in the market place.

He who cultivates the Tao *is one with the* Tao*;*
He who practices Virtue is one with Virtue;
And he who courts after Loss is one with Loss.

The way of loss is the way of whirlwind activity, of rash endeavor, of ambition, the accumulation of "extraneous growths." It is the way of aggression, of success. The way of virtue is the Confucian way of self-conscious and professional goodness, which is, in fact, a less pure form of virtue. St. Thomas would say it works *humano modo* rather than with the divine and mysterious spontaneity of the gifts of the Holy Ghost. But the way of *Tao* is just that: the way of supreme spontaneity, which is virtuous in a transcendent sense because it "does not strive."

High virtue is non-virtuous;
Therefore it has virtue.
Low virtue never frees itself from virtuousness,
Therefore, it has no virtue.

The "sage," or the man who has discovered the secret of the *Tao*, has not acquired any special esoteric knowledge that sets him apart from others and makes him smarter than they are. On the contrary, he is from a certain point of view more stupid and exteriorly less remarkable. He is "dim and obscure." While everyone else exults over success as over a sacrificial ox, he alone is silent, "like a babe who has not yet smiled." Though he has in fact "returned to the root," the *Tao*, he appears to be the "only one who has no home to return to." He is very much like the One who has nowhere to lay His head, even though the foxes may have holes and the birds of the air their nests. He who has found the *Tao* has no local habitation and no name on the earth. He is "bland like the ocean, aimless as the wafting gale." Again we remember the Gospels: "The wind blows where it pleases . . . even so is every man who is born of the Spirit" (John 3:8).

The way of the sage is the way of not-attacking, not charging at his objective, not busying himself too intently about his goals. The Chinese ideogram for this is, unfortunately, hardly able to be translated. The "active" symbol in it looks like a charging horse. *Wu wei* is a Taoist and Zen technical expression, and perhaps it is better left as it stands. Dr. John C.H. Wu coins an English expression for it: "non-ado," and one can see what is at the back of his mind. It recalls the Shakespeare title *Much Ado About Nothing*.

The Japanese Zen artist and poet Sengai has left us two Japanese characters, *Bu Ji*, which are a work of art in themselves and eloquent of the spirit of *Tao*. *Bu Ji* means "nothing doing." I can say that there is more energy, more creativity, more productiveness in these two powerful signs created by Sengai than in all the skyscrapers of New York, and yet he dashed them onto paper with four strokes of his brush.

Hence *wu wei* is far from being inactive. It is supreme activity, because it acts at rest, acts without effort. Its effortlessness is not a matter of inertia, but of harmony with the hidden power that drives the planets and the cosmos.

The sage, then, accomplishes very much indeed because it is the *Tao* that acts in him and through him. He does not act of and by himself, still less for himself alone. His action is not a violent manipulation of exterior reality, an "attack" on the outside world, bending it to his conquering will: on the contrary, he respects external reality by yielding to it, and his yielding is at once an act of worship, a recognition of sacredness, and a perfect accomplishment of what is demanded by the precise situation.

The world is a sacred vessel which must not be tampered with or grabbed after.

To tamper with it is to spoil it, and to grasp it is to lose it.

The power of the sage is then the very power which has been revealed in the Gospels as Pure Love. *Deus caritas est* is the full manifestation of the truth hidden in the nameless *Tao*, and yet it still leaves *Tao* nameless. For love is not a name, any more than *Tao* is. One must go beyond the word and enter into communion with the reality before he can know anything about it: and then, more likely than not, he will know "in the cloud of unknowing."

The sixty-seventh chapter of the *Tao Te Ching* is one of the most profound and the most akin to Christianity. In the *Tao*, "which is queer like nothing on earth," are found three treasures: mercy, frugality, and not wanting to be first in the world. And the extraordinarily profound statement is made

> *Because I am merciful, therefore I can be brave . . .*
> *For heaven will come to the rescue of the merciful and protect*
> *him with* its *mercy.*

Again one hears echoes of the Gospel: "Blessed are the merciful . . ." "Perfect love casteth out fear." Comparing Dr. Wu's translation with that of Lin Yutang in the Modern Library edition of Lao Tzu (another extremely interesting translation, with parallel passages from the poet and sage Chuang Tzu), we find new perspectives. (It is often necessary to read a translated Chinese text in two or more versions.)

> *If one forsakes love and fearlessness,*
> *forsakes restraint and reserve power,*
> *forsakes following behind and rushes in front,*
> *He is doomed!*
>
> *For love is victorious in attack*
> *And invulnerable in defense,*
> Heaven arms with love
> Those it would not see destroyed.

The word which Lin Yutang translates as "love" and Dr. Wu as "mercy" is in fact the compassionate love of the mother for the child. Once again, the sage and the wise ruler are men who do not rush forward to aggrandize themselves, but cherish, with loving concern, the "sacred" reality of persons and things which have been entrusted to them by the *Tao*.

It must be remembered that the *Tao Te Ching* is basically not a manual for hermits but a treatise on government, and much is said there on war and peace. It is a manual that our leaders might be expected to read, and doubtless some of them might do so with profit. One of its most astute sayings is that in a war the winner is likely to be the side that enters the war with the most sorrow.

> *To rejoice over a victory is to rejoice over the slaughter of men!*
> *Hence a man who rejoices over the slaughter of men cannot*
> *expect to thrive in the world of men.*
> *. . . Every victory is a funeral.*

THE CLASSIC OF FILIAL LOVE

The paradoxical brilliance of the *Tao* classic contrasts with the simplicity of the *Hsiao Ching*, a primer of Chinese Confucian ethics and one of the first texts formerly studied by Chinese schoolboys. But this makes it even more interesting, in some respects, than the better known *Tao Te Ching*. Many who would be secretly irritated by the apparent subtlety of the *Tao* classic might prefer to meditate on the "Classic of Filial Love." It is a revelation of the deepest natural wisdom, and its intuitions are surprisingly "modern." In fact, we are here on the same ground as Freud, and substantially the same conclusions that were reached by Freud more than twenty centuries later are here exposed in all simplicity and without benefit of the Oedipus complex.

One might be tempted to imagine that this treatise is designed merely to keep sons in subjection to their parents and hence to exalt parental authority for its own sake. It is doubtless true that the rigid formalism of Confucian ethics became, after two thousand years, a somewhat suffocating system. But, in its original purity, the Confucian ideal is basically *personalistic*. The fundamental justification for filial piety is that our person is received as a gift from our parents and is to be fully developed out of gratitude toward them. Hence, the astounding fact that this filial piety is not simply a cult of the parent as such, but a development of one's own gifts in honor of the parents who gave them to us. Then, when we reach manhood and our parents are old, we make a fitting return to them by loving support. This basic attitude is said to be "the foundation of virtue and the root of civilization."

If a child can enter fruitfully and lovingly into the five basic relationships, he will certainly develop into a good citizen and a worthy leader, supposing that to be his vocation. The five basic relationships are those of father to son, marked by *justice*; mother to son, marked by *compassion*, or merciful love; the son to his parents, marked by *filial love*; the elder brother to his younger brother, marked by *friendship*; and the younger to the elder, marked by *respect* for his senior.

Thus, we see a wonderful organic complex of strength from the father, warmth from the mother, gratitude from the son, and wholesome respectful friendship between brothers. "He who really loves his parents will not be proud in high station; he will not be insubordinate in an inferior position; among his equals he will not be contentious. To be proud in high station is to be ruined; to be insubordinate in an inferior position is to incur punishment; to be contentious among one's equals leads to physical violence. As long as these three evils are not uprooted, a son cannot be called filial even though he feast his parents daily on three kinds of choice meat." On such a ground grows up a love that reaches out through society and makes it the earthly image of the invisible order of heaven.

The *Hsiao Ching* then shows how this love has various ways of coming to fruitful development in all the levels of society, from the Son of Heaven down through the princes and scholars to the peasants. "From the Son of Heaven to the commoners, if filial piety is not pursued from beginning to end, disasters are sure to follow." The society of love (compare the works of Pseudo-Dionysius) is hierarchical. The lower depend on the higher in this exercise of love. The emperor is at the summit. All depends on him, and he should ideally be capable of the widest and most all-embracing love. For he must love all his subjects and care for their needs. In so doing, he embodies the "heavenly principle" on earth and imitates heaven, who loves all alike. He also has a duty to share with his subjects this knowledge of heavenly love, and this he does by means of *ritual and music*. In other words, the nation which lives by love grows in love by liturgical celebration of the mystery of love: such are the Christian terms in which we might expand this primitive intuition.

It is important to notice that in all this there is no such thing as blind subservience to age and to authority. On the contrary, one of the basic duties of filial love is to correct the father when he is wrong, and one of the basic duties of the minister is to correct his prince when he errs. This, of course, was the ideal. The pungent humor of Chuang Tzu shows us many occasions when in practice this kind of "filial love" was not appreciated.

CONCLUSIONS

Christopher Dawson has remarked on the "religious vacuum" in our education. It is absolutely essential to introduce into our study of the humanities a dimension of *wisdom* oriented to contemplation as well as to wise action. For this, it is no longer sufficient merely to go back over the Christian and European cultural traditions. The horizons of the world are no longer confined to Europe and America. We have to gain new perspectives, and on this our spiritual and even our physical survival may depend.

NELLY SACHS

FROM

O the Chimneys

[*Translated by Michael Hamburger*]

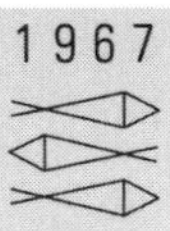

O THE CHIMNEYS

And though after my skin worms destroy this body, yet in my flesh shall I see God.
JOB, *19:26*

O the chimneys
On the ingeniously devised habitations of death
When Israel's body drifted as smoke
Through the air—
Was welcomed by a star, a chimney sweep,
A star that turned black
Or was it a ray of sun?

O the chimneys!
Freedomway for Jeremiah and Job's dust—
Who devised you and laid stone upon stone
The road for refugees of smoke?

O the habitations of death,
Invitingly appointed
For the host who used to be a guest—
O you fingers
Laying the threshold
Like a knife between life and death—

O you chimneys,
O you fingers
And Israel's body as smoke through the air!

JOAN DIDION

FROM

Slouching Towards Bethlehem

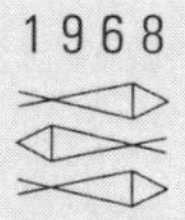
1968

ON MORALITY

As it happens I am in Death Valley, in a room at the Enterprise Motel and Trailer Park, and it is July, and it is hot. In fact it is 119°. I cannot seem to make the air conditioner work, but there is a small refrigerator, and I can wrap ice cubes in a towel and hold them against the small of my back. With the help of the ice cubes I have been trying to think, because *The American Scholar* asked me to, in some abstract way about "morality," a word I distrust more every day, but my mind veers inflexibly toward the particular.

Here are some particulars. At midnight last night, on the road in from Las Vegas to Death Valley Junction, a car hit a shoulder and turned over. The driver, very young and apparently drunk, was killed instantly. His girl was found alive but bleeding internally, deep in shock. I talked this afternoon to the nurse who had driven the girl to the nearest doctor, 185 miles across the floor of the Valley and three ranges of lethal mountain road. The nurse explained that her husband, a talc miner, had stayed on the highway with the boy's body until the coroner could get over the mountains from Bishop, at dawn today. "You can't just leave a body on the highway," she said. "It's immoral."

It was one instance in which I did not distrust the word, because she meant something quite specific. She meant that if a body is left alone for even a few minutes on the desert, the coyotes close in and eat the flesh. Whether or not a corpse is torn apart by coyotes may seem only a sentimental consideration, but of course it is more: one of the promises we make to one another is that we will try to retrieve our casualties, try not to abandon our dead to the coyotes. If we have been taught to keep our promises—if, in the simplest terms, our upbringing is good enough—we stay with the body, or have bad dreams.

I am talking, of course, about the kind of social code that is sometimes called, usually pejoratively, "wagon-train morality." In fact that is precisely what it is. For better or worse, we are what we learned as children: my own childhood was illuminated by graphic litanies of the grief awaiting those who failed in their loyalties to each other. The Donner-Reed Party, starving in the Sierra snows, all the ephemera of civilization gone save that one vestigial taboo, the provision that no one should eat his own blood kin. The Jayhawkers, who quarreled and separated not far from where I am tonight. Some of them died in the Funerals and some of them died down near Badwater and most of the rest of them died in the Panamints. A woman who got through gave the Valley its name. Some might say that the Jayhawkers were killed by the desert summer, and the Donner Party by the mountain winter, by circumstances beyond control; we were taught instead that they had somewhere abdicated their responsibilities, somehow breached their primary loyalties, or they would not have found themselves helpless in the mountain winter or the desert summer, would not have given way to acrimony, would not have deserted one another, would not have *failed.* In brief, we heard such stories as cautionary tales, and they still suggest the only kind of "morality" that seems to me to have any but the most potentially mendacious meaning.

•

You are quite possibly impatient with me by now; I am talking, you want to say, about a "morality" so primitive that it scarcely deserves the name, a code that has as its point only survival, not the attainment of the ideal good. Exactly. Particularly out here tonight, in this country so ominous and terrible that to live in it is to live with antimatter, it is difficult to believe that "the good" is a knowable quantity. Let me tell you what it is like out here tonight. Stories travel at night on the desert. Someone gets in his pickup and drives a couple of hundred miles for a beer, and he carries news of what is happening, back wherever he came from. Then he drives another hundred miles for another beer, and passes along stories from the last place as well as from the one before; it is a network kept alive by people whose instincts tell them that if they do not keep moving at night on the desert they will lose all reason. Here is a story that is going around the desert tonight: over across the Nevada line, sheriff's deputies are diving in some underground pools, trying to retrieve a couple of bodies known to be in the hole. The widow of one of the drowned boys is over there; she is eighteen, and pregnant, and is said not to leave the hole. The divers go down and come up, and she just stands there and stares into the water. They have been diving for ten days but have found no bottom to the caves, no bodies and no trace of them, only the black 90° water going down and down and down, and a single translucent fish, not classified. The story tonight is that one of the divers has been hauled up incoherent, out of his head, shouting—

until they got him out of there so that the widow could not hear—about water that got hotter instead of cooler as he went down, about light flickering through the water, about magma, about underground nuclear testing.

That is the tone stories take out here, and there are quite a few of them tonight. And it is more than the stories alone. Across the road at the Faith Community Church a couple of dozen old people, come here to live in trailers and die in the sun, are holding a prayer sing. I cannot hear them and do not want to. What I can hear are occasional coyotes and a constant chorus of "Baby the Rain Must Fall" from the jukebox in the Snake Room next door, and if I were also to hear those dying voices, those Midwestern voices drawn to this lunar country for some unimaginable atavistic rites, *rock of ages cleft for me*, I think I would lose my own reason. Every now and then I imagine I hear a rattlesnake, but my husband says that it is a faucet, a paper rustling, the wind. Then he stands by a window, and plays a flashlight over the dry wash outside.

What does it mean? It means nothing manageable. There is some sinister hysteria in the air out here tonight, some hint of the monstrous perversion to which any human idea can come. "I followed my own conscience." "I did what I thought was right." How many madmen have said it and meant it? How many murderers? Klaus Fuchs said it, and the men who committed the Mountain Meadows Massacre said it, and Alfred Rosenberg said it. And, as we are rotely and rather presumptuously reminded by those who would say it now, Jesus said it. Maybe we have all said it, and maybe we have been wrong. Except on that most primitive level—our loyalties to those we love—what could be more arrogant than to claim the primacy of personal conscience? ("Tell me," a rabbi asked Daniel Bell when he said, as a child, that he did not believe in God. "Do you think God cares?") At least some of the time, the world appears to me as a painting by Hieronymous Bosch; were I to follow my conscience then, it would lead me out onto the desert with Marion Faye, out to where he stood in *The Deer Park* looking east to Los Alamos and praying, as if for rain, that it would happen: ". . . *let it come and clear the rot and the stench and the stink, let it come for all of everywhere, just so it comes and the world stands clear in the white dead dawn.*"

•

Of course you will say that I do not have the right, even if I had the power, to inflict that unreasonable conscience upon you; nor do I want you to inflict your conscience, however reasonable, however enlightened, upon me. ("We must be aware of the dangers which lie in our most generous wishes," Lionel Trilling once wrote. "Some paradox of our nature leads us, when once we have made our fellow men the objects of our enlightened interest, to go on to make them the objects of our pity, then of our wisdom, ultimately of our coercion.") That the ethic of conscience is intrinsically insidious seems scarcely a revelatory point, but it is one raised with increasing infrequency; even those who do raise it tend to *segue* with troubling readiness into the quite contradictory position that the ethic of conscience is dangerous when it is "wrong," and admirable when it is "right."

You see I want to be quite obstinate about insisting that we have no way of knowing—beyond that fundamental loyalty to the social code—what is "right" and what is "wrong," what is "good" and what "evil." I dwell so upon this because the most disturbing aspect of "morality" seems to me to be the frequency with which the word now appears; in the press, on television, in the most perfunctory kinds of conversation. Questions of straightforward power (or survival) politics, questions of quite indifferent public policy, questions of almost anything: they are all assigned these factitious moral burdens. There is something facile going on, some self-indulgence at work. Of course we would all like to "believe" in something, like to assuage our private guilts in public causes, like to lose our tiresome selves; like, perhaps, to transform the white flag of defeat at home into the brave white banner of battle away from home. And of course it is all right to do that; that is how, immemorially, things have gotten done. But I think it is all right only so long as we do not delude ourselves about what we are doing, and why. It is all right only so long as we remember that all the *ad hoc* committees, all the picket lines, all the brave signatures in *The New York Times*, all the tools of agitprop straight across the spectrum, do not confer upon anyone any *ipso facto* virtue. It is all right only so long as we recognize that the end may or may not be expedient, may or may not be a good idea, but in any case has nothing to do with "morality." Because when we start deceiving ourselves into thinking not that we want something or need something, not that it is a pragmatic necessity for us to have it, but that it is a *moral imperative* that we have it, then is when we join the fashionable madmen, and then is when the thin whine of hysteria is heard in the land, and then is when we are in bad trouble. And I suspect we are already there.

CESARE PAVESE

FROM

The Selected Works of Cesare Pavese

[*Translated by R. W. Flint*]

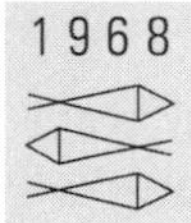

FROM

THE HOUSE ON THE HILL

The ambush had been laid between two large protecting rocks. Not one of the blackshirts saved his skin. The partisans carried off prisoners in the other truck, after lining them against a wall and threatening: "We could murder you in your own style. We prefer to keep you alive for your shame."

The local people were bundling their things and driving out their animals. Nobody would have dared to sleep at Due Rocce. Some went up to the sanctuary, hoping in the virtue of the place; others went anyway, just to go. They had until nightfall, because the boy on the bicycle who had shouted to me was running to give news of the wounded on the telephone, at the blockhouse, to save what could be saved. Tomorrow the roads and lanes would be a death trap.

The priest was inside, where someone was dying. I stayed among the dead, not daring to climb over them. I looked off at the bell tower and knew I wouldn't get home before tomorrow. Some instinct pulled me back, down the road already walked, to put between me and the coming storm the guiltless village below, the Tinella and the railway. Otino was down there; he could at least hide me. If I could get by the German stations before nightfall, I could wait with him for the fury to blow itself out.

I left, passed the peasant of the oxen, waiting with his mouth open in front of the canebrake, kept straight on, and an hour afterward I was climbing the last rise under a cool sky, beyond which lay the Tinella. Again I saw some of the morning's horizons. The church towers and farms made sense; I wondered if I would always live among terrors like this at home. Meanwhile I kept to the road, tense at the corners and crossroads, never showing myself against the skyline. Now I knew what a rifle shot was, what it sounded like.

At dusk I reached the Tinella and the tracks. While I was waiting in the mud among alder bushes, I heard the puffing of a train. A long local freight train chuffed slowly by and I noticed several burly German soldiers standing between cars. That they were traveling seemed a good sign, meaning that the zone was still quiet.

I jumped the tracks and went to Otino's hill. It was difficult finding my way among the acacias, but the hilltop stood out clearly. I took a path that seemed right and went up and listened for footsteps or rustling leaves above the shrilling of crickets. The sky overhead was brilliant with stars.

Otino wasn't there, but it was the right hill. I was tired, hungry, and dragging my feet over the furrows. I came on a small shed in a vineyard, made of solid masonry and doorless—a shelter for the man who tended the grapes. I went in and threw myself on a sack.

When I woke up much later, my back and neck were stiff and aching. A dog was barking not far away; I imagined him a stray, crazed with hunger. Not enough light came in the opening for me to see the countryside. In that darkness the dog's voice was the voice of the whole earth. I tossed around in a half sleep.

Not to be seen leaving, I went out before dawn. The moon was rising. Turning back, I realized that the "shed" had been a simple abandoned chapel. The sky brightened behind the moon and I was cold, hungry, and scared. I was crouching in a grainfield, cursing the heavy dew, thinking of those dead. "To think of them is to pray for them," I thought.

At full light I found the low houses, gave the women the news. Otino had gone into the fields. I asked permission to wait for him in the hayloft. They gave me bread and soup; while I ate I calmed the women about the probable outcome of the killings. "They will only comb that side of the Tinella," I said, "or else I wouldn't have made it here."

Days followed of high winds sweeping the slopes; from up there one could pick out the successive crests, the smallest trees, houses, vines, to the distant woods. Otino showed me the sanctuary tower and a crook of the road where the slaughter had taken place. He roamed the hilltops, saw people, made them talk. One morning we saw a column of smoke rising from the woods: that evening we heard in the village of another clash toward the Tanaro. A division of Germans and Fascists had descended on the slope and had burned, shot, and robbed.

At night I slept in the hayloft; they had lent me a blanket. The gusty wind fell toward evening and I strained my ears for the crack of shots or human cries. All of us stayed with Otino in the fields, under brighter stars than I could remember; we were all searching out distant fires. We caught sight of an ominous glow against the deep blackness of the hills. "Remember that," Otino told me. "You'll pass near there. Where they have burned, there's no more surveillance."

I wanted to pay him something for the food I had eaten. His mother didn't say no; she only sighed and wondered why the war never ended. "If it lasts a century," I said, "who is better off than you?" Under the portico one could still see a streak of blood from a skinned rabbit. "There you are," Otino said, pointing at it. "That's how we'll end."

He brought me into the vineyard I had entered the first night; I told him it seemed a fine refuge. If all you needed was to sleep in a church to be safe, Otino said, the churches would be stuffed. "There isn't a church left here," I replied. "They've stripped the nut trees and burned over the ground."

"We came here to play when we were boys."

We went in, talking of life in the district, how everyone was afraid that even along the railway one could be shot at by a German or overtaken by a troop truck. "Have they burned any churches?" I asked. "If that's all they burned," he said, "it would be nothing."

One evening we collected all the branches we could find, and adding cornhusks, we lit a fire in the corner, beneath the window. Then, sitting before the flames, we smoked like boys. We said: "We can set fires too." I was nervous at first and went out to look at the window, but the little reflection was screened by a hillock in any case. "They can't see it, no, no," Otino said. Then we discussed once more the local people, those who were more afraid than we. "They, too, aren't living any longer. That's not living. They know the moment will come."

"We're all in the trenches."

Otino laughed. Gunfire was spitting a long way off.

"Now we're beginning," I said.

We listened. The wind was quiet and the dogs were barking. "Let's go to the house," I said. I spent a bad night, trembling at my thoughts. The rustle of hay seemed to fill the world.

Again, the next day, I studied the barrier of hills that waited for me. They were white and dried by the wind and heat, clear-cut under the sky. Again I wondered if the terror had reached the forests and above. I walked up a lane to buy bread in the village. People, curious and suspicious, watched me from doorways; I nodded to some of them. From the high square one could see new hills behind, like pinkish clouds. I stopped in front of the church. The brilliant light and silence gave me a pulse of hope. The present seemed impossible; life would be taken up again as secure and solid as it was at that moment. I'd forgotten for too long that bloodshed and pillage couldn't last forever.

A girl came out. She looked around and went down the street. For a moment she also entered my hope. She stepped carefully in the wind on the rough cobbles, not looking in my direction.

On the little square there wasn't anyone to be seen, and the heaped-up, red-brown roofs that until yesterday had seemed a safe hiding place now seemed like caves from which the prey would be driven out by fire. The problem was merely to resist the flames until they were finally spent.

In the evening came rumors of action in the nearby valley, against a village of women and old men. They swore it was true. In fact, nobody had heard a single shot: the stables had been plundered and the hay barns burned. The people, huddling in ravines, heard their cattle lowing but couldn't get to them. It had been late morning, just when I had been looking out from the church.

Otino was reaping in the fields, heard the news, and went on reaping.

"Thank God," I said, "that you kept me here."

He straightened up and passed his hand over his eyes. "Go at night when it's cooler."

We talked it over again that night and I decided it would be better to follow the Tinella than to risk the hills. I left the next day and by evening was at home with my parents, beyond the woods and the Belbo.

•

Nothing has happened. I've been at home for six months and the war still goes on. Rather, as the weather gets worse, the armies on the main fronts have begun to retrench again; another winter will pass, we will see snow again, we'll make a circle around the radio by the fire. Here the November mud in roads and vineyards is beginning to slow up the partisan bands. They say that this winter no one will have the will to fight; it will be hard enough merely to exist and wait to die in the spring. If then, as they say, we get heavy snows like last year's to stop up the doors and windows, it would be better if it never thawed.

We have had our dead here too. Apart from this and the scares and our uncomfortable flights into gullies behind the property (my mother or sister thrashing me awake, snatching up shoes and trousers, running hunched-down through the vineyard, then the wait, the demoralizing wait), apart from the boredom and shame, nothing happens. Throughout September there was no day without shooting in the hills or by the iron bridge—isolated shots as in the old hunting season, but sometimes bursts of machine-gun fire. Now it is less frequent. This is the true life of the forest the way one dreams it as a boy. And sometimes I think that only a boy's unawakened conscience, his genuine unaffected unawareness could manage to see what is going on without suffering fits of repentance. The heroes of these valleys in any case are all boys; they have the straight, stubborn look of boys. But for the fact that we—who are no longer young—nursed this war in our hearts and said: "Let it come then, if it has to come," even war, *this* war, might seem a clean business. Anyway, who knows? The war is burning our houses. It is sowing our squares and streets with the dead. It drives us like hares from refuge to refuge. It will end by forcing the rest of us to fight as well, extorting our active consent. A day will come when nobody is outside the war—not the cowards or the melancholy or the solitary. We will all have agreed to make war. And then maybe we'll have peace.

Nevertheless, the corn has been gathered on the farms and the grapes harvested. Obviously, not with the cheerfulness of the old days; too many are missing, some for good. Of the people in the neighborhood, only the old or middle-aged remember me, but for me the hill remains always a childhood land—bonfires, escapades, and games. If I had Dino here, I could still give him orders, but he has gone to play a more serious part. At his age it is easy. It is more difficult for the others who have played it before and are still doing so.

Now that the countryside is bare, I go back to my walking; I go up and down the hill, reflecting on the long illusion that gave me the impulse to write this book. Where the illusion will carry me I often wonder. What else is there to think about? Here every step, nearly every hour of the day, and certainly every sudden memory confronts me with what I was—what I am and have forgotten. Obsessed by the chance encounters of this year, I keep asking myself: "What is there in common between me and the man who fled the bombs, fled the Germans, fled from remorse and pain?" Not that I don't feel a pang if I think of those who have disappeared, if I think of the nightmare figures who run the roads like bitches—I finally tell myself that it's still not enough, that to end the horror we must enter it, we the survivors must enter, even to bloodshed—but it happens that the "I," this I who sees me rummaging cautiously through the faces and manias of these recent days, feels like someone else, detached, as if everything done, said, or suffered had been merely somewhere out there—someone else's concern, ancient history. This, in other words, is the illusion: here at home I find an older reality, a life beyond my own years, beyond Elvira, Cate, beyond Dino or school, all that I have wished or hoped for as a man; and I wonder if I will ever be able to escape. I see now that throughout this year and earlier too, even during the season of my meager follies, of Anna Maria, Gallo, Cate, when we were still young and the war a distant cloud—I see that I have lived a long isolation, a useless holiday, like a boy who creeps into a bush to hide, likes it there, looks at the sky from under the leaves and forgets to come out, ever.

It is here the war has seized me and seizes me every day. If I walk the woods, if at every suspicion of raiders I duck into the gullies, if I sometimes talk to passing partisans (Giorgi has been here with his men: he threw back his head and told me: "We'll have time to talk on evenings of snow"), it's not that I don't see that the war is no game, this war that has come even up here, which seizes even our past by the throat. I don't know if Cate, Fonso, Dino, and all the others will return. Sometimes I hope so, and it scares me. But I have seen the unknown dead, those little men of the Republic. It was they who woke me up. If a stranger, an enemy, becomes a thing like that when he dies, if one stops short and is afraid to walk over him, it means that even beaten our enemy is someone, that after having shed his blood, one must placate it, give this blood a voice, justify the man who shed it. Looking at certain dead is humiliating. They are no longer other people's affairs: one doesn't seem to have happened there by chance. One has the impression that the same fate that threw these bodies to the ground holds us nailed to the spot to see them, to fill our eyes with the sight. It's not fear, not our usual cowardice. One feels humiliated because one understands—touching it with one's eyes—that we might be in their place ourselves: there would be no difference, and if we live we owe it to this dirtied corpse. That is why every war is a civil war; every fallen man resembles one who remains and calls him to account.

There are days when, walking this naked countryside, I give a sudden start; a dry tree trunk, a knot of grass, a ridge of rock seems like a stretched-out body. It might still happen. I'm sorry Belbo stayed behind in Turin. Some of the day I spend in the kitchen, in the huge kitchen with its floor of beaten earth, where my mother, my sister, the women of the house, make the preserves. My father comes and goes in the cellar as slowly as old Gregorio. At times I wonder if a reprisal, a whim, some destiny will send the house up in flames and reduce it to four gutted and blackened walls. It has happened already to many. What would my father do, what would the women say? Their tone is: "If only they would stop awhile . . ."; and for them the guerrilla war, this whole damnable business, is a game for boys, like those that used to follow the feasts of our patron saint.

If the partisans demand flour or cattle, my father says: "It's not right. They have no right. Let them ask for it as a gift."

"Who has a right then?" I ask him.

"Wait until it's over and we'll see," he says.

I don't believe that it can end. Now that I've seen what war is, what civil war is, I know that everybody, if one day it should end, ought to ask himself: "And what shall we make of the fallen? Why are they dead?" I wouldn't know what to say. Not now, at any rate. Nor does it seem to me that the others know. Perhaps only the dead know, and only for them is the war really over.

FROM

The Blue Estuaries

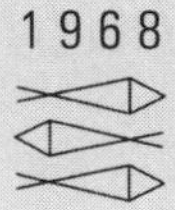

SEVERAL VOICES OUT OF A CLOUD

Come, drunks and drug-takers; come, perverts unnerved!
Receive the laurel, given, though late, on merit; to whom
    and wherever deserved.

Parochial punks, trimmers, nice people, joiners true-blue,
Get the hell out of the way of the laurel. It is deathless
    And it isn't for you.

FROM

Unspeakable Practices, Unnatural Acts

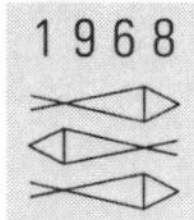

THE DOLT

Edgar was preparing to take the National Writers' Examination, a five-hour fifty-minute examination, for his certificate. He was in his room, frightened. The prospect of taking the exam again put him in worlds of hurt. He had taken it twice before, with evil results. Now he was studying a book which contained not the actual questions from the examination but similar questions. "Barbara, if I don't knock it for a loop this time I don't know what we'll do." Barbara continued to address herself to the ironing board. Edgar thought about saying something to his younger child, his two-year-old daughter, Rose, who was wearing a white terry-cloth belted bathrobe and looked like a tiny fighter about to climb into the ring. They were all in the room while he was studying for the examination.

"The written part is where I fall down," Edgar said morosely, to everyone in the room. "The oral part is where I do best." He looked at the back of his wife which was pointed at him. "If I don't kick it in the head this time I don't know what we're going to do," he repeated. "Barb?" But she failed to respond to this implied question. She felt it was a false hope, taking this examination which he had already failed miserably twice and which always got him very worked up, black with fear, before he took it. Now she didn't wish to witness the spectacle any more so she gave him her back.

"The oral part," Edgar continued encouragingly, "is A-okay. I can for instance give you a list of answers, I know it so well. Listen, here is an answer, can you tell me the question?" Barbara, who was very sexually attractive (that was what made Edgar tap on her for a date, many years before) but also deeply mean, said nothing. She put her mind on their silent child, Rose.

"Here is the answer," Edgar said. "The answer is Julia Ward Howe. What is the question?"

This answer was too provocative for Barbara to resist long, because she knew the question. "Who wrote the *Battle Hymn of the Republic*?" she said. "There is not a grown person in the United States who doesn't know that."

"You're right," Edgar said unhappily, for he would have preferred that the answer had been a little more recherché, one that she would not have known the question to. But she had been a hooker for a period before their marriage and he could resort to this area if her triumph grew too great. "Do you want to try another one?"

"Edgar I don't *believe in* that examination any more," she told him coldly.

"I don't believe in you Barbara," he countered.

This remark filled her with remorse and anger. She considered momentarily letting him have one upside the head but fear prevented her from doing it so she turned her back again and thought about the vaunted certificate. With a certificate he could write for all the important and great periodicals, and there would be some money in the house for a change instead of what they got from his brother and the Unemployment.

"It isn't you who has to pass this National Writers' Examination," he shot past her. Then, to mollify, he gave her another answer. "Brand, tuck, glave, claymore."

"Is that an answer?" she asked from behind her back.

"It is indeed. What's the question?"

"I don't know," she admitted, slightly pleased to be put back in a feminine position of not knowing.

"Those are four names for a sword. They're archaic."

"That's why I didn't know them, then."

"Obviously," said Edgar with some malice, for Barbara was sometimes given to saying things that were obvious, just to fill the air. "You put a word like that in now and then to freshen your line," he explained. "Even though it's an old word, it's so old it's new. But you have to be careful, the context has to let people know what the thing is. You don't want to be simply obscure." He liked explaining the tricks of the trade to Barb, who made some show of interest in them.

"Do you want me to read you what I've written for the written part?"

Barb said yes, with a look of pain, for she still felt acutely what he was trying to do.

"This is the beginning," Edgar said, preparing his yellow manuscript paper.

"What is the title?" Barbara asked. She had turned to face him.

"I haven't got a title yet," Edgar said. "Okay, this is the beginning." He began to read aloud. "*In the town of A——, in the district of*

Y——, there lived a certain Madame A——, wife of that Baron A—— who was in the service of the young Friedrich II of Prussia. The Baron, a man of uncommon ability, is chiefly remembered for his notorious and inexplicable blunder at the Battle of Kolin: by withdrawing the column under his command at a crucial moment in the fighting, he earned for himself the greatest part of the blame for Friedrich's defeat, which resulted in a loss, on the Prussian side, of 13,000 out of 33,000 men. Now as it happened, the château in which Madame A—— was sheltering lay not far from the battlefield; in fact, the removal of her husband's corps placed the château itself in the gravest danger; and at the moment Madame A—— learned, from a Captain Orsini, of her husband's death by his own hand, she was also told that a detachment of pandours, the brutal and much-feared Hungarian light irregular cavalry, was hammering at the château gates."

Edgar paused to breathe.

Barb looked at him in some surprise. "The beginning turns me on," she said. "More than usual, I mean." She began to have some faint hope, and sat down on the sofabed.

"Thank you," Edgar said. "Do you want me to read you the development?"

"Go ahead."

Edgar drank some water from a glass near to hand.

"The man who brought this terrible news enjoyed a peculiar status in regard to the lady; he was her lover, and he was not. Giacomo Orsini, second son of a noble family of Siena, had as a young man a religious vocation. He had become a priest, not the grander sort of priest who makes a career in Rome and in great houses, but a modest village priest in the north of his country. Here befell him a singular misfortune. It was the pleasure of Friedrich Wilhelm I, father of the present ruler, to assemble, as is well known, the finest army in Europe. Tiny Prussia was unable to supply men in sufficient numbers to satisfy this ambition; his recruiters ranged over the whole of Europe, and those whom they could not persuade, with promises of liberal bounties, into the king's service, they kidnapped. Now Friedrich was above all else fond of very tall men, and had created, for his personal guard, a regiment of giants, much mocked at the time, but nonetheless a brave and formidable sight. It was the bad luck of the priest Orsini to be a very tall man, and of impressive mien and bearing withal; he was abducted straight from the altar, as he was saying mass, the Host in his hands—"

"This is very exciting," Barb broke in, her eyes showing genuine pleasure and enthusiasm.

"Thank you," Edgar said, and continued his reading.

"—and served ten years in the regiment of giants. On the death of Friedrich Wilhelm, the regiment was disbanded, among other economies; but the former priest, by now habituated to military life, and even zestful for it, enlisted under the new young king, with the rank of captain."

"Is this historically accurate?" Barbara asked.

"It does not contradict what is known," Edgar assured her.

"Assigned to the staff of Baron A——, and much in the latter's house in consequence, he was thrown in with the lovely Inge, Madame A——, a woman much younger than her husband, and possessed of many excellent qualities. A deep sympathy established itself between them, with this idiosyncrasy, that it was never pressed to a conclusion, on his part, or acknowledged in any way, on hers. But both were aware that it existed, and drew secret nourishment from it, and took much delight in the nearness, one to the other. But this pleasant state of affairs also had a melancholy aspect, for Orsini, although exercising the greatest restraint in the matter, nevertheless considered that he had, in even admitting to himself that he was in love with Madame A——, damaged his patron the Baron, whom he knew to be a just and honorable man, and one who had, moreover, done him many kindnesses. In this humor Orsini saw himself as a sort of jackal skulking about the periphery of his benefactor's domestic life, which had been harmonious and whole, but was now, in whatsoever slight degree, compromised."

Rose, the child, stood in her white bathrobe looking at her father who was talking for such a long time, and in such a dramatic shaking voice.

"The Baron, on his side, was not at all insensible of the passion that was present, as it were in a condition of latency, between his young wife and the handsome Sienese. In truth, his knowledge of their intercourse, which he imagined had ripened far beyond the point it had actually reached, had flung him headlong into a horrible crime: for his withholding of the decisive troops at Kolin, for which history has judged him so harshly, was neither an error of strategy nor a display of pusillanimity, but a willful act, having as its purpose the exposure of the château, and thus the lovers, whom he had caused to be together there, to the blood-lust of the pandours. And as for his alleged suicide, that too was a cruel farce; he lived, in a hidden place."

Edgar stopped.

"It's swift-moving," Barbara complimented.

"Well, do you want me to read you the end?" Edgar asked.

"The end? Is it the end already?"

"Do you want me to read you the end?" he repeated.

"Yes."

"I've got the end but I don't have the middle," Edgar said, a little ashamed.

"You don't have the middle?"

"Do you want me to read you the end or don't you?"

"Yes, read me the end." The possibility of a semi-professional apartment, which she had entertained briefly, was falling out of her head with this news, that there was no middle.

"The last paragraph is this:

"During these events Friedrich, to console himself for the debacle at Kolin, composed in his castle at Berlin a flute sonata, of which the critic Guilda has said, that it is not less lovely than the sonatas of Georg Philip Telemann."

"That's ironic," she said knowingly.

"Yes," Edgar agreed, impatient. He was as volatile as popcorn.

"But what about the middle?"

"I don't have the middle!" he thundered.

"Something has to happen between them, Inge and what's his name," she went on. "Otherwise there's no story." Looking at her he thought: she is still streety although wearing her housewife gear. The child was a perfect love, however, and couldn't be told from the children of success.

Barb then began telling a story she knew that had happened to a friend of hers. This girl had had an affair with a man and had become pregnant. The man had gone off to Seville, to see if hell was a city much like it, and she had spontaneously aborted, in Chicago. Then she had flown over to parley, and they had walked in the streets and visited elderly churches and like that. And the first church they went into, there was this tiny little white coffin covered with flowers, right in the sanctuary.

"Banal," Edgar pronounced.

She tried to think of another anecdote to deliver to him.

"I've got to get that certificate!" he suddenly called out desperately.

"I don't think you can pass the National Writers' Examination with what you have on that paper," Barb said then, with great regret, because even though he was her husband she didn't want to hurt him unnecessarily. But she had to tell the truth. "Without a middle."

"I wouldn't have been great, even with the certificate," he said.

"Your views would have become known. You would have been something."

At that moment the son manqué entered the room. The son manqué was eight feet tall and wore a serape woven out of two hundred transistor radios, all turned on and tuned to different stations. Just by looking at him you could hear Portland and Nogales, Mexico.

"No grass in the house?"

Barbara got the grass which was kept in one of those little yellow and red metal canisters made for sending film back to Eastman Kodak.

Edgar tried to think of a way to badmouth this immense son leaning over him like a large blaring building. But he couldn't think of anything. Thinking of anything was beyond him. I sympathize. I myself have these problems. Endings are elusive, middles are nowhere to be found, but worst of all is to begin, to begin, to begin.

L. WOIWODE

FROM

What I'm Going to Do, I Think

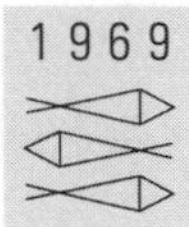

***Go** up on roof and check screens on chimneys.*

He got out the ladder and leaned it against the eave. He stepped onto its bottom rung and with bent knees bounced his weight, driving its legs deep into the loose dirt. He climbed the ladder and stepped onto the roof of the dining wing. It had a low pitch, and was covered with wide-tab shingles that looked like hundreds of E's turned on their backs and arranged in neat rows. The shingles, of asphalt composition, red in color, were littered with bits of twig and pine needles. Sand had blown into the spaces between the tabs and lay there in drifts. The dining wing was low and small, like a miniature copy of the lodge, and it formed an L at the side of the building. He walked its peak to the juncture of the L. The roof of the main building ran perpendicular to the roof of the wing, slanting down past the wing, and it was pitched as steep as the roof of a barn. From where he stood on the peak of the dining wing, its slanting overhang passed him just above the groin.

He hoisted himself onto the main roof, turned toward its peak, and started moving toward the chimney in a bent position, using his hands, like an ape, to help him forward. Sand gritted under his leather soles and he started slipping backward. He threw his body flat to get more resistance and grabbed at the tabs of shingles as he slid along. No handles. It was a ten- or twelve-foot fall, a fall he could take if he was prepared for it and didn't panic, but he didn't care to try. He flung out his elbows and pressed down hard. His shirt ripped at the elbows and finally he came to a stop, flat on his stomach, far below the point he'd started from. His cheek was resting on his hands. Should he call for her? He tested with his foot. Extending his leg and toes as far as possible, he still couldn't feel the edge of the roof. Lifting his head, he saw that he had bruised some of the shingles black. Damn.

Gripping two of the tabs, he got to his knees, splayed his lower legs out in a V, and, using the flats of his calves and the flats of his forearms, he edged up toward the chimney. It was near the peak. He passed the dining wing and when he was close to the chimney he lay down to rest.

The chimney, a small brick one, vented the cookstove. It emerged through the overhang and rose five feet above the roof. He would have to stand to see the screen, which was wired over its top. He got hold of the chimney, pulled himself around so that he was on the area of roof above it, and stood up and leaned against it at an angle. He picked the twigs, dead leaves, seed sheaths, and leaf stems off the screen. It was windowscreen and its mesh was clogged with soot. He slapped it with the flat of his hand. The soot stayed. He picked up a twig and scraped it back and forth across the screen, then slapped it again. Still it stayed clogged. Hell with it. It would be easier to hose it down, or just leave it off until they were ready to go. The heat and smoke of the stove would keep animals away. He unwired the screen and tossed it to the ground.

With the help of the chimney it was easy to make it to the peak of the roof and he sat there for a moment, straddling the peak, until his breathing and heartbeat slowed. The fireplace chimney was at the other end of the lodge. He stood, keeping one foot on either side of the peak, and walked over to the chimney. It was made of stone, was six feet in breadth at its top, as big as a door, and most of its mass extended beyond the overhang. He looked over the edge of the roof toward its base. It was built up along the outside wall of the lodge, its large stones exposed to the weather, and it stood exactly at the center of the building, so that the peak of the roof, meeting at its middle, was like a pointer indicating how well it had been placed. Its screen was of inch-square mesh and didn't need cleaning. He picked off the few twigs that were lying on it and threw them to the ground. This end of the lodge was near the woods and the roof was darkened by leaf shadow. Moss grew on the shingles. He sat on the peak near the chimney, in the coolness of the shade, and stared at the lake.

There was a slight breeze. He could see small whitecaps catching the sun. The air was damp and smelled of pine and water. He made himself more comfortable, and began rubbing his skinned elbows. Sitting like this in the kitchen. The brightness of the room, the cool shadow lying over his arms, over hers. A smell of water. Some spools on the floor, the thread gone from them. Standing the spools in a tower. Her at the stove. Water being poured, always the sound of water when she was present, water for the drinking pail, water to cook with, water to rinse the milk from the separator parts, water for dishes, water for baths and washing—the smell of water pumped from the well and the sound of it being poured. A sturdy woman. Short and well-built, with a broad forehead and eyes that he watched, so light blue. Shy and wary of him even then, though he was only five. At ease only doing chores or at the stove, her dark hair pinned up for chores and down in the house, strands of it down her back. Her hands, broad and strong, moving from vessel to vessel as she worked. Tipping her head back and shaking her hair. Then her eyes on him, then away quick. Rolling a spool toward her.

A nuthatch flew from the woods and landed close to the chimney on the log of the eave and clung there, hanging at an angle, studying him with cocked head, then walked around the eave and started tapping at the shingles with its beak, making soft buzzing chirrs of content.

She never spoke to him in a raised voice. Seldom spoke to him. His father, large and silent, his brow forever furrowed, spoke only to Grandpa or gave commands: Get away before you get hurt. Don't do that. Don't ask. There's no use trying to tell you, just watch how I do it. Button up your shirt. Stay away from there. And one summer, when Chris fell out of a tree, fell off the drawbar of a moving tractor, and wandered so close to a pile of burning trash that his pants leg caught on fire and he had to be taken to the hospital, his father said, What I'm going to do, I think, is get a new kid.

The farm was near the edge of town, and his father told him to keep from underfoot, mix with the town kids, but he liked being alone. Or in the kitchen here.

Outside, there was a series of footpaths worn in the grass. One led to the barn and one to the toolshed. Another one, bordered with lilac bushes that spotted it with blossoms, led to the outdoor toilet. Another path led to the chicken coop, and another to his rabbit hutch. Off to the side of the hutch the ground was covered with planks and there were bushes around the planks. A sewery smell rose from the planks. The cesspool. Stay away from there.

Standing on the planks one day, he and a boy from town turned a baby rabbit loose and were watching it hop, feeble and trembling, over the rough boards. It stopped and turned scared eyes on them, and the sunlight made its ears so incandescent Chris could see the delicate veins in them.

—Oh, look, he said. A halo. Oh. It came from God.

—No, siree, the boy said. It came from his mother's cut.

—Cut?

—Just like you.

—What do you mean?

—Your mother's cut. You came out of it.

—She doesn't have a cut.

—She does too. Every mother has a cut. They got to have one. That's the way you get borned.

—I wasn't born from one.

—You were too.

—My mother doesn't have a cut.

—Yes she does.

—She does not!

—You want to bet? It's right between her legs.

—She doesn't have a cut there.

—Every mother has a cut there. Girls too. Even my little sister does.

—My mother doesn't!

—She does too, you dumb hick.

—No she doesn't, I know she doesn't!

—How do you know?

—I looked once.

A lie. But, oh, what a hell of a place to hear about it, on those boards. And with all the beauty, all the essence and mystery of it missing. The softening n.

The nuthatch came pecking past him, busy, businesslike, unafraid, and climbed onto the chimney and started circling it, its quick beak searching the spaces in the mortar.

Rolling the spool toward her. Moving up to it. Rolling it closer. Her at the stove. Rolling it closer. Stopping at her heels. Then his cheek to the floor. . . . Bare legs, the calves, knees. Moving closer to see thighs. Higher, it would have to be higher. There. A dark line on the white between her legs. A tiny fissure. A hair? Finally rising up inside her skirt to see.

Her scream.

Then getting him disentangled, and the blow that sent him skidding across the linoleum.

"What's the matter with you! Don't you know how terrible that is! Don't you know it's the worst sin!"

Though he hadn't moved, the nuthatch took off with the noisy *yank-yanks* of fear.

He stood. The altitude and sudden change in position made him feel faint and displaced. He made his way slowly along the peak, eased himself into a sitting position, scooted down the roof feet first, lowered himself onto the dining wing, and came down the ladder and went into the lodge. He was pale and introverted the rest of the afternoon, and Ellen's questions and concern irritated him, confused him, and eventually made him angry. He himself wasn't sure what was wrong, and he paced around the rooms as though searching for a clue. Finally, he took the key to the pumphouse from a hook on the kitchen wall and went out the back door. He had only taken a few steps toward the meadow when he saw something that made him stop with such suddenness it was as if one of his parents had materialized.

He had left the ladder standing.

He went back into the lodge, hung up the key, and walked into the bedroom and lay down.

RANDALL JARRELL

FROM

The Complete Poems

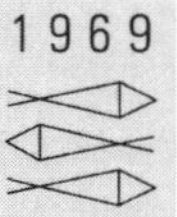

THE DEATH OF THE BALL TURRET GUNNER

From my mother's sleep I fell into the State,
And I hunched in its belly till my wet fur froze.
Six miles from earth, loosed from its dream of life,
I woke to black flak and the nightmare fighters.
When I died they washed me out of the turret with a hose.

JEAN STAFFORD

FROM

The Collected Stories of Jean Stafford

1969

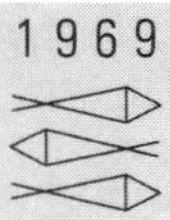

CHILDREN ARE BORED ON SUNDAY

Through the wide doorway between two of the painting galleries, Emma saw Alfred Eisenburg standing before "The Three Miracles of Zenobius," his lean, equine face ashen and sorrowing, his gaunt frame looking undernourished, and dressed in a way that showed he was poorer this year than he had been last. Emma herself had been hunting for the Botticelli all afternoon, sidetracked first by a Mantegna she had forgotten, and then by a follower of Hieronymus Bosch, and distracted, in an English room as she was passing through, by the hot invective of two ladies who were lodged (so they bitterly reminded one another) in an outrageous and expensive mare's-nest at a hotel on Madison. Emma liked Alfred, and once, at a party in some other year, she had flirted with him slightly for seven or eight minutes. It had been spring, and even into that modern apartment, wherever it had been, while the cunning guests, on their guard and highly civilized, learnedly disputed on aesthetic and political subjects, the feeling of spring had boldly invaded, adding its nameless, sentimental sensations to all the others of the buffeted heart; one did not know and never had, even in the devouring raptures of adolescence, whether this was a feeling of tension or of solution—whether one flew or drowned.

In another year, she would have been pleased to run into Alfred here in the Metropolitan on a cold Sunday, when the galleries were thronged with out-of-towners and with people who dutifully did something self-educating on the day of rest. But this year she was hiding from just such people as Alfred Eisenburg, and she turned quickly to go back the way she had come, past the Constables and Raeburns. As she turned, she came face to face with Salvador Dali, whose sudden countenance, with its unlikely mustache and its histrionic eyes, familiar from the photographs in public places, momentarily stopped her dead, for she did not immediately recognize him and, still surprised by seeing Eisenburg, took him also to be someone she knew. She shuddered and then realized that he was merely famous, and she penetrated the heart of a guided tour and proceeded safely through the rooms until she came to the balcony that overlooks the medieval armor, and there she paused, watching two youths of high-school age examine the joints of an equestrian's shell.

She paused because she could not decide what to look at now that she had been denied the Botticelli. She wondered, rather crossly, why Alfred Eisenburg was looking at it and why, indeed, he was here at all. She feared that her afternoon, begun in such a burst of courage, would not be what it might have been; for this second's glimpse of him—who had no bearing on her life—might very well divert her from the pictures, not only because she was reminded of her ignorance of painting by the presence of someone who was (she assumed) versed in it but because her eyesight was now bound to be impaired by memory and conjecture, by the irrelevant mind-portraits of innumerable people who belonged to Eisenburg's milieu. And almost at once, as she had predicted, the air separating her from the schoolboys below was populated with the images of composers, of painters, of writers who pronounced judgments, in their individual argot, on Hindemith, Ernst, Sartre, on Beethoven, Rubens, Baudelaire, on Stalin and Freud and Kierkegaard, on Toynbee, Frazer, Thoreau, Franco, Salazar, Roosevelt, Maimonides, Racine, Wallace, Picasso, Henry Luce, Monsignor Sheen, the Atomic Energy Commission, and the movie industry. And she saw herself moving, shaky with apprehensions and martinis, and with the belligerence of a child who feels himself laughed at, through the apartments of Alfred Eisenburg's friends, where the shelves were filled with everyone from Aristophanes to Ring Lardner, where the walls were hung with reproductions of Seurat, Titian, Vermeer, and Klee, and where the record cabinets began with Palestrina and ended with Copland.

These cocktail parties were a modus vivendi in themselves for which a new philosophy, a new ethic, and a new etiquette had had to be devised. They were neither work nor play, and yet they were not at all beside the point but were, on the contrary, quite indispensable to the spiritual life of the artists who went to them. It was possible for Emma to see these occasions objectively, after these many months of abstention from them, but it was still not possible to understand them, for they were so special a case, and so unlike any parties she had known at home. The gossip was different, for one thing, because it was stylized, creative (integrating the whole of the garrotted, absent friend), and all its details were precise and all its conceits were Jamesian, and all its practitioners sorrowfully saw themselves in the role of Pontius Pilate, that hero of the untoward circumstance. (It has to be done, though we don't want to do it; 'tis a pity she's a whore, when no one writes more intelligent verse than she.) There was, too, the matter of the drinks, which were much worse than those served by anyone else, and much more plentiful. They dispensed with the fripperies of olives in martinis and cherries in manhattans (God forbid! They had no sweet teeth), and half the time there was no ice, and when there was, it was as likely as not to be suspect shavings got from a bed for shad at the corner fish store. Other species, so one heard, went off to dinner after cocktail parties certainly no later than half past eight, but no one ever left a party given by an Olympian until ten, at the earliest, and then groups went out together, stalling and squabbling at the door, angrily unable to come to a decision about where to eat, although they seldom ate once they got there but, with the greatest formality imaginable, ordered several rounds of cocktails, as if they had not had a drink in a month of Sundays. But the most surprising thing of all about these parties was that every now and again, in the middle of the urgent, general conversation, this cream of the enlightened was horribly curdled, and an argument would end, quite literally, in a bloody nose or a black eye. Emma was always astounded when this happened and continued to think that these outbursts did not arise out of hatred or jealousy but out of some quite unaccountable quirk, almost a reflex, almost something physical. She never quite believed her eyes—that is, was never altogether convinced that they were really beating one another up. It seemed, rather, that this was only a deliberate and perfectly honest demonstration of what might have happened often if they had not so diligently dedicated themselves to their intellects. Although she had seen them do it, she did not and could not believe that city people clipped each other's jaws, for, to Emma, urban equaled urbane, and ichor ran in these Augustans' veins.

•

As she looked down now from her balcony at the atrocious iron clothes below, it occurred to her that Alfred Eisenburg had been just such a first-generation metropolitan boy as these two who half knelt in lithe and eager attitudes to study the glittering splints of a knight's skirt. It was a kind of childhood she could not imagine and from the thought of which she turned away in secret, shameful pity. She had been really stunned when she first came to New York to find that almost no one she met had gluttonously read Dickens, as she had, beginning at the age of ten, and because she was only twenty when she arrived in the city and unacquainted with the varieties of cultural experience, she had acquired the idea, which she was never able to shake entirely loose, that these New York natives had been deprived of this and many other innocent pleasures because they had lived in apartments and not in two- or three-story houses. (In the early years in New York, she had known someone who had not heard a cat purr until he was twenty-five and went to a houseparty on Fire Island.) They had played hide-and-seek dodging behind ash cans instead of lilac bushes and in and out of the entries of apartment houses instead of up alleys densely lined with hollyhocks. But who was she to patronize and pity them? Her own childhood, rich as it seemed to her on reflection, had not equipped her to read, or to see, or to listen, as theirs had done; she envied them and despised them at the same time, and at the same time she feared and admired them. As their attitude implicitly accused her, before she beat her retreat, she never looked for meanings, she never saw the literary-historical symbolism of the cocktail party but went on, despite all testimony to the contrary, believing it to be an occasion for getting drunk. She never listened, their manner delicately explained, and when she talked she was always lamentably off key; often and often she had been stared at and had been told, "It's not the same thing at all."

Emma shuddered, scrutinizing this nature of hers, which they all had scorned, as if it were some harmless but sickening reptile. Noticing how cold the marble railing was under her hands, she felt that her self-blame was surely justified; she came to the Metropolitan Museum not to attend to the masterpieces but to remember cocktail parties where she had drunk too much and had seen Alfred Eisenburg, and to watch schoolboys, and to make experience out of the accidental contact of the palms of her hands with a cold bit of marble. What was there to do? One thing, anyhow, was clear and that was that today's excursion into the world had been premature; her solitude must continue for a while, and perhaps it would never end. If the sight of someone so peripheral, so uninvolving, as Alfred Eisenburg could scare her so badly, what would a cocktail party do? She almost fainted at the thought of it, she almost fell headlong, and the boys, abandoning the coat of mail, dizzied her by their progress toward an emblazoned tabard.

In so many words, she wasn't fit to be seen. Although she was no longer mutilated, she was still unkempt; her pretensions needed brushing; her ambiguities needed to be cleaned; her evasions would have to be completely overhauled before she could face again the terrifying learning of someone like Alfred Eisenburg, a learning whose components cohered into a central personality that was called "intellectual." She imagined that even the boys down there had opinions on everything political and artistic and metaphysical and scientific, and because she remained, in spite of all her opportunities, as green as grass, she was certain they had got their head start because they had grown up in apartments, where there was nothing else to do but educate themselves. This being an intellectual was not the same thing as dilettantism; it was a calling in itself. For example, Emma did not even know whether Eisenburg was a painter, a writer, a composer, a sculptor, or something entirely different. When, seeing him with the composers, she had thought he was one of them; when, the next time she met him, at a studio party, she decided he must be a painter; and when, on subsequent occasions, everything had pointed toward his being a writer, she had relied altogether on circumstantial evidence and not on anything he had said or done. There was no reason to suppose that he had not looked upon her as the same sort of variable and it made their anonymity to one another complete. Without the testimony of an impartial third person, neither she nor Eisenburg would ever know the other's actual trade. But his specialty did not matter, for his larger designation was that of "the intellectual," just as the man who confines his talents to the nose and throat is still a doctor. It was, in the light of this, all the more extraordinary that they had had that lightning-paced flirtation at a party.

Extraordinary, because Emma could not look upon herself as an intellectual. Her private antonym of this noun was "rube," and to her regret—the regret that had caused her finally to disappear from Alfred's group—she was not even a bona-fide rube. In her store clothes, so to speak, she was often taken for an intellectual, for she had, poor girl, gone to college and had never been quite the same since. She would not dare, for instance, go up to Eisenburg now and say that what she most liked in the Botticelli were the human and compassionate eyes of the centurions' horses, which reminded her of the eyes of her own Great-uncle Graham, whom she had adored as a child. Nor would she admit that she was delighted with a Crivelli Madonna because the peaches in the background looked exactly like marzipan, or that Goya's little red boy inspired in her only the pressing desire to go out immediately in search of a plump cat to stroke. While she knew that feelings like these were not really punishable, she had not perfected the art of tossing them off; she was no flirt. She was a bounty jumper in the war between Great-uncle Graham's farm and New York City, and liable to court-martial on one side and death on the other. Neither staunchly primitive nor confidently *au courant*, she rarely knew where she was at. And this was her Achilles' heel: her identity was always mistaken, and she was thought to be an intellectual who, however, had not made the grade. It was no use now to cry that she was not, that she was a simon-pure rube;

not a soul would believe her. She knew, deeply and with horror, that she was thought merely stupid.

It was possible to be highly successful as a rube among the Olympians, and she had seen it done. Someone calling himself Nahum Mothersill had done it brilliantly, but she often wondered whether his name had not helped him, and, in fact, she had sometimes wondered whether that had been his real name. If she had been called, let us say, Hyacinth Derryberry, she believed she might have been able, as Mothersill had been, to ask who Ezra Pound was. (This struck her suddenly as a very important point; it was endearing, really, not to know who Pound was, but it was only embarrassing to know who he was but not to have read the "Cantos.") How different it would have been if education had not meddled with her rustic nature! Her education had never dissuaded her from her convictions, but certainly it had ruined the looks of her mind—painted the poor thing up until it looked like a mean, hypocritical, promiscuous malcontent, a craven and apologetic fancy woman. Thus she continued secretly to believe (but *never* to confess) that the apple Eve had eaten tasted exactly like those she had eaten when she was a child visiting on her Great-uncle Graham's farm, and that Newton's observation was no news in spite of all the hue and cry. Half the apples she had eaten had fallen out of the tree, whose branches she had shaken for this very purpose, and the Apple Experience included both the descent of the fruit and the consumption of it, and Eve and Newton and Emma understood one another perfectly in this particular of reality.

•

Emma started. The Metropolitan boys, who, however bright they were, would be boys, now caused some steely article of dress to clank, and she instantly quit the balcony, as if this unseemly noise would attract the crowd's attention and bring everyone, including Eisenburg, to see what had happened. She scuttered like a quarry through the sightseers until she found an empty seat in front of Rembrandt's famous frump, "The Noble Slav"—it was this kind of thing, this fundamental apathy to most of Rembrandt, that made life in New York such hell for Emma—and there, upon the plum velours, she realized with surprise that Alfred Eisenburg's had been the last familiar face she had seen before she had closed the door of her tomb.

In September, it had been her custom to spend several hours of each day walking in a straight line, stopping only for traffic lights and outlaw taxicabs, in the hope that she would be tired enough to sleep at night. At five o'clock—and gradually it became more often four o'clock and then half past three—she would go into a bar, where, while she drank, she seemed to be reading the information offered by the *Sun* on "Where to Dine." Actually she had ceased to dine long since; every few days, with effort, she inserted thin wafers of food into her repelled mouth, flushing the frightful stuff down with enormous drafts of magical, purifying, fulfilling applejack diluted with tepid water from the tap. One weighty day, under a sky that grimly withheld the rain, as if to punish the whole city, she had started out from Ninetieth Street and had kept going down Madison and was thinking, as she passed the chancery of St. Patrick's, that it must be nearly time and that she needed only to turn east on Fiftieth Street to the New Weston, where the bar was cool, and dark to an almost absurd degree. And then she was hailed. She turned quickly, looking in all directions until she saw Eisenburg approaching, removing a gray pellet of gum from his mouth as he came. They were both remarkably shy and, at the time, she had thought they were so because this was the first time they had met since their brief and blameless flirtation. (How curious it was that she could scrape off the accretions of the months that had followed and could remember how she had felt on that spring night—as trembling, as expectant, as altogether young as if they had sat together underneath a blooming apple tree.) But now, knowing that her own embarrassment had come from something else, she thought that perhaps his had, too, and she connected his awkwardness on that September day with a report she had had, embedded in a bulletin on everyone, from her sole communicant, since her retreat, with the Olympian world. This informant had run into Alfred at a party and had said that he was having a very bad time of it with a divorce, with poverty, with a tempest that had carried off his job, and, at last, with a psychoanalyst, whose fees he could not possibly afford. Perhaps the nightmare had been well under way when they had met beside the chancery. Without alcohol and without the company of other people, they had had to be shy or their suffering would have shown in all its humiliating dishabille. Would it be true still if they should inescapably meet this afternoon in an Early Flemish room?

Suddenly, on this common level, in this state of social displacement, Emma wished to hunt for Alfred and urgently tell him that she hoped it had not been as bad for him as it had been for her. But naturally she was not so naïve, and she got up and went purposefully to look at two Holbeins. They pleased her, as Holbeins always did. The damage, though, was done, and she did not really see the pictures; Eisenburg's hypothetical suffering and her own real suffering blurred the clean lines and muddied the lucid colors. Between herself and the canvases swam the months of spreading, cancerous distrust, of anger that made her seasick, of grief that shook her like an influenza chill, of the physical afflictions by which the poor victimized spirit sought vainly to wreck the arrogantly healthy flesh.

Even that one glance at his face, seen from a distance through the lowing crowd, told her, now that she had repeated it to her mind's eye, that his cheeks were drawn and his skin was gray (no soap and water can ever clean away the grimy look of the sick at heart) and his stance was tired. She wanted them to go together to some hopelessly disreputable bar and to console one another in the most maudlin fashion over a lengthy succession of powerful drinks of whisky, to compare their illnesses, to marry their invalid souls for these few hours of painful communion, and to babble with rapture that they were at last, for a little while, no longer alone. Only thus, as sick people, could they marry. In any other terms, it would be a *mésalliance*, doomed to divorce from the start, for rubes and intellectuals must stick to their own class. If only it could take place—this honeymoon of the cripples, this nuptial consummation of the abandoned—while drinking the delicious amber whisky in a joint with a jukebox, a stout barkeep, and a handful of tottering derelicts; if it could take place, would it be possible to prevent him from marring it all by talking of secondary matters? That is, of art and neurosis, art and politics, art and science, art and religion? Could he lay off the fashions of the day and leave his learning in his private entrepôt? Could he, that is, see the apple fall and not run madly to break the news to Newton and ask him what on earth it was all about? Could he, for her sake (for the sake of this pathetic rube all but weeping for her own pathos in the Metropolitan Museum), forget the whole dispute and, believing his eyes for a change, admit that the earth was flat?

It was useless for her now to try to see the paintings. She went, full of intentions, to the Van Eyck diptych, and looked for a long time at the souls in Hell, kept there by the implacable, indifferent, and genderless angel who stood upon its closing mouth. She looked, in renewed astonishment, at Jo Davidson's pink, wrinkled, embalmed head of Jules Bache, which sat, a trinket on a fluted pedestal, before a Flemish tapestry. But she was really conscious of nothing but her desire to leave the museum in the company of Alfred Eisenburg, her cousin-german in the territory of despair.

So she had to give up, two hours before the closing time, although she had meant to stay until the end, and she made her way to the central stairs, which she descended slowly, in disappointment, enviously observing the people who were going up, carrying collapsible canvas stools on which they would sit, losing themselves in their contemplation of the pictures. Salvador Dali passed her, going quickly down. At the telephone booths, she hesitated, so sharply lonely that she almost looked for her address book, and she did take out a coin, but she put it back and pressed forlornly forward against the incoming tide. Suddenly, at the storm doors, she heard a whistle and she turned sharply, knowing that it would be Eisenburg, as, of course, it was, and he wore an incongruous smile upon his long, El Greco face. He took her hand and gravely asked her where she had been all this year and how she happened to be here, of all places, of all days. Emma replied distractedly, looking at his seedy clothes, his shaggy hair, the green cast of his white skin, his deep black eyes, in which all the feelings were disheveled, tattered, and held together only by the merest faith that change *had* to come. His hand was warm and her own seemed to cling to it and all their mutual necessity seemed centered here in their clasped hands. And there was no doubt about it; he had heard of her collapse and he saw in her face that she had heard of his. Their recognition of each other was instantaneous and absolute, for they cunningly saw that they were children and that, if they wished, they were free for the rest of this winter Sunday to play together, quite naked, quite innocent. "What a day it is! What a place!" said Alfred Eisenburg. "Can I buy you a drink, Emma? Have you time?"

She did not accept at once; she guardedly inquired where they could go from here, for it was an unlikely neighborhood for the sort of place she wanted. But they were *en rapport*, and he, wanting to avoid the grownups as much as she, said they would go across to Lexington. He needed a drink after an afternoon like this—didn't she? Oh, Lord, yes, she did, and she did not question what he meant by "an afternoon like this" but said that she would be delighted to go, even though they would have to walk on eggs all the way from the Museum to the place where the bottle was, the peace pipe on Lexington. Actually, there was nothing to fear; even if they had heard catcalls, or if someone had hooted at them, "Intellectual loves Rube!" they would have been impervious, for the heart carved in the bark of the apple tree would contain the names Emma and Alfred, and there were no perquisites to such a conjugation. To her own heart, which was shaped exactly like a valentine, there came a winglike palpitation, a delicate exigency, and all the fragrance of all the flowery springtime love affairs that ever were seemed waiting for them in the whisky bottle. To mingle their pain, their handshake had promised them, was to produce a separate entity, like a child that could shift for itself, and they scrambled hastily toward this profound and pastoral experience.

CHRISTA WOLF

FROM

The Quest for Christa T.

[*Translated by Christopher Middleton*]

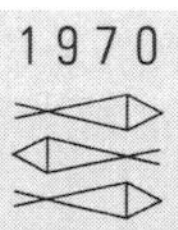

We'd forgotten how to be in readiness even for miracles to happen.

We did hope for some support from chance. Could anyone, in his immense confusion, ever have taken heart and said "It had to be thus, and only thus"? Sometimes in a place one had long been familiar with, one could raise one's head, suddenly look about, and think: So this is where it has brought me . . .

On the blackboard in the large lecture hall stood a scanned line of verse: *Úns hât der winter geschádet überál.* No writing on the wall, this, nothing in the least symbolic; and nothing in me was responding. I was listening to the lecturer, who wore a blue shirt, was red-haired and freckled, and showed great enthusiasm for the children's playground which he wanted the students of our faculty to build. No, I felt nothing, and I wasn't startled and I had no doubts. I saw Christa T. sitting in front of me. I could have put my hand on her shoulder, but didn't. It isn't her, I told myself, against my better knowledge, for it was her hand that I saw, writing. When she left, I stayed where I was. I didn't call her. I told myself: If it's her, then I'll see her every day. It was amazing, but I wasn't amazed; and the excitement I was waiting for never came.

If it was her—my God, it was her!—I wanted her to recognize me first. I knew that in seven years you can forget many names and faces, if you want to. In those days we economized strictly with our memories.

Then unexpectedly we were facing one another in the narrow aisle of a department store. Both at the same moment and spontaneously we signaled our recognition. It was her and it was me too. Yes, she too admitted that she'd recognized me at the lecture. The fact that we didn't ask one another why we had left it until now, in this place, to talk to one another, was the first sign of our old and now new intimacy.

We left the store and walked slowly through the streets of Leipzig, still a strange place for me, toward the station.

Resurrected from the dead. If miracles could happen, this was one of them; but we no longer knew the right way to accommodate a miracle. We hardly realized that a miracle can be met other than with broken phrases and mocking looks. We crossed the empty squares where the wind was still blowing, the wind that rises out of the ruins every day in cities after a war. Dust swept along the streets in front of us, gusts of wind blowing everywhere, it wasn't very comfortable; we turned up our coat collars and buried our hands in our pockets. And we used those broken phrases and temporizing looks which suit such cities best.

As Christa T. walked, she leaned slightly forward, as against some slight but permanent obstacle to which she'd grown accustomed. I supposed it was because of her height. Hadn't she always walked like this? She looked at me, smiled.

Now I knew too why I had prevented myself from talking to her straightaway. And this seemed the right moment to ask the question that occurred to me. But I didn't ask the question—either then or later; and only in my last letter, which she could no longer read, did I give a hint of it.

For the time being, the gap in our conversation had to be filled with information about ourselves: where she had ended up, and where I had. As if surprised, we shook our heads over the strange courses our lives had taken during the past six years, several times almost crossing. But almost isn't really, we knew that now, and fifty miles can be the same as five hundred. To have missed something by a lifetime is the same as missing it by a hair's breadth, we had found out about that; but we now acted as if we could still be surprised by the one mile which had prevented us from meeting earlier. Acted as if we really did want to know what had become of everything, though we didn't say much about things, and that gave us away. She now heard of our teacher's death, unless she knew of it before. Ah, Christa T. said. We gave one another a quick look. A distant death.

So there we were, asking one another about our experiences, as if conclusions could be drawn from them. Doing so, we noticed we were using and avoiding the same words. We'd both been to the same lecture; we must both have read the same books. There weren't many ways to choose among, at that time; no great choice among thoughts, hopes, doubts.

But one thing I really did want to know: was she still capable, at any moment, in the middle of the crowded street, among the hurrying, shabbily dressed people, of letting go with her shout—*hooohaahooo . . .* ? Or had I found her again in vain? Other people I had met in the meantime could do many of the other things. Only she could do that.

Had I missed feeling joy? Surprise? Suddenly the joy came. And even surprise arrived, late as usual. A miracle! If miracles could happen, this was one. And who says we weren't ready for it and met it inappropriately, with broken phrases? We stood at the streetcar stop and began to laugh. All the days ahead of us! We looked at one another and laughed, as at a successful prank, an utter trick, played on someone, perhaps on oneself. We were laughing as we said goodbye. She was laughing and waving to me as I left in the streetcar.

The laughter could stay. But we still had to travel once more the road from the store to the station, speak different words, finally find the courage to make whole sentences out of the broken ones, to eliminate the vagueness in our talk, however long it took. We have to look at one another differently, and see different things. Only the laughter at the end can stay the same: because all the days are ahead of us. All the time that will take away the vagueness, whether we like it or not. We'd better like it.

Better to travel the road twice, in that case.

Vagueness? The word may seem strange. The years we'd have had to talk about had been precise and sharp enough. But to make the precise and sharp cut-off separating "ourselves" from "the others," once and for all, that would save us. And secretly to know: the cut-off very nearly never came, because we ourselves might well have become otherwise. But how does one cut oneself away from oneself? We didn't speak of that. But she knew it, Christa T., when she walked beside me across the windy squares, or else we'd have had nothing to say. Her quick look, when we mentioned our teacher's death—a hard and distant death—proved one thing to me: she knew what it is, this innocence that comes from not being mature.

When we met and took that road a second time, Horst Binder, our railwayman neighbor's son, rose up again between us. Christa T. knew him too; I had pointed him out to her, had told her how he kept following me around. I was furious, a conquest like that doesn't do anything for one; he was creepy, he was nothing to boast about. He'd wanted to carry my book bag and I'd torn it out of his hand; I hated his wispy hair, which fell over his eyes, and most of all I hated his meaningful ardent look. I wanted to be able to laugh about him together with Christa T.; but she hadn't been able to laugh either, she'd been sorry for him.

Until one day we'd been out on parade, a huge square of white blouses and brown skirts. The one-armed troop commander bellowed a name so you could hear it all over the parade ground: Horst Binder. I knew what was coming. For he lived next door, and people on our street had been talking about him for days; but I couldn't speak his name any more, so I never mentioned him, not even to Christa T. I avoided her questioning look and wished what I shouldn't have wished: that I wasn't standing here in this troop, and that he, Horst Binder, wasn't about to be commended by the troop commander for denouncing his father, a railway workman, for listening to foreign radio stations.

I never did find out if she understood why we avoided looking one another in the eye when the time came to dismiss. Now, walking once more from the store to the station, I could tell her that in the end, before the Red Army arrived, Horst Binder had shot first his mother and then himself. We could ask one another why we'd been spared, why the opportunities had not swept us up as well. What opportunities would we have taken: all or none? And if we didn't know that, did we know anything about ourselves?

This terrible gratitude for the lack of opportunity isn't something to be forgotten. And this suspicion directed toward the adult in oneself . . . Proceed with all severity and sharpness against that adult: pour suspicion on him, accuse him, find him guilty. Don't tolerate any contradictions. Reject the defense with derision; pronounce the verdict: a life term. Accept it. Execute the verdict oneself.

Life term. Not an empty phrase.

Seven years later, walking a certain road, a broken phrase is proof enough that this too is something we both understand.

As for Christa T., she'd had a breakdown during those years. It wasn't the work, although it may have been hard going, cutting out uniforms on the Mecklenburg farm, at a scratched wooden table, while summer came on, in spite of everything. Sometimes the young Soviet lieutenant came, stood in the doorway, looked in her direction, looked at her; neither knew what the other was thinking. Once he shook her hand, before he left: Why are you so sad? Then she ran home, threw herself on the bed, bit the pillows; then nothing was any use, she screamed. Good heavens, so sensitive too! And always for no reason.

The horseman who'd done nothing but gallop across a lake that happened to be frozen over fell dead from his horse when he discovered what he'd crossed. She only screamed, it's not much. She burned her old diaries, all her vows went up in smoke, and the enthusiasms one was now ashamed of, the aphorisms and songs. There won't be time for her to speak of them again, *her* lifetime's not long enough. On that subject, meanwhile, only broken phrases.

Then came one summer when we were less than thirty miles apart, working in fields that were quite similar to one another. She must have noticed that one can breathe here too, that the lungs are also made for this new air. To live thus, straighten one's back, dripping sweat, look about oneself. This kind of country. Fields, meadow, a few bushes, the river. Lean cows with black spots, fenced enclosures. This foreign flickering heat, which leaps about between sky and earth far away on the horizon, unmitigated, uncooled by the forest which, in her deepest convictions, ought to limit the view on all sides. Vanquish the feeling that it's indecent for the land to turn to the sky, nakedly, baldly, directly, without the mediation of trees. Look up. But not into the sun, it'll kill me. It'll liquefy the blue, make it metallic and watery, it doesn't want us to have the blue, I can't bear it, this longing for the real blue, but I'll go fetch it, now, just a second . . . Yes.

They put her in a truck and drove off. You see, she's not up to it. Looks strong, but she's delicate inside, or something. She should do what the burgomaster suggested. Can't make much difference to her, to take a teacher re-training course. Can't she see what's with the children hereabouts? All right then, she says, I'll teach, why not. —She gave me a sideways look to see if I understood that she felt uneasy about grabbing the first thing to come along, especially this thing, which, as she knew, can't be done by halves. A teacher! I said. What a stroke of luck!

I have a picture of her taken at that time.

Yes, perhaps what she was looking for among the children was shelter. Their light precarious breath, their small hands holding one's own. And the fact that only important things are important to them. Love, for example, she can't help still believing in it, somewhat. When doubts came—love, what is it? can it help to shift a single speck of dust?—then sometimes she thought back on the little schoolhouse, the thirty-two children facing her, on decrepit old benches, poorly dressed, hungry, and, oh God, their shoes! But to offer them shelter with one's own unshelteredness . . .

Three years. Her attic room with the sloping walls, the piles of shoddily bound books with thick gray pages, the new names on the covers, Gorky, Makarenko, the new pamphlets which everyone was given, as important as one's daily bread, unless one's hand was shut. Curiously enough, she finds some of what she reads familiar; it dawns on her that such thoughts are possible; she doesn't understand how, after all this rational clarity, the uttermost unreason could still have been possible. She jumps up: yes, that's how it will be, this is the way to ourselves. Understood this way, her longing wouldn't be ridiculous and beside the point; it would be usable and helpful.

Not a word about this on our first walk. At most, two or three titles, sober concepts from philosophy and economics. Would I understand? Know the pain of self-expansion, also the pleasure, which is unforgettable and by which one will measure all future pleasures? How many of them will have to be rejected. But she, Christa T., on our way to the station, pushes her coat collar up, before I can get too close to her. It's understood. Now what next?

But in that earlier time, looking up from the precise and illuminating statements in the pamphlets, she walks to the window of her room. The view overlooking seventeen poplar trees. The tallest is being climbed today by the shepherd's son, a boy in my class, and he drags down the magpie's nest, to shouts of encouragement from a gang of boys at the foot of the tree. But he flings the eggs, almost ready for hatching, one after another against the big boulder which served at last week's lesson on the geology of the region. And there I stand, have read my pamphlets, look on while it's happening, and it makes me want to cry. It's such a thin surface we walk on, so close to our feet the danger of dropping through into this bogland. Hurl the tomcat against the stable wall, leave the boy lying there in the snow, throw the bird's eggs against the boulder. Every time it happens she's cut to the quick.

Her picture. The face of the teacher, Christa T., "Miss T.," twenty-one years old, among thirty-two children's faces, with the brick wall of the schoolhouse behind. At this very moment they too may be standing there to be photographed, the children of the ten-year-olds of that time, and their teacher will be twenty-one years old, but she looks different. I'd like to walk through the village and ask the people who are now around thirty: Do you remember her, know her? At least her name? Have you remembered, at least, perhaps, that she implored you not to drown the kittens in the river, not to chase the blind old dogs and throw stones at them, not to throw the young birds against the wall? Did you laugh at her? Or you girls, whose women's faces are shimmering through on this picture, didn't you find yourselves thinking of her when you held your own children in your arms?

The children's faces. Some laughing, some self-satisfied, some frightened, one with a threatening look, a few sinister, but I can't find anything that's mysterious. The teacher, top row, extreme left, is different. She has something to hide, a wound, one might think, slow to heal. She's aloof and restrained, but ready. Being depended upon, she found a foothold. Being asked a favor, she smiles. The eyes, of course . . .

Is that the place for her to stay in? Three successive years she joins her class, before the summer holidays, the photographer snaps the shutter, develops the plate, he sees no difference, delivers the pictures and takes his fee. The teacher, Christa T., goes into her room and ranges the three photos beside one another, looks at them for a long time, you couldn't notice a tremor. Finally she sits down at her desk, the pictures in front of her, and writes her application for admission to the university.

That's how she came to be in the same lecture hall as I, to face the same blackboard, the same freckled boy who insists on building a children's playground with us. His name is Günter, Christa T. says—we've almost reached the station—I know him, there's no stopping him. That's the moment we start to laugh, and we go on laughing, until my streetcar comes.

All the days ahead of us!

MICHAEL J. ARLEN

FROM

Exiles

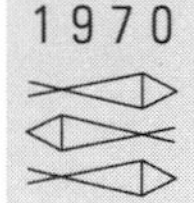

Each school vacation in New York there was the ritual of having lunch with Uncle Hugh. Uncle Hugh was not my uncle, or anywhere near it. He was a man called Hugh Payson Courtland (in point of fact, for most of his life Hugh Payson Courtland II, his father having finally, at age ninety-two, removed both himself and his roman numeral), and he was my father's new friend. My father's new American friend. Hugh was a little over six feet. Close to sixty. Silvery-haired. Bright blue eyes. One of those marvelous ruddy Episcopal faces that always looked as if it had just been scoured with a steel brush. Uncle Hugh had himself been to St. Paul's, and Harvard. He had been an aviator in the First World War. He had been some kind of a lawyer. Now he was some kind of a businessman. He was a director. He was on "boards." Uncle Hugh had lots of brothers and cousins, who lived on ancestral acres in exotic Englishy-sounding places like Beverly Farms and Bedford Village. Hugh's father apparently had been a long-ago famous New York senator, and there were countless photographs of the old gentleman all over Hugh's house, mostly on horseback. Uncle Hugh was clearly Very Old Family, the near-end-of-the-line in fact of one of those proud, rich New England families—Hugh himself, one gathered (from Hugh), represented the more or less Bohemian, or renegade, aspect of the family; mostly, it would seem, by having married a French wife, a pale, decent woman of considerable forbearance. I remember dinners at Hugh's house, a rather shambly but nicely lived-in brownstone in the East Seventies, with Marie, his wife, downstairs on the ground floor, in the kitchen, and Hugh three stories above in his elegant little library: drinks, cigars, old books on the shelves, Hugh in his evening clothes ("I think it is good for the morale to dress for dinner"), Hugh prattling on with his stories—Hugh was the only man I've ever met whose conversation consisted entirely of stories. Marie downstairs in her long dress, it always seemed to be the same dress too (a long purply thing with a couple of hopeful strands of silver), Marie down in the engine room way below, hauling up the ancient Courtland china and the ancient Courtland silver on the dumbwaiter, creak-creak-creak-clank, Hugh and his amusing stories, sounds of creaking rope, Marie hauling up the roast, Marie hauling up the veg, clank-clank, sounds of pulleys, sounds of glasses being rattled, Hugh telling us about the amusing thing that had happened to his Cousin Sandy at a Turkish bagnio in 1922, Marie finally appearing in the doorway to announce dinner, poking pins back into her hair, brushing off her dress, Marie managing a smile, Marie looking as if she had been down at the docks all afternoon unloading sacks of flour and would like just now to go to bed.

I usually felt ill-at-ease alone with Uncle Hugh, mostly because he was always trying to tell me dirty stories, and because I couldn't make much sense of him, although the last I didn't much require. I very much wanted to be friends, though, or whatever it was I was supposed to be with Uncle Hugh, because he was my father's friend; because then he was the only actual friend I was aware of my father having. Our lives, my father's life, had always been peopled for me by these dim far-off shapes of his "old friends," the barely visible outlines of such as Maugham, Noel Coward, Clark Gable, and the like. It didn't bother me that I had almost never seen these men, although naturally it would have pleased me like anything to impress my Wall Street and Oyster Bay schoolmates, sons of Merrill Lynch and Winthrop Stimson, with my acquaintance in the wider world. Mostly it bothered me that my father didn't seem to see them either, or that when he did (one might run into Gary Cooper at the theater, exchange a few words), it seemed like dinghies bumping. Noel Coward would be in town for the opening of a new play. Noel would come by for a drink. Noel admittedly was more of a genuine old friend than the others (my father, I knew, had been one of the key backers for Coward's first play, *The Vortex*), but even so, it seemed that no matter how much gossip and wit and anecdote they nudged across a coffee table at each other every few years, they remained two people clearly in private untouching worlds. I don't know what I expected—Coward and my father on a walking tour of Belgium together, or sharing a Thanksgiving turkey, or drinking a lot and cuffing each other on the shoulder. Uncle Hugh at any rate seemed to have the makings of some kind of visible ordinary friend. For one thing, he came around a lot. He professed to take an interest in our family. He may have been a grade or two off as to what year my sister was in at school, but at least he knew she was at school, and more or less where. And he seemed genuinely to like my father. He and my father "did things together." Other people's fathers, I knew, "did things together" with their friends—playing golf, or cards, or going in a large boat to fish for marlin. My father and Uncle Hugh, I think, mostly walked back from lunch together. It seemed enough. I remember seeing them together walking down Fifth Avenue. An October afternoon. Hugh in a dark suit, gray vest, a bowler on his head. My father with his cane, no hat. My father gesticulating with his hand, talking. Hugh laughing. Comrades. And then, once each school vacation, once each school vacation for at least five years, Hugh would take me to lunch at the Racquet Club. I both looked forward to these times, because having lunch with Hugh Payson Courtland at the Racquet seemed like such a nice snobby thing to do, and dreaded them, because I felt that although Hugh wanted to like me and take-an-interest in me as part of his role as my father's new friend, in fact he disapproved of me because I didn't laugh at his jokes, or worse, laughed in that awful obvious way of trying not to disappoint the teller. The routine never varied much. I'd put on my "good suit," try to find a tie without egg on it, shine the shoes, hop a bus down to Fifty-third Street, present myself at the big door always in the hope that the Swiss Guards who manned the entrance would instinctively assume me to be a member. Mr. Hugh Payson Courtland would be waiting in the bar. Much handshaking and clasping of shoulders. Drinks, a brandy and soda for Hugh, a beer for me, a brief torrent of jokes and stories about Hugh's days at St. Paul's. We would then go to the oyster bar, which I also dreaded, because I could barely look at oysters or clams in those days without wanting to throw up, but at my first lunch with Hugh I had somehow got myself into the fix of saying, Oh yes, by all means the oyster bar, I love oysters, etc. If I couldn't give him much return on the jokes, at least I wanted to cooperate on the shellfish. And then lunch. A small table by the window. Hugh sitting opposite me. Another avalanche of anecdotes, and then the jokes: I really shouldn't tell you this, Hugh would say with a giggle. And then some damn thing about American aviators and farmers' daughters. Or about President Roosevelt and his secretary. Hugh elaborating on the detail. Me sitting there, gravely, primly (desperately not wanting to be grave or prim), waiting, waiting for the punch line, I must be able to spot the punch line coming, rearrange my face so that my burst-of-helpless-laughter (in reality a sickly grin) will be vaguely plausible. The punch line. The sickly grin. Hugh giggling, giggling, I really used to hate those giggles, that pink face, soft, the eyes all squinched up, the hand reaching across to my arm. "I really shouldn't have told you that." A kind of wink. I once tried to say something of my discomfiture to my father, but it just didn't make any sense to him. Uncle Hugh after all didn't tell dirty jokes to *him*. "Hugh is very naughty," my mother would say sometimes, but I think what she mostly had in mind was Marie and the dumb-waiter. I don't know what it was my father really felt for Hugh. He liked him, I know, because he used to speak of him in a certain way, that simple offhand way that people use when they like someone. I think Hugh must have entertained him, to some degree anyway. Mostly, I'd guess that he found in Hugh, and in Hugh's place in America (Hugh's alleged place in America), some kind of solid object to hold on to, not that he ever seemed to be holding on to it very tightly. I think he probably liked to have it around. And they had good times together.

I remember sitting in class one morning up at St. Paul's, and someone coming in to say that classes were being let out for the next hour for the purpose of listening to two visiting dignitaries who had just come up to address the school. We all filed down into the big study hall, partly pleased at being let out of class, partly wary as to just what in hell was coming next—and there, seated on either side of the great glowing Rector, were Uncle Hugh and my father, grave, serious, terribly serious, in their best Supreme Court manner. And then they spoke, my father first, something about Literature and Life, at least it was supposed to be about that. I remember Aldous Huxley being mentioned, and several stories about Sam Goldwyn—I was too generally dizzy and embarrassed to listen properly, but the faces around me seemed suitably attentive. Some laughs. Applause. Then Uncle Hugh spoke, something about Paris and Business and Rebuilding Europe, which he seemed to be making up as he went along. Also a success. I went up to see them after it was over, that seeming to be the logical thing to do. They were full of good spirits—had been up in Boston the day before attending some Harvard thing Hugh had been involved in, a big party, a lot of drinking, and somewhere along the line had decided to come up to the school and lecture at it. We had lunch at the small inn nearby, my father and Hugh congratulating each other on the fine reception accorded their talks, the attentive quality of the students, the general splendidness of young-people-today, and so forth, both of them extremely pleased with themselves. It was very nice. We all had brandy after lunch, which gave me a warm buzz between the ears, and then they went back to New York. It was the first time, now that I think of it, that my father had ever been to the school.

My father had one other friend around that time, whom I've almost forgotten because after my father died he moved right out of our lives. His name was Nadal, André Nadal. He was Iranian, I think. Some generations back anyway. A dark tall man, with a bushy mustache. Thick brown curling hair. A kind face. He was an immigration inspector and he lived somewhere in Queens. I think my father had met him when he'd first arrived from England—I don't know much about the connection beyond that, except that for a long while in New York the only two people, *friends*, I could have imagined "dropping by" for Thanksgiving dinner (if one had been having Thanksgiving dinner) would have been André and Uncle Hugh. André I think of as a truly gentle man, with one of those lovely, warm, seemingly untroubled laughs. He would sometimes come by for lunch when my father kept that table at the St. Regis, taking his place quietly along with the others, the flashy talkers, the great English-suited figures, the Rockefeller Center boulevardiers—André seated there listening, saying a few words, the rumpled brown suit, the long hair, André laughing. And then when the others would leave, André would stay on with my father, and sort of gently chide him for his frivolities. Not chide him very much. I think of André as being an intelligent, sensitive man, and the only man I can myself recall who used to talk seriously to my father about "life," and things like that. André was very proud of his job; of "government"; of being in the civil service. I remember once our families all had dinner on a summer evening. André took us out to the Tavern-on-the-Green—André; his wife, a nice large lady who seemed even friendlier than André; their daughter, a girl of about ten; and the four of us. I think we may have had one or two other dinners together, but I just happen to remember that one. I don't really remember very much about it. My father talked about his brother Taki, and his family in England. André talked about Government, and the "role of Congress." Everyone seemed very happy. Some seven or eight years later, at the funeral service for my father, I remember seeing André coming into the chapel, standing alone at the back. I went over towards him—it had been a long while since I had seen him, since any of us had gotten together. He was just standing in the back, a bit the way he used to sit there in the St. Regis, the only man there as far as I could see who seemed to be shedding the kind of tears that actually make you wet.

[. . .]

By the end of my last year at St. Paul's, all the things I most wanted to be I wasn't. I wanted to be a great school athlete and win the revered Gordon medal (presented the day before graduation at a special ceremony around the flagpole by old Mr. Gordon himself). I would have settled for being what was known as "extremely popular" (a quality much admired in those days, as I guess "personality" was in girls), a leader of the school, an important figure on the student council—one of the four Sixth Form toffs who sat in special ornamented seats in chapel, just in front of the special ornamented seats of the Rector and

Vice-Rector. None of these signal honors seemed in the cards, or anywhere near it, although life there on the whole didn't seem too bad, mostly because the school was then (and I imagine now) so full of the kind of young men I admired very much: young men who could play hockey very well, or squash, or who could kick 25-yard field goals at crucial moments, and who owned cars on the side, and sometimes sailboats, and had summer houses as well as ordinary houses. There was a time, quite a long time in fact, when I think I envied nearly anyone who had a house—well, not really any house. If pressed closely on the subject, I think it would turn out that what I chiefly envied were people who had houses in places like Greenwich and Old Westbury. Marvelous desirable Greenwich! O great wondrous mowed lawns! And little boats at Indian Harbor! Club memberships! Yacht Club parties! The heady presence of older girls ("women") who went to Smith, and older men ("men") who went to Yale and Princeton. And all those beautiful red-faced, flush-nosed Wall Street Dads (no damn Daddy nonsense there), with their billowy sports coats, and fuchsia slacks, and brand-new Chryslers, and elaborate bars with electric ice-smashers, and hearty laughs, and jokes, and deep grave interest in the Yale football team—and all those blond, well blondish, Mums, or Moms, or Mothers, with their sleek county look, their cashmeres, stationwagons, teensie-weensie drinkies in the evening, *their* equally deep grave interest in the Yale football team! I stayed close to all these people, or tried to stay close. Roomed with the more lustrous athletes. On vacations, tried to be adopted by their parents in Connecticut or Long Island. About all I really thought I had going for me then was that I was a "good student," but even that I secretly believed to be a sham. Not so much the factual, the achievement part. I knew I was a good student because I had the grades to prove it. St. Paul's, in those days at any rate, was a great believer in the authority and importance of grades. Once a month the "ranking list" of each form was tacked on to the main bulletin board, the name of every boy in the school listed on immense sheets of graph paper and, beside his name, the grade he had received in each subject figured out to the nearest decimal point, such as 88.7 (being naturally a better grade than 88.6). On the whole I was very good at this sort of thing—getting good grades. In truth I had no idea, or very little idea, of whether I was intelligent or not. For the most part, I believed I wasn't—but I knew how to study very hard. I knew, for example, that if I painstakingly underlined and then wrote out the correct meaning of every word in my Latin homework I didn't know, and then looked at them over and over again, and over again, I would get them right. And then the results of all this pleased my father very much. He liked for me to do well at school, to get good grades. In fact, he counted on me to do well. Each vacation time the reports would be mailed home. "History: 84.5. He continues to show an interest in the subject and has a strong grasp of the information. But his essays lately have shown a tendency to be unsure and general . . ." I see the history is down a bit, my father would say. Yes, I guess so, I'd say. Then: It's all that stuff after Napoleon. It doesn't seem very interesting. Not interesting! he'd say. That's a curious explanation. After Napoleon? The Second Empire? I thought history was one of your best subjects, etc. And so forth. He took an interest. And I did too most of the time. But then in the spring of my last term there I began to slack off. Or rather, I just stopped taking all those pains. No special reason; maybe just being the last term, spring, sunshine, end-of-school. And then, scant weeks before examinations, I realized that my beautiful grades had dropped considerably in the past month's rankings, and that from the way things were going I wasn't going to emerge with honors at graduation even as a student, which admittedly seemed a poor third to the Gordon medal, or being on the council, but which I knew would be a good deal better than nothing.

There were a number of prizes to be awarded each graduation, and while most of them were for the high hurdles or hockey or something of the sort, a few were for "scholarship," and of these one of the better was called the Baxter Prize for History, which in some corner of my mind I had always reserved for myself. And so I decided to really study for it, because in actual fact I had had a pretty good chance of winning it, only now my monthly grades were down so that I would have to do extraordinarily well on the exam (and my rivals would have to do very much less well) for me to pull it off.

All the exams were scheduled for the final week of school, with history on the last day; and so, while paying some small attention to the other subjects, I allotted myself, each day, every day, a certain amount of time for reading over the history book. It was the standard Morison & Commager American history text: a big blue thing. Two volumes. The exam would be on the second volume. Most everyone studied in their rooms or in the library, but I would go over to the schoolhouse right after dinner, the big red-brick building with most of the classrooms, which was supposed to be unoccupied at night, and hole up in a back room—hard wooden chairs, one of those circular tables, blackboards, maps, charts of chemical elements, travel posters of the Loire. I re-read every word in Morison & Commager. And then I re-read it again. I tried to imagine what the questions might be, and then I'd seek out the relevant chapters, and just gaze at each page, page after page, late at night, sometimes no longer knowing what I was reading, what I was doing, until two or three in the morning when my eyes were so blurred, and I was so tired, that I'd pack up and go back to my room half a mile away, where my hockey-playing roommates were fast asleep. I remember taking the exam that final day, the day before the two-day graduation ceremonies began, and when my parents were due up. It didn't seem too difficult an exam, and I thought I'd done well; at least I'd written it very rapidly, which was usually a good sign, and with a sense of what I was doing. Anyway it was over. I suddenly wanted terribly much to get the prize, and I figured I had a fair chance. My mother and father were due in around noon. There was to be a track meet and crew races in the afternoon. Sometime while all that was going on, Mr. Harding was going to post the history results. I was pleased about but rather wary of my parents' arrival. Originally I hadn't wanted them to come up. Not so much because of the usual filial embarrassment, although I certainly felt some of that. Mostly because their actual physical presence reminded me that I couldn't realistically hope to be adopted into one of those beautiful county families in Greenwich or Long Island—I already had parents of my own; and in fact there they were, walking down the brick walk beside the schoolhouse, two figures clearly different from all the others who had just now come into view —no billowy sports coat on him, no B. H. Wragge on her, no Old St. Paul's blazer, no straw hats, no jolly laugh, no jolly group: a short dark man with a mustache, an excessively tailored suit, a cane (he'd brought a cane, for God's sake!), and a woman with an exotic hairdo, also a tailored suit, and a kind of presence that seemed both to advertise and disregard her total ignorance of football at Yale, or anywhere else. We went through the usual peculiar ceremonies of greeting-in-public. "What do you want to do?" I'd say. Shifting from one foot to the other. Hands thrust into pockets, thrust out of pockets. "But it's *your* school," they'd say. "You show us." Benign. Cooperative. The elders of the tribe remind the young brave that it's *his* Initiation Rite, after all. "Surely you don't want to see the crew race!" I'd say wildly. My mother would beam as if I had just proposed a moonlight visit to the Taj Mahal. "Crew race? But of course we want to see the crew race. We certainly don't want to miss that. Your uncle was once on the crew at Balliol . . ." and so forth. And off we would go, me staring at the ground, nodding distractedly at friends ("That nice boy seemed to be trying to speak to you . . ."), some yellow rented schoolbus to take us all out to the pond, hearty alumni in old crew blazers, my friends, their parents, younger brothers—and there we all were on the banks of Long Pond, my mother and father standing on a little hillock of grass, my father leaning casually on his cane. "Is there any particular boat we should cheer for?" *Cheer* for? My sense of lunacy and gloom would deepen. It seemed quite bad enough that they should suddenly be there. Visible. But audible too! Cheering! The boat races proceeded. Two little eight-oared shells nudging down the middle of the dark-blue pond. A handful of motorboats trailing behind. It was too far away to see much of anything. Loud cheering from the bank. "Come on, Shattuck! Come on, Halcyon!" (The names of the two rowing clubs.) My father was talking with Mr. Enfield, the Latin master. The importance of a Classical Education, and so forth. My mother seemed to be staring into the middle distance with a sort of contented bafflement. I looked out at the boats, privately thought they were both marvelous, and worried desperately about the history exam. Finally, the races were over, we went back to the school. I ducked my parents—they were going to some tea at the Rector's house, I didn't even bother to worry whether or not they would embarrass me there—and ran over to the schoolhouse, where the grades would be posted.

On the bulletin board there was a brand-new list. My form. History. I looked at it, found my name, felt a wild feeling of apprehension and excitement, read across the graph-paper line towards the grades. Zero. 0. I couldn't believe it. Zero. Nobody got zero. I read quickly down the column of numbers. Everyone else had done pretty much as expected. Holmes, my chief rival, had an 89. I had zero. I felt quite sick, saw some people coming, ran out the door. I wandered around the back of the schoolhouse for a bit, not knowing what to do, hoping dimly that if I wandered around enough the zero would somehow change itself, which it didn't. Then I went over to see Mr. Harding. He had a small suite of rooms in one of the Fifth Form houses. I wasn't sure whether I wanted him to be in or not. I knocked at the heavy brown door. Silence. I was about to go away, then knocked again. The door opened. Harding appeared. Gray baggy trousers. Dark vest. Gold watch chain in the vest. He must have been around fifty then, although he seemed older. Thin gray hair. Straight nose. Eyes that were very clear, and sometimes kind. "I don't understand about the exam . . ." I began. I must have been very close to tears. "What don't you understand?" said Harding. I was sitting in a small chair beside his desk. He seemed very cold, remote. "The zero," I said. "The grade." Harding reached over for a stack of blue books, riffled through them, produced what seemed to be mine. A large, unmistakable zero in red crayon had been inscribed on the cover. "I think the grade should be perfectly clear," Harding said. Then: "I am not a fool, you know." I looked at him dumbly. Then: "The answer to the essay question that you have written here is an exact word-for-word transcription of pages 94 through 97 in *The History of the American*

Republic." He more or less flung the exam book at me. I opened it, looked through it with thick fingers, not really seeing anything, even my own handwriting seemed strange to me—felt sick, felt very scared, began to cry, then eventually tried to explain. All I could say really was that I hadn't cheated. Sir, sir, I hadn't cheated. I had just studied very hard. I had (it seemed) studied so hard, or relentlessly, or stupidly, that I'd in fact memorized the bloody textbook. We went on like that for a while. Then Harding stood up and went over to a shelf. He produced a fresh exam book and put it in front of me. "All right," he said. "You will sit here and write me the same answer to the essay question that you so kindly gave me yesterday. I will now repeat the question." He leaned against the side of the small leaded window, closed his eyes, unrolled the question, which I remember had to do with Woodrow Wilson, the League of Nations, and the period just after the First War. "You have thirty minutes," he said, and left the room. For whole moments, minutes, endless minutes, I just stared dumbly at the exam book in front of me. I opened it. Stared at the blank page. The inside of my head seemed absolutely inert. Woodrow Wilson. The League of Nations. I was supposed to remember and write out a 700-word or so stretch of text that I hadn't even known I'd memorized some days ago. Eventually I began to write. I began somewhere, and just wrote. Some of the phrases seemed familiar, plausible. Some of it was blind. I wrote on and on, and finished. I called out to Mr. Harding that I was done. He was in the other room. "All right," I heard him say, but he seemed not to be coming nearer, and so I left.

I went back to try to find my parents at the Rectory. Everybody I passed or met, I felt sure, was looking at me. Everybody *knew*. My parents must surely know. I saw them talking with Mr. Francis, who was the Vice-Rector. They all looked very grave. I felt absolutely sick. "Mr. Francis has been explaining to us about the summer teaching program," my father said, in his newfound parent-teacher voice. I stayed with them, silent, fearful. Later, at dinner, the three of us in the little tearoomy inn, a din of parents, old graduates, boys around us, I longed to tell them of my misfortune, my disgrace, but couldn't bear to. "Is something wrong?" my father asked at some point. "No," I said. "He's probably tired," my mother said. Before going back to my house, my father and I took a short walk down beside the Lower School pond. It was one of the places I'd liked most at St. Paul's. Not a big pond at all, quite gardened and tended-to on the near side, where we were walking; but on the far side, full of coves and inlets, tall wild clumps of rushes, reeds, small swampy places, hidden places. In my Fifth Form year, George Brock and I had kept a small beat-up rowboat hidden there, an old thing that barely floated but that we'd patched up somehow, and spent what had seemed like most of the spring aboard it, fishing late at night, smoking, discussing the true meanings of life, hockey, sex. My father seemed intent on talking to me about a summer job. "I think it's time you began to get into something," he said. And: "Now that you're older . . ." he said. I paced beside him, trying to be manly, glancing out mournfully at the darkened pond. Ah, the simple past! George and I had bought a fishing rod in Concord one afternoon, quite an elaborate, expensive fly-fishing thing, and used to try to instruct each other in the evening, standing knee-deep in mud and swamp, the pond eventually lit only by stars and half a moon, the fly-line whistling, singing above one's head, landing inevitably in trees and bushes, landing in bulrushes, now and then, invisibly, unnoticed, upon the water. "Fantastic, fantastic," George would say. "Don't make a sound for Christ's sakes!" (I never figured out what role silence was supposed to play at those moments.) Now I walked beside this pond, beside my father, feeling him not at all, listening in a way quite placidly to his admonitions about summer work, but with only this one thought in my mind, of Harding's zero. I knew I didn't want to tell my father about it. It wasn't that I was uncertain whether he would understand or not; I didn't even take it that far. I just didn't want to tell him. We walked along. I said I agreed, a summer job would be a good thing. I said I'd thought of trying to get a job as crew aboard Dave Whitney's sloop. "That's not the kind of summer job I had in mind," he said. We talked a bit about the new apartment in New York, about my sister, about my cousin Sarkis who had been visiting, and then said good night in front of the inn. Good night, good night, a light male-to-male brush of the cheek. I went back to my room. My roommates were all up, all very cheery. I went into the bedroom, undressed, got into bed, turned towards the wall, tried all night to sleep.

The next day, graduation in the afternoon—well, the story has a happy ending, this one anyway, although when I look back on it, it all seems foolish, no one comes out of it in any strong light, except possibly for old Harding. He'd decided to believe me at any rate—the second exam I'd written had turned out to be more or less exactly like the first. This still left him, and me, with the problem of my having answered a history exam more or less by rote. He gave me a 90, which is what I'd usually had (except for the past two months), and this got me the Baxter Prize. I remember that evening sitting between my mother and father in the study hall, the cavernous Middle School study hall where the prizes were awarded. Row upon row of wooden chairs. Everybody's beautiful parents on either side of me. Masters in their black robes.

Some girls. The whole world seemed to have returned to life. My great good friend, Harry Thompson, the wondrous hockey player, sat two rows behind me, between his mother and stepfather, and stepmother and father. His father, Harry Thompson II, had also been a wondrous hockey player, although I gathered that he had been "too light for the Varsity" at Yale. We waved, exchanged cheery greetings between the awards. Charlie Prescott had already received the Gordon medal, which was no surprise to anyone. Dick Vandiver, head of the student council (reportedly so mature that he had to shave twice a day) received the Merrick Prize. Some other prizes. The Charles Henderson Hubbard Prize "for that boy who, in his qualities of sportsmanship, leadership, and school spirit, most resembles the late Charles Henderson Hubbard," and so forth. The Baxter Prize for History. Me. The Rector resplendent as the Pope of Rome upon the platform, two books thrust into my hand. My parents were very pleased. "Interesting books, too," my mother said. Afterwards, Harry Thompson, especially wondrous in his blazer, hair wetted down, huge long arms, inarticulate, introduced me to his parents, then in a wild fit of politesse introduced all his parents and semi-parents to mine. "And this is my mother, and this is Fred White . . . and this is my dad . . . and this is Jane . . ." Jane, the stepmother, an elegant suburban Theda Bara whom I greatly admired for her charm and sophistication, discussed packing and the size of suitcases with my mother. Harry Thompson II clasped my father around the shoulders and looked happy. It was all very gay. The next morning, the cars began to drive up to the dormitories. Some with chauffeurs, mostly not. Harry's father had a big green convertible. A trunk and hockey sticks and records and baseball gloves were loaded in. My mother and father and I went back by train, a nice trip really, we stopped at Boston, had lunch at the Ritz. My father talked about the importance of having a "really good education," and about the Rector, who was always trying to tell him of his deep admiration for the English people. We laughed a lot, the three of us. I remember the thick blue goblets they used as water glasses, and still think of them with pleasure.

It was several more years, well into college, before I stopped trying to memorize things, and then it wasn't by any decision, I just stopped. I guess I dimly began to be aware that my mind had a life, an existence of its own. A couple of years ago, though, one of my daughters, who was studying something in school about the War of 1812, asked me a question about the shipping trade between England and the Caribbean colonies, and I found myself answering with a column of statistics, average annual tonnage, molasses, rum, Jamaica, London, Boston, that I remember having memorized in the Fourth Form at St. Paul's, when we studied those things too. But maybe the statistics were wrong, at least I rather hope so; I stopped in mid-sentence anyway, told her I didn't know, that she should look it up. One more small thing: I wrote a story about that incident once, the incident with Harding, the prize, graduation. It was the first story I ever sold, right after college. I had it pretty much the way it all had happened, only in my story (it wasn't much of a story) the boy did manage to tell his father. They walked down along beside the pond, and then he told his father, who was angry at first, for a "brief instant." And then clasped the boy to him. The mother had blond hair, green eyes, and was called Nancy.

FROM

A Friend of Kafka and Other Stories

1970

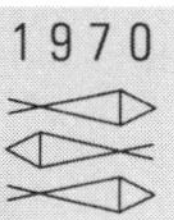

A FRIEND OF KAFKA

[*Translated by the author and Elizabeth Shub*]

I

I had heard about Franz Kafka years before I read any of his books from his friend Jacques Kohn, a former actor in the Yiddish theater. I say "former" because by the time I knew him he was no longer on the stage. It was the early thirties, and the Yiddish theater in Warsaw had already begun to lose its audience. Jacques Kohn himself was a sick and broken man. Although he still dressed in the style of a dandy, his clothes were shabby. He wore a monocle in his left eye, a high old-fashioned collar (known as "father-murderer"), patent-leather shoes, and a derby. He had been nicknamed "the lord" by the cynics in the Warsaw Yiddish writers' club that we both frequented. Although he stooped more and more, he worked stubbornly at keeping his shoulders back. What was left of his once yellow hair he combed to form a bridge over his bare skull. In the tradition of the old-time theater, every now and then he would lapse into Germanized Yiddish—particularly when he spoke of his relationship with Kafka. Of late, he had begun writing newspaper articles, but the editors were unanimous in rejecting his manuscripts. He lived in an attic room somewhere on Leszno Street and was constantly ailing. A joke about him made the rounds of the club members: "All day long he lies in an oxygen tent, and at night he emerges a Don Juan."

We always met at the club in the evening. The door would open slowly to admit Jacques Kohn. He had the air of an important European celebrity who was deigning to visit the ghetto. He would look around and grimace, as if to indicate that the smells of herring, garlic, and cheap tobacco were not to his taste. He would glance disdainfully over the tables covered with tattered newspapers, broken chess pieces, and ashtrays filled with cigarette stubs, around which the club members sat endlessly discussing literature in their shrill voices. He would shake his head as if to say, "What can you expect from such schlemiels?" The moment I saw him entering, I would put my hand in my pocket and prepare the zloty that he would inevitably borrow from me.

This particular evening, Jacques seemed to be in a better mood than usual. He smiled, displaying his porcelain teeth, which did not fit and moved slightly when he spoke, and swaggered over to me as if he were on-stage. He offered me his bony, long-fingered hand and said, "How's the rising star doing tonight?"

"At it already?"

"I'm serious. Serious. I know talent when I see it, even though I lack it myself. When we played Prague in 1911, no one had ever heard of Kafka. He came backstage, and the moment I saw him I knew that I was in the presence of genius. I could smell it the way a cat smells a mouse. That was how our great friendship began."

I had heard this story many times and in as many variations, but I knew that I would have to listen to it again. He sat down at my table, and Manya, the waitress, brought us glasses of tea and cookies. Jacques Kohn raised his eyebrows over his yellowish eyes, the whites of which were threaded with bloody little veins. His expression seemed to say, "This is what the barbarians call tea?" He put five lumps of sugar into his glass and stirred, rotating the tin spoon outward. With his thumb and index finger, the nail of which was unusually long, he broke off a small piece of cookie, put it into his mouth, and said, "*Nu ja,*" which meant, One cannot fill one's stomach on the past.

It was all play-acting. He himself came from a Hasidic family in one of the small Polish towns. His name was not Jacques but Jankel. However, he had lived for many years in Prague, Vienna, Berlin, Paris. He had not always been an actor in the Yiddish theater but had played on the stage in both France and Germany. He had been friends with many celebrities. He had helped Chagall find a studio in Belleville. He had been a frequent guest at Israel Zangwill's. He had appeared in a Reinhardt production, and had eaten cold cuts with Piscator. He had shown me letters he had received not only from Kafka but from Jakob Wassermann, Stefan Zweig, Romain Rolland, Ilya Ehrenburg, and Martin Buber. They all addressed him by his first name. As we got to know each other better, he had even let me see photographs and letters from famous actresses with whom he had had affairs.

For me, "lending" Jacques Kohn a zloty meant coming into contact with Western Europe. The very way he carried his silver-handled cane seemed exotic to me. He even smoked his cigarettes differently from the way we did in Warsaw. His manners were courtly. On the rare occasion when he reproached me, he always managed to save my feelings with some elegant compliment. More than anything else, I admired Jacques Kohn's way with women. I was shy with girls—blushed, became embarrassed in their presence—but Jacques Kohn had the assurance of a count. He had something nice to say to the most unattractive woman. He flattered them all, but always in a tone of good-natured irony, affecting the blasé attitude of a hedonist who has already tasted everything.

He spoke frankly to me. "My young friend, I'm as good as impotent. It always starts with the development of an overrefined taste—when one is hungry, one does not need marzipan and caviar. I've reached the point where I consider no woman really attractive. No defect can be hidden from me. That is impotence. Dresses, corsets are transparent for me. I can no longer be fooled by paint and perfume. I have lost my own teeth, but a woman has only to open her mouth and I spot her fillings. That, by the way, was Kafka's problem when it came to writing: he saw all the defects—his own and everyone else's. Most of literature is produced by such plebeians and bunglers as Zola and D'Annunzio. In the theater, I saw the same defects that Kafka found in literature, and that brought us together. But, oddly enough, when it came to judging the theater Kafka was completely blind. He praised our cheap Yiddish plays to heaven. He fell madly in love with a ham actress—Madam Tschissik. When I think that Kafka loved this creature, dreamed about her, I am ashamed for man and his illusions. Well, immortality is not choosy. Anyone who happens to come in contact with a great man marches with him into immortality, often in clumsy boots.

"Didn't you once ask what makes me go on, or do I imagine that you did? What gives me the strength to bear poverty, sickness, and, worst of all, hopelessness? That's a good question, my young friend. I asked the same question when I first read the Book of Job. Why did Job continue to live and suffer? So that in the end he would have more daughters, more donkeys, more camels? No. The answer is that it was for the game itself. We all play chess with Fate as partner. He makes a move; we make a move. He tries to checkmate us in three moves; we try to prevent it. We know we can't win, but we're driven to give him a good fight. My opponent is a tough angel. He fights Jacques Kohn with every trick in his bag. It's winter now; it's cold even with the stove on, but my stove hasn't worked for months and the landlord refuses to fix it. Besides, I wouldn't have the money to buy coal. It's as cold inside my room as it is outdoors. If you haven't lived in an attic, you don't know the strength of the wind. My windowpanes rattle even in the summertime. Sometimes a tomcat climbs up on the roof near my window and wails all night like a woman in labor. I lie there freezing under my blankets and he yowls for a cat, though it may be he's merely hungry. I might give him a morsel of food to quiet him, or chase him away, but in order not to freeze to death I wrap myself in all the rags I possess, even old newspapers—the slightest move and the whole works comes apart.

"Still, if you play chess, my dear friend, it's better to play with a worthy adversary than with a botcher. I admire my opponent. Sometimes I'm enchanted with his ingenuity. He sits up there in an office in the third or seventh heaven, in that department of Providence that rules our little planet, and has just one job—to trap Jacques Kohn. His orders are 'Break the keg, but don't let the wine run out.' He's done exactly that. How he manages to keep me alive is a miracle. I'm ashamed to tell you how much medicine I take, how many pills I swallow. I have a friend who is a druggist, or I could never afford it. Before I go to bed, I gulp down one after another—dry. If I drink, I have to urinate. I have prostate trouble, and as it is I must get up several times during the night. In the dark, Kant's categories no longer apply. Time ceases to be time and space is no space. You hold something in your hand and suddenly it isn't there. To light my gas lamp is not a simple matter. My matches are always vanishing. My attic teems with demons. Occasionally, I address one of them: 'Hey, you, Vinegar, son of Wine, how about stopping your nasty tricks!'

"Some time ago, in the middle of the night, I heard a pounding on my door and the sound of a woman's voice. I couldn't tell whether she was laughing or crying. 'Who can it be?' I said to myself. 'Lilith? Namah? Machlath, the daughter of Ketev M'riri?' Out loud, I called, 'Madam, you are making a mistake.' But she continued to bang on the door. Then I heard a groan and someone falling. I did not dare to open the door. I began to look for my matches, only to discover that I was holding them in my hand. Finally, I got out of bed, lit the gas lamp, and put on my dressing gown and slippers. I caught a glimpse of myself in the mirror, and my reflection scared me. My face was green and unshaven. I finally opened a door, and there stood a young woman in bare feet, wearing a sable coat over her nightgown. She was pale and her long blond hair was disheveled. 'Madam, what's the matter?' I said.

" 'Someone just tried to kill me. I beg you, please let me in. I only want to stay in your room until daylight.'

"I wanted to ask who had tried to kill her, but I saw that she was half frozen. Most probably drunk, too. I let her in and noticed a bracelet with huge diamonds on her wrist. 'My room is not heated,' I told her.

" 'It's better than to die in the street.'

"So there we were both of us. But what was I to do with her? I only have one bed. I don't drink—I'm not allowed to—but a friend had given me a bottle of cognac as a gift, and I had some stale cookies. I gave her a drink and one of the cookies. The liquor seemed to revive her. 'Madam, do you live in this building?' I asked.

" 'No,' she said. 'I live on Ujazdowskie Boulevard.'

"I could tell that she was an aristocrat. One word led to another, and I discovered that she was a countess and a widow, and that her lover lived in the building—a wild man, who kept a lion cub as a pet. He, too, was a member of the nobility, but an outcast. He had already served a year in the Citadel, for attempted murder. He could not visit her, because she lived in her mother-in-law's house, so she came to see him. That night, in a jealous fit, he had beaten her and placed his revolver at her temple. To make a long story short, she had managed to grab her coat and run out of his apartment. She had knocked on the doors of the neighbors, but none of them would let her in, and so she had made her way to the attic.

" 'Madam,' I said to her, 'your lover is probably still looking for you. Supposing he finds you? I am no longer what one might call a knight.'

" 'He won't dare make a disturbance,' she said. 'He's on parole. I'm through with him for good. Have pity—please don't put me out in the middle of the night.'

" 'How will you get home tomorrow?' I asked.

" 'I don't know,' she said. 'I'm tired of life anyhow, but I don't want to be killed by him.'

" 'Well, I won't be able to sleep in any case,' I said. 'Take my bed and I will rest here in this chair.'

" 'No. I wouldn't do that. You are not young and you don't look very well. Please, go back to bed and I will sit here.'

"We haggled so long we finally decided to lie down together. 'You have nothing to fear from me,' I assured her. 'I am old and helpless with women.' She seemed completely convinced.

"What was I saying? Yes, suddenly I find myself in bed with a countess whose lover might break down the door at any moment. I covered us both with the two blankets I have and didn't bother to build the usual cocoon of odds and ends. I was so wrought up I forgot about the cold. Besides, I felt her closeness. A strange warmth emanated from her body, different from any I had known—or perhaps I had forgotten it. Was my opponent trying a new gambit? In the past few years he had stopped playing with me in earnest. You know, there is such a thing as humorous chess. I have been told that Nimzowitsch often played jokes on his partners. In the old days, Morphy was known as a chess prankster. 'A fine move,' I said to my adversary. 'A masterpiece.' With that I realized that I knew who her lover was. I had met him on the stairs —a giant of a man, with the face of a murderer. What a funny end for Jacques Kohn—to be finished off by a Polish Othello.

"I began to laugh and she joined in. I embraced her and held her close. She did not resist. Suddenly a miracle happened. I was a man again! Once, on a Thursday evening, I stood near a slaughterhouse in a small village and saw a bull and a cow copulate before they were going to be slaughtered for the Sabbath. Why she consented I will never know. Perhaps it was a way of taking revenge on her lover. She kissed me and whispered endearments. Then we heard heavy footsteps. Someone pounded on the door with his fist. My girl rolled off the bed and lay on the floor. I wanted to recite the prayer for the dying, but I was ashamed before God—and not so much before God as before my mocking opponent. Why grant him this additional pleasure? Even melodrama has its limits.

"The brute behind the door continued beating it, and I was astounded that it did not give way. He kicked it with his foot. The door creaked but held. I was terrified, yet something in me could not help laughing. Then the racket stopped. Othello had left.

"Next morning, I took the countess's bracelet to a pawnshop. With the money I received, I bought my heroine a dress, underwear, and shoes. The dress didn't fit, neither did the shoes, but all she needed to do was get to a taxi—provided, of course, that her lover did not waylay her on the steps. Curious, but the man vanished that night and never reappeared.

"Before she left, she kissed me and urged me to call her, but I'm not that much of a fool. As the Talmud says, 'A miracle doesn't happen every day.'

"And you know, Kafka, young as he was, was possessed by the same inhibitions that plague me in my old age. They impeded him in everything he did—in sex as well as in his writing. He craved love and fled from it. He wrote a sentence and immediately crossed it out. Otto Weininger was like that, too—mad and a genius. I met him in Vienna—he spouted aphorisms and paradoxes. One of his sayings I will never forget: 'God did not create the bedbug.' You have to know Vienna to really understand these words. Yet who did create the bedbug?

"Ah, there's Bamberg! Look at the way he waddles along on his short legs, a corpse refusing to rest in its grave. It might be a good idea to start a club for insomniac corpses. Why does he prowl around all night? What good are the cabarets to him? The doctors gave him up years ago when we were still in Berlin. Not that it prevented him from sitting in the Romanisches Café until four o'clock in the morning, chatting with the prostitutes. Once, Granat, the actor, announced that he was giving a party—a real orgy—at his house, and among others he invited Bamberg. Granat instructed each man to bring a lady—either his wife or a friend. But Bamberg had neither wife nor mistress, and so he paid a harlot to accompany him. He had to buy her an evening dress for the occasion. The company consisted exclusively of writers, professors, philosophers, and the usual intellectual hangers-on. They all had the same idea as Bamberg—they hired prostitutes. I was there, too. I escorted an actress from Prague, whom I had known a long time. Do you know Granat? A savage. He drinks cognac like soda water, and can eat an omelette of ten eggs. As soon as the guests arrived, he stripped and began dancing madly around with the whores, just to impress his highbrow visitors. At first, the intellectuals sat on chairs and stared. After a while, they began to discuss sex. Schopenhauer said this . . . Nietzsche said that. Anyone who hadn't witnessed it would find it difficult to imagine how ridiculous such geniuses can be. In the midst of it all, Bamberg was taken ill. He turned as green as grass and broke out in a sweat. 'Jacques,' he said, 'I'm finished. A good place to die.' He was having a kidney or a gall-bladder attack. I half carried him out and got him to a hospital. By the way, can you lend me a zloty?"

"Two."

"What! Have you robbed Bank Polski?"

"I sold a story."

"Congratulations. Let's have supper together. You will be my guest."

II

While we were eating, Bamberg came over to our table. He was a little man, emaciated as a consumptive, bent over and bowlegged. He was wearing patent-leather shoes, and spats. On his pointed skull lay a few gray hairs. One eye was larger than the other—red, bulging, frightened by its own vision. He leaned against our table on his bony little hands and said in his cackling voice, "Jacques, yesterday I read your Kafka's *Castle*. Interesting, very interesting, but what is he driving at? It's too long for a dream. Allegories should be short."

Jacques Kohn quickly swallowed the food he was chewing. "Sit down," he said. "A master does not have to follow the rules."

"There are some rules even a master must follow. No novel should be longer than *War and Peace*. Even *War and Peace* is too long. If the Bible consisted of eighteen volumes, it would long since have been forgotten."

"The Talmud has thirty-six volumes, and the Jews have not forgotten it."

"Jews remember too much. That is our misfortune. It is two thousand years since we were driven out of the Holy Land, and now we are trying to get back in. Insane, isn't it? If our literature would only reflect this insanity, it would be great. But our literature is uncannily sane. Well, enough of that."

Bamberg straightened himself, scowling with the effort. With his tiny steps, he shuffled away from the table. He went over to the gramophone and put on a dance record. It was known in the writers' club that he had not written a word in years. In his old age, he was learning to dance, influenced by the philosophy of his friend Dr. Mitzkin, the author of *The Entropy of Reason*. In this book Dr. Mitzkin attempted to prove that the human intellect is bankrupt and that true wisdom can only be reached through passion.

Jacques Kohn shook his head. "Half-pint Hamlet. Kafka was afraid of becoming a Bamberg—that is why he destroyed himself."

"Did the countess ever call you?" I asked.

Jacques Kohn took his monocle out of his pocket and put it in place. "And what if she did? In my life, everything turns into words. All talk, talk. This is actually Dr. Mitzkin's philosophy—man will end up as a word machine. He will eat words, drink words, marry words, poison himself with words. Come to think of it, Dr. Mitzkin was also present at Granat's orgy. He came to practice what he preached, but he could just as well have written *The Entropy of Passion*. Yes, the countess does call me from time to time. She, too, is an intellectual, but without intellect. As a matter of fact, although women do their best to reveal the charms of their bodies, they know just as little about the meaning of sex as they do about the intellect.

"Take Madam Tschissik. What did she ever have, except a body? But just try asking her what a body really is. Now she's ugly. When she was an actress in the Prague days, she still had something. I was her leading man. She was a tiny little talent. We came to Prague to make some money and found a genius waiting for us—*Homo sapiens* in his highest degree of self-torture. Kafka wanted to be a Jew, but he didn't know how. He wanted to live, but he didn't know this, either. 'Franz,' I said to him once, 'you are a young man. Do what we all do.' There was a brothel I knew in Prague, and I persuaded him to go there with me. He was still a virgin. I'd rather not speak about the girl he was engaged to. He was sunk to the neck in the bourgeois swamp. The Jews of his circle had one ideal—to become Gentiles, and not Czech Gentiles but German Gentiles. To make it short, I talked him into the adventure. I took him to a dark alley in the former ghetto and there was the brothel. We went up the crooked steps. I opened the door and it looked like a stage set: the whores, the pimps, the guests, the madam. I will never forget that moment. Kafka began to shake, and pulled at my sleeve. Then he turned and ran down the steps so quickly I was afraid he would break a leg. Once on the street, he stopped and vomited like a schoolboy. On the way back, we passed an old synagogue, and Kafka began to speak about the golem. Kafka believed in the golem, and even that the future might well bring another one. There must be magic words that can turn a piece of clay into a living being. Did not God, according to the Cabala, create the world by uttering holy words? In the beginning was the Logos.

"Yes, it's all one big chess game. All my life I have been afraid of death, but now that I'm on the threshold of the grave I've stopped being afraid. It's clear, my partner wants to play a slow game. He'll go on taking my pieces one by one. First he removed my appeal as an actor and turned me into a so-called writer. He'd no sooner done that than he provided me with writer's cramp. His next move was to deprive me of my potency. Yet I know he's far from checkmate, and this gives me strength. It's cold in my room—let it be cold. I have no supper—I won't die without it. He sabotages me and I sabotage him. Some time ago, I was returning home late at night. The frost burned outside, and suddenly I realized that I had lost my key. I woke up the janitor, but he had no spare key. He stank of vodka, and his dog bit my foot. In former years I would have been desperate, but this time I said to my opponent, 'If you want me to catch pneumonia, it's all right with me.' I left the house and decided to go to the Vienna station. The wind almost carried me away. I would have had to wait at least three-quarters of an hour for the streetcar at that time of night. I passed by the actors' union and saw a light in a window. I decided to go in. Perhaps I could spend the night there. On the steps I hit something with my shoe and heard a ringing sound. I bent down and picked up a key. It was mine! The chance of finding a key on the dark stairs of this building is one in a billion, but it seems that my opponent was afraid I might give up the ghost before he was ready. Fatalism? Call it fatalism if you like."

Jacques Kohn rose and excused himself to make a phone call. I sat there and watched Bamberg dancing on his shaky legs with a literary lady. His eyes were closed, and he leaned his head on her bosom as if it were a pillow. He seemed to be dancing and sleeping simultaneously. Jacques Kohn took a long time—much longer than it normally takes to make a phone call. When he returned, the monocle in his eye shone. "Guess who is in the other room?" he said. "Madam Tschissik! Kafka's great love."

"Really."

"I told her about you. Come, I'd like to introduce you to her."

"No."

"Why not? A woman that was loved by Kafka is worth meeting."

"I'm not interested."

"You are shy, that's the truth. Kafka, too, was shy—as shy as a yeshiva student. I was never shy, and that may be the reason I have never amounted to anything. My dear friend, I need another twenty groschen for the janitors—ten for the one in this building, and ten for the one in mine. Without the money I can't go home."

I took some change out of my pocket and gave it to him.

"So much? You certainly must have robbed a bank today. Forty-six groschen! Piff-paff! Well, if there is a God, He will reward you. And if there isn't, who is playing all these games with Jacques Kohn?"

HERMANN HESSE

FROM

Stories of Five Decades

[*Translated by Ralph Manheim*]

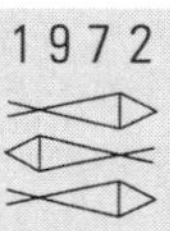

HARRY, THE STEPPENWOLF

The enterprising owner of a small menagerie had succeeded in signing up Harry, the famous Steppenwolf, for a short engagement. He had posters put up all over town, confident that they would draw a large crowd, and in this expectation he was not disappointed. Everyone had heard of the Steppenwolf, his legend had become a favorite topic of conversation in cultivated society; everyone had his bit of information to contribute, and opinions were very much divided. Some held that such an animal was under all circumstances a dangerous, unwholesome phenomenon; nothing was sacred to him, he scoffed at respectability, ripped the portraits of the great off the walls of the temples of culture and went so far as to ridicule Johann Wolfgang von Goethe; he was infecting the young with his asocial attitude, and the only solution was for all respectable citizens to band together and do away with him, for until he was dead and buried he would give the community no peace. But this simple, straightforward, and probably sound opinion was far from universal. There was a second party, which held an entirely different view, namely, that though the Steppenwolf was indeed a dangerous animal, he not only had a right to live, but also performed an ethical and social function. Each one of us, said the adherents of this party, who for the most part were highly educated, each one of us secretly and unbeknownst even to himself nurtures a Steppenwolf in his bosom. The bosoms referred to by the speakers of these words were the highly respectable bosoms of the best society, of lawyers and manufacturers, and these bosoms were covered with silk shirts and vests of the most modern cut. Deep within him, said these liberal-minded persons, each one of us has the feelings, instincts, and sufferings of the Steppenwolf; we must all come to grips with such instincts, for at heart each one of us is a poor, howling, hungry Steppenwolf. So they spoke when under cover of their silk shirts and fashionable vests they discussed the Steppenwolf, and many who publicly criticized him assented. Then the gentlemen put on their fine felt hats and sumptuous fur coats, got into their sumptuous motor cars, and rode back to their work, to their offices, editorial rooms, and factories. One evening, as a group of these eminent citizens gathered over their whiskey, one of them even suggested that they start an association of Steppenwolves.

On the day when the menagerie opened its new attraction, many curious persons came to see the notorious animal. A visit to his cage cost an extra groschen. It was a small cage, formerly inhabited by a panther who had regrettably died before his time. The enterprising owner had done his best to furnish it for the occasion, something of a problem, for this Steppenwolf was undoubtedly a rather unusual animal. Just as our friends and lawyers and industrialists allegedly had a wolf concealed beneath their shirts and frock coats, so in his hairy breast this wolf allegedly concealed a complex human soul, Mozart arias, and so on. To do justice to the unusual circumstances and the expectations of the public, the shrewd entrepreneur (who had known for years that the wildest animals are not so capricious, dangerous, and incalculable as the public) had resorted to rather startling accessories, emblems as it were of the wolf-man. It was an ordinary cage, with iron bars and a bit of straw on the floor, but on one wall hung a handsome Empire mirror and in the middle of the cage there was an open small piano, a pianette. On top of this rather wobbly piece of furniture stood a plaster bust of Goethe, the prince of poets.

As for the animal himself, who had aroused so much curiosity, there seemed to be nothing in the least remarkable about him. He looked exactly as a Steppenwolf, *Lupus campestris*, cannot help looking. Most of the time he lay motionless in a corner, as far as possible from the visitors, gnawing on his forepaws and staring into space as though he had before him not bars but the endless steppe. Now and then he stood up and strode back and forth a few times; then the piano wobbled on the uneven floor and the plaster Olympian also wobbled alarmingly. The animal paid little attention to the visitors, and most of them were rather disappointed in his looks. But here again there were divergent opinions. Many declared that he was a perfectly ordinary animal, without expression, a common dull-witted beast, and that was that; and furthermore, "Steppenwolf" was not a biological term. Others maintained on the contrary that the animal had beautiful eyes and that his whole being expressed such soulfulness that one's heart went out to him in sympathy. Only a handful of intelligent visitors realized that the remarks of both camps would have applied equally well to any other animal in the menagerie.

Early in the afternoon two children accompanied by their governess entered the room with the wolf's cage in it and stood for a long time watching him. One of the children was a pretty, rather quiet eight-year-old girl, the other a sturdy boy of about twelve. The Steppenwolf liked them both, their skin smelled young and healthy; he kept eyeing the little girl's firm, well-shaped legs. The governess, well, that was something else again; he thought it preferable to pay her as little attention as possible.

In order to be near the pretty little girl Harry lay down just behind the bars of his cage. While enjoying the children's scent, he listened to the three of them and was rather bored by their conversation. They were talking about Harry, in whom they all seemed to take a lively interest. But their attitudes were very different. The boy, a healthy, active young fellow, staunchly supported the opinion he had heard from his father at home. A cage in a menagerie, he said, was just the right place for such an animal; to let him run around loose would be irresponsible foolishness. In a pinch they could try to train him, maybe he could be taught to pull sleds like a husky, but it probably wouldn't work. No, if young Gustav were to come across this wolf, no matter where, he would not hesitate to shoot him down.

The Steppenwolf listened and licked his chops amiably. He liked the boy. "I only hope," he thought, "that if we should suddenly meet, you'll have a gun. And I hope I meet you out in the steppe, rather than surprise you by stepping out of your mirror." Yes, the boy appealed to him. He would grow up to be a spirited young man, a competent and successful engineer or manufacturer or officer, and Harry would have no objection to measuring his strength with him now and then and, if the worst came to the worst, to being shot by him.

It would have been harder to say how the pretty little girl felt about the Steppenwolf. At first she just looked at him, but much more carefully and with much more curiosity than the two others, who thought they already knew all about him. The little girl discovered that she liked Harry's tongue and teeth; she liked his eyes too, but she had misgivings about his rather unkempt coat, and his pungent animal smell aroused a strange feeling of excitement, in which revulsion, disgust, and prurient curiosity were mingled. All in all, she liked him and it did not escape her that Harry was very fond of her, that he was looking at her with admiration and desire. She breathed in his admiration with visible pleasure and from time to time asked a question.

"Fräulein, why has this wolf got a piano in his cage?" she asked. "Wouldn't he rather have something to eat?"

"He's not an ordinary wolf," said the governess. "He's a musical wolf. But you're too young to understand."

The little girl frowned and said: "There seem to be lots of things that I'm too young to understand. If the wolf is musical, of course he should have a piano, two for all I care. But that statue on top of the piano—I do think it's funny. What is he supposed to do with it?"

"It's a symbol." The governess was about to launch into an explanation, but the wolf came to the little girl's help. With a loving look at her, he jumped up so suddenly that for a moment all three were afraid, stretched voluptuously, went over to the wobbly piano, and began to rub and scrape against it. He went on rubbing more and more violently, until the wobbly bust lost its balance and fell. The floor resounded, and Goethe, like the Goethe of certain learned professors, broke into three pieces. The wolf sniffed for a moment at each of the three fragments, then turned his back on them with indifference, and went back to the vicinity of the little girl.

At this point the governess took the center of the stage. She was one of those who despite sports clothes and bobbed hair felt certain that they had discovered wolves in their bosoms. She was one of Harry's readers and admirers and regarded herself as his soul sister, for deep down inside her she too had all sorts of complicated feelings and conflicts. A faint voice told her, to be sure, that her sheltered middle-class life was not really a steppe or a wilderness, that she would never summon up the courage or despair to break out of it and like Harry to take a desperate leap into chaos. No, of course she would never do any such thing. But she would always have sympathy and understanding for the Steppenwolf, and she wished she could let him see it. The next time this Harry reverted to human form and put on a dinner jacket, she had a good mind to invite him to tea or to play Mozart with her four-handed. Yes, indeed, she would try.

Meanwhile the little eight-year-old had been giving the wolf her undivided attention. She was delighted with his cleverness in toppling the bust. She knew he had done it for her benefit; he had understood her words and clearly sided with her against her governess. Would he demolish the silly piano too? Oh, he was marvelous, she just loved him.

But Harry had lost interest in the piano. He crouched down as near as he could get to the child, and lay there like a fawning dog with his head on the floor and his muzzle thrust forward between the bars, looking up at her with rapture in his eyes. The child could not resist. Spellbound and trusting, she put out her little hand and stroked his dark nose. Harry ogled at her encouragingly and gently licked her little hand with his warm tongue.

When the governess saw this, her mind was made up. She too wanted to make herself known to Harry as an understanding sister; she too wanted to establish a bond with him. Quickly she untied the gold string on the elegant little package she was holding, unwrapped it, and peeled the silver paper from a pretty chocolate heart. Then with a glance full of deep meaning she held it out to the wolf.

Harry blinked and quietly went on licking the little girl's hand, but at the same time he kept a close eye on the governess's movements. And the instant the hand with the chocolate heart was close enough, he snapped like a flash, closing his teeth on heart and hand. The three visitors screamed in unison and recoiled, but the governess was unable to get away, for her brother wolf held her fast, and it was several anguished moments before she was able to pull back her bleeding hand and look at it. It had been bitten to the bone.

The poor young lady let out another piercing scream. But in that moment she was fully cured of her inner conflict. No, she was not a she-wolf, she had nothing in common with this loathsome brute, who was now sniffing with interest at the bloody chocolate heart. And then and there she declared war.

A bewildered group formed around the governess and she found herself face to face with the livid menagerie owner. Standing straight and firm, holding out her bleeding hand for fear of soiling her dress, she declared with breathtaking eloquence that she would not rest until this brutal assault had been avenged, and the guilty parties would be amazed to hear the amount of damages she would demand for the disfiguring of her shapely pianist's hand. And the wolf had to be killed, she wouldn't settle for less, they would see.

Quickly recovering his composure, the owner called her attention to the chocolate heart, which was still lying in front of Harry. There were signs all about, saying that it was strictly forbidden to feed the animals. Which relieved him of all responsibility. Let her sue him, no court in the world would take her part. Moreover, he had liability insurance. But right now, if the young lady knew what was good for her, she would see a doctor.

And so she did; but no sooner had the doctor dressed her wounds than she went on to see a lawyer. The next day people flocked to Harry's cage by the hundreds.

Since then the whole town has been talking about the lawsuit between the lady and the Steppenwolf. For the plaintiff is taking the position that Harry the wolf is primarily responsible and the owner of the menagerie a mere accessory. For, as the complaint explains at great length, this Harry cannot be regarded as an irresponsible animal; he is a citizen with a first and last name, he has been employed only temporarily as a wolf, and has published his memoirs. Regardless of what the lower court may decide, the case is sure to make its way through all the echelons of justice and ultimately to be set before the Reich Court.

Accordingly, the highest judicial authority in the land can be expected in the foreseeable future to provide us with a definitive decision on the question: Is the Steppenwolf, in the last analysis, an animal or a man?

FROM

Moly and My Sad Captains

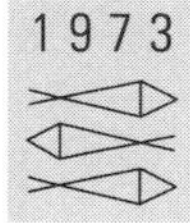

MY SAD CAPTAINS

One by one they appear in
the darkness: a few friends, and
a few with historical
names. How late they start to shine!
but before they fade they stand
perfectly embodied, all

the past lapping them like a
cloak of chaos. They were men
who, I thought, lived only to
renew the wasteful force they
spent with each hot convulsion.
They remind me, distant now.

True, they are not at rest yet,
but now that they are indeed
apart, winnowed from failures,
they withdraw to an orbit
and turn with disinterested
hard energy, like the stars.

FROM

Ninety-Two in the Shade

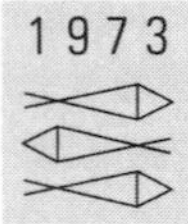

Eight-thirty and Skelton was trudging for the dock. He would have dreaded this meeting less if it had been just a meeting with Dance, though he would still have dreaded it. In any case, he was now doing not what he wished to do but what he ought to do; and getting a gentle energy return from satisfying this minor imperative. Carter would be there, however; so would Roy Soleil; maybe even Myron Moorhen. All the way to the dock, Skelton was cultivating an air of reason. He did not consider this meeting to be a showdown; which is always an encounter of meat and blades for a hamburger reason.

Faron Carter held in his hand a forged-steel nozzle at the end of a large-diameter black hose that trailed in four lazy curves all the way out to a Gulf truck at whose wheel sat a harmless footling of the oil monsters. Into a filler pipe, Carter was directing a golden rush of gasoline that (final suspiration of vanished forests, dinosaurs, and simple monocot meadows) soon enough would drive bright metal billets of cam and piston to blue whir of propeller for getting from Point A to Point B. Otherwise, the petroleum drive for hotcakes is too well known for further elucidation; it contests munitions for the winning turkey. One thinks of the opossum, a simple marsupial widely known in this land is our land. When the mother opossum is on a trip and hunger calls, she reaches into her pouch and eats a baby 'possum; until eventually mother opossum is alone in the American Night with no one to call her "Mom."

"Tom," said Carter, "you been scarce as hen's teeth. I don't know when I seen you last—"

"Last time I saw you," said Skelton, "I was laying on the bottom of the canal over there watching you and Roy Rogers driving around looking for me with a pistol."

"Is ah that an admission of guilt?"

"Not unless you have concealed a court recorder in that palmetto."

"Well, nice to have you around again," said Cart, real friendly. "Your granddad come to our Lions Club luncheon yesterday and he and

I had a chance to visit awhile. Your old granddad is some character! He told me how much he was looking forward to you joinin the dock down here. And so am I! So am I . . ."

"Where's Nichol at?"

"I'm over here!" Dance's voice from behind the sea wall; must be in his skiff. That was a break: the chance to talk in private.

Skelton walked across the springy Bermuda grass toward Dance; he could just see the curve of Dance's back as he bent over the engine, an oval of dark sweat in the center of the khaki shirt.

Faron Carter walked to the door of the bait shack and met Myron Moorhen, there risen from his desk at the sound of Skelton's voice; columns of figures still seemed to hang in his ovine eyes. Beneath his jackknife nose his lower lip bunched in concern around the bright teeth of a lemur.

"I'll be."

"You'll be what, Myron."

"I didn't nearly expect to see that incendiary show his face . . . !"

"I hadn't known you to run you a court of inquiry on the subject!"

"Well, now what is the policy then?"

"We don't have no policy. Nichol Dance had the policy. Nichol Dance you may just recall is the old boy lost his boat?" This last word soaring in ridicule.

"Okay, okay."

"So he has the policy."

"Okay."

"And we live and let live or die and let die whichever the case may be."

"I get it then," said Myron Moorhen. "Ours is a policy of non-intervention and Dance's is . . . is what?"

"Dry up, Myron."

Myron wandered dutiful to the numbers. The shrimp tank aerator bubbled; and the whole place smelled to high heaven because a customer had left a wahoo on the tournament scale all weekend and it had turned.

Myron Moorhen started his Bic at the top of the third column and ran it clear to the last figure; where he moved its point horizontally to the word "debit."

"What all is going to happen?"

"Someone is going to get killed," Carter replied. "Myron, where did you put that wahoo?"

•

"I don't see why a busted o-ring would cause the engine to quit."

"All right now," said Dance, "pay attention now." He swung the engine over to one side. "The o-ring I'm talking about is right up here at the top of the drive shaft and keeps sea water from getting up here —right?—past the crank—right?—and killing the engine."

"How did you know the o-ring was busted?"

"I figured it was, is how. Then I pulled the powerhead and there it was in pieces."

"How did the rest of it look?"

"It didn't look good. I pulled the impeller in the water pump and the rubber blades were all deteriorated."

"How does it run now?"

"Go up forward and start it."

The engine turned over and caught quickly; but idled unevenly. "Not great," Skelton was the first to say.

"Run it up another thousand." The engine came up to pitch; but still rough. It was an old-timer. "Let's see how it runs. I just changed the nineteen-inch prop it had for a twenty-one."

Skelton freed the lines and sat down in the portside chair. Then Dance sat down and wheeled the boat away from the dock. It was not an unhandsome skiff, a very old Roberts made on Tavernier.

Dance said, "Lightning struck those little keys east of the Snipes day before yesterday; I have to make a quick run over there and see. There's a lot of birds out there. I want to see how did they do."

They ran directly across Jewfish and Waltz Key basins and jumped the bank behind Old Dan Mangrove because they had the tide. Skelton studied Dance handling the tricky run. He went up behind the Mud Keys and broke through to the Gulf just northwest of the Snipes and turned east, shutting down over sandy bottom so that the shadow of the boat on the bottom swung and pivoted as the wake overtook the boat. The skiff came to rest, locked to its shadow as though on a pendulum.

Skelton jacked up the engine by hand; it had no power tilt. Dance got up on the bow and poled them toward the beach in the thunderous old storm wash that came in off the Gulf. On the reef line, green rollers poured through the surge channels.

Dance threw the anchor high up on the beach; and they went ashore. Before they walked up into the beach grass they could see a couple of wild palms shattered by lightning, some with livid streaks in their smooth gray trunks. As soon as they were up on the higher part of the key, they found a number of white herons, little blue herons, and one wood stork, killed by the lightning. "Isn't that a crime," said Dance. The birds were already throbbing and heavy with worms, perhaps ten birds scattered as the lightning had found them, long wading legs criss-crossed, beaks pointing about ridiculously in this last idleness of death.

They started back. They were halfway across Waltz Key Basin before they talked again. Dance said, "Look here, I know it wasn't much of a joke."

"You're right."

"Not that it excuses what you done."

"Yeah well."

"And you cannot guide. I gave my word."

"Well, I *am* going to guide."

"You are not."

Skelton nodded that he was, as pleasant as he could.

Two spotted rays shot out in front of the boat and coursed away on spotted wings, their white ventrals showing in their hurry: then vanished in the glare. The water was still and glassy, green over the turtle-grass bottom. There were birds everywhere now, soaring out before them—the cormorants that rested on stakes and mangroves to dry out their wings, the anhingas, gulls, frigate birds, and pelicans, the wading herons and cranes of every variation of slate, whites upon whites, emblematic black chevrons or stripes, wings finished in a taper or left rough-ended. They threaded the keys amid this aerial display over uncounted fish coursing the tidal basin, over a bottom itself home to a million kinds of animal, that walked, stalked, and scuttled by every tropism from heat to light, and lived in intermeshing layers, layer upon layer, that passed through each other like light and never touched.

A jet passed over and Skelton looked up for it; every year you had to look farther ahead of the sound. The plane made a beautiful silver line.

•

Thomas Skelton felt that simple survival at one level and the prevention of psychotic lesions based upon empirical observation of the republic depended upon his being able to get out on the ocean. Solitary floating as the tide carried him off the seaward shelf was in one sense sociopathic conduct for him; not infrequently such simplicity was one of three options; the others being berserking and smoking dope all the livelong day.

Notwithstanding the shriveling of the earth before its most singular product, Skelton's reflex to be a practicing Christian remained. His skill in sidestepping confrontation, his largest capability, left him—faith, hope, and charity—largely untried. Somewhere, he knew that. It had taken a quarter of a century to produce the combination for him: access to the space of ocean (and the mode of livelihood that would make that access constant) and an unformed vision of how he ought to live on earth with others.

So he told Nichol Dance, "I am going to guide."

But today, by the time he got to Searstown, he was looking around at the human surge and thinking how attractive it must be to go shopping at the Annual White Sales without anyone offering to murder you over the percales, or to spew your guts across the Dansk Mug Set. Even the shapely teeny-bopper whom he had zero chance of having, looked in at the new Sugarcane Harris albums without the air of impending murder for *anyone*, much less herself.

And how shall I accept my own death? A forefinger in the entrance hole while a billion protozoa redistribute my chemical components from behind where the bullet exits and kills an innocent pelican whitening a speedboat nearby.

Miranda, said Skelton to himself at Searstown, I'd feel a lot better if I could do a little barking. Imagine: The course of the bullet; its "entry" is immediately to the left of the sternum, where in its passage it disrupts the heart's determined flutter as to cause not quite immediate death. He knows what it is. There is the majesty of that surprise. His conviction that the chance against his living again is infinity minus one saves him from complete regret. Skelton's eyes, which always had a bright and fluid life, become on this sunny day quickly dry; and a place where the small insects of the empty beach can walk without . . . struggling for purchase. Gradually, his eyes become a popular trysting spot for breeding beach bugs; and by the magic geometry of mitosis, each eyeball is soon transformed into a thriving community with roots in, on the one hand, the first aeons of earth time; and, on the other, the weirdest reaches of the evolutionary space-future in which, feasibly, the products of Skelton's eyeballs might be colonizing planets of their own for reasons of civilization. By the same token, his prostate might get to the White House.

Skelton was modifying his fuselage, and shopping in the Sears hardware store for tools and parts. He bought a Craftsman variable-speed drill with a firm money-back guarantee. The magic of the electric drill was that it allowed you to take the oddly shaped hole of an electrical outlet and by running its force through a black cord and a silvery mechanism cause holes at the other end, of any size you liked.

Would Dance regret his deed? Would he look again at that delirious passage by which what is quick and numinous becomes meat, and say: Phooey? Or would he, like the television commentators before every event, "never cease to be amazed"?

The hardware department with its bins of galvanized nails, black bolts, and chromium-plated screws, its bright power tools, was presided over by six clerks in green smocks who soared among its counters, from time to time regrouping at the cash register to clinch a sale or take a quick pull of coffee from a translucent white coffee cup. Skelton knew that—embroiled as he was as a customer—hardware, generally speaking, was bad for the world.

It was among the glues, directly behind the epoxy display, to be precise, that he knew it was time to go and see why his father was asking Miranda for a date. The two-part epoxy was best for maximum adhesion between clean flat surfaces. The one-part "mock" epoxies were "just the thing," a lady clerk volunteered, for simple household repairs, including china, furniture, butter churns, ice skates, and simple treadle assemblies.

Sweet Jesus, thought Skelton, not in the least taking the Name in vain, death is in my lane tromping the passing gear.

"Ma'am," he said to the lady clerk, whose beveled white hairdo strove implacable against air and light, "have you got time to join me in a smoke? I uh won't lay a hand on you."

She broke into laughter. Here is where Skelton could serve humanity in its gloomy mission.

"Okay."

They stood outside in the mall by speeding machines and parked-auto clusters. Skelton didn't smoke tobacco. This might be tough.

"I forgot my cigarettes."

"Have one of mine, hon." She held out a pack and he took one. A granny shot past baying on a go-cart. The gramp ran behind. He had just jerked the starter, and Gran shot off like Puffed Rice from a cannon. Now it looked like she would beat him to Akron.

"So!" said Skelton. "You smoke Luckies!"

"Two packs a day and I've tried them all."

Skelton used to smoke. He had something to say here.

"I like Camels myself."

"Well, they're a rich-type cigarette like Luckies. But Camels have I don't know too *deep* a taste for me. But I *hate* Chesterfields!"

"Me too! They're so harsh!"

"Harsh isn't the word. —Have you ever smoked filters?"

"Benson and Hedges!"

"Aha!"

"Parliaments!"

"Me too! Couldn't taste a thing! —I don't know," she said, "for me it's L.S.M.F.T., Lucky Strike Means Fine Tobacco."

Skelton pulled her into his arms. His eyes were moist. "Do you want a light?" she asked. Skelton couldn't look her in the eye.

"I really don't smoke any more."

FROM

Two Citizens

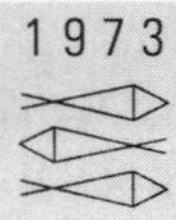

LOVE IN A WARM ROOM IN WINTER

The trouble with you is
You think all I want to do
Is get you into bed
And make love with you.

And that's not true!

I was just trying to make friends.
All I wanted to do
Was get into bed
With you and make

Love with you.

Who was that little bird we saw towering upside down
This afternoon on that pine cone, on the edge of a cliff,
In the snow? Wasn't he charming? Yes, he was, now,
Now, now,
Just take it easy.

Aha!

GRACE PALEY

FROM

Enormous Changes at the Last Minute

1974

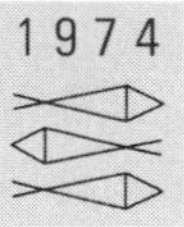

FAITH IN THE AFTERNOON

As for you, fellow independent thinker of the Western Bloc, if you have anything sensible to say, don't wait. Shout it out loud right this minute. In twenty years, give or take a spring, your grandchildren will be lying in sandboxes all over the world, their ears to the ground, listening for signals from long ago. In fact, kneeling now on the great plains in a snootful of gray dust, what do you hear? Pigs oinking, potatoes peeling, Indians running, winter coming?

Faith's head is under the pillow nearly any weekday midnight, asweat with dreams, and she is seasick with ocean sounds, the squealing wind stuck in its rearing tail by high tide.

That is because her grandfather, scoring the salty sea, skated for miles along the Baltic's icy beaches, with a frozen herring in his pocket. And she, all ears, was born in Coney Island.

Who are her antecedents? Mama and Papa of course. Her environment? A brother and a sister with their own sorrow to lead by the nose out of this life. All together they would make a goddamn quadruped bilingual hermaphrodite. Even so, proving their excellence, they bear her no rancor and are always anxious to see her, to see the boys, to take the poor fatherless boys to a picnic with their boys, for a walk, to an ocean, glad to say, we saw Mama in the Children of Judea, she sends love . . . They never say snidely, as the siblings of others might, It wouldn't hurt you to run over, Faith, it's only a subway ride . . .

Hope and Faith and even Charles—who comes glowering around once a year to see if Faith's capacity for survival has not been overwhelmed by her susceptibility to abuse—begged their parents to reconsider the decision to put money down and move into the Children of Judea. "Mother," said Hope, taking off her eyeglasses, for she did not like even that little window of glass to come between their mother and herself. "Now, Mother, how will you make out with all those *yentas*? Some of them don't even speak English." "I have spoken altogether too much English in my life," said Mrs. Darwin. "If I really liked English that much, I would move to England." "Why don't you go to Israel?" asked Charles. "That would at least make sense to people." "And leave you?" she asked, tears in her eyes at the thought of them all alone, wrecking their lives on the shoals of every day, without her tearful gaze attending.

When Faith thinks of her mother and father in any year, young or impersonally aged, she notices that they are squatting on the shore, staring with light eyes at the white waves. Then Faith feels herself so damply in the swim of things that she considers crawling Channels and Hellesponts and even taking a master's degree in education in order to exult at last in a profession and get out of the horseshit trades of this lofty land.

Certain facts may become useful. The Darwins moved to Coney Island for the air. There was not enough air in Yorkville, where the grandmother had been planted among German Nazis and Irish bums by Faith's grandfather, who soon departed alone in blue pajamas, for death.

Her grandmother pretended she was German in just the same way that Faith pretends she is an American. Faith's mother flew in the fat face of all that and, once safely among her own kind in Coney Island, learned real Yiddish, helped Faith's father, who was not so good at foreign languages, and as soon as all the verbs and necessary nouns had been collected under the roof of her mouth, she took an oath to expostulate in Yiddish and grieve only in Yiddish, and she has kept that oath to this day.

Faith has only visited her parents once since she began to understand that because of Ricardo she would have to be unhappy for a while. Faith really is an American and she was raised up like everyone else to the true assumption of happiness.

No doubt about it, squinting in any direction she is absolutely miserable. She is ashamed of this before her parents. "You should get help," says Hope. "Psychiatry was invented for people like you, Faithful," says Charles. "My little blondie, life is short. I'll lay out a certain amount of cash," says her father. "When will you be a person," says her mother.

Their minds are on matters. Severed Jerusalem; the Second World War still occupies their arguments; peaceful uses of atomic energy (is it necessary altogether?); new little waves of anti-Semitism lap the quiet beaches of their accomplishment.

They are naturally disgusted with Faith and her ridiculous position right in the middle of prosperous times. They are ashamed of her willful unhappiness.

All right! Shame then! Shame on them all!

•

That Ricardo, Faith's first husband, was a sophisticated man. He was proud and happy because men liked him. He was really, he said, a man's man. Like any true man's man, he ran after women too. He was often seen running, in fact, after certain young women on West Eighth Street or leaping little fences in Bedford Mews to catch up with some dear little pussycat.

He called them pet names, which generally referred to certain flaws in their appearance. He called Faith Baldy, although she is not and never will be bald. She is fine-haired and fair, and regards it as part of the lightness of her general construction that when she gathers her hair into an ordinary topknot, the stuff escapes around the contour of her face, making her wisp-haired and easy to blush. He is now living with a shapely girl with white round arms and he calls her Fatty.

When in New York, Faith's first husband lives within floating distance of the Green Coq, a prospering bar where he is well known and greeted loudly as he enters, shoving his current woman gallantly before. He introduces her around—hey, this is Fatty or Baldy. Once there was Bugsy, dragged up from the gutter where she loved to roll immies with Russell the bartender. Then Ricardo, to save her from becoming an old tea bag (his joke), hoisted her on the pulpy rods of his paperbacked culture high above her class, and she still administers her troubles from there, poor girl, her knees gallivanting in air.

Bugsy lives forever behind the Horney curtain of Faith's mind, a terrible end, for she used to be an ordinarily reprehensible derelict, but by the time Ricardo had helped her through two abortions and one lousy winter, she became an alcoholic and a whore for money. She soon gave up spreading for the usual rewards, which are an evening's companionship and a weekend of late breakfasts.

Bugsy was before Faith. Ricardo agreed to be Faith's husband for a couple of years anyway, because Faith in happy overindulgence had become pregnant. Almost at once, she suffered a natural miscarriage, but it was too late. They had been securely married by the state for six weeks when that happened, and so, like the gentleman he may very well be, he resigned himself to her love—a medium-sized, beefy-shouldered man, Indian-black hair, straight and coarse to the fingers, lavender eyes—Faith is perfectly willing to say it herself, to any good listener: she loved Ricardo. She began indeed to love herself, to love the properties which, for a couple of years anyway, extracted such heart-warming activity from him.

Well, Faith argues whenever someone says, "Oh really, Faithy, what do you mean—love?" She must have loved Ricardo. She had two boys with him. She had them to honor him and his way of loving when sober. He believed and often shouted out loud in the Green Coq, that Newcastle into which he reeled every night, blind with coal, that she'd had those kids to make him a bloody nine-to-fiver.

Nothing, said Faith in those simple days, was further from her mind. For her public part, she had made reasoned statements in the playground, and in the A & P while queued up for the cashier, that odd jobs were a splendid way of making out if you had together agreed on a substandard way of life. For, she explained to the ladies in whom she had confided her entire life, how can a man know his children if he is always out working? How true, that is the trouble with children today, replied the ladies, wishing to be her friend, they never see their daddies.

•

"Mama," Faith said, the last time she visited the Children of Judea, "Ricardo and I aren't going to be together so much any more."

"Faithy!" said her mother. "You have a terrible temper. No, no, listen to me. It happens to many people in their lives. He'll be back in a couple of days. After all, the children . . . just say you're sorry. It isn't even a hill of beans. Nonsense. I thought he was much improved when he was here a couple of months ago. Don't give it a thought. Clean up the house, put in a steak. Tell the children be a little quiet, send them next door for the television. He'll be home before you know it. Don't pay attention. Do up your hair something special. Papa would be more than glad to give you a little cash. We're not poverty-stricken, you know. You only have to tell us you want help. Don't worry. He'll walk in the door tomorrow. When you get home, he'll be turning on the hi-fi."

"Oh, Mama, Mama, he's tone deaf."

"Ai, Faithy, you have to do your life a little better than this."

They sat silently together, their eyes cast down by shame. The doorknob rattled. "My God, Hegel-Shtein," whispered Mrs. Darwin. "Ssh, Faith, don't tell Hegel-Shtein. She thinks everything is her business. Don't even leave a hint."

Mrs. Hegel-Shtein, president of the Grandmothers' Wool Socks Association, rolled in on oiled wheelchair wheels. She brought a lapful of multicolored wool in skeins. She was an old lady. Mrs. Darwin was really not an old lady. Mrs. Hegel-Shtein had organized this Active Association because children today wear cotton socks all winter. The grandmothers who lose heat at their extremities at a terrible clip are naturally more sensitive to these facts than the present avocated generation of mothers.

"Shalom, darling," said Mrs. Darwin to Mrs. Hegel-Shtein. "How's tricks?" she asked bravely.

"Aah," said Mrs. Hegel-Shtein. "Mrs. Essie Shifer resigned on account of her wrists."

"Really? Well, let her come sit with us. Company is healthy."

"Please, please, what's the therapy value if she only sits? Phooey!" said Mrs. Hegel-Shtein. "Excuse me, don't tell me that's Faith. Faith? Imagine that. Hope I know, but this is really Faith. So it turns out you really have a little time to see your mother . . . What luck for her you won't be busy forever."

"Oh, Celia, I beg you, be quiet," Faith's mortified mother said. "I must beg you. Faith comes when she can. She's a mother. She has two little small boys. She works. Did you forget, Celia, what it was like in those days when they're little babies? Who comes first? The children . . . the little children, they come first."

"Sure, sure, first, I know all about first. Didn't Archie come first? I had a big honor. I got a Christmas card from Florida from Mr. and Mrs. First. Listen to me, foolish people. I went by them to stay in the summer place, in the woods, near rivers. Only it got no ventilation, the whole place smells from termites and the dog. Please, I beg him, please, Mr. First, I'm a old woman, be sorry for me, I need extra air, leave your door open, I beg, I beg. No, not a word. Bang, every night eleven o'clock, the door gets shut like a rock. For a ten-minute business they close themselves up a whole night long.

"I'm better off in a old ladies' home, I told them. Nobody there is ashamed of a little cross ventilation."

Mrs. Darwin blushed. Faith said, "Don't be such a clock watcher, Mrs. Hegel-Shtein."

Mrs. Hegel-Shtein, who always seemed to know Faith better than Faith knew Mrs. Hegel-Shtein, said, "All right, all right. You're here, Faithy, don't be lazy. Help out. Here. Hold it, this wool on your hands, your mama will make a ball." Faith didn't mind. She held the wool out on her arms. Mrs. Darwin twisted and turned it round and round. Mrs. Hegel-Shtein directed in a loud voice, wheeling back and forth and pointing out serious mistakes. "Gittel, Gittel," she cried, "it should be rounder, you're making a square. Faithy, be more steadier. Move a little. You got infantile paralysis?"

"More wool, more wool," said Mrs. Darwin, dropping one completed ball into a shopping bag. They were busy as bees in a ladies' murmur about life and lives. They worked. They took vital facts from one another and looked as dedicated as a kibbutz.

•

The door to Mr. and Mrs. Darwin's room had remained open. Old bearded men walked by, thumbs linked behind their backs, all alike, the leftover army of the Lord. They had stuffed the morning papers under their mattresses, and because of the sorrowful current events they hurried up to the Temple of Judea on the sixth floor, from which they could more easily communicate with God. Ladies leaned on sticks stiffly, their articulations jammed with calcium. They knocked on the open door and said, "Oi, busy . . ." or "Mrs. Hegel-Shtein, don't you ever stop?" No one said much to Faith's mother, the vice-president of the Grandmothers' Wool Socks Association.

Hope had warned her: "Mother, you are only sixty-five years old. You look fifty-five." "Youth is in the heart, Hopey. I feel older than Grandma. It's the way I'm constituted. Anyway Papa is practically seventy, he deserves a rest. We have some advantage that we're young enough to make a good adjustment. By the time we're old and miserable, it'll be like at home here." "Mother, you'll certainly be an object of suspicion, an interloper, you'll have enemies everywhere." Hope had been sent to camp lots of years as a kid; she knew a thing or two about group living.

Opposite Faith, her mother swaddled the fat turquoise balls in more and more turquoise wool. Faith swayed gently back and forth along with her outstretched wool-wound arms. It hurt her most filial feelings that, in this acute society, Mrs. Hegel-Shtein should be sought after, admired, indulged . . .

"Well, Ma, what do you hear from the neighborhood?" Faith asked. She thought they could pass some cheery moments before the hovering shadow of Ricardo shoved a fat thumb in her eye.

"Ah, nothing much," Mrs. Darwin said.

"Nothing much?" asked Mrs. Hegel-Shtein. "I heard you correctly said nothing much? You got a letter today from Slovinsky family, your heart stuck in your teeth, Gittel, you want to hide this from little innocent Faith. Little baby Faithy. Ssh. Don't tell little children? Hah?"

"Celia, I must beg you. I have reasons. I must beg you, don't mix in. Oh, I must beg you, Celia, not to push any more, I want to say nothing much on this subject."

"Idiots!" Mrs. Hegel-Shtein whispered low and harsh.

"Did you really hear from the Slovinskys, Mama, really? Oh, you know I'm always interested in Tessie. Oh, you remember what a lot of fun Tess and I used to have when we were kids. I liked her. I never didn't like her." For some reason Faith addressed Mrs. Hegel-Shtein: "She was a very beautiful girl."

"Oh, yeh, beautiful. Young. Beautiful. Very old story. Naturally. Gittel, you stopped winding? Why? The meeting is tonight. Tell Faithy all about Slovinsky, her pal. Faithy got coddled from life already too much."

"Celia, I said shut up!" said Mrs. Darwin. "Shut up!"

(Then to all concerned a short dear remembrance arrived. A policeman, thumping after him along the boardwalk, had arrested Mr. Darwin one Saturday afternoon. He had been distributing leaflets for the Sholem Aleichem School and disagreeing reasonably with his second cousin, who had a different opinion about the past and the future. The leaflet cried out in Yiddish: "Parents! A little child's voice calls to you, 'Papa, Mama, what does it mean to be a Jew in the world today?' " Mrs. Darwin watched them from the boardwalk bench, where she sat getting sun with a shopping bag full of leaflets. The policeman shouted furiously at Mr. and Mrs. Darwin and the old cousin, for they were in an illegal place. Then Faith's mother said to him in the Mayflower voice of a disappearing image of life, "Shut up, you Cossack!" "You see," said Mr. Darwin, "to a Jew the word 'shut up' is a terrible expression, a dirty word, like a sin, because in the beginning, if I remember correctly, was the word! It's a great assault. Get it?")

"Gittel, if you don't tell this story now, I roll right out and I don't roll in very soon. Life is life. Everybody today is coddlers."

"Mama, I want to hear anything you know about Tess, anyway. Please tell me," Faith asked. "If you don't tell me, I'll call up Hope. I bet you told her."

"All stubborn people," said Mrs. Darwin. "All right. Tess Slovinsky. You know about the first tragedy, Faith? The first tragedy was she had a child born a monster. A real monster. Nobody saw it. They put it in a home. All right. Then the second child. They went right away ahead immediately and they tried and they had a second child. This one was born full of allergies. It had rashes from orange juice. It choked from milk. Its eyes swoll up from going to the country. All right. Then her husband, Arnold Lever, a very pleasant boy, got a cancer. They chopped off a finger. It got worse. They chopped off a hand. It didn't help. Faithy, that was the end of a lovely boy. That's the letter I got this morning just before you came."

Mrs. Darwin stopped. Then she looked up at Mrs. Hegel-Shtein and Faith. "He was an only son," she said. Mrs. Hegel-Shtein gasped. "You said an only son!" On deep tracks, the tears rolled down her old cheeks. But she had smiled so peculiarly for seventy-seven years that they suddenly swerved wildly toward her ears and hung like glass from each lobe.

Faith watched her cry and was indifferent. Then she thought a terrible thought. She thought that if Ricardo had lost a leg or so, that would certainly have kept him home. This cheered her a little, but not for long.

"Oh, Mama, Mama, Tessie never guessed what was going to happen to her. We used to play house and she never guessed."

"Who guesses?" screamed Mrs. Hegel-Shtein. "Archie is laying down this minute in Florida. Sun is shining on him. He's guessing?"

Mrs. Hegel-Shtein fluttered Faith's heart. She rattled her ribs. She squashed her sorrow as though it were actually the least toxic of all the world's great poisons.

However, the first one to live with the facts was Mrs. Hegel-Shtein. Eyes dry, she said, "What about Brauns? The old Braun, the uncle, an idiot, a regular Irgunist, is here."

"June Braun?" Faith asked. "My friend June Braun? From Brighton Beach Avenue? That one?"

"Of course, only, that isn't so bad," Mrs. Darwin said, getting into the spirit of things. "Junie's husband, an engineer in airplanes. Very serious boy. Papa doesn't like him to this day. He was in the movement. They bought a house in Huntington Harbor with a boat, a garage, a garage for the boat. She looked stunning. She had three boys. Brilliant. The husband played golf with the vice-president, a goy. The future was golden. She was active in everything. One morning they woke up. It's midnight. Someone uncovers a little this, a little that. (I mentioned he was in the movement?) In forty-eight hours, he's blacklisted. Good night Huntington Harbor. Today the whole bunch live with the Brauns in four rooms. I'm sorry for the old people."

"That's awful, Mama," Faith said. "The whole country's in a bad way."

"Still, Faith, times change. This is an unusual country. You'll travel around the world five times over, you wouldn't see a country like this often. She's up, she's down. It's unusual."

"Well, what else, Mama?" Faith asked. June Braun didn't sorrow her at all. What did June Braun know about pain? If you go in the dark sea over your head, you have to expect drowning cheerfully. Faith believed that June Braun and her husband whatever-his-name-could-be had gone too deeply into the air pocket of America whence all handouts come, and she accepted their suffocation in good spirit.

"What else, Mama? I know, what about Anita Franklin? What about her? God, was she smart in school! The whole senior class was crazy about her. Very chesty. Remember her, she got her period when she was about nine and three quarters? Or something like that. You knew her mother very well. You were always in cahoots about something. You and Mrs. Franklin. Mama!"

"You sure you really want to hear, Faithy, you won't be so funny afterward?" She liked telling these stories now, but she was not anxious to tell this one. Still she had warned Faith. "All right. Well, Anita Franklin. Anita Franklin also didn't guess. You remember she was married way ahead of you and Ricardo to a handsome boy from Harvard. Oh, Celia, you can imagine what hopes her mother and her father had for her happiness. Arthur Mazzano, you know, Sephardic. They lived in Boston and they knew such smart people. Professors, doctors, the finest people. History-book writers, thinking American people. Oh, Faithy darling. I was invited to the house several times, Christmas, Easter. I met their babies. Little blondies like you were, Faith. He got maybe two Ph.D.'s, you know, in different subjects. If someone wanted to ask a question, on what subject, they asked Arthur. At eight months their baby walked. I saw it myself. He wrote articles for Jewish magazines you never heard of, Celia. Then one day, Anita finds out from the horse's mouth itself, he is fooling around with freshmen. Teenagers. In no time it's in the papers, everybody in court, talking talking talking, some say yes, some no, he was only flirting, you know the way a man flirts with youngsters. But it turns out one of the foolish kids is pregnant."

"Spanish people," said Mrs. Hegel-Shtein thoughtfully. "The men don't like their wives so much. They only get married if it's a good idea."

Faith bowed her head in sorrow for Anita Franklin, whose blood when she was nine and three quarters burst from her to strike life and hope into the busy heads of all the girls in the fifth and sixth grades. Anita Franklin, she said to herself, do you think you'll make it all alone? How do you sleep at night, Anita Franklin, the sexiest girl in New Utrecht High? How is it these days, now you are never getting laid any more by clever Arthur Mazzano, the brilliant Sephardic Scholar and Lecturer? Now it is time that leans across you and not handsome, fair Arthur's mouth on yours, or his intelligent Boy Scouty conflagrating fingers.

At this very moment, the thumb of Ricardo's hovering shadow jabbed her in her left eye, revealing for all the world the shallowness of her water table. Rice could have been planted at that instant on the terraces of her flesh and sprouted in strength and beauty in the floods that overwhelmed her from that moment on through all the afternoon. For herself and Anita Franklin, Faith bowed her head and wept.

•

"Going already, Faith?" her father asked. He had poked his darling birdy head with poppy pale eyes into the sun-spotted room. He is not especially good-looking. He is ugly. Faith has often thanked the Germ God and the Gene Goddess and the Great Lords of All Nucleic Acid that none of them look like him, not even Charles, to whom it would not matter, for Charles has the height for any kind of face. They all look a little bit Teutonish, like their grandmother, who thinks she's German, just kind of light and even-featured, with Charles inclining to considerable jaw. People expect decision from Charles because of that jaw, and he has learned to give it to them—the wit of diagnosis, then inescapable treatment, followed by immediate health. In fact, his important colleagues often refer their wives' lower abdominal distress to Charles. Before he is dead he will be famous. Mr. Darwin hopes he will be famous soon, for in that family people do not live long.

Well, this popeyed, pale-beaked father of Faith's peered through the room into the glassy attack of the afternoon sun, couldn't focus on tears, or bitten lips for that matter, but saw Faith rise to look for her jacket in the closet.

"If you really have to go, I'll walk you, Faithy. Sweetheart, I haven't seen you in a long time," he said. He withdrew to wait in the hallway, well out of the circle of Mrs. Hegel-Shtein's grappling magnetism.

Faith kissed her mother, who whispered into her damp ear, "Be something, don't be a dishrag. You have two babies to raise." She kissed Mrs. Hegel-Shtein, because they had been brought up that way, not to hurt anyone's feelings, particularly if they loathed them, and they were much older.

Faith and her father walked through the light-green halls in silence to the life-giving lobby, where rosy, well-dressed families continued to arrive in order to sit for twenty minutes alongside their used-up elders. Some terrible political arguments about Jews in Russia now were taking place near the information desk. Faith paid no attention but moved toward the door, breathing deeply. She tried to keep her father behind her until she could meet the commitments of her face. "Don't rush, sweetheart," he said. "Don't rush, I'm not like these old cockers here, but I am no chicken definitely."

Gallantly he took her arm. "What's the good word?" he asked. "Well, no news isn't bad news, I hope?"

"So long, Chuck!" he called as they passed the iron gate over which, in stunning steel cursive, a welder had inscribed *The Children of Judea*. "Chuckle, chuckle," said her father, grasping her elbow more firmly, "what a name for a grown-up man!"

She turned to give him a big smile. He deserved an enormous smile, but she had only a big one available.

"Listen, Faithl, I wrote a poem, I want you to hear. Listen. I wrote it in Yiddish, I'll translate it in my head:

Childhood passes
Youth passes

Also the prime of life passes.
Old age passes.
Why do you believe, my daughters,
That old age is different?

"What do you say, Faithy? You know a whole bunch of artists and writers."

"What do I say? Papa." She stopped stock-still. "You're marvelous. That's like a Japanese Psalm of David."

"You think it's good?"

"I love it, Pa. It's marvelous."

"Well . . . you know, I might give up all this political stuff, if you really like it. I'm at a loss these days. It's a transition. Don't laugh at me, Faithy. You'll have to survive just such events some day yourself. Learn from life. Mine. I was going to organize the help. You know, the guards, the elevator boys—colored fellows, mostly. You notice, they're coming up in the world. Regardless of hopes, I never expected it in my lifetime. The war, I suppose, did it. Faith, what do you think? The war made Jews Americans and Negroes Jews. Ha ha. What do you think of that for an article? 'The Negro: Outside In at Last.' "

"Someone wrote something like that."

"Is that a fact? It's in the air. I tell you, I'm full of ideas. I don't have a soul to talk to. I'm used to your mother, only a funny thing happened to her, Faithy. We were so close. We're still friendly, don't take me the wrong way, but I mean a funny thing, she likes to be with the women lately. Loves to be with that insane, persecution, delusions-of-grandeur, paranoical Mrs. Hegel-Shtein. I can't stand her. She isn't a woman men can stand. Still, she got married. Your mother says, Be polite, Gersh; I am polite. I always loved the ladies to a flaw, Faithy, but Mrs. Hegel-Shtein knocks at our room at 9 a.m. and I'm an orphan till lunch. She has magic powers. Also she oils up her wheelchair all afternoon so she can sneak around. Did you ever hear of a wheelchair you couldn't hear coming? My child, believe me, what your mother sees in her is a shady mystery. How could I put it? That woman has a whole bag of spitballs for the world. And also a bitter crippled life."

They had come to the subway entrance. "Well, Pa, I guess I have to go now. I left the kids with a friend."

He shut his mouth. Then he laughed. "Aaah, a talky old man . . ."

"Oh no, Pa, not at all. No. I loved talking to you, but I left the kids with a friend, Pa."

"I know how it is when they're little, you're tied down, Faith. Oh, we couldn't go anywhere for years. I went only to meetings, that's all. I didn't like to go to a movie without your mother and enjoy myself. They didn't have babysitters in those days. A wonderful invention, babysitters. With this invention two people could be lovers forever.

"Oh!" he gasped, "my darling girl, excuse me . . ." Faith was surprised at his exclamation because the tears had come to her eyes before she felt their pain.

"Ah, I see now how the land lies. I see you have trouble. You picked yourself out a hard world to raise a family."

"I have to go, Pa."

"Sure."

She kissed him and started down the stairs.

"Faith," he called, "can you come soon?"

"Oh, Pa," she said, four steps below him, looking up, "I can't come until I'm a little happy."

"Happy!" He leaned over the rail and tried to hold her eyes. But that is hard to do, for eyes are born dodgers and know a whole circumference of ways out of a bad spot. "Don't be selfish, Faithy, bring the boys, come."

"They're so noisy, Pa."

"Bring the boys, sweetheart. I love their little goyish faces."

"O.K., O.K.," she said, wanting only to go quickly. "I will, Pa, I will."

Mr. Darwin reached for her fingers through the rail. He held them tightly and touched them to her wet cheeks. Then he said, "Aaah . . ." an explosion of nausea, absolute digestive disgust. And before she could turn away from the old age of his insulted face and run home down the subway stairs, he had dropped her sweating hand out of his own and turned away from her.

PHILIP LARKIN

FROM

High Windows

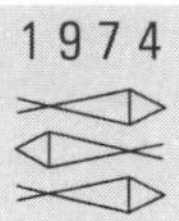

ANNUS MIRABILIS

Sexual intercourse began
In nineteen sixty-three
(Which was rather late for me)—
Between the end of the *Chatterley* ban
And the Beatles' first LP.

Up till then there'd only been
A sort of bargaining,
A wrangle for a ring,
A shame that started at sixteen
And spread to everything.

Then all at once the quarrel sank:
Everyone felt the same,
And every life became
A brilliant breaking of the bank,
A quite unlosable game.

So life was never better than
In nineteen sixty-three
(Though just too late for me)—
Between the end of the *Chatterley* ban
And the Beatles' first LP.

J. G. BALLARD

FROM

Concrete Island

1974

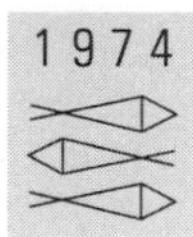

THROUGH THE CRASH BARRIER

Soon after three o'clock on the afternoon of April 22nd 1973, a 35-year-old architect named Robert Maitland was driving down the high-speed exit lane of the Westway interchange in central London. Six hundred yards from the junction with the newly built spur of the M4 motorway, when the Jaguar had already passed the 70 m.p.h. speed limit, a blow-out collapsed the front nearside tyre. The exploding air reflected from the concrete parapet seemed to detonate inside Robert Maitland's skull. During the few seconds before his crash he clutched at the whiplashing spokes of the steering wheel, dazed by the impact of the chromium window pillar against his head. The car veered from side to side across the empty traffic lanes, jerking his hands like a puppet's. The shredding tyre laid a black diagonal stroke across the white marker lines that followed the long curve of the motorway embankment. Out of control, the car burst through the palisade of pinewood trestles that formed a temporary barrier along the edge of the road. Leaving the hard shoulder, the car plunged down the grass slope of the embankment. Thirty yards ahead, it came to a halt against the rusting chassis of an overturned taxi. Barely injured by this violent tangent that had grazed his life, Robert Maitland lay across his steering wheel, his jacket and trousers studded with windshield fragments like a suit of lights.

In these first minutes as he recovered, Robert Maitland could remember little more of the crash than the sound of the exploding tyre, the swerving sunlight as the car emerged from the tunnel of an overpass, and the shattered windshield stinging his face. The sequence of violent events only micro-seconds in duration had opened and closed behind him like a vent of hell.

'. . . my God . . .'

Maitland listened to himself, recognizing the faint whisper. His hands still rested on the cracked spokes of the steering wheel, fingers splayed out nervelessly as if they had been dissected. He pressed his palms against the rim of the wheel, and pushed himself upright. The car had come to rest on sloping ground, surrounded by nettles and wild grass that grew waist-high outside the windows.

Steam hissed and spurted from the crushed radiator of the car, spitting out drops of rusty water. A hollow roaring sounded from the engine, a mechanical death-rattle.

Maitland stared into the steering well below the instrument panel, aware of the awkward posture of his legs. His feet lay among the pedals as if they had been hurriedly propped there by the mysterious demolition squad which had arranged the accident.

He moved his legs, reassured as they took up their usual position on either side of the steering column. The pedal pressure responded to the balls of his feet. Maitland ignored the grass and the motorway outside and began a careful inventory of his body. He tested his thighs and abdomen, brushed the fragments of windshield glass from his jacket and pressed his rib-cage, exploring the bones for any sign of fracture.

In the driving mirror he examined his head. A triangular bruise like the blade of a trowel marked his right temple. His forehead was covered with flecks of dirt and oil carried into the car by the breaking windshield. Maitland squeezed his face, trying to massage some expression into the pallid skin and musculature. His heavy jaw and hard cheeks were drained of all blood. The eyes staring back at him from the mirror were blank and unresponsive, as if he were looking at a psychotic twin brother.

Why had he driven so fast? He had left his office in Marylebone at three o'clock, intending to avoid the rush-hour traffic, and had ample time to cruise along in safety. He remembered swerving into the central drum of the Westway interchange, and pressing on towards the tunnel of the overpass. He could still hear the tyres as they beat along the concrete verge, boiling off a slipstream of dust and cigarette packets. As the car emerged from the vault of the tunnel the April sunlight had rainbowed across the windshield, momentarily blinding him . . .

His seat belt, rarely worn, hung from its pinion by his shoulder. As Maitland frankly recognized, he invariably drove well above the speed limit. Once inside a car some rogue gene, a strain of rashness, overran the rest of his usually cautious and clear-minded character. Today, speeding along the motorway when he was already tired after a three-day conference, preoccupied by the slight duplicity involved in seeing his wife so soon after a week spent with Helen Fairfax, he had almost wilfully devised the crash, perhaps as some bizarre kind of rationalization.

Shaking his head at himself, Maitland knocked out the last of the windshield with his hand. In front of him was the rusting chassis of the overturned taxi into which the Jaguar had slammed. Half hidden by the nettles, several other wrecks lay nearby, stripped of their tyres and chromium trim, rusty doors leaning open.

Maitland stepped from the Jaguar and stood in the waist-high grass. As he steadied himself against the roof the hot cellulose stung his hand. Shielded by the high embankment, the still air was heated by the afternoon sun. A few cars moved along the motorway, their roofs visible above the balustrade. A line of deep ruts, like the incisions of a giant scalpel, had been scored by the Jaguar in the packed earth of the embankment, marking the point where he had left the road a hundred feet from the overpass tunnel. This section of the motorway and its slip roads to the west of the interchange had been opened to traffic only two months earlier, and lengths of the crash barrier had yet to be installed.

Maitland waded through the grass to the front of his car. A single glance told him that he had no hope of driving it to a nearby access road. The front end had been punched into itself like a collapsed face. Three of the four headlamps were broken, and the decorative grille was meshed into the radiator honeycomb. On impact the suspension units had forced the engine back off its mountings, twisting the frame of the car. The sharp smell of anti-freeze and hot rust cut at Maitland's nostrils as he bent down and examined the wheel housing.

A total write-off—damn it, he had liked the car. He walked through the grass to a patch of clear ground between the Jaguar and the embankment. Surprisingly, no one had yet stopped to help him. As the drivers emerged from the darkness below the overpass into the fast right-hand bend lit by the afternoon sunlight they would be too busy to notice the scattered wooden trestles.

Maitland looked at his watch. It was three eighteen, little more than ten minutes since the crash. Walking about through the grass, he felt almost light-headed, like a man who has just witnessed some harrowing event, a motorway pile-up or public execution . . . He had promised his eight-year-old son that he would be home in time to collect him from school. Maitland visualized David at that moment, waiting patiently outside the Richmond Park gates near the military hospital, unaware that his father was six miles away, stranded beside a crashed car at the foot of a motorway embankment. Ironically, in this warm spring weather the line of crippled war veterans would be sitting in their wheel chairs by the park gates, as if exhibiting to the boy the variety of injuries which his father might have suffered.

Maitland went back to the Jaguar, steering the coarse grass out of the way with his hands. Even this small exertion flushed his face and chest. He looked round for the last time, with the deliberate gaze of a man inspecting an unhappy terrain he is about to leave for ever. Still shaken by the crash, he was already aware of the bruises across his thighs and chest. The impact had hurled him like a broken punch-bag on to the steering wheel—the second collision, as safety engineers modestly termed it. Calming himself, he leaned against the Jaguar's trunk; he wanted to fix in his mind this place of wild grass and abandoned cars where he had very nearly lost his life.

Shielding his eyes from the sunlight, Maitland saw that he had crashed into a small traffic island, some two hundred yards long and triangular in shape, that lay in the waste ground between three converging motorway routes. The apex of the island pointed towards the west and the declining sun, whose warm light lay over the distant television studios at White City. The base was formed by the southbound overpass that swept past seventy feet above the ground. Supported on massive concrete pillars, its six lanes of traffic were sealed from view by the corrugated metal splash-guards installed to protect the vehicles below.

Behind Maitland was the northern wall of the island, the thirty-feet-high embankment of the westbound motorway from which he had crashed. Facing him, and forming the southern boundary, was the steep embankment of the three-lane feeder road which looped in a north-westerly circuit below the overpass and joined the motorway at the apex of the island. Although no more than a hundred yards away, this freshly grassed slope seemed hidden behind the over-heated light of the island, by the wild grass, abandoned cars and builder's equipment. Traffic moved along the westbound lanes of the feeder road, but the metal crash barriers screened the island from the drivers. The high masts of three route indicators rose from concrete caissons built into the shoulder of the road.

Maitland turned as an airline coach passed along the motorway. The passengers on the upper deck, bound for Zurich, Stuttgart and Stockholm, sat stiffly in their seats like a party of mannequins. Two of them, a middle-aged man in a white raincoat and a young Sikh wearing a turban on his small head, looked down at Maitland, catching his eyes for a few seconds. Maitland returned their gaze, deciding not to wave at them. What did they think he was doing there? From the upper deck of the bus his Jaguar might well appear to be undamaged, and they would assume that he was a highway official or traffic engineer.

Below the overpass, at the eastern end of the island, a wire-mesh fence sealed off the triangle of waste ground from the area beyond, which had become an unofficial municipal dump. In the shadows below the concrete span were several derelict furniture vans, a stack of stripped-down billboards, mounds of tyres and untreated metal refuse. A quarter of a mile to the east of the overpass, visible through the fence, was a neighbourhood shopping centre. A red double-decker bus circled a small square, passing the striped awnings of multiple stores.

Clearly there was no exit from the island other than the embankments. Maitland removed the ignition keys from the instrument panel and unlocked the Jaguar's trunk. The chances of a wandering tramp or tinker finding the car were slight—the island was sealed off from the world around it by the high embankments on two sides and the wire-mesh fence on its third. The compulsory landscaping had yet to be carried out by the contractors, and the original contents of this shabby tract, its rusting cars and coarse grass, were still untouched.

Holding the handle of his leather overnight case, Maitland tried to lift it from the trunk. He found himself fainting from the exertion. The blood had drained instantly from his head, as if the minimum circulation was being maintained. He put down the case and leaned weakly against the open lid of the trunk.

In the polished panels of the rear wheel-housing Maitland stared at the distorted reflection of himself. His tall figure was warped like a grotesque scarecrow, and his white-skinned face bled away in the curving contours of the bodywork. A madman's grimace, one ear on a pedicle six inches from his head.

The crash had shaken him more than he realized. Maitland glanced down at the contents of the trunk—the tool-kit, a clutter of architectural journals, and a cardboard crate holding half a dozen bottles of white Burgundy which he was taking home for his wife Catherine. After the death of his grandfather the previous year Maitland's mother had been giving him some of the old man's wines.

'Maitland, you could use a drink now . . .' he told himself aloud. He locked the trunk, reached into the back of the car and picked up his raincoat, hat and briefcase. The crash had jerked loose a clutter of forgotten items from beneath the seats—a half-empty tube of sun lotion, memento of a holiday he had taken at La Grande Motte with Dr Helen Fairfax, the preprint of a paper she had given at a paediatric seminar, a packet of Catherine's miniature cigars he had hidden when trying to make her give up smoking.

Holding his briefcase in his left hand, hat on his head, raincoat over his right shoulder, Maitland set off towards the embankment. It was three thirty-one, still less than half an hour since the accident.

He looked back for the last time at the island. Already the waist-high grass, marked by the winding corridors that recorded his uncertain movements around the car, was settling itself again, almost hiding the silver Jaguar. A thin yellow light lay across the island, an unpleasant haze that seemed to rise from the grass, festering over the ground as if over a wound that had never healed.

A truck's diesel engine thundered below the overpass. Turning his back on the island, Maitland stepped on to the foot of the embankment and clambered up the soft slope. He would climb the embankment, wave down a passing car and be on his way.

THE EMBANKMENT

The earth flowed around him like a warm, alluvial river. Halfway up the embankment Maitland found himself sinking to his knees in the sliding slope. An unpacked topsoil intended only to carry the grass cover, the earth had not yet been consolidated by the seedlings sprouting through its open surface. Maitland laboured away, searching for a firm foothold and using the briefcase as a paddle. The effort of climbing the embankment had almost exhausted him, but he forced himself on.

Tasting blood in his mouth, he stopped and sat down. Squatting on the powdery slope, he took the handkerchief from his pocket and touched his tongue and lips. The red stain formed the imprint of his shaky mouth, like an illicit kiss. Maitland felt the tender skin of his right temple and cheekbone. The bruise ran from the ear as far as his right nostril. Pressing a finger into the nasal cleft, he could feel the injured sinus and gums, a loosened eye-tooth.

Waiting for his breath to return, Maitland listened to the traffic moving above his head. The sound of engines drummed ceaselessly through the tunnel of the overpass. On the far side of the island the feeder road was busy now, and Maitland waved his raincoat at the passing cars. However, the drivers were concentrating on the overhead route indicators and the major junction with the motorway.

The towers of the distant office-blocks rose into the afternoon air. Searching the warm haze over Marylebone, Maitland could almost identify his own building. Somewhere behind the glass curtain-walling on the seventeenth floor his secretary was typing the agenda for the following week's finance committee meeting, never thinking for a moment that her boss was squatting on this motorway embankment with a bloody mouth.

His shoulders began to shake, a rapid tremor that set off his diaphragm. With an effort Maitland mastered the spasm. He swallowed back the phlegm that choked his throat and stared down at the Jaguar, thinking again about the crash. It had been stupid of him to ignore the speed limit. Eager to see Catherine again, he was looking forward to relaxing in their cool, formal house with its large white rooms. After three days with Helen Fairfax, in this sensible woman doctor's warm and comfortable apartment, he had felt almost suffocated.

Standing up, Maitland edged sideways across the slope. Ten feet above him was the hard shoulder of the motorway, and the palisade of wooden trestles. Maitland tossed his briefcase up the slope. Moving like a crab on his feet and forearms, he climbed the more shallow soil, reached both hands on to the concrete shoulder and pulled himself on to the road.

Exhausted by the climb, Maitland sat down unsteadily on a wooden trestle. He brushed the dirt on his hands against his trousers. The briefcase and raincoat lay at his feet in a grimy bundle like the luggage of a tramp. Sweat bathed his shirt inside the jacket, soaking through the fabric. The blood was thick in his mouth, but he sucked it back without a pause.

He stood up and turned to face the oncoming traffic. Three lines of vehicles sped towards him. They emerged from the tunnel below the overpass and accelerated along the fast bend. The rush-hour had begun. Magnified by the roof and walls of the overpass, the noise reverberated off the concrete roadway around Maitland, drowning his first shouts. Now and then an interval of fifty feet appeared between the speeding vehicles, but even during these first minutes as Maitland stood there, waving his briefcase and raincoat, the hundreds of cars carrying their homeward drivers pressed closer together, almost bumper to bumper.

Maitland lowered the briefcase, watching the traffic roar past him. The red pinewood trestles had been knocked back by the speeding vehicles into a loose line. Lower in the western sky, the strong sun shone directly into the drivers' eyes as they emerged from the overpass into the fast right-hand bend.

Maitland looked down at himself. His jacket and trousers were stained with sweat, mud and engine grease—few drivers, even if they did notice him, would be eager to give him a lift. Besides, it would be almost impossible to slow down here and stop. The pressure of the following traffic, free at last from the long tail-backs that always blocked the Westway interchange during the rush-hour, forced them on relentlessly.

Trying to position himself more conspicuously, Maitland edged along the narrow road shoulder. No pedestrian or emergency verge had been provided along this fast bend, and the cars speeding past him at sixty miles an hour were no more than three or four feet away. Still carrying the raincoat and briefcase, he moved along the line of trestles, steering each one out of his way. He waved his hat in the exhaust-filled air, shouting over his shoulder into the engine noise.

'Emergency . . . ! Stop . . . ! Pull over . . . !'

Two trestles kicked together by a passing truck blocked his way. The lines of traffic swept by, swerving under the route indicators towards the junction ahead. Brake lights pumped, and the sunlight flared off the windshields in electric lances.

A horn blared warningly behind Maitland as he climbed around the trestles. A car plunged within inches of his right hip, an angry passenger whirling in a window. Maitland pulled himself back, and saw the white hull of a police car in the far lane. It was moving at a steady fifty miles an hour, a few feet behind the bumper of the car in front, but the driver looked over his shoulder at Maitland.

'Slow down . . . ! Police . . . !'

Maitland waved both the hat and briefcase, but the police car had been carried away by the rush of traffic. Trying to follow it on foot, Maitland was almost hit by the fender of a passing taxi. A black limousine swept towards him out of the tunnel, the uniformed chauffeur seeing Maitland at the last moment.

Realizing that he would be crushed against the trestles, Maitland moved away from them. His right hand smarted from a passing blow. The skin had been torn by a piece of sharp windshield or wing-mirror trim. He wrapped the blood-stained handkerchief around it.

Three hundred yards away, beyond the eastern entrance of the overpass, was the call-box of an emergency telephone, but he knew that he would be killed if he tried to walk through the tunnel. Maitland edged back along the hard shoulder and took up his position at the point where the Jaguar had left the road. He put on his raincoat and buttoned it neatly, straightened his hat and waved calmly at the passing vehicles.

•

He was still standing there as dusk began to fall. Headlamps swerved past him, their beams cutting across his face. Horns blared endlessly as the three lines of vehicles, tail lights flaring, moved towards the junction. The rush-hour was in full swing. As Maitland stood weakly by the roadside, waving with a feeble hand, it seemed to him that every vehicle in London had passed and re-passed him a dozen times, the drivers and passengers deliberately ignoring him in a vast spontaneous conspiracy. He was well aware that no one would stop for him, at least until the rush-hour was over at eight o'clock. Then, with luck, he might be able to attract the attention of a solitary driver.

Maitland lifted his watch into the glare of the passing headlamps. It was seven forty-five. His son would long since have reached home alone. Catherine would either have gone out or be making dinner for herself, assuming that he had decided to stay on in London with Helen Fairfax.

Thinking of Helen, ophthalmoscope in the breast pocket of her white coat, peering critically into the eyes of some small child at her clinic, Maitland looked down at the wound on his hand. He was now more tired and shaken than at any time since the crash. Even in the warm, exhaust-filled air he shivered irritably; he felt as if his entire nervous system was being scraped by invisible knives, his nerves drawn through their slings. His shirt clung to his chest like a wet apron. At the same time a cold euphoria was coming over him. He assumed that this light-headedness revealed the first symptoms of carbon monoxide poisoning. He waved at the cars lunging past him in the darkness, and tottered to and fro like a drunken man.

An articulated fuel tanker bore down on him along the outer lane, its yellow bulk almost filling the tunnel below the overpass. As it laboured around the bend the driver saw Maitland staggering between his headlamps. Air brakes hissed and slammed. Maitland side-stepped casually out of the tanker's way, took off his hat and tossed it under the massive rear wheels. Laughing to himself, Maitland watched it vanish.

'Hey . . . !' He gestured with his briefcase. 'My hat—you've got my hat . . . !'

Horns blared around him. A taxi pulled almost to a halt, the fender brushing Maitland's legs. Glaring down at Maitland, the driver tapped his forehead as he surged away. Maitland waved him on gallantly. He knew already that he was too exhausted to control himself. His one hope was that he might become so deranged that people would stop simply to prevent him from damaging their cars. He looked at the blood from his mouth on the back of his fingers, but flung the hand away and turned to the passing traffic. Gazing up at the maze of concrete causeways illuminated in the night air, he realized how much he loathed all these drivers and their vehicles.

'Stop . . . !'

He shook his blood-smeared fist at an elderly woman driver watching him suspiciously over her steering wheel.

'Yes, you . . . ! You can go! Take your damned car away! No—stop!'

He kicked a wooden trestle into the road, laughing as a passing truck knocked it back at him, jarring his left knee. He pushed out another.

His voice rose to a harsh shout above the traffic sounds, a bitter, primal scream.

'Catherine . . . ! Catherine . . . !'

With cold anger he shouted her name at the cars, screaming it like a child into the swerving headlamps. He lurched into the roadway again, blocking the outer lane and waving his briefcase like a demented race-track official. Surprisingly, the traffic responded to him, thinning out slightly. For the first time a gap appeared in the stream of vehicles, and he could see through the tunnel to the Westway interchange.

Across the road from him was the central reservation, a narrow island four feet wide with a maintenance walk between the crash barriers. Maitland leaned against a trestle, trying to rally all his powers of self-control. He was aware of half his mind revelling in this drunken tantrum, but with an effort mastered himself. If he could cross the road, he would then be able to walk back to the Westway interchange and find an emergency telephone.

He straightened himself, annoyed that he had wasted time. Clearing his head, he waited for a break in the traffic stream. A dozen cars moved towards him in procession, followed by a second group, an airline coach taking up the rear. A breakdown truck towing a damaged van roared past Maitland, blocking his vision as he leaned back in the darkness, watching the play of headlamps in the approaches to the tunnel.

The road was clear except for a two-decker car-transporter. The driver signalled to Maitland, as if prepared to offer him a lift. Maitland ignored him, waiting impatiently as the long stern section of the transporter lumbered by. The road was clear before the next set of approaching headlamps. Gripping the briefcase, he ran forward across the road.

He was halfway across the road when he heard the blare of a warning horn. Over his shoulder he saw the low hull of a white sportscar, almost invisible behind its unlit headlamps. Maitland stopped and turned back, but the skidding car was already on him, the young driver wrestling with the wheel as he lost control. Maitland felt the car rush through the air towards him. Before he could shout the car had plunged into a wooden trestle which Maitland had kicked into the road. The pinewood frame hurled against him. He felt his legs knocked away and was flung backwards through the dark air.

FROM

Geography III

1976

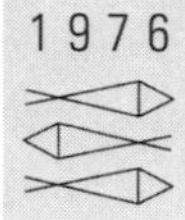

ONE ART

The art of losing isn't hard to master;
so many things seem filled with the intent
to be lost that their loss is no disaster.

Lose something every day. Accept the fluster
of lost door keys, the hour badly spent.
The art of losing isn't hard to master.

Then practice losing farther, losing faster:
places, and names, and where it was you meant
to travel. None of these will bring disaster.

I lost my mother's watch. And look! my last, or
next-to-last, of three loved houses went.
The art of losing isn't hard to master.

I lost two cities, lovely ones. And, vaster,
some realms I owned, two rivers, a continent.
I miss them, but it wasn't a disaster.

—Even losing you (the joking voice, a gesture
I love) I shan't have lied. It's evident
the art of losing's not too hard to master
though it may look like (*Write* it!) like disaster.

FROM

Sea Grapes

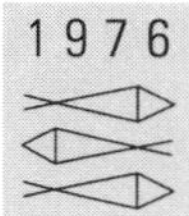

SEA GRAPES

That sail which leans on light,
tired of islands,
a schooner beating up the Caribbean

for home, could be Odysseus,
home-bound on the Aegean;
that father and husband's

longing, under gnarled sour grapes, is
like the adulterer hearing Nausicaa's name
in every gull's outcry.

This brings nobody peace. The ancient war
between obsession and responsibility
will never finish and has been the same

for the sea-wanderer or the one on shore
now wriggling on his sandals to walk home,
since Troy sighed its last flame,

and the blind giant's boulder heaved the trough
from whose groundswell the great hexameters come
to the conclusions of exhausted surf.

The classics can console. But not enough.

FRANK BIDART

FROM

The Book of the Body

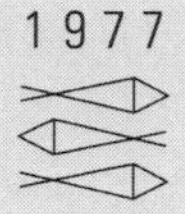

HAPPY BIRTHDAY

Thirty-three, goodbye—
the awe I feel

is not that you won't come again, or why—

or even that after
a time, we think of those who are dead

with a sweetness that cannot be explained—

but that I've read the trading-cards:
RALPH TEMPLE CYCLIST CHAMPION TRICK RIDER

WILLIE HARRADON CYCLIST
THE YOUTHFUL PHENOMENON

F. F. IVES CYCLIST
100 MILES 6 H. 25 MIN. 30 SEC.

—as the fragile metal of their
wheels stopped turning, as they

took on wives, children, accomplishments, all those
predilections which also insisted on ending,

they could not tell themselves from what they had done.

Terrible to dress in the clothes
of a period that must end.

They didn't plan it that way—
they didn't plan it that way.

CHRISTOPHER ISHERWOOD

FROM

My Guru and His Disciple

1980

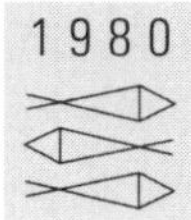

I can't remember now by what degrees and through whom I found out the facts about Prabhavananda's past life and background. This anyhow seems the right place to tell what is essential.

He was born on December 26, 1893, at Surmanagar, a village in Bengal near the town of Bankura, northwest of Calcutta. His name, during the first twenty years of his life, was Abanindra Nath Ghosh.

Abanindra's parents were normally devout Hindus. He accepted their religious beliefs, but he wasn't a deeply meditative or reclusive boy. He liked playing football and other games, and had plenty of friends.

However, by the time he was fourteen, he had read about Ramakrishna, the holy man already regarded by some as an avatar. Ramakrishna had been born in a village not very far away, and had spent his adult life at a temple just outside Calcutta. Abanindra had also read about Ramakrishna's chief disciples, Vivekananda and Brahmananda, who had founded the Ramakrishna Order of monks after Ramakrishna's death in 1886. He felt a mysterious power of attraction in their names.

Then one day, by seeming chance, Abanindra met Sarada Devi. She had been Ramakrishna's wife and was now regarded by his disciples as their spiritual mother—"Holy Mother," they called her. One of her attendants told Abanindra who she was; otherwise, he would have taken her for an ordinary countrywoman, sitting barefoot, without the slightest air of self-importance, outside a village inn. When he approached and bowed down to touch her feet in reverence, she said, "Son, haven't I seen you before?"

When Abanindra was eighteen and a student in Calcutta, he visited the Belur Math, the chief monastery of the Ramakrishna Order, which is beside the Ganges, on the outskirts of the city. He wanted to see the room in which Vivekananda used to stay; since his death in 1902, it had been maintained as a public shrine. When Abanindra left the Vivekananda Room, he found himself for the first time face to face with

Brahmananda. And Brahmananda said to him, "Haven't I seen you before?"

The effect of this encounter upon Abanindra was far too powerful and subtle to be described in a few words. I shall keep referring to it throughout this book. All I need say here is that Abanindra longed to meet Brahmananda again. So, a few months later, he impulsively spent the money he had been given for tuition fees on a ticket to Hardwar, because he knew that Brahmananda was visiting a monastery there. He arrived in the middle of the night, unannounced, but Brahmananda didn't seem at all surprised to see him. He allowed Abanindra to stay a month, accepted him formally as his disciple, and then sent him back to Calcutta to continue his education.

[· · ·]

What I have just written is misleading in one respect; it suggests that my relationship with Prabhavananda was now established and continuous. Well, in a sense, it was. I thought about him many times every day, taking it for granted that he would be available whenever I needed him. But the astonishing fact remains that, during the rest of the year and the spring and summer of 1940, I very seldom went to see him.

I will try to explain why.

•

Sometime in July 1939, Berthold Viertel, the poet and film director, had returned home from England via New York. I had first met him in 1933 in London, where we had worked together on the script of a film he was to direct (see *Christopher and His Kind*). We had become close friends.

Berthold, his wife, Salka, and their three sons had a house near the beach in Santa Monica Canyon. Though Berthold and Salka were both Jews from Central Europe, they couldn't exactly be called refugees, since they had settled in the United States several years before Hitler came into power. Both had worked for the Hollywood studios, Salka as an actress as well as a writer.

Berthold had now been commissioned to direct a film and wanted me to help him with the script. It was to be about a young German officer who becomes a Nazi and is later disillusioned; quite ordinary stuff for those days, but when Berthold began to improvise on it, it sounded thrilling—what stuff didn't? I agreed eagerly, although he warned me that there would be very little money in it for either of us—the producer was of the kind called "independent," a more ominous word then than now. (Indeed, the film was never made and ended in a lawsuit—which I had to settle out of my own pocket.)

Since 1933, refugees from Hitler's Reich had been arriving in Los Angeles. Salka, because of her connections at the studios and elsewhere, was able to find many of them work, especially the writers, actors, and musicians. Her home had become one of their favorite meeting places.

I myself belonged to this refugee world by adoption, having lived in it during my wanderings through various European countries, between 1933 and 1938. In those days, I had known a lot of its inhabitants, some intimately, and had been accepted by them almost as one of themselves, all the more so because I was traveling with an anti-Nazi German, Heinz. As far as an outsider could, I empathized with their self-mocking, witty despair and nearly sane paranoia.

These people were already dwelling in a future, a wartime, which very few native Californians could even imagine. To myself, as a European, the war atmosphere which the refugees breathed was more native than the ignorant peacefulness of the California air. They drew me into their midst by an overwhelming psychological suction. While I was with them, I actually worried less, because I felt that they were all sharing my worry with me. I took to spending more and more time in their depressing yet comforting company and became reluctant to leave it.

In September, a week or two after the outbreak of war in Europe, Vernon and I moved from the house we had been renting in Hollywood, into furnished rooms. These rooms were in Santa Monica Canyon, only a short walk from the Viertels but a long drive from where Chris Wood and Gerald Heard lived, and an even longer drive from the Vedanta Center.

•

Early in 1940, I got a job at M-G-M. This was chiefly thanks to the Viertels, who knew a producer there, Gottfried Reinhardt, one of Max Reinhardt's sons. We were to make a film out of James Hilton's novel *Rage in Heaven*. My fellow screenwriter was Robert Thoeren, an Austrian. So I remained within the refugee world even at the studio. Gottfried, Robert, and I often spoke German together when we were discussing the script.

Looked at from outside, my life could have been described as busy, successful, and social. I was earning five hundred dollars a week, low-bracket pay by movie standards, Arabian Nights wealth by mine. I wasn't inspired by my film work but I was fond of my fellow workers and enjoyed our parlor game of plot construction. In the evenings, at the Viertels' and elsewhere, I mingled with famous and fascinating people: Aldous and Maria Huxley (who had a house nearby), Garbo, Charlie Chaplin, Anita Loos, Thomas Mann and his family, Bertrand Russell.

And yet, deep down, I was miserable. I felt steeped in that dull brutish inertia which the Hindus call *tamas*, the lowest condition of the psyche. My misery expressed itself in various minor ailments. These were being treated by a doctor, whose large fees I could now easily afford.

The days go by and I don't see the Swami, don't start meditating. This isn't mere laziness. The opposition is enormously strong. Incredible as it seems, part of me actually wants to wallow in black lazy misery, like a pig in filth.

My diary adds that Vernon has finally caught my depression, "like a South Sea islander who nearly dies of a common cold imported by a trader."

March 6, 1940. I've seen the Swami. He says if I'm too busy to meditate I should think about the word Om, which is God. But I can only become aware of God by thinking all around him. Om says nothing. It's just a comic noise. I'm afraid the Swami is altogether too Indian for me. I must talk to Gerald again.

The Sanskrit word *Om* is used by Hindus as the basic name of God, because it is thought of as being the most comprehensive of all human sounds. Fully pronounced, it combines utterance by the throat, the mouth, and the lips—approximately *Ah-oo-mm*. This I already knew. But there were moods in which my anti-Hindu prejudice made me rhyme *Om* with *Tom*, thus turning it into "just a comic noise"—as in om-tiddly-om-pom.

•

In July, I went at least twice to a class Prabhavananda was giving on the Upanishads (those portions of the Vedas which contain the teachings of Vedanta philosophy; the rest contain prayers, hymns, rules of conduct, and instructions for the performance of rituals).

Seated on a cushion, he smilingly exposed the ignorance of his class. He is gentle, persuasive, and humorous. He speaks quietly, with an absolute, matter-of-fact authority. To him, spiritual truths are unanswerable facts, like the facts of geography. You don't have to get excited about them, or argue or defend. You just state them . . . I notice that he has a taste for very elegant, pointed shoes.

Someone mentioned the Holy Ghost. The Swami was asked to explain It, and said that he couldn't, he wasn't a Christian. So everybody present had a try, and the difference in our definitions was a sufficient comment on the muddle of Christian theology. To every suggestion, the Swami replied, "No—that is too far-fetch-ed." At last he sent one of the girls out for Webster's Dictionary. Some of the class were quite scandalized. "You won't find it there," they told him. But the Swami was confident: "Webster's Dictionary can tell you everything." He was wrong, however. Webster said only: "Comforter, Paraclete." The Swami promised to "ask Mr. Hard." He seems to have great confidence in Gerald.

On July 29, I got further instructions from Prabhavananda. He told me to meditate on the *Atman*, the indwelling God, "this thing" within each one of us: "Imagine that there is a cavity within you. In the middle of this cavity there is a throne, in the form of a red lotus. In the middle of this lotus, a golden light is burning. Approach this light and say 'Oh Self, reveal Yourself to me.' "

My comment on this was:

My imagination revolts from this: it sounds like a stage scene at the Radio City Music Hall. But I shall try to do it. I have put myself into the Swami's hands and I must follow his instructions, just as I follow Dr. K.'s. We always want to choose our own medicine. A rose, for example, wouldn't seem nearly so silly to me. But perhaps the lotus is better, just because I don't like it.

"The Swami is too Indian for me" was a complaint I would return to, again and again. But, even while persisting in my prejudice, I had to admit to myself that the very Indianness of Vedanta was helpful to me. Because of my other, anti-Christian set of prejudices, I was repelled by the English religious words I had been taught in childhood and was grateful to Vedanta for speaking Sanskrit. I needed a brand-new vocabulary and here it was, with a set of philosophical terms which were exact in meaning, unemotive, untainted by disgusting old associations with clergymen's sermons, schoolmasters' pep talks, politicians' patriotic speeches.

•

I had now met Aldous Huxley many times—usually with Maria, but occasionally by himself at M-G-M, while we were both working there. (*He* was earning fifteen hundred dollars a week, and sending most of it to help relatives and friends in wartime Europe.) I already felt at ease with Maria, who was charmingly outspoken; she asked me frank questions about my personal life, which I answered with equal frankness. When the three of us were together, we behaved like intimate friends. When Aldous and I were alone, I felt uneasy because I was aware—indeed, it was Gerald who had made me aware—that Aldous, with all his liberalism, found homosexuality and the homosexual temperament deeply distasteful. I am sure that he liked me personally and that he fought against his prejudice. He was a nobly fair-minded man. Nevertheless, my uneasiness remained.

That Aldous and I were both officially disciples of Prabhavananda didn't strengthen the bond between us, as far as I was concerned. I was beginning to realize that Aldous and Prabhavananda were temperamentally far apart. Prabhavananda was strongly devotional. Aldous was much more akin to his friend Krishnamurti, who was then living at Ojai, a couple of hours' drive from Los Angeles. Krishnamurti expounded a philosophy of discrimination between the real and the unreal; as a Hindu who had broken away from Hinduism, he was repelled by devotional religion and its rituals. He also greatly disapproved of the guru-disciple relationship.

According to my diary (July 31), I must have told Aldous at least something about Prabhavananda's latest instructions to me, thus prompting Aldous to tell me that Krishnamurti never meditated on "objects"—such as lotuses, lights, gods, and goddesses—and even believed that doing so might lead to insanity.

This conversation disturbed me very much. Suppose Gerald is barking up the wrong tree? But I'm also aware that these doubts are not quite candid; they are being prompted by the Ego as part of its sabotage effort.

My indiscretion in talking to Aldous about Prabhavananda's instructions was inexcusable. Indeed, it was worse than an indiscretion, since I must have known in advance that Aldous would be critical, and would thus disturb me and strengthen my doubts.

•

The refugees weren't the only ones who drew me into their midst and away from Prabhavananda. There was also an assortment of men and women whom I will call "Seekers," because many of them would have so described themselves. I met them through Gerald, who had now become a central figure in their circles, not only in Los Angeles, but throughout the country. Chris Wood protected him from the Seekers' phone calls by refusing to take messages for him, but his mail was enormous and urgent. "It's funny," I once said to him, "how these people invariably write to you airmail special delivery, when all their questions are about eternity."

Some of the Seekers had unquestionable integrity and courage—even perhaps saintliness: a man who had become a clergyman because he had had a vision of Christ when he was fighting in World War I, a Japanese who had been persecuted by his countrymen for his pacifism, an ex-burglar who had practiced mental non-violence while being beaten up by prison guards. As for the rest, many might have been called cranks but almost none of them fakes. I couldn't imagine any of them as disciples of Prabhavananda—some because they were too exclusively Christian, others because they put the need for social action before spiritual training, others because they were entangled in the occult, others because they were trying to use what they called religion to heal sickness, promote longevity, ensure success in business and joy in marriage—all this with perfect confidence in the purity of their motives.

What was I looking for, amidst these people? What made me sit through their lectures and join them in hours of earnest discussion? I might have answered truthfully that I was interested in some of them as practitioners of pacifism. I could have claimed that the rest were at least teaching me tolerance: during my pre-California life I wouldn't have been seen dead with them. Their earnest air of dedication, their gently persuasive voices, and their pious vocabulary would have turned my atheistic stomach.

But I had to admit to a deeper motive. I was associating with the Seekers in order to find weaknesses in their faith and contradictions in their creeds; to prove to myself, if possible, that they were seeking a non-existent treasure. If their treasure was non-existent, then Prabhavananda's might be, too.

Thus I kept rediscovering in myself an active underground force of opposition to Prabhavananda's way of life—insofar as it threatened to influence mine. In my diary, I called this force my ego—what I actually meant was my self-will. "Nothing burns in Hell except self-will" was a favorite quotation of Gerald's, from the *Theologia Germanica*, XXXIV.

Speaking of hell, I am thankful that I at least had the good sense not to personify my self-will as the Devil and imagine myself to be the prey of an awesomely malign superpower, whose strength I couldn't be expected to resist. What I was struggling with was something quite intimate and unalarming, something that had an animal, not a superhuman nature; something that was partly a monkey, partly a dog, partly a peacock, partly a pig. One must be firm with it, one must keep an eye on it always, but there was no reason to hate it or be afraid of it. Its plans for my future weren't devilish, they weren't even clever. It merely wanted to maintain the usual messy aimless impulse-driven way of life to which it was accustomed. It would actually rather wallow in "lazy black misery" than be interfered with by Prabhavananda.

FROM

The Morning of the Poem

1980

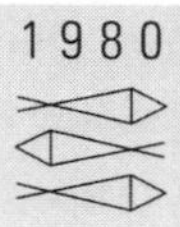

SONG

The light lies layered in the leaves.
Trees, and trees, more trees.
A cloud boy brings the evening paper:
The Evening Sun. It sets.
Not sharply or at once
a stately progress down the sky
(it's gilt and pink and faintly green)
above, beyond, behind the evening leaves
of trees. Traffic sounds and
bells resound in silver clangs
the hour, a tune, my friend
Pierrot. The violet hour:
the grass is violent green.
A weeping beech is gray,
a copper beech is copper red.
Tennis nets hang
unused in unused stillness.
A car starts up and
whispers into what will soon be night.
A tennis ball is served.
A horsefly vanishes.
A smoking cigarette.
A day (so many and so few)
dies down a hardened sky
and leaves are lap-held notebook leaves
discriminated barely
in light no longer layered.

MARILYNNE ROBINSON

FROM

Housekeeping

1980

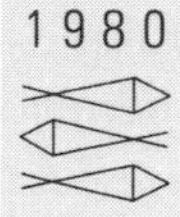

I walked after Sylvie [the narrator Ruth's aunt] down the shore, all at peace, and at ease, and I thought, We are the same. She could as well be my mother. I crouched and slept in her very shape like an unborn child.

"Wait here," Sylvie said when we came to the shore. She walked down to a place where trees grew near the water. After a few minutes she came back. "The boat is not where I left it!" she said. "Well, we'll have to look for it. I'll find it. Sometimes it takes a while, but I always find it." She climbed up onto a rock that stood out from the hillside, almost to the water, and looked up and down the shore. "I'll bet it's over there." She climbed down from the rock and began walking south. "See those trees? I found it once before, in a place just like that, all covered with branches."

"Someone was trying to hide it," I suggested.

"Can you imagine? I always put it right back where I find it. I don't care if someone else uses it. You know, so long as they don't damage it."

We walked down to where a stand of birch and aspen trees sheltered a little inlet. "This would be a perfect place for it," Sylvie said, but it was not there. "Don't be discouraged," she said. "We're so early. No one could have got to it first. Wait." She walked up into the woods. Behind a fallen log, and behind a clump of fat, low-growing pines, was a heap of pine boughs with poplar branches and brown needles and leaves. Here and there an edge or a corner of tarpaulin showed. "Look at that," Sylvie said. "Someone went to a lot of trouble." She kicked away the branches until on one side the tarpaulin and the shape of the rowboat were exposed. Then she lifted the side of the boat until it fell over upright on the heap of branches. She pulled at the tarpaulin that had been spread under the boat until she found the oars. She stuck them under the seat. The boat made a thick, warm sound as we pushed it through the pine needles. It scraped dully across some big rocks, then dragged through the sand. We pushed it into the water. "Get in," Sylvie said. "Hurry." I climbed in and sat down on a narrow, splintery plank, facing the shore. "There's a man yelling at us," I said.

"Oh, I know!" Sylvie pushed the boat out in two long strides, and then, with a hand on each gunwale, half leaped and half pulled herself into it. The boat wallowed alarmingly. "I have to sit in that seat," she said. She stood up and turned around and stooped to hold the gunwales, and I crawled under her body and out between her legs. A stone splashed the water inches from my face, and another rattled into the bottom of the boat. Sylvie swung an oar over my head, settled it into the lock, crouched, and pulled us strongly away from the shore. A stone flew past my arm. I looked back and saw a burly man in knee boots and black pants and a red plaid jacket. I could see that he was wearing one of those shapeless felt hats that fishermen there decorate with preposterous small gleams and plumes and violent hooks. His voice was full of rage. "Just ignore him," Sylvie said. She pulled again, and we were beyond reach. The man had followed us into the water until he was up to his boot tops in it. "Lady!" he bawled. "Ignore him," Sylvie said. "He always acts like that. If he thinks someone's watching him, he just carries on more."

I turned around and watched Sylvie. Her handling of the boat was strong and easy. When we were about one hundred yards from the shore she turned the boat toward the north. The man, now back on the beach, was still yelling and dancing his wrath and pitching stones after us. "It's pitiful," Sylvie said. "He's going to have a heart attack someday."

"It must be his boat," I suggested.

Sylvie shrugged. "Or he might just be some sort of lunatic," she said. "I'm certainly not going to go back and find out." She was unperturbed by our bare escape and by her drenched loafers and the soggy skirts of her coat. I found myself wondering if this was why she came home with fish in her pockets.

"Aren't you cold, Sylvie?"

"The sun's coming up," she said. The sky above Fingerbone was a floral yellow. A few spindled clouds smoldered and glowed a most unfiery pink. And then the sun flung a long shaft over the mountain, and another, like a long-legged insect bracing itself out of its chrysalis, and then it showed above the black crest, bristly and red and improbable. In an hour it would be the ordinary sun, spreading modest and impersonal light on an ordinary world, and that thought relieved me. Sylvie continued to pull, strongly and slowly.

"You wouldn't believe how many people live out here on the islands and up in the hills," Sylvie said. "I bet there are a hundred. Or more. Sometimes you'll see a little smoke in the woods. There might be a cabin there with ten children in it."

"They just hunt and fish?"

"Mostly."

"Have you ever seen any of them?"

"I think I have," Sylvie said. "Sometimes if I think I see smoke I go walking toward it, and now and then I'm sure there are children around me. I can practically hear them."

"Oh."

"That's one reason I keep crackers in my pockets."

"I see."

Sylvie rowed on through the gilded water, smiling to herself.

"I'll tell you something. You'll probably think I'm crazy. I tried to catch one once." She laughed. "Not, you know, trap it, but lure it out with marshmallows so I could see it. What would I do with another child?"

"So you did see someone."

"I just stuck marshmallows on the twigs of one of the apple trees, almost every day for a couple of weeks. Then I sat sort of out of sight—there's still a doorstep there with lilacs growing on both sides of it. The house itself fell into the cellar hole years ago, of course. I just sat there and waited, but it never came. I was a little bit relieved," she said. "A child like that might claw or bite. But I did want to look at it."

"This was at the place we're going to now."

Sylvie smiled and nodded. "Now you're in on my secret. Maybe you'll have better luck. And at least we don't have to hurry. It was so hard to get home in time for you and Lucille."

Sylvie pulled and then pulled, and we slid heavily through the slosh and jostle of the water. Sylvie looked at the sky and said no more. I peered over the side now and then, into the murky transparencies of the upper waters, which were clouded and crude as agate. I saw gulls' feathers and the black shapes of fish. The fragmented image of jonquil sky spilled from top to top of the rounding waves as the shine spills on silk, and gulls sailed up into the very height of the sky, still stark white when they could just be seen. To the east the mountains were eclipsed. To the west they stood in balmy light. Dawn and its excesses always reminded me of heaven, a place where I have always known I would not be comfortable. They reminded me of my grandfather's paintings, which I have always taken to be his vision of heaven. And it was he who brought us here, to this bitter, moon-pulled lake, trailing us after him unborn, like the infants he had painted on the dresser drawers, whose garments swam in some ethereal current, perhaps the rim of the vortex that would drag them down out of that enameled sky, stripped and screaming. Sylvie's oars set off vortices. She swamped some leaves and spun a feather on its curl. The current that made us sidle a little toward the center of the lake was the draw of the river, and no vortex, though my grandfather's last migration had settled him on the lake floor. It seemed that Sylvie's boat slipped down the west side of every wave. We would make a circle, and never reach a shore at all, if there were a vortex, I thought, and we would be drawn down into the darker world, where other sounds would pour into our ears until we seemed to find songs in them, and the sight of water would invade our eyes, and the taste of water would invade our bowels and unstring our bones, and we would know the seasons and customs of the place as if there were no others. Imagine my grandfather reclined how many years in his Pullman berth, regarding the morning through a small blue window. He might see us and think he was dreaming again of flushed but weightless spirits in a painted sky, buoyant in an impalpable element. And when our shadow had passed he might see the daylit moon, a jawless, socketed shard, and take it for his image in the glass. Of course he was miles away, miles south, at the foot of the bridge.

At last she pulled us toward a broad point that lay out into the lake. I could see that the mountain standing behind and against the one from which the point extended had a broken side. Stone showed pink as a scar on a dog's ear. "You can see where it is from here," Sylvie said. "They built right beside those cliffs." She brought us up against the shore and we climbed out of the boat and dragged it up on the beach. I followed Sylvie inland along the side of the point.

The mountains that walled the valley were too close, the one upon the other. The rampages of glaciers in their eons of slow violence had left the landscape in a great disorder. Out from the cleft or valley the mountains made spilled a lap of spongy earth, overgrown with brush. We walked up it along the deep, pebbly bed left by the run-off and the rain, and there we came upon the place Sylvie had told me about, stunted orchard and lilacs and stone doorstep and fallen house, all white with a brine of frost. Sylvie smiled at me. "Pretty, isn't it?"

"It's pretty, but I don't know how anyone could have wanted to *live* here."

"It's really pretty in the sunlight. You'll see in a little while."

"Well, let's not wait here, though. It's too cold."

Sylvie glanced at me, a little surprised. "But you'll want to watch for the children."

"Yes. All right."

"Well, I think you better just stay in one place and be very quiet."

"Yes, but it's too cold here."

Sylvie shrugged. "It's still early." We walked back down to the shore, and found some rocks against which we could sit, out of the wind, facing the sun. Sylvie crossed her ankles and folded her arms. She appeared to fall asleep.

After a while I said, "Sylvie?"

She smiled. "Shhh."

"Where's our lunch?"

"Still in the boat. You're probably right. It would be good if they saw you eating."

I found a bag of marshmallows among the odds and ends that Sylvie had bundled into a checkered tablecloth and brought along for lunch —a black banana, a lump of salami with a knife through it, a single yellow chicken wing like an elegant, small gesture of defeat, the bottom fifth of a bag of potato chips. I ripped the cellophane and took out marshmallows to fill my pockets. Then I sat down by Sylvie and made a small fire of driftwood and skewered one through its soft belly with a stick and held it in the flame until it caught fire. I let it burn until it was as black as a lump of coal, then I pulled off the weightless husk with my fingers and ate it, and held the creamy part that still clung to the stick in the flame until it caught fire; and so the morning passed.

Sylvie stood up and stretched, and nodded at the sun, which was a small, white, wintery sun and stood askant the zenith although it was surely noon. "We can go up there now," she said. I followed her up into the valley again and found it much changed. It was as if the light had coaxed a flowering from the frost, which before seemed barren and parched as salt. The grass shone with petal colors, and water drops spilled from all the trees as innumerably as petals. "I told you it was nice," Sylvie said.

Imagine a Carthage sown with salt, and all the sowers gone, and the seeds lain however long in the earth, till there rose finally in vegetable profusion leaves and trees of rime and brine. What flowering would there be in such a garden? Light would force each salt calyx to open in prisms, and to fruit heavily with bright globes of water—peaches and grapes are little more than that, and where the world was salt there would be greater need of slaking. For need can blossom into all the compensations it requires. To crave and to have are as like as a thing and its shadow. For when does a berry break upon the tongue as sweetly as when one longs to taste it, and when is the taste refracted into so many hues and savors of ripeness and earth, and when do our senses know any thing so utterly as when we lack it? And here again is a foreshadowing—the world will be made whole. For to wish for a hand on one's hair is all but to feel it. So whatever we may lose, very craving gives it back to us again. Though we dream and hardly know it, longing, like an angel, fosters us, smooths our hair, and brings us wild strawberries.

Sylvie was gone. She had left without a word, or a sound. I thought she must be teasing, perhaps watching me from the woods. I pretended not to know I was alone. I could see why Sylvie thought children might come here. Any child who saw once how the gleaming water spilled to the tips of branches, and rounded and dropped and pocked the softening shadows of frost at the foot of each tree, would come to see it again.

If there had been snow I would have made a statue, a woman to stand along the path, among the trees. The children would have come close, to look at her. Lot's wife was salt and barren, because she was full of loss and mourning, and looked back. But here rare flowers would gleam in her hair, and on her breast, and in her hands, and there would be children all around her, to love and marvel at her for her beauty, and to laugh at her extravagant adornments, as if they had set the flowers in her hair and thrown down all the flowers at her feet, and they would forgive her, eagerly and lavishly, for turning away, though she never asked to be forgiven. Though her hands were ice and did not touch them, she would be more than mother to them, she so calm, so still, and they such wild and orphan things.

•

I walked out of the valley and down the little apron of earth at its entrance. The shore was empty and, after its manner, silent. Sylvie must be up at the point, I thought. I imagined her hiding the boat more securely. That would be a reasonable precaution for her to take, convinced as she was that these woods were peopled. I sat on a log and whistled and tossed stones at the toe of my shoe. I knew why Sylvie felt there were children in the woods. I felt so, too, though I did not think so. I sat on the log pelting my shoe, because I knew that if I turned however quickly to look behind me the consciousness behind me would not still be there, and would only come closer when I turned away again. Even if it spoke just at my ear, as it seemed often at the point of doing, when I turned there would be nothing there. In that way it was persistent and teasing and ungentle, the way half-wild, lonely children are. This was something Lucille and I together would ignore, and I had been avoiding the shore all that fall, because when I was by myself and obviously lonely, too, the teasing would be much more difficult to disregard. Having a sister or a friend is like sitting at night in a lighted house. Those outside can watch you if they want, but you need not see them. You simply say, "Here are the perimeters of our attention. If you prowl around under the windows till the crickets go silent, we will pull the shades. If you wish us to suffer your envious curiosity, you must permit us not to notice it." Anyone with one solid human bond is that smug, and it is the smugness as much as the comfort and safety that lonely people covet and admire. I had been, so to speak, turned out of house now long enough to have observed this in myself. Now there was neither threshold nor sill between me and these cold, solitary children who almost breathed against my cheek and almost touched my hair. I decided to go back up and wait for Sylvie by the cellar hole, where she could not help but find me.

FROM

A Part of Speech

1980

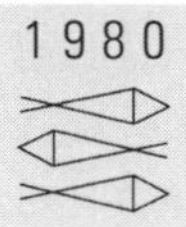

ODYSSEUS TO TELEMACHUS

[*Translated by George L. Kline*]

My dear Telemachus,
                                        The Trojan War
is over now; I don't recall who won it.
The Greeks, no doubt, for only they would leave
so many dead so far from their own homeland.
But still, my homeward way has proved too long.
While we were wasting time there, old Poseidon,
it almost seems, stretched and extended space.

I don't know where I am or what this place
can be. It would appear some filthy island,
with bushes, buildings, and great grunting pigs.
A garden choked with weeds; some queen or other.
Grass and huge stones . . . Telemachus, my son!
To a wanderer the faces of all islands
resemble one another. And the mind
trips, numbering waves; eyes, sore from sea horizons,
run; and the flesh of water stuffs the ears.
I can't remember how the war came out;
even how old you are—I can't remember.

Grow up, then, my Telemachus, grow strong.
Only the gods know if we'll see each other
again. You've long since ceased to be that babe
before whom I reined in the plowing bullocks.
Had it not been for Palamedes' trick
we two would still be living in one household.
But maybe he was right; away from me
you are quite safe from all Oedipal passions,
and your dreams, my Telemachus, are blameless.

CZESLAW MILOSZ

FROM

The Issa Valley

[*Translated by Louis Iribarne*]

1981

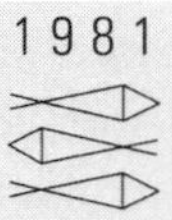

Whenever Thomas went into the library, he had to put on his little sheepskin against the cold; the room was never heated and his hands turned blue as he leafed through the sheets of parchment in the hope of finding something on plants or animals. Often, he grabbed a couple of volumes and took refuge in a warmer part of the house. One of the tomes abducted in this manner bore a title whose contorted, snakelike letters he had difficulty deciphering: "On the Office of Swordbearing . . ." Unable to cope with the rest, he went to his grandfather for an explanation of the contents. His grandfather—but not before putting on his pince-nez—read the title aloud: *The doctrines of the Church of Our Lord Jesus Christ/ being in Lithuania/ briefly summarized/ according to Holy Scripture. The defense of said office against all its adversaries having been written by Simon Budny. On the question of what is clearly prescribed by Holy Scripture/ that a Christian may own subjects, both freemen and slaves/ so long as they be treated in a God-fearing manner. This being the 1583d year A.D.*

Tapping the leather pince-nez case against the volume's musty cover, his grandfather began turning the pages. After a while he cleared his throat. "This is not a Catholic book. You see, Thomas, long, long ago there lived a man named Hieronymous Surkont. This book was his; he was a Calvinist."

Thomas knew that the word Calvinist connoted something bad, that it was even a derogatory term. But they, those infidels, who didn't go to a church but to a *Kirche*, belonged to the far-off world of cities, railroads, and machines. Protestants? Here in Gine? He regarded it as an honor to have been initiated into such a shameful secret.

"A heretic?"

Grandfather's fingers slipped the pince-nez back into its case. He looked out the window and stared at the snow. "Hm? Yes, yes, a heretic . . ."

"And this Hieronymous Surkont used to live here?"

Grandfather suddenly perked up. "Did he live here? Probably, but we know very little about him. He spent most of his time in Kedainiai, at the court of Prince Radziwiłł. That's where the Calvinists had their parish and school."

Thomas sensed some reticence on his grandfather's part, some resistance, the sort of deliberate ambiguity the grownups used when they spoke of certain family members in hushed voices, falling silent the moment anyone entered the room. The faces of these outcasts, impossible to visualize, disappeared into the dark background as in some faded photograph, with not a trace of a brow or facial blemish left behind as a reminder. Whatever sins they had committed—grave enough to bring shame to their descendants—the age in which they lived, the degree of kinship dissolved into whispers or mild reproaches directed at the intruder. But this time it was different.

"There is a German side to the Surkont family. They are all descendants of Hieronymous. Nearly three hundred years ago, in 1655, the Swedes invaded our land. Hieronymous went over to the side of the Swedish king, Karl Gustav."

"Then he was a traitor?"

Grandfather liked to pinch the end of his purple-veined nose, puff his nostrils, then suddenly let go, producing a *pff-pff* sound.

"That he was"—*pff-pff*—"but if he'd fought against the Swedes, he would have betrayed the Prince he served. Either way, he would have been a traitor."

Thomas frowned as he contemplated the complexities of the dilemma. "So it was Prince Radziwiłł's fault," he declared at last.

"Now *there* was an ambitious man," said his grandfather. "He thought that once Karl Gustav made him a Grand Duke he would no longer be a vassal of the Polish king. As ruler of Lithuania, he could then force everyone to convert."

"And if he had," said Thomas, "we would all be Calvinists, right?"

"Probably." He scrutinized his grandson's face, grinning in a way that suggested he saw through the boy's questions, to the awareness gradually taking hold: Why are we what we are? Who or what decides? What would he have become if he were someone else? "But Hieronymous Surkont wasn't exactly a Calvinist. He was a Socinian, another—uh—species of those who refused to recognize the Pope."

And he began telling him of the Socinians, or Arians, as they were also called, and of the new set of doctrines they had propagated—doctrines prohibiting, among other things, the holding of public office, whether that of voivode, judge, or soldier, a practice expressly condemned by Christ; and the ownership of serfs. This last point had been a cause of much dissension, many arguing that the Bible sanctioned it —this being the position of the book he had taken from the library. As for Hieronymous, following the expulsion of the Swedes he left the country, never to return, eventually settling in Prussia, somewhere around Königsberg.

Thus was the seed sown, and his grandfather had no way of knowing how long it would be nurtured in the vegetable sleep of seeds that patiently bide their time. The seed was sown: in it were contained the squeaking of wooden boards, the sound of footsteps slipping along bookshelves and numbered folios that glow among dark rows of leather bindings; elbows propped on the table in a ring of light cast by a green shade; a pencil bobbing up and down in mimicry of thought, which in the beginning is nothing but a haze, a blur without shape or outline . . . No one lives alone; he is speaking with those who are no more, their lives are incarnated in him; he is retracing their footsteps, climbing the stairs to the edifice of history. Their hopes and defeats, the signs left behind, be it a single letter carved in stone—here is the way to peace, to mitigating the judgments he imposed on himself. Happiness is given to those who have the gift. Never and nowhere will they feel alone, as they are comforted by the memory of all who have struggled, like themselves, for something unattainable. Whether or not Thomas was rewarded, such moments as those spent in the company of his grandfather abided with him, anticipating an age when voices muted by time would become precious.

•

It took the Spaniard Michael Servetus more than two hours to die. It took so long because not enough wood had been piled, and through the flames he chastised the city of Geneva for its frugality. "Poor me, I can't even die a proper death! Surely the two hundred ducats and the gold chain they confiscated should have bought enough wood to burn me alive!"*

Meanwhile, Calvin had sat unbendingly in his chair, reading the Bible in the penumbra of his room, while his vicar, Guillaume Farel, his eyes smarting from the smoke, had shouted up at the burning heretic: "Believe in Jesus Christ, the everlasting Son of God!"

Such was the fate of Michael Servetus, after his having hidden

* A record of Servetus's last days, based on no longer extant sources, is given by Wiszowaty. See Stanislaw Kot's "L'influence de Michel Servet sur le mouvement antitrinitarien en Pologne et en Transylvanie," in the collection *Autour de Michel Servet et de Sébastien Castellion* (Alphen aan den Rijn, The Netherlands: H. D. Tjeenk Willink, 1953).

among the papists in France for twenty years—a fate willed by the very man with whom he had secretly exchanged letters and in whom he had sought refuge. But Servetus had an indomitable spirit, the tongue in his charred mouth still stirred, and his weak voice could yet testify to the sacrilegious truth: "I believe that Christ was the true Son of God, but not that he was everlasting."

He was survived by a rumor that spread from country to country, that caused goose quills to scratch in Basel, Tübingen, Wittenberg, Strasbourg, and Cracow as they went about copying theses secretly obtained from friends attacking the Trinity. When copies of Servetus's banned writings were discovered on some Polish students in Tübingen, the Prince sneered: "*Schwärmerei!*"; the university trembled and tried to hush up the whole affair. Servetus's name was never mentioned, and even Petrus Gonesius, now returned from Padua to propagate the new doctrine among the Protestant sects in Poland and Lithuania, was careful not to utter his master's name in public. But Melanchthon wasn't fooled. "I have been reading the work of a Lithuanian who means to summon Servetus from hell," he wrote. In Transylvania and Moravia, meanwhile, Jacob Paleologus was composing his great work *Contra Calvinum pro Serveto*—quite clearly written in defense of the Spaniard. But the chest containing his manuscripts was sealed by the hand of the Holy Inquisition, following his arrest and journey to Rome, where he died a martyr's death.

In the writing of any chronicle, people and events are re-created from certain minor details. Now, it would be dishonest to say that Hieronymous Surkont was a short or tall man, dark-haired or fair, when not the slightest physical description of him, not even the dates of his birth and death, has survived. This much was certain: that Rome was for him the seat of the Antichrist; that as he rode horseback in his elkskin jacket along the road skirting the Issa, he had contemplated with sadness this people incapable of embracing the true faith. For theirs was a fake Christianity aptly fitting popish superstitions: after singing hymns in church, the women ran and offered sacrifice to snakes, convinced that if they didn't their men would not be up to fulfilling their conjugal duties. Fables took the place of Holy Scripture, fables about a god of water and a god of wind who shook the world. And pagan rites, such as those observed when hunters assembled before the hunt. And furtive meetings under the oaks.

An inquisitive man, driven by what must have been a powerful thirst for knowledge, he had probably sought out those like himself, finding them in Kedainiai. He must have studied diligently to have felt an equal in those disputes held by candlelight, supporting his arguments with quotations from the Bible: "Your reasoning, my good sir, is fallacious, more properly deserving of the name of sophistry, because that passage in Hebrew can be interpreted otherwise." Or: "Fellow brother, is not the intent clearly evident in the Greek and Latin commentaries?" This was at a time when the Trinitarians, still loyal to Calvin, and the ditheists, and even those who, following the example of Simon Budny, refused to worship Christ, still tolerated one another, thanks to the moderating influence of Radziwiłł, who, even though he took as his model the Church of Geneva, refrained from banning theological disputes and was even inclined toward novelties. Not a few Arians from Poland had found a haven on his estate, though, to be sure, at the price of exercising a certain caution.

Was Hieronymous Surkont submerged; that is, was he baptized as an adult, in the manner prescribed by the Brethren, who were strictly opposed to the baptism of infants? No telling, though it is known that he ceased to be a Trinitarian, remaining loyal to the memory of Servetus, nearly a hundred years after that martyr's death. That the three-headed Cerberus substituted for the One God was a heinous insult to reason he took as self-evident. He embraced the revolutionary thesis that God was one, as was Holy Scripture, which was clear and unequivocal and did not require any official exegesis; one had only to read the Gospels, to return to the age of the Apostles, to traverse centuries during which Scholasticism had sought to obscure the simple words of the prophets and of Christ. Calvin had gone only halfway, killing Servetus in fear of the truth. Whoever failed to destroy Cerberus would never be entirely free of all the hocus-pocus, indulgences, Masses for the dead, pleas for the intercession of the saints, and all other things of a magical nature.

One can infer, from the scarcity of facts available, that in that religious controversy which for many decades divided the Brethren, Hieronymous Surkont leaned in favor of the legacy bequeathed by Petrus Gonesius. Placing all hope in Jesus Christ for the salvation of his soul ("I am a vile worm in the eyes of my Lord," Thomas deciphered in one of his books), he would have argued that Christ did not share in God's divinity; that the Logos, the invisible and immortal Word, became flesh in the Virgin's womb; in other words, that Christ was conceived of the Logos. He had embraced Christ's humanity with awe, gratitude, and joy, but not like the nonworshippers, who did not distinguish between Jeremiah, Isaiah, and Jesus, and who were more apt to invoke the Old Testament than the New.

But what of his thoughts on Gonesius's *De primatu Ecclesiae Christianae*, which he surely must have studied, and on the works of his disciples? Hieronymous Surkont could hardly have dismissed their arguments in the practical realm, arguments that had long reverberated in the synods of Lithuania. Their demands, after all, were given credence by the Gospels. For was it not written: "And unto him that smiteth thee on one cheek offer also the other; and him that taketh away thy cloak forbid not to take thy coat also." Was it not written: "Jesus said unto him, Follow me; and let the dead bury their dead." Was it not written: "And every one that heareth these sayings of mine, and doeth them not, shall be likened unto a foolish man, which built his house upon the sand: And the rain descended, and the floods came, and the winds blew, and beat upon that house; and it fell: and great was the fall of it." Jews, Greeks, slaves, and masters are equal; all are brothers. A Christian does not shed blood, but divests himself of the sword. He frees his serfs from bondage, sells his earthly goods, and distributes his wealth among the poor. Only thus does he become worthy of salvation; only thus does he distinguish himself from the hypocrites, whose actions give the lie to their words.

The period in question came after the synods of Lithuania had rejected these uncompromising demands, giving rise to bitter dissension among the Brethren. Surkont had set out to refute their arguments with the aid of the Old Testament, as well as with examples taken from his own experience. Granted, the serfs had endured great poverty and oppression—but free them from bondage? That would have been to invite paganism, barbarism, and banditry. Look what happened during the emancipation under Rekut, starosty of Samogitia: the serfs took cover in the forests, emerging only to murder and maraud. Then, too, there was the example of their own peasant rebellion with its revival of the old gods, serving notice on the landowners inhabiting the Issa Valley. Unbelt one's sword? The disciples of Gonesius had chosen a bad time to propose so drastic a measure: to the east, beyond the Dnieper, the wars with Ivan the Terrible were still going on unabated. Outvoted in the synods, they never recovered from their defeat.

Then came Karl Gustav of Sweden, brandishing the sword on behalf of an Imperium for Protestants. And Hieronymous Surkont? Did he suffer moments of vacillation? Of indecision? His Prince had painted a powerful vision of Lithuanians living under the protection of a Swedish king; stripping the papists of both land and serfs, they were to become bearers of light to the east and to the south, all the way to the Ukraine, wherever the black robes, their mouths full of holy Byzantium but not knowing a word of Greek themselves, had succeeded in keeping the people in ignorance. They had no choice: they were being threatened by a Jesuit invasion—the Jesuits, with their cunning methods of seduction, their theaters, schools, every year luring more and more of the faithful away; the desecration of temples, funeral processions being attacked by student mobs . . . Before long, nothing would be left of the Reformed Church in Lithuania. The Prince had played his last card, obedient to his vocation as protector of the faith. And to another ambition, off in the distance: the crown. And, who knows, even visions of Swedish, Lithuanian, and Polish armies standing at the gates of Moscow.

One suspects that he was driven not only by his loyalty to the Prince but also by his contempt for the blusterous nobility, roused by the priests to a holy war against the heretics. Never applying cold reason, never opening the Bible, guided only by blind, elemental instinct.

Faithful to the end. And the horror of it all: the initial reverses, the vacillation of even the most fervent believers, a fratricidal war, a country laid waste, the sinister indifference of allies . . . Death came to the Prince as the papists stormed the fortress, the last outpost. Then, for Hieronymous, the final hour of reckoning, the time when each man repeats after Christ: "Lord, why hast thou forsaken me," the final dissolution of pride and will.

We can assume that he found consolation in the Bible, or in the memory of their own Anti-Trinitarian martyr—his head crowned with straw drenched in sulphur; his body chained to the stake; his book, waiting for the first lick of the flames, bound to his foot. A detailed account of Servetus's death has survived, thanks to Hieronymous Surkont's co-religionists from the Protestant sects of Poland and Lithuania. It was they who copied the manuscript, otherwise not extant, bearing the title *Historia de Serveto et eius morte*, whose author was Petrus Hyperphragmus Gandavus. No, exile could not compare with bodily torture.

Surkont, nonetheless, had endured spiritual torture, the stigma of a traitor, the burden of self-doubt that came from not knowing whether he had made the right choice. Between his fealty to the King, the Res Publica, and to his Prince, who never begrudged him their theological differences. Between his contempt for the papists and his aversion for the invaders, whose successes—not defeats—he was obliged to wish for. A heretic in the eyes of the Catholics. A barely tolerated outcast among the Protestants. All he could do, in fact, was to repeat: "I am a vile worm in the sight of my Lord."

Quite by accident, it was discovered that Hieronymous's last descendant, a Lieutenant Johann von Surkont, student of theology, was killed in the year 1915, in the Vogesen. If his body lies on a slope facing the east, where thick rows of crosses descend into the valley of the Rhine, crosses that from a distance might be mistaken for vineyards, then the grass on his grave is brushed by the dry winds coming from his native Lithuania.

HEBERTO PADILLA

FROM

Legacies

[*Translated by Alastair Reid and Andrew Hurley*]

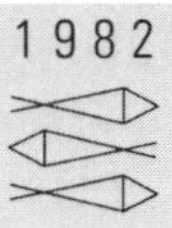

SONG OF THE JUGGLER

General, dein Tank ist ein
starker Wagon.
—BRECHT

General, there's a battle
between your orders and my songs.
It goes on all the time:
night, day.
It knows neither tiredness nor sleep—
a battle that has gone on for many years,
so many that my eyes have never seen a sunrise
in which you, your orders, your arms, your trenches
did not figure.

A rich battle
in which, aesthetically speaking, my rags
and your uniform face off.
A theatrical battle—
it only lacks dazzling stage sets
where comedians might come on from anywhere
raising a rumpus as they do in carnivals,
each one showing off his loyalty and valor.

General, I can't destroy your fleets or your tanks
and I don't know how long this war will last
but every night one of your orders dies without
being followed,
and, undefeated, one of my songs survives.

ELIAS CANETTI

FROM

The Torch in My Ear

[*Translated by Joachim Neugröschel*]

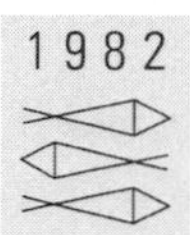

A few months after I had moved into my new room, something occurred that had the deepest influence on my subsequent life. It was one of those not too frequent public events that seize an entire city so profoundly that it is no longer the same afterwards.

On the morning of July 15, 1927, I was not at the Chemical Institute on Währingerstrasse as usual; I happened to be at home. I was reading the morning newspaper at the coffeehouse in Ober Sankt Veit. Today, I can still feel my indignation when I took hold of *Die Reichspost*: the giant headline said: "A JUST VERDICT." There had been shootings in Burgenland; workers had been killed. The court had declared the murderers not guilty. This acquittal had been termed, nay, trumpeted, as a "just verdict" in the organ of the government party. It was this mockery of any sense of justice rather than the verdict itself that triggered an enormous agitation among the workers of Vienna. From all districts of the city, the workers marched in tight formations to the Palace of Justice, whose sheer name embodied the unjust verdict for them. It was a totally spontaneous reaction: I could tell how spontaneous it was just by my own conduct. I quickly biked into the center of town and joined one of these processions.

The workers, usually well disciplined, trusting their Social Democratic leaders and satisfied that Vienna was administered by these leaders in an exemplary manner, were acting *without* their leaders on this day. When they set fire to the Palace of Justice, Mayor Seitz mounted a fire engine and raised his right hand high, trying to block their way. His gesture had no effect: the Palace of Justice was *burning*. The police were ordered to shoot; there were ninety deaths.

Fifty-three years have passed, and the agitation of that day is still in my bones. It was the closest thing to a revolution that I have physically experienced. Since then, I have known quite precisely that I would not have to read a single word about the storming of the Bastille.

I became a part of the crowd, I fully dissolved in it, I did not feel the slightest resistance to what the crowd was doing. I am amazed that despite my frame of mind, I was able to grasp all the concrete individual scenes taking place before my eyes. I would like to mention one such scene.

In a side street, not far from the burning Palace of Justice, yet out of the way, stood a man, sharply distinguished from the crowd, flailing his hands in the air and moaning over and over again: "The files are burning! All the files!"

"Better files than people!" I told him, but that did not interest him; all he could think of was the files. It occurred to me that he might have some personal involvement in the files, be an archivist. He was inconsolable. I found him comical, even in this situation. But I was also annoyed. "They've been shooting down people!" I said angrily, "and you're carrying on about files!" He looked at me as if I weren't there and wailed repeatedly: "The files are burning! All the files!" He was standing off to the side, but it was not undangerous for him; his lament was not to be missed—after all, I too had heard him.

In the following days and weeks of utter dejection, when you could not think of anything else, when the events you had witnessed kept recurring over and over again in your mind, haunting you night after night even in your sleep, there was still *one* legitimate connection to literature. And this connection was Karl Kraus. My idolization of him was at its highest level then. This time it was gratitude for a specific public deed; I don't know whom I could ever be more thankful to for such an action. Under the impact of the massacre on that day, he put up posters everywhere in Vienna, demanding the voluntary resignation of Police Commissioner Johann Schober, who was responsible for the order to shoot and for the ninety deaths. Kraus was alone in this demand; he was the only public figure who acted in this way. And while the other celebrities, of whom Vienna has never had a lack, did not wish to lay themselves open to criticism or perhaps ridicule, Kraus alone had the courage of his indignation. His posters were the only thing that kept us going in those days. I went from one poster to another, paused in front of each one, and I felt as if all the justice on earth had entered the letters of Kraus's name.

Some time ago, I set down this account of July 15 and its aftermath. I have quoted it here verbatim. Perhaps, although brief, it can offer a notion of the gravity of what happened.

Ever since, I have often tried to approach that day, which may have been the most crucial day of my life after my father's death. I have to say "approach," for it is very hard to get at this day; it is an outspread day, stretching across an entire city, a day of movement for me too, for I biked all over Vienna. My feelings on that day were all focused in *one direction.* It was the most *unambiguous* day that I can remember, unambiguous only because one's feelings could not be diverted from the day as it went by.

I don't know *who* made the Palace of Justice the goal of the tremendous processions from all parts of the city. One could think that the choice was spontaneous, even though this cannot be true. Someone must have blurted out the words "to the Palace of Justice." But it is not important to know who it was, for these words were taken in by everybody who heard them; they were accepted without qualms, waverings, or deliberation, without delay or demur, and they pulled everybody in one and the same direction.

Perhaps the substance of July 15 fully entered *Crowds and Power.* If this is so, then it would be impossible to trace anything back completely to the original experience, to the sensory elements of that day.

There was the long bike ride into town. I cannot remember the route. I do not know where I first bumped into people. I cannot *see* myself clearly on that day, but I still feel the excitement, the advancing, and the fluency of the movement. Everything is dominated by the word *fire*, then by actual fire.

A *throbbing* in my head. It may have been sheer chance that I did not personally see any attacks upon policemen. But I did see the throng being shot at and people falling. The shots were like whips. I saw people run into the side streets and I saw them reemerge and form into crowds again. I saw people fall and I saw corpses on the ground, but I wasn't right next to them. I was dreadfully frightened, especially of these corpses. I went over to them, but *avoided* them as soon as I got closer. In my excitement, they seemed to be *growing bigger.* Until the Republican Defense Corps arrived to carry them away, the corpses were surrounded by empty space, as if people expected bullets to strike here again.

The mounted Defense Corps made an extremely horrible impression, perhaps because they were frightened themselves.

A man in front of me spat and pointed his right thumb halfway back: "Someone's hanging there! They've pulled his pants off!" What was he spitting at? The victim? Or the murder? I couldn't see what he was pointing at. A woman in front of me shrieked: "Peppi! Peppi!" Her eyes were closed and she was reeling. Everyone began to run. The woman fell down. However, she hadn't been shot. I heard galloping horses. I didn't go over to the woman, who was lying on the ground. I ran with the others. I sensed that I had to run with them. I wanted to flee into a doorway, but I couldn't get away from the running throng. A very big, strong man running next to me banged his fist on his chest and bellowed as he ran: "Let them shoot me! Me! Me! Me!" Suddenly, he was gone. He hadn't fallen down. Where was he?

This was perhaps the eeriest thing of all: you saw and heard people in a powerful gesture that ousted everything else, and then those very people had vanished from the face of the earth. Everything yielded and invisible holes opened everywhere. However, the overall structure did not disappear; even if you suddenly found yourself alone somewhere, you could feel things tugging and tearing at you. The reason was that you *heard* something everywhere: there was something rhythmic in the air, an evil music. You could call it music; you felt elevated by it. I did not feel as if I were moving on my own legs. I felt as if I were in a resonant wind. A crimson head popped up in front of me, at various points, up and down, up and down, rising and dropping, as if floating on water. I looked for it as though I were to follow its directives; I thought it had red hair, then I recognized a red kerchief and no longer looked for it.

I neither met nor recognized anyone; any people I spoke to were unknown to me. However, there were few people I spoke to. I heard a great deal; there was always something to hear; most cutting of all were the boohs when the police fired into the throng and people fell. At such moments, the boohs were relentless, especially the female boohs, which could be made out distinctly. It seemed to me as if the volleys of gunfire were elicited by boohs. But I also noticed that this impression was wrong, for the volleys continued even when no more boohs could be heard. You could hear the gunfire everywhere, even farther away, whiplashes over and over.

The persistence of the crowd, which, driven away, instantly erupted from the side streets. The fire would not let the people go; the Palace of Justice burned for hours, and the time of the burning was also the time of utmost agitation. It was a very hot day; even if you did not see the fire, the sky was red for a great distance, and the air smelled of burned paper, thousands and thousands of files.

The Defense Corps, which you saw everywhere, recognizable by their windbreakers and armbands, contrasted with the police force: the Corps was unarmed. Its weapons were stretchers on which the wounded and the dead were carried off. Its eagerness to help was obvious; its members stood out against the fury of the boohs as though they were not part of the crowd. Also, they turned up everywhere; their emergence often signaled victims before these victims were seen by anyone else.

I did not personally see the Palace of Justice being set on fire, but I learned about it before I saw flames: I could tell by a change of tone in the crowd. People shouted at one another about what had happened; at first, I did not understand; it sounded joyous, not shrill, not greedy; it sounded liberated.

The fire was what held the situation together. You felt the fire, its presence was overwhelming; even if you did not see it, you nevertheless had it in your mind, its attraction and the attraction exerted by the crowd were one and the same. The salvoes of gunfire by the police aroused boohs, the boohs new salvoes. But no matter where you happened to be under the impact of the gunfire, no matter where you seemingly fled, your connection with others (an open or secret connection, depending on the place) remained in effect. And you were drawn back into the province of the fire—circuitously, since there was no other possible way.

This day, which was borne by a uniform feeling (a single, tremendous wave surging over the city, absorbing it: when the wave ebbed, you could scarcely believe that the city was still there)—this day was made up of countless details, each one etched in your mind, none slipping away. Each detail exists in itself, memorable and discernible, and yet each one also forms a part of the tremendous wave, without which everything seems hollow and absurd. The thing to be grasped is the wave, not these details. During the following year and then again and again later on, I tried to grasp the wave, but I have never succeeded. I could not succeed, for nothing is more mysterious and more incomprehensible than a crowd. Had I fully understood it, I would not have wrestled with the problem of a crowd for thirty years, trying to puzzle it out and trying to depict it and reconstruct it as thoroughly as possible, like other human phenomena.

Even were I to assemble all the concrete details of which this day consisted for me, bring them together hard and unadorned, neither reducing nor exaggerating—I could not do justice to this day, for it consisted of more. The roaring of the wave was audible all the time, washing these details to the surface; and only if this wave could be rendered in words and depicted, could one say: really, nothing has been reduced.

Instead of approaching individual details, however, I could speak about the effects that this day had on my later thinking. This day was responsible for some of my most important insights in my book on crowds. Anything I looked for in widely separate source works, repeating, testing, taking notes, reading, and then subsequently rereading in slow motion, as it were, I was able to compare with the memory of that central event, which remained fresh—notwithstanding subsequent events, which occurred on a greater scale, involving more people, with greater consequences for the world. For later years, when agitation and indignation no longer had the same weight, the isolation of the Fifteenth of July, its restriction to Vienna, gave it something like the character of a model: an event limited in both space and time, with an indisputable cause and taking a clear and unmistakable course.

Here, once and for all, I had experienced something that I later called an *open* crowd, I had witnessed its formation: the confluence of people from all parts of the city, in long, steadfast, undeflectable processions, their direction set by the position of the building that bore the name *Justice*, yet embodied injustice because of a miscarriage of justice. I had come to see that a crowd has to fall apart, and I had seen it fearing its disintegration; I had watched it do everything it could to prevent it; I had watched it actually see itself in the fire it lit, hindering its disintegration so long as this fire burned. It warded off any attempt at putting out the fire; its own longevity depended on that of the fire. It was scattered, driven away, and sent fleeing by attacks; yet even though wounded, injured, and dead people lay before it on the streets, even though the crowd had no weapons of its own, it gathered again, for the fire was still burning, and the glow of the flames illuminated the sky over the squares and streets. I saw that a crowd can flee without panicking; that mass flight and panic are distinguishable. So long as the fleeing crowd does not disintegrate into individuals worried only about themselves, about their own persons, then the crowd still exists, although fleeing; and when the crowd stops fleeing, it can turn and attack.

I realized that the crowd needs no *leader* to form, notwithstanding all previous theories in this respect. For one whole day, I watched a crowd that had formed *without a leader*. Now and then, very seldom, there were people, orators, giving speeches that supported the crowd. Their importance was minimal, they were anonymous, they contributed nothing to the formation of the crowd. Any account giving them a central position falsifies the events. If anything did loom out, sparking the formation of the crowd, it was the sight of the burning Palace of Justice. The salvoes of the police did not whip the crowd apart: they whipped it together. The sight of people escaping through the streets was a mirage: for even when running, they fully understood that certain people were falling and would not get up again. These victims unleashed the wrath of the crowd no less than the fire did.

During that brightly illuminated, dreadful day, I gained the true picture of what, as a crowd, fills our century. I gained it so profoundly that I kept going back to contemplate it anew, both compulsively and willingly. I returned over and over and watched; and even today, I sense how hard it is for me to tear myself away, since I have managed to achieve only the tiniest portion of my goal: to understand what a crowd is.

MARIO VARGAS LLOSA

FROM

Aunt Julia and the Scriptwriter

[*Translated by Helen R. Lane*]

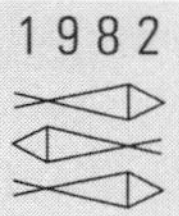

Just as Pedro Camacho was the closest thing to a writer that I'd ever seen in my short life, among all my acquaintances Javier was the one whose generosity and exuberance made him most resemble a Renaissance prince. Moreover, he was a very efficient planner: he'd already informed Aunt Julia [the narrator Mario's aunt-in-law] and Nancy of what was awaiting us that night, and he already had the theater tickets in his pocket. His program couldn't have been more enticing, and it immediately dispelled my gloomy reflections on the vocation and the miserable fate that awaited the man of letters in Peru. Javier was also very happy: he'd been going out with Nancy for a month now, and their keeping company together was taking on the proportions of a real romance. My having confessed my feelings toward Aunt Julia to my cousin had been very useful to him because, on the pretext of helping us hide our secret and making it easier for us to go out together by double-dating, he'd been managing to see Nancy several times a week. My cousin and Aunt Julia were inseparable now: they went out shopping and to the movies together and exchanged confidences. My cousin had become an enthusiastic fairy godmother of our romance, and one afternoon she raised my morale by remarking to me: "Julita has a way about her that cancels out any difference in age, Marito."

The grandiose program for that Sunday (a day on which, I firmly believe, a large part of my future was determined by the stars) got off to an excellent start. In Lima in the fifties we had very few chances to see first-rate theater, and the Argentine company of Francisco Petrone brought us a series of modern works that had never been performed before in Peru. Nancy went by Aunt Olga's to get Aunt Julia and the two of them came downtown in a taxi. Javier and I were waiting for them at the door of the Teatro Segura. Javier, who was a great believer in the grand gesture, had rented an entire box, which turned out to be the only one occupied, so that there were almost as many eyes focused on us as on the stage. My guilty conscience made me quite certain that any number of relatives and acquaintances would see us and immediately suspect the truth. But the moment the performance began, my fears evaporated. They were doing *Death of a Salesman*, by Arthur Miller, the first nontraditional play, violating the conventions of time and space, that I'd ever seen. I was so excited and so enthused that during the intermission I began to talk a blue streak, praising the work to the skies, commenting on its characters, its technique, its ideas, and later, as we were eating sausages and drinking dark beer in the Rincón Toni on La Colmena, I went on raving about it and got so absorbed in what I was saying that Javier later told me: "You would have thought you were a parrot that had been slipped a dose of Spanish fly." My cousin Nancy, who had always thought my literary inclinations were as peculiar as the odd hobby that fascinated our Uncle Eduardo—a little old man, my grandfather's brother, now a retired judge, whose life was centered on the unusual pastime of collecting spiders—after hearing my interminable peroration on the work we had just seen, suspected that my literary bent might lead me off the deep end. "You're going off your rocker, my boy," she warned me.

Javier had chosen the Negro-Negro to end the evening because it had a certain intellectual-bohemian atmosphere—on Thursdays they gave little shows, one-act plays, monologues, recitals, and it was a favorite gathering place for painters, musicians, and writers—but besides that, it was also the darkest *boîte* in Lima, a basement in the arcades of the Plaza San Martín that had twenty tables at most, with a decor we thought was "existentialist." It was a night spot that, the few times I had been there, gave me the illusion that I was in a *cave* in Saint-Germain-des-Prés. They seated us at a little table on the edge of the dance floor, and Javier, more princely than ever, ordered four whiskies. He and Nancy immediately got up to dance, and there in that tiny, crowded basement, I went on talking to Julia about theater and Arthur Miller. We were sitting almost on top of each other, holding hands, she was patiently listening to me, and I went on and on about how that night I had discovered the theater: it could be something as complex and profound as the novel, and because it was something living, requiring the participation of flesh-and-blood beings in order to take on material form, and other arts, painting, music, it was perhaps even superior.

"I've decided all of a sudden that I'm going to change genres and start writing plays instead of stories," I told her, all excited. "What do you say to that?"

"There's no reason you shouldn't, as far as I'm concerned," Aunt

Julia answered, rising to her feet. "But now, Varguitas, come dance with me and whisper sweet nothings in my ear. Between pieces, if you like, you have my permission to talk to me about literature."

I followed her instructions to the letter. We held each other very tightly and kissed as we danced, I told her that I was in love with her, and she answered that she was in love with me, and aided by the intimate, exciting, sensuous atmosphere and Javier's whiskies, for the very first time I made no effort to hide the desire that she aroused in me; as we danced, my lips nuzzled her neck, my tongue stole into her mouth and sipped her saliva, I held her very close so as to feel her breasts, her belly, and her thighs, and then, back at the table, under cover of the darkness, I fondled her legs and breasts. That's what we were doing, so happy we were giddy, when Nancy came back to the table, during a break between two boleros, and made our blood run cold by blurting out: "Good Lord, just look who's here: Uncle Jorge."

It was a danger we ought to have thought of. Uncle Jorge, our youngest uncle, daringly combined, in a superfrenetic life, all sorts of business affairs and commercial ventures and an intense night life filled with wine, women, and song. A tragicomic story about him had made the rounds, the scene of which was another *boîte*: the Embassy. The show had just begun, the girl who was singing couldn't go on because a drunk sitting at one of the tables kept interrupting her by shouting insults. Uncle Jorge had risen to his feet in the middle of the crowded nightclub, roaring like a Don Quixote: "Shut your mouth, you wretch, I'm going to teach you to respect a lady," and with his fists raised like a boxer had started to move in on the idiot, only to discover a moment later that he was making a fool of himself since the pseudo-customer's interruption of the chanteuse was part of the show. And there he was, sitting just two tables away from us, looking very elegant, his face just barely visible in the light of the matches being struck by the smokers in the place and the waiters' flashlights. I recognized his wife, my Aunt Gaby, sitting next to him, and despite the fact that they were only a few feet away from us, both of them were deliberately avoiding looking in our direction. It was all quite obvious: they'd seen me kissing Aunt Julia, they'd immediately guessed everything, and had opted for a diplomatic blindness. Javier asked for the check, we left the Negro-Negro almost at once, and Uncle Jorge and Aunt Gaby carefully looked the other way even when we rubbed elbows as we passed their table on the way out. In the taxi on the way back to Miraflores, the four of us just sat there with long faces, not saying a word, till Nancy finally summed up what all of us were thinking: "All that scheming for nothing; the fat's in the fire now."

But, as in a good suspense film, nothing at all happened during the next few days. There was not the slightest sign that the family clan had been alerted by Uncle Jorge and Aunt Gaby. Uncle Lucho and Aunt Olga didn't say one word to Aunt Julia that would lead her to think that they knew, and that Thursday, when I screwed up my courage and turned up for lunch at their house as usual, they were as outgoing and affectionate with me as always. Nor was Cousin Nancy the object of a single captious question on the part of Aunt Laura and Uncle Juan. And at my house, my grandparents seemed to be lost in daydreams and kept asking me, with the most angelic innocence imaginable, whether I was still taking Aunt Julia to the movies ("So nice of you—Julita's such a film fan"). Those were anxious days, during which, taking extra precautions, Aunt Julia and I decided not to see each other, even in secret, for at least a week. We nonetheless talked to each other on the telephone. Aunt Julia would go out to the grocery store on the corner to phone me at least three times a day, and we would exchange our respective observations regarding the dreaded family reaction and entertain all sorts of hypotheses. Could Uncle Jorge possibly have decided to keep our secret to himself? I knew that this was unthinkable, in view of the family's usual habits. So what in the world was happening? Javier advanced the thesis that Aunt Gaby and Uncle Jorge had downed so many whiskies that night that they hadn't really realized what was going on, that the only thing that lingered in their memory was a vague suspicion, and that they hadn't wanted to unleash a scandal over something that was not absolute proven fact. More or less out of curiosity, but also out of masochism, I made the rounds and dropped in at the homes of the entire clan that week so as to know what to expect. I noted nothing out of the ordinary, save for an omission that intrigued me and set off a pyrotechnical explosion of speculation on my part. Aunt Hortensia, who had invited me to come have tea and biscuits with her, didn't mention Aunt Julia once in the course of a two-hour conversation. "They know everything and have plans afoot," I assured Javier, who was sick and tired of hearing me talk of nothing else. "When you come right down to it, you're dying to get your whole family up in arms so as to have something to write about," he commented.

During that eventful week I also found myself unexpectedly involved in a street fight and playing the part of Pedro Camacho's bodyguard, so to speak. I had gone one day to San Marcos University, where the results of an exam in criminal law had just been posted, and was full of remorse at having discovered that I had received a higher grade than my friend Velando, who was the one who had had everything down pat. As I was crossing the Parque Universitario, I ran into Genaro Sr., the patriarch of the phalanx that owned Radio Panamericana and Radio

Central, and the two of us walked as far as the Calle Belén together, talking as we strolled along. He was a gentleman who always dressed in black and was always very solemn, and the Bolivian scriptwriter sometimes referred to him—for reasons not at all difficult to guess—as The Slave Driver.

"Your friend the genius is still giving me headaches," Genaro Sr. said to me. "I've had it up to here with him. If he weren't so productive, I'd have booted him out long before this."

"Another protest from the Argentine embassy?" I asked.

"I don't know what sort of a hopeless mess he's cooking up," he complained. "He's taken to pulling people's leg, shifting characters from one serial to an entirely different one or changing their names all of a sudden so as to get our listeners all confused. My wife had already told me what was going on, and now we're starting to get phone calls, and we've even received two letters. It seems that the priest from Mendocita now has the name of the Jehovah's Witness and vice versa. I'm far too busy to listen to serials. Do *you* ever listen to them?"

We had reached La Colmena and were heading toward the Plaza San Martín, past buses leaving for the provinces and little Chinese cafés, and I remembered that Aunt Julia, speaking of Pedro Camacho a few days before, had made me laugh and confirmed my suspicions that the scriptwriter was secretly a humorist at heart. "Something really weird has happened. The young wife had her kid, but it died at birth, and they buried it with all the rites of the Church. So how do you explain the fact that in this afternoon's chapter they took the baby to the Cathedral to be baptized?"

I told Genaro Sr. that I didn't have time to listen to them either and that perhaps these interchangeable characters and mixed-up plots were Pedro Camacho's highly original way of telling a story.

"We aren't paying him to be original; we're paying him to entertain our listeners," Genaro Sr. informed me, making it quite plain that he for his part was not a progressive-minded impresario but a thoroughgoing traditionalist. "If he keeps on with jokes like that, he's going to make us lose our listeners, and sponsors will withdraw their commercials. You're his friend: pass the word on to him to cut out these modernist gimmicks, or else he's liable to end up without a job."

I suggested that he tell him so himself: since he was the boss, the threat would carry more weight.

But Genaro Sr. shook his head, with an air of compunction that Genaro Jr. had inherited. "He won't even let me speak to him. Success has gone to his head, and every time I try to have a word with him, he's disrespectful."

Genaro Sr. had gone to his cubicle to tell him, as politely as possible, that the station had been receiving phone calls, and show him the letters of complaint. Without saying a single word in reply, Pedro Camacho had taken the two letters, torn them to pieces without opening them, and tossed them in the wastebasket. He then began typing, as though there were no one present, and as Genaro Sr., on the edge of apoplexy, was leaving that hostile lair, he heard him mutter: "Let the cobbler stick to his last."

"I can't put up with any more insults like that; I'd have to kick him out, and that wouldn't be realistic either," he concluded with a weary gesture. "But you don't have anything to lose. He's not going to insult you—you're more or less a writer too, aren't you? Give us a hand, do it for the corporation, talk to him."

I promised him I would, and in fact, to my misfortune, I went down after the twelve o'clock Panamericana newscast to invite Pedro Camacho to come have a cup of verbena-and-mint. We were leaving Radio Central when two big strapping young men blocked our path. I recognized them immediately: the barbecue cooks, two brothers with big bushy mustaches, from the Argentina Grill, a restaurant located on the same street, across from the school run by the Little Sisters of Bethlehem; dressed in white aprons and tall chef's toques, they were the ones who prepared the rare steaks and grilled tripe that were the specialty of the restaurant.

The two of them surrounded him, looking as though they were out for trouble, and the older and fatter one said to him in a threatening tone of voice: "So we're child-killers, are we, Camacho, you bastard? Did you think there was nobody in this country who could teach you a little respect, you bum?"

He grew more and more excited as he spoke, turning bright red and stumbling over his words. The younger brother kept nodding in agreement, and as his elder paused for a moment, choking with rage, he too put in his two cents' worth. "And what about the lice? So you think, do you, that women where we come from eat the vermin they pull out of their kids' hair as a special treat, you fucking son of a bitch? Do you think I'm going to let you get away with insulting my mother?"

The Bolivian scriptwriter hadn't backed away an inch and stood there listening to them with a magisterial air, his exophthalmic eyes slowly shifting from one to the other. Then, with a characteristic little bow from the waist, mindful of a master of ceremonies, and in a very solemn tone of voice, he suddenly asked them the most civil question imaginable. "Are you by any chance Argentines?"

The fat barbecue chef, foaming at the mustache now, his face only a few inches away from Pedro Camacho's (a confrontation that had forced him to bend way over), roared patriotically: "Yes, you bastard, we're Argentines—and proud of it!"

Once he had received this confirmation—really quite unnecessary since the moment they had spoken two words it was obvious from their accent that they were Argentines—I saw the Bolivian turn deathly pale, as though something had exploded inside him; his eyes blazed, he assumed a threatening expression, and whipping the air with his index finger, he apostrophized them thus: "I suspected as much. Well, then: clear out of here immediately and go sing tangos!"

The order was not meant humorously; his tone of voice was deadly serious. For a second the barbecue chefs just stood there, at a loss for words. It was plain to see that the scriptwriter wasn't joking: despite the fact that he was absolutely defenseless physically, the tiny little man was stubbornly holding his ground, his fierce eyes glaring at them scornfully.

"What was that you said?" the fat one finally blurted out, nonplussed and beside himself with rage. "Huh, huh? What was that again?"

"Go sing tangos and wash your ears!" Pedro Camacho said, enlarging on his order, in his impeccable accent. And then, after the briefest of pauses, with the audacity that was to be our downfall, he said slowly and distinctly, in a glacially calm voice: "If you don't want a beating."

This time I was even more surprised than the barbecue cooks. That this little man, scarcely taller than a dwarf and with the physique of a third-grade schoolchild, was threatening to thrash two Samsons weighing well over two hundred pounds apiece was not only mad but suicidal. But the fatter one was already going into action: he grabbed the Bolivian by the collar and, amid the laughter of the crowd that had gathered round, lifted him off his feet as though he were a feather, and shouted: "*You're* going to give *me* a beating? Well, we'll see about that, shorty . . ."

When I saw that the older brother was about to send Pedro Camacho flying with a straight right to the jaw, I was obliged to intervene. I grabbed the Samson's arm, trying at the same time to free the scriptwriter, who was suspended in midair, purple-faced and jerking his legs like a spider, and I managed to say something like: "Listen, don't be a bully, let him go," when suddenly, without warning, the younger brother gave me a punch that sent me sprawling on the ground. As I struggled to my feet in a daze and prepared to put into practice the philosophy taught me by my grandfather, a gentleman of the old school, who held that no Arequipan worthy of the name ever refuses an invitation to fight (and above all an invitation as clear as a sock in the jaw), I saw that the older brother was soundly boxing the artist's ears (he had mercifully chosen to cuff him rather than punch him, in view of his adversary's

Lilliputian stature). Then, after that, as I traded rights and lefts with the younger barbecue cook (in defense of art, I thought to myself), I didn't see much else. The fight didn't last very long, but when people from Radio Central finally rescued us from the hands of the two hulking brutes, I had bumps and bruises all over and Pedro Camacho's face was so puffy and swollen that Genaro Sr. had to take him to the public emergency clinic. That afternoon, instead of thanking me for having risked my neck defending his exclusive star, Genaro Jr. bawled me out for a news item that Pascual, taking advantage of all the confusion, had managed to slip into two successive bulletins; the paragraph in question began (with a certain amount of exaggeration) as follows: "Thugs from the Río de la Plata today criminally attacked our news director, the celebrated journalist . . ."

When Javier turned up that afternoon in my shack at Radio Panamericana, he roared with laughter on hearing the story of the fight, and went with me to ask the scriptwriter how he felt. They'd put a pirate's patch over his right eye, and he was wearing two adhesive bandages, one on his neck and another under his nose. How did he feel? He gave a disdainful wave of his hand, dismissing the entire incident as of no importance, and made no attempt to thank me for having plunged into the fray out of solidarity with him.

His one and only comment delighted Javier. "It saved the lives of those two when people separated us. If it had gone on a few minutes more, the crowd would have recognized me and then they'd have lynched the poor things."

We went to the Bransa, where he told us that one day in Bolivia a soccer player "from *that* country" who'd heard his programs had turned up at the studio armed with a revolver, which luckily the guards had detected in time.

"You're going to have to be careful," Javier warned him. "Lima is full of Argentines now."

"It's a matter of little moment. Sooner or later, worms are going to eat all three of us," Pedro Camacho philosophized.

And he delivered us a lecture on the transmigration of souls, an article of faith with him. He told us a secret: if it were left to him to choose, he would like to be some calm, long-lived marine animal, such as a tortoise or a whale, in his next reincarnation. I took advantage of his good spirits to exercise my *ad honorem* role of intermediary between him and the Genaros that I had assumed some time ago and gave him Genaro Sr.'s message about the phone calls, the letters, the episodes in his serials that a number of people didn't understand. The old man begged him not to complicate his plots, to take into account the level of intelligence of the average listener, which was quite low. I tried to sugarcoat the pill by siding with him (as a matter of fact, I really was on his side, moreover): this urgent request was absurd, naturally, one should be free to write as one pleased, and I was merely repeating what they had asked me to tell him.

He heard me out in such silence and with such an impassive expression on his face that he made me feel very uncomfortable. And when I finished, he still didn't say a word. He swallowed the last sip of his verbena-and-mint tea, rose to his feet, muttered that he had to get back to his office, and left without even saying goodbye. Had he taken offense because I'd talked to him about the phone calls in front of someone he didn't know? Javier thought so, and advised me to offer him my apologies. I promised myself never to act as an intermediary for the Genaros again.

During that week I spent without seeing Aunt Julia, I went out at night several times with old friends from Miraflores whom I hadn't bothered to look up since the beginning of my secret romance. They were former schoolmates of mine or kids I'd known in the neighborhood, youngsters who were now studying engineering, like Blackie Salas, or medicine, like Pinky Molfino, or had gotten jobs, like Coco Lanas, pals with whom I'd shared wonderful things since I'd been knee-high to a grasshopper: pinball games and the Parque Salazar, going swimming at the Terrazas and the beaches of Miraflores, parties on Saturday nights, crushes on girls, movies. But on going out with them, after months of not seeing them, I realized that we were no longer the bosom buddies we'd once been; we were still great friends, but we no longer had as many things in common. On the nights we went out together during that week, we did the same daring things together that we'd done in the past: going to the old run-down Surco cemetery to prowl around in the moonlight amid the tombstones that had toppled over in some earthquake, trying to find a skull to make off with; skinny-dipping in the enormous Santa Rosa swimming pool near Ancón, still under construction; making the rounds of the gloomy, depressing brothels on the Avenida Grau. My pals were still the same as ever, cracking the same jokes, talking of the same girls, but I couldn't share with them the things that mattered most to me: literature and Aunt Julia. If I'd told them that I was writing stories and dreamed of being a writer, they would doubtless have thought, just as my cousin Nancy did, that I had a screw loose. And if I'd told them about my romance—as they told me about their conquests—with a divorcée, who was not my mistress but my sweetheart, my *enamorada* (in the most Miraflorine sense of that word), they would have taken me for (as a poetic, esoteric, very popular expression of those days went) a *cojudo a la vela*—an ass under full sail. I didn't feel the slightest scorn for them for not reading literature, nor did I consider myself superior because I was having a romance with a real, grownup woman who'd had lots of experience, but the truth of the matter was that on those nights, as we poked around graves under the eucalyptus and pepper trees of Surco, or splashed about beneath the stars of Santa Rosa, or drank beer and haggled over prices with the whores at Nanette's, I was bored, and found my thoughts dwelling more on my "Dangerous Games" (which had not appeared in *El Comercio* this week either) and on Aunt Julia than on what they were saying.

When I told Javier about my disappointing reunion with my old neighborhood gang of buddies, he stuck out his chest and replied: "It's because they're still just kids. But you and I are men now, Varguitas."

WILLIAM GOLDING

FROM

A Moving Target

1982

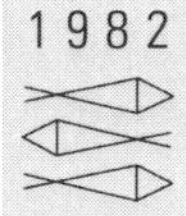

AN AFFECTION FOR CATHEDRALS

Among the virtues and vices that make up the British character, we have one vice, at least, that Americans ought to view with sympathy. For they appear to be the only people who share it with us. I mean our worship of the antique. I do not refer to beauty or even historical association. I refer to age, to a quantity of years. Provided a public man is old enough, we forgive him any folly. Provided a building is old enough, we discount ugliness, discomfort, dirt, and employ a special government department to shore it up. All the religious revolutions of the last five hundred years have affected only the top half of our minds, and left us with a little of the medieval attitude towards relics deep in our British unconscious. This is the most harmless thing left there; but still, it conditions our aesthetic attitudes.

For what is a work of art? Is it the form or the substance? 'Both,' we feel, when we think about it at all, 'but if we must choose, give us the substance.'

There was much outcry when our National Gallery began to clean the dirt of centuries off the old masters. We had got used to being able to catch no more than a glimpse of the original, and to viewing great art, as it were, on a dark and foggy night. Perhaps we felt the Master had said, 'It looks rather gaudy now—but wait for five hundred years till it's really dirty and then you'll be able to enjoy it properly.'

Stone that has mouldered out of shape is left just so. We do not believe that a reconstruction, a filling of the old form with new material, would result in anything genuine. We prefer a lump of the original stone, against which we lean a notice saying: 'Such a work of art as this is irreplaceable. Please do not touch.' On the other hand, one of the most beautiful churches in my part of the country, for which we have to thank an eccentric nobleman of the nineteenth century, is an accurate reproduction of an eleventh century church in the south of France. Yet no one goes to see it; as if we ought to be moved, not by repeated performances of a symphony, but only by the first, with the composer conducting.

A ludicrous belief, you will agree; and yet I must admit, against all sense and reason, that I share it. The truth is, we have a primitive belief that virtue, force, power—what the anthropologist might call *mana*—lie in the original stones and nowhere else. Yet we must know these stones; they must be part of daily life so that we may have adjusted some sensor to the correct wavelength for reception, as you might adjust your eyes to a dim light.

Our old churches are full of this power. I do not refer to their specifically religious function or influence. There is a whole range of other feelings that have, so to speak, coagulated around them. These feelings are worth analysing and the analysis might help us to understand ourselves. I think particularly of the two English cathedrals I know well—Winchester and Salisbury. I can hold models of them each in my head, weighing them against each other. Let me give Winchester every advantage I can think of.

Winchester has had three cathedrals on the same site; and probably a pagan temple before that, since there is a sacred and pre-Christian well in the crypt. Even the present building, begun in the eleventh century, is the accretion of at least four hundred years of construction and four styles of architecture. The city was once England's capital; so the cathedral is stocked with the graves of kings, queens, cardinals and archbishops—a most distinguished crowd who contribute historical perspective. In a desire—which we British understand if no one else does—to share a roof with these top people, hundreds of commoners and minor nobilities have crowded in and got themselves buried in the less fashionable parts of the building. Here, the very stones speak to you in English or Latin or Greek. What they have to say varies from the pathetic to the mildly funny. What precisely is implied by the inscription to Davis Williams D.C.L.? All we are told of him is that

IN THIS CATHEDRAL
HIS POWERFUL AND MELODIOUS VOICE
WAS SINGULARLY IMPRESSIVE.

But I must confess that my favourite is a Royal Navy inscription, stiff-upperlipped, a masterpiece of understatement to

WILLIAM CARMICHAEL FORREST
1ST LIEUTENANT H.M.S. DOTEREL
WHO LOST HIS LIFE BY THE ACCIDENTAL

EXPLOSION OF THE SHIP'S MAGAZINE
AND CONSEQUENT FOUNDERING
OF THE SHIP.

To saunter and read these is a quiet pleasure. One does not need much scholarship to feel the pathos in the memorial of those children

IN ORIENTALI INDIA HEU! LONGE
A PARENTIBUS SEPULTARUM.

You may find your lips twitching at the quotation thought apt for Jane Austen, our demure satirist of English life:

'SHE OPENETH HER MOUTH WITH WISDOM;
AND IN HER TONGUE IS THE LAW OF KINDNESS.'

Doctor Johnson gave it as his opinion that in a lapidary inscription, no man is on oath, but one feels that Miss Austen might have been better accommodated with some other quotation from the Scriptures.

For a Winchester man, might *mana* reside in the statuary? Winchester is crowded with statues. Like the inscriptions, some of them are funny. Those marble parliamentarians, those gesticulating statesmen of the eighteenth century seem to have nothing to do with religion or death. Are they perhaps persons who stepped inside to shelter from sudden rain and had so gross an ignorance of the nature of the place that they harangued the high altar; and were struck so, justly, as an example to those who come after? Sometimes the dust of commoners has taken a revenge and lies on those aristocratic noses to make clowns or masks of them, so that a whole splendid monument seems to hold up nothing but the face of zany. Time has taken an even neater revenge on my favourite Winchester statue. He is a seventeenth century nobleman, just about to set out on a stroll or enter some drawing room. You can see every hair of his wig, every thread of his lace, see even the pattern woven into his silk coat—see, still, the narcissistic smugness written in every line of his complacent face. Below him is the inscription which was to proclaim his lineage and his virtues. But here is the joke: you cannot read a word of it. Some statues carry modern, explanatory notices; but no one has cared to tamper with the anonymity of this alabaster gentleman. There is a gleeful conspiracy to keep him in the state to which the decay of monuments has called him.

Of course, not all Winchester statues are laughable. At the east end is a tiny bronze statue of William Walker, raised by public subscription. He was a diver; and at the beginning of this century when the building was in danger of collapsing into its own soggy foundations, he worked daily for six years, in slime and stinking darkness, until he had underpinned the walls and made the cathedral safe. Winchester thinks highly of him.

Then there is a figure in its own chantry—a small room or chapel where it was intended that mass should be said in perpetuity for the owner's soul. The whole thing looks like a gigantic four-poster; and the figure lies there in bed, apparently asleep. No expense has been spared. The figure is not only carved but enamelled and deceives the eye, as do the waxworks of Madame Tussaud. Even the cardinal's red hat is exact, though stone. To the thoughtful eye, this is not a Christian tomb at all. It resembles an Egyptian one, with a figure provided as an eternal home for the *ka*, the life spirit. Indeed, the apparent security of the figure is no more than a desperate attempt to cheat death, a last throw made by a man who had some considerable acquaintance with sin. This is the tomb of Henry Beaufort, a political churchman, chancellor of England, and so on, whose deathbed in 1447 was one of the most terrible recorded. He tried, in his delirium, to bribe death to pass him by. Shakespeare makes articulate what lies behind the calm figure and the cardinal's hat:

If thou be'st death, I'll give thee England's treasure,
Enough to purchase such another island,
If thou wilt let me live—

It is an eerie tomb; and not all its huddling as near as possible to the shrine of Saint Swithin can keep me comfortable if I stand in that part of the cathedral. If this is *mana*—and I do not think it is—I can do without it. Not the tomb of William Rufus, placed with kingly indifference to the convenience of others, on the centre line of the building so that processions have to divide around it; not those blue-and-gilt coffers with their loads of ecclesiastical and royal bones placed on the surround of the sanctuary; indeed not even Winchester City with its Round Table, its ancient school and holy well can give me what I get from more familiar stones in Salisbury.

I am not the only one who feels so. A few days ago I walked in Winchester Cathedral behind two people from Salisbury. The cathedrals are only twenty-five miles apart and Winchester is the richer. But these ladies from Salisbury did not find it so. Somewhere on the downland road that links the two cities, they had passed an invisible barrier and found themselves outside their own diocese. Winchester, they felt—

Winchester, once England's capital—was provincial. What were cardinals and Kings to put against Poore, Longespee, Herbert and Hooker? The stones of Winchester were the wrong shape and the wrong sort. I had begun to eavesdrop in a spirit of kindly amusement, but I found myself to my astonishment agreeing with them. I had come, as I often do, to admire Winchester and be affectionate to it; and it took these ladies to bring me to my senses. I knew I had always felt as they did but had never had the self-awareness to admit it. Winchester *is* made of the wrong stone. It is the wrong shape. It stands on a slope, and it has no spire.

Driving home across the downs, I was now prepared for the invisible barrier, and heard a distinct 'Ping!' as I passed through it. The barrier was the exact point where Salisbury and Winchester influences were balanced. Like a space probe passing from moon's gravity to earth's gravity I was now hurrying faster and faster towards my own experiences of *mana*. I do not live in the close; but I was going home, and I was going home to the cathedral.

Fifteen miles away you can feel the cathedral begin to pull. It seems ageless as the landscape. You sense that the rivers run towards it, the valleys opening out, each to frame the spike of the spire. As for the roads, where else should they lead? Even today, though motor traffic is imposing a new pattern on the old one, you can see how the tracks make deeply for the spire and draw together at the ancient bridge just outside the close. It has been a long, steady work, this influencing of the landscape, this engraving and rubbing out, this adjusting and twitching of a whole country into place. And *mana*, however subtle, however indefinable, has at least one quality that aligns it with other forces: it varies inversely as the square of the distance. Fifteen miles away it begins to pull; but stand close to the walls and you feel you might click against them like a nail to a magnet.

A critic may bring up the sane, sad theory that you feel this way because the cathedral has become part of your life, and that *mana* is no more than familiarity. Of course there is something in this. Your mind becomes stocked with memories enough to fill the huge building itself. There are vistas you remember as a graded series of pictures, because you first walked there when you clung to your mother's hand. A particular Salisbury monument comes to my mind in three sizes; one when I looked up to it, one when I saw it at eye level, and one, alas, when I stand and look down. There have been the great occasions, celebrations of victory, when orchestras have played and massed choirs sung. There are grotesque memories too—one of a flooded cathedral with a punt moving solemnly up the nave. There are memories of inexpressible beauty: a floodlit cathedral, a magic cathedral under the full moon; a bonewhite spire against the smoke from burning Dunkirk, with the lightning conductors glittering like emeralds; a rose-coloured cathedral, yet washed from below with the reflected whiteness of a million open daisies. There are memories of the cathedral when it seemed no more impressive than a barn. It is a splendid instrument for meteorology to play on, and never looks the same two days running. Yet meteorology is not *mana*.

Does it lie in our statues? We have not so many as Winchester since we have never been so central to affairs. What statues we have are mostly imperfect. The left wing of religion is always knocking our cathedrals about and the right wing makes them over-elaborate. The left wing, the iconoclasts of the seventeenth century, have left their trademark in the painted glass—or rather in the absence of it. What enraged them was a face; and sometimes you can see a saint in a window with plain glass where his face used to be. This must have been tremendous fun of course—think of breaking things and being virtuous into the bargain! You can see *their* like any day of the week in a newsreel, turning over cars and breaking shopwindows. One iconoclast was so famous he even got the nickname 'Blue Dicky' for his skill in smashing painted glass with a pike, going from window to window, and as the chronicler says, 'rattling down their glassy bones'.

But there has been another specialist at work in Salisbury. He is nameless and timeless, but you can identify him by his individual psychosis. He cannot see a stone projection without wanting to break it off. Why, in Athens, in the year 415 BC, he was up all night, bashing away at—but that is another story and too indelicate for an essay on cathedrals. In a church he has to be content with noses. It is no good when you walk round Salisbury Cathedral and look at our maimed figures to think of a slow decay. Stone noses don't fall off, particularly when an effigy lies on its back and its nose points at the vaulting. Each of these breakages represents an episode, a moment of time. It was darkish, I believe, and the cathedral as nearly deserted as may be, when the little man stole out of the shadows with his hammer. Bash! Clitter clatter! and he is away over the downs, fingering the stung place on his cheek where a minute fragment of Bishop Poore hit him, but giggling and jerking with a possibly sexual excitement which dies down gradually so that he broods on the great days in Italy and Greece, and that wonderful *young* time he had in Egypt, when statues were statues and you had to use a sledgehammer. He left our cathedral with hardly a nose in the place.

Yet he did not injure the building as much as indifference has injured it. In the eighteenth century the fabric was wholly neglected. Anyone who took his religion seriously was dismissed as an 'enthusiast', as damning a label as 'communist' is today. Significantly enough, the cross on the top of our spire was replaced by a useful weather-cock in that century; a mechanism, perhaps, by which the venal and indifferent canons regulated their affairs. If you read the statutes of the cathedral you will find that, during the eighteenth century, not one addition was made. Round about 1760, however, the canons got people to build houses in the close, and gave them a 199-year lease for nothing but the condition that when the lease expired the houses should become cathedral property. Today, these leases are running out and the exquisite houses reverting to the chapter. It was a superbly long-sighted stroke of business that makes Wall Street look like a kindergarten. But these same canons so neglected the cathedral structure that during a storm of about the same date as the leases, the great west window bellied like a sail in the wind, then burst.

Even so, it is arguable that restoration has done more harm to Salisbury Cathedral than indifference. In the late eighteenth century there came a man called James Wyatt. He swept away monuments or altered their position. We had chantries—Beauchamp and Hungerford—clapped like earmuffs on each side of the Lady Chapel. He took them away and re-erected them, one in a public park where children have kicked it to bits, the other in the grounds of a laundry. He pushed the old choir screen into a side chapel. He tore down and threw away the acres of painted glass that the iconoclasts had not reached, and filled the windows with clear glass that lets the daylight in; as if inviting anyone who should pray in the cathedral to do so with eyes open, lest he should be led astray by some sense of awe and mystery, and the feeling that a church is a different sort of place from anywhere else. Wyatt opened vistas in the vast interior as though the building were a gentleman's estate. He was part of the Gothic revival, which was neither Gothic nor a revival but a misunderstanding of a church's function and a misreading of history. The only good thing he did was to reveal the bones of the building itself. Salisbury Cathedral is unique in England because it was built all in one style, like Blenheim or the Crystal Palace.

Round about the year 1200, Bishop Poore was standing on a hill overlooking the confluence of the local rivers, according to legend, when the mother of Jesus appeared to him, told him to shoot an arrow and build her a church where the arrow fell. The arrow flew more than a mile and fell in the middle of a swamp. There, with complete indifference to such things as health, foundations, access and general practicability, the cathedral was built. Eighty years later, with a technological gamble which makes space travel seem child's play, the builders erected the highest spire in the country on top of it, thousands of tons of lead and iron and wood and stone. Yet the whole building still stands. It leans. It totters. It bends. But it still stands; and Wyatt stripped the building to the point where we can see the members of that ancient engineering as clearly as they may be seen in a bridge; so that a model of the cathedral, however small, is a pretty, even an exquisite thing. I have heard rumour that there is in fact a weight-bearing stratum in the swamp; but if there is, and the thing does not float by some miracle, the builders could not have known about it. So it stands, a perpetual delight, a perpetual wonder, with the whole of our little body politic shrugged into shape about it.

Perhaps the wonder is not so visible inside. There, you may be more conscious of the bending pillars, of Wyatt's daylight emptiness in which the soaring stone is too naked, too austere. Yet a Gothic cathedral is never quite without the quirkish and personal. The noseless bishops and knights on their tomb slabs preserve a timeless dignity; but a hundred feet above them squint the faces in which the medieval stonecutter recorded his opinion of the boss. It was never a flattering opinion, but always full of life, always contemporary, with the mordant immediacy of a political cartoon. Tourists seldom examine these faces because they have not the time; and some of these cartoons are nearly inaccessible. But if you have the hardihood to use your binoculars, it is astonishing how the faces leap down. You are looking straight at the life of seven hundred years ago, the life of the tavern and street, the sweaty, brawling, cruelly good-humoured life that later congregated on the Left Bank or in Greenwich Village; and still later was to be debauched finally by television and mass sales into respectability. You can look straight at the work of artists who would never be knighted or win an international prize. In these carvings is the integrity of an art that did not know temptation.

The tourists walk through. Conducted parties group to listen. Sightseers wander. At moments when there is no other noise, you hear always the showering sound of heels on stone. This slow drift goes on all day. If one of the daily services is in progress, part of the building is cut off symbolically by ropes of red silk stretched between pillars. Far off, inside the rope, the choir sings, or you hear the echoing versicles said, not sung, to a congregation of three or four in a dim side chapel. When the major services are held, such visitors as do not wish to take part but are only there to see what the inside of a cathedral looks like, stand grouped under the west windows, with wary vergers to see they don't turn their backs on the high altar. At these times you may see such richness and ritual as the church has retained or renewed from medieval times: gold crosses, candles, a robed choir, priests in glittering copes, bishops and deans in mitres. There will be processions: but in general they will reach the altar by the shortest route. For though the ambulatory is still there, its stones worn by the feet of ancient pomp, the church has rid itself of all that; and there is a perpetual wing of the church that regards even the lighting of one candle as a step towards the fires of Smithfield. When your meditation has got as far as that, you may turn back to the thought of Bishop Poore and his shining faith, with relief. Yes. Let Winchester keep its mixed architecture, its King Alfred, King William Rufus and Saint Swithin. Even though we have only Saint Osmund, a junior saint of whom next to nothing is known, and whose canonization was so much in debate it took centuries of diplomacy at Rome to get him recognized, nevertheless our building is a miracle of faith.

Yet this may have nothing to do with *mana*. A few years ago, when shapeless stones from Salisbury spire were piled on the cloisters, their replacements already in position four hundred feet overhead, you could have seen me stand and regard them with a strange and slightly sheepish, even furtive respect. They were just stone, you might say, that was all. They were not art, they were not architecture. They were a formless substance but I could not take my eyes off them. Did I not say we British prefer the substance if we must choose? The historian of religion might mutter about the stones that they were 'relics by contact'. But contact with what? It was *mana*, indescribable, unaccountable, indefinable, impossible *mana*. I think somewhat wryly how I stood the other day in the nave of Salisbury Cathedral, near a local cleric. He watched, with a kind of benevolent suspicion, as I held my hand close to a pillar, then moved it forward and back, like a man trying to find out if he has switched on the bars of an electric fire; but suspicion seemed to be winning over benevolence—so I went away.

COLETTE

FROM

The Collected Stories of Colette

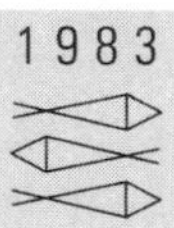

THE RESPITE

[*Translated by Matthew Ward*]

"How's your arm tonight?"

"Not bad, not bad."

"Oh, you always say that. And your knee? I know, 'not bad, not bad' . . . The wind is blowing terribly outside. God only knows what I must have looked like on the Pont des Arts. Holding on to my hat like this; my pleated skirt—you'll never catch me in a pleated skirt again —blown up against my back, my purse without a handle, and me clutching it under my arm like this, no, no, women are just too foolish to dress in a way that's so . . . And as for my hair, just look at it!"

She exaggerated her disarray with a kind of artistry, raising one shoulder up to her ear, screwing up her mouth, wrinkling the skin on her forehead to help keep her hat in place, and squeezing her short skirt between her thighs. She had never been afraid of making faces; she indulged in extreme and grotesque mimicry and somehow remained beyond reproach. Already past thirty, she would imitate Chevalier, improvise an old general's mustache out of wads of cotton, stuff a pillow under her skirt, and exclaim: "Allow me to present to you the pregnant concierge!"

"Does she deliberately make herself ugly out of modesty or pride?" Brice wondered, watching his wife walk pigeon-toed, run into the corner of the table, and rub her thigh. "It's a kind of lie, too."

"You didn't pick up my medicine?"

She looked over her shoulder at her husband, and winked as if to say: "Child!"

"Yes, I did. Got you this time!"

"Oh, a phone call would have been enough to replenish my stock. I'm afraid about tonight . . ."

On his desk he set his big expert's magnifying glass, that venerable old tool dethroned by other newer methods of investigation. Antique, set in copper, it superimposed three lenses which could be used with one over the other or be opened out into a trefoil.

"Were you studying something?" asked Marcelle.

"Nothing," he sighed. "Who cares about painting these days, genuine or fake? Speaking of which, the Tiepolo drawings Myrtil Schwabe bought are fakes. Of course, I gave her ample warning."

Do you think it is that e-e-easy
To fool an expert such as me-e-e . . .

sang Marcelle.

"She's got her nerve . . ." thought Brice indignantly. With his left hand he grabbed his upper right arm, and smiled the way patients who flaunt a certain stoic aplomb smile. Marcelle's tall figure leaned over him.

"Is it very bad? Try to hold out for another thirty or forty minutes. Let's save the ammunition for tonight. Can you?"

"Can I? Come on, it's a game for me . . ."

He shut his eyes so that she would not read in them an overwhelming fact which he himself did not as yet believe: for the second time since that morning, the neuritis had just deserted his right shoulder and his arm as far as the elbow. So total was the reprieve becoming, so eager were the muscles to move, and so astonished were they to feel themselves free and light, that he nearly betrayed himself, nearly groaned with ease. "Not to suffer," thought Brice, "what pleasure can compare with this inner silence, this perfection of one's whole being? Do I even have a left arm? Where is my left arm, its burning right shoulder, the shooting pains of a probe being helped along with a stylet, replaced from time to time by a heavy roller which crushes half the forearm, leaving the other half bound down, in spasms, pulling on its chains?"

He stretched his leg out gingerly. "Nothing in the leg anymore. My knee is being a dear, like a young boy's knee, the knee of a runner . . ." Meanwhile, his wife, in the next room, was speaking to him.

"What did you say, Marcelle?" he shouted. "What square are you talking about?"

"St. Julien-le-Pauvre," she answered from the other bedroom. "What they've done with that little corner is just wonderful. I'm also going to go see the Jardins des Gobelins, apparently they've kept the old fruit trees. Can you imagine? Open-wind apricot trees in Paris . . ."

He heard her laugh.

"Talk about wind, they're getting plenty of it today!"

She reappeared in the doorway of his room. Brice had just enough time to draw in his arm, which he had been stretching, bending, stretching with underhanded exhilaration. Marcelle gave her husband a searching look.

"You're suffering like a poor little baby and hoping I won't be able to tell."

"It's impossible to hide anything from you," said Brice, taking on the jerky delivery, the smile of the discreet martyr.

She stopped twisting around her finger the ringlets of her hair tangled by the gusting wind, knelt down next to the armchair, put her big, careful arm around Brice's neck, and leaned over gently, cheek to cheek.

"Poor, poor baby."

"Marcelle," Brice said grimly, "you're wearing your hair too long, I've told you so a hundred times."

"Yes, darling."

"You should change that idiotic hairdo, those curly wood shavings, and that flat part on the back of your head!"

"Yes, darling."

"You say, 'Yes, darling,' but you're just making fun of me!"

"Yes, darling."

He freed his head with an exasperated gesture, and Marcelle stood up.

"Careful now, you silly goose," she said tenderly. "No acrobatics. What if I put a nice hot towel on your shoulder while you're waiting for your medicine?"

"Hot and useless . . ."

"So it will mix the pointless with the unpleasant. One more word and you'll get my Michel Simon imitation."

She stood in front of him, too tall, long-armed, but well proportioned, and built simply from head to feet. Maturity rested lightly on her, without excess weight, reddening her face a bit, heightening the clear blue of her eyes. Marcelle judged her nose, her mouth, the shape of her chin strictly: "It's not very finely made, but it's good and solid."

For the moment she felt useless and was trying not to show her pity. She pulled the little peplum of her dark green jacket down over her short green-, gray-and-brown-plaid skirt. "It's the same outfit she's wearing in the photograph," thought Brice. "The square buttons, the little Scotch trim on the pockets and collar, everything's the same . . . Photography really is a fine art!" He was overcome with rage, afraid of losing his composure, and asked to be left alone.

"I'd like to try to sleep a little before dinner, you understand."

Puzzled, Marcelle did not respond right away.

"I'd be happy if you slept, of course, but . . . what about tonight?"

"Tonight, tonight . . . One sleepless night more or less, for the last eight days . . ."

"Seven days, Georges . . ."

"Seven days, then! They obviously haven't seemed long to you!"

As he grew more upset, she was quick to give in.

"I'm going, I'm going. Something to drink? Are you comfortable like that? You don't want me to take away the big cushion?" His only response was a shake of his head, and before she left, he had still to endure the caress of a cool hand on his.

Left alone, he tested his arm and his leg, both feeling as new and impatient as himself. He closed his fist firmly around his bunch of keys to keep them from jingling. He took the page torn from the newspaper, the photograph he had studied twenty times, back out of the drawer, and placed the triple lens over it. Blurred faces came into focus and seemed to rise up toward him. *If you recognize yourself as the person in the circle, please stop by our offices; you will receive the sum of* . . . In the center of the white circle, the features of a fat lady peered questioningly at the photographer, as she was starting down the stairs to the métro. Above her, two lovers were bidding each other an avid goodbye, with a passionate kiss which bent the woman back over the iron railing; the man could barely be seen, behind a pleated plaid skirt, a dark jacket, and a pointed felt hat. Beneath the hat's wide brim Brice recognized the straight, somewhat large nose, the overly long ringlets of hair, and the religiously lowered eyelids. "I've never seen the shape of her jaw so clearly before. How long has she had that chin? It's like an animal's, really. She's like all women; once out of their usual companion's sight, they change . . ."

He felt keen, shrewd, filled with hatred. He started to undo, to take off his long, blue, flannel invalid's robe. "Too soon. She wouldn't believe the attack subsided so quickly. I'll take care of this dirty business tomorrow . . ."

At first he used the information provided by the newspaper itself: *Photograph taken in the Xth arrondissement*, and the name of the station, Château-Landon. He was proud of himself for not having asked his wife any questions, but he had her followed. In her presence, he had no trouble grasping his upper right arm with his left hand, as if overcome by a brief, sharp pain, and into his limping around the apartment he put all the casualness of the cripple reconciled to his lameness.

He experienced the strange vigor of the suspicious, their physical immunity, but also a jealous torment which at times made him tremble all over, especially at night, and against which he cowardly asked for help.

"Ask them to fix me a hot-water bottle, Marcelle. Would you hand me the vicuña blanket?"

He found out nothing, neither around the entrance to the métro nor in his wife's mail, and having called off the too-costly gumshoe after a week, he ventured a vague but direct inquiry: "What would make you really happy, Marcelle?"

She turned her prominent eyes toward him and answered without having to think: "Lots of money, to buy a house in the country with, a complete fishing outfit, and the best bootmaker for sport shoes. And another apartment that wouldn't be so close to the Seine."

"She's stupid," thought Brice. "Stupid or very clever."

"And another husband, Marcelle? What would you think of a brand-new husband? New, handsome, robust?"

He laughed, but Marcelle wrinkled up her nose.

"That, my dear, is what I call humor for men only. Little games that go over big in certain government offices. Take my Uncle Auguste, you know what he and his colleagues used to do in the offices for Air Purification? When they weren't telling stories about their wedding nights, they were staining pieces of paper with ink and folding them in half to make designs, or else they'd play at what-would-you-do-if-you-won-a-million."

"Customs of a bygone age," said Brice vexedly.

"Thank God! Ever since women started working in government offices, the men have been behaving a little better!"

In the end, Brice lost his patience. One day he even admitted to himself that his interrogation humiliated himself most of all. Surprised by an unexpected hug from Marcelle—"Do you still like my big monkey's arms around your neck?"—he was unable to hide his sudden emotion and his wet eyes.

"It's my nerves. You know, now that the worst is over . . . it's easing up . . ."

She kissed him, and boisterously celebrated the departure of the fickle pain. But when they were apart, he was once again seized with rage, became overexcited while out walking, rushed home, and did not wait any longer to thrust in front of his wife's eyes the crumpled page from the newspaper which never left him. He had considered accompanying his action with some accusatory remark, but all he could come up with was: "Can you see anything, here, in the way of a resemblance?"

Sitting down, Marcelle smoothed out the creases in the paper with the palm of her hand.

"Oh, well, yes," she said slowly. "Well, yes, yes . . ."

Brice suddenly felt very tired and sat down.

"I can see," Marcelle continued, "that a Scotch plaid is almost always prettier when it's worn on the bias than when it's worn straight. I can see that my saleslady is right when she says a design altered to a client's taste is always less pretty . . . This'll teach me . . . Compare the square shapes of my plaid to the diamonds on this woman here . . ."

She broke off to laugh. "Say, Georges, by the way, look at these two in the photograph, they're really putting their hearts into it, did you see? And *coram populo*!"

Speechless, Brice grabbed his upper right arm with his left hand.

"What is it, Georges? Hurting again?"

He tightened his lips, stricken from his shoulder to his elbow, called back to the burning, capricious, throbbing pain. His neuritis kept him awake till morning. Toward dawn, exhausted, he reached the point of surrender and vague prayers, and he begged: "My suspicions, let me have my suspicions back . . . Let me have last week's misery back, the torture that was easing my pain—a truce, a respite, that's all, a respite."

FROM

Edisto

1984

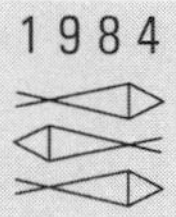

A QUESTION OF HEREDITY

It didn't take a genius to know it was big, not after I knew Theenie had been at the house and thrown down the laundry and wasn't back at her shack and had left my cake out there without her wax paper sealed to it like peritoneum—you know, she has a thing about freshness. She can sit down with some chicken she found in tin foil about two weeks old and heat it up by letting it sit on the table while she irons and then eat it with a Co'-Cola, bouncing the bones in her hand to check for meat she hadn't sucked off, and be perfectly happy. And she could cook mullet brought in head down in a pickle bucket of pink fish slime and worm goo, fry them, and bounce those bones a little too, but when it comes to making something like a cake, which, considering its components (like water and flour and other powders), can't be too foul, at least not like mullet in a bucket sat on by a fat lady in the sun until they stopped biting—it comes to making a bakery-clean white thing like a cake and she's got to have fresh eggs, fresh real butter, sweet milk, and you can't even walk around the house while it cooks lest it fall, and she won't run the vacuum cleaner while it's in there either. She can only sit down with another Co'-Cola and a Stanback powder to virtually pray for it, and then it's out, it will have to cool, and nine times out of ten, before you can touch it, she has grafted to it wax paper set into the hot buttery sugary crust of the cake and welded there by a fusion of wax and cake, and that cake you could throw in the ocean and it would float like a crab-pot marker for years, and the day it washed up on a beach and was found by an islander he could take it to his hut and with great-eyed delight peel off the wax paper with his skinning knife and devour the rich, golden flesh inside. And as soon as you slice up this memorial, this baby, and make your smacky fuss about how good it is, she starts making her fuss about how much trouble it is, and she's not making any more, she's too old, you're too old, too old for *her* to have to work that hard, why, she *raised* you. (She raised two other sets of white kids before me. And she's not through until she hears they got married.) You smile and smack and smile away, she sitting at the kitchen table in her white uniform, hair bluing and legs swollen, fingering an aspirin onto a toothache, complaining and complaining before rising and completing without another idle breath the rest of the cleaning or ironing or bed-making or whatever kind of tracking after the mess of white folks that afternoon presents, and she shows up the next morning with a silent assault on the breakfast detail, fresh and renewed somehow against a thousand cigarette butts in amber dregs of whiskey, and strewn clothes, and crap, crap from the high life.

So I knew it didn't take no genius to know something big was about, and from the way the Doctor took in Taurus like the bright kid they'd heard had decided to be an English major, from the way she toyed with him, the crap about servants, his hanging around, an obvious bid for a surrogate father for me—it isn't the first time she has solicited the attentions of your notably masculine types, at least partly I am sure for some father image around the house—and from what Taurus told me about her (Theenie) bolting out of the shack with jets of terror into the palms waving around like big testifying arms at a revival, from this I knew something was up, particularly for Theenie, old Theenie, who says to me, "Sim, you ain't *got* to do but two things. One is die, and thuther is live *till* you die." I turn my head like a beagle at the novelty of this suggestion coming from her. "Ain' I right?" she says. "I guess you are," I say. "You *believe* it, then."

And I suppose you begin to. You certainly have to think she must believe it, odd as it seems at first that she can believe she has freedom, but then it looks like that belief might be her support in her heavy old world. She must say deep down somewhere very quietly while standing on those swelling brown-scaled legs ironing again and again the brocade this, the fancy that, that she can stand it, stand the steam rising off the board into her face, hot fingers manipulating the coverlets and slipcases just out of range of the iron, steam rising to her sweaty face before the fan turns and blows it off her, because she doesn't *have* to, she likes Simons, he all right, but I ain' got to do it for him neither, I *will* is all. I only got to do two things. Die and live till.

So what makes her pour out of her house and job like water downhill because a man who might be a simple bill collector, some fool, interrupts her at cake baking?

You don't ask an old soothsayer like Theenie herself, who in this case could not be asked because she didn't stop running, save for the brief talk she had with the Doctor, until she got safely back on John's Island. You ask a great old earthy philosopher like Theenie something truly mysterious too directly and the answer you get, if you get one, will be as evasive as your question was blunt. I'm sitting on the commode one day and look off at the trash can by my knee and see some gauze, a bandage, and open it up and there's blood on it, with black flecks like pepper in it—I about faint. "Theeeenie!" I yell. "Thee*nee*!" I'm buckling up in a white fine sweat and pointing at the can when she opens the door. "Who got cut?"

"Hmmp!" she says. "No one." And slams the door, leaving me there in the surgical chamber.

That leaves the Doctor sole heiress to the fortune of secrecy that has her quietly jubilant about losing her maid and welcoming into the house *the* man who chased off her maid, and she gives him the maid quarters when he doesn't ask for them, and charges him with taking me to school. It leaves the Doctor, who had quite a little chat with Theenie, it would seem.

There was nothing for it but direct questions, no one but the new man and the Doctor to ask.

"How'd you scare her that bad?"

"I don't know."

"See you tomorrow."

I took my cake back to the Cabana, where the Doctor was perfectly blumbery. I took her drink and freshened it without being asked (she holds the glass out and says, "Do me?").

"How come that dude scared Theenie?"

"Have you been writhing?"

"Yes ma'am, a whole story just today. But tell me how he scared her."

"She believes she's her grandson—he's. *He's* her grandson. He's come to avenge them for leaving him in New York."

"Who?"

"Her daughter. Her daughter and she did."

"A *baby*?" I asked. Didn't sound like Theenie at all.

She nodded.

"Because he was not . . ."

"Half," she said. "And she says it was sick. Anyway, I'm not sure she's right."

"But she's scared," I said.

"Yes, she's scared," she confirmed, with a slow, exaggerated nodding of her head.

"Well, good night."

"Sleep tight," she said. "Sweet dreams." It wouldn't do to ask any more. I can make it up just as true as she can. So I got out my spiral notebook and corrected for the lie I told about writing a story that day.

BETWEEN LIVING AND DYING
by Simons Manigault

Between living and dying, she had made two mistakes. One was letting her daughter go to New York to be a singer, and the other was letting them take her daughter's baby from its grandmother, herself, who got there in time to get it and take it home and raise it right, whether he was half white or not and sick. It was the sick that got him away from her, the sick that her daughter gave it, junk in it. Her daughter in New York messed up on drugs and taking things called fixes got the baby away from her and got her half convinced he was going to die so she let them take him and then she was never able to get him back and her fool daughter crazy enough to go to a place like that was too crazy to want him if she could have had him and she was just an old colored lady a long way from home and she left. It grinded her up to think about it and she never forgot it and she knew it was not true about having only to die and live till you die. You had to be careful somewhere in between or you could be chased by something like losing your daughter's baby because you weren't careful somewhere else, and you lost your daughter herself or she lost her sense, which is the samc. You could be chased by it and even caught up with.

And it would come for you, not your daughter who had no sense, but you who did, who knew better all along, you the wrong one in it. You would have to leave Simons and Mizmanigo and weave baskets again, but that would be the pricc.

So Theenie and Taurus never talked, not after her terrible recognition, trundling *kawhoosh* past him, floorboards bending and springing her off the porch over the steps she would have stumbled down, her crooked-worn and polished pump heels flying in the sand. And her turning the yellow-and-white eyes on him for one last look and whirling at last into the ushering arms of thc rat palms. I call them rat palms because we were pulling them off, the dead butts of branches, one night for a fire, and because you must pull very hard to rip them loose, I learned the hard way that whatever is between the husk and the coconut-hair bark of the tree comes down on your arm, and that night in the dark my whatever-in-between was no drowsy rumpled sparrow or polite silken tree frog but a rat about the size of possum and texture of armadillo, and it landed all over my arm from hand to shoulder in one shuddering rush, and I nearly shook my arm out of socket and got a chronic case of girls' fear of rats from that and still have it, and you would too.

So he goes in the house and reads W.P.A. stories on the walls where the roaches have eaten away the flour but not the ink of the newspapers, and he naps, wakes, and emerges into the old, bored heat of this named but never discovered small place of the South and hears the tin roof *tic*, *tic* in that heat.

So they never talk. One runs calf-eyed into the woods from the other, who later watches her on Sony monitors in a wall bank of federally funded TV sets. *On a tape* he sees what he sees of her, what he sees of—I found out—of his only known or at least speculative origins, watches as calmly as a surgeon an operation.

What would she have told him if she could have stayed? Probably the usual speech she would make to coroners courting the Doctor.

"She got a *double* use for *you*, mister. If you cain' see that, why you scudgin' us all. Ever since Mr. M. left, it's been a trile with that Simons. Because iss onliess us here. He roundbunction, *in* trouble, fallin' out of *buses*, *ekk*setra. All she wont is somebody to keep him right. Even *she* know that. And Law knows I do, I see enough of that in my own. Somebody got to hep that boy kotch up. He so far ahead he's *behine*. Yes, he *is*." Her head nodding, in a rhythm like a small, gentle locomotive; her whole head rolling on the syllables. "Yes*suh*."

A fine speech and well-intended. But she'd tell it to every coroner and tennis attorney aiding and abetting Arabs to come around here. A wonderful bunch of suitors. Penelope never figured on such a healthy run of dudes when the Progenitor bagged it, I hope.

Taurus came in the house, played a game, accepted an invitation to spend a while with us, told me everything I asked, and otherwise kept his eyes open and his mouth shut. He was somebody you figured knew something. And he was supposed, as Theenie would have put it, to "rescure" me.

I was going to have to modify the Boy Act. He was definitely modifying the Coroner Act.

WE SEE A FIGHT IN CHARLESTON

I told him nothing ever happens here but he wouldn't listen, and couldn't we hike in the woods, he wants to know. The woods, I say. What woods?

"All that dark close noise I passed coming down here," he says. "The black changing sound."

So I had to tell him they was no woods, they was leftovers.

"From what?"

"From, number one, from nothing happening to them except heat and afternoons of Negroes in white shirts with their eyes turning yellow looking at the road. And from, two, from the heat and the rain making so much grow that since no planters or even Sherman ever got here to weed anything out, it became a giant unpruned greenhouse festering in its very success," I said. "Burning up in an excess of youth, like city slums," I said. "Only this city is a rich unturned city of no lights.

"And it became a bog of verdure and got scurvy sort of and the big oaks became turkey oaks and the palm trees became palmettos, and *then* the Arabs landed.

"And they bought the choicest squats what were touched by wind or water, and hired some American scalawags who somehow got that tennis-ball-velvet grass to grow on sand and so converted sand dunes to sand traps, and they cemented the rest and painted it green and so the tennis pros showed up next (not the big ones, only ones like Rod Laver and I saw a college kid beat him), and then the tennis groupies in their German cars and then the Germans themselves came, BASF chemical conglomerate, but an old-time referendum took care of them and sent them home. They didn't hide their intentions.

"So after the tennis groupies got moved into their exclusive condominia, their dogs came, replacing the natural old squatters like skunks and possum with Irish setters, a new breed of them that ignores birds for Frisbees, and then they shored it all up with fake redwood and yardmen disguised as gardeners and attorneys as world travelers on their sailing yachts that never leave the marina. That leaves the scurvy woods and the rickets people right where they were. Right here."

We had walked into this anemic scrub a ways. Before us I showed him an old homesite I call the Frazier ruins.

"Because I forgot a few details," I said. "Before the Arabs, but in the same choice sites they bought, the Marines bought the very first island, and for one simple and sufficient reason: it contained an adequate, maybe the largest, population of the region's first and final indigenous denizen: the sand flea. So grunts get out there on Parris Island at attention and they tell them not to move a muscle on pain of whomp upside the head, and they become hamburger, and it probably won World War II. Because sitting in a foxhole with Jap bullets zinging all over Guam or shooting a flame thrower into a cave or walking waist-deep over a half mile of razor coral reefs because the LSTs ran aground and seeing half of you shot wasn't as bad as doing pushups in sand fleas, so we won.

"And one other detail. Joe Frazier."

The homesite was little pine trees coming up through powdery old two-by-fours and rusty tin panels in the hot sand. Taurus was already looking at the skinks. Skinks are lizards made for speed.

"And the skinks." He already knew how to hold them in place with eye contact. You can walk right up on skinks sometimes if they know you are looking right at them and you do not break eye contact, but if you look away to take a step, they are gone, because they know you don't know which way they went.

"This could have been where he trained," I said.

"Who?"

"Frazier."

"Oh."

"Maybe right under this tin is the rotten old croker sack, just resting in the sand after the hard work of getting Joe on his way to Everlast leather bags and Philadelphia and the big time and—"

"What croker sack?"

He stopped me, but of course he didn't really want to know. I think he hadn't been paying attention to me. And he was right: Who knows if Joe hit a croker sack? He might have just torn up a nightclub or something and somebody got him to a gym in time to put his natural destructiveness to work. But the time I took a Dixie cup of the Doctor's Early Times out here to see what she saw in it, I was sure about Joe and the bag.

He was at the bag in his snot-dauber routine. On a short arm of rope swayed the bag, as large and solid as a piece of ocean, as heavy as tide. Joe hit it and it veered and he blew snot out of his left nostril and hit it coming back and stopped it still. Joe got on a bus. The bag hung there, the beam held it, the barn held on, the town, the heat. The green browned, Joe won.

In Philadelphia they had canvas bags with pockets worn in them by professional punches. They tied a rope across the gym chest-high to Joe and made him step across the gym under it, bobbing from side to side. They said, "Touch it with your ears, Frazier, but don't make the rope move or you'll do it all day." Joe got so good and fast at it that it sometimes seemed the rope moved, not his head, like you think only the cloth moves but a sewing machine needle doesn't. He got so good he threw in extra touches: rolled his shoulders, hooked the snot off his nose, went *hinh hinh* to keep time, faked and mimicked punches. Off this motion would spin his success, would come long looping punches that would have busted croker sacks to pieces. The rope was steady; he followed it. It led him to the Heavyweight Championship of the World. The liquor didn't make me numby or anything, but I did eat the wax out of the Dixie cup, which was a childhood thing of mine, and the liquory, stainy wax tasted much better than the snort itself.

"You want to see him fight?"

"What?" I said. "Who?"

"Frazier."

"Where?"
"Charleston."
"Sure if we—"
"I'll get tickets."

I was a goofball not to know about the fight; it was the Ali fight. Taurus just stood there in the sun, smiling. We walked all over the ruin, the tin breaking in great *ka-thunks*, spurting the skinks out of and back into their jillion million corrugated bunkers. The little bastards had it made: pinstriped miniature monitor dragons, gun-blue survivors, pen-and-ink leftover pygmies of the dinosaur days, living in modern galvanized tunnels buried in the sand like long Quonset huts shrunk down so small even the government lost them.

•

We drove half the night that night, up Highway 17, watching all the flintzy old motels with names like And-Gene Motel that are about closed for good since I-95 opened up and drained the blood out of the old roads. And clubs, or joints, or *jernts*, the Negroes say, umpteen eleven jernts with neon tubes running all over them, broken so the color and the gas leaked out with the road blood. It's very sad. There's one place built like a mosque or something, with this bulbous outline like a fancy sundae, and the neon still works: purple and red. We stopped to get some beer because Taurus said you needed beer to go to a fight because you had to understand the people who might get carried away after it and start a fight with you. In the jernt was a gritty floor and a jukebox and some red booths. A woman in tight black pants and a red stretchy shirt sitting by the cash register got the beer, took the money, rung it in, got back on the stool, picked up a cigarette, blew smoke up at the ceiling, and we left.

Well, I took one. Taurus looked in the sack when I did, as if to count the remainder, but he didn't say anything.

It was awful, but I used it to hurry up and get there with.

We stopped at the Piggly Wiggly and got some food. They had Hoppin' John so I got some in a square carton with a nifty wire handle and intricate closing designs cut into the flaps like a goldfish carton at a fair.

We finally got there. It was in a gym, a big blood-colored thing probably built by the W.P.A., because it had those heavy, square, useless blocks of stone all over so you couldn't tell if it was a museum or what. It was as big as an airplane hangar, with third-story windows they open with chains and pulleys from the floor, and fans in the windows the size of propellers.

Five thousand people were in there on bleachers and metal folding chairs around a boxing ring in which a Negro who looked like a moose was trying to box a pink-white dude with a snow-white flat-top haircut. I say white, but he had green-and-blue tattoos all over his body—a standing bruise. I never had seen any real boxing before and what got me was how nobody seemed to get hit and they spent a lot of time hugging each other until the referee would tell them none of that. The Negro was as big as James Earl Jones and as bald and looked scared, and the white man was bobbing all the time and sliding and grinning all the while like he knew a private secret.

"The black guy's with the promoter's stable," Taurus told me.

"Stable?" I said. "Like horses?"

"The other guy's from prison."

"You mean like Sonny Liston? He learned to box there and got out—"

"No," he said. "He's *in* there. He lives there."

"How do you know?"

"I saw their bus."

"Wha'd it say?"

"C.C.I."

"Charleston Cornhole Idiots."

"Columbia Correctional Institution."

Well, that made all the difference in the world. Now I saw the white guy's secret. He was grinning because he was on the town, out of stir for the night, chained up and bused down and unchained for a night of freedom. And the Negro twice his size was scared because he was in the ring with a *convict.*

Behind the boxers loomed an almost drive-in-sized luminescent screen, white as the moon. The real fight would come on that. You could see a big cable running across the floor away from it that I guess the broadcast had to come through. The moose and the bruise performed their bobbing and hugging, their tiny terrors like mortal shadows against the very sky.

"What's that fireman doing here?"

"He's the fire marshal. I don't know."

We watched the fire marshal talk to a dude with pointy shoes and skinny pants near the door. Then the dude sort of held his hands up in the air and pushed it several times like he was saying "All right" or "Calm down" to the fireman. Then the fireman left and they began closing the doors, but people pushed through. Then they locked them with chains around the handles, the bar kind you press to open school doors. People hit the doors with chairs, which you could tell were chairs because their legs came popping through the glass, that thick, glue-colored glass in school doors with chicken wire set inside. It sounded like guns.

When the first flicker of light hit the screen, it threw up the boxers' shadows bigger than Olympic giants and the whole crowd shut up. Like that. We must have looked like a photograph of a crowd, faces silent, still, looking through blue cigarette smoke.

One more tiny flicker and the hum-drum cranked up louder than ever and I didn't hear any more chairs go off. It flickered a bunch and the fighters started sort of ducking from the light, crouching down and taking a peek at the screen so not to miss anything. When it flickered off they were huddled in a little clench, taking a peek, and when it came on it cast their shadows up on the screen, and we laughed, because you'd see tiny mortals in a huddle and then they'd start fighting and it would come on and they'd be bigger than Godzilla for a couple of crazy, huge hooks; then sloppy amateurs again, then *bir*UP: Killers on the Skyline, the biggest sluggers of all time.

The crowd started booing, so the promoter threw in the towel on his moose, who was glad, and they got out of the ring and everyone just watched the screen. A second or two of faraway light like heat lightning kept hitting it, notching up the noise with every moon-like vision; the audience a bunch of primitives getting giddy because they can't figure out the television, don't know whether to watch the fantastic little men *in* it or to watch *it*, weirded out by the promise of the spectacle but also by this queer satellite light or whatever pouring a faraway world into this hot, smoky gym.

A flash of something real: Ali! and cheers go up. Coppery and gliding, done up in white shoe tassels, eyes bright as a squirrel's, dancing like skip-to-the-music. Those tassels whipping around, wrapping and unwrapping, cracking like whips, *violent*-looking things, snapping and fibrous and lashing his solid legs. You can't hear yourself.

And Joe! *Louder* cheers. He chugs in wearing pedal pushers, big green paisley bloomers, already snot-daubing, a million hunkering little ducks and hooks in the perfect rhythm of the taut rope, buoy down and buoy up, and *hinh* and *hinh*, Joe's got the sound going already.

"You know what he is?" I say.

"Who?"

"He's a renascent smart ass."

Taurus looked at me.

"But now Joe," I said. "There is *business* in Joe." I had him smiling.

A rumor comes by that Joe's family is in the gym and people are looking for them, but fat chance of that because there's every dude with a wallet between Denmark and Olar in the joint, pimps and bankers and city *muh-fuh* gentlemen in colorful undershirts, and country cane pole ones in flannel shirts, but Taurus is looking at one bunch up top I decide might as well be them. There are three or four heavyset kind-of-old ladies in Cossack hats like fur bowls on their heads—probably their Sunday rigs. And behind them stand some men a bit younger and thin-looking in cigar-brown suits with their white shirts very bright, and dark, skinny ties. Their faces are dark and narrow too. Overall they look a bit unsure about things, like it's church.

That's about how Joe looks, bouncing in his corner as if he'd like to kneel down in a pew. And Ali orbiting, advertising, selling, leering like he ought to have on an Elvis Presley costume instead of a terry robe, and Joe snot-daubing, and if they were his people in there, they drove up in probably one big Buick and planned to drive all the way back that night just to see their boy on a drive-in movie screen beamed in by a radio contraption in space a million miles away, and Joe is worried about them driving that far, as if he doesn't have enough to worry about with, I have to admit, a majestic-looking machine of a man assholing all around the ring, and Ali, Mr. *ex*-Cassius Clay, is worried about a woman at ringside he's going to leave his sweet wife for named Veronica Porshe. I read that later.

Well, there's a bunch of circus barking, and *ding* and they're off. Whatever it is that goes on, goes on punctuated by *ding*s and the yelling becomes *who won that one i don't know i don't know either who won that one* and *ding* and yelling again. Five thousand fire-code violators yelling, elbowing, stomping, craning, holding their heads when they can't stand it, lusting for their chosen hero on this living moonscape of escape when—

Silence.

Ali is going over, going over like, like a tree—

All noise.

We see only then, before he hits the deck, Joe's extra-special message to Mr. Smart Ass, looping out of the dark like one of those mace balls, Ali's eyes skittering toward it white like a horse's. All the people are in the air.

In the air they grab each other and shake each other like their stepchildren, and make noise like children being shaken, hysterical garbling and nonsense, jerking each other silly, agape at a fallen god.

And Taurus wasn't even *looking*. He stood there as if an anthem were playing and looked at the Cossack ladies. And they were looking straight ahead, not at the screen.

"He *south*pawed him," I screamed, but he didn't seem to hear.

"I never knew what that word meant until—" But he wasn't listening.

We left and drove again, half until ever, and did not stop at a jernt or talk or anything, and I made it to school the next day on time.

FROM

The Lamplit Answer

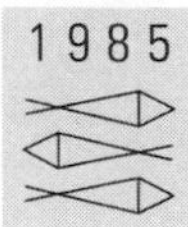

SNOW MELTING

Snow melting when I left you, and I took
This fragile bone we'd found in melting snow
Before I left, exposed beside a brook
Where raccoons washed their hands. And this, I know,

Is that raccoon we'd watched for every day.
Though at the time her wild human hand
Had gestured inexplicably, I say
Her meaning now is more than I can stand.

We've reasons, we have reasons, so we say,
For giving love, and for withholding it.
I who would love must marvel at the way
I know aloneness when I'm holding it,

Know near and far as words for live and die,
Know distance, as I'm trying to draw near,
Growing immense, and know, but don't know why,
Things seen up close enlarge, then disappear.

Tonight this small room seems too huge to cross.
And my life is that looming kind of place.
Here, left with this alone, and at a loss
I hold an alien and vacant face

Which shrinks away, and yet is magnified—
More so than I seem able to explain.
Tonight the giant galaxies outside
Are tiny, tiny on my windowpane.

FROM

The Counterlife

1986

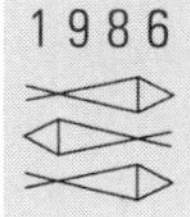

When I located him at his newspaper, Shuki couldn't at first understand who I said was calling—when he did, he pretended to be stupefied. "What's a nice Jewish boy like you doing in a place like this?"

"I come regularly every twenty years to be sure everything's okay."

"Well, things are great," Shuki replied. "We're going down the drain six different ways. It's too awful even to joke about."

We'd met eighteen years earlier, in 1960, during my only previous visit to Israel. Because *Higher Education*, my first book, had been deemed "controversial"—garnering both a Jewish prize and the ire of a lot of rabbis—I'd been invited to Tel Aviv to participate in a public dialogue: Jewish-American and Israeli writers on the subject "The Jew in Literature."

Though only a few years older than I, Shuki back in 1960 had already completed a ten-year stint as an army colonel and just been appointed Ben-Gurion's press attaché. One day he'd taken me up to the Prime Minister's office to shake the hand of "the Old Man," an event that, however special, turned out to be nowhere near so instructive as our lunch beforehand with Shuki's father in the Knesset dining room. "You might learn something meeting an ordinary Israeli working man," Shuki said; "and as for him, he loves coming down here to eat with the big shots." Of course why he especially liked coming to eat at the Knesset was because his son was now working there for his political idol.

Mr. Elchanan was in his mid-sixties then and still employed as a welder in Haifa. He'd emigrated to mandate Palestine from Odessa in 1920, when the Soviet revolution was proving to be more hostile to Jews than its Russian-Jewish supporters had foreseen. "I came," he told me, in the good if heavily accented English that he'd learned as a Palestinian Jew under the British, "and I was already an old man for the Zionist movement—I was twenty-five." He was not strong, but his hands were strong—his hands were the center of him, the truly exceptional thing in his whole appearance. He had kind, very mild, soft brown eyes, but otherwise plain, ungraspable features set in a perfectly round and gentle face. He was not tall like Shuki but short, his chin was not protruding heroically but slightly receding, and he was a little stooped from a lifetime of physical work forming joints and connections. His hair was grayish. More than likely you wouldn't even see him if he sat down across from you on a bus. How intelligent was he, this unprepossessing welder? Intelligent enough, I thought, to raise a very good family, intelligent enough to bring up Shuki and his younger brother, an architect in Tel Aviv, and of course intelligent enough to understand in 1920 that he had better leave Russia if he was intent upon remaining a socialist and a Jew. In conversation, he displayed his share of forceful wit, and even a playful, poetic imagination of sorts when it came time to put me through my paces. I myself couldn't see him as a worker who was nothing more than "ordinary," but then I wasn't his offspring. In fact, it wasn't at all difficult to think of him as an Israeli counterpart to my own father, who was then still practicing chiropody in New Jersey. Despite the difference in professional status, they would have got on well, I thought. That may even be why Shuki and I got on so well.

We were just beginning our soup when Mr. Elchanan said to me, "So you're going to stay."

"Am I? Who said so?"

"Well, you're not going back there, are you?"

Shuki kept spooning the soup—this was obviously a question he wasn't startled to hear.

I figured at first that Mr. Elchanan was joking with me. "To America?" I said, smiling. "Going next week."

"Don't be ridiculous. You'll stay." Here he put down his spoon and came over to my side of the table. With one of those extraordinary hands of his he lifted me by the arm and steered me over to a window of the dining room that looked out across modern Jerusalem to the old walled city. "See that tree?" he said. "That's a Jewish tree. See that bird? That's a Jewish bird. See, up there? A Jewish cloud. There is no country for a Jew but here." Then he set me back down where I could resume eating.

Shuki said to his father, once he was over his plate again, "I think that Nathan's experience makes him see things differently."

"What experience?" The voice was brusque as it hadn't been with me. "He needs us," Mr. Elchanan pointed out to his son, "—and even more than we need him."

"Is that so," Shuki said softly, and continued eating.

However earnest I may have been at twenty-seven, however dutifully, obstinately sincere, I really didn't want to tell my friend's well-meaning, stoop-shouldered old father just how wrong he was, and in response to their exchange I merely shrugged.

"He lives in a museum!" Mr. Elchanan said angrily. Shuki half-nodded—this too he seemed to have heard before—and so Mr. Elchanan turned to say it again directly to me. "You are. We are living in a Jewish theater and you are living in a Jewish museum!"

"Tell him, Nathan," said Shuki, "about your museum. Don't worry, he's been debating with me since I was five—he can take it."

So I did as Shuki said and, for the remainder of the lunch, I told him—as was my style in my twenties (with fathers particularly), told him overpassionately and at enormous length. I wasn't improvising, either: these were conclusions I'd been reaching on my own in the last few days, the result of traveling for three weeks through a Jewish homeland that couldn't have seemed to me more remote.

To be the Jew that I was, I told Shuki's father, which was neither more nor less than the Jew I wished to be, I didn't need to live in a Jewish nation any more than he, from what I understood, felt obliged to pray in a synagogue three times a day. My landscape wasn't the Negev wilderness, or the Galilean hills, or the coastal plain of ancient Philistia; it was industrial, immigrant America—Newark where I'd been raised, Chicago where I'd been educated, and New York where I was living in a basement apartment on a Lower East Side street among poor Ukrainians and Puerto Ricans. My sacred text wasn't the Bible but novels translated from Russian, German, and French into the language in which I was beginning to write and publish my own fiction—not the semantic range of classical Hebrew but the jumpy beat of American English was what excited me. I was not a Jewish survivor of a Nazi death camp in search of a safe and welcoming refuge, or a Jewish socialist for whom the primary source of injustice was the evil of capital, or a nationalist for whom cohesiveness was a Jewish political necessity, nor was I a believing Jew, a scholarly Jew, or a Jewish xenophobe who couldn't bear the proximity of goyim. I was the American-born grandson of simple Galician tradesmen who, at the end of the last century, had on their own reached the same prophetic conclusion as Theodor Herzl—that there was no future for them in Christian Europe, that they couldn't go on being themselves there without inciting to violence ominous forces against which they hadn't the slightest means of defense. But instead of struggling to save the Jewish people from destruction by founding a homeland in the remote corner of the Ottoman Empire that had once been biblical Palestine, they simply set out to save their own

Jewish skins. Insomuch as Zionism meant taking upon oneself, rather than leaving to others, responsibility for one's survival as a Jew, this was their brand of Zionism. And it worked. Unlike them, I had not grown up hedged in by an unnerving Catholic peasantry that could be whipped into a Jew-hating fervor by the village priest or the local landowner; even more to the point, my grandparents' claim to legitimate political entitlement had not been staked in the midst of an alien, indigenous population that had no commitment to Jewish biblical rights and no sympathy for what a Jewish God said in a Jewish book about what constitutes Jewish territory in perpetuity. In the long run I might even be far more secure as a Jew in my homeland than Mr. Elchanan, Shuki, and their descendants could ever be in theirs.

I insisted that America simply did not boil down to Jew and Gentile, nor were anti-Semites the American Jew's biggest problem. To say, Let's face it, for the Jews the problem is always the goyim, may have a ring of truth about it for a moment—"How can anyone dismiss that statement out of hand in this century? And if America should prove to be a place of intolerance, shallowness, indecency, and brutality, where all American values are flushed into the gutter, it could have more than just the ring of truth—it could turn out to be so." But, I went on, the fact of it was that I could not think of any historical society that had achieved the level of tolerance institutionalized in America or that had placed pluralism smack at the center of its publicly advertised dream of itself. I could only hope that Yacov Elchanan's solution to the problem of Jewish survival and independence turned out to be no less successful than the unpolitical, unideological "family Zionism" enacted by my immigrant grandparents in coming, at the turn of the century, to America, a country that did not have at its center the idea of exclusion.

"Though I don't admit this back in New York," I said, "I'm a little idealistic about America—maybe the way that Shuki's a little idealistic about Israel."

I wasn't sure if the smile I saw wasn't perhaps a sign of how impressed he was. He ought to be, I thought—he certainly doesn't hear stuff like this from the other welders. I was even, afterwards, a little chagrined that I had said quite so much, fearing that I might have demolished *too* thoroughly the aging Zionist and his simplifications.

But he merely continued smiling away, even as he rose to his feet, came around the table, and once again lifted me by my arm and led me back to where I could look out on his Jewish trees and streets and birds and clouds. "So many words," he finally said to me, and with just a trace of that mockery that was more recognizably Jewish to me than the clouds—"such brilliant explanations. Such deep thoughts, Nathan.

I never in my life saw a better argument than you for our never leaving Jerusalem again."

His words were our last words, for before we could even eat dessert Shuki rushed me upstairs for my scheduled minute with another stocky little gentleman in a short-sleeve shirt who, in person, also looked to me deceptively inconsequential, as though the model of a tank that I spotted among the papers and family photos on his desk could have been nothing more than a toy constructed for a grandchild in his little workshop.

Shuki told the Prime Minister that we'd just come up from lunch with his father.

This amused Ben-Gurion. "So you're staying," he said to me. "Good. We'll make room."

A photographer was already there, poised to take a picture of Israel's Founding Father shaking hands with Nathan Zuckerman. I am laughing in the photograph because just as it was to be snapped, Ben-Gurion whispered, "Remember, this isn't yours—it's for your parents, to give them a reason to be proud of you."

He wasn't wrong—my father couldn't have been happier if it had been a picture of me in my Scout uniform helping Moses down from Mount Sinai. This picture wasn't merely beautiful, it was also ammunition, to be used primarily, however, in his struggle to prove to *himself* that what leading rabbis were telling their congregations from the pulpit about my Jewish self-hatred couldn't possibly be true.

Framed, the photograph was exhibited for the remaining years of my parents' lives atop the TV console in the living room, alongside the picture of my brother receiving his dental diploma. These to my father were our greatest achievements. And his.

FROM

Break It Down

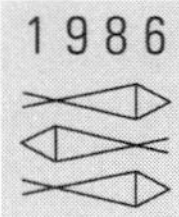

BREAK IT DOWN

He's sitting there staring at a piece of paper in front of him. He's trying to break it down. He says:

I'm breaking it all down. The ticket was $600 and then after that there was more for the hotel and food and so on, for just ten days. Say $80 a day, no, more like $100 a day. And we made love, say, once a day on the average. That's $100 a shot. And each time it lasted maybe two or three hours so that would be anywhere from $33 to $50 an hour, which is expensive.

Though of course that wasn't all that went on, because we were together almost all day long. She would keep looking at me and every time she looked at me it was worth something, and she smiled at me and didn't stop talking and singing, something I said, she would sail into it, a snatch, for me, she would be gone from me a little ways but smiling too, and tell me jokes, and I loved it but didn't exactly know what to do about it and just smiled back at her and felt slow next to her, just not quick enough. So she talked and touched me on the shoulder and the arm, she kept touching and stayed close to me. You're with each other all day long and it keeps happening, the touches and smiles, and it adds up, it builds up, and you know where you'll be that night, you're talking and every now and then you think about it, no, you don't think, you just feel it as a kind of destination, what's coming up after you leave wherever you are all evening, and you're happy about it and you're planning it all, not in your head, really, somewhere inside your body, or all through your body, it's all mounting up and coming together so that when you get in bed you can't help it, it's a real performance, it all pours out, but slowly, you go easy until you can't anymore, or you hold back the whole time, you hold back and touch the edges of everything, you edge around until you have to plunge in and finish it off, and when you're finished, you're too weak to stand but after a while you have to go to the bathroom and you stand, your legs are trembling, you hold on to the door frames, there's a little light coming in through the window, you can see your way in and out, but you can't really see the bed.

So it's not really $100 a shot because it goes on all day, from the start when you wake up and feel her body next to you, and you don't miss a thing, not a thing of what's next to you, her arm, her leg, her shoulder, her face, that good skin, I have felt other good skin, but this skin is just the edge of something else, and you're going to start going, and no matter how much you crawl all over each other it won't be enough, and when your hunger dies down a little then you think how much you love her and that starts you off again, and her face, you look over at her face and can't believe how you got there and how lucky and it's still all a surprise and it never stops, even after it's over, it never stops being a surprise.

It's more like you have a good sixteen or eighteen hours a day of this going on, even when you're not with her it's going on, it's good to be away because it's going to be so good to go back to her, so it's still here, and you can't go off and look at some old street or some old painting without still feeling it in your body and a few things that happened the day before that don't mean much by themselves or wouldn't mean much if you weren't having this thing together, but you can't forget and it's all inside you all the time, so that's more like, say, sixteen into a hundred would be $6 an hour, which isn't too much.

And then it really keeps going on while you're asleep, though you're probably dreaming about something else, a building, maybe, I kept dreaming, every night, almost, about this building, because I would spend a lot of every morning in this old stone building and when I closed my eyes I would see these cool spaces and have this peace inside me, I would see the bricks of the floor and the stone arches and the space, the emptiness between, like a kind of dark frame around what I could see beyond, a garden, and this space was like stone too because of the coolness of it and the gray shadow, that kind of luminous shade, that was glowing with the light of the sun falling beyond the arches, and there was also the great height of the ceiling, all this was in my mind all the time though I didn't know it until I closed my eyes, I'm asleep and I'm not dreaming about her but she's lying next to me and I wake up enough times in the night to remember she's there, and notice, say, once she was lying on her back but now she's curled around me, I look at her closed eyes, I want to kiss her eyelids, I want to feel that soft skin under my lips, but I don't want to disturb her, I don't want to see her frown as though in her sleep she has forgotten who I am and feels just that something is bothering her and so I just look at her and hold on to it all, these times when I'm watching over her sleep and she's next to me and isn't away from me the way she will be later, I want to stay awake all night just to go on feeling that, but I can't, I fall asleep again, though I'm sleeping lightly, still trying to hold on to it.

But it isn't over when it ends, it goes on after it's all over, she's still inside you like a sweet liquor, you are filled with her, everything about her has kind of bled into you, her smell, her voice, the way her body moves, it's all inside you, at least for a while after, then you begin to lose it, and I'm beginning to lose it, you're afraid of how weak you are, that you can't get her all back into you again and now the whole thing is going out of your body and it's more in your mind than your body, the pictures come to you one by one and you look at them, some of them last longer than others, you were together in a very white clean place, a coffeehouse, having breakfast together, and the place is so white that against it you can see her clearly, her blue eyes, her smile, the colors of her clothes, even the print of the newspaper she's reading when she's not looking up at you, the light brown and red and gold of her hair when she's got her head down reading, the brown coffee, the brown rolls, all against that white table and those white plates and silver urns and silver knives and spoons, and against that quiet of the sleepy people in that room sitting alone at their tables with just some chinking and clattering of spoons and cups in saucers and some hushed voices her voice now and then rising and falling. The pictures come to you and you have to hope they won't lose their life too fast and dry up though you know they will and that you'll also forget some of what happened, because already you're turning up little things that you nearly forgot.

We were in bed and she asked me, Do I seem fat to you? and I was surprised because she didn't seem to worry about herself at all in that way and I guess I was reading into it that she did worry about herself so I answered what I was thinking and said stupidly that she had a very beautiful body, that her body was perfect, and I really meant it as an answer, but she said kind of sharply, That's not what I asked, and so I had to try to answer her again, exactly what she had asked.

And once she lay over against me late in the night and she started talking, her breath in my ear, and she just went on and on, and talked faster and faster, she couldn't stop, and I loved it, I just felt that all that life in her was running into me too, I had so little life in me, her life, her fire, was coming into me, in that hot breath in my ear, and I just wanted her to go on talking forever right there next to me, and I would go on living, like that, I would be able to go on living, but without her I don't know.

Then you forget some of it all, maybe most of it all, almost all of it, in the end, and you work hard at remembering everything now so you won't ever forget, but you can kill it too even by thinking about it too much, though you can't help thinking about it nearly all the time.

And then when the pictures start to go you start asking some questions, just little questions, that sit in your mind without any answers, like why did she have the light on when you came in to bed one night, but it was off the next, but she had it on the night after that and she had it off the last night, why, and other questions, little questions that nag at you like that.

And finally the pictures go and these dry little questions just sit there without any answers and you're left with this large heavy pain in you that you try to numb by reading, or you try to ease it by getting out into public places where there will be people around you, but no matter how good you are at pushing that pain away, just when you think you're going to be all right for a while, that you're safe, you're kind of holding it off with all your strength and you're staying in some little bare numb spot of ground, then suddenly it will all come back, you'll hear a noise, maybe it's a cat crying or a baby, or something else like her cry, you hear it and make that connection in a part of you you have no control over and the pain comes back so hard that you're afraid, afraid of how you're falling back into it again and you wonder, no, you're terrified to ask how you're ever going to climb out of it.

And so it's not only every hour of the day while it's happening, but it's really for hours and hours every day after that, for weeks, though less and less, so that you could work out the ratio if you wanted, maybe after six weeks you're only thinking about it an hour or so in the day altogether, a few minutes here and there spread over, or a few minutes here and there and half an hour before you go to sleep, or sometimes it all comes back and you stay awake with it half the night.

So when you add up all that, you've only spent maybe $3 an hour on it.

If you have to figure in the bad times too, I don't know. There weren't any bad times with her, though maybe there was one bad time, when I told her I loved her. I couldn't help it, this was the first time this had happened with her, now I was half falling in love with her or maybe completely if she had let me but she couldn't or I couldn't completely because it was all going to be so short and other things too, and so I told her, and didn't know of any way to tell her first that she didn't have to feel this was a burden, the fact that I loved her, or that she didn't have to feel the same about me, or say the same back, that it was just that I had to tell her, that's all, because it was bursting inside me, and saying it wouldn't even begin to take care of what I was feeling, really I couldn't say anything of what I was feeling because there was so much, words couldn't handle it, and making love only made it worse because then I wanted words badly but they were no good, no good at all, but I told her anyway, I was lying on top of her and her hands were up by her head and my hands were on hers and our fingers were locked and there was a little light on her face from the window but I couldn't really see her and I was afraid to say it but I had to say it because I wanted her to know, it was the last night, I had to tell her then or I'd never have another chance, I just said, Before you go to sleep, I have to tell you before you go to sleep that I love you, and immediately, right away after, she said, I love you too, and it sounded to me as if she didn't mean it, a little flat, but then it usually sounds a little flat when someone says, I love you too, because they're just saying it back even if they do mean it, and the problem is that I'll never know if she meant it, or maybe someday she'll tell me whether she meant it or not, but there's no way to know now, and I'm sorry I did that, it was a trap I didn't mean to put her in, I can see it was a trap, because if she hadn't said anything at all I know that would have hurt too, as though she were taking something from me and just accepting it and not giving anything back, so she really had to, even just to be kind to me, she had to say it, and I don't really know now if she meant it.

Another bad time, or it wasn't exactly bad, but it wasn't easy either, was when I had to leave, the time was coming, and I was beginning to tremble and feel empty, nothing in the middle of me, nothing inside, and nothing to hold me up on my legs, and then it came, everything was ready, and I had to go, and so it was just a kiss, a quick one, as though we were afraid of what might happen after a kiss, and she was almost wild then, she reached up to a hook by the door and took an old shirt, a green and blue shirt from the hook, and put it in my arms, for me to take away, the soft cloth was full of her smell, and then we stood there close together looking at a piece of paper she had in her hand and I didn't lose any of it, I was holding it tight, that last minute or two, because this was it, we'd come to the end of it, things always change, so this was really it, over.

Maybe it works out all right, maybe you haven't lost for doing it, I don't know, no, really, sometimes when you think of it you feel like a prince really, you feel just like a king, and then other times you're afraid, you're afraid, not all the time but now and then, of what it's going to do to you, and it's hard to know what to do with it now.

Walking away I looked back once and the door was still open, I could see her standing far back in the dark of the room, I could only really see her white face still looking out at me, and her white arms.

I guess you get to a point where you look at that pain as if it were there in front of you three feet away lying in a box, an open box, in a window somewhere. It's hard and cold, like a bar of metal. You just look at it there and say, All right, I'll take it, I'll buy it. That's what it is. Because you know all about it before you even go into this thing. You know the pain is part of the whole thing. And it isn't that you can say afterwards the pleasure was greater than the pain and that's why you would do it again. That has nothing to do with it. You can't measure it, because the pain comes after and it lasts longer. So the question really is, Why doesn't that pain make you say, I won't do it again? When the pain is so bad that you have to say that, but you don't.

So I'm just thinking about it, how you can go in with $600, more like $1,000, and how you can come out with an old shirt.

FROM

The Haw Lantern

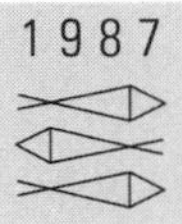

THE HAW LANTERN

The wintry haw is burning out of season,
crab of the thorn, a small light for small people,
wanting no more from them but that they keep
the wick of self-respect from dying out,
not having to blind them with illumination.

But sometimes when your breath plumes in the frost
it takes the roaming shape of Diogenes
with his lantern, seeking one just man;
so you end up scrutinized from behind the haw
he holds up at eye-level on its twig,
and you flinch before its bonded pith and stone,
its blood-prick that you wish would test and clear you,
its pecked-at ripeness that scans you, then moves on.

SCOTT TUROW

FROM

Presumed Innocent

1987

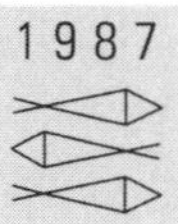

Three a.m. When I awake my heart is racing and cool traces of sweat are abrading my neck, so that in the idiocy of sleep I am trying to loosen my collar. I grope; then lie back. My breath is short, and my heartbeat thunders intermittently in the ear against the pillow. My dream is still clear to me: my mother's face in agony; that worn cadaverous image as she neared the end, and worse, her look of lost, unspeaking terror.

When my mother became sick, and quickly died, she was in the most peaceful period of her adult life. She and my father were no longer living together, although they still worked side by side each day in the bakery. He had moved in with a widow, Mrs. Bova, whose urgent bearing when she came into the shop I can remember even from the years before her husband died. For my mother, whose life with my father had been a dominion of fear, this arrangement became a kind of liberation. Her interest in the world outside her suddenly increased. She became one of the first of the regular callers on those listener-participation talk shows. Tell us what you think about interracial dating, legalizing marijuana, who killed Kennedy. She stacked the dining-room table with old newspapers and magazines, pads and index cards on which she made notations to herself, preparing for tomorrow's programs. My mother, who was phobic about venturing beyond our apartment building or the shop, who had to begin her preparations early in the morning if she was going to depart her home sometime that afternoon, who from the time I was eight sent me to the market so that she could avoid leaving the house —my mother became a local personality of sorts for her outspoken views about various worldly controversies. I could not reconcile this development with the accommodations I had made long before with myself to accept her wildly verging eccentricities, or the narrow margins of her former life.

She had been twenty-eight, four years my father's senior, when they were married, the sixth daughter of a Jewish union organizer and a lass from Cork. My father wed, I'm sure, for her savings, which allowed him to open up the shop. Nor was there ever any sign that my mother had married for love. She was an old maid and, I would guess, far too peculiar to gather other suitors. Her behavior, as I witnessed it, was apt to be excessive and ungovernable, with manic tours from pinnacles of rosy hilarity to hours of brooding looks. Sometimes she became frantic. She was forever running to ransack her crowded dresser drawers, rummaging in her sewing box as she made high-pitched excited noises. Because she seldom left home, her sisters made it a habit to look after her. This was a brave endeavor. When my aunts visited, my father would assail them in loud conversation with himself as busybodies, and he was not above actual threats of violence if they came when he was drunk. The two who ventured most often, my Aunts Flo and Sarah, were both bold, determined women, their father's daughters, and they were apt to control my father with stern looks and fearless demeanor, not much different than if they were confronting some barking cur. They were undeterred in their unannounced mission to protect the meek—Rosie (my mother) and, especially, me. For me these sisters were a hovering presence throughout my childhood. They brought me candies; they took me for haircuts and bought my clothes. They supervised my upbringing in such routine fashion that I was in my twenties before I recognized their intentions—or their kindness. And somehow, without ever realizing it had happened, I grew to know there were two worlds, my mother's and the other one dwelled in by her sisters, the one to which I eventually recognized I, as well, belonged. It was a fixed star of my youth to think that my mother was not, as I put it to myself, regular; to know that my adoration of her was a purely private matter, unintelligible to others and beyond my power to explain.

Do I really care what she would think now? I suppose. What child would not? I am almost glad she did not live to witness this. In her last few months she was with us. We were still living in the city in a one-bedroom apartment, but Barbara refused to see my mother anywhere else. She slept on a daybed in the living room from which she seldom rose. Barbara, most of the time, sat on a hard wooden chair drawn close. Near the end, my mother spoke constantly to Barbara. Her head was laid on her pillow, her face sadly reduced by disease, her eyes narrowly focused, their light growing weak. Barbara held her hand. They murmured. I could not make out the words—but the sound was constant, like a running tap. Barbara Bernstein, daughter of a sleek suburban matron, and my mother, of roaming mind and indelibly sweet disposition, voyaged to one another, crossed the straits of loneliness, while I, as ever, was too full of private grief to make my own approach. I watched them from the door: for Barbara, the mother who made no demands; for Rosie, a child who would not disregard her. When I took Barbara's place, my mother held my hand. I had the decency to tell her often that I loved her; she smiled weakly, but seldom spoke. Near the end, it was Barbara who gave her the shots of Demerol. A few of the syringes are still downstairs in a box of odd keepsakes of my mother that Barbara maintains: antique bobbins and index cards; the gold-tipped Parker pen she used to make notes for her radio appearances.

I walk through the dark to find my slippers, slide my robe from the closet. In the living room, I sit, feet up, huddled in a rocking chair. Lately I have been thinking of taking up cigarettes again. I feel no cravings, but it would give me something to do in these abject hours in the dead of night when I am now so often awake.

A game I play with myself is called What Is the Worst Part? So many things seem trivial. I do not care much now about the way the women gape at me when I walk around in the village center. I do not worry about my reputation, or the fact that for the rest of my life, even if charges are dropped tomorrow, many people will cringe reflexively whenever they hear my name. I do not worry about how hard it will be for me to find work as an attorney if I am acquitted. But the steady emotional erosion, the sleeplessness, the manic anxiety I cannot pretend about or minimize. What is worst are these midnight wakings and the instants before I can gather myself, when I am sure that the terror is never going to end. It is like groping for the switch plate in the dark, but I am never certain—and here the terror is the worst—I am never sure that I will find it. As the search becomes more and more prolonged, the little bit of sense that holds forth in me erodes, gives way, bubbles off like a tablet dropped into water, and the wild blackness of some limitless and everlasting panic begins to swallow me.

That is what is worst; that and my worries about Nathaniel. On Sunday, we will put him on a train for Camp Okawaka near Skageon, where he is scheduled to remain for the three weeks the trial is projected to last. Recalling this, I quietly tread the stairs and stand in the dark hall outside his door. I listen until I can catch the rhythm of his breath, and then force my own breathing down to that same measure. As I watch Nat sleep, the weirdness of science overcomes me: I think of atoms and molecules, skin and veins, muscle and bones. I try to comprehend my son for an instant as a compilation of parts. But that fails. We cannot ever enlarge the realm of our final understanding. I know Nathaniel as the hot mass of my feelings for him; I behold him as something no smaller or more finite or reducible than my passions. He will not piece or parse. He is my boy, gentle and beautiful in sleep, and I am grateful, grateful so that my heart is sore and breaking, that in this rough life I have felt such tenderness.

If I am convicted, they will take me away from him. Even Larren Lyttle will send me to prison for many years, and the thought of missing the remainder of his young life shatters me, breaks me into pieces. Oddly, I feel little conscious fear of prison itself. I dread the exile and the separation. The thought of confinement can make me ill at ease. But the actual physical horrors I am sure to suffer are seldom in my mind, even when I pierce myself with the thought of the extreme consequences I may face.

And yet I know. I have spent days at Rudyard, the state pen, where every murderer is sent. I have been there usually to interview a witness, but the sights are chilling. The bars are heavy iron slats, painted flat black, two inches deep, one-half inch wide, and behind them are all these bastards who now—now it strikes you—are so much the same. The black guys chattering their manic raging stuff. The white guys in their rolled-up stocking caps. The Latinos who look out with pointy-eyed rage. They are collectively every man you have avoided in a hallway or a bus station, every kid you picked out in high school as destined to be a bum. They are the ones who always wore their deficits like scars, headed here almost as certainly as a skyward-shot arrow plunging back to earth.

About this group it is no longer possible to harbor any kind of sentiment. I have heard every horror story. And I know that these grisly anecdotes are some of the unseen ink that blackens my dreams. For me this will not be far from torture. I know about the nighttime shivs, about the showers where blow jobs are given in the open. I know about Marcus Wheatley, one of the guys I tried to get to talk in Night Saints, who hosed somebody on a dope deal down there, and was laid on his back in the weight room, told to put up his hands, and then given a barbell with 250 pounds on each end, which asphyxiated him, even while it acted half like a guillotine. I know about the demographics of that neighborhood, 16 percent murderers, and more than half the inmates there for some form of violent crime. I know about the gray food. The four men in a cell. The odor of excrement that is overpowering on certain tiers. I know that every month there are areas where the gang control becomes so complete that the guards refuse to walk through for days. I know about the guards themselves and the eight of them who were convicted in the federal court for a New Year's party they threw in which they used shotguns to line up twelve black prisoners whom they took turns beating with flagstones and bricks.

I know about what happens to men like me there, because I know what happened to some I helped to send. I know about Marcy Lupino, who, whenever my thoughts loiter here, is the person most likely to come to mind. Marcello was a regular type, your basic hustling American, a C.P.A. who early in his career did a little work setting odds for some of the boys from his old neighborhood. Eventually Marcy's accounting practice prospered and he determined that he no longer required outside employment, at which time John Conte, one of the Boys, informed him that his was not the kind of job that he was free to quit. And that's the way it went. Marcy Lupino, respected C.P.A., PTA president, and member of the board of directors of two banks, a guy who wouldn't monkey with the books of his biggest client, left his office every afternoon at 3:30 p.m. sharp to set the spread on ball games, to tote the odds for tomorrow's ponies. All well and good, until one day when a federal snitch gave away a wire room. The IRS came through the door and found Marcy Lupino among half a dozen other people and three million dollars in betting slips. The feds wanted him to talk in the worst way. But Marcy was very good at arithmetic. Two years on a gambling beef, mail fraud, wire fraud, racketeering charges, whatever the feds could put to him, was not worth ten minutes of what John Conte and the Boys would do. They would cut out his testicles and feed them to him, make him chew. And this, Marcy Lupino knew, was not a figure of speech.

So Mike Townsend from the Organized Crime Strike Force called me. He wanted to provide Marcy with incentives. We charged Marcy stateside, and when he was convicted he went to Rudyard instead of the federal overnight camp he had been counting on, a place with a salad bar and tennis courts, a place where he would teach bookkeeping to inmates working on college degrees and copulate with Mrs. Lupino every ninety days as part of the furlough program. Instead, we sent him off in manacles, chained to a man who had put out his infant daughter's eyes with his keys.

Six months later Townsend called and we took a trip north to see if Lupino had responded. We found him in a field with a hoe. He was scraping at the ground. We reintroduced ourselves, hardly a necessity. Marcy Lupino took his hoe, propped it under his arm, and leaned on it as he wept. He cried like I have never seen a man cry; he shook from head to toe, his face turned purple, and the water poured from his eyes, truly, as from a faucet. A little fat bald-headed forty-eight-year-old man, crying as hard as he could. But he would not talk. He said one thing to us: 'I got no teet'.' Nothing else.

As we were walking back, the guard explained.

Big buck nigger, Drover, wanted Lupino as his babe. He's the kind, man, nobody says no, not even the Italians in this joint. He gets himself into Lupino's cell one night, takes out his dingus, and tells Lupino to suck. Lupino won't, so Drover takes Lupino's face and bangs it on the bunk rail until there is not a whole tooth left in Lupino's head; some aching roots, some pieces, but not one tooth.

Warden's got a rule, the guard says. You get bandages for your wounds, we'll sew you up, but no special treatment unless you talk. Fuckin Lupino ain't getting his false teeth until he tells who did the tap dance on him. And fuckin Lupino, he ain't tellin, he knows what's good for him, nobody here is that dumb. No, the guard says, he ain't tellin. And ol' Drover, he is laughin, he says he done a real good job, and that his big Johnson goes in there now, smooth as silk; he says he been in many pussies that don't feel that good. The guard, a fine humanitarian, leaned on his shotgun and laughed. Crime, he reported to Townsend and me, sure don't pay.

Run, I think now as I sit in the dark contemplating Marcy Lupino. Run. The thought always comes that suddenly: run. As a prosecutor, I could never understand why they stayed around to let it fall, to face trial, sentencing, prison. But they remained for the most part, as I have. There is $1600 in my checking account and I have no other money in the world. If I looted Barbara's trust, I would have enough to go, but then I would probably lose the only real motive I have for freedom—the chance to see Nat. And even if I could spend summers with him in Rio or Uruguay or wherever it is that they do not extradite for murder, the powers of even a desperate fancy are too meager to imagine how I would survive without a language I know or a skill those cultures would recognize. I could simply disappear to the center of Cleveland or Detroit, become somebody different, and never see my son again. But the fact is that none of these are visions of what I recognize as life. Even in these lightless hours, I want the same things I wanted when I got off the bus at night in the village green in Nearing. We are so simple sometimes, and fortified so strangely. I sit here in the dark with my heels drawn against me, and as I shiver, I imagine the odor of the smoke of cigarettes.

CHRISTOPHER LOGUE

FROM

War Music

1987

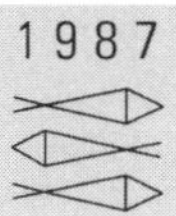

Now I shall ask you to imagine how
Men under discipline of death prepare for war.
There is much more to it than armament,
And kicks from those who could not catch an hour's sleep,
Waking the ones who dozed like rows of spoons;
Or those with everything to lose, the kings,
Asleep like pistols in red velvet.
Moments like these absolve the needs dividing men.
Whatever caught and brought and kept them here,
Under Troy's ochre wall for ten burnt years,
Is lost: and for a while they join a terrible equality;
Are virtuous, self-sacrificing, free;
And so insidious is this liberty
That those surviving it will bear
An even greater servitude to its root:
Believing they were whole, while they were brave;
That they were rich, because their loot was great;
That war was meaningful, because they lost their friends.
They rise!—the Greeks with smiling iron mouths.
They are like Nature; like a mass of flame;
Great lengths of water struck by changing winds;
A forest of innumerable trees;
Boundless sand; snowfall across broad steppes at dusk.
As a huge beast stands and turns around itself,
The well-fed, glittering army, stands and turns.

TOM WOLFE

FROM

The Bonfire of the Vanities

1987

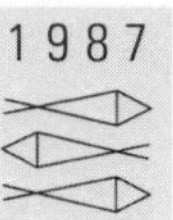

The investment-banking firm of Pierce & Pierce occupied the fiftieth, fifty-first, fifty-second, fifty-third, and fifty-fourth floors of a glass tower that rose up sixty stories from out of the gloomy groin of Wall Street. The bond trading room, where Sherman worked, was on the fiftieth. Every day he stepped out of an aluminum-walled elevator into what looked like the reception area of one of those new London hotels catering to the Yanks. Near the elevator door was a fake fireplace and an antique mahogany mantelpiece with great bunches of fruit carved on each corner. Out in front of the fake fireplace was a brass fence or fender, as they called it in country homes in the west of England. In the appropriate months a fake fire glowed within, casting flickering lights upon a prodigious pair of brass andirons. The wall surrounding it was covered in more mahogany, rich and reddish, done in linen-fold panels carved so deep, you could *feel* the expense in the tips of your fingers by just looking at them.

All of this reflected the passion of Pierce & Pierce's chief executive officer, Eugene Lopwitz, for things British. Things British—library ladders, bowfront consoles, Sheraton legs, Chippendale backs, cigar cutters, tufted club chairs, Wilton-weave carpet—were multiplying on the fiftieth floor at Pierce & Pierce day by day. Alas, there wasn't much Eugene Lopwitz could do about the ceiling, which was barely eight feet above the floor. The floor had been raised one foot. Beneath it ran enough cables and wires to electrify Guatemala. The wires provided the power for the computer terminals and telephones of the bond trading room. The ceiling had been lowered one foot, to make room for light housings and air-conditioning ducts and a few more miles of wire. The floor had risen; the ceiling had descended; it was as if you were in an English mansion that had been squashed.

No sooner did you pass the fake fireplace than you heard an ungodly roar, like the roar of a mob. It came from somewhere around the corner. You couldn't miss it. Sherman McCoy headed straight for it, with relish. On this particular morning, as on every morning, it resonated with his very gizzard.

He turned the corner, and there it was: the bond trading room of Pierce & Pierce. It was a vast space, perhaps sixty by eighty feet, but with the same eight-foot ceiling bearing down on your head. It was an oppressive space with a ferocious glare, writhing silhouettes, and the roar. The glare came from a wall of plate glass that faced south, looking out over New York Harbor, the Statue of Liberty, Staten Island, and the Brooklyn and New Jersey shores. The writhing silhouettes were the arms and torsos of young men, few of them older than forty. They had their suit jackets off. They were moving about in an agitated manner and sweating early in the morning and shouting, which created the roar. It was the sound of well-educated young white men baying for money on the bond market.

"Pick up the fucking phone, please!" a chubby, pink-faced member of the Harvard Class of 1976 screamed at someone two rows of desks away. The room was like a newspaper city room in that there were no partitions and no signs of visible rank. Everyone sat at light gray metal desks in front of veal-colored computer terminals with black screens. Rows of green-diode letters and numbers came skidding across.

"I said please pick up the fucking phone! I mean holy shit!" There were dark half-moons in the armpits of his shirt, and the day had just begun.

A member of the Yale Class of 1973 with a neck that seemed to protrude twelve inches out of his shirt stared at a screen and screamed over the telephone at a broker in Paris: "If you can't see the fucking screen . . . Oh, for Christ's sake, Jean-Pierre, that's the *buy*er's five million! The *buy*er's! Nothing further's coming in!"

Then he covered the telephone with his hand and looked straight up at the ceiling and said out loud to no one, except Mammon, "The frogs! The fucking frogs!"

Four desks away, a member of the Stanford Class of 1979 was sitting down, staring at a sheet of paper on his desk and holding a telephone to his ear. His right foot was up on the stirrup of a portable shoeshine stand, and a black man named Felix, who was about fifty—or was he about sixty?—was humped over his foot, stropping his shoe with a high-shine rag. All day long Felix moved from desk to desk, shining the shoes of young bond traders and salesmen as they worked, at three dollars per, counting the tip. Seldom was a word exchanged; Felix scarcely registered on their maculae. Just then Stanford '79 rose from his chair, his eyes still fastened on the sheet of paper, the telephone still at his ear—and his right foot still on the shoeshine stirrup—and he shouted: "Well then, why do you think everybody's stripping the fucking twenty-years?"

Never took his foot off the shoeshine stand! What powerful legs he must have! thought Sherman. Sherman sat down before his own telephone and computer terminals. The shouts, the imprecations, the gesticulations, the fucking fear and greed, enveloped him, and he loved it. He was the number one bond salesman, "the biggest producer," as the phrase went, in the bond trading room of Pierce & Pierce on the fiftieth floor, and he loved the very roar of the storm.

"This Goldman order really fucked things up good!"

"—step up to the fucking plate and—"

"—bid 8½—"

"I'm away by two thirty-seconds!"

"Somebody's painting you a fucking picture! Can't you see that?"

"I'll take an order and buy 'em at 6-plus!"

"Hit the five-year!"

"Sell five!"

"You couldn't do ten?"

"You think this thing continues up?"

"Strip fever in the twenty-year! That's all these jerks keep talking about!"

"—a hundred million July-nineties at the buck—"

"—naked short—"

"Jesus Christ, what's going on?"

"I don't fucking believe this!"

"Holy fucking shit!" shouted the Yale men and the Harvard men and the Stanford men. "Ho-lee fuc-king shit."

How these sons of the great universities, these legatees of Jefferson, Emerson, Thoreau, William James, Frederick Jackson Turner, William Lyons Phelps, Samuel Flagg Bemis, and the other three-name giants of American scholarship—how these inheritors of the *lux* and the *veritas* now flocked to Wall Street and to the bond trading room of Pierce & Pierce! How the stories circulated on every campus! If you weren't making $250,000 a year within five years, then you were either grossly stupid or grossly lazy. That was the word. By age thirty, $500,000—and that sum had the taint of the mediocre. By age forty you were either making a million a year or you were timid and incompetent. *Make it now!* That motto burned in every heart, like myocarditis. Boys on Wall Street, mere boys, with smooth jawlines and clean arteries, boys still able to blush, were buying three-million-dollar apartments on Park and Fifth. (Why wait?) They were buying thirty-room, four-acre summer places in Southampton, places built in the 1920s and written off in the 1950s as white elephants, places with decaying servants' wings, and they were doing over the servants' wings, too, and even adding on. (Why not? We've got the servants.) They had carnival rides trucked in and installed on the great green lawns for their children's birthday parties, complete with teams of carnival workers to operate them. (A thriving little industry.)

And where did all of this astonishing new money come from? Sherman had heard Gene Lopwitz discourse on that subject. In the Lopwitz analysis, they had Lyndon Johnson to thank. Ever so quietly, the U.S. had started printing money by the billions to finance the war in Vietnam. Before anyone, even Johnson, knew what was happening, a worldwide inflation had begun. Everyone woke up to it when the Arabs suddenly jacked up oil prices in the early 1970s. In no time, markets of all sorts became heaving crapshoots: gold, silver, copper, currencies, bank certificates, corporate notes—even bonds. For decades the bond business had been the bedridden giant of Wall Street. At firms such as Salomon Brothers, Morgan Stanley, Goldman Sachs, and Pierce & Pierce, twice as much money had always changed hands on the bond market as on the stock market. But prices had budged by only pennies at a time, and mostly they went down. As Lopwitz put it, "The bond market has been going down ever since the Battle of Midway." The Battle of Midway (Sherman had to look it up) was in the Second World War. The Pierce & Pierce bond department had consisted of only twenty souls, twenty rather dull souls known as the Bond Bores. The less promising members of the firm were steered into bonds, where they could do no harm.

Sherman resisted the thought that it had been even thus when he entered the bond department. Well, there was no more talk about Bond Bores these days . . . Oh no! Not at all! The bond market had caught fire, and experienced salesmen such as himself were all at once much in demand. All of a sudden, in investment houses all over Wall Street, the erstwhile Bond Bores were making so much money they took to congregating after work in a bar on Hanover Square called Harry's, to tell war stories . . . and assure one another this wasn't dumb luck but, rather, a surge of collective talent. Bonds now represented four-fifths of Pierce & Pierce's business, and the young hotshots, the Yalies, Harvards, and Stanfords, were desperate to get to the bond trading room of Pierce & Pierce, and at this very moment their voices ricocheted off Eugene Lopwitz's linen-fold mahogany walls.

Masters of the Universe! The roar filled Sherman's soul with hope, confidence, esprit de corps, and righteousness. Yes, righteousness! Judy understood none of this, did she? None of it. Oh, he noticed her eyes glazing over when he talked about it. Moving the lever that moves the world was what he was doing—and all she wanted to know was why he never made it home for dinner. When he did make it home for dinner, what did she want to talk about? Her precious interior-decorating business and how she had gotten their apartment into *Architectural Digest*, which, frankly, to a true Wall Streeter was a fucking embarrassment. Did she commend him for the hundreds of thousands of dollars that made her decorating and her lunches and whatever the hell else she did possible? No, she did not. She took it for granted . . .

. . . and so forth and so on. Within ninety seconds, emboldened by the mighty roar of the bond trading room of Pierce & Pierce, Sherman managed to work up a good righteous head of resentment against this woman who had dared make him feel guilty.

He picked up the telephone and was ready to resume work on the greatest coup of his young career, the Giscard, when he spotted something out of the corner of his eye. He *detected* it—righteously!—amid that great bondscape of writhing limbs and torsos. *Arguello was reading a newspaper.*

Ferdinand Arguello was a junior bond salesman, twenty-five or -six years old, from Argentina. He was leaning back in his chair nonchalantly reading a newspaper, and even from here Sherman could see what it was: *The Racing Form. The Racing Form!* The young man looked like a caricature of a South American polo player. He was slender and handsome; he had thick wavy black hair, combed straight back. He was wearing a pair of red silk moiré suspenders. *Silk moiré.* The bond department of Pierce & Pierce was like an Air Force fighter squadron. Sherman knew it even if this young South American didn't. As the number one bond salesman, Sherman had no official rank. Nevertheless, he occupied a moral eminence. You were either capable of doing the job and willing to devote 100 percent to the job, or you got out. The eighty members of the department received a base salary, a safety net, of $120,000 a year each. This was regarded as a laughably small sum. The rest of their income came from commissions and profit-sharing. Sixty-five percent of the department's profits went to Pierce & Pierce. But 35 percent was split among the eighty bond salesmen and traders themselves. All for one and one for all, and lots for oneself! And therefore . . . no slackers allowed! no deadwood! no lightweights! no loafers! You headed straight for your desk, your telephone, and your computer terminal in the morning. The day didn't start with small talk and coffee and perusals of *The Wall Street Journal* and the financial pages of the *Times*, much less *The Racing Form.* You were expected to get on the telephone and start making money. If you left the office, even for lunch, you were expected to give your destination and a telephone number to one of the "sales assistants," who were really secretaries, so that you could be summoned immediately if a new issue of bonds came in (and had to be sold fast). If you went out for lunch, it better have something directly to do with selling bonds for Pierce & Pierce. Otherwise—sit here by the telephone and order in from the deli like the rest of the squadron.

Sherman walked to Arguello's desk and stood over him. "What are you doing, Ferdi?"

From the moment the young man looked up, Sherman could tell he knew what the question meant and that he knew he was wrong. But if there was one thing an Argentine aristocrat knew, it was how to brazen it out.

Arguello locked a level gaze onto Sherman's eyes and said, in a voice just slightly louder than necessary: "I'm reading *The Racing Form.*"

"What for?"

"What for? Because four of our horses are racing at Lafayette today. That's a track outside of Chicago."

With this he resumed reading the newspaper.

It was the *our* that did it. *Our* was supposed to remind you that you were in the presence of the House of Arguello, lords of the pampas. Besides that, the little shit was wearing a pair of red silk moiré suspenders.

"Look . . . sport," said Sherman, "I want you to put that sheet away."

Challengingly: "What did you say?"

"You heard me. I said put that fucking sheet away!" It was supposed to come out calmly and firmly, but it came out furiously. It came out furiously enough to finish off Judy, Pollard Browning, the doorman, and a would-be mugger.

The young man was speechless.

"If I ever see you with a *Racing Form* in here again, you can go sit outside Chicago and make your money! You can sit on the clubhouse turn and bet perfectas! This is Pierce & Pierce, not OTB!"

Arguello was crimson. He was paralyzed with anger. All he could do was beam a ray of pure hatred at Sherman. Sherman, the righteous wrathful one, turned away, and as he did, he noticed with satisfaction that the young man was slowly closing the open expanse of *The Racing Form.*

Wrathful! Righteous! Sherman was elated. People were staring. Good! Idleness was a sin not against the self or against God but against

Mammon and Pierce & Pierce. If he had to be the one to call this greaseball to accounts, then—but he regretted the *greaseball*, even in his thoughts. He considered himself as part of the new era and the new breed, a Wall Street egalitarian, a Master of the Universe who was a respecter only of performance. No longer did Wall Street or Pierce & Pierce mean Protestant Good Family. There were plenty of prominent Jewish investment bankers. Lopwitz himself was Jewish. There were plenty of Irishmen, Greeks, and Slavs. The fact that not one of the eighty members of the bond department was black or female didn't bother him. Why should it? It didn't bother Lopwitz, who took the position that the bond trading room at Pierce & Pierce was no place for symbolic gestures.

"Hey, Sherman."

He happened to be passing Rawlie Thorpe's desk. Rawlie was bald, except for a fringe of hair around the back of his head, and yet he still looked youthful. He was a great wearer of button-down shirts and Shep Miller suspenders. The button-down collars had a flawless roll.

"What was that all about?" he asked Sherman.

"I couldn't believe it," said Sherman. "He's over there with *The Racing Form*, working on fucking horse charts." He felt compelled to embellish the offense a bit.

Rawlie started laughing. "Well, he's young. He's probably had it with electric doughnuts."

"Had it with what?"

Rawlie picked up his telephone and pointed to the mouthpiece. "See that? That's an electric doughnut."

Sherman stared. It did look sort of like a doughnut, with a lot of little holes instead of one big one.

"It just dawned on me today," said Rawlie. "All I do all day is talk to other electric doughnuts. I just hung up from talking to a guy over at Drexel. I sold him a million and a half Joshua Tree bonds." On Wall Street you didn't say *a million and a half dollars' worth of bonds*. You said *a million and a half bonds*. "That's some goddamned outfit in Arizona. His name is Earl. I don't even know his last name. Over the past two years I bet I've done a couple dozen transactions with him, fifty, sixty million bonds, and I don't even know his last name, and I've never met him, and I probably never will. He's an electric doughnut."

Sherman didn't find this amusing. In some way it was a repudiation of his triumph over the shiftless young Argentinian. It was a cynical denial of his very righteousness itself. Rawlie was a very amusing man, but he hadn't been himself since his divorce. Maybe he was no longer such a great squadron warrior, either.

"Yeah," said Sherman, managing a half smile for his old friend. "Well, I gotta go call some a *my* doughnuts."

Back at his desk Sherman settled down to the work at hand. He stared at the little green symbols trucking across the computer screen in front of him. He picked up the telephone. The French gold-backed bond . . . A weird, very promising situation, and he had discovered it when one of the fellows, quite casually, mentioned the bond, in passing, one evening at Harry's.

Back in the innocent year 1973, on the eve of the heaving crap-shoot, the French government had issued a bond known as the Giscard, after the French President, Giscard d'Estaing, with a face value of $6.5 billion. The Giscard had an interesting feature: it was backed by gold. So as the price of gold went up and down, so did the price of the Giscard. Since then the price of both gold and the French franc had shot up and down so crazily, American investors had long since lost interest in the Giscard. But lately, with gold holding firm in the $400 range, Sherman had discovered that an American buying Giscards stood to make two to three times the interest he could make on any U.S. government bond, plus a 30 percent profit when the Giscard matured. It was a sleeping beauty. The big danger would be a drop in the value of the franc. Sherman had neutralized that with a scheme for selling francs short as a hedge.

The only real problem was the complexity of the whole thing. It took big, sophisticated investors to understand it. Big, sophisticated, *trusting* investors; no newcomer could talk anybody into putting millions into the Giscard. You had to have a track record. You had to have talent—genius!—mastery of the universe!—like Sherman McCoy, biggest producer at Pierce & Pierce. He had convinced Gene Lopwitz to put up $600 million of Pierce & Pierce's money to buy the Giscard. Gingerly, stealthily, he had bought the bonds from their various European owners without revealing the mighty hand of Pierce & Pierce, by using various "blind" brokers. Now came the big test for a Master of the Universe. There were only about a dozen players who were likely buyers of anything as esoteric as the Giscard. Of these Sherman had managed to start negotiations with five: two trust banks, Traders' Trust Co. (known as Trader T) and Metroland; two money managers; and one of his best private clients, Oscar Suder of Cleveland, who had indicated he would buy $10 million. But by far the most important was Trader T, which was considering taking half the entire lot, $300 million.

The deal would bring Pierce & Pierce a 1 percent commission up front—$6 million—for conceiving of the idea and risking its capital. Sherman's share, including commissions, bonuses, profit-sharing, and resale fees, would come to about $1.75 million. With that he intended to pay off the horrendous $1.8 million personal loan he had taken out to buy the apartment.

So the first order of business today was a call to Bernard Levy, a Frenchman who was handling the deal at Trader T; a relaxed, friendly call, the call of a biggest-producing salesman (Master of the Universe), to remind Levy that although both gold and the franc had fallen in value yesterday and this morning (on the European exchanges), it meant nothing; all was well, very well indeed. It was true that he had met Bernard Levy only once, when he made the original presentation. They had been conferring on the telephone for months . . . but *electric doughnut*? Cynicism was such a cowardly form of superiority. That was Rawlie's great weakness. Rawlie cashed his checks. He wasn't too cynical to do that. If he wanted to belly up because he couldn't deal with his wife, that was his sad problem.

As Sherman dialed and waited for Bernard Levy to come on the line, the rousing sound of the greed storm closed in about him once again. From the desk right in front of his, a tall bug-eyed fellow (Yale '77): "Thirty-one bid January eighty-eights—"

From a desk somewhere behind him: "I'm short seventy million ten-year!"

From he knew not where: "They got their fucking buying shoes on!"

"I'm in the box!"

"—long 125—"

"—a million four-years from Midland—"

"Who's fucking around with the W-Is?"

"I tell you, I'm in the box!"

"—bid 80½—"

"—buy 'em at 6-plus—"

"—pick up 2½ basis points—"

"Forget it! It's nut-cutting time!"

•

At ten o'clock, Sherman, Rawlie, and five others convened in the conference room of Eugene Lopwitz's suite of offices to decide on Pierce & Pierce's strategy for the main event of the day in the bond markets, which was a U.S. Treasury auction of 10 billion bonds maturing in twenty years. It was a measure of the importance of the bond business to Pierce & Pierce that Lopwitz's offices opened right out into the bond trading room.

The conference room had no conference table. It looked like the lounge in the English hotel for the Yanks where they serve tea. It was full of small antique tables and cabinets. They were so old, brittle, and highly polished, you got the feeling that if you flicked one of them hard with your middle finger, it would shatter. At the same time, a wall of plate glass shoved a view of the Hudson River and the rotting piers of New Jersey into your face.

Sherman sat in a George II armchair. Rawlie sat next to him, in an old chair with a back shaped like a shield. In other antique or antiqued chairs, with Sheraton and Chippendale side tables beside them, were the head government trader, George Connor, who was two years younger than Sherman; his deputy, Vic Scaasi, who was only twenty-eight; the chief market analyst, Paul Feiffer; and Arnold Parch, the executive vice president, who was Lopwitz's first lieutenant.

Everyone in the room sat in a classic chair and stared at a small brown plastic speaker on top of a cabinet. The cabinet was a 220-year-old Adam bowfront, from the period when the brothers Adam liked to paint pictures and ornate borders on wooden furniture. On the center panel was an oval-shaped painting of a Greek maiden sitting in a dell or grotto in which lacy leaves receded fuzzily in deepening shades of green into a dusky teal sky. The thing had cost an astonishing amount of money. The plastic speaker was the size of a bedside clock radio. Everyone stared at it, waiting for the voice of Gene Lopwitz. Lopwitz was in London, where it was now 4:00 p.m. He would preside over this meeting by telephone.

An indistinct noise came out of the speaker. It might have been a voice and it might have been an airplane. Arnold Parch rose from his armchair and approached the Adam cabinet and looked at the plastic speaker and said, "Gene, can you hear me all right?"

He looked imploringly at the plastic speaker, without taking his eyes off it, as if in fact it *were* Gene Lopwitz, transformed, the way princes are transformed into frogs in fairy tales. For a moment the plastic frog said nothing. Then it spoke.

"Yeah, I can hear you, Arnie. There was a lotta cheering going on." Lopwitz's voice sounded as if it were coming from out of a storm drain, but you could hear it.

"Where are you, Gene?" asked Parch.

"I'm at a cricket match." Then less clearly: "What's the name a this place again?" He was evidently with some other people. "Tottenham Park, Arnie. I'm on a kind of a terrace."

"Who's playing?" Parch smiled, as if to show the plastic frog that this wasn't a serious question.

"Don't get technical on me, Arnie. A lot of very nice young gentlemen in cable-knit sweaters and white flannel pants, is the best I can tell you."

Appreciative laughter broke out in the room, and Sherman felt his own lips bending into the somehow obligatory smile. He glanced about the room. Everyone was smiling and chuckling at the brown plastic speaker except for Rawlie, who had his eyes rolled up in the Oh Brother mode.

Then Rawlie leaned over toward Sherman and said, in a noisy whisper: "Look at all these idiots grinning. They think the plastic box has eyes."

This didn't strike Sherman as very funny, since he himself had been grinning. He was also afraid that Lopwitz's loyal aide, Parch, would think he was Rawlie's confederate in making sport of the maximum leader.

"Well, everybody's here, Gene," Parch said to the box, "and so I'm gonna get George to fill you in on where we stand on the auction as of now."

Parch looked at George Connor and nodded and walked back to his chair, and Connor got up from his and walked over to the Adam cabinet and stared at the brown plastic box and said: "Gene? This is George."

"Yeah, hi, George," said the frog. "Go ahead."

"Here's the thing, Gene," said Connor, standing in front of the Adam commode, unable to take his eyes off the plastic box, "it feels pretty good. The old twenties are trading at 8 percent. The traders are telling us they'll come in on the new ones at 8.05, but we think they're playing games with us. We think we're gonna get action right down to 8. So here's what I figure. We'll scale in at 8.01, 8.02, 8.03, with the balance at 8.04. I'm ready to go 60 percent of the issue."

Which, translated, meant: he was proposing to buy $6 billion of the $10 billion in bonds offered in the auction, with the expectation of a profit of two thirty-seconds of a dollar—6¼¢—on every one hundred dollars put up. This was known as "two ticks."

Sherman couldn't resist another look at Rawlie. He had a small, unpleasant smile on his face, and his gaze seemed to pass several degrees to the right of the Adam commode, toward the Hoboken docks. Rawlie's presence was like a glass of ice water in the face. Sherman resented him all over again. He knew what was on his mind. Here was this outrageous arriviste, Lopwitz—Sherman knew Rawlie thought of him that way—trying to play the nob on the terrace of some British cricket club and at the same time conduct a meeting in New York to decide whether Pierce & Pierce was going to stake two billion, four billion, or six billion on a single government bond issue three hours from now. No doubt Lopwitz had his own audience on hand at the cricket club to watch this performance, as his great words bounced off a communications satellite somewhere up in the empyrean and hit Wall Street. Well, it wasn't hard to find something laughable in it, but Lopwitz was, in truth, a Master of the Universe. Lopwitz was about forty-five years old. Sherman wanted nothing less seven years down the line, when he was forty-five. To be astride the Atlantic . . . with billions at stake! Rawlie could snigger . . . and sink into his kneecaps . . . but to think what Lopwitz now had in his grasp, to think what he made each year, just from Pierce & Pierce, which was at least $25 million, to think of the kind of life he led—and what Sherman thought of first was Lopwitz's young wife, Snow White. That was what Rawlie called her. Hair as dark as ebony, lips as red as blood, skin as white as snow . . . She was Lopwitz's fourth wife, French, a countess, apparently, no more than twenty-five or twenty-six, with an accent like Catherine Deneuve doing a bath-oil commercial. She was something . . . Sherman had met her at a party at the Petersons'. She had put her hand on his forearm, just to make a point in conversation—but the way she kept the pressure on his arm and stared at him from about eight inches away! She was a young and frisky animal. Lopwitz had taken what he wanted. He had wanted a young and frisky animal with lips as red as blood and skin as white as snow, and that was what he had taken. What had ever happened to the other three Mrs. Eugene Lopwitzes was a question Sherman had never heard brought up. When you had reached Lopwitz's level, it didn't even matter.

"Yeah, well, that sounds all right, George," said the plastic frog. "What about Sherman? Are you there, Sherman?"

"Hi, Gene!" said Sherman, rising from the George II armchair. His own voice sounded very odd to him, now that he was talking to a plastic box, and he didn't dare even take a quick glance at Rawlie as he walked over to the Adam commode and took his stance and stared, rapt, at the machine on top.

"Gene, all my customers are talking 8.05. My gut feeling, though, is that they're on our side. The market has a good tone. I think we can bid ahead of the customer interest."

"Okay," said the voice in the box, "but just make sure you and George stay on top a the trading accounts. I don't wanna hear about Salomon or anybody horsing around with shorts."

Sherman found himself marveling at the frog's wisdom.

Some sort of throttled roar came over the speaker. Everybody stared at it.

Lopwitz's voice returned. "Somebody just hit the hell outta the ball," he said. "The ball's kinda dead, though. Well, you kinda hadda be there." It wasn't clear what he meant by that. "Well, look, George. Can you hear me, George?"

Connor hopped to it, rose from his chair, hustled over to the Adam commode.

"I can hear you, Gene."

"I was just gonna say, if you feel like stepping up to the plate and taking a good whack at it today, go ahead. It sounds okay."

And that was that.

At forty-five seconds before the auction deadline of 1:00 p.m., George Connor, at a telephone in the middle of the bond trading room, read off his final scaled-in bids to a Pierce & Pierce functionary sitting at a telephone at the Federal Building, which was the physical site of the auction. The bids averaged $99.62643 per $100 worth of bonds. Within a few seconds after 1:00 p.m., Pierce & Pierce now owned, as planned, $6 billion worth of the twenty-year bond. The bond department had four hours in which to create a favorable market. Vic Scaasi led the charge on the bond trading desk, reselling the bonds mainly to the brokerage houses—by telephone. Sherman and Rawlie led the bond salesmen, reselling the bonds mainly to insurance companies and trust banks—by telephone. By 2:00 p.m., the roar in the bond trading room, fueled more by fear than greed, was unearthly. They all shouted and sweated and swore and devoured their electric doughnuts.

By 5:00 p.m. they had sold 40 percent—$2.4 billion—of the $6 billion at an average price of $99.75062 per $100 worth of bonds, for a profit of not two but four ticks! *Four ticks!* That was a profit of twelve and a half cents per one hundred dollars. *Four ticks!* To the eventual retail buyer of these bonds, whether an individual, a corporation, or an institution, this spread was invisible. But—*four ticks!* To Pierce & Pierce it meant a profit of almost $3 million for an afternoon's work. And it wouldn't stop there. The market was holding firm and edging up. Within the next week they might easily make an additional $5 to $10 million on the 3.6 billion bonds remaining. *Four ticks!*

By five o'clock Sherman was soaring on adrenaline. He was part of the pulverizing might of Pierce & Pierce, Masters of the Universe. The audacity of it all was breathtaking. To risk $6 billion in one afternoon to make *two ticks*—six and a quarter cents per one hundred dollars—and then to make four ticks—*four ticks!*—the audacity!—the audacity! Was there any more exciting power on the face of the earth? Let Lopwitz watch all the cricket matches he wants to! Let him play the plastic frog! Master of the Universe—the audacity!

The audacity of it flowed through Sherman's limbs and lymph channels and loins. Pierce & Pierce was the power, and he was wired into the power, and the power hummed and surged in his very innards.

[· · ·]

Sherman leaned back in his chair and surveyed the bond trading room. The processions of phosphorescent green characters still skidded across the faces of the computer terminals, but the roar had subsided to something more like locker-room laughter. George Connor stood beside Vic Scaasi's chair with his hands in his pockets, just chatting. Vic arched his back and rolled his shoulders and seemed about to yawn. There was Rawlie, reared back in his chair, talking on the telephone, grinning and running his hand over his bald pate. Victorious warriors after the fray . . . Masters of the Universe . . .

FROM

The Yellow Wind

[*Translated by Haim Watzman*]

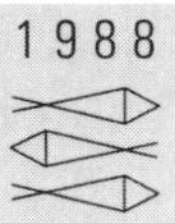

On a day of turbid rain, at the end of March, I turn off the main road leading from my house in Jerusalem to Hebron, and enter the Deheisha refugee camp. Twelve thousand Palestinians live here in one of the highest population densities in the world; the houses are piled together, and the house of every extended family branches out in ugly cement growths, rooms and niches, rusty iron beams spread throughout as sinews, jutting like disconnected fingers.

In Deheisha, drinking water comes from wells. The only running water is the rainwater and sewage flowing down the paths between the houses. I soon give up picking my way between the puddles; there is something ridiculous—almost unfair—about preserving such refinement here, in the face of a few drops of filth.

Beside each house—a yard. They are small, fenced in with corrugated aluminum, and very clean. A large *jara* filled with springwater and covered with cloth stands in each yard. But every person here will tell you without hesitation that the water from the spring of his home village was sweeter. "In Ain Azrab"—she sighs (her name is Hadijah, and she is very old)—"our water was so clear and healthy that a dying man once immersed himself, drank a few mouthfuls, and washed—and was healed on the spot." She cocks her head, drills me with an examining gaze, and mocks: "So, what do you think of that?"

I discover—with some bafflement, I admit—that she reminds me of my grandmother and her stories about Poland, from which she was expelled. About the river, about the fruit there. Time has marked both their faces with the same lines, of wisdom and irony, of great skepticism toward all people, both relatives and strangers.

"We had a field there. A vineyard. Now see what a flowering garden we have here," and she waves her brown, wrinkled hand over the tiny yard.

"But we made a garden," murmurs her daughter-in-law, a woman of wild, gypsy, unquiet beauty. "We made a garden in tin cans." She nods toward the top of the cinder-block fence, where several pickle cans bring forth red geraniums, in odd abundance, as if drawing their life from some far source of fruitfulness, of creation.

A strange life. Double and split. Everyone I spoke to in the camp is trained—almost from birth—to live this double life: they sit here, very much here, because deprivation imposes sobriety with cruel force, but they are also there. That is—among us. In the villages, in the cities. I ask a five-year-old boy where he is from, and he immediately answers, "Jaffa," which is today part of Tel Aviv. "Have you ever seen Jaffa?" "No, but my grandfather saw it." His father, apparently, was born here, but his grandfather came from Jaffa. "And is it beautiful, Jaffa?" "Yes. It has orchards and vineyards and the sea."

And farther down, where the path slopes, I meet a young girl sitting on a cement wall, reading an illustrated magazine. Where are you from? She is from Lod, not far from Ben-Gurion International Airport, forty years ago an Arab town. She is sixteen. She tells me, giggling, of the beauty of Lod. Of its houses, which were big as palaces. "And in every room a hand-painted carpet. And the land was wonderful, and the sky was always blue."

I remembered the wistful lines of Yehuda Halevy, "The taste of your sand—more pleasant to my mouth than honey," and Bialik, who sang to the land which "the spring eternally adorns," how wonderfully separation beautifies the beloved, and how strange it is, in the barrenness of the gray cement of Deheisha, to hear sentences so full of lyric beauty, words spoken in a language more exalted than the everyday, poetic but of established routine, like a prayer or an oath: "And the tomatoes there were red and big, and everything came to us from the earth, and the earth gave us and gave us more."

"Have you visited there, Lod?" "Of course not." "Aren't you curious to see it now?" "Only when we return."

This is how the others answer me also. The Palestinians, as is well known, are making use of the ancient Jewish strategy of exile and have removed themselves from history. They close their eyes against harsh reality, and stubbornly clamping down their eyelids, they fabricate their Promised Land. "Next year in Jerusalem," said the Jews in Latvia and in Cracow and in San'a, and the meaning was that they were not willing to compromise. Because they had no hope for any real change. He who has nothing to lose can demand everything; and until his Jerusalem becomes real, he will do nothing to bring it closer. And here also, again and again, that absolute demand: everything. Nablus and Hebron and

Jaffa and Jerusalem. And in the meantime—nothing. In the meantime, abandoned physically and spiritually. In the meantime, a dream and a void.

•

It's all bolitics, the Palestinians say. Even those who can pronounce the "p" in "politics" will say "bolitics," as a sign of defiance, in which there is a sort of self-mocking; "bolitics," which means that whole game being played over our heads, kept out of our hands, crushing us for decades under all the occupations, sucking out of us life and the power to act, turning us into dust, it's all bolitics, the Turks and the British, and the son-of-a-whore Hussein who killed and slaughtered us without mercy, and now all of a sudden he makes himself out to be the protector of the Palestinians, and these Israelis, who are willing to bring down a government because of two terrorists they killed in a bus, and with the considered cruelty of an impeccably meticulous jurist they change our laws, one thousand two hundred new laws they issued, and deprive us of our land and of our tradition and of our honor, and construct for us here some kind of great enlightened prison, when all they really want is for us to escape from it, and then they won't let us return to it ever—and in their proud cunning, which we are completely unable to understand, they bind their strings to us, and we dance for them like marionettes.

"It's all bolitics," laughs the ironic woman, who reminds me slightly of my grandmother, and slightly of the cunning, old, loud Italian from *Catch-22*, the one who explains to proud American Nately why America will lose the war in the end, and poor Italy will not win, but survive. "The strongest weapon the Arabs in the occupied territories can deploy against us," a wise man once said, "is not to change." And it is true—when you walk through the Deheisha camp you feel as if that conception has internalized itself unconsciously here, seeped its way into the hearts of the people and become power, defiance: we will not change, we will not try to improve our lives. We will remain before you like a curse cast in cement.

She suddenly remembers: "There, in the village, in Ain Azrab, we baked bread over a straw fire. Not here. Because here we don't have livestock, and none of their leavings." She falls silent and hugs herself. Her forehead wrinkles repeatedly in a spasm of wonder. The brown, wrinkled fingers go, unconsciously, through the motions of kneading.

Everything happens elsewhere. Not now. In another place. In a splendid past or a longed-for future. The thing most present here is absence. Somehow one senses that people here have turned themselves voluntarily into doubles of the real people who once were, in another place. Into people who hold in their hands only one real asset: the ability to wait.

And I, as a Jew, can understand that well.

"When a person is exiled from his land," a Jewish-American author once said to the Palestinian writer from Ramallah, Raj'a Shehade, "he begins to think of it in symbols, like a person who needs pornography. And we, the Jews, have also become expert pornographers, and our longings for this land are woven of endless symbols." The author was speaking of the Jews of hundreds of years ago, but on the day I went to Deheisha the Knesset was storming in fierce debate over the symbolism of the name "Judea and Samaria," and Knesset member Geula Cohen demanded that this remain the only legal designation, and that the terms "West Bank" and "territories" in all their permutations not be used. "Judea and Samaria" really sounds more significant and symbolical, and there are many among us for whom the phrase activates a pleasant historical reflex, a sort of satisfying shiver reaching into the depths of the past, there spreading ripples of longing for other sleeping phrases as well—the Bashan, the Gilad, the Horan, all parts of the ancient Greater Israel and today parts of Syria and Jordan.

About half a million Palestinian refugees live today in the Gaza Strip. In the West Bank there are about 400,000. (We are speaking here only of refugees, and not of the entire Arab population under Israeli rule.) In Jordan there are about 850,000. In Lebanon, some 250,000. Syria also has about 250,000. A total of about two and a quarter million refugees. Even if the problem of the refugees living under Israeli rule is solved, the bitterness of their more than a million brothers in the Arab countries, living in no less appalling conditions, will remain. This is why the feeling of despair is so deep among all those who know this problem well. This is why the refugees allow themselves to become addicted to their dreams.

Raj'a Shehade, writer and lawyer, admits that he, too, was a pornographer of views in his youth. Of the view of Jaffa and the coastal plain, about which he has heard stories and legends. When he hikes today over the hills next to Ramallah, it happens that he forgets himself for a minute and he can enjoy the contact with the earth, smell the thyme, gaze upon an olive tree—and then he understands that he is looking at an olive tree, and before his eyes the tree transmutes, and becomes a symbol, the symbol of struggle, of loss, "and at that very same moment the tree is stolen from me," says Shehade, "and in its place is a void, filling up with pain and anger."

The void. The absence, which for decades has been filling with hatred.

A.N., whom I met another time, in Nablus, told me: "Of course I hate you. Maybe at the beginning I didn't hate and only feared. Afterwards, I began to hate." A.N., thirty years old, is a resident of the Balata refugee camp. He spent ten years of his life in jail (the Ashkelon and Nafha prisons) after being found guilty of belonging to the Popular Front for the Liberation of Palestine. ("I didn't actually take part in operations. They only taught me to shoot.") "Before I went to jail, I didn't even know I was a Palestinian. There they taught me who I am. Now I have opinions. Don't believe the ones who tell you that the Palestinians don't really hate you. Understand: the average Palestinian is not the fascist and hating type, but you and the life under your occupation push him into hatred. Look at me, for example. You took ten years of my life from me. You exiled my father in '68. He hadn't done anything. He wasn't even a PLO supporter. Maybe even the opposite. But you wanted to kick out anyone who had an opinion about anything. So that we would be here completely without leaders. Even without leaders who were a little bit for you. And my mother—for six years you did not allow her to go to visit him. And I—after prison, you don't let me build a house, or leave here to visit Jordan, nothing. And you constantly repeat: See what progress we have brought you. You forget that in twenty years everything has progressed. The whole world strides forward. True, you helped us a little, but you aren't willing to give us the most important thing. True, we progressed a little, but look how much you progressed during that time. We remained way behind, and if you check it out, maybe you'll see that we are even worse off in a relative sense than we were in '67." (The standard of living may be measured by personal consumption per capita and GNP per capita. I checked the facts with Dr. Meron Benvenisti, author of *The West Bank Data Project.* In his study, private consumption per capita in the West Bank is estimated at about 30 percent of that of Israel; GNP per capita in the West Bank is four times smaller than in Israel.)

"Then," the young man from Balata continued, restrained in his expression but transmitting cold, tight-lipped anger, "then you say under the Jordanians it was bad for you. Maybe so. But the Jordanians took only our national identity from us, and you took everything. National identity, and the identity of every one of us who fears you and depends on you for his livelihood, you took everything. You made us into living dead. And me, what remains for me? Only the hatred of you and thoughts of *siyassah* [politics]. That's another evil you brought upon us, that you made every man here, even the most ordinary fellah, into a politician."

•

I drink tea with three women in Deheisha. One hears the most penetrating things from the women. The men are more afraid of imprisonment and intimidation. It is the women who march at the head of the demonstrations, it is the women who shout, who scream out the bitterness in their hearts before the television cameras. Brown women, with sharp features, women bearing suffering. Hadijah is seventy-five years old, her mind sharp and her narrow body healthy. "*Allah yikhalik*," I say to her, may God be with you, and she laughs to herself, a thin chuckle of bare gums, and says: "What is it to Him?" and explains to me that a man is like a stalk of wheat: when he turns yellow, he bends.

She has lived in this house, a standard refugee house, for forty years. The United Nations Welfare and Relief Agency (UNWRA) built it, and the UN symbol can still be found on the walls and doors. At the head of each refugee camp in the West Bank and Gaza Strip stands an UNWRA-appointed director. He serves as middleman between the agency and the residents. He is himself a former refugee and lives in the camp. He has the authority to distribute food and welfare payments, to grant the right to live in the camp, and to recommend students for university admissions.

The house consists of two small rooms and does not have running water. The electricity is usually out. Today it is raining outside, and the house is almost completely dark. Hadijah and her elderly sister sit on a straw mat and examine the medicines the camp doctor has prescribed for the sister. She suffers from asthma. The teachers and doctors who work in the refugee camps come, in general, from outside, from the nearby cities. The simplest jobs, cleaning and sanitation and construction, are filled by the camp residents. In the house in which I now sit live five people. In the room in which we drink our tea there is one cabinet, a suitcase on top. Half open. As if waiting to move on. A few wooden chairs made by an untrained hand, a few shelves holding vegetables. The young woman, tense, offers oranges and a paring knife. Another item of furniture found in every house here is the dowry chest of the woman of the house, made from the soft trunk of the Judas tree. Here she keeps her dowry, the bedsheets, the wedding dress, and perhaps some childish luxury, a toy, a pretty handkerchief—after all, she was no more than a girl when she was married.

"And if someone were to offer you today a dunam [one-quarter acre, the standard measure of land in countries once under Turkish rule] of land in a nice place, with light, in the open air?"

Yes, yes—she laughs—of course, but only on my own land. There.

She also declaims this, like the politicians, like those purveyors of her fate over all these years. She, at least, has the right to do so. I try to remember how many times Palestinian leaders missed opportunities to gain themselves a homeland: there was the partition proposal of '36 and the second proposal of '47, and maybe there were other chances.

They—in their blindness—rejected them all. We drink silently. The men are at work. On the wall, two nails. They serve as a wardrobe. On one hangs the black *'igal* (headband) of a kaffiyeh.

Whoever has served in the army in the "territories" knows how such rooms look from the inside during the night. Whoever has taken part in searches, in imposing curfews, in capturing a suspect at night, remembers. The violent entry into rooms like this one, where several people sleep, crowded, in unaired stench, three or four together under scratchy wool blankets, wearing their work clothes still in their sleep, as if ready at any moment to get up and go wherever they are told. They wake in confusion, squinting from the flashlight, children wail, sometimes a couple is making love, soldiers surround the house, some of them—shoes full of mud after tramping through the paths of the camp—walking over the sleep-warm blankets, some pounding on the tin roof above.

The old woman follows, it seems, my gaze to the bare cement walls, the heating lamp, the wool blankets rolled up on the floor. Suddenly she boils over: "Do we look like gypsies, do we? Miserable, are we? Ha? We are people of culture!" Her sister, the sick woman, nods rapidly, her sharp chin stabbing her sunken chest: "Yes, yes, people of culture!" They fall silent, wheezing. The young woman, of the wild, exotic presence, wants to say something and is silent. Her hand literally clamps her mouth closed. Within the arabesque filigree of manners and considered delicacy, of conversation and the protection of hospitality, the wires suddenly go taut. I am confused. The young woman tries to make amends. Change the subject. Is her mother-in-law willing to tell this Israeli here about, for instance, her childhood in Ain Azrab? No. Is she willing to recall the days when she worked the land? No, no. Salt on a wound. Would you be willing, *ya mama*, to sing the songs the fellahin, the winegrowers, the shepherds sang then? No. She only tightens her cracked lips stubbornly, her balding head shaking, but again, out of the conquering power of absence, her left foot begins to tap to a far-off rhythm, and her body moves silently forward and back, and as she traps my cautious gaze, she slaps her thigh with a trembling hand, and her nose reddens with rage: "Culture! You people don't know that we have culture! You can't understand this culture. It's not a culture of television!" Suddenly she is completely emptied of her anger: once again her face takes on an expression of defeat, of knowing all, the ancient signs written on the faces of the old: "The world is hard, hard . . ." She nods her head in bitter sorrow, her eyes close themselves off from the small, dark room: "You can't understand. You can't understand anything. Ask, maybe, your grandmother to tell you."

JONATHAN FRANZEN

FROM

The Twenty-Seventh City

1988

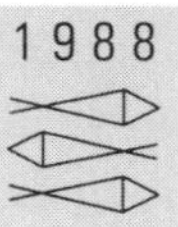

The room was evasive. On the first morning, Barbara had awakened from the drugging she'd received in the car to find herself on a standard-sized mattress, on a fitted bottom sheet with the kitty-litter smell of package-fresh linens, her face aching where he'd hit her, and her ankle bound. This was New York.

Or so she assumed. It could have been anywhere. The skylight diffused a light that seemed to fall, not shine, powdery and pure, free light, unreflected by a landscape. Her ankle was locked in a fetter, an iron ring attached by a ¾-inch cable to a tremendous eyebolt anchored in the wall. At the foot of the bed was a camping toilet, which she used, and then retched over, bringing up nothing.

When she awoke a second time she believed the light had changed, but only because that was the nature of light (to change) and the brain (to expect it). The carpeting had the color and texture of moss that hadn't been rained on for a while. Her suitcase stood across the room from her, by the only door, in the center of which was a peephole. A small framed portrait of the dead Shah of Iran hung on one of the walls adjacent to hers. The fourth wall was bare. That was the catalogue of her medium-sized rectangular room, the sum of its contents and features. With anything more, it might have had a personality; with anything less, it would have been bare, and bareness, too, was a kind of personality. She could only assume that Nissing was insane.

But when he opened the door and said, "Breakfast of astronauts!" she began to wonder. He handed her a tray bearing raspberry Pop-Tarts and a tall glass of Tang. His pistol was stuck under the waist of his bluejeans, half buried in his shirt. Through the door, which he'd left ajar, she saw that a black curtain completely filled the outer door frame. She asked where she was. Captive, he said. What was he going to do with her? They'd see.

He brought her three meals a day, breakfast always Pop-Tarts and

Tang with seconds and even thirds if she asked; lunches lukewarm soup and Saltines; dinners TV-dinners. He watched her eat, which didn't really bother her. At 236 Sherwood Drive, in the bedroom, he'd had to drag her to her feet by her hair. But when he'd drugged her, in his car, her instincts of flight and resistance had gone to sleep, and they had not reawakened. The pain in her bedroom had been terrible to her. Nissing's physical dominance was complete, monolithic. She was happy to believe that further resistance would only feed his sadism, because she didn't want to feel that pain again.

For a while she lived by natural light and natural time. When darkness fell she sat or lay or did exercises in darkness. She asked for a lamp and a clock. He said no. But when she asked for books and he brought them, new Penguin paperbacks, he brought a reading lamp, too. She asked for magazines, a newspaper. He said no. She asked to take a bath or a shower, and on the third night, a few hours after darkness fell, he came in, unlocked the fetter, and tied a black hood over her head. He led her through two rooms that she could tell were empty from the way his voice twanged in the corners. He unhooded her in a newly redone bathroom and sat on the toilet, gun in hand, while she undressed, showered, and put on clean clothes. He led her back and refastened her fetter. She was allowed to do this every three days. Every two days, after she complained about the smell of the porta-potty, Nissing took it away and returned it clean. Eventually she realized it was more than clean; each time, it was brand-new.

"We're at Sardi's, a 'whim' of yours, a kind of tourist thing. Those peas you're eating are escargots in garlic butter. I'm savoring pâté with toast points. Three tables over, you can see Wallace Shawn waving his fork over a plate of spaghetti and talking with his mouth full. It's Valentine's Day. You spent the afternoon at the Modern on a bench facing a Mondrian. On your lap was a spiral notebook. In your hand was a black felt-tip pen. Everyone wants to be an artist. The thought was on your mind and it paralyzed you, the problem of originality, of individuality qua commodity. You'd thought you could start small, start concrete, describe a painting on a wall in the museum. You were thinking about the roots of modern writing, both literature and the other sort, my sort. Liberated men and women confronting the new art and learning new methods of vision. But the only thing you were able to write was the letter T. A capital T. At the top of the page. You didn't dare scratch it out, but what would it become? This? The? They? Today? Tomorrow? You felt the problem. You were thinking about me and my sort of writing, my facile typewriting in the study, in that favorite chair of yours. I was the problem. *I* had liberated you. You hadn't done it yourself. An hour passed. In a stupor you watched the postures and paces of the visitors. A guard told you a little-known fact about that particular Mondrian and walked on. Now that a guard had spoken to you, you couldn't stay."

"This is very clever, John, but I'm trying to eat."

"Is it my fault your story isn't new? That piece of fried chicken is your prime rib. The last time you had prime rib—it must have been January fourth at the Port of St. Louis."

All his statements about her were true. From the very first moments of their new relationship, when he'd given her a typewritten letter to Martin for her to copy onto her stationery, he'd displayed—flaunted—a criminal familiarity with her private life. He knew exactly what had happened on Martin's birthday, three days before she'd even met him. She asked him how he knew. He reminded her that since they'd seen each other nearly every day in early January, she'd had plenty of time to tell him the story of her life. She asked again: how did he know what had happened on Martin's birthday? He reminded her that they'd met in October when he came to photograph the garden. He reminded her that they'd necked and petted like schoolchildren in the leaves behind the garage.

"After the waiter takes our plates, I reach across the table with a velvet box for you. You think of your first lunch with me, my first gift. I say Happy Valentine's Day. This time, you're gracious. You open the box. This time, it's a watch, a Cartier, with a silver band."

He dropped a silver watch on her lap. The hands showed ten of two, the jeweler's magic hour. She put it on her wrist.

"This time, you're gracious, and you're prepared. You give me a black silk tie you bought secondhand on East Eighth Street. We order champagne. We are the paragons of ostensible romance. But we're ruthless, almost trembling with cynicism as we go through the motions of an extramarital affair, the motions that every modern man and woman craves. Self-expression. Individuality. The youth that hasn't seen or read it all before. The dousing of the fires of doubt with bucket after bucket of dollars. We're united in pain—"

"This watch doesn't work."

"Dead? Dead? Dead?"

Nissing leaped to his feet and fired. Barbara saw black, smelled smoke, felt a peppery burn on her neck, and sound returned; she heard the bang. Nissing had shot the wall behind her head. She touched the hole in the plaster. It was hot.

"Back at the apartment, we make savage love."

He couldn't fool her. She saw how all his sudden pirouettes and shouting, the Hamletesque free associations, were merely steps towards madness and not at all the thing itself. She'd taken those kinds of steps herself when she was younger and feeling "crazy" and trying to impress her friends with her complexity and danger. His steps were the same, only a little larger. Obviously no one could formulate an airtight definition of sanity, but he met all of her intuitive requirements. So why had he stalked her and kidnapped her? The question might never have come up if he'd kept his mouth shut. But he opened it and she heard a mind like her own. The question clung. She nursed it. She tried to keep her mind clear. It was the perfect time, she joked, for her to read *The Faerie Queene* and *Moby-Dick*. Then John came in and fed her and told her what they'd done that day in New York. If she got bored, she began her evening sit-ups and leg-lifts before he finished.

She found it impossible to think about Martin. He was locked in their past, rattling the bars of conditions that now never got an update, pacing between walls of activities and scenes that aged like inorganic matter, fading rather than changing. Their weekly conversations confirmed this. It was the conclusion reached by some students of the supernatural: you could speak to the dead, but they had nothing to say.

At first she'd believed that captivity couldn't alter her if she developed a routine and kept her mind active. But it altered her. Towards the end of the first week she noticed she'd begun to wring her hands in the darkness. She was shocked. And increasingly often she fell into a deep confusion, in the small light of her lamp, about the time of day. Was it early morning or was it late evening? She couldn't remember. But how could a person not remember what she'd been doing one hour earlier? And then the spatial disorientations. Nissing freed her ankle only on the nights she showered. The cable, about six feet long, allowed her some play but not enough to move far from the mattress or reverse herself on it. She therefore slept and read and ate always with her head closer to the wall with the Shah's portrait. She'd come to associate this wall with East. Suddenly it would be West, when all she'd done was turn a page. The frightening thing was that she cared which way was East. Trying to jostle her internal compass needle back to its correct setting, she'd pinch herself, blink, bang her head on the wall, kick her legs in a frenzy.

"Sunday morning," Nissing said, entering with the telephone and folding chairs. "I'm out for my morning run in the park. You haven't talked to Luisa for a while."

"And I don't feel like it this morning. I just wrote her a letter."

"I'm afraid that letter was lost in the mail."

She threw aside her book. "*What the hell was wrong with that letter?*"

Nissing blinked. "Nothing!"

"Then why did it get lost in the mail?"

He unfolded the chairs. "I don't control the mails, my darling. That's the postmaster's job. I'm sure if you asked him he'd tell you that a certain percentage of articles, a low percentage of course, do get lost, inevitably, in the mail. Perhaps a machine tore the address off. Perhaps the letter blew into a sewer while the postal service employee was emptying the box on Fifth Avenue, honey, where you mailed it."

"You just never get tired of yourself, do you?"

"Our first quarrel!"

"FUCK YOU. FUCK YOU."

"It's becoming inescapable that you call Luisa. After a fight like this? You get tired of my steady talking, my steady self-confidence, and we quarrel. I lose my cool a bit. Yes, I do. I shout. Why don't you go back to your husband, someone you can subjugate? And then I slam the door and go out running. You think of me and my concern with bodily perfection, the joyous agony on my face as I enter the fourth mile of my run. You're heaving. Sunday morning. February 18."

"I asked you a question." She stood and wrung her hands. "I asked you what was wrong with that letter."

"Don't try to reason with a madman, honey."

"You aren't any madman."

"Oh yes I am!" He shoved her into the wall. "Oh yes I am! I'm madder than the arms race!" His free hand reached out of space and closed below her jaw and squeezed. She smelled clove smoke on his fingers. They tightened on her throat. She couldn't swallow, and then he squeezed harder. "You're a piece of meat. I'd kill you right now and enjoy it but not as much as I will when you're fat and ripe and I beat the life out of you and you're mooing for more."

Her certitude wavered, but she held on to the words of the assertion in her head. "No you won't," she squeaked. " 'Cause you're not."

He let go. She fell, coughing, to her knees.

" 'Cause you have to work these things up," she said. "You have to do exercises. You have to find the impulse 'cause it isn't in you. I know you. You cannot be. Credit me with some sense. Of human personality."

"Oh, credit you. You think I have to stand here and argue with you?"

"Yes." She coughed. "I think that. You're doing it. Aren't you."

"Do your gagging and then speak normally."

She looked up at him. "You can't prove—"

"Because when you're dead, dear, when you're a pile of garbage, you won't be around to have it proved to. You don't know what goes on behind that door, what goes on in me. You may think otherwise, because I am pleasant, to a degree, in this room with you, you may have a 'sense' of me, a 'gut feel' for my sanity, but you only get what I give you on this side of the door."

His eyes were black and tan, his skin tanned deeper, from underneath, from a brightness inside him. He looked like a well-read Mediterranean beach bum. If she could prove him rational then she could begin to figure out why he'd done this. She remembered Dostoevsky, and the willed wildness of students. She thought of the Iranian students. But was he even Iranian? The picture of the Shah had been seeming more and more like a joke. John was a nihilist, not a royalist. Could he have dared himself to kidnap her? As an experiment in evil? In revolution? Oh! This was the worst pain of all, that the world seethed with motives she could never grasp. Even if this captivity were clearly political she still wouldn't understand it, how a political demon or even ordinary pragmatism could lead a person to take risks like this. And politics stood for all the other motives she couldn't grasp.

"Why did you single me out?" she said.

"Out of all the women I've met? I guess it's natural you think you're the first."

And the small mystery—it was large to her but small in the larger scheme—merely stood for the larger mystery, the unconditional ignorance: why had she been born?

"Time for a phone call."

"No."

"Aw honey. Will you promise to do it later?"

He was trying to look drowningly pathetic. But he couldn't make his face as wild as his words, which didn't count as proof of insanity, because anyone could learn to speak wildly. And what did he care, anyway, whether she believed him insane? The question led into briars.

"Be nice to me, John," she said.

"It isn't me, it's the postal service. Soon this becomes a motto of our home. We make up and we make love, savage love."

"Be nice to me."

IAN FRAZIER

FROM

Great Plains

1989

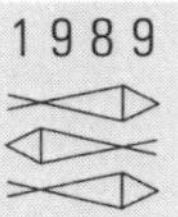

Away to the Great Plains of America, to that immense Western short-grass prairie now mostly plowed under! Away to the still-empty land beyond newsstands and malls and velvet restaurant ropes! Away to the headwaters of the Missouri, now quelled by many impoundment dams, and to the headwaters of the Platte, and to the almost invisible headwaters of the slurped-up Arkansas! Away to the land where TV used to set its most popular dramas, but not anymore! Away to the land beyond the hundredth meridian of longitude, where sometimes it rains and sometimes it doesn't, where agriculture stops and does a double take! Away to the skies of sparrow hawks sitting on telephone wires, thinking of mice and flaring their tail feathers suddenly, like a card trick! Away to the air shaft of the continent, where weather fronts from two hemispheres meet, and the wind blows almost all the time! Away to the fields of wheat and milo and sudan grass and flax and alfalfa and nothing! Away to parts of Montana and North Dakota and South Dakota and Wyoming and Nebraska and Kansas and Colorado and New Mexico and Oklahoma and Texas! Away to the high plains rolling in waves to the rising final chord of the Rocky Mountains!

A discount airplane ticket from New York City to the middle of the Great Plains—to Dodge City, Kansas, say, which once called itself Queen of the Cowtowns—costs about $420, round trip. A discount ticket over the plains—to the mountains, to Salt Lake City, to Seattle, to Los Angeles—is much cheaper. Today, most travellers who see the plains do it from thirty thousand feet. A person who wanted to go from New York to California overland in 1849, with the Gold Rush, could take a passenger ship to Baltimore, the B & O Railroad to Cumberland, Maryland, a stagecoach over the Allegheny Mountains to the Monongahela River, a steamboat to Pittsburgh, another steamboat down the Ohio to the Mississippi to St. Louis, another from St. Louis up the Missouri to Independence or St. Joseph or Council Bluffs, and an ox-drawn wagon west from there. If you left the East in early April, you might be on the plains by mid-May, and across by the Fourth of July. Today, if you leave Kennedy Airport in a 747 for Los Angeles just after breakfast, you will be over the plains by lunch. If you lean across the orthopedist from Beverly Hills who specializes in break-dancing injuries and who is in the window seat returning from his appearance on *Good Morning America*, you will see that the regular squares of cropland below you have begun to falter, that the country is for great distances bare and puckered by dry watercourses, that big green circles have begun to appear, and that often long, narrow rectangles of green alternate with equal rectangles of brown.

Chances are, nothing in the seat pocket in front of you will mention that those green circles are fields watered by central-pivot irrigation, where a wheeled span of irrigation pipe as much as a quarter mile long makes a slow circuit, like the hand of a clock. If you ask the flight attendant about those green and brown rectangles, chances are he or she will not say that in the spring of 1885 a wheat farmer on the Canadian plains named Angus Mackay was unable to plant a field which had already been plowed when his hands left to help suppress a rebellion of frontiersmen of French and Indian ancestry against the Dominion of Canada, and so he left the field fallow, cultivating it occasionally to kill the weeds; that when he planted it the following year, it weathered a drought to produce thirty-five bushels of wheat per acre, thirty-three bushels more than continuously cropped land; that the practice he had initiated, called summer fallow, was an effective way to conserve moisture in the soil in a semi-arid climate, and many other farmers adopted it; that the one problem with summer fallow was the tendency of fields with no crop cover sometimes to dry up and blow away; that in 1918 two other Canadian farmers, Leonard and Arie Koole, experimented successfully with crops planted in narrow sections at right angles to the prevailing winds, to protect sections of fallow ground in between; and that this refinement, called strip farming, turned out to be the best way to raise wheat on the northern plains.

Crossing high and fast above the plains, headed elsewhere, you are doing what rain clouds tend to do. You are in a sky which farmers have cursed and blasted with dynamite barrages and prodded with hydrogen balloons and seeded with silver-iodide crystals and prayed to in churches every day for months at a time, for rain. Usually the clouds wait to rain until they are farther west or east—over the Rockies, or the Midwest. Probably, as you look out the airplane window, you will see the sun. On the plains, sunshine is dependable. Most of the buildings on the plains have roofs of galvanized metal. As dawn comes up, and the line of sunlight crosses the land, the roofs of barns and equipment sheds and grain silos and Department of Agriculture extension stations and grain elevators and Air Force barracks and house trailers and pipe warehouses and cafes and roadside-table shelters start to tick and pop in scattered unison, all the way from Canada to Texas.

The Great Plains are about 2,500 miles long, and about 600 miles across at their widest point. The area they cover roughly parallels the Rocky Mountains, which make their western boundary. Although they extend from the Southwestern United States well into Canada, no single state or province lies entirely within them. North to south, the states of the Great Plains are:

Montana	North Dakota
Wyoming	South Dakota
Colorado	Nebraska
New Mexico	New Mexico
	Kansas
	Oklahoma

Texas

The Great Plains include the eastern part of the first column, the western part of the second column, some of west Texas, and all of the Texas panhandle. In Canada, they include southern Alberta, Saskatchewan, and Manitoba. They are five hundred to a thousand miles inland from the Pacific Ocean, and over a thousand miles inland from the Atlantic. The Texas plains are about five hundred miles from the Gulf of Mexico.

Just where the Great Plains begin and end is not always certain. To the west, they sometimes continue past the Rocky Mountain front through gentle foothills all the way to the Continental Divide. To the north, flatlands stretch past the Arctic Circle, but the open prairie has given way to boreal pine forests long before that. In the Southwest, a change from semi-arid grassland to true desert is sudden in some places, slow in others. Of all the Great Plains boundaries, the eastern one is the hardest to fix. Many geographers and botanists have said that the Great Plains begin at the hundredth meridian, because that is the approximate limit of twenty-inch annual rainfall. Before Europeans came, it was more or less where the tall grasses of the East stopped and the Western short grasses started. (The hundredth meridian is the eastern line of the Texas panhandle; a map of the lower forty-eight states folds in half a little bit to the right of it.) Since the same amount of rain never falls two years in a row, this eastern boundary always changes. Sometimes it happens to coincide at certain points with the Missouri River;

the eastern side of the river will be green and lush, and the western side will be a tan and dusty cowboy-movie set. Farmers can't grow corn, or raise dairy cattle, or do much European-style agriculture at all on sub-twenty-inch rainfall, and when they first moved out onto the Great Plains, they sometimes had difficulty borrowing money. Many banks and insurance companies had a policy of not lending money for the purposes of agriculture west of the hundredth meridian. So, whether or not the rain stopped exactly at the hundredth meridian, at one time lots of Eastern loan officers did. If you were beyond their help, you knew you were on the Great Plains.

It makes sense that traditional finance would balk there, because the Great Plains don't exactly qualify as real estate. In fact, the Great Plains are probably better described in terms of the many things they aren't. They aren't woodlands; their subsoil doesn't have enough moisture for tree roots. You can go a long way out there without seeing a single tree. They aren't mountains (although they contain the Black Hills in South Dakota and the Bearpaw Mountains in Montana and the Cypress Hills in Canada), and they aren't Land of a Thousand Lakes (although they used to have many sweetwater springs, and hundreds of rivers and streams, and an underground aquifer the volume of Lake Huron), and they aren't standard farmland (although they export two-thirds of the world's wheat, and could export more). And although they have suffered droughts about every twenty years since white people first settled there, and millions of acres have gone to blowing sand, and although Zebulon Pike, who happened to pick a route that led through the sandhills region when he explored for the government in 1806–7, compared the Great Plains to the deserts of Africa, and although the members of a later expedition, in 1819–20, agreed with Pike, and published a map with the words "Great Desert" across the southern plains, and although a popular atlas of 1822 extended the label over more territory and in another edition changed it to "Great American Desert," and although that appeared in the middle of North America on maps and globes for fifty years afterwards, and generations of geography students wondered about it and dreamed of going there, the Great Plains are not a desert.

White people did not consider moving onto the Great Plains in any numbers until after the Civil War. When they did, railroad promoters, governors of empty Western states, syndicates with land to sell, emigration societies, scientists, pretend scientists, politicians in crowded Eastern states, U.S. Geological Survey officials, Walt Whitman, *The New York Times*, *The New York Tribune*, all loudly advertised the Great Plains as a garden spot. The idea of the Great American Desert came in for much scoffing and debunking. Strangely, the Great Plains greened up with good rains several times just as another wave of homeseekers was about to go there. People thought they'd harvest a couple of good crops and pay off their starting costs and be in business. In the 1870s and '90s, and in 1918–24, and, most spectacularly, in the 1930s, drought knocked parts of these waves back. Since their days as a Great Desert, the Great Plains have also been the Frontier (supposedly of such importance in the formation of the American character), the "newer garden of creation" (Whitman's phrase), the Breadbasket of the World, the Dust Bowl, Vanishing Rural America. The Great Plains are like a sheet Americans screened their dreams on for a while and then largely forgot about. Since 1930, two-thirds of the counties on the Great Plains have lost population. About fifteen years ago, the Great Plains reappeared, briefly, as part of the New Energy Frontier. The Great Plains contain more than fifty percent of America's coal reserves. When we finally do run out of oil, somebody will probably think up yet another name for the Great Plains.

•

In the fall of 1982, I moved from New York to Montana. I sublet my apartment to my sister, packed my van, and headed west. On the way, I stopped in Cleveland to usher at my other sister's wedding. At the reception, to entertain the bridesmaids, I ate a black cricket the size of my thumb. Later, I was driving around the city's west side by myself singing "Jerusalem" with the windows open, tears streaming down my face. The next morning I wanted to call the hangover ambulance and go to the hangover hospital. The singing, and the feel of the cricket's toothpicky legs between my teeth, replayed in my mind on a tight tape loop. I took my van to Mike's Sohio Service Center for a tune-up, and when they were done I drove to Chicago. I stayed with friends there for one night, and then I drove on through Wisconsin, Minnesota, South Dakota, and didn't really stop until I crossed the Montana state line. At the edge of a little town, I pulled off the road, took off my shoes, moved some stuff from the mattress, and fell asleep, the gasoline still sloshing back and forth gently in the tank.

America is like a wave of higher and higher frequency toward each end, and lowest frequency in the middle. When the ticking of the car roof in the sun woke me, I looked out the windshield and saw nothing. A Hefty trash bag against a barbed-wire fence, maybe, torn to pennants by the wind; a metal prefab building in the distance; bunch grass blowing; a road as straight as a string. I started the car and went on. I didn't pass a single place that looked as if it was in any way expecting me: no landscaped residential communities, no specialty sporting-goods stores, no gourmet delis offering many kinds of imported beers. Just grain silos, and flat brown fields with one cow on them, and wheat fields, and telephone poles, and towns with four or six buildings and a "No U-Turn" sign at each end. In the larger town of Shelby, Montana, I went to a cafe called Ma's, and people looked at me. I bought a newspaper to see about houses for rent, and from a picture at the top of a column recognized the columnist, a man with a large waxed mustache, sitting one table away. I continued west, across the Blackfeet Indian Reservation, into the foothills of the Rocky Mountains, and then up through the mountain canyons. All at once a low-slung '67 Pontiac full of long-haired Indians passed me, going about ninety. Then a Montana state highway cop, with no sirens going. Then several more cars of Indians, then another highway cop, then more Indians. Just across the Flathead River and inside the boundary of Glacier National Park, I came upon the cars again. They were now pulled every which way off the road; policemen and Indians, both, were just standing there, hands in pockets. Some were looking off into the brush. Nobody's mouth was moving.

On the other side of the mountains, in the city of Kalispell, Montana, I finally saw a few people who looked kind of like me. I parked my van and took a $15-a-week room in the Kalispell Hotel. The bathroom was down the hall; the walls were thin. I spent several hours listening to a man in the next room trying to persuade another man to trade him five dollars for five dollars' worth of food stamps. Daily, I looked at houses to rent—shotgun cottages by the rail yards, ski chalets with circular fireplaces, and a house that was built under a small hill, for energy reasons. Finally I found one I liked, a cedar A-frame cabin with a wood stove and a sleeping loft and a flower box with marigolds. The house was on a long road that went from pavement to dirt and back to pavement. Beyond the road were foothills, clear-cut of timber in patches, like heads shaved for surgery, and beyond the hills were mountains. At the rental agency, I overheard a secretary giving someone else directions to the house. I mentioned to the agent that I could pay a two- or three-month security deposit in cash. The next morning, the agent left a message for me at the Kalispell Hotel and I called her back and she said I had the house.

I did not know one person in Montana. I sat in the house and tried to write a novel about high school; I went for walks, drank quarts of Coors beer, listened to the radio. At night, a neighbor's horse shifted his weight from hoof to hoof out in the trees, and sometimes cropped grass so near I could hear him chew. The first snowstorm blew in from the north, and crows crossed the sky before it like thrown black socks.

For years in New York I had dreamed of Montana. Actually, I had also dreamed of joining the Army, going to truck-driving school in New Jersey, building a wooden sailboat, playing the great golf courses of the world, and moving to Fiji. I had examined all those ideas and then rejected them. Montana made the most sense to me. I saw the movie *Rancho Deluxe* (filmed in Livingston, Montana) eight or nine times. At parties, I told people, "Well, I'm going to be moving to Montana soon." Now here I was. Suddenly I no longer had any place to dream about.

So I started to dream about the Great Plains. For fantasies, the Great Plains are in many respects the perfect place. They're so big that you could never know all there is to know about them—your fantasies could never wear them out. Even the plural in their name seems to make them extend farther into a distant romantic haze. Also, they are a place where I will probably never live. This is important, because anyplace I move, I ruin. Look at the north side of Chicago. Look at SoHo. I move in, the rents go up, coffee shops become French restaurants, useful stores close. Don't ask me how I do it—it's just a talent I have. A hundred years ago, it was not unusual to hear of single men and women and young couples with families moving out to start farms on the Great Plains. Today you hear of people my age being urban pioneers in some neglected neighborhood, or moving to the suburbs, or moving to Northern California or Washington or northwest Montana, like me. You never hear of us moving to the Great Plains.

Whenever money and the weather allowed, I would cross the mountains and drive around on the plains. A friend came to visit in the spring, and the first thing I did was take her there. My friend is from the West Indies; she had never seen the American West, except for California. We followed U.S. Highway 2 to Glacier National Park, and then we went up the Going-to-the-Sun Highway, past the standing dead trees burned in the lightning fire of 1967, through tunnels in the rock, past precipitous drops on the passenger side, past cliffs dripping water, past old snowdrifts with graffiti scratched on them, past our own chilled breath blowing out the car windows, past mountains with white, sharp tops, and then across Logan Pass, on the Continental Divide. I kept telling my friend I wanted her to see the Great Plains. The road began to descend, and at the turn of each switchback another mountain range would disappear, like scenery withdrawn into the wings, while the sky that replaced it grew larger and larger. We left the park and turned onto U.S. Highway 89. A driver coming down this road gets the most dramatic first glimpse of the Great Plains I've ever seen. For some miles, pine trees and foothills are all around; then, suddenly, there is nothing across the road but sky, and a sign says HILL TRUCKS GEAR DOWN, and you come over a little rise, and the horizon jumps a hundred miles away in an instant. My friend's jaw—her whole face, really—fell, and she said, "I had no idea!"

We came through the lower foothills, with vertebrae of rock sticking through their brown backs, and soon we were driving on a straight dirt road through unfenced wheat fields. We stopped the car and got out. The wheat—of a short-stemmed variety bred to mature at a height convenient for harvesting machinery—stretched in rows for half a mile in either direction. Through the million bearded spikes the wind made an "s" sound bigger than we could hear. We drove on, and birds with long, curved bills (Hudsonian godwits, the bird book said) flew just above us, like gulls following a ship. The sky was 360 degrees of clouds, a gift assortment of mares' tails and cumulus and cirrus, with an occasional dark storm cloud resting on a silvery-gray pedestal of rain. We could see the shadows of the clouds sliding along beneath them far into the distance. I said that when early travellers on the plains came through a big herd of buffalo, they could watch the human scent move through it on the wind, frightening animals eight and ten miles away. Suddenly we crossed the path of one of the rainclouds, and the hard dirt road turned to glue. Mud began to thump in the wheel wells, and the car skidded sideways, went off the road, and stuck. We got out in cement-colored mud over our ankles. Two pieces of harvesting machinery sat in a field nearby; other than that, there was no sign of people anywhere. I tried to drive while my friend pushed, then she drove while I pushed, then I left it in gear and we both pushed. We whipped the mud to peaks. It clotted on the wheels until they became useless mudballs. Finally I took a flat rock and got down on all fours and scraped the mud off each wheel. Then my friend drove carefully in reverse for one wheel turn until the wheels were covered again. Then I scraped the mud off again, and we drove another revolution. We kept doing this over and over until we made it back to dry ground. It took about two hours. Another event early travellers mentioned in their diaries was miring their wagons in the gumbo mud of the Great Plains. Now I knew what they meant. When I got back in the car, I was all-over mud and my fingernails were broken. From her purse, my friend produced a freshly laundered white cotton handkerchief.

For hours we drove on roads which Rand McNally & Company considers unworthy of notice. A moth glanced off the edge of the windshield, and in the sunset the dust its wings left sparkled like mascara. That night, my friend said on a gas-station pay phone, "I'm on the Great Plains! It's amazing here! The sky is like a person yawned and never stopped!"

Eventually, over several summers, I drove maybe 25,000 miles on the plains—from Montana to Texas and back twice, as well as many shorter distances. I went to every Great Plains state, dozens of museums, scores of historic sites, numerous cafes. When I couldn't travel, I borrowed books about the plains from the Kalispell Public Library—*Curse Not His Curls*, by Robert J. Ege (a ringing defense of General Custer), and *Crow Killer: The Saga of Liver-Eating Johnson*. I also watched the local newspapers for items about the plains, and finally I learned why the Indians and policemen I had seen by the road the day I first arrived were standing that way. They were at the place where the bodies of two missing Blackfeet Indians, Thomas Running Rabbit and Harvey Mad Man, had been found earlier in the afternoon.

Police in Eureka, California, had arrested two Canadians for robbing a convenience store, and had discovered that the Canadians' car was the same one the young Blackfeet men were driving when they disappeared. In custody, one of the Canadians, a nineteen-year-old named André Fontaine, said that they and another man had hitchhiked down from Red Deer, Alberta, to West Glacier, Montana; that there the three met two Indians in a bar; that they drove west with them in the Indians' car; that the Indians stopped the car; that his companions took the Indians into the woods; that he heard two shots; that his companions came running from the woods; that the three then drove away. Aided by this information, police soon caught the third man, a Canadian named Ronald Smith, in Wyoming. All three were returned to Montana and held in the Flathead County Jail. At first, they pleaded not guilty, but then Ronald Smith confessed to shooting both the young men. Smith was twenty-four, and he said he had always wanted to see what it felt like to kill somebody. He said that it felt like nothing. While awaiting trial as an accomplice, André Fontaine was asked to appear as a guest on F. Lee Bailey's television show, *Lie Detector*. The Flathead County Attorney, a county sheriff's detective, a local police detective, and a court-appointed defense attorney accompanied André Fontaine back to California for the taping. The show put them up in North Hollywood at the Beverly Garland Hotel, except for the prisoner, who stayed in the Los Angeles County Jail. When Ronald Smith confessed, he had requested the death penalty. He had said that he felt he was beyond rehabilitation, and that the Indians in the Montana prisons would probably kill him anyway. Shortly before his execution date, he changed his mind. Lawyers took his appeal through the county and state courts, which denied it, and to the U.S. Supreme Court, which refused to hear it. Then they filed another appeal in the federal courts challenging the constitutionality of the death penalty. Three years after the crime, while the appeal was still at the state level, I moved from Montana back to New York.

[. . .]

In the Black Hills, near the town of Custer, South Dakota, sculptors are carving a statue of Crazy Horse from a six-hundred-foot-high mountain of granite. The rock, called Thunderhead Mountain, is near Mt. Rushmore. The man who began the statue was a Boston-born sculptor named Korczak Ziolkowski, and he became inspired to the work after receiving a letter from Henry Standing Bear, a Sioux chief, in 1939. Standing Bear asked Ziolkowski if he would be interested in carving a memorial to Crazy Horse as a way of honoring heroes of the Indian people. The idea so appealed to Ziolkowski that he decided to make the largest statue in the world: Crazy Horse, on horseback, with his left arm outstretched and pointing. From Crazy Horse's shoulder to the tip of his index finger would be 263 feet. A forty-four-foot stone feather would rise above his head. Ziolkowski worked on the statue from 1947 until his death in 1982. As the project progressed, he added an Indian museum and a university and medical school for Indians to his plans for the grounds around the statue. Since his death, his wife and children have carried on the work.

The Black Hills, sacred to generations of Sioux and Cheyenne, are now filled with T-shirt stores, reptile gardens, talking wood carvings, wax museums, gravity mystery areas ("See and feel COSMOS—the only gravity mystery area that is family approved"), etc. Before I went there, I thought the Crazy Horse monument would be just another attraction. But it is wonderful. In all his years of blasting, bulldozing, and chipping, Ziolkowski removed over eight million tons of rock. You can just begin to tell. There is an outline of the planned sculpture on the mountain, and parts of the arm and the rider's head are beginning to emerge. The rest of the figure still waits within Thunderhead Mountain—Ziolkowski's descendants will doubtless be working away in the year 2150. This makes the statue in its present state an unusual attraction, one which draws a million visitors annually: it is a ruin, only in reverse. Instead of looking at it and imagining what it used to be, people stand at the observation deck and say, "Boy, that's really going to be great someday." The gift shop is extensive and prosperous; buses with "Crazy Horse" in the destination window bring tourists from nearby Rapid City; Indian chants play on speakers in the Indian museum; Boy Scouts, Girl Scouts, local residents, and American Indians get in free. The Crazy Horse monument is the one place on the plains where I saw lots of Indians smiling.

Korczak Ziolkowski is not the only person ever to feel strong emotion at the thought of Crazy Horse. Some, both Indian and non-Indian, regard him with a reverence which borders on the holy. Others do not get the point at all. George Hyde, who has written perhaps the best books about the western Sioux, says of the admirers of Crazy Horse, "They depict Crazy Horse as the kind of being never seen on earth: a genius in war, yet a lover of peace; a statesman, who apparently never thought of the interests of any human being outside his own camp; a dreamer, a mystic, and a kind of Sioux Christ, who was betrayed in the end by his own disciples—Little Big Man, Touch the Clouds . . . and the rest. One is inclined to ask, what is it all about?"

Personally, I love Crazy Horse because even the most basic outline of his life shows how great he was; because he remained himself from the moment of his birth to the moment he died; because he knew exactly where he wanted to live, and never left; because he may have surrendered, but he was never defeated in battle; because, although he was killed, even the Army admitted he was never captured; because he was so free that he didn't know what a jail looked like; because at the most desperate moment of his life he only cut Little Big Man on the hand; because, unlike many people all over the world, when he met white men he was not diminished by the encounter; because his dislike of the oncoming civilization was prophetic; because the idea of becoming a farmer apparently never crossed his mind; because he didn't end up in the Dry Tortugas; because he never met the President; because he never rode on a train, slept in a boardinghouse, ate at a table; because he never wore a medal or a top hat or any other thing that white men gave him; because he made sure that his wife was safe before going to where he expected to die; because although Indian agents, among themselves, sometimes referred to Red Cloud as "Red" and Spotted Tail as "Spot," they never used a diminutive for him; because, deprived of freedom, power, occupation, culture, trapped in a situation where bravery was invisible, he was still brave; because he fought in self-defense, and took no one with him when he died; because, like the rings of Saturn, the carbon atom, and the underwater reef, he belonged to a category of phenomena which our technology had not then advanced far enough to photograph; because no photograph or painting or even sketch of him exists; because he is not the Indian on the nickel, the tobacco pouch, or the apple crate. Crazy Horse was a slim man of medium height with brown hair hanging below his waist and a scar above his lip. Now, in the mind of each person who imagines him, he looks different.

I believe that when Crazy Horse was killed, something more than a man's life was snuffed out. Once, America's size in the imagination was limitless. After Europeans settled and changed it, working from the coasts inland, its size in the imagination shrank. Like the center of a dying fire, the Great Plains held that original vision longest. Just as people finally came to the Great Plains and changed them, so they came to where Crazy Horse lived and killed him. Crazy Horse had the misfortune to live in a place which existed both in reality and in the dreams of people far away; he managed to leave both the real and the imaginary place unbetrayed. What I return to most often when I think of Crazy Horse is the fact that in the adjutant's office he refused to lie on the cot. Mortally wounded, frothing at the mouth, grinding his teeth in pain, he chose the floor instead. What a distance there is between that cot and the floor! On the cot, he would have been, in some sense, "ours": an object of pity, an accident victim, "the noble red man, the last of his race, etc. etc." But on the floor Crazy Horse was Crazy Horse still. On the floor, he began to hurt as the morphine wore off. On the floor, he remembered Agent Lee, summoned him, forgave him. On the floor, unable to rise, he was guarded by soldiers even then. On the floor, he said goodbye to his father and Touch the Clouds, the last of the thousands that once followed him. And on the floor, still as far from white men as the limitless continent they once dreamed of, he died. Touch the Clouds pulled the blanket over his face: "That is the lodge of Crazy Horse." Lying where he chose, Crazy Horse showed the rest of us where we are standing. With his body, he demonstrated that the floor of an Army office was part of the land, and that the land was still his.

FROM

The Mambo Kings Play Songs of Love

1989

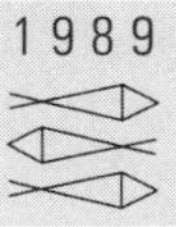

It was a Saturday afternoon on La Salle Street, years and years ago when I was a little kid, and around three o'clock Mrs. Shannon, the heavy Irish woman in her perpetually soup-stained dress, opened her back window and shouted out into the courtyard, "Hey, Cesar, yoo-hoo, I think you're on television, I swear it's you!" When I heard the opening strains of the *I Love Lucy* show I got excited because I knew she was referring to an item of eternity, that episode in which my dead father and my Uncle Cesar had appeared, playing Ricky Ricardo's singing cousins fresh off the farm in Oriente Province, Cuba, and north in New York for an engagement at Ricky's nightclub, the Tropicana.

This was close enough to the truth about their real lives—they were musicians and songwriters who had left Havana for New York in 1949, the year they formed the Mambo Kings, an orchestra that packed clubs, dance halls, and theaters around the East Coast—and, excitement of excitements, they even made a fabled journey in a flamingo-pink bus out to Sweet's Ballroom in San Francisco, playing on an all-star mambo night, a beautiful night of glory, beyond death, beyond pain, beyond all stillness.

Desi Arnaz had caught their act one night in a supper club on the West Side, and because they had perhaps already known each other from Havana or Oriente Province, where Arnaz, like the brothers, was born, it was natural that he ask them to sing on his show. He liked one of their songs in particular, a romantic bolero written by them, "Beautiful María of My Soul."

Some months later (I don't know how many, I wasn't five years old yet) they began to rehearse for the immortal appearance of my father on this show. For me, my father's gentle rapping on Ricky Ricardo's door has always been a call from the beyond, as in Dracula films, or films of the walking dead, in which spirits ooze out from behind tombstones and through the cracked windows and rotted floors of gloomy antique halls: Lucille Ball, the lovely redheaded actress and comedienne who played Ricky's wife, was housecleaning when she heard the rapping of my father's knuckles against that door.

"I'm commmmmming," in her singsong voice.

Standing in her entrance, two men in white silk suits and butterfly-looking lace bow ties, black instrument cases by their side and black-brimmed white hats in their hands—my father, Nestor Castillo, thin and broad-shouldered, and Uncle Cesar, thickset and immense.

My uncle: "Mrs. Ricardo? My name is Alfonso and this is my brother Manny . . ."

And her face lights up and she says, "Oh, yes, the fellows from Cuba. Ricky told me all about you."

Then, just like that, they're sitting on the couch when Ricky Ricardo walks in and says something like "Manny, Alfonso! Gee, it's really swell that you fellas could make it up here from Havana for the show."

That's when my father smiled. The first time I saw a rerun of this, I could remember other things about him—his lifting me up, his smell of cologne, his patting my head, his handing me a dime, his touching my face, his whistling, his taking me and my little sister, Leticia, for a walk in the park, and so many other moments happening in my thoughts simultaneously that it was like watching something momentous, say the Resurrection, as if Christ had stepped out of his sepulcher, flooding the world with light—what we were taught in the local church with the big red doors—because my father was now newly alive and could take off his hat and sit down on the couch in Ricky's living room, resting his black instrument case on his lap. He could play the trumpet, move his head, blink his eyes, nod, walk across the room, and say "Thank you" when offered a cup of coffee. For me, the room was suddenly bursting with a silvery radiance. And now I knew that we could see it again. Mrs. Shannon had called out into the courtyard alerting my uncle: I was already in his apartment.

With my heart racing, I turned on the big black-and-white television set in his living room and tried to wake him. My uncle had fallen asleep in the kitchen—having worked really late the night before, some job in a Bronx social club, singing and playing the horn with a pickup group of musicians. He was snoring, his shirt was open, a few buttons had popped out on his belly. Between the delicate-looking index and forefingers of his right hand, a Chesterfield cigarette burning down to the filter, that hand still holding a half glass of rye whiskey, which he used to drink like crazy because in recent years he had been suffering from bad dreams, saw apparitions, felt cursed, and, despite all the women he took to bed, found his life of bachelorhood solitary and wearisome. But I didn't know this at the time, I thought he was sleeping because he had worked so hard the night before, singing and playing the trumpet for seven or eight hours. I'm talking about a wedding party in a crowded, smoke-filled room (with bolted-shut fire doors), lasting from nine at night to four, five o'clock in the morning, the band playing one-, two-hour sets. I thought he just needed the rest. How could I have known that he would come home and, in the name of unwinding, throw back a glass of rye, then a second, and then a third, and so on, until he'd plant his elbow on the table and use it to steady his chin, as he couldn't hold his head up otherwise. But that day I ran into the kitchen to wake him up so that he could see the episode, too, shaking him gently and tugging at his elbow, which was a mistake, because it was as if I had pulled loose the support columns of a five-hundred-year-old church: he simply fell over and crashed to the floor.

A commercial was running on the television, and so, as I knew I wouldn't have much time, I began to slap his face, pull on his burning red-hot ears, tugging on them until he finally opened one eye. In the act of focusing he apparently did not recognize me, because he asked, "Nestor, what are you doing here?"

"It's me, Uncle, it's Eugenio."

I said this in a really earnest tone of voice, just like that kid who hangs out with Spencer Tracy in the movie of *The Old Man and the Sea*, really believing in my uncle and clinging on to his every word in life, his every touch like nourishment from a realm of great beauty, far beyond me, his heart. I tugged at him again, and he opened his eyes. This time he recognized me.

He said, "You?"

"Yes, Uncle, get up! Please get up! You're on television again. Come on."

One thing I have to say about my Uncle Cesar, there was very little he wouldn't do for me in those days, and so he nodded, tried to push himself off the floor, got to his knees, had trouble balancing, and then fell backwards. His head must have hurt: his face was a wince of pain. Then he seemed to be sleeping again. From the living room came the voice of Ricky's wife, plotting as usual with her neighbor Ethel Mertz about how to get a part on Ricky's show at the Tropicana, and I knew that the brothers had already been to the apartment—that's when Mrs. Shannon had called out into the courtyard—that in about five more minutes my father and uncle would be standing on the stage of the Tropicana, ready to perform that song again. Ricky would take hold of the microphone and say, "Well, folks, and now I have a real treat for you. Ladies and gentlemen, Alfonso and Manny Reyes, let's hear it!"

And soon my father and uncle would be standing side by side, living, breathing beings, for all the world to see, harmonizing in a duet of that *canción.*

As I shook my uncle, he opened his eyes and gave me his hand, hard and callused from his other job in those days, as superintendent, and he said, "Eugenio, help me. Help me."

I tugged with all my strength, but it was hopeless. Still he tried: with great effort he made it to one knee, and then, with his hand braced on the floor, he started to push himself up again. As I gave him another tug, he began miraculously to rise. Then he pushed my hand away and said, "I'll be okay, kid."

With one hand on the table and the other on the steam pipe, he pulled himself to his feet. For a moment he towered over me, wobbling as if powerful winds were rushing through the apartment. Happily I led him down the hallway and into the living room, but he fell over again by the door—not fell over, but rushed forward as if the floor had abruptly tilted, as if he had been shot out of a cannon, and, wham, he hit the bookcase in the hall. He kept piles of records there, among them a number of the black and brittle 78s he had recorded with my father and their group, the Mambo Kings. These came crashing down, the bookcase's glass doors jerking open, the records shooting out and spinning like flying saucers in the movies and splintering into pieces. Then the bookcase followed, slamming into the floor beside him: the songs *"Bésame Mucho," "Acércate Más," "Juventud,"* "Twilight in Havana," "Mambo Nine," "Mambo Number Eight," "Mambo for a Hot Night," and their fine version of "Beautiful María of My Soul"—all these were smashed up. This crash had a sobering effect on my uncle. Suddenly he got to one knee by himself, and then the other, stood, leaned against the wall, and shook his head.

"Bueno," he said.

He followed me into the living room, and plopped down on the couch behind me. I sat on a big stuffed chair that we'd hauled up out of the basement. He squinted at the screen, watching himself and his younger brother, whom, despite their troubles, he loved very much. He seemed to be dreaming.

"Well, folks," Ricky Ricardo said, "and now I have a real treat for you . . ."

The two musicians in white silk suits and big butterfly-looking lace bow ties, marching toward the microphone, my uncle holding a guitar, my father a trumpet.

"Thank you, thank you. And now a little number that we composed . . ." And as Cesar started to strum the guitar and my father lifted his trumpet to his lips, playing the opening of "Beautiful María of My Soul," a lovely, soaring melody line filling the room.

They were singing the song as it had been written—in Spanish. With the Ricky Ricardo Orchestra behind them, they came into a turnaround and began harmonizing a line that translates roughly into English as: "What delicious pain love has brought to me in the form of a woman."

My father . . . He looked so alive!

"Uncle!"

Uncle Cesar had lit a cigarette and fallen asleep. His cigarette had slid out of his fingers and was now burning into the starched cuff of his white shirt. I put the cigarette out, and then my uncle, opening his eyes again, smiled. "Eugenio, do me a favor. Get me a drink."

"But, Uncle, don't you want to watch the show?"

He tried really hard to pay attention, to focus on it.

"Look, it's you and Poppy."

"Coño, sí . . ."

My father's face with his horsey grin, arching eyebrows, big fleshy ears—a family trait—that slight look of pain, his quivering vocal cords, how beautiful it all seemed to me then . . .

And so I rushed into the kitchen and came back with a glass of rye whiskey, charging as fast as I could without spilling it. Ricky had joined the brothers onstage. He was definitely pleased with their performance and showed it because as the last note sounded he whipped up his hand and shouted *"Olé!,"* a big lock of his thick black hair falling over his brow. Then they bowed and the audience applauded.

The show continued on its course. A few gags followed: a costumed bull with flowers wrapped around its horns came out dancing an Irish jig, its horn poking into Ricky's bottom and so exasperating him that his eyes bugged out, he slapped his forehead and started speaking a-thousand-words-a-second Spanish. But at that point it made no difference to me, the miracle had passed, the resurrection of a man, Our Lord's promise which I then believed, with its release from pain, release from the troubles of this world.

[. . .]

1980

"I said, do you like California?"

"Yes."

"It's beautiful. I chose this climate here because it reminds me of Cuba. Here grow many of the same plants and flowers. You know, me and your father and uncle came from the same province, Oriente. I haven't been back there in over twenty years. Could you have imagined what Fidel would have made of Desi Arnaz going back to Cuba? Have you ever been there?"

"No."

"Well, that's a shame. It's a little like this." He stretched and yawned.

"Tell you what we'll do, boy. We'll set you up in the guest room, and then I'll show you around. Do you ride horses?"

"No."

"A shame." He winced, straightening up his back. "Do me a favor, boy, and give me a hand up."

Arnaz reached out and I pulled him to his feet.

"Come on, I'll show you my different gardens."

Beyond the patio, down a few steps, was another stairway, and that led to another patio, bounded by a wall. A thick scent of flowers in the air.

"This garden is modeled after one of my favorite little plazas in Santiago. You came across it on your way to the harbor. I used to take my girls there." And he winked. "Those days are long gone.

"And from this *placita* you could see all of Santiago Bay. At sunset the sky burned red, and that's when, if you were lucky, you might steal a kiss. Or make like Cuban Pete. That's one of the songs that made me famous."

Nostalgically, Arnaz sang, "My name is Cuban Pete, I'm the King of the Rumba Beat!"

Then we both stood for a moment looking at how the Pacific seemed to go on forever and forever.

"One day, all this will either be gone or it will last forever. Which do you think?"

"About what?"

"The afterlife. I believe in it. You?"

I shrugged.

"Maybe there's nothing. But I can remember when life felt like it would last forever. You're a young man, you wouldn't understand. You know what was beautiful, boy? When I was little and my mother would hold me in her arms."

I wanted to fall on my knees and beg him to save me. I wanted to hold him tight and hear him say, "I love you," just so I could show Arnaz that I really did appreciate love and just didn't throw it back into people's faces. Instead, I followed him back into the house.

"Now I have to take care of some telephone calls. But make yourself at home. The bar's over there."

Arnaz disappeared, and I walked over to the bar and fixed myself a drink. Through the big window, the brilliant blue California sky and the ocean.

Sitting in Desi Arnaz's living room, I remembered the episode of the *I Love Lucy* show in which my father and uncle had once appeared, except it now seemed to be playing itself out right before me. I blinked my eyes and my father and uncle were sitting on the couch opposite me. Then I heard the rattle of coffee cups and utensils and Lucille Ball walked into the living room. She then served the brothers their coffee.

When I thought, Poppy, my father looked up at me and smiled sadly.

"I'm so happy to see you again."

"And, son, I'm happy to see you."

My uncle smiled, too.

That's when Arnaz came in, but he wasn't the white-haired gentleman with the jowlish face and kind, weary eyes who had led me around the grounds. It was the cocky, handsome Arnaz of youth.

"Gee, fellows," he said. "It's nice to see you again. How are things down in Cuba?"

And I couldn't help myself. I walked over and sat on the couch and wrapped my arms around my father. Expected to find air, but hit on solid flesh. And his neck was warm. His expression pained and timid, like a hick off the boat. He was alive!

"Poppy, but I'm glad to see you."

"It is the same for me, son. It will always be the same."

Embracing him, I started to feel myself falling through an endless space, my father's heart. Not the heart of flesh and blood that had stopped beating, but this other heart filled with light and music, and I felt myself being pulled back into a world of pure affection, before torment, before loss, before awareness.

•

Later, an immense satin heart dissolved and through a haze appeared the interior of the Tropicana nightclub. Facing a dance floor and stage, about twenty tables set with linen and candles at which sat ordinary but elegantly dressed people—your nightclub clientele of that day. Pleated curtains hanging down from the ceiling, potted palms here and there. A tuxedoed maître d' with an oversize black wine list in hand, a long-legged cigarette girl, and waiters going from table to table. Then the dance floor itself, and finally the stage, its apron and wings painted to resemble African drums, with birds and squiggly voodoo lines, these patterns repeated on the conga drums and on the music stands, behind which sat the members of the Ricky Ricardo Orchestra, twenty or so musicians seated in four tiered rows, each man decked out in a frilly-sleeved mambo shirt and vest decorated with sequined palms (with the exception of a female harpist in long-skirted dress and wearing rhinestone glasses), the musicians looking very human, very ordinary, wistful, indifferent, happy, poised, and ready with their instruments.

At center stage, a large ball microphone, spotlight, drumroll, and Ricky Ricardo.

"Well, folks, tonight I have a special treat for you. Ladies and gentlemen, I am pleased to present to you, direct from Havana, Cuba, Manny and Alfonso Reyes, singing a bolero of their own composition, 'Beautiful María of My Soul.' "

The brothers walked out in white suits and with a guitar and trumpet in hand, bowed to the audience, and nodded when Ricky Ricardo faced the orchestra and, holding his thin conductor's wand ready to begin, asked them, "Are you ready?"

The older brother strummed an A-minor chord, the key of the song; a harp swirled in as if from the clouds of heaven; then the bassist began to play a habanera, and then the piano and horns played a four-chord vamp. Standing side by side before the big ball microphone, brows creased in concentration, expressions sincere, the brothers began to sing that romantic bolero, "Beautiful María of My Soul." A song about love so far away it hurts; a song about lost pleasures, a song about youth, a song about love so elusive a man can never know where he stands; a song about wanting a woman so much death does not frighten you, a song about wanting that woman even when she has abandoned you.

As Cesar sang, his vocal cords trembling, he seemed to be watching something profoundly beautiful and painful happening in the distance, eyes passionate, imploring, his earnest expression asking, "Can you see who I am?" But the younger brother's eyes were closed and his head was tilted back. He looked like a man on the verge of falling through an eternal abyss of longing and solitude.

For the final verses they were joined by the bandleader, who harmonized with them and was so happy with the song that at the end he whipped his right hand up into the air, a lock of thick black hair falling over his brow. Then he shouted, *"Olé!"* The brothers were now both smiling and taking bows, and Arnaz, playing Ricky Ricardo, repeated, "Let's give them a nice hand, folks!" My uncle and my father bowed again and shook Arnaz's hand and walked offstage, waving to the audience.

Oh, love's sadness,
Why did you come to me?
I was happy before you
entered my heart.

How can I hate you
if I love you so?
I can't explain my torment,
for I don't know how to live
without your love . . .

What delicious pain
love has brought to me
in the form of a woman.
My torment and ecstasy,
María, my life. . . .
Beautiful María of my soul,

Why did she finally mistreat me so?
Tell me, why is it that way?
Why is it always so?
María, my life,
Beautiful María of my soul.

And now I'm dreaming, my uncle's heart swelling to the size of the satin heart on the *I Love Lucy* show, and floating free from his chest over the rooftops of La Salle, so enormous it can be seen for blocks and blocks. Cardinal Spellman has come to the parish to administer confirmation to the sixth-graders, and my friends and I are hanging out across the street, watching the hoopla, which has been announced in all the newspapers; limousines, reporters, clergy of every rank, from novitiates to bishops, crowded outside the church. And as they file into the church, I notice the enormous satin heart, and it makes me afraid, so I go into the church even when my friends, tough hoods in sleeveless black T-shirts, call me a little girl for doing it, and yet, when I'm inside, there's no confirmation ceremony going on, it's a funeral. A beautiful flower-covered coffin with brass curlicue handles is set out in the center aisle, and the Cardinal has just finished saying Mass and is giving his blessing. That's when the organist starts to play, except, out of each key, instead of pipe-organ music, instead of Bach, what sounds is a mambo trumpet, a piano chord, a conga, and suddenly it's as if there's a whole mambo band in the choir stall, and when I look, there is a full-blown mambo orchestra straight out of 1952 playing a languid bolero, and yet I can hear the oceanic scratching, the way you do with old records. Then the place is very sad, as they start carrying out the coffin, and once it's outside, another satin heart escapes, rising out of the wood, and goes higher and higher, expanding as it reaches toward the sky, floating away, behind the other.

LEONARD MICHAELS

FROM

Shuffle

1990

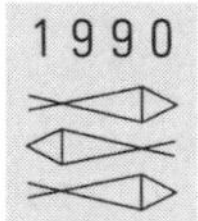

TO FEEL THESE THINGS

My mother, Anna Czeskies, was seventeen when she married and said goodbye to her parents in Brest Litovsk. She sailed to New York, settled in Coney Island, and moved later to a tenement in Manhattan, near my father's barbershop. Soon afterwards, the year Hitler came to power and Roosevelt was elected President, I was born. These names, intoned throughout my childhood, belonged to mythical deities. One was evil. The other was the other.

My mother's family intended to follow her to America, but the day my grandfather went to get their emigration papers there was a pogrom. He was attacked in the street by a mob and left for dead. He didn't recover quickly. Then it was too late to get out of Poland.

In photos he is pale and thin. Skin pulls tight across sharp bones in a narrow face. He has the alert, hypersensitive look of an ill-nourished person, but sits correctly, posing in the old style, as if a photo is serious business. He was a tailor who made uniforms for Polish army officers and had a feeling for posture. My mother says they threw his unconscious body into a cellar. I heard the story around the time children hear fairy tales. Once upon a time my grandfather was walking in the street . . .

Years later I would hear that organized terrorism had been reported for centuries in Europe, Russia, and the Middle East. Rabbinical commentaries engaged questions as to whether the community should surrender a few to save the rest, die with the few, or resist. Rabbis consulted the commentaries while the SS prepared gas chambers and worked out train schedules. When the Nazis seized Brest Litovsk, my grandfather, grandmother, and their youngest daughter, my mother's sister, were buried in a pit with others.

As my mother sat in the living room at night, waiting for my father to come home from work, she sometimes cried. This was my personal experience of the Holocaust, in a three-room apartment on the Lower

East Side of Manhattan, amid claw-footed furniture covered by plastic to protect the fabric.

I had no concrete understanding of her grief. I'd never met my grandparents, uncles, or aunt. I had to imagine things—the story about my grandfather, the danger of streets . . . Eventually, I figured it was bad for Jews the way *it* is said to be raining. I didn't know what *it* was, only that *it* was worse than Hitler, older, absolutely unreasonable, strong, able to do things like fix the plumbing and paint the walls. *It* was like animals and trees, what lives outside, more physical than a person, though *it* appeared in persons. With this understanding, I was slow to perform simple, childhood actions—riding a bicycle, throwing a ball, running like other bodies—which expressed one's being-at-home-in-the-world.

My mother—without parents, siblings, friends, or English—was generally intimidated by America, even fearful of going out alone in the streets. She had black hair which she wore in long braids. Her eyes were blue. Strange men wanted to approach and talk to her. She kept me close. We were constantly together. Her many fears nourished mine, especially because I was sickly, susceptible to respiratory diseases and ear infections; colds, bronchitis, pleurisy, and pneumonia twice. Through feverish delirium, I heard my mother at my bedside saying, *"Meir far deir,"* which means: Let me die rather than you. Her phrase, repeated like a radio signal, kept me from drifting out of life.

I learned English, mainly from the woman who lived next door. Her name was Lynn Nations. She came from Texas and was married to a Jew, Arthur Kleinman, a furrier and lefty intellectual. They had no children. She worked at Saks Fifth Avenue, a tall, slender woman with fine features and light brown hair. She was proud of her legs, and she flaunted a tough, classy manner. I remember the clack of her high heels on the marble floor of the outside hallway. I was often in her apartment and she in ours, telling us the smart things she'd said that day at Saks, how she corrected her customers' taste and sold them half the store. We understood her idea of herself, if not always what she said, but she talked at us for years, teasing us toward English. To her, my Yiddish was hilarious. "Arthur, did you hear what he called the telephone wire? A *shtrik*. No wonder he's afraid of it."

Arthur, fluent in Yiddish, looked at me with astonishment. *"Das iz nisht a shtrik. Das iz a telephone vyeh."* I see his Slavic face leaning down, thick in nose and lip, winking at me, compromising English and Yiddish to assure me that meaning is greater than words.

When I came crying from the playground after some kid hit me, Lynn's eyes contracted into icy dots of rage. She snatched me from my mother by the back of my neck—"You let go of your child"—and steered me into the playground and thrust me toward the kid. Still crying, I started swinging, and it was good, it was excellent, for a scrawny sickly kid to hear his blubbering become curses and to be a piece of nature in a playground fistfight. Lynn hated my crying, seeing it as pogrom-obsessed *Yiddishkeit.* For her better opinion, I made small beginnings, used my fists, spoke English. During the war I changed further.

I put a big map of Europe on my bedroom wall. When I read about Allied bombing raids in Germany, Italy, or elsewhere, I found the city and stuck a red pin into it. I imagined myself a B-17 pilot or bombardier. In movies, I saw the doors of the bomb bay swing open and long bombs with tails and sticklike incendiaries fall away toward factories, railroad tracks, and whole cities. This great work was being done by regular guys from America. My mother took me to the movies on Friday afternoons after school. Before we left, I had to drink a glass of milk. I hated its whiteness, the whiteness of its taste. "Finish the whole glass. It's good for you." But then came the B-17, stuck with machine guns in ribs, nose, belly, and tail, a primordial reptile dragging long flaps and lugubrious claws for landing gear, lumbering up into the gray dawn among its thousand sisters, each bearing a sacred gift of bombs.

After the war, her brothers' names appeared in the *Forward*, published a few blocks from us, in a white building opposite the Seward Park Library that I'd passed many times on the way to my father's barbershop around the corner on Henry Street. The distant, the exotic, the fairy tale of evil and a murdered family was suddenly in these familiar streets, even in the Garden Cafeteria near the foot of the *Forward* building, where I sometimes sat with my father and ate whitefish on black bread with onion, amid the dark Jewish faces of taxi drivers, pickle salesmen, dry-goods merchants, journalists, and other urban beings who sipped coffee or borscht, and smoked cigarettes and argued, joked, or complained in Yiddish, or in such English as had been mutilated into the nuances required by Yiddish, grammatical niceties flung aside so that meaning and feeling could walk on the earth.

The names of my uncles, Yussel and Srulke Czeskies, had appeared among those of survivors gathered in camps for displaced persons who now sought relatives in America. One uncle had been in the Russian army, the other in the Polish army. I was happy. I was also worried. Would my mother be held responsible for what they had endured? When her brothers actually stood in our apartment, I retreated to corners, absorbed in shadowy thought, like a neighborhood cat. A strange mechanism of feeling drew me from happiness toward internal complications; early notions of guilt as fundamental to life.

The father of a friend of mine developed his own religious practices, reducing life to secret study and his tuxedo-renting business. He was a big gloomy man with a high rounded back, black brows, and a reproachful glare. During the day, he worked. At night, he studied. He sought the deepest meaning of things, the fate of the Jews. There had been a tragic mistake. He would discover, in holy books, how to understand the Holocaust.

Even as a child, I thought Jews were obsessed with meaning. We didn't just eat, sleep, work, study, play, but needed the meaning of these things and everything. Meaning as such, as if it had practical value, like wood or gold. We sought it with brain fingers, loved how it feels in the elaborations of talk. At the heart of all meaning was the religion, the law, forever established, yet open to perpetual analysis and explication. But I knew that beneath all meaning was the general complicity with murder. In the sidewalks, the grass, the weather, and the human heart: the need to murder.

And yet, outside, in murderous nature, I could see that colors never clash and the world is everywhere beautiful. I feared its allure.

I remember pictures of President Roosevelt, the long handsome face with its insouciant smile, his cigarette holder aloft in a white aristocratic hand, perhaps in the manner of SS officers outside the windows of the gas chambers, chatting and smoking as we died in agony visible to them. Of course, I wasn't there. I had only a sense of ubiquitous savagery, the inchoate, nightmarish apprehensions of a child, much like insanity or the numinousness of a religious vision where ideas have the force of presence, overriding logic. Yiddish-speaking relatives discussed the President's tepid reaction to Kristallnacht and his decision to turn away a ship of Jewish refugees from American shores. From those who could make a difference, I figured, came indifference. Knowing nothing about immigration laws or the isolationist politics of America, I understood only a weird mixture of comfort and sadism in the President's smile. In his capacity to do something lived the frisson of doing nothing. I couldn't have articulated this understanding any more than I could have said how I tie my shoelaces.

"Take care," writes Primo Levi, "not to suffer in your own homes what is inflicted on us here." He means don't let his experience of Auschwitz become yours. I read the sentence repeatedly before I understood that is all he means, and that he doesn't mean: DON'T FEEL THESE THINGS IN THE DAILINESS OF YOUR LIFE OR IT WILL POISON EVERYTHING ELSE—running in the playground, speaking English, knowing it's time to make a fist.

Thus, misreading a few words, I rediscover my primitive apprehensions long after the Holocaust. I literally remind myself that I wasn't with my grandparents in Poland, or with the children packed into cattle trains to the death camps. I can't claim too little. Nothing happened to me. I was a sickly kid, burdened by sweaters and scarves and winter coats buttoned to the neck. If I loosened my scarf or undid a coat button, my mother would fly into a state of panic, as though millions of germs were shooting through the gap I'd made in my clothing.

MICHAEL CUNNINGHAM

FROM

A Home at the End of the World

1990

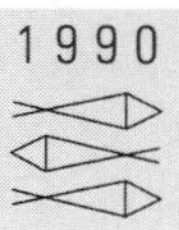

We gathered at dusk on the darkening green. I was five. The air smelled of newly cut grass, and the sand traps were luminous. My father carried me on his shoulders. I was both pilot and captive of his enormity. My bare legs thrilled to the sandpaper of his cheeks, and I held on to his ears, great soft shells that buzzed minutely with hair.

My mother's red lipstick and fingernails looked black in the dusk. She was pregnant, just beginning to show, and the crowd parted for her. We made our small camp on the second fairway, with two folding aluminum chairs. Multitudes had turned out for the celebration. Smoke from their portable barbecues sharpened the air. I settled myself on my father's lap, and was given a sip of beer. My mother sat fanning herself with the Sunday funnies. Mosquitoes circled above us in the violet ether.

That Fourth of July the city of Cleveland had hired two famous Mexican brothers to set off fireworks over the municipal golf course. These brothers put on shows all over the world, at state and religious affairs. They came from deep in Mexico, where bread was baked in the shape of skulls and virgins, and fireworks were considered to be man's highest form of artistic expression.

The show started before the first star announced itself. It began unspectacularly. The brothers were playing their audience, throwing out some easy ones: standard double and triple blossomings, spiral rockets, colored sprays that left drab orchids of colored smoke. Ordinary stuff. Then, following a pause, they began in earnest. A rocket shot straight up, pulling a thread of silver light in its wake, and at the top of its arc it bloomed purple, a blazing five-pronged lily, each petal of which burst out with a blossom of its own. The crowd cooed its appreciation. My father cupped my belly with one enormous brown hand, and asked if I was enjoying the show. I nodded. Below his throat, an outcropping of dark blond hairs struggled to escape through the collar of his madras shirt.

More of the lilies exploded, red yellow and mauve, their silver stems lingering beneath them. Then came the snakes, hissing orange fire, a dozen at a time, great lolloping curves that met, intertwined, and diverged, sizzling all the while. They were followed by huge soundless snowflakes, crystalline bodies of purest white, and those by a constellation in the shape of Miss Liberty, with blue eyes and ruby lips. Thousands gasped and applauded. I remember my father's throat, speckled with dried blood, the stubbly skin loosely covering a huge knobbed mechanism that swallowed beer. When I whimpered at the occasional loud bang, or at a scattering of colored embers that seemed to be dropping directly onto our heads, he assured me we had nothing to fear. I could feel the rumble of his voice in my stomach and my legs. His lean arms, each lazily bisected by a single vein, held me firmly in place.

•

I want to talk about my father's beauty. I know it's not a usual subject for a man—when we talk about our fathers we are far more likely to tell tales of courage or titanic rage, even of tenderness. But I want to talk about my father's frank, unadulterated beauty: the potent symmetry of his arms, blond and lithely muscled as if they'd been carved of raw ash; the easy, measured grace of his stride. He was a compact, physically dignified man; a dark-eyed theater owner quietly in love with the movies. My mother suffered headaches and fits of irony, but my father was always cheerful, always on his way somewhere, always certain that things would turn out all right.

When my father was away at work my mother and I were alone together. She invented indoor games for us to play, or enlisted my help in baking cookies. She disliked going out, especially in winter, because the cold gave her headaches. She was a New Orleans girl, small-boned and precise in her movements. She had married young. Sometimes she prevailed upon me to sit by the window with her, looking at the street, waiting for a moment when the frozen landscape might resolve itself into something ordinary she could trust as placidly as did the solid, rollicking Ohio mothers who piloted enormous cars loaded with groceries, babies, elderly relations. Station wagons rumbled down our street like decorated tanks celebrating victory in foreign wars.

"Jonathan," she whispered. "Hey, boy-o. What are you thinking about?"

It was a favorite question of hers. "I don't know," I said.

"Tell me anything," she said. "Tell me a story."

I was aware of the need to speak. "Those boys are taking their sled to the river," I told her, as two older neighborhood boys in plaid caps—boys I adored and feared—passed our house pulling a battered Flexible Flyer. "They're going to slide it on the ice. But they have to be careful about holes. A little boy fell in and drowned."

It wasn't much of a story. It was the best I could manage on short notice.

"How did you know about that?" she asked.

I shrugged. I had thought I'd made it up. It was sometimes difficult to distinguish what had occurred from what might have occurred.

"Does that story scare you?" she said.

"No," I told her. I imagined myself skimming over a vast expanse of ice, deftly avoiding the jagged holes into which other boys fell with sad, defeated little splashes.

"You're safe here," she said, stroking my hair. "Don't you worry about a thing. We're both perfectly safe and sound right here."

I nodded, though I could hear the uncertainty in her voice. Her heavy-jawed, small-nosed face cupped the raw winter light that shot up off the icy street and ricocheted from room to room of our house, nicking the silver in the cabinet, setting the little prismed lamp abuzz.

"How about a *funny* story?" she said. "We could probably use one just about now."

"Okay," I said, though I knew no funny stories. Humor was a mystery to me—I could only narrate what I saw. Outside our window, Miss Heidegger, the old woman who lived next door, emerged from her house, dressed in a coat that appeared to be made of mouse pelts. She picked up a leaf of newspaper that had blown into her yard, and hobbled back inside. I knew from my parents' private comments that Miss Heidegger was funny. She was funny in her insistence that her property be kept immaculate, and in her convictions about the Communists who operated the schools, the telephone company, and the Lutheran church. My father liked to say, in a warbling voice, "Those Communists have sent us another electric bill. Mark my words, they're trying to force us out of our homes." When he said something like that my mother always laughed, even at bill-paying time, when the fear was most plainly etched around her mouth and eyes.

That day, sitting by the window, I tried doing Miss Heidegger myself. In a high, quivering voice not wholly different from my actual voice I said, "Oh, those bad Communists have blown this newspaper right into my yard." I got up and walked stiff-legged to the middle of the living room, where I picked up a copy of *Time* magazine from the coffee table and waggled it over my head.

"You Communists," I croaked. "You stay away now. Stop trying to force us out of our homes."

My mother laughed delightedly. "You are *wick*ed," she said.

I went to her, and she scratched my head affectionately. The light from the street brightened the gauze curtains, filled the deep blue candy dish on the side table. We were safe.

•

My father worked all day, came home for dinner, and went back to the theater at night. I do not to this day know what he did all those hours—as far as I can tell, the operation of a single, unprosperous movie theater does not require the owner's presence from early morning until late at night. My father worked those hours, though, and neither my mother nor I questioned it. He was earning money, maintaining the house that protected us from the Cleveland winters. That was all we needed to know.

When my father came home for dinner, a frosty smell clung to his coat. He was big and inevitable as a tree. When he took off his coat, the fine hair on his forearms stood up electrically in the soft, warm air of the house.

My mother served the dinner she had made. My father patted her belly, which was by then round and solid as a basketball.

"Triplets," he said. "We're going to need a bigger house. Two bedrooms won't do it, not by a long shot."

"Let's just worry about the oil bill," she said.

"Another year," he said. "A year from now, and we'll be in a position to look at real estate."

My father frequently alluded to a change in our position. If we arranged ourselves a certain way, the right things would happen. We had to be careful about how we stood, what we thought.

"We'll see," my mother said in a quiet tone.

He got up from the table and rubbed her shoulders. His hands covered her shoulders entirely. He could nearly have circled her neck with his thumb and middle finger.

"You just concentrate on the kid," he said. "Just keep yourself healthy. I'll take care of the rest."

My mother submitted to his caresses, but took no pleasure in them. I could see it on her face. When my father was home she wore the same cautious look she brought to our surveys of the street. His presence made her nervous, as if some part of the outside had forced its way in.

My father waited for her to speak, to carry us along in the continuing conversation of our family life. She sat silent at the table, her shoulders tense under his ministrations.

"Well, I guess it's time for me to get back to work," he said at length. "So long, sport. Take care of the house."

“Okay,” I said. He patted my back, and kissed me roughly on the cheek. My mother got up and started to wash the dishes. I sat watching my father as he hid his muscled arms in his coat sleeves and returned to the outside.

Later that night, after I’d been put to bed, while my mother sat downstairs watching television, I snuck into her room and tried her lipstick on my own lips. Even in the dark, I could tell that the effect was more clownish than alluring. Still, it revised my appearance. I made red spots on my cheeks with her rouge, and penciled black brows over my own pale blond ones.

I walked light-footed into the bathroom. Laughter and tinkling music drifted up through the stairwell. I put the bathroom stool in the place where my father stood shaving in the mornings, and got up on it so I could see myself in the mirror. The lips I had drawn were huge and shapeless, the spots of crimson rouge off-center. I was not beautiful, but I believed I had the possibility of beauty in me. I would have to be careful about how I stood, what I thought. Slowly, mindful of the creaky hinge, I opened the medicine cabinet and took out my father’s striped can of Barbasol. I knew just what to do: shake the can with an impatient snapping motion, spray a mound of white lather onto my left palm, and apply it incautiously, in profligate smears, to my jaw and neck. Applying makeup required all the deliberation one might bring to defusing a bomb; shaving was a hasty and imprecise act that produced scarlet pinpoints of blood and left little gobbets of hair—dead as snakeskin—behind in the sink.

When I had lathered my face I looked long into the mirror, considering the effect. My blackened eyes glittered like spiders above the lush white froth. I was not ladylike, nor was I manly. I was something else altogether. There were so many different ways to be a beauty.

•

My mother grew bigger and bigger. On a shopping trip I demanded and got a pink vinyl baby doll with thin magenta lips and cobalt eyes that closed, when the doll was laid flat, with the definitive click of miniature window frames. I suspect my parents discussed the doll. I suspect they decided it would help me cope with my feelings of exclusion. My mother taught me how to diaper it, and to bathe it in the kitchen sink. Even my father professed interest in the doll’s well-being. “How’s the kid?” he asked one evening just before dinner, as I lifted it stiff-limbed from its bath.

“Okay,” I said. Water leaked out of its joints. Its sulfur-colored hair, which sprouted from a grid of holes punched into its scalp, had taken on the smell of a wet sweater.

"Good baby," my father said, and patted its firm rubber cheek with one big finger. I was thrilled. He loved the baby so.

"Yes," I said, holding the lifeless thing in a thick white towel.

My father hunkered down on his huge hams, expelling a breeze spiced with his scent. "Jonathan?" he said.

"Uh-huh."

"You know boys don't usually play with dolls, don't you?"

"Well. Yes."

"This is your baby," he said, "and that's fine for here at home. But if you show it to other boys they may not understand. So you'd better just play with it here. All right?"

"Okay."

"Good." He patted my arm. "Okay? Only play with it in the house, right?"

"Okay," I answered. Standing small before him, holding the swaddled doll, I felt my first true humiliation. I recognized a deep inadequacy in myself, a foolishness. Of course I knew the baby was just a toy, and a slightly embarrassing one. A wrongful toy. How had I let myself drift into believing otherwise?

"Are you all right?" he asked.

"Uh-huh."

"Good. Listen, I've got to go. You take care of the house."

"Daddy?"

"Yeah?"

"Mommy doesn't want to have a baby," I said.

"Sure she does."

"No. She told me."

"Jonathan, honey, Mommy and Daddy are both very happy about the baby. Aren't you happy, too?"

"Mommy hates having this baby," I said. "She told me. She said you want to have it, but she doesn't want to."

I looked into his gigantic face, and could see that I had made some sort of contact. His eyes brightened, and the delta of capillaries that spread over his nose and cheeks stood out in sharper, redder relief against his pale skin.

"It's not true, sport," he said. "Mommy sometimes says things she doesn't mean. Believe me, she's as happy about having the baby as you and I are."

I said nothing.

"Hey, I'm late," he said. "Trust me. You'll have a little sister or brother, and we're all going to be crazy about her. Or him. You'll be a big brother. Everything'll be great."

After a moment he added, "Take care of things while I'm gone, okay?" He stroked my cheek with one spatulate thumb, and left.

That night I awoke to the sound of a whispered fight being conducted behind the door of their bedroom at the end of the hall. Their voices hissed. I lay waiting for—what? Soon I had fallen asleep again, and do not know to this day whether or not I dreamed the sound of the fight. It is still sometimes difficult to distinguish what happened from what might have happened.

•

When my mother delivered one evening in December I was left behind with Miss Heidegger, the neighbor woman. She was a milky-eyed, suspicious old soul who had worried her hair to a sparse gray frazzle through which the pink curve of her skull could be seen.

As I watched my parents drive away together Miss Heidegger stood behind me, smelling mildly of wilted rose perfume. When the car was out of sight I told her, "Mommy's not really going to have the baby."

"No?" she said pleasantly, having no idea how to talk to children when they began speaking strangely.

"She doesn't want to," I said.

"Oh, now, you'll love the baby, dear," Miss Heidegger said. "Just you wait. When Momma and Poppa bring it home, you'll see. It'll be the sweetest little thing you can imagine."

"She doesn't like having a baby," I said. "We don't want it."

At this poor Miss Heidegger's remaining blood rushed to her face, and she went with a sound like rustling tissue to the kitchen to see about dinner. She put together something limp and boiled, which I with my child's devotion to bland food liked enormously.

My father telephoned from the hospital after midnight. Miss Heidegger and I reached the phone at the same moment. She answered and stood erect in her blue bathrobe, nodding her withered head. I could tell something was wrong from her eyes, which took on a thinness and brilliance like that of river ice just before it melts, when it is no more than the memory of ice lingering another moment or two over bright brown water.

The baby would be described to me as a canceled ticket, a cake taken too soon from the oven. Only as an adult would I piece together the true story of the snarled cord and ripped flesh. My mother had died for nearly a minute, and miraculously come back. Most of her womb had had to be scooped out. The baby, a girl, had lived long enough to bleat once at the fluorescent ceiling of the delivery room.

I suppose my father was in no condition to talk to me. He left that to Miss Heidegger, who put the telephone down and stood before me with an expression of terrified confusion like that with which I imagine we must greet death itself. I knew something dreadful had happened.

She said in a whisper, "Oh, those poor, poor people. Oh, you poor little boy."

Although I did not know exactly what had happened, I knew this to be an occasion for grief. I tried feeling inconsolable, but in fact I was enlivened and rather pleased by the chance to act well in a bad situation.

"Now, don't you worry, dear," Miss Heidegger said. There was true horror in her voice, a moist gargling undertone. I tried leading her to a chair, and found to my astonishment that she obeyed me. I ran to the kitchen and got her a glass of water, which was what I believed one offered somebody in a state of emotional agitation.

"Don't you worry, I'll stay with you," she said as I got a coaster for the glass and set it on the end table. She tried pulling me onto her lap but I had no interest in sitting there. I remained standing at her feet. She petted my hair and I stroked the thin, complicated bones of her flannel-covered knee.

She said helplessly, almost questioningly, "Oh, she was so healthy. She just looked perfectly fine."

Emboldened, I took one of her brittle, powdery old hands in mine.

"Oh, you poor thing," she said. "Don't you worry now, I'm here."

I continued standing at her feet, holding the bones of her hand. She smiled at me. Was there some aspect of pleasure in her smile? Probably not; I suspect I imagined it. I gently kneaded her hand. We stayed that way for quite a while, bowed and steadfast and vaguely satisfied, like a pair of spinsters who have learned to find solace in the world's unfathomable grief.

•

My mother came back over a week later, reserved and rather shy. Both she and my father looked around the house as if it were new to them, as if they had been promised something grander. In my mother's absence Miss Heidegger had instituted a smell of her own, compounded of that watery rose perfume and the odor of unfamiliar cooking. She squeezed my parents' hands and left discreetly, hurriedly. She might have been told privately that at any moment the house would catch fire.

After she had gone my mother and father both kneeled down and held me. They surrounded me, all but buried me, with their flesh and their brisk, known smells.

My father wept. He had never before shed a single tear in my presence and now he cried extravagantly, great phlegmy sobs that caught in his throat with the clotted sound of a stopped pipe. Experimentally, I placed my hand on his forearm. He did not brush it off, or reprimand me. His pale hairs sprouted up raucously between my fingers.

"It's okay," I whispered, though I don't believe he heard me over his keening. "It's okay," I said again, in full voice. He did not derive any visible comfort from my reassurances.

I glanced at my mother. She was not crying. Her face was drained not only of color but of expression as well. She might have been a vacant body, waiting dumbfounded to be infused with a human soul. But when she felt my eyes on her she managed, in a strong-limbed, somnambulistic fashion, to draw me to her breast. Her embrace caught me off guard, and I lost my hold on my father's forearm. As my mother crushed my face into the folds of her coat I lost track of my father entirely. I felt myself being pulled down into the depths of my mother's coat. It filled my nose and ears. The sound of my father's laments grew muffled and remote as I was impelled deeper into my mother's clothes, through the outer layer of cold toward the scented, familiar-smelling core. I resisted a moment, tried to return to my father, but she was too strong. I disappeared. I left my father, and gave myself over to my mother's more ravenous sorrow.

•

Afterward she was more reluctant than ever to go outdoors. Sometimes in the mornings she took me into bed with her and kept me there, reading or watching television, until mid-afternoon. We played games, told stories. I believed I knew what we were doing together during those long, housebound days. We were practicing for a time when my father would no longer be with us; when it would be just we two.

To make my mother laugh I did imitations, although I no longer felt inclined to imitate Miss Heidegger. I settled into doing my mother herself, which sometimes made her screech with laughter. I would put on her scarves and hats, speak in my own version of her New Orleans accent, which I made half Southern and half Bronx. "What are you thinking?" I'd drawl. "Honey, tell me a story."

She always laughed until her eyes shone with tears. "Sweetheart," she would say, "you're a natural. What do you say we put you on the stage, you can support your old mama in her dotage?"

When finally we got up she dressed hurriedly, and set about cooking and cleaning with the relentlessness of an artist.

My father no longer massaged her shoulders when he came home at night. He did not plant exaggerated, smacking kisses on her forehead or the tip of her nose. He couldn't. A force field had grown up around her, transparent and solid as glass. I could see it go up when he came home, with the rampant smells of the outside world clinging to his coat. When the field was up my mother looked no different—her face remained clever and slightly feverish, her movements exact as a surgeon's as she laid out the perfect dinner she had made—but she could not be touched. We knew it, both my father and I, with a visceral certainty that was all the more real for its inexplicability. My mother had powers. We ate our dinner (her cooking got better and better, she hit ever more elaborate heights), talked of usual things, and my father kissed the air in our vicinity as he readied himself to return to the outside.

•

One night in late spring, I was awakened by the sound of a proper fight. My parents were downstairs. Even in rage they kept their voices down, so that only an occasional word or phrase worked its way up to my room. The effect was like that of two people screaming inside a heavy sack. I heard my father say, "*pun*ishment," and, nearly a full minute later, my mother answer, "what *you* want . . . something . . . *sel*fish."

I lay in the dark, listening. Presently I heard footsteps—my father's—mounting the stairs. I believed he would come into my room, and I feigned elaborate, angelic sleep, my head centered on the pillow and my lips slightly parted. But my father did not come to me. He went instead to the room he shared with my mother. I heard him go in, and heard nothing more.

Minutes passed. My mother did not follow him. The house was silent, filled with a gelid, wintery hush even as lilac and dogwood leaves brushed darkly against the windowpanes. I lay carefully in my own bed, uncertain of what was expected and what allowed on a night like this. I thought I would just go back to sleep, but that refused to happen.

Finally, I got out of bed and walked down the hall to my parents' room. The door stood ajar. Light from their bedside lamp—a pink-gold light tinted by the parchment shade—hung with a certain weight in the semidarkness of the hall. From the kitchen my mother could be heard shelling pecans, a series of sharp, musical cracks.

My father lay diagonally across the double bed, in an attitude of refined, almost demure, abandon. His face was turned toward the wall on which a blue-and-green Paris street, unpeopled, hung in a silver frame. One of his arms was draped over the edge of the mattress, the large fingers dangling extravagantly. His rib cage rose and fell with the steady rhythm of sleep.

I stood in the doorway for a while, contemplating my position. I had expected him to hear me, to look up and commence worrying over the fact that I had been disturbed. When he maintained his posture on the bed I stepped quietly into the room. It was time for me to speak but I could not think of what to say. I had thought my simple presence would cause a next thing to happen. I looked around the room. There were the twin bureaus, with my mother's makeup and perfumes arranged on a mother-of-pearl tray. There was the oak-framed mirror, displaying a rectangle of flowered wallpaper from the opposite wall. Empty-handed, without an offering, I crept to the bed and cautiously touched my father's elbow.

He lifted his head and looked at me as if he didn't recognize me; as if we had met once, long ago, and now he was trying to summon up my name. His face nearly stopped my heart. For a moment it seemed he had left us after all; his fatherly aspect had withdrawn and in its place was only a man, big as a car but blank and unscrupled as an infant, capable of anything. I stood in the sudden glare of his new strangeness, shyly smiling in yellow pajamas.

Then he brought himself back. He reoccupied his face and laid a gentle hand on my shoulder. "Hey," he whispered. "What are you doing up?"

I shrugged. Even today, as an adult, I can't remember a time when I did not pause and consider before telling the truth.

He could have picked me up and taken me onto the bed with him. That gesture might have rescued us both, at least for the time being. I ached for it. I'd have given everything I imagined owning, in my greediest fantasies, to have been pulled into bed with him and held, as he'd held me while the sky exploded over our heads on the Fourth of July. But he must have been embarrassed at having been caught fighting. Now he was a man who had awakened his child by yelling at his wife, and had then flung himself across the bed like a heartbroken teenage girl. He could become other things, but he would always be that as well.

"Go back to sleep," he said, in a voice gruffer than he may have intended it to be. I believe he hoped the situation could still be undone. If he acted forcefully enough, we could jump back in time and restitch the fabric of my sleep. I would wake in the morning with nothing more than dimly recollected dreams.

I refused. I would settle for nothing less than consoling him. My father ordered me back to bed and I grew balky and petulant. I hovered at the edge of tears, which strained his patience. I wanted him to require my presence. I needed to know that by my kindness and perseverance I was victorious in the long contest for his love.

"Jonathan," he said. "Jonathan, come on."

I let myself be taken back to my room. I had no options. He picked me up and for the first time I did not exult in his touch or his spicy smell, the broad curving shine of his forehead. At that moment I came to know my mother's reticence, her delicate-boned sense of remove. I had practiced imitating her and now, in a rush, I could do nothing else. If my father rubbed my weary shoulders I would tense up; if he stomped in from the snow I would think nervously of the collapse of my spinach soufflé.

He put me into bed tenderly enough. He pulled the covers over me, told me to get some shut-eye. He did not act badly. Still, in a fury, I slipped out of bed and ran across the room to my toy chest. Unfamiliar feelings racketed in my ears, made me light-headed. "Jonathan," my father said sharply. He started after me, but I was too quick for him. I dug to the bottom of the chest, knowing just where to reach. I pulled the doll out by her slick rubber leg and held her roughly in my arms.

He hesitated, half standing over my miniature bed. On my headboard, a cartoon rabbit danced ecstatically on a field of four-petaled pink flowers.

"This is mine," I said, in a nearly hysterical tone of insistence. The floor of my bedroom felt unsteady beneath my feet, and I clung to the doll as if it alone could keep me from losing my balance and slipping away.

My father shook his head. For the single time in my recollection, his kindness failed. He had wanted so much, and the world was shrinking. His wife shunned him, his business was not a success, and his only son—there would be no others—loved dolls and quiet indoor games.

"Jesus Christ, Jonathan," he hollered. "Jesus H. Christ. What in the hell is the matter with you? *What?*"

I stood dumb. I had no answer to that question, although I knew one was expected.

"This is mine" was all I could offer by way of an answer. I held the doll so close to my chest her stiff eyelashes gouged me through my pajamas.

"Fine," he said more quietly, in a defeated tone. "Fine. It's yours." And he left.

I heard him go downstairs, get his jacket from the hall closet. I heard my mother fail to speak from the kitchen. I heard him close the front door, with a caution and deliberateness that implied finality.

He would return in the morning, having slept on the couch in his office at the theater. After an awkward period we would resume our normal family life, find our cheerfulness again. My father and mother would invent a cordial, joking relationship that involved neither kisses nor fights. They would commence living together with the easy, chaste familiarity of grown siblings. He would ask me no more unanswerable questions, though his singular question would continue crackling in the back of my head like a faulty electrical connection. My mother's cooking would become renowned. In 1968, our family would be photographed for the Sunday supplement of the Cleveland *Post*: my mother cutting into a shrimp casserole while my father and I looked on, proud, expectant, and perfectly dressed.

EDNA O'BRIEN

FROM

Lantern Slides

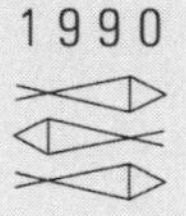

BROTHER

Bad cess to him. Thinks I don't know, that I didn't smell a rat. All them bachelors swaggering in here, calling him out to the haggart in case I twigged. "Tutsy this and Tutsy that." A few readies in it for them, along with drives and big feeds. They went the first Sunday to reconnoitre, walk the land and so forth. The second Sunday they went in for refreshments. Three married sisters, all gawks. If they're not hitched up by now there must be something wrong; harelip or a limp or fits. He's no oil painting, of course. Me doing everything for him: making his porridge and emptying his worshipful Po, for God knows how many years. Not to mention his lumbago, and the liniment I rubbed in.

"I'll be good to you, Maisie," he says. Good! A bag of toffees on a holy day. Takes me for granted. All them flyboys at threshing time trying to ogle me up into the loft for a fumble. Puckauns. I'd take a pitchfork to any one of them; so would he if he knew. I scratched his back many's the night and rubbed the liniment on it. Terrible aul smell. Eucalyptus.

"Lower . . . lower," he'd say. "Down there." Down to the puddingy bits, the lupins. All to get to my Mary. He had a Mass said in the house after. Said he saw his mother, our mother; something on her mind. I had to have grapefruit for the priest's breakfast, had to de-pip it. These priests are real gluttons. He ate in the breakfast room and kept admiring things in the cabinet, the china bell and the bog-oak cabin, and so forth. Thought I'd part with them. I was running in and out with hot tea, hot water, hot scones; he ate enough for three. Then the big handshake; Matt giving him a tenner. I never had that amount in my whole life. Ten bob on Fridays to get provisions, including sausages for his breakfast. Woeful the way he never consulted me. He began to get hoity-toity, took off those awful trousers with the greasy backside from all the sweating and lathering on horseback, tractor, and bike; threw them in the fire cavalier-like. Had me airing a suit for three days. I had it on a clotheshorse, turning it round every quarter of an hour, for fear of it scorching.

Then the three bachelors come into the yard again, blabbing about buying silage off him. They had silage to burn. It stinks the countryside. He put on his cap and went out to talk to them. They all leant on the gate, cogitating. I knew 'twas fishy, but it never dawned on me it could be a wife. I'd have gone out and sent them packing. Talking low they were, and at the end they all shook hands. At the supper he said he was going to Galway Sunday.

"What's in Galway?" I said.

"A greyhound," he said.

First mention of a greyhound since our little Deirdre died. The pride and joy of the parish she was. Some scoundrels poisoned her. I found her in a fit outside in the shed, yelps coming out of her, and foam. It nearly killed him. He had a rope that he was ruminating with for months. Now this bombshell. Galway.

"I'll come with you, I need a sea breeze," I said.

"It's all male, it's stag," he said, and grinned.

I might have guessed. Why they were egging him on I'll never know, except 'twas to spite me. Some of them have it in for me; I drove bullocks of theirs off our land, I don't give them any haults on bonfire night. He went up to the room then and wouldn't budge. I left a slice of griddle bread with golden syrup on it outside the door. He didn't touch it. At dawn I was raking the ashes and he called me, real soft-soapy, "Is that you, Maisie, is that you?" Who in blazes' name did he think it was—Bridget or Mary of the Gods! "Come in for a minute," he said. "There's a flea or some goddamn thing itching me, maybe it's a tick, maybe they've nested." I strip the covers and in th'oul candlelight he's like one of those saints that they boil, thin and raky. Up to then I only ventured in the dark, on windy nights when he'd say he heard a ghost and I had to go to him. I reconnoitre his white body while he's muttering on about the itch, says, "Soldiers in the tropics minded itch more than combat." He read that in an almanac.

"Maisie," he says in a watery voice, and puts his hand on mine and steers me to his shorthorn. Pulled the stays off of me. Thinking I don't know what he was after. All pie. Raving about me being the best sister in the wide world and I'd give my last shilling and so forth. Talked about his young days when he hunted with a ferret. Babble, babble. His limbs were like jelly, and then the grunts and him burying himself under the red flannel eiderdown, saying God would strike us.

The next Sunday he was off again. Not a word to me since the tick mutiny, except to order me to drive cattle or harness the horse. Got a new pullover, a most unfortunate colour, like piccalilli. He didn't get home that Sunday until all hours. I heard the car door banging. He boiled himself milk, because the saucepan was on the range with the skin on it. I went up to the village to get meal for the hens and everyone was gassing about it. My brother had got engaged for the second time in two weeks. First it was a Dymphna and now it was a Tilly. It seemed he was in their parlour—pictures of cows and millstreams on the wall—sitting next to his intended, eating cold ox tongue and beetroot, when he leans across the table, points to Tilly, and says, "I think I'd sooner her."

Uproar. They all dropped utensils and gaped at him, thinking it a joke. He sticks to his guns, so much so that her father and the bachelors dragged him out into the garden for a heart-to-heart. Garden. It seems it's only high grass and an obelisk that wobbles. They said, "What the Christ, Matt?" He said, "I prefer Tilly, she's plumper." Tilly was called out and the two of them were told to walk down to the gate and back, to see what they had in common.

In a short time they return and announce that they understand one another and wish to be engaged. Gink. She doesn't know the catastrophe she's in for. She doesn't know about me and my status here. Dymphna had a fit, shouted, threw bits of beetroot and gizzard all about, and said, "My sister is a witch." Had to be carried out and put in a box room, where she shrieked and banged with a set of fire irons that were stored there. Parents didn't care, at least they were getting one Cissy off their hands. Father breeds French herds, useless at it. A name like Charlemagne. The bachelors said Matt was a brave man, drink was mooted. All the arrangements that had been settled on Dymphna were now transferred to Tilly. My brother drank port wine and got maudlin. Hence the staggers in the yard when he got home and the loud octavias. Never said a word at the breakfast. I had to hear it in the village. She has mousey hair and one of her eyes squints, but instead of calling it a squint the family call it a "lazy eye." It is to be a quiet wedding. He hasn't asked me, he won't. Thinks I'm too much of a gawk with my gap teeth, and that I'd pass remarks and say, "I've eaten to my satisfaction and if I ate any more I'd go flippety-floppety," a thing he makes me say here to give him a rise in the wet evenings.

All he says is "There'll be changes, Maisie, and it's for the best." Had the cheek to ask me to make an eiderdown for the bed, rose-coloured satin. I'll probably do it, but it will only be a blind. He thinks I'm a softie. I'll be all pie to her at first, bringing her the tea in bed and asking her if she'd like her hair done with the curling tongs. We'll pick elder flowers to make jelly. She'll be in a shroud before the year is out. To think that she's all purty now, like a little bowerbird, preening herself. She won't even have the last rites. I've seen a photo of her. She sent it to him for under his pillow. I'll take a knife to her, or a hatchet. I've been in Our Lady's once before, it isn't that bad. Big teas on Sundays and fags. I'll be out in a couple of years. He'll be so morose from being all alone, he'll welcome me back with open arms. It's human nature. It stands to reason. The things I did for him, going to him in the dark, rubbing in that aul liniment, washing out at the rain barrel together, mother-naked, my bosoms slapping against him, the stars fading and me bursting my sides with the things he said—"Dotey." Dotey no less. I might do for her out of doors. Lure her to the waterfall to look for eggs. There're swans up there and geese. He loves the big geese eggs. I'll get behind her when we're on that promontory and give her a shove. It's very slippery from the moss. I can just picture her going down, yelling, then not yelling, being swept away like a newspaper or an empty canister. I'll call the alarm. I'll shout for him. If they do smell a rat and tackle me, I'll tell them that I could feel beads of moisture on my brother's poll without even touching it, I was that close to him. There's no other woman could say that, not her, not any woman. I'm all he has, I'm all he'll ever have. Roll on, nuptials. Daughter of death is she.

FROM

Wolfwatching

1991

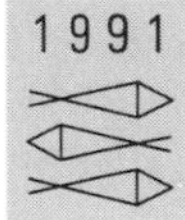

A SPARROW HAWK

Slips from your eye-corner—overtaking
Your first thought.

Through your mulling gaze over haphazard earth
The sun's cooled carbon wing
Whets the eye-beam.

Those eyes in their helmet
Still wired direct
To the nuclear core—they alone

Laser the lark-shaped hole
In the lark's song.

You find the fallen spurs, among soft ashes.

And maybe you find him

Materialized by twilight and dew
Still as a listener—

The warrior

Blue shoulder-cloak wrapped about him,
Leaning, hunched,
Among the oaks of the harp.

ALEKSANDR SOLZHENITSYN

FROM

One Day in the Life of Ivan Denisovich

[*Translated by H. T. Willetts*]

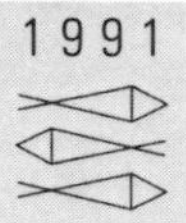

Shukhov sprang down nimbly, holding the cigarette he'd just rolled and had been wanting so long, thrust his feet into his boots and was ready to go—but he took pity on Tsezar. Not that he wanted to earn a bit more from Tsezar, he just pitied the man with all his heart: Tsezar might think a lot of himself, but he didn't know the first thing about the facts of life. When you got a parcel, you didn't sit gloating over it, you rushed it off to the storeroom before roll call. Eating could wait. But what could Tsezar do with his parcel now? If he turned out for roll call carrying that great big bag, what a laugh that would be—five hundred men would be roaring with laughter. If he left the stuff where it was, it would very likely be pinched by the first man back from roll call. (In Ust-Izhma the system was even tougher: the crooks would always be home from work first, and by the time the others got in, their nightstands would be cleaned out.)

Shukhov saw that Tsezar was in a panic—but he should have thought about it sooner. He was shoving the fatback and sausage under his shirt—if nothing else, he might be able to take them out to roll call and save them.

Shukhov took pity on him and told him how it was done:

"Sit tight, Tsezar Markovich—lie low, out of the light, and go out last. Don't stir till the warder and the orderlies come around the beds looking in every nook and cranny—then you can go out. Tell 'em you aren't well! And I'll go out first and hop back in first. That's the way to do it."

And off he dashed.

He had to be pretty rough to start with, shoving his way through the crowd (taking good care, though, of the cigarette in his clenched hand). But there was no more shoving in the corridor shared by both halves of the hut and near the outer door. The crafty lot stuck like flies to the walls, leaving free passage for one at a time between the ranks: go out in the cold if you're stupid enough, we'll hang on here a bit! We've been freezing outside all day as it is, why freeze for an extra ten minutes now? We aren't that stupid, you know. You croak today—I'll wait till tomorrow!

Any other time, Shukhov would have propped himself up against the wall with the rest. But now he strode by, sneering.

"What are you afraid of, never seen a Siberian frost before? The wolves are out sunbathing—come and try it! Give us a light, old man!"

He lit up just inside the door and went out on the porch. "Wolf's sunshine" was what they jokingly called the moonlight where Shukhov came from.

The moon had risen very high. As far again and it would be at its highest. Sky white with a greenish tinge, stars bright but far between. Snow sparkling white, barracks walls also white. Camp lights might as well not be there.

A crowd of black jackets was growing thicker outside the next hut. They were coming out to line up. And outside that other one. From hut to hut the buzz of conversation was almost drowned out by the crunch of snow under boots.

Five men went down the steps and lined up facing the door. Three others followed them. Shukhov took his place in the second rank with those three. After a munch of bread and with a cig in his mouth, it wasn't too bad standing there. The Latvian hadn't cheated him—it was really good tobacco, heady and sweet-smelling.

Men gradually trickled through the door, and by now there were two or three more ranks of five behind Shukhov. Those already out were in a foul temper. What did the lousy bastards think they were doing, hanging around in the corridor instead of coming outside? Leaving us to freeze.

No zek ever lays eyes on a clock or watch. What good would it do him, anyway? All a zek needs to know is—how soon is reveille? How long till work parade? Till dinnertime? Till lights-out?

Anyway, evening roll call is supposed to be at nine. But that's not the end of it, because they can make you go through the whole rigmarole twice or three times over. You can't get to sleep before ten. And reveille, they figure, is at five. Small wonder that the Moldavian fell asleep just now before quitting time. If a zek manages to get warm, he's asleep right away. By the end of the week there's so much lost sleep to make up for that if you aren't bundled out to work on Sunday the hut is one great heap of sleeping bodies.

Aha—zeks were pouring down from the porch now—the warder

and the hut orderly were kicking their behinds. Give it to them, the swine!

"What the hell are you playing at up there?" the front ranks yelled at them. "Skimming the cream from shit? If you'd come out sooner, they'd have finished counting long ago."

The whole hut came tumbling out. Four hundred men—eighty ranks of five. They lined up—neat fives to begin with, then higgledy-piggledy.

"Sort yourselves out at the back there!" the hut orderly roared from the steps.

They don't do it, the bastards.

Tsezar came out hunched up, acting the invalid, followed by two orderlies from the other half of the hut, two from Shukhov's, and another man with a limp. These five became the front rank, so that Shukhov was now in the third. Tsezar was packed off to the rear.

After this, the warder came out onto the porch. "Form up in fives," he shouted at the rear ranks. He had a good pair of tonsils.

"Form up in fives," the hut orderly bellowed. His tonsils were even healthier.

Still they don't move, damn their eyes.

The hut orderly shot down the steps, hurled himself at them, cursing and thumping backs.

He took care which backs he thumped, though. Only the meek were lambasted.

They finally lined up properly. He went back to his place, and shouted with the warder: "First five! Second! Third!"

Each five shot off into the hut as its number was called. Finished for the day.

Unless there's a second roll call, that is. Any herdsman can count better than those good-for-nothings. He may not be able to read, but the whole time he's driving his herd he knows whether all his calves are there or not. This lot are supposed to be trained, but it's done them no good.

The winter before, there'd been no drying rooms in the camp and everybody kept his boots in the barracks overnight—so they'd chased everybody out for a second, a third, or even a fourth count. The men didn't even dress, but rolled out wrapped in their blankets. Since then, drying rooms had been built—not for every hut, but each gang got a chance to dry its boots every third day. So now they'd started doing second counts inside the huts: driving the men from one half to the other.

Shukhov wasn't first in, but he ran without taking his eyes off the one man in front. He hurried to Tsezar's bed, sat on it, and tugged his boots off. Then he climbed up onto a handy bunk and stood his boots on the stove to dry. You just had to get in first. Then back to Tsezar's bed. He sat with his legs tucked under him, one eye watching to see that Tsezar's sack wasn't whipped from under his pillow, the other on the lookout for anybody storming the stove and knocking his boots off their perch.

He had to shout at one man. "Hey! You there, Ginger! Want a boot in your ugly mug? Put your own boots up, but don't touch other people's!"

Zeks were pouring into the hut now. In Gang 20 there were shouts of "Hand over your boots!"

The men taking the boots to the drying room would be let out and the door locked behind them. They'd come running back, shouting: "Citizen warder! Let us in!"

Meanwhile, the warders would gather in the HQ hut with their boards to check their bookkeeping and see whether anyone had escaped.

None of that mattered to Shukhov at present. Ah—here comes Tsezar, diving between the bunks on his way home.

"Thanks, Ivan Denisovich."

Shukhov nodded and scrambled up top like a squirrel. He could finish eating his two hundred grams, he could smoke a second cigarette, or he could just go to sleep.

Only, he was in such high spirits after such a good day he didn't really feel much like sleeping.

Making his bed wasn't much of a job: he just whisked off his blackish blanket, lay down on the mattress (he couldn't have slept on a sheet since he'd left home in '41—in fact, he couldn't for the life of him see why women bothered with sheets, it just made extra washing), laid his head on the pillow stuffed with shavings, shoved his feet into his jerkin, spread his jacket over his blanket, and—

"Thanks be to Thee, O God, another day over!"

He was thankful that he wasn't sleeping in the punishment cell. Here it was just about bearable.

Shukhov lay with his head toward the window, Alyoshka on the other half of the bunk with his head at the other end, where light from the bulb would reach him. He was reading his Testament again.

The lamp wasn't all that far away. They could read or even sew.

Alyoshka heard Shukhov thank God out loud, and looked around.

"There you are, Ivan Denisovich, your soul is asking to be allowed to pray to God. Why not let it have its way, eh?"

Shukhov shot a glance at him: the light in his eyes was like candle flame. Shukhov sighed.

"Because, Alyoshka, prayers are like petitions—either they don't get through at all, or else it's 'complaint rejected.' "

Four sealed boxes stood in front of the staff hut, and were emptied once a month by someone delegated for that purpose. Many prisoners dropped petitions into those boxes, then waited, counting the days, expecting an answer in two months, one month . . .

There would be no answer. Or else—"complaint rejected."

"That's because you never prayed long enough or fervently enough, that's why your prayers weren't answered. Prayer must be persistent. And if you have faith and say to a mountain, 'Make way,' it will make way."

Shukhov grinned, rolled himself another cigarette, and got a light from the Estonian.

"Don't talk rot, Alyoshka. I never saw mountains going anywhere. Come to think of it I've never seen any mountains. But when you and your whole Baptist club did all that praying in the Caucasus, did one single mountain ever move over?"

Poor devils. What harm does their praying do anybody? Collected twenty-five years all around. That's how things are nowadays: twenty-five is the only kind of sentence they hand out.

"We didn't pray for anything like that, Denisych," Alyoshka said earnestly. He moved around with his Testament until he was almost face to face with Shukhov. "The Lord's behest was that we should pray for no earthly or transient thing except our daily bread. 'Give us this day our daily bread.' "

"Our ration, you mean?" Shukhov asked.

Alyoshka went on undeterred, exhorting Shukhov with his eyes more than his words, patting and stroking his hand.

"Ivan Denisovich! We shouldn't pray for somebody to send us a parcel, or for an extra portion of skilly. What people prize highly is vile in the sight of God! We must pray for spiritual things, asking God to remove the scum of evil from our hearts."

"No, you listen to me. There's a priest at our church in Polomnya . . ."

"Don't tell me about your priest!" Alyoshka begged, his brow creased with pain.

"No, you just listen." Shukhov raised himself on his elbow. "In our parish, Polomnya, nobody was better off than the priest. If we got a roofing job, say, we charged other people thirty-five a day but we charged him a hundred. And there was never a peep out of him. He was paying alimony to three women in three different towns and living with his fourth family. The local bishop was under his thumb, our priest greased his palm well. If they sent any other priest along, ours would make his life hell, he wasn't going to share with anybody."

"Why are you telling me about this priest? The Orthodox Church has turned its back on the Gospels—*they* don't get put inside, or else they get off with five years because their faith is not firm."

Shukhov calmly observed Alyoshka's agitation, puffing on his cigarette.

"Look, Alyoshka"—smoke got into the Baptist's eyes as Shukhov pushed his outstretched hand aside—"I'm not against God, see. I'm quite ready to believe in God. But I just don't believe in heaven and hell. Why do you think everybody deserves either heaven or hell? What sort of idiots do you take us for? That's what I don't like."

Shukhov lay back again, after carefully dropping his ash into the space behind his head, between the bunk and the window, so as not to burn the captain's belongings. Lost in thought, he no longer heard Alyoshka's muttering.

"Anyway," he concluded, "pray as much as you like, but they won't knock anything off your sentence. You'll serve your time from bell to bell whatever happens."

Alyoshka was horrified. "That's just the sort of thing you shouldn't pray for! What good is freedom to you? If you're free, your faith will soon be choked by thorns! Be glad you're in prison. Here you have time to think about your soul. Remember what the Apostle Paul says, 'What are you doing, weeping and breaking my heart? For I am ready not only to be imprisoned but even to die in Jerusalem for the name of the Lord Jesus.' "*

Shukhov stared at the ceiling and said nothing. He no longer knew whether he wanted to be free or not. To begin with, he'd wanted it very much, and counted up every evening how many days he still had to serve. Then he'd got fed up with it. And still later it had gradually dawned on him that people like himself were not allowed to go home but were packed off into exile. And there was no knowing where the living was easier—here or there.

The one thing he might want to ask God for was to let him go home.

But *they* wouldn't let him go home.

Alyoshka wasn't lying, though. You could tell from his voice and his eyes that he was glad to be in prison.

* Acts 21:13.

"Look, Alyoshka," Shukhov explained, "it's worked out pretty well for you. Christ told you to go to jail, and you did it, for Christ. But what am I here for? Because they weren't ready for the war in '41—is that the reason? Was that my fault?"

"No second roll call, by the look of it," Kildigs growled from his bed. He yawned.

"Wonders never cease," Shukhov said. "Maybe we can get some sleep."

At that very minute, just as the hut was growing quiet, they heard the rattle of a bolt at the outer door of the hut. The two men who'd taken the boots to be dried dashed into the hut shouting, "Second roll call!"

A warder followed them, shouting, "Out into the other half!"

Some of them were already sleeping! They all began stirring, grumbling and groaning as they drew their boots on (very few of them were in their underpants—they mostly slept as they were, in their padded trousers—without them, your feet would be frozen stiff even under a blanket).

Shukhov swore loudly. "Damn them to hell!" But he wasn't all that angry, because he hadn't fallen asleep yet.

Tsezar's hand reached up to place two biscuits, two lumps of sugar, and one round chunk of sausage on Shukhov's bed.

"Thank you, Tsezar Markovich," Shukhov said, lowering his head into the gangway between bunks. "Better give me your bag to put under my pillow for safety." (A passing zek's thieving hands wouldn't find it so quickly up there—and anyway, who would expect Shukhov to have anything?)

Tsezar passed his tightly tied white bag up to Shukhov. Shukhov tucked it under his mattress and was going to wait a bit until more men had been herded out so that he wouldn't have to stand barefoot on the corridor floor so long. But the warder snarled at him: "You over there! In the corner!"

So Shukhov sprang to the floor, landing lightly on his bare feet (his boots and foot rags were so cozy up there on the stove it would be a pity to move them). He had cobbled so many pairs of slippers—but always for others, never for himself. Still, he was used to it, and it wouldn't be for long.

Slippers were confiscated if found in the daytime.

The gangs who'd handed in their boots for drying were all right now if they had slippers, but some had only foot rags tied around their feet, and others were barefoot.

"Get on with it! Get on with it!" the warder roared.

The hut orderly joined in: "Want a bit of the stick, you scum?"

Most of them were crammed into the other half of the hut, with the last few crowding into the corridor. Shukhov stood against the partition wall by the night bucket. The floor was damp to his feet, and an icy draft blew along it from the lobby.

Everybody was out now, but the warder and the hut orderly went to look yet again to see whether anybody was hiding, or curled up asleep in a dark spot. Too few or too many at the count meant trouble—yet another recheck. The two of them went around and around, then came back to the door.

One by one, but quickly now, they were allowed back in. Shukhov squeezed in eighteenth, dashed to his bunk, hoisted his foot onto a bracket, and—heave-ho!—up he went.

Great. Feet into his jerkin sleeve again, blanket on top, jacket over that, and we're asleep! All the zeks in the other half of the barracks would now be herded into our half—but that was their bad luck.

Tsezar came back. Shukhov lowered the bag to him.

Now Alyoshka was back. He had no sense at all, Alyoshka, never earned a thing, but did favors for everybody.

"Here you are, Alyoshka!" Shukhov handed him one biscuit.

Alyoshka was all smiles. "Thank you! You won't have any for yourself!"

"Eat it!"

If we're without, we can always earn something.

He himself took the lump of sausage—and popped it into his mouth. Get the teeth to it. Chew, chew, chew! Lovely meaty smell! Meat juice, the real thing. Down it went, into his belly.

End of sausage.

The other stuff he planned to eat before work parade.

He covered his head with the skimpy, grubby blanket and stopped listening to the zeks from the other half crowding in between the bunks to be counted.

•

Shukhov felt pleased with life as he went to sleep. A lot of good things had happened that day. He hadn't been thrown in the hole. The gang hadn't been dragged off to Sotsgorodok. He'd swiped the extra gruel at dinnertime. The foreman had got a good rate for the job. He'd enjoyed working on the wall. He hadn't been caught with the blade at the search point. He'd earned a bit from Tsezar that evening. And he'd bought his tobacco.

The end of an unclouded day. Almost a happy one.

Just one of the 3,653 days of his sentence, from bell to bell.

The extra three were for leap years.

FROM

Canvas

[*Translated by Renata Gorczynski, Benjamin Ivry, C. K. Williams*]

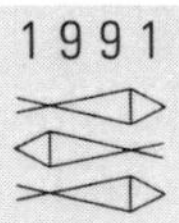

CANVAS

I stood in silence before a dark picture,
before a canvas that might have been
coat, shirt, flag,
but had turned instead into the world.

I stood in silence before the dark canvas,
charged with delight and revolt and I thought
of the arts of painting and living,
of so many blank, bitter days,

of moments of helplessness
and my chilly imagination
that's the tongue of a bell,
alive only when swaying,

striking what it loves,
loving what it strikes,
and it came to me that this canvas
could have become a winding-sheet, too.

FROM

The Death of Artemio Cruz

[*Translated by Alfred Mac Adam*]

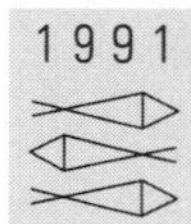

You must feel proud that you could impose your will on them. Confess it: you imposed yourself so they would let you in as their equal. You've rarely felt happier, because from the time you began to be what you are, from the time you learned to appreciate the feel of fine cloth, the taste of fine liquors, the scent of fine lotions, all those things that for the past few years have been your isolated and only pleasure, from that time on you turned your eyes northward and lived with the regret that a geographical error kept you from being part of them in everything. You admire their efficiency, their comforts, their hygiene, their power, their will, and you look around you and the incompetence, the misery, the filth, the languor, the nakedness of this poor country that has nothing, all seem intolerable to you. And what pains you even more is knowing that no matter how much you try, you cannot be like them, you can only be a copy, an approximation, because after all, say it now: was your vision of things, in your worst or your best moments, ever as simplistic as theirs? Never. Never have you been able to think in black and white, good guys versus bad guys, God or the Devil: admit that always, even when it seemed just the opposite, you've found the germ, the reflection of the white in the black. Your own cruelty, when you've been cruel, hasn't it always been tinged with a certain tenderness? You know that all extremes contain their opposites: cruelty and tenderness, cowardice and bravery; life, death. In some way—almost unconsciously, because of who you are, because of where you've come from, because of what you've lived through—you know this, and for that reason you can never resemble them who don't know these things. Does that bother you? Of course it does, it's uncomfortable, annoying. It's much easier to say: this is good and that is evil. Evil. You could never say, "That is evil." Perhaps because we are more forsaken, we do not want to lose that intermediate, ambiguous zone between light and shadow, that zone where we can find forgiveness. Where you may be able to find it. Isn't everyone, in a single moment of his life, capable of embodying—as you do—good and evil at the same time, letting himself be simultaneously led by two mysterious, different-colored threads that unwind from the same spool, so that the white thread ascends and the black one descends and, despite everything, the two come together again in his very fingers? You won't want to think about all that. You will detest me for reminding you of it. You would like to be like them, and now, an old man, you almost achieve that goal. Almost. Only almost. You yourself will block oblivion; your bravery will be the twin of your cowardice, your hatred will have been born from your love, all your life will have contained and promised your death. Therefore, you will not have been either good or evil, generous or selfish, faithful or a traitor. You will let the others affirm your good qualities and your faults; but you yourself, how will you deny that each of your affirmations will be negated, that each of your negations will be affirmed? No one will know about it, except perhaps you. That your existence will be woven of all the threads on the loom, like the lives of all men. That you will have neither too few nor too many chances to make of your life what you wish it to be. And if you become one thing and not another, it will be because, despite it all, you will have to choose. Your choices will not negate the rest of your possible life, all that you will leave behind each time you choose: they will only hone it, hone it to the point that today your choice and your destiny will be one and the same. The coin will no longer have two sides: your desire will be identical with your destiny. Will you die? It won't be the first time. You will have lived so much dead life, so many moments of mere gesticulation. When Catalina puts her ear to the door that separates you and listens to your movements; when you, on the other side of the door, move without knowing you're being listened to, without knowing that someone lives dependent on the sounds and silences of your life behind the door, who will live in that separation? When both of you realize one single word would be enough and yet you keep silent, who will live in that silence? No, you won't want to remember that. You'd like to recall something else; that name, that face the passage of time will wear away. But you will know that if you remember these things, you will save yourself, you will save yourself too easily. You will first remember the things that condemn you, and having been saved there, you will find out that the other, what you think will save you, will be your real condemnation: remembering what you want. You will remember Catalina when she was young, when you met her, and you will compare her with the faded woman of today. You will remember and remember why. You will incarnate what she, and all of them, thought then. You won't know it. You will have to incarnate it. You will never listen to what others say. You will have to live what they say. You will shut your eyes: you will shut them. You will not smell that incense. You will not listen to that weeping. You will remember other things, other days. Days that will reach you at night—your night of eyes shut. You will only recognize them by their voice, never by sight. You will have to give credit to the night and accept it without seeing it, believe it without recognizing it, as if it were the God of all your days: the night. Now you must be thinking that all you'll have to do to have it is to close your eyes. You will smile, despite the pain that reasserts itself. You will try to stretch your legs a little. Someone will touch your hand, but you will not respond to that—what? caress? care? anguish? calculated move? Because you will have created the night with your closed eyes, and from the depth of that ocean of ink, a stone boat—which the hot and sleepy midday sun will cheer in vain—will sail toward you: thick blackened walls raised to protect the Church from Indian attacks and also to link the religious conquest to the military conquest. The rough soldiers, Spanish, the troops of Queen Isabella the Catholic, advance toward your closed eyes with the swelling din of their fifes and drums, and in sunlight you will traverse the wide esplanade with a stone cross at its center and with exterior chapels, the prolongation of the native religion, theatrical and open-air, at its corners. At the top of the church built at the end of the esplanade, the vaults made of *tezontle* stone will rest on forgotten Moorish scimitars, sign of yet one more bloodline imposed on that of the conquistadors. You will advance toward the portal of the early, still Castilian, baroque, already rich in columns wound with profuse vines and aquiline keystones; the portal of the Conquest, severe and playful, with one foot in the old, dead world and the other in the new world that didn't begin here but on the other side of the sea: the new world arrived with them, with a redoubt of austere walls to protect their sensual, happy, greedy hearts. You will go further and will penetrate into the nave of the ship, its Castilian exterior conquered by the macabre, smiling plenitude of this Indian heaven of saints, angels, and indigenous gods. A single, enormous nave will run toward the altar of gilt foliage, somber opulence of masked faces, lugubrious and festive prayer, always urgent, for this freedom, the only one granted, to decorate a temple and fill it with tranquil astonishment, with sculpted resignation, with the horror of emptiness, the terror of the dead times, of those who prolonged the slow deliberateness of free labor, the unique instants of autonomy in color and form, far from that exterior world of whips and branding irons and smallpox. You will walk to the conquest of your new world through a nave devoid of blank spaces:

angel heads, luxuriant vines, polychrome flowers, red, round fruits captured in trellises of gold, white saints in chains, saints with astonished faces, saints in a heaven invented by Indians in their own image and likeness: angels and saints wearing the face of the sun and the moon, with the hand to protect harvests, with the index finger of the hounds, with the cruel, unnecessary, alien eyes of the idol, with the rigorous face of the cycles. The faces of stone behind the pink, kindly, ingenuous masks, masks that are, however, impassive and dead: create the night, fill the black sails with wind, close your eyes, Artemio Cruz . . .

NADINE GORDIMER

FROM

Jump and Other Stories

1991

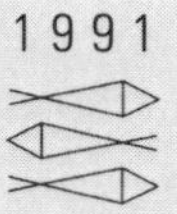

THE MOMENT BEFORE THE GUN WENT OFF

Marais Van der Vyver shot one of his farm labourers, dead. An accident, there are accidents with guns every day of the week—children playing a fatal game with a father's revolver in the cities where guns are domestic objects, nowadays, hunting mishaps like this one, in the country—but these won't be reported all over the world. Van der Vyver knows his will be. He knows that the story of the Afrikaner farmer—regional Party leader and Commandant of the local security commando—shooting a black man who worked for him will fit exactly *their* version of South Africa, it's made for them. They'll be able to use it in their boycott and divestment campaigns, it'll be another piece of evidence in their truth about the country. The papers at home will quote the story as it has appeared in the overseas press, and in the back-and-forth he and the black man will become those crudely-drawn figures on anti-apartheid banners, units in statistics of white brutality against the blacks quoted at the United Nations—he, whom they will gleefully be able to call 'a leading member' of the ruling Party.

People in the farming community understand how he must feel. Bad enough to have killed a man, without helping the Party's, the government's, the country's enemies, as well. They see the truth of that. They know, reading the Sunday papers, that when Van der Vyver is quoted saying he is 'terribly shocked', he will 'look after the wife and children', none of those Americans and English, and none of those people at home who want to destroy the white man's power will believe him. And how they will sneer when he even says of the farm boy (according to one paper, if you can trust any of those reporters), 'He was my friend, I always took him hunting with me.' Those city and overseas people don't know it's true: farmers usually have one particular black boy they like to take along with them in the lands; you could call it a kind of friend, yes, friends are not only your own white people, like yourself, you take into your house, pray with in church and work with on the Party committee. But how can those others know that? They don't want to know it. They think all blacks are like the big-mouth agitators in town. And Van der Vyver's face, in the photographs, strangely opened by distress—everyone in the district remembers Marais Van der Vyver as a little boy who would go away and hide himself if he caught you smiling at him, and everyone knows him now as a man who hides any change of expression round his mouth behind a thick, soft moustache, and in his eyes by always looking at some object in hand, leaf of a crop fingered, pen or stone picked up, while concentrating on what he is saying, or while listening to you. It just goes to show what shock can do; when you look at the newspaper photographs you feel like apologizing, as if you had stared in on some room where you should not be.

There will be an inquiry; there had better be, to stop the assumption of yet another case of brutality against farm workers, although there's nothing in doubt—an accident, and all the facts fully admitted by Van der Vyver. He made a statement when he arrived at the police station with the dead man in his bakkie. Captain Beetge knows him well, of course; he gave him brandy. He was shaking, this big, calm, clever son of Willem Van der Vyver, who inherited the old man's best farm. The black was stone dead, nothing to be done for him. Beetge will not tell anyone that after the brandy Van der Vyver wept. He sobbed, snot running onto his hands, like a dirty kid. The Captain was ashamed, for him, and walked out to give him a chance to recover himself.

•

Marais Van der Vyver left his house at three in the afternoon to cull a buck from the family of kudu he protects in the bush areas of his farm. He is interested in wildlife and sees it as the farmers' sacred duty to raise game as well as cattle. As usual, he called at his shed workshop to pick up Lucas, a twenty-year-old farmhand who had shown mechanical aptitude and whom Van der Vyver himself had taught to maintain tractors and other farm machinery. He hooted, and Lucas followed the familiar routine, jumping onto the back of the truck. He liked to travel standing up there, spotting game before his employer did. He would lean forward, braced against the cab below him.

Van der Vyver had a rifle and .300 ammunition beside him in the cab. The rifle was one of his father's, because his own was at the gunsmith's in town. Since his father died (Beetge's sergeant wrote 'passed on') no one had used the rifle and so when he took it from a cupboard he was sure it was not loaded. His father had never allowed a loaded gun in the house; he himself had been taught since childhood never to ride with a loaded weapon in a vehicle. But this gun was loaded. On a dirt track, Lucas thumped his fist on the cab roof three times to signal: look left. Having seen the white-ripple-marked flank of a kudu, and its fine horns raking through disguising bush, Van der Vyver drove rather fast over a pot-hole. The jolt fired the rifle. Upright, it was pointing straight through the cab roof at the head of Lucas. The bullet pierced the roof and entered Lucas's brain by way of his throat.

That is the statement of what happened. Although a man of such standing in the district, Van der Vyver had to go through the ritual of swearing that it was the truth. It has gone on record, and will be there in the archive of the local police station as long as Van der Vyver lives, and beyond that, through the lives of his children, Magnus, Helena and Karel—unless things in the country get worse, the example of black mobs in the towns spreads to the rural areas and the place is burned down as many urban police stations have been. Because nothing the government can do will appease the agitators and the whites who encourage them. Nothing satisfies them, in the cities: blacks can sit and drink in white hotels, now, the Immorality Act has gone, blacks can sleep with whites . . . It's not even a crime any more.

Van der Vyver has a high barbed security fence round his farmhouse and garden which his wife, Alida, thinks spoils completely the effect of her artificial stream with its tree-ferns beneath the jacarandas. There is an aerial soaring like a flag-pole in the back yard. All his vehicles, including the truck in which the black man died, have aerials that swing their whips when the driver hits a pot-hole: they are part of the security system the farmers in the district maintain, each farm in touch with every other by radio, twenty-four hours out of twenty-four. It has already happened that infiltrators from over the border have mined remote farm roads, killing white farmers and their families out on their own property for a Sunday picnic. The pot-hole could have set off a land-mine, and Van der Vyver might have died with his farm boy. When neighbours use the communications system to call up and say they are sorry about 'that business' with one of Van der Vyver's boys, there goes unsaid: it could have been worse.

It is obvious from the quality and fittings of the coffin that the farmer has provided money for the funeral. And an elaborate funeral means a great deal to blacks; look how they will deprive themselves of the little they have, in their lifetime, keeping up payments to a burial society so they won't go in boxwood to an unmarked grave. The young wife is pregnant (of course) and another little one, wearing red shoes several sizes too large, leans under her jutting belly. He is too young to understand what has happened, what he is witnessing that day, but neither whines nor plays about; he is solemn without knowing why.

Blacks expose small children to everything, they don't protect them from the sight of fear and pain the way whites do theirs. It is the young wife who rolls her head and cries like a child, sobbing on the breast of this relative and that.

All present work for Van der Vyver or are the families of those who work; and in the weeding and harvest seasons, the women and children work for him, too, carried—wrapped in their blankets, on a truck, singing—at sunrise to the fields. The dead man's mother is a woman who can't be more than in her late thirties (they start bearing children at puberty) but she is heavily mature in a black dress between her own parents, who were already working for old Van der Vyver when Marais, like their daughter, was a child. The parents hold her as if she were a prisoner or a crazy woman to be restrained. But she says nothing, does nothing. She does not look up; she does not look at Van der Vyver, whose gun went off in the truck, she stares at the grave. Nothing will make her look up; there need be no fear that she will look up; at him. His wife, Alida, is beside him. To show the proper respect, as for any white funeral, she is wearing the navy-blue-and-cream hat she wears to church this summer. She is always supportive, although he doesn't seem to notice it; this coldness and reserve—his mother says he didn't mix well as a child—she accepts for herself but regrets that it has prevented him from being nominated, as he should be, to stand as the Party's parliamentary candidate for the district. He does not let her clothing, or that of anyone else gathered closely, make contact with him. He, too, stares at the grave. The dead man's mother and he stare at the grave in communication like that between the black man outside and the white man inside the cab the moment before the gun went off.

•

The moment before the gun went off was a moment of high excitement shared through the roof of the cab, as the bullet was to pass, between the young black man outside and the white farmer inside the vehicle. There were such moments, without explanation, between them, although often around the farm the farmer would pass the young man without returning a greeting, as if he did not recognize him. When the bullet went off what Van der Vyver saw was the kudu stumble in fright at the report and gallop away. Then he heard the thud behind him, and past the window saw the young man fall out of the vehicle. He was sure he had leapt up and toppled—in fright, like the buck. The farmer was almost laughing with relief, ready to tease, as he opened his door, it did not seem possible that a bullet passing through the roof could have done harm.

The young man did not laugh with him at his own fright. The farmer carried him in his arms, to the truck. He was sure, sure he could not be dead. But the young black man's blood was all over the farmer's clothes, soaking against his flesh as he drove.

How will they ever know, when they file newspaper clippings, evidence, proof, when they look at the photographs and see his face—guilty! guilty! they are right!—how will they know, when the police stations burn with all the evidence of what has happened now, and what the law made a crime in the past. How could they know that *they do not know*. Anything. The young black callously shot through the negligence of the white man was not the farmer's boy; he was his son.

ROSELLEN BROWN

FROM

Before and After

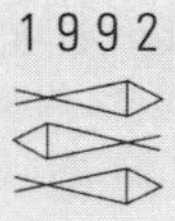

I'm going to talk about that day. I'm going to ease through the ordinary motions of the ordinary day, trying to remember: young winter in Hyland, the snow falling the way I like it best, so quietly, no wind, no noise like rain—you look out the window after long concentration, or, better, open the door, and there it is, everything changed, covered with softness, every angle forgiven, every eyesore pile of junk or ugly car fender hidden. And the smell of it—do you know snow smells sweet when it's falling? It's a little sweet, a little harsh, acid in the nostrils, but that's the cold and the damp, and your wet hat and gloves. The snow's like sugar.

All right—I'm coming toward it slowly. I can't rush up on the seam between before and after. (Not seam, no way. Excuse me. Chasm.) It's not fair to our whole long lives *before*. I didn't know *before* was over already. I didn't, and Carolyn didn't either.

[. . .]

When Mickey Tuohy left I stood in the doorway looking out, feeling warm and snug, the way you do when the lamps are on and the cold is right out there but your feet are dry. I was looking forward to the whole long evening: I'd picked up a video while I was in town, a movie about Van Gogh, and we were going to crowd into the den later and watch it together. I had to book time with the kids, which was getting harder and harder, especially with Jacob, who was always busy these days, on principle. (If he could substitute the flick for homework, of course, he might work up some enthusiasm.) There'd be a lot to talk about, I thought: Van Gogh's madness, his talent, whether it was necessary to suffer the way he did. And the good adolescent question: Who was responsible for his pain—himself, the world? Jacob and I loved to skirmish. Sometimes I think we'd choose sides just to have colors to fight under. He was getting sharp and fearless; Judith was still too young to mix it up, but she had promise. I felt like I had them in training, a luscious feeling to counter the snow-shocked, inarticulate friends they spent too much time with. (I loved Hyland for a hundred reasons, but the intellectual life of its high-school population was not one of them.)

I made dinner. This has always been part of our deal—Carolyn gets to put the house out of her head every day and go off into the clear fluorescent spaces of her office and the hospital. I get to answer to nobody, but in return I do the housewifely duties (which I like) and amuse the hell out of some of the guys I know downtown. They don't exactly say I'm pussywhipped—their word, not mine—but I'm pretty sure they tell it to each other. But what the hell. My best dish was red snapper Veracruzana—green olives, sauce a little spicy—and it could have been on a menu anywhere. In New Hampshire you can hardly eat ethnic, so you have to do it yourself, and I have conquered three or four cuisines tolerably. Jacob and Judith were game and Carolyn, I think, was relieved that I'd made a project out of duty and therefore took some pride in it. ("Your cooking is competitive," she says, implying that that's what you have to expect of a man in the kitchen. "You learn recipes and come up with methods as if you're climbing a mountain." I don't know if that's true or good or bad; it isn't something I have to argue.)

She came in while I was setting the table—the best placemats for Friday night, a little special something for the Sabbath we don't otherwise keep. She called out to me from the hall. "I'm going to have to speak to Jacob about how sloppy his parking is getting." She came into the kitchen pink-faced. The hair around her face was wet—it must have been dewed with snowflakes. She gave me a little hug of greeting. "His car is all over the garage, Ben, I swear I could hardly get in there at all."

"Ah, lady," I said, and caught hold of her. "Between thee and me let not mere circumstance intrude. Come bring thy body to the Sabbath bed, where we—"

"Ben! Are you crazy?"

I pretended to take offense. "What, then? Art thou affronted?"

She gave me a friendly little shove. "What are we eating, lovey? Something warm like stew, I hope, or soup?"

We really don't do too badly at that reversal, but every now and then, more in the presence of friends than when we're alone where we can take care of it, Carolyn seems a little self-conscious about expecting to be served like a husband. This is a small town with a lot of very traditional expectations, milk and cookies after school and guess who bakes them? But not today.

"Chili."

"Terrific." I got a kiss for that. "Is Judith upstairs?" She bent to pull her boots off. Even now, routine or not, I always find it provocative to see her calves, her lovely pale calves, suddenly unsheathed like that.

"We had a little set-to about her piano practicing. We're going to have to sit down with her and find out if she really wants to go on with her lessons."

She had gone to the cupboard where we keep the wine. "I need a little of this today." She poured generous glasses for both of us, though she hadn't asked and I hadn't answered. Then she told me about Martha Taverner. "I'm surprised you haven't heard all the wretched details on your CB."

"It hasn't been on," I said, and I was nearly dizzy with the shock of it, "except for a second when I was showing Mickey Tuohy the shaman." I knew Martha's father from slow-pitch softball. I didn't know him well, but he was more than a face to me—a smallish, wiry banty-man. Second baseman, his legs slightly bowed, his color and energy high. When we lost he got sullen and tried to fix the blame. But when we won he would get drunk on the joy of it. He was an infectious laugher. I couldn't say anything but "Jesus, Jesus," as if that might clear my head of the vision of his daughter dead.

Just then Judith called downstairs. I guess she had heard her mother.

"Where's the Boy?" Carolyn asked. I had to think for a second. She had said his car was in the garage, but I realized I hadn't seen him.

"Does he have those damn tapes turned up?" she asked. "I can't *bear* them."

"No, Judith was here when I got back, but he must be—well, I don't know. Maybe he's sleeping."

Teenagers sleep. They tell me it's normal. Sometimes I thought he went up there, lay down for an hour or so in the late-afternoon dark, and came downstairs two inches taller, with a doubled shoe size.

"Well, give him a little longer. This stuff needs to thicken. It hasn't reached its, mm—quintessence—yet." I looked under the lid; the steam of the chili came up and surrounded both our faces like a warm, sharp-sweet cloud.

Then the bell rang.

It rang into the ordinary noises of our day. It rasped so harshly that when I tried to go back to it, or just before, it sounded like the gong they ring at boxing matches, urgent, a rip through space and time, promising cruelty and pain.

I've heard about stories, how they're really just a finely strung architecture of *the way things were* and *the way things turned out*, held together—or divided, would be better—by the most terrible word, the word that lifts the roof off, lands the ax blow, curdles the milk. The blood. All the world's change, its doom, its fatality, is in it: *Then* . . . But that doesn't mean you know it when it comes.

Carolyn put her glass down on the round table I had begun to set. I remember finding it later and guzzling the last of her abandoned wine when I was beyond feeling anything, its heat, its cool, its flavor. By then, it was dregs left over from a century ago.

I figured it was someone who couldn't get up the hill. We have to take our tow chain out when the weather's mean and yank our neighbors up; it happens a couple of times each winter.

"Fran," I heard her say, surprised. They were walking into the kitchen, she was laughing a little girlishly—he makes her nervous. "You haven't called me Dr. Reiser since we first moved here! What in the world does *that* mean?"

Fran Conklin came in behind her in his parka, his navy-blue wool hat to his eyes, his snowmobile boots leaving serious puddles, dirty ones, in his wake. He grabbed at the hat, pulled it off, and stood holding it like a scolded boy. "Ben," he said and shook my hand earnestly.

"Hey there, Chief. A visit out of uniform! Don't tell me they've got you collecting for the Policeman's Fund in the snow."

The police chief and I have had our moments. You have to understand that the police aren't viewed out here in the country—near-country, whatever you want to call it—quite as suspiciously as they are in the city. If there's any Establishment, it's not one that includes them, only the rich and the old families (which are usually the same). They're just local boys, not particularly violent, who have a steady necessary job; they have to buy their own guns, their uniforms. They have to plead with the town every time the department needs a new cruiser, and then get a used one someplace. But even at that the chief is a man to deal with, and we've had our hostilities. I put a sculpture up one time, for example, in the town park down near the falls—this was for the 4th of July celebration, and it was supposed to be the American Family, made of pickup parts, complete with a little wooden dog and cat on wheels. People loved it, kids climbed on it like it was a playground toy. It made them laugh. I was really tickled. For the first time I thought, Okay, I've crossed a line, they *get* it. But the chief didn't. He got Yahoo on me and pronounced it Refuse or Rubbish or something, I don't remember how he insulted it exactly, but he said I had to move it, dismantle it, it was an eyesore—unpainted wood with the detritus of the moment varnished into it, the non-biodegradables: McDonald's containers, one Adidas hightop, a hubcap, a button that said FREE LYNDON LAROUCHE. Fran won, all the power on his side, but not before the newspaper gave me their editorial blessing: *"Lighten up, Mr. Police Chief. Art these days is in the eye of the beholder"*—and he'd been made to feel like a heavy.

Nonetheless, we were not unfriendly. If he was overzealous in his line of work, I knew I was equally zealous in mine—we were both fanatics, so we had something in common, and by now we could laugh about it. But today, in our kitchen, standing in the sharp aura of chili and woodsmoke, he was not at ease.

"Keeping busy, you two? You've been working hard, Carolyn."

"Oh, I've got enough to do, I suppose." She smiled, a little bewildered, I could see that, around the eyes.

"Get you anything, Fran?" I asked. "A beer if you're not working?"

"No, that's okay, Ben. You managing to keep busy in this season? You must be snug in that workshop of yours."

"Right. Just bought a neat little stove—one of those kind of miniature Fishers with the deer and stuff on the side? Really nice piece of craftsmanship. Keeps the place so hot all I want to do is sleep." I realized, as I spoke, that when I talk to Fran or Mickey I start everything I say in the middle, casually discarding the "I" as if complete sentences were pretentious.

Anyway, Fran nodded perfunctorily, since it was clear he hadn't come up here in a snowstorm to find out how we were feeling. I saw him take a deep breath. "Jacob around?"

Oh. "Don't know, actually. We both just got in a little while ago —the car's here."

"Would you like me to see if he's here?" Carolyn volunteered. "I'll just have a look to see if he's up there asleep, Fran. You—need him for something?"

He pursed his lips a little, as if he was running something around in his mouth. "Why don't you do that, Carolyn," he said, rather too gently. He sounded like a man who was afraid he might break something.

I looked at him hard while Carolyn went upstairs. He hummed for a second or two, absurd, and kept his hands in his pockets. He was a broad-faced man with a forehead ruled like a music staff with creases. Just in the last year or two he'd started growing dewlaps.

Carolyn came back down looking troubled. "No, he hasn't been up there as far as I can see. Judith hasn't seen him. What is this, Fran? What's the matter?"

"I'm going to—" He stopped short. "He's—" And stopped again.

The more he shuffled, the longer I went without breathing. If Jacob was hurt, Fran would be telling us, not looking for him. "All right." He looked resigned. "Something happened up on Poor Farm Road a little while ago. Something pretty bad." His face was bright red with the effort of this. "And we're trying to find some people to talk to about it."

"What? What happened?" We both said that. We both knew.

"Carolyn—" He turned to her. "A girl got herself killed."

"I know. I saw her." She didn't miss a beat.

Her abruptness seemed to take him by surprise. I could see his face harden. "You saw her."

"In ER. They had her in there—beyond saving, I mean." She was twisting her hands in a way I'd never seen. "It was awful. *You* know. But they called us all down."

Fran cleared his throat. At least he was very uncomfortable. "Then you have an idea—And you know who it was."

"But why do you want to talk to Jacob? What does—"

He looked away from us; he looked at the shaman in his corner, startled for a second, and then back. "I don't like to have to tell you this," he said simply. "I really don't. There are days I swear I wish I was back directing traffic instead of running this show." He put his hands together and cracked his knuckles. That always drives me berserk, I don't know why people think they have the right to make others listen. I restrained my anger but it wasn't easy. "Okay. Jacob was seen with this girl. He picked her up from work, she makes ice-cream cones at Jacey's after school." He flushed again. "Made. Even in winter—doesn't seem to slow anyone down." A small laugh. An attempt, to be generous, at shared humanity with the victims. "He came by with the car and they took off like they've been doing."

"They have?" I said, a little too vociferous. "Martha *Taverner*?"

Maybe he never mentioned it, Fran said. You know kids. And so on. But they'd been seen together by a lot of people, today and other days. And somebody called headquarters who'd seen the mess in front of Tuttle's fence, the smashed, the finished girl. And he needed to talk to Jacob. When the chief himself comes to your door, I suddenly realized, and I wondered where my head had been, you'd better believe you're in trouble. So I blew up at him.

"Look, Ben. I don't want to jump ahead, okay? Jacob's the last person I'd like to think about with a murder on my hands. This is a bludgeon death we've got here, a girl with her skull—well, I don't have to say. Carolyn, you saw it, dear. There isn't anybody I want to suspect of doing that, your son or anybody else's."

"Or someone passing through," I prompted him.

He was trying to be obliging. "Or someone passing through."

And then we went into second gear. I am making myself dredge all this up because, I suppose, it still has the little shreds of our innocence in it, the poor rags of our not-knowing. We struggled to stay dumb.

"And you don't know where he is," Fran said.

Carolyn frowned the way she does when she's studying something that won't yield. "The car's in the garage. I just—" She stopped because there was nothing else to say.

He wanted to see the car.

She moved to get her keys.

"No, wait," I said, so suddenly I didn't know it was coming. "You can't just do that."

"Do what?" Fran asked me, caught off-guard.

"I don't think you can just do that, go search somebody's car. You don't have a warrant."

Carolyn was aghast. She is a good girl sometimes, too often, maybe, under her take-charge cool. "*Ben*jamin," she said in a tone I didn't like. "This is *Fran*. We know him, he isn't just some cop in off the street."

I told her I knew who he was, thank you. I assured him I trusted him and knew he had a job to do. (Later, I thought, I will try to suggest that she doesn't have to speak that way to me in public, like I'm a little patient of hers who's been feeding his medicine to the cat.) "A warrant," I repeated. "Yes, a warrant, to come nosing around. What's so strange about that?"

I was trying to picture Jacob, my son, and I couldn't even see his face. I saw his body instead, the shiny blue jacket he has from the wrestling team—he wrestles at 120 pounds—his shoulders in a T-shirt broadening finally after years of being too small, too skinny. His Adam's apple that sticks out these days, exaggerated, like an erection. He's a nice-looking boy, not a knockout (just as well, I tell him, though of course he disagrees). But I couldn't conjure up his features, it was as if I hadn't seen him for months. The mystery of desperation, that seizing-up of the heart and brain. It just put a lock on memory. *Gone*, utterly gone. I needed to see him for myself, and fast.

Then I called Wendell, the only friend we have who's also a lawyer. (One of the many good things about Hyland is how few lawyers you have to know.) It was too late for the office, but he wasn't home either; only his inane machine gave out its syrup, which I blamed on Steph: "Wendell and Stephanie regret that they can't come to the phone now but they want you to know they *value* your call." Steph, breathless: she got it from church, he got it from est. I liked them anyway, but they sometimes strained at the edges of my patience, and one of these days, I thought, rather ungenerously, given that I needed Wendell right now, they're going to find themselves outside it. I told him to call me instantly when he got in.

Judith had come downstairs while I was on the phone. She took one look at us, her eyes widening, and went to her mother, who put an arm protectively around her shoulders. I wished she were young enough to be sent out of the room to be spared this scene. I wished we were all too young, at least by a day, so that we could be back on the other side of *Then*. But she is twelve. She's one of us.

We wrangled, Fran and I. He said he needed to have a look at the condition of Jacob's car. I told him it was my car and, as far as I could remember these things, he'd need a "show-cause order," something like that. He told me that playing hotshot lawyer would only make things (I suspect he meant feelings) harder, slow things down. "I know you're his father," he said soothingly. "You want to protect him. I've got kids, too, you know." But he had to ask me again. "Do you know where he might be? Did he have any special plans for today? Ben? Do you know anything you're not telling me?"

He looked at Judith. "Have you seen your brother, dear?"

Judith opened her mouth, but I yelled, "Hey, off-limits! Leave her out of this, okay? I'll tell you what I know that I'm not telling you. I know my son—"

"Please," Carolyn said as if I was the crazy one here. *"Please,* Ben."

But the man was affronting my kitchen, my family, my day, my sight. He was suggesting something unimaginably insulting, and he was doing it in my own house. "I told you I haven't seen him since he went to school this morning, all right? We ate breakfast—Carolyn's gone already by the time we eat. Frozen waffles, right, Jude?" She nodded; she was still speechless, like someone who'd been kidnapped and wasn't sure it was all right to talk to her captors. "Real maple syrup, okay? Our own. Grade B, but good. Coffee for him. Or sugar, actually, with a little coffee in it. Tea for me. Hot chocolate for Judith. His lunch in a bag, I know because I packed it: tuna sandwich on rye, apple, very good chocolate-chip cookies. Some junk he chews, Sunbursts or something, he always throws those in—"

"Starbursts," Judith breathed softly.

"Starbursts. He says they keep him awake in class. That's it. That's what I know."

Carolyn, not helping, said, "Then what are you afraid of?"

"Who says I'm afraid of anything?" We were glaring at each other.

She wheedled at me a little. "What are you so angry at? I mean, why make an adversary out of poor Fran?" Somewhere along the way Fran had gotten poor. "I'm sure Jacob can explain why he wasn't with the girl. Maybe she got out of the car and walked away, maybe he dropped her somewhere, a thousand—Fran!" she suddenly said and put her hand to her mouth. It was a rough, much-used hand, I saw, focusing sharply, but she did the best she could with it, its neat nails, fingers modestly ringed. "How do we know *he's* all right? We haven't thought —what if some madman did something to *both* of them! Maybe Jacob's hurt, or been kidnapped or—"

"Look," the chief said, ignoring her idea. "Can you think where he'd be—just—well, say it's an ordinary afternoon, what would he do?"

We looked at each other. "His friends," Judith offered. She may have been the calmest of us, as if having to sound adult pulled her up to a higher level, while the rest of us slipped backward with shocking speed. "Why don't you call Frodo and Jackie." She is a resourceful child, I thought gratefully, an oasis of cool. She had short fairish hair, cut like a Dutch boy's; she had the beginnings of a chest, but she was a dancer and a gymnast, a girl whose legs were always expressing a life of their own, turning and turning, the spokes of a lovely wheel, so the rest of her would probably stay like a washboard, flat but nicely inflected. "I'll call them if you want."

Fran's two-way radio gave out a sudden bleat. He listened to something so garbled it was like aggressive Chinese, and he muttered something back, and turned to go. "Please, Ben," he said to me at the door. "Please do your best not to obstruct this thing. Your son may have a perfect—there may be no problem at all. Chances are good. I'd be glad if he was out of it altogether, I don't know why you don't trust me. But don't put yourself in front of the law, okay? 'Cause it won't do anybody any good. Get your lawyer if you want, but don't block the law yourself, okay?"

"Of course," Carolyn assured him. Hostess to the bitter end. "He knows. He—"

"Also, do me a favor, both of you? Just think for one blessed minute about Terry and Mike Taverner over there in their kitchen. Well, you saw, Carolyn. I don't have to tell you. They had to put Terry under heavy sedation. Hostages to fortune, that's all we've got, our kids are—"

I wasn't feeling very tolerant. "What weekend criminal-justice course did you pick that up from?" It was less than decent of me. I deserved the look my wife shot me.

But Fran had dignity, along with chutzpah. "My priest, if you want to know. Just this past Sunday, he called his sermon 'Hostages to Fortune,' about how we're living dangerously when we love anybody, even ourselves, he said. Then he asked—"

"Weren't they looking for you back there on your beeper, Fran?" Maybe if he left we'd be back where we were.

I knew I'd regret my shortness with him somewhere down the line. But the way I understood it he came in out of the cold to announce that he suspected my son had murdered a girl and was hiding either here or somewhere else. Maybe here. Maybe he really believed we might have him upstairs, or down in the cellar crouched behind the furnace, so that while he talked with us he looked and listened very carefully, feeling the atmosphere, reading our body movements, trying to pick up the sound of creaking floorboards, weight shifting out of sight. It had been the most offensive and unreal half hour of my life—all I could do, finally, was open the door for him and banish him gratefully, without even the friendly pretense of a goodbye.

•

I still had the cold door latch in my hand—it was black hammered wrought iron, part of the colonial history we'd restored to the house, and it felt hard and elemental against my palm, like part of a shotgun. I stood there clutching it and looking at the old wood of the door, with its long, striated cracks no cold miraculously came through. I was thinking how totally implausible this was—in a funny way (or maybe not so funny, maybe dangerous), I don't think I believe in *reality* much. I mean this, even if it sounds demented. Events don't seem as real to me as imaginings. I live inside my head in a way Carolyn doesn't live in hers, and just as well, I suppose, for the agitated parents who call up when their baby's choking or screaming with pain and she has to decide what's wrong and how to fix it. I live for making things up. A real event, for me, is the good fit of two pieces of wood I have to glue, or finding two matched stones to set in for one of my creatures' eyes. So this was all doubly unreal to me. First, it was impossible to imagine Jacob on the run, Jacob even remotely in trouble, let alone guilty of—I don't have the words. An atrocity. When I last saw him he was in deep trouble with me for running up a couple of three-dollar overdue bills on his library books. I couldn't imagine him making real footsteps in the real world. I mean, I couldn't really believe anything any of us did made a *difference*. So this all felt like someone else's nightmare: I refused to believe it was mine, or, rather, ours. His.

•

But Carolyn disabused me of that. I made myself walk back into the kitchen and face her. Judith was standing in front of the woodstove holding up her hands as if she'd taken a chill.

"You should have let him look at the car," Carolyn said.

"The hell I should have. Not without a lawyer telling me I have to. And don't go telling me he's my friend, either. No police chief is my friend when he comes around on the goddamn job."

She came to me to put her arms around me, or maybe be taken into mine. One way or another, we fell together. "Please, Ben," she said into my chest. "Whatever this is, it's not a conspiracy." She put her ear against my breastbone, turning her head. "Sometimes your anxiety unhinges you."

I couldn't believe it. "It isn't anxiety, it's anger. Nobody ever gets murdered around here, so he's getting carried away. He thinks he's on *Hill Street Blues* or something."

Judith stirred where she was standing. "Maybe he's covering up for one of those dumb friends of his, they're so weird. Maybe they ran away together."

We considered it—boys being boys together?—but it didn't make things much better. Anyway, he wasn't that kind of boy.

We stood like that, and then Judith came in with us, the three of us leaning against each other, until we had to *do* something. At least I did. I had no place to go, but that didn't mean I could stand still. I went to the desk where I kept my wallet and keys when I was in the house. The keys felt strange in my hand, my hand was strange to me. If you'd told me the molecules of the world had rearranged themselves, a little dance of basic structures all turned over and settled differently, I'd have believed it.

•

It gets dark shockingly early in January, although it had already turned a little on the cusp of the solstice. There was a moon and it was cruelly beautiful, I thought (at the same time that I thought how goddamn unoriginal, how melodramatic). But it was a taunt anyway, how it laid out a shimmering path, diamond dust, straight up to the garage that sat beside the workshop I'd made in the barn, a couple of hundred feet from the house.

The snow was lavender where the light came down on it, like the weird illumination you see in planetariums that changes every color and makes white electric blue. Jacob and I loved to go to the science museum in Boston—not that long ago he had been at that age when the noisy saga of whirling planets and inexplicable anti-gravitational feats, narrated by a man with a deep official-facts voice, was thrilling. He was easily, unstintingly thrilled, or used to be. Not now, though. Boys of seventeen aren't thrilled about much besides their muscles and their victories against everyone else's brains and bodies.

It was cold enough to collapse my nostrils, and damp, way below freezing. Carolyn's car tracks into the open garage were fresh, some new snow fallen into them but not enough to soften their edges much. I could see the tracks of Jacob's car were muted—they had taken a lot of snow, had long since lost their definition. Carolyn was right about the way he parked. The car, crooked, and half over the unmarked center line, didn't look aimed so much as abandoned.

Holy Jesus, what was the story? I put on the frail garage light and used my flashlight. The car was a roomy old brown Dodge, old-fashioned-feeling inside, like an empty rumpus room, too big ever to have been handsome. It was littered, as always—candy wrappers, a couple of pink and green mimeographed notices from school on the floor, a paperback about computers, in a mangled cover. If Fran had seen this, he'd have wondered what we were haggling about. I ran the flashlight up and down in stripes—some butts in the ashtray, stuck together with gum that was gray in this light. (He says he doesn't smoke. Right now I'd settle for a little disobedience, even a little flat-out lying.)

The backseat was rubble-strewn, too. Amazing, I was thinking, how the spirit of disorganization infects everything it touches, like the mildew that must be crawling under there. It was a triumph not to have sweat socks or wet towels to make it look even more like his room. His textbooks lay splayed on the seat, and a greasy bag with a crumpled napkin in it—doughnuts, probably. It smelled fried. I finished raking the seat with my little beam. Okay, Fran, I thought. Okay. You can have it.

At the last instant I thought I'd have a look at the trunk. I was beginning to feel relief wash over me like that moon-white air outside—a mystery, still, where he might be, but nothing suspicious. The trunk snapped open and rose with the slow deliberation of a drawbridge, and then I thought I'd fall over for lack of breath. Because I knew I was looking at blood. It wasn't red, or even brown—the world was a thousand grays out here, like a black-and-white movie. But I could see the shape of the splotches and worse, the little splatters that had flown off something. The something, I suspected, was the jack.

It was lying loose, out from under the cover that hides the spare and the tire-changing equipment; it had been flung, fast and sloppy, onto a mess of—I couldn't tell what, exactly. I thought I saw a beach towel, something like a Garfield cartoon, words and picture. I know I saw a backpack, and there might have been a T-shirt. I was wearing heavy gloves—I picked it up with my padded fingers. The screw part looked wet, maybe oil. (Impossible. Who oils a jack?) I held it out of the dark of the garage into the moonlight like something whose neck had been wrung. Then I took off one glove and held the glove in my teeth the way a dog would, and I touched the huge splashes of dark on the gnarled-up terry cloth, and in the valleys of the shiny nylon backpack. They were wet, undeniably, deeply wet, and when I rubbed hard the pads of my fingers came up rusty brown.

And when I turned, dry-mouthed, I saw that something was caught on the lip of the old battered ash can that stood in the corner. It was a woolen glove—not a kid's mitten, I mean large, gray, floppy-fingered. I recognized it before I even touched it, where it had snagged on the raggedy metal rim. *Please*, I prayed. *Please.*

But it was his, and it was dark with blood that had begun to freeze. I sniffed it—sour, that funny damp-wool, itchy smell you get used to in this weather where you're always spreading out your cap and gloves on the steaming radiator to stiffen up, drying. I knew he wore these gray ones, he kept saying "They don't match my jacket, they look dumb," but hadn't wanted to part with the money to buy new ones. (I wasn't buying, they were still good enough. If he cared that much, I told him, he knew what to do about it.) They stained my fingers. Down in the basket, on top of a mess of moist papers and an empty oil can, I found the other one and balled it up in my hand. So much, I thought, for saying *Please.*

Then I looked at the ground and saw where footprints, not mine, led away from the car. You couldn't hide anything with snow on the ground, it was like the deer tracks dogs can follow. It was what made winter such a cruel tracking season, why they gave out summonses to people who didn't keep their dogs tied up. The prints went out to the paddock, toward the open field. Slowly, as if I was stalking something myself, I followed them at a distance so I wouldn't confuse them with my own. They stopped at the fence—second thoughts here, maybe, about where he'd get to if he went into the woods. (*Nowhere* is where. The trees, thick in a lot of places, up hills and down, go for a few miles but eventually you're out on the blacktop, on Route 48. He would know that; he walked these woods, he skiied them, he had them in his head the way city kids know their block.) So they stopped at the fence; stymied, I suppose, they circled around and came back to the road, where they disappeared into a mess of tire marks and footprints. What the snow hadn't already obliterated, traffic took away, and my son with it.

Our lives are over, I thought, standing and looking down the road to where it disappeared into the bad curve. It was just like that: I thought it in words, like a sign, or like something I could read that was already printed out in black and white. It was a simple sentence—a *sentence*—and it felt final. Everything else was going to be detail, horrible, humiliating, maybe even justifying. But the fact, an act in the real world that believed in itself even if I didn't believe in it, was that our lives as just another family were done.

Later, when things got very bad, Carolyn accused me of airbrushing the truth away, of manufacturing miraculous salvation, of not accepting what I knew Jacob had done. No. I say that right here, early, totally. No. She didn't understand and that was one of the worst things. I had no illusions. But he was my son, and my love is not provisional upon his actions or his goodness.

All I said was that our lives as a family—no, our *life* as a family, our single life as an eight-legged graceful animal alive under a single pelt—was over.

FROM

A Dream of Mind

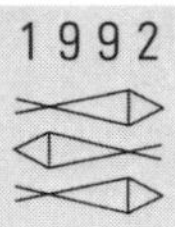

YOU

Such longing, such urging, such warmth towards, such force towards,
so much ardor and desire;
to touch, touch into, hold, hold against, to feel, feel against and long
towards again,
as though the longing, urge, and warmth were ends in themselves, the
increase of themselves,
the force towards, the ardor and desire, focused, increased, the incar-
nation of themselves.
All this in the body of dream, all in the substance of dream; allure,
attraction, and need,
the force so consumed and rapt in its need that dream might have
evolved it from itself,
except the ardor urges always towards the other, towards you, and without you it decays,
becomes vestige, reflex, the defensive attempt to surmount instinctual
qualms and misgivings.
No qualms now, no misgivings; no hesitancy or qualifications in longing
towards you;
no frightened wish to evolve ideals to usurp qualm, fear or misgiving,
not any longer.
The longing towards you sure now, ungeneralized, certain, the urge now
towards you in yourself,
your own form of nearness, the surface of desire multiplied in the need
that urges from you,
your longing, your urging, the force and the warmth from you, the sure
ardor blazing in you.

DENIS JOHNSON

FROM

Jesus' Son

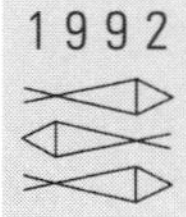

WORK

I'd been staying at the Holiday Inn with my girlfriend, honestly the most beautiful woman I'd ever known, for three days under a phony name, shooting heroin. We made love in the bed, ate steaks at the restaurant, shot up in the john, puked, cried, accused one another, begged of one another, forgave, promised, and carried one another to heaven.

But there was a fight. I stood outside the motel hitchhiking, dressed up in a hurry, shirtless under my jacket, with the wind crying through my earring. A bus came. I climbed aboard and sat on the plastic seat while the things of our city turned in the windows like the images in a slot machine.

Once, as we stood arguing at a streetcorner, I punched her in the stomach. She doubled over and broke down crying. A car full of young college men stopped beside us.

"She's feeling sick," I told them.

"Bullshit," one of them said. "You elbowed her right in the *gut*."

"He did, he did, he did," she said, weeping.

I don't remember what I said to them. I remember loneliness crushing first my lungs, then my heart, then my balls. They put her in the car with them and drove away.

But she came back.

This morning, after the fight, after sitting on the bus for several blocks with a thoughtless, red mind, I jumped down and walked into the Vine.

The Vine was still and cold. Wayne was the only customer. His hands were shaking. He couldn't lift his glass.

I put my left hand on Wayne's shoulder, and with my right, opiated and steady, I brought his shot of bourbon to his lips.

"How would you feel about making some money?" he asked me.

"I was just going to go over here in the corner and nod out," I informed him.

"I decided," he said, "in my mind, to make some money."

"So what?" I said.

"Come with me," he begged.

"You mean you need a ride."

"I have the tools," he said. "All we need is that sorry-ass car of yours to get around in."

•

We found my sixty-dollar Chevrolet, the finest and best thing I ever bought, considering the price, in the streets near my apartment. I liked that car. It was the kind of thing you could bang into a phone pole with and nothing would happen at all.

Wayne cradled his burlap sack of tools in his lap as we drove out of town to where the fields bunched up into hills and then dipped down toward a cool river mothered by benevolent clouds.

All the houses on the riverbank—a dozen or so—were abandoned. The same company, you could tell, had built them all, and then painted them four different colors. The windows in the lower stories were empty of glass. We passed alongside them and I saw that the ground floors of these buildings were covered with silt. Sometime back a flood had run over the banks, cancelling everything. But now the river was flat and slow. Willows stroked the waters with their hair.

"Are we doing a burglary?" I asked Wayne.

"You can't burgulate a forgotten, empty house," he said, horrified at my stupidity.

I didn't say anything.

"This is a salvage job," he said. "Pull up to that one, right about there."

The house we parked in front of just had a terrible feeling about it. I knocked.

"Don't do that," Wayne said. "It's stupid."

Inside, our feet kicked up the silt the river had left here. The watermark wandered the walls of the downstairs about three feet above the floor. Straight, stiff grass lay all over the place in bunches, as if someone had stretched them there to dry.

Wayne used a pry bar, and I had a shiny hammer with a blue rubber grip. We put the pry points in the seams of the wall and started tearing away the Sheetrock. It came loose with a noise like old men coughing. Whenever we exposed some of the wiring in its white plastic jacket, we ripped it free of its connections, pulled it out, and bunched it up. That's what we were after. We intended to sell the copper wire for scrap.

By the time we were on the second floor, I could see we were going to make some money. But I was getting tired. I dropped the hammer, went to the bathroom. I was sweaty and thirsty. But of course the water didn't work.

I went back to Wayne, standing in one of two small empty bedrooms, and started dancing around and pounding the walls, breaking through the Sheetrock and making a giant racket, until the hammer got stuck. Wayne ignored this misbehavior.

I was catching my breath.

I asked him, "Who owned these houses, do you think?"

He stopped doing anything. "This is my house."

"It is?"

"It was."

He gave the wire a long, smooth yank, a gesture full of the serenity of hatred, popping its staples and freeing it into the room.

We balled up big gobs of wire in the center of each room, working for over an hour. I boosted Wayne through the trapdoor into the attic, and he pulled me up after him, both of us sweating and our pores leaking the poisons of drink, which smelled like old citrus peelings, and we made a mound of white-jacketed wire in the top of his former home, pulling it up out of the floor.

I felt weak. I had to vomit in the corner—just a thimbleful of grey bile. "All this work," I complained, "is fucking with my high. Can't you figure out some easier way of making a dollar?"

Wayne went to the window. He rapped it several times with his pry bar, each time harder, until it was loudly destroyed. We threw the stuff out there onto the mud-flattened meadow that came right up below us from the river.

It was quiet in this strange neighborhood along the bank except for the steady breeze in the young leaves. But now we heard a boat coming upstream. The sound curlicued through the riverside saplings like a bee, and in a minute a flatnosed sports boat cut up the middle of the river going thirty or forty, at least.

This boat was pulling behind itself a tremendous triangular kite on a rope. From the kite, up in the air a hundred feet or so, a woman was suspended, belted in somehow, I would have guessed. She had long red hair. She was delicate and white, and naked except for her beautiful hair. I don't know what she was thinking as she floated past these ruins.

"What's she doing?" was all I could say, though we could see that she was flying.

"Now, that is a beautiful sight," Wayne said.

•

On the way to town, Wayne asked me to make a long detour onto the Old Highway. He had me pull up to a lopsided farmhouse set on a hill of grass.

"I'm not going in but for two seconds," he said. "You want to come in?"

"Who's here?" I said.

"Come and see," he told me.

It didn't seem anyone was home when we climbed the porch and he knocked. But he didn't knock again, and after a full three minutes a woman opened the door, a slender redhead in a dress printed with small blossoms. She didn't smile. "Hi," was all she said to us.

"Can we come in?" Wayne asked.

"Let me come onto the porch," she said, and walked past us to stand looking out over the fields.

I waited at the other end of the porch, leaning against the rail, and didn't listen. I don't know what they said to one another. She walked down the steps, and Wayne followed. He stood hugging himself and talking down at the earth. The wind lifted and dropped her long red hair. She was about forty, with a bloodless, waterlogged beauty. I guessed Wayne was the storm that had stranded her here.

In a minute he said to me, "Come on." He got in the driver's seat and started the car—you didn't need a key to start it.

I came down the steps and got in beside him. He looked at her through the windshield. She hadn't gone back inside yet, or done anything at all.

"That's my wife," he told me, as if it wasn't obvious.

I turned around in the seat and studied Wayne's wife as we drove off.

What word can be uttered about those fields? She stood in the middle of them as on a high mountain, with her red hair pulled out sideways by the wind, around the green and grey plains pressed down flat, and all the grasses of Iowa whistling one note.

I knew who she was.

"That was her, wasn't it?" I said.

Wayne was speechless.

There was no doubt in my mind. She was the woman we'd seen flying over the river. As nearly as I could tell, I'd wandered into some sort of dream that Wayne was having about his wife, and his house. But I didn't say anything more about it.

Because, after all, in small ways, it was turning out to be one of the best days of my life, whether it was somebody else's dream or not. We turned in the scrap wire for twenty-eight dollars—each—at a salvage yard near the gleaming tracks at the edge of town, and went back to the Vine.

Who should be pouring drinks there but a young woman whose

name I can't remember. But I remember the way she poured. It was like doubling your money. She wasn't going to make her employers rich. Needless to say, she was revered among us.

"I'm buying," I said.

"No way in hell," Wayne said.

"Come on."

"It is," Wayne said, "my sacrifice."

Sacrifice? Where had he gotten a word like sacrifice? Certainly I had never heard of it.

I'd seen Wayne look across the poker table in a bar and accuse —I do not exaggerate—the biggest, blackest man in Iowa of cheating, accuse him for no other reason than that he, Wayne, was a bit irked by the run of the cards. That was my idea of sacrifice, tossing yourself away, discarding your body. The black man stood up and circled the neck of a beer bottle with his fingers. He was taller than anyone who had ever entered that barroom.

"Step outside," Wayne said.

And the man said, "This ain't school."

"What the goddamn fucking piss-hell," Wayne said, "is that suppose to mean?"

"I ain't stepping outside like you do at school. Make your try right here and now."

"This ain't a place for our kind of business," Wayne said, "not inside here with women and children and dogs and cripples."

"Shit," the man said. "You're just drunk."

"I don't care," Wayne said. "To me you don't make no more noise than a fart in a paper bag."

The huge, murderous man said nothing.

"I'm going to sit down now," Wayne said, "and I'm going to play my game, and fuck you."

The man shook his head. He sat down too. This was an amazing thing. By reaching out one hand and taking hold of it for two or three seconds, he could have popped Wayne's head like an egg.

And then came one of those moments. I remember living through one when I was eighteen and spending the afternoon in bed with my first wife, before we were married. Our naked bodies started glowing, and the air turned such a strange color I thought my life must be leaving me, and with every young fiber and cell I wanted to hold on to it for another breath. A clattering sound was tearing up my head as I staggered upright and opened the door on a vision I will never see again: Where are my women now, with their sweet wet words and way, and the miraculous balls of hail popping a green translucence in the yards?

We put on our clothes, she and I, and walked out into a town flooded ankle-deep with white, buoyant stones. Birth should have been like that.

That moment in the bar, after the fight was narrowly averted, was like the green silence after the hailstorm. Somebody was buying a round of drinks. The cards were scattered on the table, face up, face down, and they seemed to foretell that whatever we did to one another would be washed away by liquor or explained away by sad songs.

Wayne was a part of all that.

The Vine was like a railroad club car that had somehow run itself off the tracks into a swamp of time where it awaited the blows of the wrecking ball. And the blows really were coming. Because of Urban Renewal, they were tearing up and throwing away the whole downtown.

And here we were, this afternoon, with nearly thirty dollars each, and our favorite, our very favorite, person tending bar. I wish I could remember her name, but I remember only her grace and her generosity.

All the really good times happened when Wayne was around. But this afternoon, somehow, was the best of all those times. We had money. We were grimy and tired. Usually we felt guilty and frightened, because there was something wrong with us, and we didn't know what it was; but today we had the feeling of men who had worked.

The Vine had no jukebox, but a real stereo continually playing tunes of alcoholic self-pity and sentimental divorce. "Nurse," I sobbed. She poured doubles like an angel, right up to the lip of a cocktail glass, no measuring. "You have a lovely pitching arm." You had to go down to them like a hummingbird over a blossom. I saw her much later, not too many years ago, and when I smiled she seemed to believe I was making advances. But it was only that I remembered. I'll never forget you. Your husband will beat you with an extension cord and the bus will pull away leaving you standing there in tears, but you were my mother.

ALICE MCDERMOTT

FROM

At Weddings and Wakes

1992

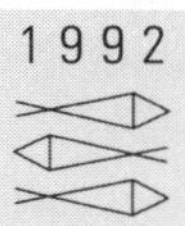

Veering, their mother led them away from the subway and down a series of unfamiliar streets where the gray sidewalks were plastered with wet black leaves and the stone red and deep gray stairs that rose up to the apartment houses beside them seemed both steeper and narrower than those that led to Momma's. A woman stood in a long window just above the sidewalk, framed from head to foot by thick velvet curtains, so that she appeared to be looking down on them from the edge of a stage. The trees here, placed evenly on the outer edge of the sidewalk, were all caged in narrow spokes of black wrought iron and the black street showed not only bits of yellow cobblestone in worn spots here and there but the occasional steely shine of old trolley tracks as well. Underneath their feet the sidewalk rose and fell in jagged rifts where, she had told them, the growing roots of the trees had risen up and cracked the concrete.

The city, it sometimes seemed to the children, was full of ancient, buried things struggling to resurface.

The church was on a narrow corner, behind a graying stone wall stained like the building itself with dirt black and mossy green. They followed her up the shallow steps and through a heavy wooden door she had only to pull open to know that the Sanctuary beyond the narrow vestibule was empty. She seemed to slump a little. She had hoped for a noon Mass. The vestibule itself was lined with doors, the two through which they had come, the four that led into the church itself, and two more on either end that led no doubt to the hidden, holy places reserved for priests and nuns and souls in transit. There were brown racks of pamphlets and holy cards and Catholic newspapers scattered between them. She paused for a moment to open her purse, which still hung in the crook of her arm, and to extract from beneath her elbow a white chapel cap for herself and two lace handkerchiefs for her daughters, and these she placed on their heads with a delicate flourish, as if preparing to make them disappear.

She held open the inner door and let them pass before her into the church, where they dipped their fingertips into the cold water in the cold stone font, touching bare forehead and woolen shoulders and chest, and following her to the first wooden pew, knelt and blessed themselves again. She stood for a moment before sliding in beside them, stood to survey the high ceiling and the stone walls. The stone here was a paler, cooler gray than that on the outside, a white gray that made the air itself seem bleached.

Just beside the altar there was a huge, certainly life-sized, chalk-white carving of Christ on the cross, and seeing this the children realized that they had been to this church before. Perhaps a number of times before. And that this, then, was the church where their parents had been married.

(It was part of all they knew that calla lilies had been placed on the altar then, to match the white satin lily Aunt Agnes had designed into the tulle skirt of their mother's gown, and the deep blue velvet one in her own.)

Kneeling beside her, they watched their mother dip her head and press her folded hands into her brow. There was black velvet on the collar and the cuffs of her short tweed coat, a bright gold clasp on the black pocketbook that hung from her arm. She'd been a bride in this church years and years before they were born, when she was still thin and their father wore a khaki uniform. Aunt Agnes had selected this church, not their parish church at all, but, she had claimed, the loveliest, the loftiest in the city, what with its pale stone and rosetta glass and soft, bleached light. Bombs were already falling and young soldiers dying in fields across the ocean, but because Aunt Agnes had taken control the day was perfect. "One perfect day at least" was what their mother said Aunt Agnes had called it. And if during the months of preparation it had seemed at times that Agnes had forgotten that this was a day meant to celebrate love, not elegance—there had been fights, the children understood, terrible rows, right up until the morning of the wedding—then she was forgiven each time their mother recounted for them the glory of that perfect day when she was young and thin and fearless.

When she blessed herself again the children followed her out of the pew and around to the back of the empty church, the boy listening to the sound of his black shoes against the stone floor and imagining himself a priest in a long, black cassock, gifted through his ordination with both the power to change bread and wine into Christ's body and blood and the privilege to stride across his church like this at any hour; the older girl praying furiously—one Our Father, one Hail Mary, one

Glory Be—raising with each trio of prayers another soul out of purgatory and into heaven, as the old nun at her school had told her she had, on this day alone, the power to do; the youngest watching her mother carefully as she again reached into her purse, this time extracting three quarters. The children slipped the coins into the metal slot beside the flickering rows of candles (the sound of the coins somehow the exact same taste and texture of the cold air itself), solemnly chose a thin stick from its container of white sand, and with much debate and hesitation, took the flame from one candle and lit another. They knelt and blessed themselves yet again and when enough time had passed stood to join their mother at the side altar where, with their own solemn deliberateness, she was writing her parents' names in the parish book of the dead.

•

In Momma's rooms the heat was turned up too high and the radiator dripped and hissed with the effort to sustain it.

"I can't imagine," Aunt May told their mother, "how any marriage can outlast so much remembering. Every slight and insult. You remember everything."

The children turned the pages of their dull magazines. "If I didn't," their mother said steadily, "I would have come back here a long time ago."

The older girl rolled from her stomach to her back, her magazine held in the air. It was a new *Playbill*, but for a play that featured only three actors, and so after she'd read through their biographies and studied the list of scenes (a drawing room late one morning, afternoon of the same day, and later that evening, assuring her that time moved no faster on that stage than this one) and then had chosen from the many advertisements the restaurant she preferred—French, three steps down, with strolling violins—she'd begun studying the magazine from various angles and directions, imagining how it would appear to her if she had one eye, was half blind, was bedridden and forced to read with it held straight-armed above her head.

Beside her, her brother turned the pages of another new addition to the magazine pile, a shiny report to stockholders that showed pictures of oil wells and ships at sea and workmen in white helmets. Next to him her sister slept with her cheek on *Life* magazine's portrait of Mr. Kennedy, her lips pressed into a puffy *o*, her small fingers moving.

She rolled over again, onto her elbows, and turning her head studied the pale green wall that had not been there when her aunts and her mother were born, when this living room and Momma's bedroom were one, or before that, long before that, when a single family lived in all the apartments as one big house. She imagined the city streets had been mostly empty then, rooms everywhere as underpopulated as the one in Aunt Agnes's new play. How else would it be possible for a single family to afford the luxury of four floors and all this space? She thought it a shame, actually, that the city had become so crowded, ships arriving day after day, as she had learned in school, spilling all kinds of people into the streets and the apartment buildings so that walls had had to be built, large rooms made smaller, just to accommodate them all. She thought it a shame that more of these immigrants hadn't simply stayed home, stayed where they belonged. Made the best, as her mother was always telling her to do, of a bad situation.

She stood and crossed the rug to the small bare entry that led to Momma's bedroom door. Before there was a wall there was only a curtain, which Momma had declared shanty Irish the moment she'd arrived as their father's wife, no longer merely their mother's sister. It was a part of everything the girl knew about the place, the curtains before the wall and the mother dying in her bed beyond it while Momma and another woman slept head to foot on the couch. While the father sat up in a chair in another corner and then collapsed sometime later on the floor of the hallway outside where the bags of shoes and old hats, the this-and-that and bric-a-brac, might have yielded some perfect touch to yesterday's Halloween costume (she'd been a flapper) if only she'd been able to sort through it on her last visit. As it was, the costume had been a disappointment, an old clown suit her mother had shredded into a flapper's dress, and a tissue rose pinned to a headband that kept slipping over her eyebrows and into her eyes. A disappointment when she considered what might have been resurrected from the shopping bags in the dark hallway, from the piles of coats and clothes and magazines that had accumulated there because, their father said, the Towne girls could not bear to part with anything.

("And hadn't we," their mother had once shouted at him, "hadn't we from the very beginning been parted from enough?")

She moved the chintz curtain that hung over the shelves built into the narrow foyer. There were rows of towels and sheets and tablecloths and napkins and a shoebox filled with ointments and medicines, a row of Aunt Agnes's books, none of which, with their thick brown spines and skimpy lettering, promised to be any more colorful or interesting than her magazines.

The child turned and, seeing that Momma's door was not closed tightly, pushed it quietly with her fingertips. Gone from her awareness and, perhaps for all time, her memory were the souls she had sent like doves into the air this morning in church, although the triumph of her achievement (she was certain they numbered well into the fifties) had stayed with her all the long walk back to Momma's and the climb up the stairs, so that she had entered the apartment just a few hours ago with the brave stride of one of the girl heroines in her own books: fifty souls admitted to the feast because of her prayers. Fifty souls forgotten now, perhaps for all time, as she pushed open the bedroom door with no other inclination than to fill the afternoon with small movements (this one somewhat better than most because it was, perhaps, forbidden) and saw through the narrow gap in the door Momma stretched out on the high bed, under the white counterpane, and Aunt Veronica in a long, pale robe standing beside her, her face turned to the window and the gray light from it falling on her in such a way that had she still remembered them the older girl might have thought that one of the souls she'd freed this morning had, on the way from purgatory to paradise, revisited the earth.

She turned again and found her brother watching her. "Aunt Veronica's awake," she whispered as she knelt close to him among the magazines, whispered because all of Aunt Veronica's movements struck the children as furtive and unpredictable.

(Too many women in too small a place, they would say later when they were making some effort to understand her; or, later still, too much repression, too much pity, too much bad luck. And then finally, convinced they'd hit the mark at last, too much drink.)

In the dining room Aunt May was saying that she hadn't told another soul and hoped she hadn't tempted fate by speaking too soon. On the floor beside them their little sister slept heavily, her fingers moving. And in the bedroom beyond the wall that hadn't always been there, Aunt Veronica stood beside Momma in the high bed and turned her face toward the window just as Momma, standing beside her dying sister, had turned (part of everything they knew) when from the sudden menacing stillness there arose an awful, lovely, distant cry that had made her scalp bristle.

"It's wonderful," their mother said softly. "No, I mean it. It's wonderful." And except for the hiss of the steam pipes and the careful clink of teacup and spoon, the apartment fell silent.

And then the boy lifted a magazine and bent it at its center. He caught his sister's eye, made a feint at throwing it, and then threw it for real, launching it across the room. It hit the brass bucket and fell away. He lifted another one and his sister, seeing the game, took one as well. The magazines opened in midair each time and then slapped to the floor. The younger girl opened her eyes. Her brother and her sister began to retrieve the magazines that had already been thrown and to toss them again, the competition really begun now that two or three magazines stood on edge inside the bucket or against the side. They moved back and forth on their knees, launching, grabbing, launching again. The little one crawled forward to join them and now it was who could get to each end of the room faster, gather the most magazines, or get the most magazines away from the others.

They began to laugh and slip and giggle. A cover ripped and a *National Geographic* hit the coffee table and made the wax flowers jingle. Their mother and Aunt May appeared together in the doorway and said, "Children," but the game had its own momentum now and the rug was a dark field and the long, long afternoon had suddenly lifted so that all that could stop them, and did stop them as their mother and Aunt May advanced into the room, determined, perhaps, to pin their arms, was, in the midst of their wild joy, a sudden black and starry crack of all three heads against one another. The three of them sat back for a few seconds as if struck by dark lightning and then the youngest one, the pain having finally seeped fully into her consciousness, began to wail. The other two felt their eyes fill with tears.

"That's what happens," Aunt May said, bending down to them. Their mother pulled the younger girl into her arms. "You see?" she said, by way of comfort. "That's what happens."

Half an hour later when Momma emerged from her room, she listened indifferently to the tale, her eyes on the potato and the peeler in her dirty hands. More than forty years ago she had stood above her sleeping sister, who was feverish but not yet dangerously so, still exhausted, they'd assumed, by a difficult birth, and had seen the light grow flat and felt the air become hollow and had heard the distant but unmistakable cry of what no one in the family, retelling the story, would call a banshee, knowing how foolish it would sound. But now she told the three children as they rolled and stretched and braided the pie dough she had set aside for them, "That's a lesson for you. That was the hand of God."

•

In her ledger book their mother had written, "If it's another girl then I'd like Veronica," and so named her for the saint who the nuns said was without vanity, who touched the bloodied face of Christ with her veil. A good thing, too, as Momma told it, since their father in his worry and then his grief could think of nothing to call her. Momma herself had found the book beside her sister's bed, had found the name written on the last page, and, had there been more peace in the household in those days, might have foreseen the girl's need to someday read it for herself. She might have made some effort to preserve the book in which her mother had named her. But Agnes told of long nights of weeping just after their mother's death, and after their father and

Momma had married, long and boisterous arguments that woke May and Agnes both in their bed.

Veronica. The nuns had told the four sisters, and in another decade the three children as well, that in Christ's day a poor woman would have owned only one veil and it would have taken her a great deal of time to weave and sew its cloth, yet Veronica had offered hers without hesitation to comfort the face of our suffering Lord.

When Aunt Veronica was fifteen, another story went, Momma had taken her to the Red Cross clinic where they studied her own ravaged face and then set her before the humming coils of a sunlamp. Five minutes it was supposed to have been, but thirty had passed before Momma rose from her chair in the waiting room. When the three sisters returned from work that evening they found Veronica stretched out on the green couch, a thin towel that had been soaked in tea covering her face. The burn would eventually peel, Momma told them. They watched her change the cloth, her hands gentle and her voice a whisper as she told Veronica to close her eyes and, if she wished, turn her head away.

Later, the men and women who interviewed her in the tall Manhattan office buildings where the other girls had found work saw a thin and nervous young woman with a certain bearing and lovely thick hair and a face scarred red and purple. Out on the street, drunks called after her, asking who had won the fight. On the subway as she rode home they leaned closer, their red-rimmed eyes touched with sympathy, and said that she was beautiful, despite her face, beautiful anyway.

The nuns at school had said that from her patron saint we learn the difference between a kind of pity that involves only a helpless, sorrowful shake of the head and the kind that makes us step forward to offer whatever we can in the way of relief.

It was Agnes who finally found her a position with a man in her own company, a Mr. Pierce, who was just coming back from retirement. He'd told Agnes that he could not say how long his return to the office would last but he would be willing to take on her untried and, he gathered, somewhat troubled younger sister as his secretary. At the end of her first day he approached Veronica's desk and took both her hands in his and told her as her cheeks blazed that she should not worry, she'd do fine. He described for Agnes when she asked how the girl's hands had trembled all day long, and yet her work, even her shorthand, was precise and neat. He said it was a shame about her skin, how it seemed to make her shy, and then added that in his day (Agnes concluded he meant in his class) a girl like Veronica would have stayed home to write poetry or cultivate a garden, to read and sew. Would have had, anyway, the luxury of being left alone.

Tracing backwards through incident and circumstance the way

other families with a more accessible history might trace bloodlines, it was concluded that Mr. Pierce had had a soft and generous heart that had perhaps caused more harm than good in the long run. Veronica worked for him for five years and when he retired permanently he gave her the opportunity to do the same, offering her a severance—from his own pocket, it was said—that seemed a small fortune in those days.

On the last day she worked she celebrated this good fortune with the office friends she had made. They were a disparate group, the girls either loud and chubby or shy like herself, or homely, or too thin, the men all kept out of the service by bad thyroids or widowed mothers or neighborhood quotas they'd been grateful to see fulfilled. Agnes didn't approve of them, said they weren't doing Veronica any favor, taking her to bars and two-bit nightclubs. Lucy and May preferred the local crowd that gathered at the brightly lit dances given by the church or the K of C, where Lucy had met her beau. But Veronica by then had begun to like a drink. She'd begun to like those dark and smoky rooms in those out-of-the-way corners of the city where with the veil of her hat pulled down over her cheeks and a drink in her hand she could speak comfortably to strangers, her words and her thoughts moving easily and the earth not quite so solid beneath her feet.

On the last day she worked, her office friends led her quietly across the dawn-lit landing and eased her in through the front door, making an escape well before Momma could do more than cluck her tongue at them. That evening when Veronica woke there was only Momma alone in her chair in the dining room. Agnes was at a show, May, by then, in the novitiate, and Lucy had only recently gone to live with her husband, six months after he'd returned from the war. Johnny had already left for good.

Veronica went to the cocktail cart that Agnes had brought home to lend some sophistication to the newly spacious apartment. She poured herself a little something. As she raised the glass Momma began to speak and Veronica turned her scarred face toward her. At the time Momma truly believed that only men could be drunkards, that the women who took a few too many, while foolish and weak-willed, usually had just cause, so she spoke to the girl now not in anger, as she had once spoken to her son, but out of sympathy, as much aware of foolishness and weak will as she was of just cause. She said she was grateful her sister hadn't lived to see this.

She said: "I stood by her bed, you know, just after you were born. It was hot, hotter than Hades. Your father had taken the girls for a stroll, toward the river, he'd said, where they might catch a breeze. You were in the cradle in the other room. I stood by the bed. She was feverish, but who wasn't in that heat. In a day or two, I figured, she'd be back to herself. And then the light just flattened out, like the life had gone out of it. I looked out the window. The world had never been so quiet. And then I began to hear one sound. I saw the curtain move, although I can tell you there was no breeze. I turned back to Annie. I stood right next to her. She was thirty-eight years old and she had three children and a new baby and a husband, and I had waited seven years to be with her. You and your sisters can talk about your newspaper tragedies, your camps and refugees, but for me this was no less than any of it. For me this was the worst thing. When Mrs. Power came up she scolded me for shutting the window, the old biddy, but all I cared about by then was that she get the doctor. Who would have believed that a time would come when I'd say it was just as well, just as well that Annie died young and missed seeing this, her own last child, the girl she'd named, throwing away the very life she'd given her."

•

At her dressing table, Aunt Veronica brushed her hair and then smoothed it into place with a black velvet band. Her reflection was pale and showed the same large eyes and long firm neck that could be seen in the few childhood photographs scattered throughout the apartment: the same large eyes and long neck that the three children would remember years later when they said, "Too much drink," hitting the mark at last.

Even on the brightest days her bedroom was dim, but now in the early and still unaccustomed darkness of All Saints', the walls seemed to draw themselves in behind her. The room was strewn with cloth, as it had been each time the children had seen it: the heavy drapes at the one window, the sheets and blankets of the unmade bed, the scattered bureau scarves and head scarves and dressing gowns, the various lengths of material that were to become a skirt or a dress. It was where the younger girl believed her fortune remained and Veronica might have believed it too, for all the time she spent there.

Veronica sat on the embroidered chair before the glass-topped dressing table, her hands held firmly in her lap to keep them steady. If a girl, then Veronica, her mother had written, for the saint who had offered comfort. And then had borne forever the indelible image of his suffering on her veil.

In the bright light of the living room she squinted a little and smiled and said, "Hello, all," before accepting the drink from Agnes and taking the youngest child into her arms.

FROM

Dog Fox Field

1992

DOG FOX FIELD

The test for feeblemindedness was, they had to make up a sentence using the words dog, fox *and* field.

JUDGEMENT AT NUREMBERG

These were no leaders, but they were first
into the dark on Dog Fox Field:

Anna who rocked her head, and Paul
who grew big and yet giggled small,

Irma who looked Chinese, and Hans
who knew his world as a fox knows a field.

Hunted with needles, exposed, unfed,
this time in their thousands they bore sad cuts

for having gaped, and shuffled, and failed
to field the lore of prey and hound

they then had to thump and cry in the vans
that ran while stopped in Dog Fox Field.

Our sentries, whose holocaust does not end,
they show us when we cross into Dog Fox Field.

DALE PECK

FROM

Martin and John

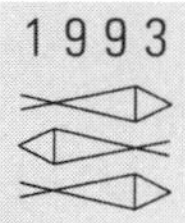

I remember little of my seven months in high school, save that, at fourteen, in gym, my sexuality and sexual preference were both revealed to me by a sudden erection in the showers. I don't know why but I panicked, and ran away across the slick tiled floor. The other boys' laughter followed me; they were the last people ever to do that. Brown bricks make the building: brown bricks and straight walls and square corners, and it seems that the plain mess just fell here, that human hands couldn't possibly have constructed such a lifeless husk. Inside, the halls reverberate with the sound of my footsteps, and an occasional laugh comes from behind the closed door of a summer school class. A silver-haired woman dressed in a gray polyester skirt and matching sleeveless sweater, her fat feet swelling from red high-heeled pumps, hobbles up to me. She looked the same twelve years ago, though even then I didn't know her name. "May I help you?" she says, and I quickly answer, "Just reminiscing." "Just what?" she says, cupping an ear toward me, though I doubt she's hard-of-hearing. "Remembering," I say loudly, giving her the benefit of the doubt. "Strolling down memory lane." I put an arm around her shoulder and pull out a long-unused smile and give it to her. She steps along with me, I at her pace. She's confused, I can tell, and flattered, as I point out my homeroom, show off the locker where I kissed my first girlfriend, and stop outside the glass-walled cafeteria where another boy and I once got into it. I don't tell her that he chased me here from the gym, nor do I mention that I pushed his face through the plate glass door; I call it a scrap, and laugh, and she says, "Boys will be boys," and laughs with me. There is the exit, I think, through which I once ran in fear. Today I stop in the doorway and wave at an old woman whose name I still don't know. "Come back some time," she says. "Sure," I say: the criminal always returns to the scene of the crime.

•

My stepmother rarely cooks. She drinks spring water through the morning and afternoon, and then orders out for dinner, usually something that can be delivered and eaten from its own disposable container: Chinese food, Italian food, things like that. Sunday comes and goes, then Monday and Tuesday, Wednesday and Thursday, Friday and another Saturday. How my parents divide their possessions I don't know. My stepmother comes in after meeting with him at his office in town. "Well," she says, "he'll keep the business, but I'll get forty percent of anything it makes and fifty percent if he ever sells it." That's only fair, considering her inheritance financed its start. "He'll keep the Lincoln, of course, and I'll keep the Jeep." The sticky point seems to be the house. "If we sell it, we'll split it sixty/forty, my way." She looks at me. "But that's only if we sell it. We'd like to give it to you, but we both think you should live here if we do. We don't want it to fall to ruins, and there's no sense paying to keep it up if no one's here. Do you want it?" she asks bluntly. I look at the family pictures mounted on the walls of the new living room, hoping that in one of them I'll find a reason to accept the house or decline it. But the images are hidden behind glass frames which reflect the lamplight like puddles catching the morning sun. "I don't think you should sell it," I say. "Why don't one of you keep it?" My stepmother sighs. "John, that's a moot point by now. Your father and I have been over and over this. We both put a lot into this place, and it wouldn't be fair if one of us got it at the expense of the other. The only fair thing to do is give it to you or sell it."

She lets me think about it for a while, and one week consumes another, and then another. Summer clamps down like a vise, wringing us dry, and the leaves on the catalpas flap like dry laundry on the line. The sprinkler system cuts off even faster now, and it can be used only during the evenings, since the combination of water and sunlight during the afternoons only magnifies the heat, singeing the grass. My stepmother works in the garden less and less each day. We sit around the house for hours; Bea listens to Vivaldi and Bartók, humming absently under her breath and starting new needlepoint or knitting projects that she'll shove in a drawer as soon as the hot spell breaks. Her cigarette smoke drives me from the living room, first to my bedroom, but that room swelters in the old, un-air-conditioned part of the house, so I retreat to the basement. There, I sift through boxes labeled John's Things, boxes filled with toys that grow progressively larger and more masculine. Lincoln Logs give way to a stainless steel Erector set; a rusted tricycle finds its replacements in a BMX motocross bike and a racing ten-speed. There are bats and rackets and hockey sticks and all sorts of balls, and all of them are alike in their dusty age. Two boxes contain only war toys: fake guns and knives and combat fatigues, and a folding shovel still crusty with dirt from its last long-ago use. In the bottom of one box I find a doll my real mother gave to me. My father had shaken the bead-stuffed thing in Bea's face one night and screamed, "This is what destroyed my little boy!" I sneered at him and swatted the doll from his hand, telling him I didn't even remember its name. This was right before he'd given me the car. My father looked at the doll, its long dress folded above desexed legs by the force of its landing. "Pretty Boy," he said. "You called it Pretty Boy when your mother was alive."

•

Barclay died today. Martin calls and says, "He was done up like a French whore." "What finally did it?" I ask. He'd seemed on a rebound when I left. "Was it the pneumonia?" "No," Martin says, and I can't tell if his voice is leering or saddened over the telephone. "It was the rat poison you bought." He starts to ask me about moving in again, but I cut him off. "Listen to me, Martin, listen to me for just a second." Martin tries to say something, but I cut him off again, keep talking. "Barclay used to bathe me. Do you see what I'm saying, Martin? He used to wash the smell of them off me. He'd fill the tub with water that was almost boiling—he'd spike it with pots of water he'd cooked on the stove to get it that hot. He used to steal the best soaps and shampoos and stuff, for me, he never used them on himself, only on me. He even had a little brush that he used under my fingernails, and when he finished washing me, he had clean clothes for me, and he put them on me and combed my hair and sent me out again. And I always knew I was done for the night when instead of clothes he'd wrap me in this robe he'd got somewhere, probably stole it too, this beautiful silk robe that was too small for me. Fits you like a miniskirt, Barclay'd say, and he'd put this on me just to walk me ten feet from the tub to the bed and take it off me and tuck me in, and then, after I was asleep, he'd get in bed too and wake me up with his kisses, and with him I never had to do anything but I always wanted to no matter how many, what kind I'd done that night. Something Barclay did always had me wanting him. After we were finished he washed me again, this would be my fourth or fifth bath of the night and I'd tell him it was okay, let's just sleep, but he always insisted, he said, Honey, if you don't know it by now, then let me set you straight: this girl ain't no better than the rest of 'em." I stop then, not because that's all there is but because I know I've said too much and because Martin is crying on the other end of the line. My own cheeks are dry. "Martin?" I say. His voice snuffles out, wet and angry, "But he was sick, John, sick, don't you see that?"

At first I think he means AIDS, and then, when I realize he doesn't, I hang up. I want to say something, just one thing that will sum it all up—I want to tell Martin he's wrong, and I want to tell him he's right too—but I realize that saying what's right and what's wrong isn't enough in this case. And it's not important either, now. Barclay's dead. There's only one thing, really, that I still want to tell Martin. The rat poison, I'll say some time: I bought it for the rats.

•

My father takes me to dinner again. We go to the same Italian restaurant and order the same food, and over dinner it seems he re-explains the situation to me using the same words as last time. As we drive back to his girlfriend's house in the climate-controlled shell of his Lincoln, he says, "One thing you have to remember, John, before you judge me, is that I love her. I'll always love her." Who does he mean? I wonder, for there are three candidates here. I'm about to ask, when he stops at a red light. In the car next to us two high school girls with wild hair and tan breasts bursting from their bikinis stare at my father's car, either in admiration or because they are preening, using his tinted windows as a mirror. My father stares at them behind the safety of his one-way glass wall. What would he do, I think, if I suddenly pressed the button that unrolls the window? Even as I make my move, the light turns green and he floors it, blowing the Toyota off the road —again, Barclay's phrase—and the force of his acceleration knocks my hand away from the button, so I never get the chance to expose him. Looking at my hand, I feel relieved that I was prevented from acting rashly. It would only have led to trouble. Beside me, my father raises his eyebrows in a minute, whimsical gesture, and surprises me by murmuring, "Ah, the beauty that does not belong to me."

•

Out of bed early one morning and I feel like my old self again, though which self that is I don't know. It's rained while I slept and the pale water sluicing down the windowpanes mixes with sunlight to form transparent shadows on the floor. I pull on a pair of shorts and wander outside. My stepmother works in the yard with a pair of garden shears in her ungloved hands. I watch her and see that she's cutting dandelions. They've finally bloomed, thanks to the rain, and thousands of bright gold suns litter the lawn, and they're vaguely beautiful, though Bea has always abhorred them. I set up a lawn chair and watch her attack the dandelions with the shears all morning and afternoon, cutting and cutting, reminding me of the mother of Dinesen's "Sorrow-Acre." By evening, somehow, she has finished the entire lawn, and rakes the wet dandelions in a huge pile. Today was cooler than days past, overcast, but the sun's invisible rays, amplified by the rain-laden clouds, have burned both our skins. Now my stepmother stands at the pile, and its dimensions dwarf hers for the moment; now she douses it with gasoline from a can; now it's alight, spewing dank smoke, and the flames seem to magnify the gold of the dandelion heads before consuming them. I walk over to her with the hose. "Don't you want this, just in case?" "No," she says, holding her stiff-fingered hands away from her body. "Let it burn itself out." She turns to me. "And I don't care if it takes everything with it." The look in her eyes frightens me; they challenge me to a reply which I can't offer. "Besides," she says, thrusting out her hands, "I couldn't hold the hose anyway." In the light from the flames I can see her palms are covered with blisters, most of them ripped open. She turns back to the pyre, face glowing and rapturous, and says, "We're selling the house. Go back to your man. You don't really want to be here." I barely hear her, staring at her hands, which seem to be letting go of something, setting it down and pushing it far away. Water from the hose dribbles to the ground and soaks my feet. I reach for what she's setting down, reach and reach—my hands grip the hose so tightly—but I can't find it. Eventually I abandon the effort, turn the water off. Just as the fire burns out, Bea says, "I didn't get them by the roots, you know. They'll be back next year." She speaks as though we'll still be here, but then I think, The roots she speaks of, they stretch far beyond the borders of this house.

•

Martin calls me and demands an answer. Here is his story: I've known you for over a year, John, and all you ever let me do is kiss you on the lips with a closed mouth. You cook me overspiced food and I buy you new books which you refuse to read. I tell you what plays are worth seeing, but you take me to the beach instead and don't go in the water. I tell you I love you, and I have to wring a response from you, but you always say you love me too. You won't take anything from me, and you won't give me anything; you beg me not to leave, but you offer me no reason to stay. You call when you wake up sweating in the middle of the night, and I listen to you cry on the phone and wish I could hold you and wipe the dampness from your skin. I buy the magazines and videos that still have you in them, and I use them to get off, and then I burn them. You tell me all about Barclay, and I tell you nothing about Henry, save that he exists. Over a year and your dinners have become incredibly elaborate, hours-long productions and your bookshelves are overflowing and Barclay is dead. You didn't even make his funeral. I made Henry move out. This doesn't mean things have changed, really, just that they could. Change. Just know that I'm not afraid of it, John, whatever it is, okay?

So there's that.

Henry is Martin's lover, but I am the one Martin loves. I sleep with no one but I care for Barclay. Years ago, when I was fourteen and newly run away from home—from school, really, where Eric Johnson's slashed face probably still bled—Barclay dressed me in a child's tuxedo and top hat and presented me at the first of many Harvest Balls, "where the fruit is you." He watched and hummed Judy as I gave it to an aging drag queen named Anisette, "like the drink, darling." Barclay's hot hand clapped me on the shoulder when I'd finished; I sweated but felt dried out. "That was so marvelous, dear, for your first time, but now let me show you how it's really done." He upended me, and Anisette sat on my chest while he did it, sipping a cocktail, her Scarlett O'Hara gown pulled above her hairy waist and choking me with its dusty ruffles. I've been thirsty ever since. Anisette still straddled me when she handed Barclay several crumpled bills from her purse, and I remember growing confused then: behind the dry mountain of her body my inner thighs still twitched with pleasure, but in front of her bulk I sucked in vain for the air and water that poured, without my control, from my mouth and eyes and nose, forced out by Anisette's unbearable weight on my chest. And I must tell you: this is the hollow center of my being, the one thing in my life I don't understand, and from it I've learned not to trust my instincts, not to act, because I know that I have no control over the consequences of those actions. "Oh, baby," Barclay had leaned close and whispered to me: "Don't cry. I love you, I really do. I'll love you till the day I die." And then, laughing, he walked away. And it's not that Barclay could joke about his own death that bothered me, not then, when death was a new thing, nor later, when his ice-cold skeletal hand clutched mine through three bouts of pneumonia and he still laughed when he could summon the breath. It's just that when he placed his hands on my body, squeezing in all the places that used to belong to him, and kissed me with his cracked tongue, it seemed he laughed at mine as well. "No," I told him, "it's not the old days anymore." "Don't act like a little boy," he said. "There never were any old days. There's no difference between then and now."

•

And perhaps he's right, for when I return to my school the woman still hobbles the hallways in her gray skirt and sweater and garish pumps. She looks at me and smiles quickly; her hands flutter to touch her dyed hair, and she asks me what I'm doing here. "I'd like to take you for coffee," I say, and she glances around to see if anyone else has heard my offer. She protests for a moment—"Well, I don't know, I hardly know you"—but soon says yes. In a small bright café we drink coffee and she tells me her name is Mrs. Enniger. I let her talk for an hour, and then, walking at her snail's pace toward her house, we pass a shoe store. "Shoes," I say. "I want to buy you shoes." "What?" she says as I whisk her inside. I point to her pumps and say, "If you keep wearing those, you'll be on a cane in five years." She says, "No, no, I'm fine," but when I ease her shoes off she sighs audibly; her feet are swollen and misshapen, and it takes several minutes before they appear normal. I slip a pair of rubber-soled, orthopedic shoes on her. "Try these," I say. She stands, takes a few tentative steps. "I feel funny," she says. "I've been walking on stilts for too long. But these are so comfortable!" She smiles at me, sits down, looks at her feet, says, "But they're old lady's shoes." Look, look, look in the mirror, I want to say: You're not old. Mrs. Derkman was old, Barclay was old. But I only say, "I won't force them on you." "Are they expensive?" she asks. "They cost me nothing." She wears them home. At her house, old habits send me walking in behind her, a hand on her waist slipping lower. I stop before she really notices, but one hand flutters to her hip where mine had been. She jokes, "You've changed my life," and perhaps I have, but mine, I realize, is still the same.

•

The smell of tempura and soy sauce fills Martin's apartment one evening. Boxes labeled John's Things flood the floor. Toy pistols and pots and pans mix like childhood and adulthood all around me. They are the legacy of both my parents: though my father bought everything, it was my stepmother who saved each item. If it was just this one thing and nothing more—just these boxes—then I would puzzle it through until I understood it. But it's not: it's this and it's everything. Henry found his own place in no time, and I planted a few flowers on Barclay's grave, thinking that my mother's lies untended somewhere in Kansas. When I fed him, I ask myself now, did I really want to keep him alive, or just some memory of my past? My stepmother has moved to the West Coast with a boyfriend and my father has gone alone to Colorado. They'll call me, I imagine, or I'll call them: it's inevitable. Here is Martin, his arms on my body, saying, I love you, make love to me. Bring me a glass of water, I say; I was going to drink it but then I dip my fingers in the glass like a young shoot and trace patterns on Martin's body with my water fingers, and it's okay, because he hasn't seen the movie where I did it first, following a script, watched by a camera, burned under sun-bright lamps, having sex with a man who would be dead in six months. Behind me now, Martin says he'll take care of me no matter what, and I say, but not to him, "No."

PETER HØEG

FROM

Smilla's Sense of Snow

[*Translated by Tiina Nunnally*]

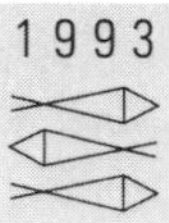

My father was in his early thirties when he came to Greenland and met my mother.

The Inuit Aisivak told Knud Rasmussen that in the beginning the world was inhabited only by two men, who were both great sorcerers. Since they wanted to multiply, one of them transformed his body in such a way that he could give birth; and then the two of them created many children.

In the 1860s the Greenland catechist Hanseeraq recorded in the diary of the Brethren Congregation, *Diarium Friedrichstal*, many examples of women who hunted as men did. There are examples in Rink's collection of legends, and in *Reports from Greenland*. It has certainly never been commonplace, but it *has* happened. Caused by the excessive number of women, by death and necessity, and by the natural acceptance in Greenland that each of the sexes contains the potential to become its opposite.

As a rule, however, women have then had to dress like men, and they have had to renounce any sort of family life. The collective could tolerate a change in sex, but not a fluid transition state.

It was different with my mother. She laughed and gave birth to her children and gossiped about her friends and cleaned skins like a woman. But she shot and paddled a kayak and dragged meat home like a man.

When she was about twelve years old, she went out on the ice with her father in April, and there he shot at an *uuttoq*, a seal sunning itself on the ice. He missed. For other men there might be various reasons why they would miss. For my grandfather there was only one. Something irreversible was about to happen. Calcification of the optic nerve. A year later he was totally blind.

On that day in April my mother stayed behind while her father walked on to check a long line. There she had time to ponder the various possibilities for her future. Such as the welfare assistance which even today is below subsistence level in Greenland and at that time was a kind of unintentional joke. Or death by starvation, which was not uncommon, or a life of depending on kinfolk who didn't even have enough for themselves.

When the seal popped up again, she shot it.

Before, she had jigged for sea scorpions and Greenland halibut, and hunted for grouse. With this seal she became a hunter.

I think it was rare for her to step outside herself and take an objective look at her role. But it happened once when we were living in tents at the summer encampment near Atikerluk, a mountain that is invaded by auks in the summertime, by so many black, white-breasted birds that only someone who has seen it can fully grasp the vast numbers. They defy measurement.

We had come from the north, where we were fishing for narwhals from small, diesel-powered cutters. One day we caught eight animals. Partly because the ice had trapped them in a restricted area, partly because the three boats lost contact with each other. Eight narwhals are far too much meat, even for dog food. Far too much meat.

One of them was a pregnant female. The nipple is located right above the genital opening. When my mother opened the abdominal cavity with a single cut to remove the intestines, an angel-white, perfectly formed pup two and a half feet long slid out onto the ice.

For close to four hours the hunters stood around in virtual silence, gazing out at the midnight sun, which at that time of year brings perpetual light, and ate *mattak*, narwhal skin. I couldn't eat a single bite.

One week later we are camping out near the bird mountain, and we haven't eaten for twenty-four hours. The technique is to melt into the landscape, waiting, and take the bird with a large net. On the second try I get three.

They were females, on their way to their young. They nest on ledges on the steep slopes, where the young make an infernal racket. The mothers hide the worms they find in a kind of pouch in their beaks. You kill them by pressing on their heart. I had three birds.

There had been so many before these. So many birds killed, cooked in clay, and eaten; so many that I couldn't remember them all. And yet I suddenly see their eyes as tunnels, at the end of which their young are waiting, and the babies' eyes are in turn tunnels, at the end of which is the narwhal pup, whose gaze in turn leads inward and away. Ever so slowly I turn over the net, and with a great explosion of sound, the birds rise into the air.

My mother is sitting next to me, quite still. And she looks at me as if seeing something for the first time.

I don't know what it was that stopped me. Compassion is not a virtue in the Arctic. It amounts to a kind of insensitivity: a lack of feeling for the animals, the environment, and the nature of necessity.

"Smilla," she says, "I have carried you in *amaat*."

It's the month of May, and her skin has a deep brown sheen, like a dozen layers of varnish. She is wearing gold earrings and a chain with two crosses and an anchor around her neck. Her hair is pulled into a bun at the nape of her neck, and she is big and beautiful. Even now, when I think of her, she is the most beautiful woman I have ever seen.

I must have been around five years old. I don't know exactly what she means, but this is the first time I understand that we are of the same sex.

"And yet," she says, "I am as strong as a man."

She has on a red-and-black-checked cotton shirt. Now she rolls up one sleeve and shows me her lower arm, which is as broad and hard as a paddle. Then she slowly unbuttons her shirt. "Come, Smilla," she says quietly. She never kisses me, and she seldom touches me. But at moments of great intimacy, she lets me drink from the milk that is always there, beneath her skin, just as her blood is. She spreads her legs so I can come between them. Like the other hunters, she wears pants made of bearskin given only a rudimentary tanning. She loves ashes, sometimes eating them straight from the fire, and she has smeared some underneath her eyes. In this aroma of burned coal and bearskin, I go to her breast, which is brilliantly white, with a big, delicate rose aureole. There I drink *immuk*, my mother's milk.

Later she once tried to explain to me why one month there are 3,000 narwhals gathered in a single fjord seething with life. The next month the ice traps them and they freeze to death. Why there are so many auks in May and June that they color the cliffs black. The next month half a million birds are dead of starvation. In her own way she wanted to point out that behind the life of the Arctic animals there has always been this extreme fluctuation in population. And that in these fluctuations, the number we take means less than nothing.

I understood her, understood every word. Then and later on. But that didn't change a thing. The year after—the year before she disappeared—I began to feel nauseated when I went fishing. I was then about six years old. Not old enough to speculate about the reason. But old enough to understand that it was a feeling of alienation toward nature. That some part of it was no longer accessible to me in the natural way that it had been before. Perhaps I had even then begun to want to understand the ice. To want to understand is an attempt to recapture something we have lost.

[. . .]

I don't know how my mother and father met. I do know that he came to Greenland because this hospitable land has always been the site of scientific experiments. He was in the process of developing a new technique for the treatment of trigeminal neuralgia, an inflammation of the facial sensory nerve. Previously, this condition was assuaged by killing the nerve with injections of alcohol, which led to partial facial paralysis and loss of sensation on one side of the musculature of the mouth, the so-called drooping lip. This can afflict even the best and richest of families, which is why my father had become interested in it. There were many incidences of that illness in North Greenland. He had come to treat them with his new technique—a partial heat-denaturing of the affected nerve.

There are photographs of him. Wearing his Kastinger boots and his down clothing, with ice ax and glacier goggles, in front of the house they put at his disposal on the American base. With his hands on the shoulders of the two short, dark men who are to interpret for him.

For him, North Greenland was truly the outermost Thule. Not for a minute did he imagine that he would stay more than the one required month in a windblown ice desert, where there wasn't even a golf course.

You might have some clue to the white-hot energy between him and my mother if you consider the fact that he stayed there four years. He tried to get her to move onto the base, but she refused. For my mother, just like everyone born in North Greenland, any suggestion of being cooped up was intolerable. Instead, he followed her out to one of the barracks made of plywood and corrugated tin that were put up when the Americans drove the Inuits out of the area where the base was built. Even today I still ask myself how he managed it. The answer, of course, is that as long as she was alive, he would have left his golf bag and clubs behind at a moment's notice to follow her, even right into the searing center of black hell.

"*They* had a child," people say. In this case that wouldn't be correct. I would say that *my mother* had my little brother and me. Outside of this scenario was my father, present without being able to take any real part, dangerous as a polar bear, imprisoned in a land that he hated by a love that he did not understand and that held him captive, over which he seemed to have not even the slightest influence. The man with the syringes and the steady hands, the golf player Moritz Jaspersen.

When I was three years old, he left. Or rather, his own character drove him away. Deep within every blind, absolute love grows a hatred toward the beloved, who now holds the only existing key to happiness. I was, as I said, only three years old, but I remember how he left. He left in a state of seething, pent-up, livid, profane rage. As a form of energy this was surpassed only by the longing that flung him back again. He was stuck to my mother with a rubber band that was invisible to the rest of the world but which had the effect and physical reality of a drive belt.

He didn't have much to do with us children when he was there. From my first six years I remember only traces of him. The smell of the Latakia tobacco he smoked. The autoclave in which he sterilized his instruments. The interest he aroused whenever he would occasionally put on his cleats, take up a stance, and shoot a bucket of balls across the new ice. And the mood he brought with him, which was the sum of the feelings he had for my mother. The same kind of soothing warmth that you might expect to find in a nuclear reactor.

What was my mother's role in this? I don't know, and I will never find out. Those who understand such things say that the two spouses must always assist each other if a relationship is truly to founder and turn to flotsam. That's possible. Like everybody else, from the age of seven I have painted my childhood with lots of false colors, and some of this may have rubbed off on my mother as well. But in any case, she was the one who stayed where she was, and set out her nets and braided my hair. She was there, a huge presence, while Moritz with his golf clubs and beard stubble and syringes oscillated between the two extremes of his love: either a total merging or putting the entire North Atlantic between him and his beloved.

•

No one who falls into the water in Greenland comes up again. The sea is less than 39° F, and at that temperature all the processes of decomposition stop. That's why fermentation of the stomach contents does not occur here; in Denmark, however, it gives suicides renewed buoyancy and brings them to the surface, to wash up on shore.

But they found the remains of her kayak, which led them to conclude that it must have been a walrus. Walruses are unpredictable. They can be hypersensitive and shy. But if they come a little farther south, and if it's autumn, when there are few fish, they can be transformed into some of the swiftest and most meticulous killers in the great ocean. With their two tusks they can stave in the side of a ship made of ferrocement. I once saw hunters holding a cod up to a walrus that they had captured alive. The walrus puckered up his lips as for a kiss and then sucked the meat right off the bones of the fish.

CALVIN TRILLIN

FROM

Remembering Denny

1993

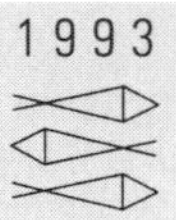

When Denny and I arrived in New Haven, in the fall of 1953, Yale could strike a high-school boy from the provinces as something like a foreign country—a rather intimidating foreign country. Years after this, in reviewing a book by Peter Prescott about his first year at Harvard and recalling a couple of other memoirs published by Ivy League graduates of the mid-fifties, I wrote that "in my official capacity as Corresponding Secretary of the Ivy League Society of Public High School Rubes," I had a question to ask: "If all of these Eastern prep-school types like Prescott and Michael Arlen (who went from St. Paul's School to Harvard in *Exiles*) and John Gregory Dunne (who went from Portsmouth Priory to Princeton in *Vegas*) were not actually as self-assured and sophisticated as they appeared to be, why did they have to wait twenty years to tell us so?" In our entering class at Yale the ratio of private-school graduates to public-school graduates was sixty-one to thirty-nine in favor of private schools. The Eastern boarding-school people had their own way of dressing—what was called the Ivy look did not spread to the rest of the country until a year or two later—and their own way of talking, a drawl through the teeth that provoked me to concoct the theory that the man who had previously made his living stunning the cows at a Kansas City slaughterhouse just before the knife came down had been hired by St. Paul's School to break the jaw of every entering boy, in a courteous and understated way.

Some of the boarding-school people had been to Europe. Some of them had boarding-school reputations as boy leaders that were enough to carry them through Yale. Some of them had taken courses that sounded to someone from public high school like college courses—courses in philosophy, or courses in foreign languages that were neither Spanish nor French. Some of our classmates came from the sort of backgrounds we had simply never contemplated. Although I have told the story for years as a joke, one of my roommates—I call him Thatcher

Baxter Hatcher in the joke, since a lot of people in our class seemed to have three last names—actually did tell me that after the war his family no longer dressed for dinner, and I actually did think he meant that they were allowed to come to the table in their undershirts. There were people in our class I came to think of as package people: you could go into a store and find their family names on packages, wrapped around candy bars or flour or beer. One of the roommates Denny was assigned to freshman year was John Mars, whose family produced Mars bars. My boyhood friend from Kansas City who had enrolled in Princeton the same autumn I showed up at Yale—Eddie Williams, whose father was an English teacher at Southwest—had a roommate I never heard him address as anything but Eberhard Faber the Pencil King, as in "Could you please pass the salt, Eberhard Faber the Pencil King?" There were, of course, at Yale as well as Princeton, boarding-school types you wouldn't joke with the way Eddie Williams could joke with Eb Faber—people who seemed to resent the presence of people they didn't recognize from the cotillion. For them, Eddie used a Princeton phrase that I've mentioned ever since when the subject of evocative epithets comes up: tweedy shitballs.

High-school boys from the provinces may have felt ignorant of some things that the Eastern boarding-school people took for granted—I remember realizing in my sophomore year that I had arrived at Yale never having heard of either Dostoevsky or Greenwich—but most of us, I think, got the feeling that a lot of the rich Eastern people were at Yale because of some entitlement of family or class or money and that we were there because, in ways that were perhaps not immediately apparent, we somehow deserved to be. Many years after I left Yale, I realized that we had been bolstered by a belief that we would have never uttered out loud and may not even have articulated to ourselves: there was widespread circumstantial evidence that, on the whole, we were smarter than they were. Even now, nearly forty years later, I'm reminded regularly that I accepted this proposition as a given: if I meet someone who is easily identifiable as being from what was once called a St. Grottlesex background, my gut expectation—kicking in fast enough to override my beliefs about judging people as individuals, slipping in well below the level of rational thinking—is that he's probably a bit slow.

Still, at first glance, Yale seemed very much *their* place. They set the tone: cool, understated, wearing through at the elbows. Most freshmen everywhere must have moments of feeling alone and far from home, but I doubt if I found that fact of any comfort when I arrived at the New Haven station one rainy day, after having sat up on a train from Kansas City for thirty hours—suffering from some awful flu symptoms brought on by the train air conditioning, lugging a huge trunk, and thinking wistfully of my high-school pals at the University of Missouri sitting down together for a few beers and a few laughs. Remarkably, the entering Class of 1957 at Yale had two people from Southwest High School—a fact of no small comfort, the two of us found, in times of celebration or trouble. Denny was the sole representative of Sequoia Union High School. There were sixty-two from Andover.

I was aware of Denny that first year—I see him in my memory walking across the Old Campus, where all freshmen lived—but I didn't really know him. I remember seeing his picture in the *Yale Daily News* as one of the two people elected as our class's representatives to an advisory group called the Undergraduate Affairs Committee. It was an honor, of sorts, although any truly acclimated Yale undergraduate knew to treat anything that smacked even slightly of student government with some disdain; the *News* story gave precedence to the twelve people elected to the Freshman Prom Committee at the same time. (Serious student government would have required overt campaigning for office—an impossibility in a place where those who wore letter sweaters wore them inside out. Achievement was admired at Yale in the fifties, but you didn't want to be caught trying.) I assumed that Denny's election had been the result of people confusing him with the football-playing Roger Hansen—in later years, naturally, I lost no opportunity to remind him of that possibility—but eventually I learned that, not having become close to his roommates, he spent a lot of time on the Old Campus, where freshmen tossed footballs around or leaned up against the fences to talk about how far behind they were with the reading, and where Denny's smile and his charm and his wit had attracted a small coterie. Much later, I also learned that he had often been homesick that year, as the only representative of Sequoia Union High School, but by the time I got to know him, at the end of junior year, there was no sign of that. By the time I got to know him, he was, well, Denny.

As Denny, he seemed to have a limitless future. We emerged from Yale in June of the year that has since been called a high point in American prosperity. With the peacemaking general in the White House and the Cold War having settled into what seemed to us to be a more or less permanent struggle between the good guys and the bad guys, there were reasons to see limitless futures for a lot of people. When I talked to André Schiffrin after Denny's death, he said the picture that comes into his mind when he thinks about how Yale undergraduates viewed the future in those days is *Stairway to Heaven*—moving up through the clouds on a blissful escalator. We had the usual problems of deciding what we wanted to do, of course, but those problems came partly from the assumption that very little was shut off. As I was reminded by Van Ooms, an economist I met at Tersh's after Denny's memorial service, we were demographically blessed: we were white males who were born in a baby bust during the Depression and came of age at a time when the privileged position of white males was so deeply embedded in the structure of the society that we didn't even think much about it. (In those days, nobody ever asked why my father hadn't put away some of the bread-company rebate for my sister to go to Radcliffe or Wellesley.) People graduating from Yale not many years after us had to face the possibility of not being able to get into a first-rank law school or of going to graduate school and then finding that no tenure-track positions on university faculties existed; people graduating from Yale not many years before us had to face the possibility that they might not survive a war. However much we complained about the draft or about the difficulty of deciding what to do, we were greatly privileged. Under the circumstances, it didn't seem so odd to be talking about what each of us would do in Denny Hansen's cabinet.

[· · ·]

In 1977, Denny was heard from again. "HANSEN sent a prompt reply to my plea for news, as he was on the eve of a trip to the Far East in his capacity as a Senior Staff Member of the National Security Council. In September, he will 'retire' to become Jacob Blaustein Professor of International Organization at the Johns Hopkins School of Advanced International Studies in Washington. He was hoping to finish by December a book for the Council on Foreign Relations' '1980s Project.' The subject is the evolving relations between the developed and developing nations." Then, having announced a move to the institution he was to be with for the rest of his life, Denny disappeared from the Class of 1957 class letter. As far as I can tell, his name didn't appear again until the spring of 1991, when the secretary—by then Don Smith, the Grinnell historian—wrote, "While preparing this letter, I received the sad news of Roger HANSEN's death by suicide early in the year. 'Denny' had two ebullient years at Magdalen, and those who knew him there will be grateful for those years and for his warm-hearted friendship."

·

For those who had gathered the evening of the memorial service in Tersh Boasberg's living room—even those who agreed with Rocky Suddarth that Denny had been in trouble from the start—analyzing Denny's life seemed to be partly a matter of trying to isolate the moment when, as a couple of people had put it, he began to lose his direction.

Most of the people in the room had themselves been highly directed since grade school. They were not just Denny people, they were fifties people—fifties high achievers, mainly, who had grown up thinking that the life of a fifties golden boy had the smooth trajectory of an airliner rising from the ground. If things didn't work out that way, it's natural for them to look for the moment when the motor started sputtering.

Somebody at Tersh's had said that the problem facing people who breeze through high school and college the way Denny did is that they get no training in losing, so the first defeat can be devastating. Denny did have some training—for instance, he had apparently been deeply disappointed that his performance as a swimmer at Yale did not match the record-breaking swimming he had done for the Sequoia Cherokees—but he also had the awful insecurity that had been present even when he seemed to be a person who could lose at nothing. George E. Vaillant's longitudinal study of members of a Harvard class twenty years ahead of us begins with the proposition that mental health is measured in how well someone adapts to the setbacks that are bound to occur; the book is called *Adaptation to Life*. There are those who believe that at some point Denny was unable to adapt because, as one of them put it, "something happened and he decided his life was worthless." The stories of failed golden boys all of us heard just after Denny died tended to have such moments—the career path mistake, the panic that cost the golden boy his confidence. For some of the people who interpret Denny's life that way, Oxford was the moment.

It seems clear that Denny had been concerned about the possibility that Oxford would be the place where he would be revealed at last as unworthy of his glories. When I spoke to Howard Lamar about Denny, he said, "I think the Rhodes Scholarship produced a great deal of worry: 'I have handled this subculture. Can I handle another one?' " As the 1957 Rhodes Scholars sailed to Southampton from New York—they all went over together, through an arrangement with the United States Lines—it was assumed that all of them had read a piece in *Life* called "A Farewell to Bright College Years?" That must have swollen the trepidation Denny would have already been feeling. The follow-up piece that *Life* did on Denny two or three months after he arrived at Oxford—a short picture spread headlined MAN OF ELI AT OXFORD—was hardly reassuring. One sentence says, "Surrounded by British undergraduates whose erudition often staggers him, Hansen could not keep up with their practice of reading books in French and German, and had to ask his tutor to assign books only in English."

After mentioning Denny's complaints about the accommodations and the food, the piece does say that "Hansen is happily getting into the spirit of Oxford life." The pictures and captions, though, are not happy. The full-page shot that opens the piece is the picture of Denny riding his bicycle on the sidewalk. Seeing that picture brought back memories of listening to Denny's complaints—we were in a café in London, if I remember correctly—about the perfidy of the *Life* crew in setting up a shot that made him look like a hick who didn't even know that bicycles were for the street. One of the pictures shows Denny pouring tea into some cups arrayed on the floor of his room while some other Americans, smiling self-consciously, watch him with great care, as if observing a mildly antic science experiment. "He had learned how to make tea only the day before," the caption says. The other picture of Denny's attempt to acclimate shows him playing darts at a pub, and notes that while the other American students drank mild and bitter ("a mixture of light and dark ale") Hansen had orangeade. The picture that outraged him almost as much as the bicycle shot shows him sitting in a chair with a blanket across his lap. "Muffled against cold in his damp rooms in Magdalen College," it says, "Hansen does his studying sustained by Ovaltine and bread filched from dining hall." Not just a boob and a prig, as Denny read it, but also a petty thief.

When that follow-up piece came out in *Life*, I was working at Time Inc. in London, in a temporary job that had emerged accidentally from a summer job as I was about to leave for Europe to wait for the draft. I could hardly have been further from the center of the company's editorial power. I spent a lot of my time answering queries from the researchers of various Time Inc. magazines in New York—queries that all seemed to begin "Need soonest," in the pigeon cable-ese then favored for communication over the leased wire, and all seemed to ask for information that nobody could possibly ever need soonest or any other time. (My favorite one read—in its entirety, as I remember—"*Fortune* needs soonest name of longest street in London uninterrupted by intersections.") But I was the target of opportunity for any complaints Denny had about how he had been treated by *Life*. I tried to respond the way any jaded reporter would have responded; I had, after all, been in the game a good three weeks. I probably told him it was routine for someone portrayed in a magazine to be sensitive about little things that readers wouldn't even notice—especially someone dumb enough to pose riding a bicycle on the sidewalk. Rereading the piece after Denny's death, though, I had to admit that, particularly compared with the "*Life* Goes to a Commencement" tone of the original article, there was something snide about it. I also realized that it may have represented the first time that adults had commented on his activities in terms that were anything but completely glowing. It may have been, in Denny's view, the first time someone had managed to see what was under the mask.

I also realized, after talking about Denny with some of the other people who were Rhodes Scholars at the time, that the *Life* reporter who had visited Denny at Oxford was, if not absolutely prescient, at least closer to the truth than Denny realized at the time. When Robert Tucker and I spoke, not long after the memorial service, about what he called Denny's sense of "not being up to things," he said, "My feeling is that this was enormously exacerbated at Oxford. He worked under people like A.J.P. Taylor—that's enough to give you an inferiority complex. They'd say, 'This is a good effort. Not top drawer, of course.' I think at Oxford it became blindingly clear that there were levels that he couldn't attain. A lot of Rhodes Scholars have suffered this reaction to Oxford." Other Rhodes Scholars tend to remember Denny as a sort of loner at Oxford—someone who didn't make a lot of friends, particularly among the English. In those days, there were always Americans at Oxford who took on English airs—people who carried tightly rolled umbrellas at all times and got fussy about their scones and began using enough English slang and English inflection to blur the American in their speech. Denny, everyone agrees, was not one of them. He may have learned to make tea and to order brown and bitter, but he remained an unreconstructed American. "He was sort of a California sunshine kid," Dick Pfaff, who was in Magdalen College with Denny and also read history, told me. "There was a lot of gee-whizzery about him." He didn't hang around with the intellectual set. Unlike a lot of Rhodes Scholars, he didn't compete for his college in sports. "Oxford was a downer for Denny," Joc Clayton wrote in his letter to Don Smith. "He had no captive audience in a community of prima donnas and he was too far from the California sun. Thereafter, he just couldn't seem to get it together."

But Smith had said "two ebullient years at Magdalen," and when I spoke to him he seemed to remember someone who was closer to the Denny of Yale—someone who still had that sense of discovery, about opera, for instance, and travel. "I think in some ways maybe I feel kind of lucky to know him when I did," Smith, who was a close friend of Denny's during their second year at Oxford, told me not long after Denny's death. "That is, maybe if I had been a student with him at Yale I would have seen the kind of icon, the golden boy from California. Later on, if he became morose and difficult, if you had gotten to know him then it might have been 'Hey, what's the big deal about this guy?' But in the second year at Oxford, I saw the sort of charm and the appeal and the good humor, but I saw this extraordinarily appealing kind of vulnerability. Which in some ways was gratifying for a kid from Tennessee who had never been out of the South until I went over there. I sort of fell in love with operatic music and so on, and here was this guy who liked the same things." Also, the notion that Oxford is where Denny confirmed his fears of not being able to measure up to the next challenge are contradicted by his academic performance. Rhodes Scholars rarely get Firsts—there were only four in the Class of 1957—but apparently Denny, despite having fallen so ill that he had to take his oral examination in the hospital, barely missed one. In an obituary of Denny written for *The American Oxonian*, Van Ooms, a Rhodes Scholar one year earlier, quoted a friend of Denny's who said, "Who knows what might have happened had he been sitting up?"

Years later, I found out that Howard Lamar had been concerned by the tone of Denny's letters from Oxford. "He was very much the visitor, the observer," Lamar told me. "They were not written as a participant. They were letters from someone on a trip." In fact, Lamar told me during that conversation, five undergraduates he had known well had become Rhodes Scholars, and he thought three had been badly damaged by the experience—partly because of becoming ensnared in a British academic culture that makes it hard to fit in back in the United States, partly because of the burden of expectations they had to carry. Don Smith believes that the burden of expectations is a problem for almost all Rhodes Scholars, and particularly Denny, because of the *Life* articles. "I have vivid memories of saying once to a friend, 'The worst thing that ever happened to me was getting the Rhodes Scholarship' or 'If I hadn't gotten the Rhodes Scholarship I wouldn't have had some of the advantages but maybe things would have been easier for me,' " he told me. "It would be very surprising to me if the ordinary recipient of the Rhodes had not had thoughts like that at one time or the other." Smith hadn't seen Denny for many years before Denny's death; he had been conscious of Denny's distancing himself from his Oxford friends even in the seventies. But when Denny died, Smith said, "I thought, Oh my God, what if I was, in a sense, the problem? What if I was one of those people he thought he was accountable to—one of those people in Oxford who was some kind of judge . . . Because he didn't have anything to live up to as far as I was concerned except to be himself."

JAMES FENTON

FROM

Out of Danger

1994

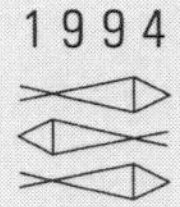

FOR ANDREW WOOD

What would the dead want from us
Watching from their cave?
Would they have us forever howling?
Would they have us rave
Or disfigure ourselves, or be strangled
Like some ancient emperor's slave?

None of my dead friends were emperors
With such exorbitant tastes
And none of them were so vengeful
As to have all their friends waste
Waste quite away in sorrow
Disfigured and defaced.

I think the dead would want us
To weep for what *they* have lost.
I think that our luck in continuing
Is what would affect them most.
But time would find them generous
And less self-engrossed.

And time would find them generous
As they used to be
And what else would they want from us
But an honoured place in our memory,
A favourite room, a hallowed chair,
Privilege and celebrity?

And so the dead might cease to grieve
And we might make amends
And there might be a pact between
Dead friends and living friends.
What our dead friends would want from us
Would be such living friends.

IAN BURUMA

FROM

The Wages of Guilt

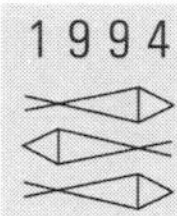

One of the most beautiful metaphors of history is Walter Benjamin's description of Paul Klee's painting *Angelus Novus*. The Angelus Novus is the angel of history; he has a human face, but the wings and feet of a bird: "His face is turned toward the past. Where we perceive a chain of events, he sees one single catastrophe which keeps piling ruin upon ruin and hurls it in front of his feet. The angel would like to stay, awaken the dead, and make whole what has been smashed. But a storm is blowing from Paradise; it has got caught in his wings with such violence that the angel can no longer close them. The storm irresistibly propels him into the future, to which his back is turned, while the pile of debris before him grows skyward. The storm is what we call progress."

The idea of progress, as well as British bombs, turned Dresden into a city of ruins and monstrosities. Walking through the hideous streets of central Dresden, seeing the few bits and pieces of the old city, like fragments of a beautiful antique jar, produced in me precisely the irrational feeling of guilt by association that I have argued against in the cases of Auschwitz and Hiroshima. The reason had little to do with the respective death tolls (roughly 30,000 in Dresden), for mass killing is shocking, whatever the actual numbers. (As Christopher Isherwood said to the man who pointed out that more Jews were murdered than homosexuals: "What are you, in real estate?") And the feeling of special regret was not particularly noble. For what is so shocking about the bombing of Dresden is that it smashed in one night the accumulated beauty of centuries. Dresden, like Prague or Venice, was one of the architectural wonders of the world. Its destruction was an act of perversity, like putting an ax to a Chippendale chair, or knifing a Michelangelo, or burning a priceless library. It was all the more perverse since there was no compelling strategic reason for it. Which is not to say that the bombing of ugly slums is any less ghastly, in human terms, than the destruction of Dresden's baroque heart. It's just that being in the new, empty hole of Dresden, where there once was a heart, is to be constantly aware of what was lost.

Parts of the old city could have been saved after the war. Enough was left of some of the palaces and churches to make restoration feasible, as in Nuremberg or Munich. But the first Communist leader of East Germany, Walter Ulbricht, decided that the past had to be eradicated. "Dresden, More Beautiful Than Ever" (*"Dresden, schöner als je"*) was his slogan, and for the second time the city fell victim to perversity: art historians were forced to draw up plans for the final destruction of Dresden's remains, and party hacks took commissions to design the frightful city that was to be the showcase of socialism. The Sophienkirche, opposite the eighteenth-century Zwinger Palace, was the finest Gothic church in Dresden. It was torn down and a squat concrete bunker, housing a workers' canteen, was built in its place. This was Ulbricht's idea of progress.

But not all the rubble was cleared. The Zwinger Palace was restored in the 1960s, as were one or two other ruins, and the remains of the eighteenth-century Frauenkirche were left as they were, because neither Ulbricht nor anybody else could agree on what to build in its place. Thus the sad pile of stones became a warning place, a memorial (to cite the official plaque) "to the tens of thousands of dead, and an inspiration to the living in their struggle against imperialist barbarism and for the peace and happiness of man."

I asked the new curator of the municipal museum, Matthias Griebel, what exactly was meant by imperialist barbarism. Griebel answered: "They meant every imperialist war: Israel in the Sinai, America in Vietnam, everything but socialist wars."

Griebel, whose shaven head and luxuriant whiskers made him resemble a great German eagle, was one of the small number of people who had tried to keep historical consciousness alive in Dresden, by organizing lectures and informal exhibitions. At first the Communist government opposed this kind of thing, for Dresden's "feudal" past belonged in the dustbin of history. It was only in the 1980s, when Communist dogma had utterly lost its popular appeal, that the regime tried to bolster its credentials by claiming a historical legitimacy: from Thomas Münzer, the peasant rebel, to Frederick of Prussia. Even Karl May, the nineteenth-century romantic, whose novels about Old Shatterhand, the German hero of the Wild West, were read avidly by Hitler and Einstein alike, was declared to be one of us. His house, "Villa Shatterhand," can be visited just down the Elbe, northwest of Dresden.

A few miles up the Elbe, on the other side of town, is Pirna, a crumbling but quaint little town with fine nineteenth-century villas and the odd bit of late Gothic architecture. I went there in search of a historical site which is not mentioned in any guidebook of the Dresden region. There was an old hospital there, once used for mental patients. I knew it was still there for I had seen photographs of it. And Griebel confirmed its existence. The mental hospital was not insignificant, for it was there that doctors first experimented on their patients with the murderous gas known as Zyklon B. More than 10,000 people died at the Sonnenstein Euthanasia Institute.

I had some trouble locating the place. An old lady cheerfully sent me up a hill, but then I got lost. "What did you say it was?" The former Euthanasia Institute. "When was this?" The Hitler period. "Sorry, I wouldn't know about that."

But I found it in the end. In a pleasant park next to Sonnenstein Castle were several turn-of-the-century buildings. I entered a villa with yellow walls which had a sign that said: "Sauna facilities for sick and old people." A young woman asked me what I wanted. I told her. She winced and said: "No, it wasn't here. We only deal with patients for specialized treatment here. You want the other building over there where they used to have a turbine factory."

The "building over there" had a rusted wire fence around it. It looked sinister enough to have been a Euthanasia Institute. And there was a plaque which commemorated one Albert Barthel, "our party comrade, murdered by the Nazis in 1942."

Yet this wasn't it either. I walked into a room and saw several young people having their lunch. They turned out to be deacons who looked after retarded children. "The former Euthanasia Institute? No, no, thank God it wasn't in this room. No, it was in the building next door."

I peered into the cellars of the building next door, a rather elegant French-style villa. There was no plaque anywhere. The grass grew wild and high around the bolted door. I listened to the birds sing in the rustling trees and I thought of the pile of teddy bears I had seen lying about in the hall of the house of deacons.

Architecture, said Mr. Griebel, is time expressed in stone. The thing about Dresden is that the stones remind its citizens of times they would like to forget. The Third Reich is but a ghostly nightmare, but the dictatorship from Ulbricht to Honecker is still visible in every jerry-built housing project and concrete workers' canteen. You cannot blame people for feeling a deep nostalgia for the old Dresden of palaces and spires. As Griebel said, "we live in the rump of a city, which we'd dearly love to restore."

I paid a last visit to the ruins of the Frauenkirche, to make a note of the memorial plaque. But I found that it had gone. Instead, there was a fence around the rubble. A man in a blue uniform was giving orders to some workmen. I climbed over the fence to get a closer look. The uniformed man, a stocky little figure, spotted me and rushed over in great strides, flushed with anger, and shouted in a thick Saxon accent that I had no business being there: it was *streng verboten*! How typically German, I thought, as every childhood prejudice flooded back in an instant. But I obeyed his orders and retreated across the fence, away from the man, who was still sputtering with rage. I took one more look at the workmen, who were piling stone upon stone. In a year or two, the Frauenkirche would be there again, fully restored in its old glory, as though nothing had happened at all.

[. . .]

If *The Tin Drum* is the world's most famous fictional chronicle of World War II, then its main character, Oskar Matzerath, the boy who stopped growing when he was three, is the war's most famous literary witness. Oskar Matzerath, with his tin drum and his glass-shattering voice, is the ideal memorialist. He has the magical wonder of a precocious child. Nothing, however embarrassing to adults, escapes his gaze. And the beat of his drum bears witness to the horrors he has seen. At the same time, Oskar embodies adult fears and longings, above all the longing for shelter in the dark, warm, womblike world under the voluminous skirts of his grandmother, Anna Bronski, sitting at the edge of a potato field in Kashubia. There, under the "wide skirt," the child is in a world where there is nothing yet to remember, and the adult can forget that anything ever happened.

[. . .]

After the war, Oskar Matzerath and his friend Klepp start a jazz band. Their tour of West Germany takes them to Düsseldorf, or, to be exact, the stretch of the Rhine between Düsseldorf and Kaiserswerth, where they play ragtime music on the riverbank. The time is 1949, one year after the currency reform which saw the birth of the Deutsche Mark. They are asked to play at an expensive, "high-class" nightclub called the Onion Cellar. It is done up in a fake old German style, with bull's-eye windowpanes, and an enamel sign outside, hanging from wrought-iron gallows. When the club is full, the main entertainment begins. The guests are handed little chopping boards with paring knives and an onion. And what does the onion do? "It did what the world and the sorrows of the world could not do: it brought forth a round human tear. It made them cry. At last they were able to cry again. To cry properly, without restraint, to cry like mad."

The Onion Cellar is, of course, an expensive and temporary cure for the "inability to mourn," the moral and spiritual numbness that overcame the German people after the war. Many thoughtful Germans I have met are irritated by this phrase: inability to mourn. Mourn what? they ask. Mourn whom? You mourn loved ones you have lost. But, say my liberal German friends, how can you mourn for the victims you have murdered? Reflection, yes; apology, certainly; compensation, of course; but mourning, surely not. And so, in liberal, thoughtful circles (the circles expected to welcome nosy foreigners in their midst) there has been—still is—much reflection and apology. But the mourning of the German dead—the soldiers, and the civilians killed by Allied bombs, or by vengeful Polish, Czech, or Slovak neighbors, who drove them from their homes—such mourning was an embarrassing affair, left largely to right-wing nationalists and nostalgic survivors, pining for their lost homelands.

In village squares and churchyards in the western half of Germany there are many memorials to the war dead of World War I. There are very few reminders of those who died in the second war, except in the rancid cellars of provincial beer halls, where foreigners are less than welcome. In fact, there appear to be more World War II memorials in the East, perhaps because guilt was never an issue in the Democratic Republic.

Helmut Kohl tried to redress the balance, clumsily, tactlessly, by dragging Ronald Reagan to the cemetery in Bitburg. He was rightly condemned. But traveling through Germany, I often felt that too much apology could become a form of self-abasement. Mourning, after all, has its purpose. The ritual expression of grief and loss strengthens the sense of continuity and community. Yet it was precisely these things that thoughtful, liberal Germans were wary of: the national community, the *Gemeinschaft*, had been twisted into murderous racism, and cultural continuity had become a delicate matter in a nation whose history was smeared with blood.

I also detected, during my year in Berlin, in 1991 and 1992, an interesting generational shift in German philosemitism. Guilt was at least a partial explanation for the Israeli calendars one saw on the walls of Germans who lived through the war. But what were those young German Gentiles doing in the new "Jewish" cafés that sprang up around the façade of the old synagogue in East Berlin? Why did some young Germans go so far as to adopt the Jewish family names of their grandfathers or great-uncles? Wasn't there something odd about the way almost any Central European Jewish writer was showered with literary prizes? Residual or inherited feelings of guilt might have had something to do with this, but I believe there was something else at work: nostalgia for a culture that is lost to Germany, an attempt to identify with a past that was erased: in short, a gesture of mourning.

Marlene Dietrich was not Jewish, but she belonged to the ruined world of Jewish Berlin. The mourners who filed past her grave, after her modest burial in Berlin, were almost all under forty. This stood in contrast to the small-minded refusal of the city authorities to give her an official funeral. Dietrich, whom some Germans never forgave for wearing an American uniform when German cities were bombed, represented another Germany, with which those young mourners wished to identify.

The supposed lack of identity, of community feeling, was a cause of much soul-searching in the Federal Republic—the problem, it seemed, was that there was no more soul to search. Which is why some romantics, of both the right and the left, looked toward the eastern half of Germany as the repository of German identity. But, to me, it was the suspicion of historical mythmaking and national romanticism that made the Federal Republic intellectually bracing. I like the idea of "constitutional patriotism." Maybe it isn't enough. Perhaps more is needed to transform a once dangerous nation. But I found it hard to share the playwright Arthur Miller's worries, expressed during Germany's unification, that Germans lacked "very transcendent feelings toward the Federal Republic" and that "it does not seem to have imbued them with sublime sensations, even among those who regard it as a triumph of German civic consciousness risen from the ruins of war." Surely, Germans have had enough sublime sensations during the last hundred years. Miller was anxious that Germans might not defend their democracy in a crisis, because "it came to life without one drop of blood being shed in its birth" and it was invented by foreigners.

There will always be Germans (and their counterparts elsewhere) who would wish, in the words of a long-forgotten Nazi ideologue, to "select the stones from the ruins of German mythology, to serve, after cleaning and polishing, as the building blocks of a new German shrine [and] to build a new German *Weltanschauung* from the remains of fallen walls." But I believe there have been enough German shrines already. Let the ruins be.

Günter Grass was not the only one to worry about German unification. Most liberal anxieties on this score were the exact opposite of the worry that West Germany lacked a soul. Unification, many warned, would revive German nationalism; the brakes were off, the dangerous German people would start to shift their bulk. There was no immediate evidence of this, however. I was in Frankfurt on the night of unification, and apart from the odd firecracker popping off in the cold sky, I saw no sign of nationalist rejoicing. Comedians in a fashionable nightclub cracked feeble jokes about sacred Deutsche Marks and banana democracy. But most people stayed home, in front of the television, a night like any other. I had seen more popular enthusiasm when the German soccer team won the world cup the year before.

Then came the neo-Nazis, the shaven-headed youths screaming "*Sieg Heil!*" and waving the old battle flags. They were nasty and brutal and murderous. In 1992 there were 4,587 attacks on foreigners. Seventeen people were killed. The year before, 7,780 racist attacks were reported in Britain, but the swastikas, the slogans, the *Sieg Heil*'s, made historical comparisons in Germany irresistible. There was a hint of *Schadenfreude* in European press reports of racist German youth crimes. It was Us and Them again.

I spent one day in Halle, a broken-down East German town, waiting to see a parade of neo-Nazis. It was November 9, the anniversary of the *Kristallnacht*, as well as of the fall of the Berlin Wall. The people of Halle were terrified. The police had blocked off every main street. An old man in the main square shouted at the mayor that it was just like Hitler's time all over again. The owner of a café locked his door after letting me in and proudly showed his gun. And finally, there they were, the neo-Nazis, the young men with heads shaved on back and sides and the young women in white socks, with their long blond hair in plaits, the look of the Hitler Maidens. They were spoken to by a pudgy figure with a Viennese accent and by the British historian David Irving. The old trams of prewar design screeched on their rusty rails. Fat men in undershirts leaned from their windows and the abolished couplet of the *Deutschlandlied* ("From the Maas up to the Memel, from the Bug up to the Belt, *Deutschland, Deutschland über alles . . .*") filled the air. It was unpleasant and utterly ludicrous—violent children dressed up in their grandparents' clothes, history repeating itself as Grand Guignol.

But it wasn't all theater. The behavior of the extremists—who, a year later, went on to burn down refugee hostels in West and East Germany, killing people, as the police stood helplessly by—proved that Germans were still capable of barbarous deeds. It was a revolting spectacle to see screaming German youths smash their boots into the faces of helpless foreigners, as the neighbors cheered and jeered. But similar or worse events in the rest of Europe—not to speak of other continents—proved that nationality, race, and culture are inadequate explanations for barbarousness. People are dangerous everywhere, when leaders acquire unlimited power and followers are given license to bully others weaker than themselves. Unbridled power leads to barbarousness, in individuals and in mobs. Auschwitz and Nanking, despite the differences in scale and style, will always stand as proof of that. But such is not the situation in the German Federal Republic, or indeed in Japan, today. Human nature has not changed, but politics have. In both countries, the rascals can be voted out. Those who choose to ignore that, and look instead for national marks of Cain, have learned nothing from the past.

PAUL MULDOON

FROM

The Annals of Chile

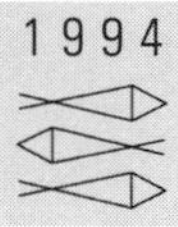

MILKWEED AND MONARCH

As he knelt by the grave of his mother and father
the taste of dill, or tarragon—
he could barely tell one from the other—

filled his mouth. It seemed as if he might smother.
Why should he be stricken
with grief, not for his mother and father,

but a woman slinking from the fur of a sea-otter
in Portland, Maine, or, yes, Portland, Oregon—
he could barely tell one from the other—

and why should he now savour
the tang of her, her little pickled gherkin,
as he knelt by the grave of his mother and father?

He looked about. He remembered her palaver
on how both earth and sky would darken—
'You could barely tell one from the other'—

while the Monarch butterflies passed over
in their milkweed-hunger: 'A wing-beat, some reckon,
may trigger off the mother and father

of all storms, striking your Irish Cliffs of Moher
with the force of a hurricane.'
Then: 'Milkweed and Monarch "invented" each other.'

He looked about. Cow's-parsley in a samovar.
He'd mistaken his mother's name, 'Regan', for 'Anger':
as he knelt by the grave of his mother and father
he could barely tell one from the other.

FROM

And the Stars Were Shining

1994

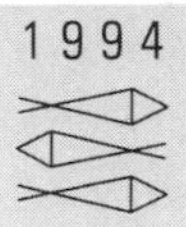

MYRTLE

How funny your name would be
if you could follow it back to where
the first person thought of saying it,
naming himself that, or maybe
some other persons thought of it
and named that person. It would
be like following a river to its source,
which would be impossible. Rivers have no source.
They just automatically appear at a place
where they get wider, and soon a real
river comes along, with fish and debris,
regal as you please, and someone
has already given it a name: St. Benno
(saints are popular for this purpose) or, or
some other name, the name of his
long-lost girlfriend, who comes
at long last to impersonate that river,
on a stage, her voice clanking
like its bed, her clothing of sand
and pasted paper, a piece of real technology,
while all along she is thinking, I can
do what I want to do. But I want to stay here.

PETER HANDKE

FROM

The Jukebox

AND OTHER ESSAYS ON STORYTELLING

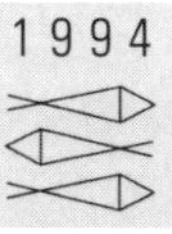

FROM

ESSAY ON THE SUCCESSFUL DAY

[*Translated by Ralph Manheim*]

A self-portrait by William Hogarth, an eighteenth-century moment, showing a palette divided approximately in the middle by a gently curving line, the so-called Line of Beauty and Grace. And on my desk a flat, rounded stone found on the shore of Lake Constance, dark granite, traversed diagonally by a vein of chalky white, with a subtle, almost playful bend, deviating from the straight line at exactly the right moment and dividing the stone into two halves, while at the same time holding it together. And that trip in a suburban train through the hills to the west of Paris, at the afternoon hour when as a rule the fresh air and clean light of certain early-morning departures are vitiated, when nothing is natural any longer and it seems likely that only the coming of darkness can bring relief from the closeness of the day, then suddenly the tracks swing out in a wide arc, strangely, breathtakingly high above the city, which unexpectedly, along with the crazy reality of its enigmatic structures, opens out into the fluvial plain—there on the heights of Saint-Cloud or Suresnes, with that unforeseen curve, an instant transition changed the course of my day, and my almost abandoned idea of a "successful day" was back again, accompanied by a heartwarming impulse to describe, list, or discuss the elements of such a day and the problems it raises. The Line of Beauty and Grace on Hogarth's palette seems literally to force its way through the formless masses of paint, seems to cut between them and yet to cast a shadow.

Who has ever experienced a successful day? Most people will say without thinking that they have. But then it will be necessary to ask: Do you mean "successful" or only "happy"? Are you thinking of a successful day or only of a "carefree" one, which admittedly is just as unusual. If a day goes by without confronting you with problems, does that, in your opinion, suffice to make it a successful day? Do you see a distinction between a happy day and a successful one? Is it essentially different to speak of some successful day in the past, with the help of memory, and right now after the day, which no intervening time has transfigured, to say not that a day has been "dealt with" or "got out of the way," but that it has been "successful"? To your mind, is a successful day basically different from a carefree or happy day, from a full or busy day, a day struggled through, or a day transfigured by the distant past—one particular suffices, and a whole day rises up in glory—perhaps even some Great Day for Science, your country, our people, the peoples of the earth, mankind? (And that reminds me: Look—look up—the outline of that bird up there in the tree; translated literally, the Greek verb for "read," used in the Pauline epistles, would signify a "looking up," even a "perceiving *upward*" or "recognizing *upward*," a verb without special imperative form, but in itself a summons, an appeal; and then those hummingbirds in the jungles of South America, which in leaving their sheltering tree imitate the wavering of a falling leaf to mislead the hawk . . .)—Yes, to me a successful day is not the same as any other; it *means* more. A successful day is more. It is more than a "successful remark," more than a "successful chess move" (or even a whole successful game), more than a "successful first winter ascent," than a "successful flight," a "successful operation," a "successful relationship," or any "successful piece of business"; it is independent of a successful brushstroke or sentence, nor should it be confused with some "poem, which after a lifetime of waiting achieved success in a single hour." The successful day is incomparable. It is unique.

[. . .]

Have you ever experienced a successful day? Everyone I know has experienced one; most people have actually had many. One was satisfied if the day hadn't been too long. Another said something like: "Standing on the bridge, with the sky over me. In the morning, laughed with the children. Just looking, nothing special. There's happiness in looking." And in the opinion of a third, simply the village street through which he had just passed—with the raindrops dripping from the enormous key of the locksmith's sign, with the bamboo shoots cooking in somebody's front garden, with the three bowls on a kitchen windowsill containing tangerines, grapes, and peeled potatoes, with the taxi parked as usual outside the driver's house—was in itself a "successful day." The priest, whose pet word was "longing," considered a day when he heard a friendly voice successful. And hadn't he himself, who longed time and again for an hour in which nothing had happened, except that a bird turned about on a branch, that a white ball lay at the bottom of a bush, and that schoolchildren were sunning themselves on the station platform, thought in spite of himself: Has this been the whole day? And often in the evening, when he called the events of the past day to mind—yes, it was a kind of "calling"—didn't the things or places of a mere moment occur to him as names for it. "That was the day when the man with the baby carriage went zigzagging through the piles of leaves." "That was the day when the gardener's banknotes were mixed with grass and leaves." "That was the day when the café was empty when the refrigerator rumbled and the light went out . . ." So why not content ourselves with a single successful hour? Why not simply call the moment a day?

Ungaretti's poem "I illuminate myself with the immeasurable" is entitled "Morning." Couldn't those two lines just as well be about the "afternoon"? Were a fulfilled moment or a fulfilled hour really enough to make you stop asking if you had failed again that day? No use attempting a successful day—why not content ourselves with a "not entirely unsuccessful one"? And if your successful day existed, wasn't your fantasy, however richly and wonderfully it whirred, accompanied by a strange fear of something like an alien planet, and didn't your usual unsuccessful day appear to you as part of the planet earth, as a kind of—possibly detested—home? As though nothing here below could succeed; except perhaps in grace? in mercy? in grace *and* mercy—if nowadays that didn't imply something improper, undeserved, perhaps even accomplished at someone else's expense? Why now does "successful day" remind me of my dead grandfather, who in his last days did nothing but scratch the wall of his room with his fingernails, lower down from hour to hour. In view of all the general failure and loss, what does a single success amount to?

Not nothing.

The day of which I can say it was "a day," and the day when I was only passing the time. At the crack of dawn. How have people handled their days up to now? How is it that in old stories we often find "Many days were fulfilled," in place of "Many days passed"? Traitor to the day: my own heart. It drives me out of the day, it beats, it hammers me out of it, hunter and hunted in one. Be still! No more secret thoughts. Leaves in my garden shoes. Out of the cage of revolving thought. Be still. Bend down under the apple tree. Go into a crouch. The crouching reader. At knee height, things coalesce to form an environment. And he prepares for the daily injury. Spreads his toes. "The seven days of the garden." That's what the unwritten sequel to *Don Quixote* should be called. To be in the garden, to be on earth. The rate of the earth's rotation is irregular, that's why the days are of unequal length, especially in view of the mountain ranges' resistance to the wind. The success of the day and passivity. Passivity as action. He let the fog drift outside the window; he let the grass blow behind the house. Letting the sun shine on one was an activity; now I'm going to let my forehead be warmed, now my eyeballs, now my knees—and now it's time for teddy-bear warmth between my shoulder blades. The sunflower head does nothing but follow the sun. Compare the successful day with Job's day. Instead of "value the moment," it should be "heed" the moment. The course of the day—thanks precisely to its rough spots, if taken to heart—is in itself a kind of transubstantiation—more than anything else, it can tell me *what I am*. Pause in your endless restlessness, and you will find rest in your flight. And by resting in his flight, he began to hear. Hearing, I am at my peak. Thanks to my keen hearing, I can hear the whirring of a sparrow's wing through the noise. When a leaf falls on the line of the distant horizon, I hear it deep inside me as a ringing. Listening as a safecracker with his jimmy listens for the clicking of the gears. Slowed by flight, the blackbird's hop-skip-jump over the hedge is humming a tune for me. Just as some people hum when reading a book. (But the most you can expect of a newspaper reader is a whistling between the teeth.) "Seeing you are dull of hearing," stormed the zealot in one of his epistles, and in another: "Stop disputing over mere words, it does no good and only bedevils those who listen." A pure tone. If only I could produce a pure tone once for a whole day. Perhaps more important than hearing is pure presence—Picasso's last wife, for example, is said to have done nothing, just to have been present in his studio. A successful day, a hard day. Suddenly, as I was raking the garden leaves, a rooster's foot gleamed candlelight yellow from out of the pile of brownish leaves. Colors darken, form brightens. In the shady corner, where the ground is still frozen hard, my footsteps sound as they did that day in the rushes. When I look up, the sky is a vault. What did "snow cloud" mean? Rich whiteness with a blue cast. Cracking hazelnuts in the palm of my hand, three of them. In Greek there used to be a word for "I am," which was simply a long-drawn-out "O"; it occurred in such sentences as "While I am in the world, I am the light of the world." And the word for what just passed through the cypress tree was: "lightwave." Look and keep looking with the eyes of the right word. And it began to snow. It is snowing. Il neige. To be silent. There was silence. He was silent in the sign of the dead. One should not say: "He (she) blessed the temporal world" (He [she] passed away) but: "He, she, the dead, bless the temporal world for me, provided I leave them alone." And at the same time wanting to stammer: he wanted to stammer. In the suburbs everything is supposedly so "individual" (a suburbanite speaking). The one-legged stance of the garbage collector at the back of his truck. The bumps placed on the roads at regular intervals were called "decelerators." A single day may not have been sufficiently far-reaching as a model; perhaps it was a model only to itself—which gave pleasure? During the lunch break I help the roofers carry slats down from the ridge. Shouldn't I have stayed home all day, doing nothing but "dwelling"? Bring about a successful day by pure dwelling? To dwell, to sit, to look up, to excel in uselessness. What did you do today? I heard. What did you hear? Oh, the house. Ah, beneath the tent of my book. But why are you going out now, instead of staying in the house, where you were in your place with your book? Because what I've read—I want to digest it out of doors. And look at the corner of the house, which is called "Travels": a small suitcase, a dictionary, hiking shoes. The ringing of bells in the belfry of the village church: the pitch is just right for this noon hour, and up here in the dark dormer window all that can be seen of them is a whirring as of bicycle spokes. Deep within the earth, there are occasional tremors, the so-called slow tremors, and for a while, so it is said, the planet reverberates with them: "the bell movement," the ringing of the earth. The silhouettes of a man and a child with a back satchel sway in the railroad underpass, as if the man were riding on a donkey. According to Goethe, life is short but the day is long, and I seem to remember Marilyn Monroe singing a song that went: "One day too long, one life too short . . ." and another: "Morning becomes evening under my body." Let the quick ellipse described by the last of the leaves of the plane tree in falling provide the line for the ending of my attempted successful day—Abbreviation! Hogarth's Line of Beauty is not actually engraved in the palette; it is stretched over it like a curved rope or a whiplash. The successful day and succinctness. (And, alongside it, the desire to postpone the end—as though I, I in particular, could learn more from my essay with each passing day.) The successful day and joyful expectation. The successful day and the discoverer's aberrations. Morning a still life—afternoon a muddle: a mere pseudolaw? Don't let yourself be ruled by these daily pseudolaws. And once again St. Paul. For him "the day" is the Day of Judgment—and for you? The day of measurement; it will not judge, but measure you; you are its people. Who here is talking to whom? I'm talking to myself. The dead silence of the afternoon. Nevertheless, the sound of children running, heard through the wind. And high up there the flower heads of the plane trees are still dangling: "his (her) heart is in it" (from the French). And at any moment, in the rustling of the withered dwarf oaks, now, for instance, I become you. What would we be without that rustling? And what word goes with it? The (toneless) yes. Stay with us, rustling. Keep pace with the day—speak in cadence with the day (homology). What became of that day on the curve high above all Paris, between Saint-Cloud and Suresnes, not far from the Val d'Or station. It hung in the balance. The bright-dark shimmer that day when the swallows veered in the summer sky, and the black-white-blue moment now: the magpies and the winter sky. The S-line again, a few days ago, on the shoulder, neck, and throat of John the Evangelist at the Last Supper over the portal of Saint-Germain-des-Près, his whole trunk lies there on the table next to the Lord Jesus—for, like the other stone figures, he had been beheaded by the Revolution. The successful day and again history's glorious forgetfulness: instead, the endless lozenge pattern of human eyes—on the streets, in the corridors of the Métro, in the trains. The gray of the asphalt, the blue of the evening sky. The shakiness of my day, the solid and enduring? Set your footprint upon the snow of the station platform beside the print of a bird's foot. A hard day once began to teeter when a single raindrop struck my inner ear. The shoe brush on the wooden stairs at sunset. A child writing its name for the first time. Keep going until the first star. Van Morrison in his song doesn't sing about "fishing in the mountains," but "out all day," about bird watching. He lets his tongue sing, and barely begun, his song is at an end. The moment of the mud-spattered forester's car in the row of clean cars. The doors of the forest open with a creak. Revolving door of a successful day: in it, things as well as people flare up as *beings*. The successful day and the will to divide it. Constant, wild obligation to be fair. Oh, hard day! Successful? Or "saved"? Unexpectedly, still in the dark, the thrust of joy in carrying on. Yes, a modified word—a proof correction that stands for the day: "thrust" instead of your usual "jolt." Stop on your night walk: the path is brightening—for once you can say "my path"—and increasing awareness of secrecy, "behold, she comes with the clouds," comes with the wind. Triad of the screech owl. Blue moment of the boat in one woodland pond, black moment of the boat in the next pond. For the first time in this suburb, behind the Heights of the Seine that hide the lights of Paris, caught sight of Orion high in the winter night, behind it parallel columns of smoke from factory chimneys, and under it the five stone steps, leading up to a door in a wall, and Ingrid Bergman in *Stromboli*, who collapses after an almost fatal night on the black, rocky slopes of the volcano, revives at sunrise, and can't get over her amazement. "How beautiful! What beauty!" In the 171 night bus a lone passenger, standing. The burned-out telephone booth. Collision between two cars at the Pointe de Chaville: from one of them leaps a man with a pistol. Glaring television lights in the front windows of the Avenue Roger Salengro, the house numbers on which go up to over 2000. The thunder of the bombers taking off from the military airfield in Villacoublay, just beyond the wooded hills, more frequently from day to day with the approach of war.

"But now you're losing the line completely. Go home to your book, to writing and reading. To the original texts, in which for example it is said: 'Let the word resound, stand by it—whether the moment be favorable or not.' Have you ever experienced a successful day? With which for once a successful moment, a successful life, perhaps even a successful eternity might coincide?"

"Not yet. Obviously!"

"Obviously"?

"If I had experienced anything even remotely resembling that, I imagine, I should have to fear not only a nightmare for the following night but the cold sweats."

"Then your successful day is not even an idea, but only a dream?"

"Yes, except that instead of *having* it, I've *made* it in this essay. Look at my eraser, so black and small, look at the pile of pencil shavings below my window. Phrases and more phrases in the void, to no good purpose, addressed to a third incomprehensible something, though the two of us are not lost. Time and again in his epistles, not to the congregations, but to individuals, his helpers, Paul, from his prison in Rome, wrote about winter. For example, 'Do try to get here before winter. And when you come, bring the cloak I left with Carpus at Troas . . .' "

"And where is the cloak now? Forget the dream. See how the snow falls past the empty bird's nest. Arise to transubstantiation."

"To the next dream?"

CHARLES WRIGHT

FROM

Chickamauga

1995

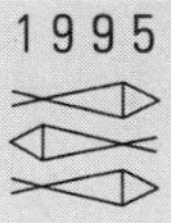

PAESAGGIO NOTTURNO

Full moon, the eighth of March; clouds
Cull and disperse; dog's bark, moon
Tracking stage left to stage right;
Maple ganglia, Munch sky.

Small night that pulls me inside,
Fingerless, fatherless; night
Crystalline, sleep-shaped and sharp,
The bulb tufts odd teeth; nightmouth.

All things are found in all things,
Wind in the peach trees, time's dust:
It's in light that light exists.
All flesh, at last, comes to you.

FROM

The Autobiography of My Mother

1996

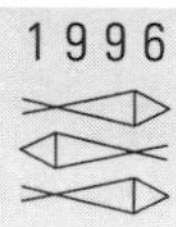

What makes the world turn?

Who would need an answer to such a question?

A man proud of the pale hue of his skin cherishes it especially because it is not a fulfillment of any aspiration, it is his not through any effort at all on his part; he was just born that way, he was blessed and chosen to be that way and it gives him a special privilege in the hierarchy of everything. This man sits on a plateau, not the level ground, and all he can see—fertile meadows, vast plains, high mountains with treasure buried deep within, turbulent seas, calm oceans—all this he knows with an iron certainty should be his own. What makes the world turn is a question he asks when all that he can see is securely in his grasp, so securely in his grasp that he can cease to look at it from time to time, he can denounce it, he can demand that it be taken away from him, he can curse the moment he was conceived and the day he was born, he can go to sleep at night and in the morning he will wake up and all he can see is still securely in his grasp; and he can ask again, What makes the world turn, and then he will have an answer and it will take up volumes and there are many answers, each of them different, and there are many men, each of them the same.

And what do I ask? What is the question I can ask? I own nothing, I am not a man.

I ask, What makes the world turn against me and all who look like me? I own nothing, I survey nothing, when I ask this question; the luxury of an answer that will fill volumes does not stretch out before me. When I ask this question, my voice is filled with despair.

There are seven days in a week, and why, I do not know. If I were to find myself in need of such things, days and weeks and months and years, it is not clear to me that I would arrange them the way I now find them. But all the same, here they are.

It was a Sunday in Roseau; the streets were disturbing, half-empty, quiet, clean; the water in the harbor was still, as if it were in a bottle, the houses were without the usual quarrelsome voices, the sky was a blue that was at once overwhelming and ordinary. The population of Roseau, that is, the ones who looked like me, had long ago been reduced to shadows; the forever foreign, the margins, had long ago lost any connection to wholeness, to an inner life of our own invention, and since it was a Sunday, some of them now were walking in a trance, no longer in their right minds, toward a church or away from a church. This activity—going to church, coming from church—had about it the atmosphere of a decree. It also signified defeat yet again, for what would the outcome have been of all the lives of the conquered if they had not come to believe in the gods of the people who had conquered them? I walked by a church. The church itself, a small beautiful structure, was meant to imitate in its simplicity and unworldliness a similar structure in a tiny village in some dark corner of England. But this church, typical of its time and place in every way, was built, inch by inch, by enslaved people, and many of the people who were slaves died while building this church, and their masters then had them buried in such a way that when the Day of Judgment came and all the dead were risen, the enslaved faces would not be turned toward the eternal light of heaven but toward the eternal darkness of hell. They, the slaves, were buried with their faces turned away from the east. But did the slaves have an interest in seeing eternal light in the first place, and what if the slaves preferred eternal darkness? The pitiful thing is, an answer to these questions is no longer of use to anybody.

And so again, what makes the world turn? Most of the people inside that church would want to know. They were singing a hymn. The words were: "O Jesus I have promised,/To serve Thee to the end;/Be Thou forever near me,/My Master and my Friend." I wanted to knock on the church door then. I wanted to say, Let me in, let me in. I wanted to say, Let me tell you something: This Master and Friend business, it is not possible; a master is one thing and a friend is something else altogether, something completely different; a master cannot be a friend. And who would want such a thing, master and friend at once? A man would want that. It is a man who would ask, What makes the world turn, and then would find in his own reply fields of gravity, imaginary lines, tilts and axes, reason and logic, and, quite brazenly, a theory of justice. And when he is done with that, he will say, yes, but what really makes the world turn? and his mouth, grim with scorn for himself, will say the words: Connive, deceive, murder.

This man is not completely ignorant of the people inside the church, or those same people inside their small houses. His name is

John or William, or something like that; he has a wife, her name is Jane or Charlotte, or something like that; he shoots plovers, he eats their eggs. His life is simple, he shuns excess because he wants to; or his life is an elaborate web of events, rituals, ceremonies because he wants it so. He is not ignorant of the many people in his thrall, this man; sometimes he likes the condition they are in and he would even die to keep them in it; sometimes he does not like the condition they are in and he would even die to remove them from it. He is not ignorant of them, he is not ignorant of them completely. They plant a field, they harvest its yield; he calculates with his sharp eye the fruits of their labor, which are tied up uniformly in bundles and lying on docks waiting to be shipped. This man makes a profit, sometimes larger than he expected, sometimes less than he expected. It is with this profit that the reality these many people represent is kept secret. For this man who says "My Master and my Friend" builds a large house, warms the rooms, sits in a chair made from a fabric that is very valuable because its origins are distant, obscure, and involves again the forced labor, the crippling, the early death of the unnamed many; sitting in this chair, he looks out a window; his forehead, his nose, his thin lips press against the glass; it is winter (something I will never see, a climate I will never know, and since I do not know it and since it holds nothing that is beautiful to me, I regard it with suspicion; I look down on people who are familiar with it but I, Xuela, am not in a position to do more than that). The grass is alive but not actively growing (dormant), the trees are alive but not actively growing (dormant); the hedge, its severely clipped shape a small monument to misery, separates two fields; the sun shines, but the light is pale and weak as if a great effort is being made. He is not looking at a graveyard; he is looking at a small part of all that he possesses, and the irregular mounds, gravelike in shape, caused by the earth first hardening then softening then hardening again, already holding his ancestors and their deeds, have ample room for him and all that he will do and for all who come from him and all that they will do. His forehead, his nose, his thin lips are pressed ever harder against the window; in his mind the still earth becomes a blue sea, a gray ocean, and on the blue sea and on the gray ocean are ships, and the ships are filled with people, and the ships filled with people sink to the bottom of the blue sea and the gray ocean again and again. The blue sea and the gray ocean are also a small part of all he possesses, and they, with their surfaces smooth and tranquil, are a sign of covenants made, inviolable promises, but even so, the irregular mounds, gravelike in shape, appear, small swell swallowing up small swell, hiding a depth whose measure can be taken but the knowledge of it cannot overcome the fear. The impartiality of the dormant field outside his window is well known to him; it will accept a creature he finds a pest, it will accept his most revered ancestor, it will accept him; but the dormant field is carved up and it is spring (I am not familiar with this, I cannot find any joy in this, I think people associated with it are less than I am but I, Xuela, am not in a position to make my feeling have any meaning) and the field can be made to do something he wants it to do. The impartiality of the blue sea, the gray ocean, is well known to him also, but these cold, vast vaults of water cannot be carved up and no season can influence them in his favor; the blue sea, the gray ocean, will take him along with all that represents his earthly happiness (the ship full of people) and all that represents his unhappiness (the ship full of people).

It is an afternoon in winter, the sky above him is a blue that is at once overwhelming and ordinary, there is a moon of pure white and not quite full in the middle of it. He is afraid. His name is John, he is the master of the people in the ship that sails on the blue sea, the gray ocean, but he is not master of the sea or the ocean itself. In his position as master, his needs are clear and paramount and so he is without mercy, he is without compassion, he is without tenderness. In his position as a Man, unclothed, unfed, as a testament to ordinariness without his house with the warmed rooms, he meets the same fate as all he used to be master of; the ground outside his window will take him in; so will the blue sea, so will the gray ocean. And so it is that at the moment he finds himself in this position, the position of a man, an ordinary man, he asks that master be friend, he asks for himself the very thing that he cannot give; he asks and he asks, even though he knows such a thing is not possible; *such a thing is not possible,* but he cannot help himself, for always the first person you feel sorry for is your own self. And it is this person, this man, who says at a moment he needs to, God does not judge; and when he is saying this, God does not judge, he places himself in a childlike pose; his knees are crossed, his hands are clasped around them, and he will repeat to himself a parable, The Sower and the Wheat, and he gives it an interpretation favorable to himself: God's love shines equally on all the wheat wherever it may grow, between the rocks, on shallow ground, on good soil.

This short, bitter sermonette that I delivered to myself was not new to me. There was hardly a day of my life that I did not observe some incident to add fresh weight to this view, for to me history was not a large stage filled with commemoration, bands, cheers, ribbons, medals, the sound of fine glass clinking and raised high in the air; in other words, the sounds of victory. For me history was not only the past: it was the past and it was also the present. I did not mind my defeat, I only minded that it had to last so long; I did not see the future, and that is perhaps as it should be. Why should anyone see such a thing; that is beyond presumption, that has the mark of uncalled-for vanity. And yet . . . and yet, it made me sad to know that I did not look straight ahead of me, I always looked back, sometimes I looked to the side, but mostly I looked back.

The church outside which I stood on that Sunday was very familiar to me, I had been baptized in it; my father had become such an outstanding member of it that he was now allowed to read the lesson during Sunday-morning service. As if obeying my summons, the congregation erupted from the church, and among them were my father, who no longer bore so much as a trace of the treachery he had committed by joining such a group of people, and Philip, the man I worked for but did not hate and who at the same time was a man I slept with but did not love and whom I would eventually marry but still not love. They were, this congregation, just then in a state of deep satisfaction, though they were not all in identical states of deep satisfaction; my father was less satisfied than Philip, his position in the group less secure, his complexion a problem, not because it was dark (it was not very dark), but because in church, a place where they tried to forget who they really were and what they had really done, my father, just by his presence alone, was a reminder that they lived and breathed criminality. But my father was an incredible mimic and knew well how to make an ordinary person miserable and how to turn the merely miserable person into the person who cries out in the middle of the night, "What makes the world turn against me?" with a wail of anguish so familiar to the night itself, yet so strange to the person from whose being these words have made an involuntary escape. Just a glance in the distance would have provided a substantial example; at the far end of the cemetery, which abutted the churchyard, stood a man named Lazarus and he was making a hole in the ground, he was making a grave; the person to be buried in this grave so far away from the church would be a poor person, perhaps one of the merely miserable. I knew of Lazarus—his name would have been given to him in a moment of innocent hope; his mother would have thought that such a name, rich and powerful as it was with divine second chance, would somehow protect him from the living death that was his actual life; but it had been of no use, he was born the Dead and he would die the Dead. He was one of the many people with whom my father maintained a parasitic existence (even as the people my father went to church with maintained a parasitic existence with my father), and I knew of him because my mother was buried in this graveyard (I could not see it now from where I stood), and once when I was visiting her grave I came upon him face to face in the graveyard, carrying a bottle (pint size) of white rum in one hand and holding up the waist of his trousers with the other; an insect kept trying to feed from a small pool of saliva that had settled at the corner of his mouth, and he at first used the hand that held the bottle of rum to brush it away, but the insect persisted, and so, instinctively, without calculation, he let go of his pants waist and firmly brushed the insect away. The insect did go away, the insect did not return, but his trousers fell down to his ankles, and again instinctively, without calculation, he reached down to pull them back up and he became as he was before, a poor man driven out of his mind by a set of events that the guilty and the tired and the hopeless call life. He looked like an overworked beast, he looked like a living carcass; the bones in his body were too prominent, they were too close to his skin, he smelled sour, he smelled stink, he smelled like something rotting, when it's in that sweet stage that can sometimes pass for a delicacy, just before real decay sets in; before his trousers met his waist again, I saw the only alive thing left of him; it was his pubic hair: it covered a large area of his crotch, growing in a wide circle, almost hiding all his private parts; its color was red, the red of a gift or the red of something burning rapidly. This brief meeting of a grave-digger and myself had no beginning and so it could have no end; there was only a "Good day" from me and an "Eh-eh" from him, and these things were said at exactly the same time, so that he did not really hear what I said and I did not really hear what he said, and that was the point. The idea of him and me really hearing each other was out of the question; from the pain of it, we might have murdered ourselves or put in motion a chain of events that would have come to an end only with our hanging from the gallows at midday in a public square. He disappeared inside the Dead House, where he kept the tools of his trade: shovels, ladders, ropes.

The congregation stood on the church steps, basking in the heat, now strong, as if they knew with certainty that it held blessings, though only for them; they spoke to one another, they listened to one another, they smiled at one another; it was a pretty picture they made, like ants from the same nest; it was a pretty picture, for Lazarus was left out of it, I was left out of it. They bade each other goodbye and returned to their homes, where they would drink a cup of English tea, even though they were quite aware that no such thing as a tea tree grew in England, and later that night, before they went to bed, they would drink a cup of English cocoa, even though they were quite aware that no such thing as a cocoa tree grew in England.

FROM

The Figured Wheel

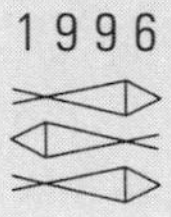

WAKING UP

But what woke just now at fifty-two years in narrow
Dormitory bed, clock on a chair, underpulse
Air-conditioning, damp tangle of dream plumage

Its afterbirth nimbus—night thong and mandible?
Possibly for a few seconds not more professor or
Poet or parent or writing conference pooh-bah

Than animal emigrant from those featherlands—the screen
Of boxes, the alleyway weeping, the black iceberg,
The garden deception, the fuck, the floating

Manhattan. Or naked, possibly for a second this vivid
Green moth smaller than a numeral, distinct, animula,
Alert visionless trembler, blundering in the light.

FARRAR, STRAUS AND GIROUX

BOOKS FOR YOUNG READERS

GEORGE SELDEN

PICTURES BY GARTH WILLIAMS

FROM

The Cricket in Times Square

1960

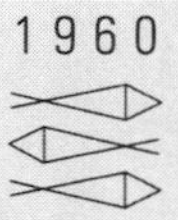

Mario heard the sound too. He stood up and listened intently. The noise of the shuttle rattled off into silence. From the streets above came the quiet murmur of the late traffic. There was a noise of rustling nothingness in the station. Still Mario listened, straining to catch the mysterious sound . . . And there it came again.

It was like a quick stroke across the strings of a violin, or like a harp that has been plucked suddenly. If a leaf in a green forest far from New York had fallen at midnight through the darkness into a thicket, it might have sounded like that.

Mario thought he knew what it was. The summer before he had gone to visit a friend who lived on Long Island. One afternoon, as the low sun reached long yellow fingers through the tall grass, he had stopped beside a meadow to listen to just such a noise. But there had been many of them then—a chorus. Now there was only one. Faintly it came again through the subway station.

Mario slipped out of the newsstand and stood waiting. The next time he heard the sound, he went toward it. It seemed to come from one corner, next to the stairs that led up to Forty-second Street. Softly Mario went toward the spot. For several minutes there was only the whispering silence. Whatever it was that was making the sound had heard him coming and was quiet. Silently Mario waited. Then he heard it again, rising from a pile of waste papers and soot that had blown against the concrete wall.

He went down and very gently began to lift off the papers. One by one he inspected them and laid them to one side. Down near the bottom the papers became dirtier and dirtier. Mario reached the floor. He began to feel with his hands through the dust and soot. And wedged in a crack under all the refuse, he found what he'd been looking for.

It was a little insect, about an inch long and covered with dirt. It

had six legs, two long antennae on its head, and what seemed to be a pair of wings folded on its back. Holding his discovery as carefully as his fingers could, Mario lifted the insect up and rested him in the palm of his hand.

"A cricket!" he exclaimed.

Keeping his cupped hand very steady, Mario walked back to the newsstand. The cricket didn't move. And he didn't make that little musical noise anymore. He just lay perfectly still—as if he were sleeping, or frightened to death.

Mario pulled out a Kleenex and laid the cricket on it. Then he took another and started to dust him off. Ever so softly he tapped the hard black shell, and the antennae, and legs, and wings. Gradually the dirt that had collected on the insect fell away. His true color was still black, but now it had a bright, glossy sheen.

When Mario had cleaned off the cricket as much as he could, he hunted around the floor of the station for a matchbox. In a minute he'd found one and knocked out one end. Then he folded a sheet of Kleenex, tucked it in the box, and put the cricket in. It made a perfect bed. The cricket seemed to like his new home. He moved around a few times and settled himself comfortably.

Mario sat for a time, just looking. He was so happy and excited that when anyone talked through the station, he forgot to shout "Newspapers!" and "Magazines!"

Then a thought occurred to him: perhaps the cricket was hungry. He rummaged through his jacket pocket and found a piece of a chocolate bar that had been left over from supper. Mario broke off one corner and held it out to the cricket on the end of his finger. Cautiously the insect lifted his head to the chocolate. He seemed to smell it a moment, then took a bit. A shiver of pleasure went over Mario as the cricket ate from his hand.

MADELEINE L'ENGLE

FROM

A Wrinkle in Time

1962

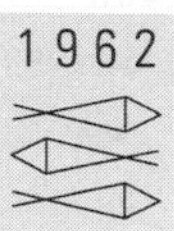

"Meg!" Calvin cried, and he turned around, looking about wildly.

"Mrs Which, you haven't left Meg be*hind*, have you?" Charles Wallace shouted.

"If you've hurt Meg, any of you—" Calvin started, but suddenly Meg felt a violent push and a shattering, as though she had been thrust through a wall of glass.

"Oh, *there* you are!" Charles Wallace said, and rushed over to her and hugged her.

"But *where* am I?" Meg asked breathlessly, relieved to hear that her voice was now coming out of her in more or less a normal way.

She looked around rather wildly. They were standing in a sunlit field, and the air about them was moving with the delicious fragrance that comes only on the rarest of spring days when the sun's touch is gentle and the apple blossoms are just beginning to unfold. She pushed her glasses up on her nose to reassure herself that what she was seeing was real.

They had left the silver glint of a biting autumn evening; and now around them everything was golden with light. The grasses of the field were a tender new green, and scattered about were tiny multicolored flowers. Meg turned slowly to face a mountain reaching so high into the sky that its peak was lost in a crown of puffy white clouds. From the trees at the base of the mountain came a sudden singing of birds. There was an air of such ineffable peace and joy all around her that her heart's wild thumping slowed.

"When shall we three meet again,
In thunder, lightning, or in rain,"

came Mrs Who's voice. Suddenly the three of them were there, Mrs Whatsit with her pink stole askew; Mrs Who with her spectacles gleaming; and Mrs Which still little more than a shimmer. Delicate multi-colored butterflies were fluttering around them, as though in greeting.

Mrs Whatsit and Mrs Who began to giggle, and they giggled until it seemed that, whatever their private joke was, they would fall down with the wild fun of it. The shimmer seemed to be laughing, too. It became vaguely darker and more solid; and then there appeared a figure in a black robe and a black peaked hat, beady eyes, a beaked nose, and long gray hair; one bony claw clutched a broomstick.

"Wwell, jusstt ttoo kkeepp yyou girrlls happpy," the strange voice said, and Mrs Whatsit and Mrs Who fell into each other's arms in gales of laughter.

"If you ladies have had your fun, I think you should tell Calvin and Meg a little more about all this," Charles Wallace said coldly. "You scared Meg half out of her wits, whisking her off this way without any warning."

"Finxerunt animi, raro et perpauca loquentis," Mrs Who intoned. "Horace. *To action little, less to words inclined.*"

"Mrs Who, I wish you'd stop quoting!" Charles Wallace sounded very annoyed.

Mrs Whatsit adjusted her stole. "But she finds it so difficult to verbalize, Charles dear. It helps her if she can quote instead of working out words on her own."

"Anndd wee mussttn'tt looose ourr sensses of hummorr," Mrs Which said. "Thee onnlly wway ttoo ccope withh ssometthingg ddeadly sseriouss iss ttoo ttry ttoo trreatt itt a llittlle lligghtly."

"But that's going to be hard for Meg," Mrs Whatsit said. "It's going to be hard for her to realize that we *are* serious."

"What about me?" Calvin asked.

"The life of your father isn't at stake," Mrs Whatsit told him.

"What about Charles Wallace, then?"

Mrs Whatsit's unoiled-door-hinge voice was warm with affection and pride. "Charles Wallace knows. Charles Wallace knows that it's far more than just the life of his father. Charles Wallace knows what's at stake."

"But remember," Mrs Who said, "Αεηπου οὐδὲν, πὰντα δ' επἰζειν χρεωτ. Euripides. *Nothing is hopeless; we must hope for everything.*"

"Where are we now, and how did we get here?" Calvin asked.

"Uriel, the third planet of the star Malak in the spiral nebula Messier 101."

"This I'm supposed to believe?" Calvin asked indignantly.

"Aas yyou llike," Mrs Which said coldly.

ELIZABETH BORTON DE TREVIÑO

FROM

I, Juan de Pareja

1965

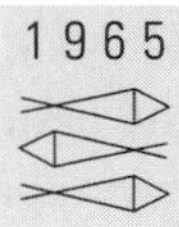

It was late in the afternoon. Master was not painting, but sitting at his desk making out some accounts and writing to order special pigments from Flanders. The door of the studio opened quietly and His Majesty stepped in, looking around in his uncertain, apologetic way. He was dressed for some court ceremony: black velvet shoes and long black silk stockings, black velvet trousers, but instead of a doublet he wore only a white shirt of thin cotton, and a dressing gown of dark silk brocade. I supposed that after contemplating a picture he meant to return to his rooms, put on his doublet, call the barber to shave him and curl his hair and mustache, and then attach his big white starched ruff at the last moment.

He pulled out his chair, sat, and stretched his long legs with a deep sigh. He smiled amiably at Master, who smiled back warmly, affectionately, and then went on with his accounts.

After a short time the King rose and went toward the wall. He stood hesitating a moment, and then turned a canvas toward him. It was mine. In the late light, the faithful hounds shone out from the dark background, sunlight on their glistening hides, light in their big, loving, dark eyes. His Majesty stood transfixed; he had never seen that canvas before. I could watch his always-slow mind adjusting to the fact that this was a portrait of his own favorite hounds.

I threw myself on my knees before him.

"I beg mercy, Sire," I pleaded. "The painting is mine. I have been working secretly all these years, with bits of canvas and color, copying the works of Master, to learn from them, and trying some original subjects by myself. I know very well that this is against the law. Master has never even suspected and has had nothing to do with my treachery. I am willing to endure whatever punishment you mete out to me."

I remained on my knees, begging the Virgin to remember my promise, praying and asking her forgiveness and her help. Opening my eyes,

I saw the feet of His Majesty moving nervously about. Evidently he did not know what to reply. Then he cleared his throat and took a deep breath. The feet in the velvet shoes remained quiet.

"What . . . what shall we do . . . with this . . . this . . . disobedient slave?" I heard his voice lisping and stuttering, as he turned toward Master.

Still on my knees, I saw Master's neat small feet, in their shoes of Cordovan leather, approach and place themselves in front of my picture. He studied it some time in silence, and the King waited.

Then Master spoke. "Have I your Majesty's leave to write an urgent letter before I answer?"

"You have it."

Master returned to his desk and I heard his quill scratching against the paper. His Majesty returned to his chair and threw himself into it. I remained where I was, praying with all my might.

Master rose, and his feet moved toward me.

"Get up, Juan," he said. He put a hand under my elbow and helped me to my feet. He was looking at me with the gentle affection he had always shown me.

He took my hand and put a letter into it. I have worn that letter sewed into a silk envelope and pinned inside my shirt ever since. The letter said:

TO WHOM IT MAY CONCERN

I have this day given freedom to my slave Juan de Pareja, who shall have all the rights and honors of a free man, and further, I hereby name him my Assistant, with the duties and salary thereto pertaining.

DIEGO RODRÍGUEZ DE SILVA Y VELÁZQUEZ

Master took the letter gently from my hand, after I had read it, and took it to the King who, reading, smiled radiantly. It was the first time in all those years that I had seen His Majesty smile. His teeth were small and uneven, but that smile seemed to me as beautiful as any I had ever seen.

The letter was given back to me, and I stood there, tears of joy streaming from my eyes.

"You were saying, Sire, something about a slave?" inquired Master softly. "I have no slave."

M. B. GOFFSTEIN

FROM

Brookie and Her Lamb

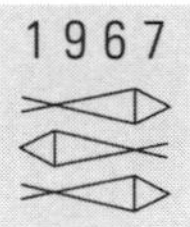

She made the lamb a cozy place where he could sit and read,

and all his books said
Baa baa baa

so he liked them very much.

ARTHUR RANSOME

PICTURES BY URI SHULEVITZ

FROM

The Fool of the World and the Flying Ship

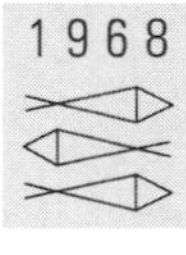
1968

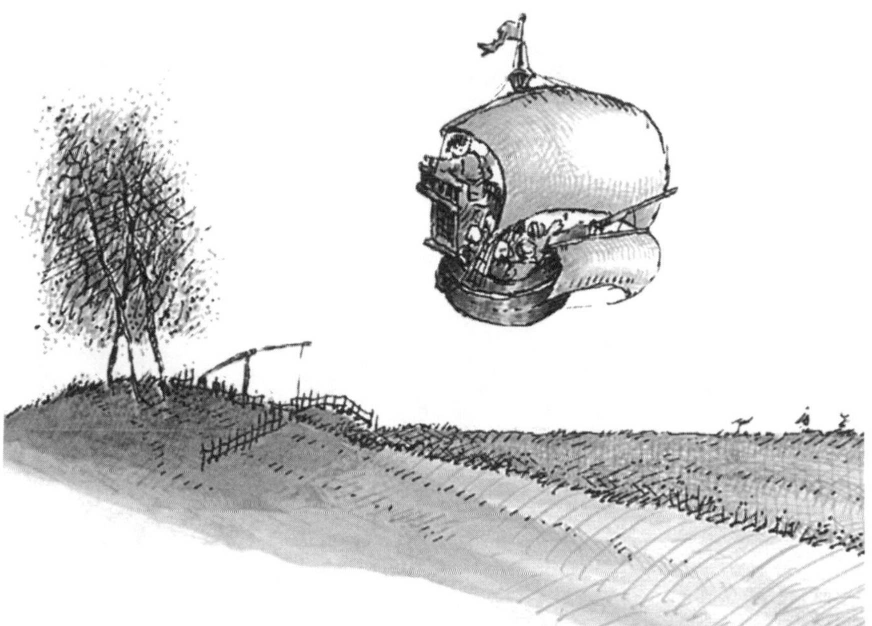

They flew on and on, and looked down, and there was a man carrying a sack of straw.

"Good health to you, uncle," says the Fool. "And where are you taking your straw?"

"To the village."

"Why, are they short of straw in your village?"

"No; but this is such straw that if you scatter it abroad in the very hottest of the summer, instantly the weather turns colder, and there is snow and frost."

"There's a place here for you too," says the Fool.

"Very kind of you," says the man, and steps in and sits down, and away they all sail together, singing like to burst their lungs.

THE BROTHERS GRIMM

TRANSLATED BY RANDALL JARRELL

PICTURES BY NANCY EKHOLM BURKERT

FROM

Snow-White and the Seven Dwarfs

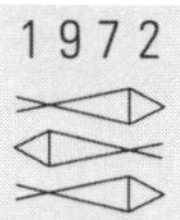

Now the poor child was all, all alone in the great forest, and so terrified that she stared at all the leaves on the trees and didn't know what to do. She began to run, and ran over the sharp stones and through the thorns, and the wild beasts sprang past her, but they did her no harm.

FROM

Duffy and the Devil

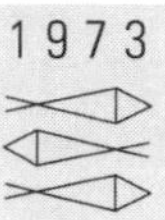
1973

"How much do I have to pay you?" asked Duffy.

"Not a penny," replied the devil. "Listen: I'll knit and I'll spin as much as you like—to me it's just a game. But at the end of three years *I'll take you away*—unless you can tell me my name!"

"Your name?" said Duffy.

"That's right. Unless you can tell me my name—or my daddy's name, either will do, they're both the same! You have three whole years to guess what it is. You get as many guesses as you please. And meanwhile, all the spinning and knitting gets done without your lifting a finger. Think it over." And suddenly as he had come, he disappeared.

NATALIE BABBITT

FROM

Tuck Everlasting

1975

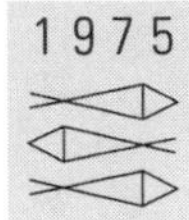

"It was real nice," said Jesse with a sigh. "It looked just the way it does now. A clearing, lots of sunshine, that big tree with all those knobby roots. We stopped and everyone took a drink, even the horse."

"No," said Mae, "the cat didn't drink. That's important."

"Yes," said Miles, "don't leave that out. We all had a drink, except for the cat."

"Well, anyway," Jesse went on, "the water tasted—sort of strange. But we camped there overnight. And Pa carved a T on the tree trunk, to mark where we'd been. And then we went on."

They had come out of the forest at last, many miles to the west, had found a thinly populated valley, had started their farm. "We put up a house for Ma and Pa," said Miles, "and a little shack for Jesse and me. We figured *we'd* be starting families of our own pretty soon and would want our own houses."

"That was the first time we figured there was something peculiar," said Mae. "Jesse fell out of a tree . . ."

"I was way up in the middle," Jesse interrupted, "trying to saw off some of the big branches before we cut her down. I lost my balance and I fell . . ."

"He landed plum on his head," said Mae with a shudder. "We thought for sure he'd broke his neck. But come to find out, it didn't hurt him a bit!"

"Not long after," Miles went on, "some hunters come by one day at sunset. The horse was out grazing by some trees and they shot him. Mistook him for a deer, they said. Can you fancy that? But the thing is, they didn't kill him. The bullet went right on through him, and didn't hardly even leave a mark."

"Then Pa got snake bite . . ."

"And Jesse ate the poison toadstools . . ."

"And I cut myself," said Mae. "Remember? Slicing bread."

But it was the passage of time that worried them most. They had worked the farm, settled down, made friends. But after ten years, then twenty, they had to face the fact that there was something terribly wrong. None of them was getting any older.

"I was more'n forty by then," said Miles sadly. "I was married. I had two children. But, from the look of me, I was still twenty-two. My wife, she finally made up her mind I'd sold my soul to the Devil. She left me. She went away and she took the children with her."

"I'm glad *I* never got married," Jesse put in.

"It was the same with our friends," said Mae. "They come to pull back from us. There was talk about witchcraft. Black magic. Well, you can't hardly blame them, but finally we had to leave the farm. We didn't know where to go. We started back the way we come, just wandering. We was like gypsies. When we got this far, it'd changed, of course. A lot of the trees was gone. There was people, and Treegap—it was a new village. The road was here, but in those days it was mostly just a cow path. We went on into what was left of the wood to make a camp, and when we got to the clearing and the tree and the spring, we remembered it from before."

"*It* hadn't changed, no more'n we had," said Miles. "And that was how we found out. Pa'd carved a T on the tree, remember, twenty years before, but the T was just where it'd been when he done it. That tree hadn't grown one whit in all that time. It was exactly the same. And the T he'd carved was as fresh as if it'd just been put there."

Then they had remembered drinking the water. They—and the horse. But not the cat. The cat had lived a long and happy life on the farm, but had died some ten years before. So they decided at last that the source of their changelessness was the spring.

"When we come to that conclusion," Mae went on, "Tuck said—that's my husband, Angus Tuck—he said he had to be sure, once and for all. He took his shotgun and he pointed it at hisself the best way he could, and before we could stop him, he pulled the trigger." There was a long pause. Mae's fingers, laced together in her lap, twisted with the tension of remembering. At last she said, "The shot knocked him down. Went into his heart. It *had* to, the way he aimed. And right on through him. It scarcely even left a mark. Just like—*you* know—like you shot a bullet through water. And he was just the same as if he'd never done it."

"After that we went sort of crazy," said Jesse, grinning at the memory. "Heck, we was going to live forever. Can you picture what it felt like to find that out?"

"But then we sat down and talked it over . . ." said Miles.

"We're still talking it over," Jesse added.

VALERIE WORTH

PICTURES BY NATALIE BABBITT

FROM

More Small Poems

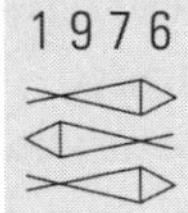

PUMPKIN

After its lid
Is cut, the slick
Seeds and stuck
Wet strings
Scooped out,
Walls scraped
Dry and white,
Face carved, candle
Fixed and lit,

Light creeps
Into the thick
Rind: giving
That dead orange
Vegetable skull
Warm skin, making
A live head
To hold its
Sharp gold grin.

WILLIAM STEIG

FROM

The Amazing Bone

1976

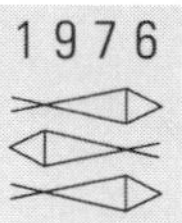

Later she sat on the ground in the forest between school and home, and spring was so bright and beautiful, the warm air touched her so tenderly, she could almost feel herself changing into a flower. Her light dress felt like petals.

"I love everything," she heard herself say.

"So do I," a voice answered.

Pearl straightened up and looked around. No one was there. "Where are you?" she asked.

"Look down," came the answer. Pearl looked down. "I'm the bone in the violets near the tree by the rock on your right."

Pearl stared at a small bone. "You talk?" she murmured.

"In any language," said the bone.

JILL PATON WALSH

FROM

Unleaving

1976

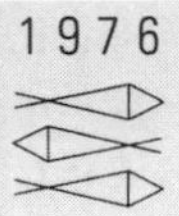

The sea is smooth and tranquil. The waves are so small and late they hardly look real. Rising from the sun-shot shallows like little jade lions, they arch green, glossy backs, come rearing and pawing a little way, and break foaming, tossing their suddenly tawny manes. Behind them in the glass-clear green water lie shimmering golden nets of floating light. In the distance Godrevy light, haze-softened, looks like a stick of blackboard chalk against the sky, and the sea lies quiet all the way there, like the waters of some limitless lake.

Molly finds a shell, a crab's claw, and shows it to her mother, tugging her skirt. Mrs. Tregeagle shoos her gently. "Go and play with the others, Molly," she says. Patrick stiffens, and turns his head to watch. Molly staggers toward the little Jones boy, playing nearest. His castle has battlements now, and windows made of pressed-on mussel shells. He stands up as she comes, and gets between her and it, arms stretched wide to stop her. "You walk on my castle and I'll hit you!" he says. "You *get*, or you'll be sorry."

Molly trots down the beach toward the others. They are whirling at the run around the scribbled paths they have drawn. Molly begins to run, too, treading on all the lines, and blurring them. She laughs her low-pitched chuckle. Soon she is circling alone; the others have withdrawn without a word spoken, have left their spiraling mazes to her trampling naked feet, and migrated yards along the beach to the edge of the stream. It is a little stream of fresh water, disgorged onto the sand by a rusty pipe through a grille; where it falls it has cut a whirlpool that bubbles thick with sand. Overflowing from that, it runs down into the sea, making channels and shallows and meanders, cutting little gorges and rapids like a geography lesson. The two Jones girls begin to dam its flow. Molly wheels drunkenly on, alone. Soon she sits down alone, and looks at the sea.

The two women are talking about college houses. One will be available when old Grimbly retires; there will be a shuffle and change about.

"I'd like the one in Walton Street," says Mrs. Jones. "But we'll never get it. Not unless Hugh is made Dean. But the college doesn't really appreciate him. Perhaps if he became Dean, though, we could do better than Walton Street."

"We couldn't have Walton Street. We need a garden. And a fence. A high one. Molly can climb these days." And here is Molly again, returning to tug at her mother's skirts.

"Oh, do go and play!" says Mrs. Tregeagle, sharply. Molly starts off toward the stream. And Patrick lies still tense, watching, with Madge beside him. He is watching so intently that Madge, still serene and sleepy, and lulled by looking into vast lovely distances, watches too. They see Molly's dumpy figure in the distance, reaching the dam-builders. They see the two girls, bent over their labors and digging frantically, straighten for a moment as she comes, and face her. Then she turns around, and comes away, retreating.

Patrick gets up, and strides down the beach toward her. He takes her hand, and leads her back to them. And Madge jumps up too, and follows, sure he is making a mistake, and yet not quite wanting to call out to him, not wanting to speak, just to catch his eye, and glance, "Be careful; are you sure?"

A big pool of water is building up behind the sand dam. It brims it, sneaks around the ends till choked off with another pile of sand. It licks at and topples the crests of the sandy battlements. Patrick leads Molly by the hand right up to the bank of the pool. "Surely she could help?" he asks, and so catches, full-face, the expression of revulsion which crosses the pretty, knowing countenance of Prudence Jones, flecked with sandy splashes from her struggle with the pent-up stream. Her sister avoids looking; simply flushes and turns away. They all stand frozen for a moment; and the meek and tiny stream has built up enough ferocity at its confinement to overbrim the barrier, and scour through it with joyous speed. The defeated engineers gaze at Patrick with sullen reproach. He turns on his heel, and marches back to the deck chairs, still leading Molly by the hand.

"*Don't* send her to play with them, Mother!" he says.

"Why ever not?" says Mrs. Tregeagle in a pained voice, and Mrs. Jones says at the same time, "Oh, no! Were they unkind?" And Patrick says, choking and furious, "You know why!" and suddenly races away from them down the beach, plunging into the sea, and swimming, head down, arms flailing, boring his way out far, beyond the diving raft, and on and on, as though to reach the horizon.

ARANKA SIEGAL

FROM

Upon the Head of the Goat: A Childhood in Hungary 1939–1944

1981

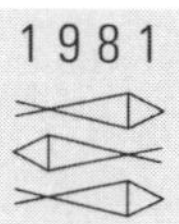

As I was walking home alone from school one day late in October, a woman with an infant in her arms approached me and asked in a wavering voice, "Do you speak Yiddish?"

I nodded.

"I'm running away from Slovakia, and we are hungry. Can you point me to a Jewish door?"

"Follow me, I'm on my way home. I'm sure my mother will give you something to eat," I said in Yiddish.

The woman followed me, walking close to the houses. When we reached our kitchen, I started to explain to Mother, but she pushed me aside and lifted the infant out of the black peasant shawl around the woman's shoulders.

"The child needs water," she said, cradling the infant in one arm, while with her free hand she scooped up a small cup of water from the bucket and forced a little of it into the child's mouth. Lilli spooned some of the vegetable soup simmering on the stove into a dish and set it on the table.

"God bless you, pretty lady," the Slovakian woman said in Yiddish as she sat down on a stool and began to gulp down the steaming soup. Mother asked Lilli to fill a washbasin with water so she could wash the baby. We watched the infant come back to life, kicking and enjoying the sensation of the warm bath. Then Mother lifted the infant out of the basin, wrapped her in a towel, and left the kitchen, taking the baby with her.

The woman began to talk. "I had no time to take anything. I just ran."

"Where were you being sent?" Lilli asked.

"Only God above knows and I hope he is keeping track of what is taking place."

"Piri," Mother said, as she came back into the kitchen, "I want you to take this woman and the baby over to Mrs. Silverman's. You know where she lives?"

"Yes."

Mother had dressed the baby in one of Joli's old dresses, and she held, along with the baby, an armful of Joli's baby clothes and diapers. She handed the child back to the woman.

"You must leave here," Mother said to the woman, "but I'm sending you to a place where you will be safe for a while. It is a shelter that some of us set up. My daughter will lead you. Take off your head scarf and try not to look Jewish. We'll give you a hat."

After an emotional farewell and many mentions of God, we walked to the gate. Mother looked out to make sure no one was watching. "Piri, you walk ahead, and if somebody stops her, keep walking; you don't know them. After you've left her at Mrs. Silverman's, I want you to come right back. You understand?"

"Yes, Anyuka."

I walked with a normal stride several paces ahead of the woman. No one noticed us, and soon I was at Mrs. Silverman's gate, the woman with her infant still behind me. I hesitated a moment, then rang the bell. Mrs. Silverman appeared almost instantly, opening her gate just enough to let me through. I started to explain why I was there, but she interrupted, "Come to the point, child. What is it you want?" I closed my mouth and motioned the woman to come up. As soon as she got close enough, Mrs. Silverman pulled her into the yard and leaned out over the gate, checking both sides of the street. Then she pushed me out. "You've never been here," were her parting words to me. I walked home swiftly.

"Everything go all right?" Mother asked, turning from the stove to look at me as I came in.

"She is there. What is Mrs. Silverman going to do with them? Does she hide people in her house?"

"Piri, Hungary is the last place for them to run to, it is the last refuge. Don't you have any homework to do?"

I realized then that Mother was involved in things I knew nothing about, and was reminded of how much she was like Babi; when she changed the subject, that was the end of the discussion. But I could not get that woman and her baby out of my mind and sometimes when I thought or dreamed about her, the woman's face became Mother's or Lilli's.

NANCY GARDEN

FROM

Annie on My Mind

1982

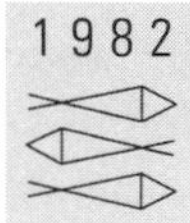

Hearing Annie sing in the recital was nothing like hearing her sing in the museum that first day, or hearing her hum around her apartment or mine or on the street the way I had a few times since then. I knew she had a lovely voice, and I knew from the time in the museum that she could put a lot of feeling behind what she sang—but this was more than all those things combined. The other kids in the recital were good—maybe the way I'd expected Annie to be—but right before Annie sang, she looked out at the audience as if to say, "Listen, there's this really beautiful song I'd like you to hear"—as if she wanted to make the audience a present of it. The audience seemed to know something unusual was coming, for when Annie looked at them, they settled back, calm and happy and expectant, and when she started singing, you couldn't even hear anyone breathe. I glanced at Dad and Mom and Chad to see if maybe it was my loving Annie that made me think she was so good, but I could see from their faces, and from the faces of the other people—not just her family, who looked about ready to burst with pride—that everyone else thought she was as good as I did.

I'm not sure how to describe Annie's voice, or if anyone really could, except maybe a music critic. It's a low soprano—mezzo-soprano is its technical name—and it's a little husky—not gravelly husky, but rich—and, according to my mother, it's one hundred percent on pitch all the time. It's also almost perfectly in control; when Annie wants to fill a room with her voice, she can, but she can also make it as soft as a whisper, a whisper you can always hear.

But none of that was what made the audience sit there not moving every time Annie sang. It was the feeling again, the same thing that first drew me to Annie in the museum, only much, much more so. Annie's singing was so spontaneous, and she gave so much of herself, that it sounded as if she'd actually written each song, or was making each one up as she went along, the way she'd done in the museum. When she sang something sad, I wanted to cry; when she sang something happy, I felt myself smiling. Dad said he felt the same, and Mom had a long serious talk with Annie the next afternoon about becoming a professional—but Annie said she wasn't sure yet if she wanted to, although she knew she wanted to major in music and continue singing no matter what else she did. Chad, even though he was shy with girls, gave her a big hug after the performance and said, "There's nothing to say, Annie, you were so good."

I couldn't think of anything to say, either. Mostly I just wanted to put my arms around her, but at the same time I felt in awe of her—this was a whole new Annie, an Annie I hardly knew. I don't remember what I did or said—squeezed her hand, I think, and said something lame. But she said later that she didn't care what anyone thought except me.

•

I had the flu that winter, badly, some time late in January, I think it was. The night before, I was fine, but the next morning I woke up with my throat on fire and my head feeling as if a team of Clydesdales were galloping through it. Mom made me go back to bed and came in every couple of hours with something for me to drink. I think the only reason I remember the doctor's making one of his rare house calls is because I nearly choked on the pills that Mom gave me to take after he'd left.

Some time that first afternoon, though, I heard voices outside my door. Mom had let Chad wave to me from the threshold earlier, and it was too early for Dad to be home, so I knew it couldn't be either of them. And then Annie was beside me, with Mom protesting from the door.

"It's okay, Mrs. Winthrop," she was saying. "I had the flu this year already."

"Liar," I whispered, when Mom finally left.

"Last year, this year," said Annie, turning the cloth on my head to its cooler side. "It's all the same." She put her hand on my cheek. "You must feel rotten."

"Not so much rotten," I said, "as not here. As if I were floating, very far away. I don't want to be far away from you," I said, reaching for her hand, "but I am." I really must have been pretty sick, because I could barely concentrate, even on Annie.

Annie held my hand, stroking it softly. "Don't talk," she said. "I won't let you float away. You can't go far with me holding on to you. I'll keep you here, love, shh." She began to sing very softly and sweetly, and although I was still floating, I was riding on clouds now, with Annie's voice and her hand gently anchoring me to Earth.

FROM

The BFG

1982

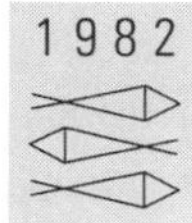

The Big Friendly Giant picked Sophie off the table and carried her to the cave entrance. He rolled the huge stone to one side and said, "Peep out over there, little girl, and tell me what you is seeing."

Sophie, sitting on the BFG's hand, peeped out of the cave.

The sun was up now and shining fiery-hot over the great yellow wasteland with its blue rocks and dead trees.

"Is you seeing them?" the BFG asked.

Sophie, squinting through the glare of the sun, saw several tremendous tall figures moving among the rocks about five hundred yards away. Three or four others were sitting quite motionless on the rocks themselves.

"This is Giant Country," the BFG said. "Those is all giants, every one."

It was a brain-boggling sight. The giants were all naked except for a sort of short skirt around their waists, and their skins were burned brown by the sun. But it was the sheer size of each one of them that boggled Sophie's brain most of all. They were simply colossal, far taller and wider than the Big Friendly Giant upon whose hand she was now sitting. And oh how ugly they were! Many of them had large bellies. All of them had long arms and big feet. They were too far away for their faces to be seen clearly, and perhaps that was a good thing.

"What on earth are they doing?" Sophie asked.

"Nothing," said the BFG. "They is just moocheling and footcheling around and waiting for the night to come. Then they will all be galloping off to places where *people* is living to find their suppers."

"You mean to Turkey," Sophie said.

"Bonecrunching Giant will be galloping to Turkey, of course," said the BFG. "But the others will be whiffling off to all sorts of flungaway places like Wellington for the booty flavor and Panama for the hatty taste. Every giant is having his own favorite hunting ground."

"Do they ever go to England?" Sophie asked.

"Often," said the BFG. "They say the English is tasting ever so wonderfully of crodscollop."

"I'm not sure I quite know what that means," Sophie said.

"Meanings is not important," said the BFG. "I cannot be right all the time. Quite often I is left instead of right."

"And are all those beastly giants over there really going off again tonight to eat people?" Sophie asked.

"All of them is guzzling human beans every night," the BFG answered. "All of them excepting me. That is why you will be coming to an ucky-mucky end if any of them should ever be getting his gogglers upon you. You would be swalloped up like a piece of frumpkin pie, all in one dollop!"

"But eating people is horrible!" Sophie cried. "It's frightful! Why doesn't someone stop them?"

"And who please is going to be stopping them?" asked the BFG.

"Couldn't you?" said Sophie.

FROM

When Sheep Cannot Sleep: The Counting Book

1986

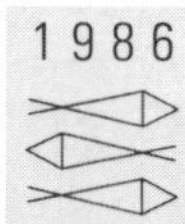

Woolly climbed to the top of a hill to look at the view. Suddenly, flashing lights zipped across the sky. Woolly was very scared.

ARTHUR YORINKS

PICTURES BY RICHARD EGIELSKI

FROM

Hey, Al

1986

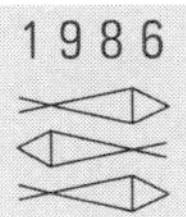

One morning, while Al was shaving, a voice called to him. "Hey, Al," it said. Al turned and saw a bird. A large bird.

"Al," said the bird, "are you working too hard? Still struggling and going nowhere? *Hmmm?* Listen. Have I got a place for you. No worries, no cares—it's terrific."

"Huh?" Al said. He was confused.

"Al, Al, *Al!* You need a change. Tomorrow, come and be my guest. Eddie, too. You'll see, you'll *love* it!"

Then, with a few flaps, the bird was gone.

BROCK COLE

FROM

The Goats

1987

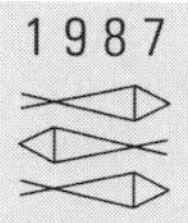

At the top of the island was an old tent platform. It had a canvas roof and sides of wood and screening. He stood at the edge of the clearing and looked at the tent platform and listened, but he couldn't hear anything except leaves rubbing against one another and the little slapping noises the waves made on the shore below. He crossed the clearing quickly and fumbled with the latch of the screen door. He was suddenly anxious to have the four walls around him.

He wasn't ready when someone inside said, "Go away."

His legs bounced him across the clearing before he could stop them, but there was nowhere to go. There was absolutely nowhere to go. He took a deep breath and walked quietly back to the door. He sat down on the steps, keeping his front hidden. He could hear someone crying inside. It sounded like a girl. She was gulping and crying at the same time.

"Hey," he said.

"I said go away."

"Hey, I can't. They took my clothes."

He waited, but there was no response.

"The mosquitoes are killing me. They really are."

Again there was no answer, but he heard a brief scuffling inside, and then the catch being released. As he pushed open the door, something black and shapeless scuttled into a corner. He didn't know what to do. He was glad it was dark inside.

"Did they leave anything?" he asked finally.

"There're some sandwiches and stuff on the table."

"I mean some blankets or clothes. I'm freezing."

"There's just one blanket."

And *she* had that, he thought. He felt his way to the table in the center of the room and ran his hand lightly over the surface. There was a package done up in plastic wrap, a box of matches, and something that felt like a candle lantern.

He left the table and groped his way toward a corner as far from the girl as possible. He found a cot there with a bare, damp mattress and a heavy pillow smelling of mildew. He sat down on the cot, holding the pillow on his lap.

"What are we going to do?" he asked.

"Nothing. Sit here."

"They'll probably come back in the morning."

"I know it."

He wondered what that would be like. Would they sneak up and try to peek through the screens, or would they be yelling and dancing around? He didn't know what went on in their heads. Sometimes he thought he knew, but then it turned out that he didn't.

"Hey. There's a candle lantern. I'm going to light it."

"Don't."

"I'm freezing, I tell you."

Holding the pillow to his front, he felt his way back to the table. By leaning against it he could keep the pillow in place while he lit the candle in the lantern.

She was huddled on the floor, completely wrapped up in a ratty old army blanket. Her face was turned away, so he couldn't see it. Her hair was stringy and damp-looking. He wondered if she was naked under the blanket. Probably she was. That would be the joke, wouldn't it? Bryce must think they would jump all over each other if they didn't have any clothes on.

He held his hands over the lantern. They burned but didn't seem to get warm. On the table beside the sandwiches was a deck of playing cards. They were the dirty ones that Arnold Metcalf showed around to his friends. The boy had never seen them up close. He hadn't wanted anyone to know he was interested. Now he didn't want to look at them. The top card had a picture of a man and a woman crumpled together. It had nothing to do with him. It was about as interesting as a picture of a dentist drilling a tooth.

Bryce must be crazy. Arnold Metcalf and Murphy—they were all crazy. Trying to guess what went on in their crazy heads was wearing him out. He retreated to the bed and sat down again, still holding the pillow over his front.

"We're the goats, I guess," he said, hoping she could explain what was happening to them.

"So?"

"So nothing."

WILHELM GRIMM
TRANSLATED BY RALPH MANHEIM
PICTURES BY MAURICE SENDAK

FROM

Dear Mili

1988

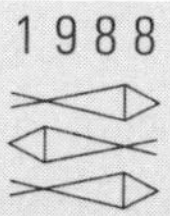

And, in her great fear, she decided to send the child into the forest, where no enemy could follow. "Come," she said, putting a piece of cake left over from Sunday in the child's pocket. "Come, child. I will take you to the forest. Then go straight ahead until you are quite safe; wait three days and come home; God in His mercy will show you the way."

She took the child to the edge of the forest, kissed her, and let her go.

FROM

Rosie and the Rustlers

1989

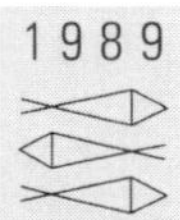

Where the mountains meet the prairie, where the men are wild and hairy,
There's a little ranch where Rosie Jones is boss.
It's a place that's neat and cozy, and the boys employed by Rosie
Work extremely hard, to stop her getting cross.

Next to Rose is Fancy Dan, on his left is Salad Sam,
One-Leg Smith and Singing Sid and Mad McGhee.
And then there's Utah Jim, who looks nice but rather dim—
Quite a decent bunch of boys they seem to me.

ALEXANDRA DAY

FROM

Carl's Christmas

1990

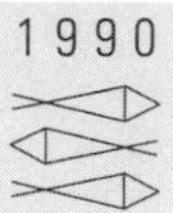

CHARLES PERRAULT

TRANSLATED BY MALCOLM ARTHUR

PICTURES BY FRED MARCELLINO

FROM

Puss in Boots

1990

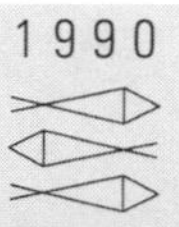

Then one day, when he knew the King would be going for a ride along the river with his daughter, who was the most beautiful Princess in the whole world, Puss said to his master: "Do as I say, and your fortune is made. Just go for a swim in the river—I'll show you the exact spot—and leave the rest to me."

The Marquis of Carabas followed Puss's instructions to the letter, though he couldn't imagine what good it would do him. While he was swimming, the King passed by and Puss shouted with all his might: "Help! Help! The Marquis of Carabas is drowning!"

SARAH STEWART

PICTURES BY DAVID SMALL

FROM

The Library

1995

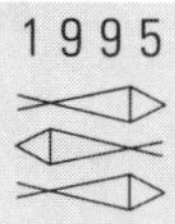

Elizabeth Brown
Walked into town
Summer, fall, winter, and spring.

Elizabeth Brown
Walked into town
Looking for only one thing.

She didn't want potato chips,
She didn't want new clothes.
She went straight to the bookstore.
"May I have one of *those*?"

HONORS

BOOKS PUBLISHED BY FARRAR, STRAUS AND GIROUX 1946–1996

ACKNOWLEDGMENTS

NOBEL PRIZES

Knut Hamsun (1920)
Hermann Hesse (1946)
T. S. Eliot (1948)
Pär Lagerkvist (1951)
François Mauriac (1952)
Juan Ramón Jiménez (1956)
Salvatore Quasimodo (1959)
Nelly Sachs (1966)
Aleksandr Solzhenitsyn (1970)
Pablo Neruda (1971)
Isaac Bashevis Singer (1978)
Czeslaw Milosz (1980)
Elias Canetti (1981)
William Golding (1983)
Wole Soyinka (1986)
Joseph Brodsky (1987)
Camilo José Cela (1989)
Nadine Gordimer (1991)
Derek Walcott (1992)
Seamus Heaney (1995)

PULITZER PRIZES

77 Dream Songs by John Berryman (1965)
The Fixer by Bernard Malamud (1967)
The Collected Stories by Jean Stafford (1970)
The Dolphin by Robert Lowell (1974)
Lamy of Santa Fe by Paul Horgan (1976)
The Morning of the Poem by James Schuyler (1981)
The Mambo Kings Play Songs of Love by Oscar Hijuelos (1990)

NATIONAL BOOK AWARDS

The Magic Barrel by Bernard Malamud (1959)
Life Studies by Robert Lowell (1960)
The Fixer by Bernard Malamud (1967)
His Toy, His Dream, His Rest by John Berryman (1969)
The Complete Poems by Elizabeth Bishop (1970)
A Day of Pleasure: Stories of a Boy Growing Up in Warsaw by Isaac Bashevis Singer (1970)

The Slightly Irregular Fire Engine or the Hithering Thithering Djinn by Donald Barthelme (1972)
The Complete Stories by Flannery O'Connor (1972)
A Crown of Feathers and Other Stories by Isaac Bashevis Singer (1974)
The Life of Emily Dickinson by Richard B. Sewall (1975)
Passage to Ararat by Michael J. Arlen (1976)
A Swiftly Tilting Planet by Madeleine L'Engle (1980)
The Right Stuff by Tom Wolfe (1980)
A Place Apart by Paula Fox (1983)
Doctor De Soto by William Steig (1983)
Paco's Story by Larry Heinemann (1987)
From Beirut to Jerusalem by Thomas L. Friedman (1989)

NATIONAL BOOK CRITICS CIRCLE AWARDS

Geography III by Elizabeth Bishop (1976)
Day by Day by Robert Lowell (1977)
On Photography by Susan Sontag (1977)
The Habit of Being: Letters by Flannery O'Connor (Ivan Sandrof/Board Award) (1979)
Less Than One: Selected Essays by Joseph Brodsky (1986)
The Counterlife by Philip Roth (1987)
Flesh and Blood by C. K. Williams (1987)
Encounters and Reflections: Art in the Historical Present by Arthur C. Danto (1990)

NEWBERY MEDALS

A Wrinkle in Time by Madeleine L'Engle (1963)
I, Juan de Pareja by Elizabeth Borton de Treviño (1966)

NEWBERY HONORS

The Cricket in Times Square by George Selden. Illustrated by Garth Williams (1961)
When Shlemiel Went to Warsaw and Other Stories by Isaac Bashevis Singer. Illustrated by Margot Zemach (1969)
Kneeknock Rise by Natalie Babbitt (1971)
Abel's Island by William Steig (1977)
A Ring of Endless Light by Madeleine L'Engle (1981)
Upon the Head of the Goat: A Childhood in Hungary 1939–1944 by Aranka Siegal (1982)
Doctor De Soto by William Steig (1983)

CALDECOTT MEDALS

The Fool of the World and the Flying Ship by Arthur Ransome. Illustrated by Uri Shulevitz (1969)

Duffy and the Devil by Harve Zemach. Illustrated by Margot Zemach (1974)

Hey, Al by Arthur Yorinks. Illustrated by Richard Egielski (1987)

CALDECOTT HONORS

The Judge: An Untrue Tale by Harve Zemach. Illustrated by Margot Zemach (1970)

Snow-White and the Seven Dwarfs by Jacob and Wilhelm Grimm. Translated by Randall Jarrell. Illustrated by Nancy Ekholm Burkert (1973)

The Amazing Bone by William Steig (1977)

It Could Always Be Worse by Margot Zemach (1978)

The Treasure by Uri Shulevitz (1980)

Puss in Boots by Charles Perrault. Illustrated by Fred Marcellino (1991)

BOOKS PUBLISHED BY FARRAR, STRAUS AND GIROUX 1946–1996

It is remarkably hard to make an accurate chronology of books published by a large trade house with a long history. The following list was compiled first from the Farrar, Straus and Giroux catalogues. As anyone in the business knows, however, catalogues are an unreliable indicator of what gets published when. We have therefore also made use of the library and card catalogues at Union Square, incomplete as they are, to give some approximation of the thousands of titles published by the firm over five decades. Any errors are ours and any corrections are welcome.—ED.

SUMMER AND FALL 1946

There Were Two Pirates, James Branch Cabell
Forlorn Sunset, Michael Sadleir
Tell Your Sons, Willa Gibbs
Anna Zenger: Mother of Freedom, Kent Cooper
Inside Your Home, Dan Cooper
United Nations: A Handbook on the New World Organization, Louis Dolivet
Never Let Weather Interfere, Messmore Kendall
The Island, Francis Brett Young
Powerful Long Ladder, Owen Dodson
The Last Circle, Stephen Vincent Benét
The Dim View, Basil Heatter
Francis, David Stern
Yank: The GI Story of the War, Staff members of *Yank: The Army Weekly*
The Gifts of Love, Andrina Iverson
Punch with Care, Phoebe Atwood Taylor
Deadly Weapon, Wade Miller
I Meet Such People!, Gurney Williams, ed.
How Much Do You Know? or An Evening at Home, Sylvan Hoffman, ed.
The Psychological Problems of Religion, Theodor Reik

SUMMER AND FALL 1947

Ghosts in Irish Houses, James Reynolds
Wax Fruit: The Antimacassar Trilogy, Guy McCrone
Pray Love, Remember, Consolata Carroll
Christ Stopped at Eboli, Carlo Levi
The Golden Voice, M. M. Marberry
Nuremberg Diary, G. M. Gilbert
The Lights Are Low, Jack Aistrop
The Iron Clew, Alice Tilton
Murder in the Town: Mr. Dixon's First Case, Mary Richart
Gourmet's Guide to Good Eating 1947, Editors of *Gourmet*
Bookman's Pleasure, Holbrook Jackson
Why I Am for the Church, Charles P. Taft
Katish, Our Russian Cook, Wanda L. Frolov
Howe & Hummel: Their True and Scandalous History, Richard H. Rovere
The Pleasures of Peacock, Ben Ray Redman, ed.
Awake to Darkness, Richard McMullen
The Philippine Story, David Bernstein
Heaven's Tableland, Vance Johnson
The Strange Life of Lady Blessington, Michael Sadleir
The Island in the Square, William DuBois
Cry Cadence, Howard Griffin
The Prodigal Never Returns, Hugh Chisholm
Yankee Pasha, Edison Marshall
The Great Light, Larry Barretto
Pop Goes the Queen, Bob Wade and Bill Miller
Feast of the Jesters, Manuel Komroff
The Case of Mr. Crump, Ludwig Lewisohn
Two Per Cent Fear, John D. Burgan
Shikar and Safari, Edison Marshall

WINTER AND SPRING 1948

Anniversary, Ludwig Lewisohn
Man: A Citizen of the Universe, John O'Hara Cosgrave
All the Girls We Loved, Prudencio de Pereda
Fatal Step, Wade Miller
Cooking by the Clock, Jean and Clarke Mattimore
The Road through the Wall, Shirley Jackson
The Tender Men, Willa Gibbs
Unclouded Summer, Alec Waugh
The Best Is None Too Good, Ralph G. Martin
Among the Nations: Three Tales and a Play about Jews, W. Somerset Maugham, Jacques de Lacretelle, John Galsworthy, and Thomas Mann Ludwig Lewisohn, ed.
I Am the Cat, Rosemary Kutak
A Collection of Travel in America, George Bradshaw, ed.
Someday, Boy, Sam Ross
The Shrouded Woman, María Luisa Bombal
Diamond Head, Houston Branch and Frank Waters
Eisenhower Speaks, Rudolph L. Treuenfels
Seven by Chance, Peter Levin
Listening with the Third Ear, Theodor Reik
A Stylish Marriage, Alec Rackowe
The Intemperate Season, Blythe Morley

The Mouse with Red Eyes, Elizabeth Eastman
The Witch-Woman Trilogy, James Branch Cabell
Red Plush, Guy McCrone

SUMMER AND FALL 1948

What Today's Woman Should Know about Marriage, Editors of *Today's Woman*
Maelstrom, Howard Hunt
State of Mind: A Boston Reader, Robert N. Linscott, ed.
The King and the Corpse, Max Murray
Last of the Conquerors, William Gardner Smith
The Pleasures of the Jazz Age, William Hodapp, ed.
Uneasy Street, Wade Miller
Into the Labyrinth, Bentz Plagemann
They Move with the Sun, Daniel Taylor
Francis Goes to Washington, David Stern
The World from Jackson Square: A New Orleans Reader, Etolia S. Basso, ed.
The Story of American Golf, Herbert Warren Wind
Laughter from Downstairs, Czenzi Ormonde
Castle in the Swamp: A Tale of Old Carolina, Edison Marshall
The Fall of Mussolini: His Own Story, Benito Mussolini
Max Ascoli, ed.
Uncle Edgar and the Reluctant Saint, Margaret Cousins
The House without a Roof, Joel Sayre
Echo of Evil, Manuel Komroff
Pilgrims in a New Land, Lee M. Freidman
The Day They Gave Babies Away, Dale Eunson

WINTER AND SPRING 1949

Information Please Almanac, 1949, John Kieran, ed.
U.S. Stories: Regional Stories from the Forty-eight States, Martha Foley and Abraham Rothberg, eds.
A Traveler's Guide to Roadside Wildflowers, Shrubs and Trees of the U.S., Kathryn S. Taylor, ed.
The Power of Freedom, Max Ascoli
The Sugar Islands, Alec Waugh
The Valley of St. Ives, Arthur Herbert Bryant
A Cook's Tour of the Eastern Shore of Maryland, Junior Auxiliary of Memorial Hospital, Easton, Maryland
Masochism in Modern Man, Theodor Reik
Murder City, O. M. Hall
The Oblong Blur and Other Odysseys, Philip Hamburger
Southbound, Barbara Anderson
Metal Magic: The Story of the American Smelting and Refining Company, Isaac F. Marcosson
The Lottery, Shirley Jackson
The Devil's Own Dear Son, James Branch Cabell
The North Star Is Nearer, Evelyn Eaton
Briton Hadden: His Life and Time, Noel F. Busch
Goethe: The Story of a Man, Ludwig Lewisohn
Four Centuries of Fine Printing, Stanley Morison
A Dictionary of Gastronomy, André L. Simon
Play-A-Bed Book for Boys and Girls (Number Two), Frances and John Casman, eds.
Aunt Bel, Guy McCrone
Atlantic Reef Corals, F. G. Walton Smith
Key West Cook Book, Women's Club of Key West

FALL AND WINTER 1949

Conditioned Reflex Therapy, Andrew Salter
The Vatican: Behind the Scenes in the Holy City, Ann Carnahan
I Hear in My Heart, Consolata Carroll
Headaches: What Causes Them—How to Get Relief, Noah D. Fabricant, M.D.
The Queen and the Corpse, Max Murray
Why Are You Single?, Hilda Holland, ed.
The Magnificent MacInnes, Shepherd Mead
Inherit the Night, Robert Christie
My Place to Stand, Bentz Plagemann
Lydia Pinkham Is Her Name, Jean Burton
Bimini Run, Howard Hunt
Intergroup Relations Centers, Everett R. Clinchy
Hear This Woman!, Ben and Ann Pinchot
The World Next Door, Fritz Peters
Fragment of a Great Confession: A Psychoanalytic Autobiography, Theodor Reik
The Bulldog Has the Key, F. W. Bronson
The Woman of Rome, Alberto Moravia
The Science of Culture, Leslie A. White
Gypsy Sixpence, Edison Marshall
Devil on Two Sticks, Wade Miller
Soviet Gold: An Eyewitness Account by a Slave Laborer in the Siberian Mines, Vladimir Petrov
Conversational Drawing, Edward H. Freedman
With a Jug of Wine, Morrison Wood
The Education of Free Men, Horace M. Kallen
A Handbook on Human Relations, Everett R. Clinchy
Pencil Fun Book for Boys and Girls, Frances W. Keene
How to Plan a Successful Children's Party, Frances W. Keene
The Keene Party Book: Parties for Children Ages 1 to 14, Frances W. Keene
Hangover, Alex Kenné
The Voice of the Corpse, Max Murray

WINTER AND SPRING 1950

The Captain's Lady, Basil Heatter
Of Fear and Freedom, Carlo Levi
Dreamers of Dreams, Holbrook Jackson
Corydon, André Gide
It Happens Every Spring, Valentine Davies
Play-A-Bed Book for Boys and Girls (Number Three), Frances and John Casman, eds.
The Sidewalks Are Free, Sam Ross
Eating Together: A Cookbook for Diabetics and Their Families, Camille Macaulay
Look Younger, Live Longer, Gayelord Hauser
Forty Forensic Fables, "O"
Shakespeare's Hamlet, Dr. Max Huhner
The Hand of Alexander, George Peterson Cherakis
The Little World of Don Camillo, Giovanni Guareschi
The Long Discovery, John Burgan
Herbert Hoover: American Quaker, David Hinshaw

The Magic Word: Studies in the Nature of Poetry, Ludwig Lewisohn
Love Stories of India, Edison Marshall
Jerusalem Has Many Faces, Judah Stampfer
The Psychoanalyst and the Artist, Daniel E. Schneider
Troubled Spring, John Brick
Fertility in Marriage: A Guide for the Childless, Louis Portnoy, M.D., and Jules Saltman
The Neat Little Corpse, Max Murray
Courtroom: The Story of Samuel S. Leibowitz, Quentin Reynolds
A Segment of My Times, Joseph M. Proskauer
How to Stay Rich: The Story of American Democratic Capitalism, Ernest L. Klein
The Sunnier Side: Twelve Arcadian Tales, Charles Jackson
Calamity Fair, Wade Miller
The Greater Trumps, Charles Williams
The Little Blue Light, Edmund Wilson

SUMMER AND FALL 1950

The Anatomy of Bibliomania, Holbrook Jackson
The Good Tidings, William Sidney
A Little Tour in France, Henry James
White Pine and Blue Water: A State of Maine Reader, Henry Beston, ed.
You and Your Marriage, Edward Kaufmann
Democracy in Politics and Economics, Charles P. Taft
Two Adolescents, Alberto Moravia
The Man Who Lived Backward, Malcolm Ross
The Truth about Your Eyes, Derrick Vail, M.D.
Flaubert and Madame Bovary, Francis Steegmuller
The Possum That Didn't, Frank Tashlin
The Darlingtons, Sylvia Brooke
Faith, Purpose and Power, James P. Warburg
Anger at Innocence, William Gardner Smith
Classics and Commercials: A Literary Chronicle of the Forties, Edmund Wilson
The Infinite Woman, Edison Marshall
The Cautious Revolution: Britain Today and Tomorrow, Ernest Watkins
The Theory and Practice of Hell, Eugen Kogon
Dogs, Ylla
The American Jew, Ludwig Lewisohn
The Traitor, William L. Shirer
Behind the Gold Curtains: The Story of the Metropolitan Opera, 1883–1950, Mary Ellis Peltz
The Ascending Line, E. Godfrey Hoare
Celebration at Dark, William Jay Smith
Murder Charge, Wade Miller
Credo, Garry Davis
Road Without Turning, Rev. James Robinson

WINTER AND SPRING 1951

The New Barbarian, Winthrop Palmer
Finistere, Fritz Peters
Boy at the Window, Owen Dodson
Love Is the One with Wings, Philip Van Doren Stern
Baseball and Mr. Spalding, Arthur Bartlett
Give Me Your Golden Hand, Evelyn Eaton
Man Is Not Alone, Abraham Joshua Heschel
All About H. Hatterr, G. V. Desani
The Right Honorable Corpse, Max Murray
The Raid, John Brick
Wine of Violence, Ralph Ingersoll
Walk on the Water, Ralph Leveridge
Holland's Handbook for Southern Gardeners, Ben Arthur Davis
Conjugal Love, Alberto Moravia
China Station, Donald R. Morris
Hangsaman, Shirley Jackson
The Selected Letters of John Keats, Lionel Trilling, ed.
Men and Gods, Rex Warner
The Catholic Book of Marriage, Rev. Philip Christopher M. Kelly
Inuk, Roger Buliard
Beyond the Windy Place: Life in the Guatemalan Highlands, Maud Oakes
A Fuchsia Survey, W. P. Wood
The Coming of the Flowers, A. W. Anderson
The Hospital, Frederick Boyden
Abel Anders, Frank Borden Hanes
Lone and Level Sands: The Story of an Air Force Colonel, Cornelius Vanderbilt Whitney
Pius XII: Eugenio Pacelli, Pope of Peace, Oscar Halecki and James F. Murray, Jr.

SUMMER AND FALL 1951

Miracle at Kitty Hawk: The Letters of Wilbur and Orville Wright, Fred Kelly, ed.
The Daughter, Arthur Markowitz
Umberto's Circus, Eduard Bass
The Watch, Carlo Levi
Head Over Heals: A Guide for the Better Self, Rt. Rev. Maurice S. Sheehy
I Killed Stalin, Sterling Noel
The Catholic Shrines of the Holy Land, Paschal Kinsel, O.F.M., and Leonard Henry, O.F.M. Photographs by Alfred Wagg
Atlantic City Cantata, Hugh Chisholm
Man's Vast Future, A. Powell Davies
The Integration of the Negro into the U.S. Navy, Lt. Dennis D. Nelson
The Selected Letters of William Cowper, Mark Van Doren, ed.
Americana Calendar, Evelyn Curro
The Face of Spain, Gerald Brenan
Protestant Panorama, Clarence W. Hall and Desider Holisher
The Writer's Workshop Companion, Gorham Munson
Apuleius' The Golden Ass, Robert Graves, trans.
The General and the President, Richard H. Rovere and Arthur M. Schlesinger, Jr.
Judaism and Modern Man, Will Herberg
Sugar on the Slate, Don Fontaine
Gentians in the Garden, G. H. Berry
Street Music, Theodora Keogh
What the Jews Believe, Philip S. Bernstein

The Sabbath: Its Meaning for Modern Man, Abraham Joshua Heschel
Ilya Schor, illus.
Creatures Great and Small, Colette
The Sound of Sleighbells, Russell McCracken
The Viking, Edison Marshall
Scirocco, Romualdo Romano
Your Siamese Cat, Hettie Gray Baker
Isle of the Damned, George John Seaton
What of the Night?: A Review of World Affairs, Ernest L. Klein
Good Luck to the Corpse, Max Murray
Where the Clock Strikes Twice, Alec Waugh
The Conformist, Alberto Moravia
The Selected Letters of Henry Adams, Newton Arvin, ed.
Murder, Inc., Burton B. Turkus, with Sid Feder
Shoot to Kill, Wade Miller
The Only War We Seek, Arthur Goodfriend
The Georgian Literary Scene, Frank Swinnerton
Fabled Shore: From the Pyrenees to Portugal, Rose Macaulay
Planned Meals, Jean Joy Campbell
Cooking with Wholegrains, Vrest and Mildred Ellen Orton

SPRING 1952

Mr. President: The First Publication from the Personal Diaries, Private Letters, Papers and Revealing Interviews of Harry S. Truman, William Hillman
Alfred Wagg, illus.
Leopard in the Grass, Desmond Stewart
Subtropical Gardening in Florida, Nixon Smiley
New Footprints of the Trojan Horse, Herbert Carlton Mayer
Quiet, Please, James Branch Cabell
The Hayburn Family, Guy McCrone
Water Wagon: Through Florida Waterways by Scow and Outboard, Rube Allyn
A Husband in the House, Stuart Engstrand
Unambo, Max Brod
They Want to Know: Answers from Business to Questions All the American People Are Asking, Earl Bunting and Edward Maher
The Wages of Fear, Georges Arnaud
Solving the High Cost of Eating, Ida Bailey Allen
In the Bright April Weather, Susanna Valentine Mitchell
Imagination Unlimited: Science-Fiction and Science, Everett F. Bleiler and T. E. Dikty
Friends and Vague Lovers, Jack Dunphy
Tibetan Sky Lines, Robert B. Ekvall
After All, Sir Norman Angell
John Bonwell: A Novel of the Ohio River Valley—1818 to 1862, Charles K. Pulse
The Trouble with Cinderella, Artie Shaw
Maeve, the Huntress, James Reynolds
The Life and Times of Kin Hubbard, Creator of Abe Martin, Fred C. Kelly
Contemporary Swedish Design, Sven Eric Skawonius and Arthur Hald
The Spendthrifts, Benito Pérez Galdós

FALL 1952

The Reader's Digest Murder Case, Fulton Oursler
The Perfect Joy of St. Francis, Felix Timmermans
A Bachelor's Establishment, Honoré de Balzac
The Selected Letters of Thomas Gray, Joseph Wood Krutch, ed.
Adlai E. Stevenson of Illinois, Noel F. Busch
Plant Propagation, E. J. King
Hagar, Ben and Ann Pinchot
At the Turning, Martin Buber
The Big Rape, James Wakefield Burke
The Illusionist, Françoise Mallet-Joris
The Fancy Dress Party, Alberto Moravia
Dynamic Dissonance: In Nature and the Arts, Louis Danz
Democracy, Henry Adams
The Western Gate: A San Francisco Reader, Joseph Henry Jackson, ed.
The Tartar Steppe, Dino Buzzati
Daughter of Confucius, Wong Su-Ling and Earl Herbert Cressy
Six O'Clock Mass, Rev. Maurice S. Sheehy
What Can a Man Believe, Arthur Goodfriend
Midcentury Journey, William L. Shirer
The Temptation to Be Good, A. Powell Davies
Homer Crist, John Brick
The Pythoness and Other Poems, Kathleen Raine
The Center of the Stage, Gerald Sykes
Guy Renton: A London Story, Alec Waugh
The Secret Self, Theodor Reik
The Shores of Light, Edmund Wilson
Don't Be Afraid of Your Child, Hilde Bruch, M.D.
The Descent, Fritz Peters
Designing for TV, Robert J. Wade
The TV Writer's Guide, Margaret R. Weiss
Design for Point-of-Sale, Ladislav Sutnar
Design with Type, Carl Dair
No Secret Is Safe: Behind the Bamboo Curtain, Mark Tennien
The Doctor and the Corpse, Max Murray
Our Appointment with Destiny, Ernest L. Klein
Gigi, Julie de Carneilhan, Chance Acquaintances, Colette
Be Happier, Be Healthier, Gayelord Hauser
More Power for Your Church, Willard A. Pleuthner
Bolívar, Salvador de Madariaga
The Immaculate Heart, Father John De Marchi
William Fay, ed.

WINTER AND SPRING 1953

Peace Through Strength: Bernard Baruch and a Blueprint for Security, Morris Victor Rosenbloom
Franz Rosenzweig: His Life and Thought, Nahum Glatzer, ed.
Stalin, A Self Portrait, Anonymous
The World of Li'l Abner, Al Capp
The Tattooed Heart, Theodora Keogh

Five Gentlemen of Japan, Frank Gibney
4000 Years of Service: The Story of the Wholesale Tobacco Industry and Its Pioneers, Joseph Kolodny
Europa and the Bull, W. R. Rodgers
What Can a Man Do?, Arthur Goodfriend
The Television Manual, William Hodapp
The Handbook of TV and Film Technique, Charles W. Curran
Restless House, Emile Zola
The Bat Brothers, Frank Borden Hanes
Encyclopedia of Biblical Interpretations: A Millennial Anthology/Genesis: Volume I, Menahem M. Kasher
A Treasury of Jewish Letters: Letters from the Famous and the Humble, Franz Kobler, ed.
The Passover Haggadah, Nahum N. Glatzer, ed.
Seed of Mischief, Willa Gibbs
"I, Willie Sutton," Quentin Reynolds
The Complete Book of the Gladiolus, Lee S. Fairchild
Low and Inside, Robert Osborn
Prince Bart: A Novel of Our Times, Jay Richard Kennedy
Caravan to Xanadu: A Novel of Marco Polo, Edison Marshall
The Legendary Mizners, Alva Johnston
The Time of Indifference, Alberto Moravia
Wedding Dance, Anne de Tourville
Food to Make You Famous, Mary Hill and Irene Radcliffe
Charlotte Turgeon, ed.
The Moon and the Bonfires, Cesare Pavese
The Drama of Display, Jim Buckley
Penrose Annual, Vol. 47, R. B. Fishenden, ed.
A Day of Impatience, Raffaele La Capria
I Thought of Daisy, Edmund Wilson
Chéri and *The Last of Chéri*, Colette
Few Die Well, Sterling Noel
The Naked Heart, John L. Weldon
Mr. Nicholas, Thomas Hinde
Life Among the Savages, Shirley Jackson
Torment, Benito Pérez Galdós
History of the Jewish People, Cecil Roth

SUMMER AND FALL 1953

The Selected Letters of Lord Byron, Jacques Barzun, ed.
Martha Crane, Charles Gorham
Reap the Whirlwind, Jean Hougron
The Bold Saboteurs, Chandler Brossard
The Redeemers, Leo W. Schwarz
Love Is My Vocation, Tom Clarkson
The Bold Women, Helen Beal Woodward
Hitler's Secret Conversations: His Private Thoughts and Plans in His Own Words, 1941–1944, Adolf Hitler
Botteghe Oscure XI, Marguerite Caetani, ed.
Proud Youth, Alexander Eliot
The Year One and Other Poems, Kathleen Raine
The Dead Boy and the Comets, Goffredo Parise
Silent Years: An Autobiography with Memoirs of James Joyce and Our Ireland, J. F. Byrne
Earthly Creatures, Charles Jackson
The American Drink Book, S. S. Field
Ballads Migrant in New England, Helen Hartness Flanders and Marguerite Olney
The Right Playmate, James Broughton and Gerard Hoffnung
The Hive, Camilo José Cela
195 Cat Tales, Hettie Gray Baker
The Haunting Melody, Theodor Reik
James Reynolds' Ireland, James Reynolds
My Mother's House and *Sido*, Colette
My Lord America, Alec Rackowe
The Blonde Corinthian, Herbert T. Cobey
Earthquake, Heinz Risse
The Growing Year, Clifton Lisle
Bring the Jubilee, Ward Moore
Hymns for Children and Grownups, Lee Hastings Bristol, Jr., and Harold W. Friedell, eds.
Deep Is the Night, James Wellard
The House That Nino Built, Giovanni Guareschi
The Mask of Innocence, François Mauriac
Interludes, Dorothy Quick
More Than Human, Theodore Sturgeon
Accents on Opera, Boris Goldovsky
32nd Annual of Advertising and Editorial Art, Art Directors Club of New York
Graphis Annual of International Advertising Art 1953/54, Walter Herdeg and Charles Rosner, eds.
Israel's History in Coins, A. Reifenberg

ARIEL CHILDREN'S BOOKS

The White Ox, Leon W. Dean
Tom Leamon, illus.
Suzy and the Dog School, Esther MacLellan and Catherine Schroll
Margaret Bradfield, illus.
Glory Boy, Frank Waldman
Harve Stein, illus.
Hide-and-Seek Voyage, Erling Gunnar Fischer
The Signal Net, Kenneth Andler
C. L. Hartman, illus.
Gravel Gold, Harriet H. Carr
C. L. Hartmen, illus.
Sheba, George Cory Franklin
L. D. Cram, illus.
Ten Gallon Hat, Shannon Garst
William Moyers, illus.
Summer Date, Margaretta Brucker
Beano, Circus Dog, Helen Orr Watson
Marie C. Nichols, illus.
The Mexican Story, May NcNeer
Lynd Ward, illus.

WINTER AND SPRING 1954

Stay On, Stranger!, William S. Dutton
The Selected Letters of Gustave Flaubert, Francis Steegmuller, ed.
The Magnificent Bastards, Lucy Herndon Crockett
The Fire-Raisers, Marris Murray
Botteghe Oscure XII, Marguerite Caetani, ed.
Bishop Healy: Beloved Outcast, Albert S. Foley, S.J.
The Fascinator, Theodora Keogh

A Rake and His Times: George Villiers, 2nd Duke of Buckingham, John Harold Wilson
Time to Come: Science-Fiction Stories of Tomorrow, August Derleth, ed.
Five Plays, Edmund Wilson
The Unmarried Mother in Our Society, Sara B. Edlin
Bernadette and Lourdes, Michel de Saint-Pierre
The Apprenticeship of Ernest Hemingway, Charles A. Fenton
The Twelfth Physician, Willa Gibbs
The Bulls of San Isidro, Saint-Paulien
The Penrose Annual, Vol. 48, 1954: A Review of the Graphic Arts, R. B. Fishenden, ed.

ARIEL CHILDREN'S BOOKS

Biggity Bantam, T. L. McCready, Jr.
Tasha Tudor, illus.
Trouble on the Trace, Tom Person
Joshua Tolford, illus.
All Aboard for the Beach, Verna Hills
Joshua Tolford, illus.
The Piebald Princess, Joan Balfour Payne
Deadmen's Cave, Leonard Wibberley
Tom Leamon, illus.
Catherine's Bells, Florence Musgrave
Zhenya Gay, illus.

FALL 1954

Don Camillo's Dilemma, Giovanni Guareschi
The Bird's Nest, Shirley Jackson
Pius XII: Eugenio Pacelli, Pope of Peace, revised, Oscar Halecki and James F. Murray, Jr.
Shrines to Our Lady Around the World, Zsolt Aradi
The Unsuitable Englishman, Desmond Stewart
Yossele Rosenblatt, Samuel Rosenblatt
Blaze of the Sun, Jean Hougron
Botteghe Oscure XIII, Marguerite Caetani, ed.
Salazar in Portugal, Christine Garnier
Solomon and the Queen of Sheba, Czenzi Ormonde
Memoirs of Hadrian, Marguerite Yourcenar
South Street, William Gardner Smith
Industrial Design in America, 1954, Society of Industrial Designers
The Kill, Emile Zola
The Deliverance of Sister Cecilia, As told to William Brinkley
Dinosaurs and Violins, Hy Sobiloff
New Guide to Intelligent Reducing, Gayelord Hauser
33rd Annual of Advertising and Editorial Art, Art Directors Club of New York
Make New Banners, Susanna Valentine Mitchell

ARIEL CHILDREN'S BOOKS

Aldo's Tower, Priscilla Carden
Kurt Werth, illus.
Pete and the Old Ford, Sanford Tousey
The Hidden Spring Mystery, Mary Adrian
Harve Stein, illus.
Chris Turner, Magician, James Brady
Lloyd Coe, illus.
The Epics of Everest, Leonard Wibberley
Genevieve Vaughan-Jackson, illus.
Almena's Dogs, Regina Woody
Elton C. Fax, illus.
The Dead Seagull, George Barker
The Swans of Ballycastle, Walter Hackett
Bettina, illus.

SPRING 1955

The Intelligent Heart: The Story of D. H. Lawrence, Harry T. Moore
Assignment: Churchill, Inspector Walter Henry Thompson of Scotland Yard
Cardinal O'Connell of Boston, Dorothy G. Wayman
Something Is Missing, Arthur Goodfriend
A Ghost at Noon, Alberto Moravia
The Vagabond, Colette
Aspects of Progressive Jewish Thought, Rabbi Israel I. Mattuck
The Innocent Sailor, Anne de Tourville
The Children of Light, Gerald Sykes
The Bishop Finds a Way, Michael Cunningham
The Third Pillar, Soma Morgenstern
Keats, John Middleton Murry
What Is Hypnosis, Andrew Salter
Maracaibo, Stirling Silliphant
Flesh and Blood, François Mauriac
Botteghe Oscure XIV, Marguerite Caetani, ed.
The Selected Letters of Anton Chekhov, Lillian Hellman, ed.
Tents Against the Sky, Robert B. Ekvall
Adventures in Brotherhood, James E. Pitt
God's Men of Color, Albert S. Foley, S.J.
First Aid for Flowers, Mary Reynolds Babcock
In a Summer Season, Ludwig Lewisohn
Catholic Approaches to Modern Dilemmas and Eternal Truths, Elizabeth Pakenham, ed.
The Botteghe Oscure Anthology, Marguerite Caetani, ed.
The Great American Heritage, Bela Kornitzer
Island in the Sun, Alec Waugh

ARIEL CHILDREN'S BOOKS

Trailer Tribe, Florence Musgrave
Genevieve Vaughan-Jackson, illus.
The One and Only, Margaretta Brucker
Pekin White, T. L. McCready, Jr.
Tasha Tudor, illus.
Pompon, Dorothy K. L'Hommedieu
Marie C. Nichols, illus.
On Your Own Two Feet, Bessie F. White
Joshua Tolford, illus.

FALL 1955

Twenty-one Stayed, Virginia Pasley
Daughters of Changing Japan, Earl Herbert Cressy
Everything and the Kitchen Sink: A Chronicle of the Makers of Progress, as Exemplified by the First Century of Crane Co., Crane Book Company
The Scimitar, Samuel Edwards
How to Live without Liquor, Ralph A. Habas, Ph.D.

Katrina, Jeramie Price
An Autobiography from the Jesuit Underground, William Weston
Never Plead Guilty, John Wesley Noble and Bernard Averbuch
Judaism for the Modern Age, Robert Gordis
Journey to the Future, Lillian Everts
Botteghe Oscure XV, Marguerite Caetani, ed.
Botteghe Oscure XVI, Marguerite Caetani, ed.
The Secret Roads, Jon and David Kimche
Five Novels by Alberto Moravia, Alberto Moravia
God in Search of Man, Abraham Joshua Heschel
The Saintmaker's Christmas Eve, Paul Horgan
Israel, the Eternal Ideal, Rabbi Irving Miller
The Popes: The Story of How They Are Chosen, Elected, and Crowned, Zsolt Aradi
Ghosts in American Houses, James Reynolds
Seven by Colette, Colette
Opera Stars in the Sun, Mary Jane Matz
Eggs I Have Known, Corinne Griffith
The Selected Letters of Henry James, Leon Edel, ed.
34th Annual of Advertising and Editorial Art, Art Directors Club of New York
Jews from Germany in the United States, Eric E. Hershler, ed.
Storm Over Paris, Sterling Noel

ARIEL CHILDREN'S BOOKS
Borghild of Brooklyn, Harriett H. Carr
The Wound of Peter Wayne, Leonard Wibberley
The Secret of the Old Salem Desk, Anne Molloy
Arline K. Thomson, illus.
Snow Birthday, Helen Kay
Barbara Cooney, illus.
Who Rides By?, Margaret Leighton
Mikko's Fortune, Lee Kingman
Arnold Edwin Barc, illus.
The Junior Sheriff Mystery, Mary Adrian
Lloyd Coe, illus.

VISION BOOKS
St. John Bosco and the Children's Saint, Dominic Savio, Catherine Beebe
St. Thérèse and the Roses, Helen Walker Homan
Father Marquette and the Great Rivers, August Derleth
St. Francis of the Seven Seas, Albert J. Nevins, M.M.

WINTER AND SPRING 1956
The Lamb, François Mauriac
The Gentleman, Edison Marshall
The Search Within, Theodor Reik
The Acceptance World, Anthony Powell
Forbidden Planet, W. J. Stuart
The Living Bread, Thomas Merton
Affairs of State: The Eisenhower Years, Richard H. Rovere
The Language of the Heart, A. Powell Davies
The Reward, Michael Barrett
Friday's Child, Wilfred Watson
Orchestral Accents, Richard Korn
Underworld U.S.A., Joseph F. Dinneen
Deliver Us From Evil: The Story of Viet Nam's Flight to Freedom, Thomas A. Dooley, M.D.
The Right to Know: An Exposition of the Evils of News Suppression and Propaganda, Kent Cooper
The Priestly Heart, Maurice S. Sheehy
An End to Dying, Sam Astrachan
Bernie Becomes a Nun, Sister Maria del Rey
Charlotte and Dr. James, Guy McCrone
A Walk on the Wild Side, Nelson Algren
Sights and Spectacles, Mary McCarthy
Three White Veils for Sandra, Lucy Prario
Brainwashing: The Story of Men Who Defied It, Edward Hunter
The Ripening Seed, Colette
The King's Messenger, Samuel Edwards
Gorilla Hunter, Fred G. Merfield, with Harry Miller
Weddings in the Family, Dale Fife
Pastures New, Clifton Lisle
The Grand Mademoiselle, Francis Steegmuller

ARIEL CHILDREN'S BOOKS
Wyatt Earp: Marshal of the Old West, Olga W. Hall-Quest
The Life of Winston Churchill, Leonard Wibberley
High Flying Hat, Nanda Ward
Lynd Ward, illus.
Marged: The Story of a Welsh Girl in America, Florence Musgrave
Arline K. Thomson, illus.
Big, Brave and Handsome, Margaretta Brucker

VISION BOOKS
Bernadette and the Lady, Hertha Pauli
Georges Vaux, illus.
St. Isaac and the Indians, Milton Lomask
Leo Manso, illus.
Fighting Father Duffy, Virginia Lee Bishop and Jim Bishop
H. Lawrence Hoffman, illus.
St. Pius X, the Farm Boy Who Became Pope, Walter Diethelm, O.S.B.
George Thompson, illus.
St. Ignatius and the Company of Jesus, August Derleth
John Lawn, illus.
John Carroll: Bishop and Patriot, Milton Lomask
Joshua Tolford, illus.

FALL 1956
A House on the Rhine, Frances Faviell
The Red Room, Françoise Mallet-Joris
A Report on the American Jesuits, John LaFarge, S.J.
Photographs by Margaret Bourke-White
The Lyndon Johnson Story, Booth Mooney
Bitter Honeymoon and Other Stories, Alberto Moravia
The Tight Corner, Sam Ross
In Silence I Speak: The Story of Cardinal Mindzenty Today and of Hungary's "New Order," George N. Shuster
The Urge to Punish, Henry Weihofen

St. Ignatius of Loyola: The Pilgrim Years, 1491–1538, James Brodrick, S.J.
The Business of Crime, Robert Rice
When the Wind Blows, Leon Phillips
The Selected Letters of Charles Lamb, T. S. Matthews, ed.
The Life of Robert Southwell: Poet and Martyr, Christopher Devlin, S.J.
The Cultivation of Christmas Trees, T. S. Eliot
A Piece of My Mind: Reflections at Sixty, Edmund Wilson
Homage to Mistress Bradstreet, John Berryman
Psychology and the Spirit, Gregory Zilboorg
Discovery and Conquest of Mexico, Bernal Díaz del Castillo
Genaro García, ed.
More Recipes with a Jug of Wine, Morrison Wood
More Ghosts in Irish Houses, James Reynolds
Thomas Merton: A Bibliography, Frank Dell'Isola
Mirage, Ruth McKenney
The Book of Catholic Quotations, John Chapin, ed.
The Mermaids, Eva Boros
Selected Writings of Sydney Smith, W. H. Auden, ed.
My Name Is Rose, Theodora Keogh
A Gallery of Zionist Profiles, Louis Lipsky
Your Nation's Capital, Morgan Beatty
The Will to Think: A Treasury of Ideas from the Pages of Think, Thomas J. Watson, ed.
The Book of Miracles, Zsolt Aradi
Stories, Jean Stafford, John Cheever, Daniel Fuchs, and William Maxwell
35th Annual of Advertising and Editorial Art, Art Directors Club of New York

ARIEL CHILDREN'S BOOKS
The Magic Christmas Tree, Lee Kingman
Bettina, illus.
Topper and Madam Pig, Dorothy K. L'Hommedieu
Marie C. Nichols, illus.
Mr. Stubbs, T. L. McCready, Jr.
Tasha Tudor, illus.
Adventure at Table Mountain, Edna Anne Hall
Carry On, Grumms!, Bessie F. White
Grace Paull, illus.

VISION BOOKS
St. Dominic and the Rosary, Catherine Beebe
Robb Beebe, illus.
The Cross in the West, Mark Boesch
H. Lawrence Hoffman, illus.
Champions in Sports and Spirit, Ed Fitzgerald
De Wolfe Hotchkiss, illus.
My Eskimos: A Priest in the Arctic, Roger Buliard, O.M.I.
Leonard Fisher, illus.
Francis and Clare, Saints of Assisi, Helen Walker Homan
John Lawn, illus.
Christmas and the Saints, Hertha Pauli
Russ Anderson, illus.
Modern Crusaders, John Travers Moore and Rosemarian V. Staudacher

WINTER AND SPRING 1957
The Silent Life, Thomas Merton
Raising Demons, Shirley Jackson
Claudine at School, Colette
I Remember Flores, Tasuko Sato and Mark Tennien
The Last Flowers, Michael Barrett
Transfigured World, Sister M. Laurentia Digges, C.S.J.
Background with Chorus, Frank Swinnerton
The Life of Hilaire Belloc, Robert Speaight
The Legion of the Damned, Sven Hassel
The Victory of Father Karl, Otto Pies, S.J.
The Story of Mary Liu, Edward Hunter
Little Brother Fate, Mary-Carter Roberts
Priest of the Plague: Henry Morse, S.J., Philip Caraman
The Towers of Trebizond, Rose Macaulay
The Assistant, Bernard Malamud
Opera Caravan: Adventures of the Metropolitan Company on Tour, Quaintance Eaton
The Complete Works of Nathanael West, Nathanael West
Edwin Vincent O'Hara: An American Prelate, J. G. Shaw
Don Camillo Takes the Devil by the Tail, Giovanni Guareschi
Close to Colette: An Intimate Portrait of a Woman of Genius, Maurice Goudeket
The Flower Drum Song, C. Y. Lee
Far to Go, Mary Louise Aswell
Drama in Diamonds, Dennis Craig and Brian Parkes

ARIEL CHILDREN'S BOOKS
Susan's Secret, Hildreth C. Wriston
W. T. Mars, illus.
Kevin O'Connor and the Light Brigade, Leonard Wibberley
Three Boys and a Girl, Margaretta Brucker
Powhatan and Captain John Smith, Olga W. Hall-Quest
Douglas Gorsline, illus.
Floorburns, John F. Carson

VISION BOOKS
Edmund Campion, Hero of God's Underground, Harold C. Gardiner, S.J.
Rose Goudeket, illus.
Modern Crusaders, John Travers Moore and Rosemarian V. Staudacher
John Lawn, illus.
Our Lady Came to Fatima, Ruth Fox Hume
Leo Manso, illus.
The Bible Story: The Promised Lord and His Coming, Catherine Beebe
Robb Beebe, illus.
St. Augustine and His Search for Faith, Milton Lomask
Johannes Troyer, illus.
St. Joan, the Girl Soldier, Louis de Wohl

FALL 1957

Of Love and Lust, Theodor Reik
Soviet Russia in China, Chiang Kai-shek
Secret Servants, Ronald Seth
Coup de Grâce, Marguerite Yourcenar
The Tichborne Claimant, Douglas Woodruff
A History of France, André Maurois
Adenauer and the New Germany, Edgar Alexander
Hercules, My Shipmate, Robert Graves
Lines of Life, François Mauriac
Mach I: A Story of the Planet Ionus, Allen Adler
The Will to Think, Norman Cousins, ed.
My Friends, the Huskies, Robert Dovers
Selected Writings of Juan Ramón Jiménez, Eugenio Florit, ed.
36th Annual of Advertising and Editorial Art, Art Directors Club of New York
My Partner-in-Law, Martin W. Littleton and Kyle Crichton
From an Altar Screen, Fray Angelico Chavez, O.F.M.
On Poetry and Poets, T. S. Eliot
The Called and the Chosen, Monica Baldwin
The Fabric of Memory, Eleanor Robson Belmont
Modern Miraculous Cures, François Leuret and Henri Bon
South from Granada, Gerald Brenan
The Selected Writings of John Jay Chapman, Jacques Barzun, ed.
Give Me Possession, Paul Horgan
Thalia, Frances Faviell
The Disinherited Mind, Erich Heller
Memoirs of a Revolutionist, Dwight Macdonald
Roman Tales, Alberto Moravia
House of Lies, Françoise Mallet-Joris
Vatican Journal, Anne O'Hare McCormick
Marion Turner Sheehan, ed.
St. Anthony Claret, Fanchón Royer

ARIEL CHILDREN'S BOOKS

Beau, Nanda Ward
Bob Haynes, illus.
The Bound Girl, Nan Denker
Comanche of the Seventh, Margaret Leighton
Elliott Means, illus.
John Barry, Father of the Navy, Leonard Wibberley
Shark Fishing Off the Great Barrier Reef, Horace Mazet
Russell Peterson, illus.
The Terrible Game, Dan Tyler Moore

COVENANT BOOKS

Major Mordecai, Robert D. Abrahams

VISION BOOKS

St. Thomas More of London, Elizabeth M. Ince
Mother Seton and the Sisters of Charity, Alma Power-Waters
John Lawn, illus.
St. Thomas Aquinas and the Preaching Beggars, Brendan Larnen, O.P., and Milton Lomask
Father Damien and the Bells, Arthur and Elizabeth Odell Sheehan
Columbus and the New World, August Derleth
St. Philip of the Joyous Heart, Francis X. Connolly

WINTER AND SPRING 1958

The Diary of "Helena Morley," Elizabeth Bishop
The Selected Letters of D. H. Lawrence, Diana Trilling, ed.
The First Christian, A. Powell Davies
Titian, Dario Cecchi
The Missouri Traveler Cookbook, Mary Hosford
The Moonlight Jewelers, Albert Vidalie
Thoughts in Solitude, Thomas Merton
Mitsou and *Music-Hall Sidelights*, Colette
A Belgian Cookbook, Juliette Elkon
The Sundial, Shirley Jackson
A Family Lawsuit, S. A. Mitchell
The Woman Gardener, Frances Perry
The Antiphon, Djuna Barnes
The Passionate Exiles, Maurice Levaillant
Home to Poland, Christine Hotchkiss
A Terrible Beauty, Arthur J. Roth
The Edge of Tomorrow, Thomas A. Dooley, M.D.
Lover's Point, C. Y. Lee
Turgenev's Literary Reminiscences, David Magarshack, ed.
My Thirty-third Year, Gerhard A. Fittkau
Two Women, Alberto Moravia
The Magic Barrel, Bernard Malamud
From the N.R.F., Justin O'Brien, ed.
A History of England, André Maurois
My Secret Diary, Giovanni Guareschi
Crack of Doom, Willi Heinrich

ARIEL CHILDREN'S BOOKS

The Spy and the Atom Gun, Ronald Seth
The Twenty-third Street Crusaders, John F. Carson
Increase Rabbit, T. L. McCready, Jr.
Tasha Tudor, illus.

COVENANT BOOKS FOR JEWISH YOUTH

Silversmith of Old New York: Myer Myers, William Wise
Border Hawk: August Bondi, Lloyd Alexander

VISION BOOKS FOR CATHOLIC YOUTH

Lydia Longley, the First American Nun, Helen A. McCarthy
St. Anthony and the Christ Child, Helen Walker Homan
Lili Réthi, illus.
St. Elizabeth's Three Crowns, Blanche Jennings Thompson
Katharine Drexel, Friend of the Neglected, Helen Tarry
Donald Bolognese, illus.

SUMMER AND FALL 1958

Satan in Goray, Isaac Bashevis Singer
A Question of Character, Jean Hougron

I Met a Traveller: The Triumph of Father Phillips, Kurt Becker, S.J.
The Last Year of Thomas Mann, Erika Mann
Words Are Stones, Carlo Levi
An American Amen, John LaFarge, S.J.
Engaged in Writing, Stephen Spender
The Criminal Mind, Philip Q. Roche, M.D.
The Young Ones, Bishop James E. Walsh of Maryknoll
Claudine in Paris, Colette
T. S. Eliot: A Symposium for His Seventieth Birthday, Neville Braybrooke, ed.
37th Art Directors Annual, Art Directors Club of New York
The Tall Man, A. M. Harris
T.R.: Champion of the Strenuous Life, William Davison Johnson, ed.
The Secret Name, Lin Yutang
The Genius of Paul, Samuel Sandmel
The Unmarried Sisters, Dale Fife
Eastern Exposure, Marvin L. Kalb
Saint Catherine Labouré of the Miraculous Medal, Joseph I. Dirvin, C.M.

ARIEL CHILDREN'S BOOKS
The Canadian Story, May McNeer
Lynd Ward, illus.
New Boy in Town, Margaretta Brucker
Little Black Chaing, Dorothy K. L'Hommedieu
Theresa Sherman, illus.
The Secret of Grandfather's Diary, Milton Lomask
W. T. Mars, illus.
Putt-Putt Skipper, Hildreth T. Wriston
Albert Orbaan, illus.
Wes Powell: Conqueror of the Grand Canyon, Leonard Wibberley

COVENANT BOOKS FOR JEWISH YOUTH
The World of Jo Davidson, Lois Harris Kuhn
Leonard Everett Fisher, illus.
Jubal and the Prophet, Frieda Clark Hyman
Bernard Krigstein, illus.

VISION BOOKS FOR CATHOLIC YOUTH
St. Louis and the Last Crusade, Margaret Ann Hubbard
Kateri Tekakwitha, Mohawk Maid, Evelyn M. Brown
St. Benedict, Hero of the Hills, Mary Fabyan Windeatt
The Curé of Ars: The Priest Who Outtalked the Devil, Milton Lomask
Johannes Troyer, illus.
Catholic Campuses, Rosemarian V. Staudacher
St. Helena and the True Cross, Louis de Wohl

WINTER AND SPRING 1959
Rivers in the Desert, Nelson Glueck
Phonemanship, William A. Garrett
The Secular Journal of Thomas Merton, Thomas Merton
Brotherhood of Evil: The Mafia, Frederic Sondern, Jr.
Chaim Weizmann, Isaiah Berlin
The Compulsion to Confess, Theodor Reik
Rome Eternal, Paul Horgan
Love and the Caribbean, Alec Waugh
More Power for Your Church & Building Up Your Congregation, Willard A. Pleuthner
Mark of Shame, Willi Heinrich
Life Studies, Robert Lowell
The Elder Statesman, T. S. Eliot
The American Bridge to the Israel Commonwealth, Bernard A. Rosenblatt
Great Companions: Critical Memoirs of Some Famous Friends, Max Eastman
A History of Spain, Max Livermore
Israel's Odyssey, Abraham Mayer Heller
The Sawbwa and His Secretary, C. Y. Lee
Reaching for the Moon and Other Addresses, Julius Mark
General Sherman's Son, Joseph T. Durkin

ARIEL CHILDREN'S BOOKS
The Little Bear's Mother, Carl Memling
Eugene Fern, illus.
The Secret of Smuggler's Cove, Margaret Leighton
Mary L. Thomson, illus.
The Elephant That Galumphed, Nanda Ward
Bob Haynes, illus.

COVENANT BOOKS FOR JEWISH YOUTH
The Uncommon Soldier, Robert D. Abrahams
Morton Garchik, illus.
The Voice of Liberty: The Story of Emma Lazarus, Eve Merriam
Charles W. Walker, illus.

VISION BOOKS FOR CATHOLIC YOUTH
Governor Al Smith, Hon. James A. Farley and James C. G. Conniff
Kit Carson of the Old West, Mark Boesch
Rose Hawthorne: The Pilgrimage of Nathaniel's Daughter, Arthur and Elizabeth Odell Sheehan
The Ursulines: Nuns of Adventure, Harnett T. Kane

SUMMER AND FALL 1959
Pope John XXIII: An Authoritative Biography, Zsolt Aradi, Msgr. James I. Tucek, and James C. O'Neill
The Tender Shoot and Other Stories, Colette
The Frozen Revolution, Poland: A Study in Communist Decay, Frank Gibney
Questions of Precedence, François Mauriac
What Is the Stars?, Arthur J. Roth
Across the Threshold: A Guide for the Jewish Homemaker, Shonie B. Levi and Sylvia R. Kaplan
Malcolm, James Purdy
The Diners' Club Cookbook, Myra Waldo
Station Wagon in Spain, Frances Parkinson Keyes
The Meaning and Matter of History, M. C. D'Arcy, S.J.
The Birthday of the World, Moshe Davis and Victor Ratner
Marc Chagall, illus.

Make the Way Known: The History of the Dominican Congregation of St. Mary of the Springs, Katherine Burton
Café Céleste, Françoise Mallet-Joris
The Mind of an Assassin, Isaac Don Levine
The Pyx, John Buell
The Private Life of Mr. Pepys, John Harold Wilson
Corsicana, Henry Barsha
Jane Austen, Elizabeth Jenkins
38th Art Directors Annual, Art Directors Club of New York
Pray, Sister: Prie-Dieu Thoughts for Nuns, John E. Moffatt, S.J.
Memoirs of Hecate County, Edmund Wilson

ARIEL CHILDREN'S BOOKS
John Treegate's Musket, Leonard Wibberley
Trovato, Bettina
Adventures of a Beagle, T. L. McCready, Jr.
Tasha Tudor, illus.
A Pony for the Winter, Helen Kay
Ingrid Fetz, illus.

COVENANT BOOKS FOR JEWISH YOUTH
Keys to a Magic Door: Isaac Leib Peretz, Sylvia Rothchild
Aboab: The First Rabbi of the Americas, Emily Hahn

VISION BOOKS FOR CATHOLIC YOUTH
Mother Cabrini, Missionary to the World, Frances Parkinson Keyes
More Champions in Sports and Spirit, Ed Fitzgerald

SPRING 1960
Fuel for the Flame, Alec Waugh
The Wayward Wife and Other Stories, Alberto Moravia
The Owl of Minerva, Gustav Regler
The Violent Bear It Away, Flannery O'Connor
Our Times: The Best from The Reporter, Max Ascoli, ed.
The Other One, Colette
The Torrents of Spring, Ivan Turgenev
Apologies to the Iroquois, Edmund Wilson
A History of Russia, John Lawrence
The Mind of the Murderer, Manfred S. Guttmacher, M.D.
Through Dooms of Love, Karl Stern
The Selected Letters of Charles Dickens, F. W. Dupee, ed.
What It Means to Be a Christian, Dr. Robert W. Youngs
Myra Waldo's Travel Guide to Europe, Myra Waldo
Lament for a Generation, Ralph de Toledano
The Night They Burned the Mountain, Thomas A. Dooley, M.D.
Like a Big Brave Man, Celso Al. Carunungan
The Pageant of Medicine, Félix Marti-Ibañez, M.D., ed.
Dune House, Geraldine Trotta
A Distant Trumpet, Paul Horgan
The Rascal and the Pilgrim, Joseph Anthony
The Third Mystic of Avila: The Self-Revelation of María Vela, a Sixteenth-Century Nun, Frances Parkinson Keyes, with Muna Lee
The Selected Writings of Salvatore Quasimodo, Allen Mandelbaum, ed.
Sunset, Isaac Babel, Cecil Hemley, and Dwight W. Webb, eds.

ARIEL CHILDREN'S BOOKS
The Coach Nobody Liked, John F. Carson
Pepito's Story, Eugene Fern
Peter Treegate's War, Leonard Wibberley

COVENANT BOOKS FOR JEWISH YOUTH
Northwest Pioneer: The Story of Louis Fleischner, Alfred Apsler
Morton Garchik, illus.
Albert Einstein: Citizen of the World, William Wise
Simon Jeruchim, illus.

VISION BOOKS FOR CATHOLIC YOUTH
St. Margaret Mary, Apostle of the Sacred Heart, Ruth Fox Hume
Johannes Troyer, illus.
When Saints Were Young, Blanche Jennings Thompson
John Lawn, illus.

FALL 1960
Madame Goldenflower, C. Y. Lee
Rebel Against the Light, Alexander Ramati
No Compromise!, Arnold Whitridge
A Ballad of Love, Frederic Prokosch
Selected Writings: An Introduction to Orgonomy, Wilhelm Reich
The Christening Party, Francis Steegmuller
Disputed Questions, Thomas Merton
The Indomitable John Scott, Lilian T. Mowrer
S. Z. Mitchell and the Electrical Industry, Sidney Alexander Mitchell
The Seduction, Susan Yorke
Andrew Johnson: President on Trial, Milton Lomask
The Chess Players, Frances Parkinson Keyes
Sex in Man and Woman, Theodor Reik
39th Art Directors Annual, Art Directors Club of New York
The Nephew, James Purdy
Claudine Married, Colette
Doctor Tom Dooley's Three Great Books, Thomas A. Dooley, M.D.
Step This Way, Sister: Reflections for Nuns, Young and—Less Young, John E. Moffatt, S.J.
A Reader's Guide to Joseph Conrad, Frederick R. Karl
Complete Poems of Michelangelo
Joseph Tusiani, trans.
The Magician of Lublin, Isaac Bashevis Singer

ARIEL CHILDREN'S BOOKS

Journey for a Princess, Margaret Leighton
The Secret of the Marmalade Cat, Milton Lomask
Lili Cassel, illus.
Andy and the Red Canoe, Hildreth T. Wriston
W. T. Mars, illus.
The Cricket in Times Square, George Selden
Garth Williams, illus.

COVENANT BOOKS FOR JEWISH YOUTH

Builders of Jerusalem: In the Times of Nehemiah, Frieda Clark Hyman
Donald Bolognese, illus.
The Flagship Hope: Aaron Lopez, Lloyd Alexander
Bernard Krigstein, illus.

VISION BOOKS FOR CATHOLIC YOUTH

Frances Warde and the First Sisters of Mercy, Sister Marie Christopher, R.S.M.
John Lawn, illus.
Vincent de Paul, Saint of Charity, Margaret Ann Hubbard
Harry Barton, illus.

SPRING 1961

Love and Mrs. Sargent, Virginia Rowans
Mémoires Intérieurs, François Mauriac
Everyman's St. Paul, Vincent P. McCorry, S.J.
Dear Newlyweds: Pope Pius XII Speaks to Young Couples, James F. Murray, Jr., and Bianca M. Murray, eds.
The Man with the Miraculous Hands, Joseph Kessel
Gettysburg, Stephen Longstreet
Citizen of New Salem, Paul Horgan
100 Years and Millions of Boys: The Dynamic Story of the Boys' Clubs of America, William Edwin Hall
Jenny by Nature, Erskine Caldwell
It Always Rains in Rome, John F. Leeming
The Selected Letters of William James, Elizabeth Hardwick, ed.
The Lost Footsteps, Silviu Craciunas
Special People, Jacques Serguine
Phaedra and Figaro, Robert Lowell and Jacques Barzun
No Easy Answers, Philip M. Klutznick
My Place in the Bazaar, Alec Waugh
Power and Responsibility: The Life and Times of Theodore Roosevelt, William Harbaugh
The Fleet Rabble, Frank Borden Hanes
A Reader's Guide to Literary Terms, Karl Beckson and Arthur Ganz
The Glass Bees, Ernst Jünger
Character Analysis, revised, Wilhelm Reich

ARIEL CHILDREN'S BOOKS

Mystery at Land's End, Marg Nelson
Kendy's Monkey Business, Helen Kay
Theresa Sherman, illus.
Sea Captain from Salem, Leonard Wibberley
Enrico Arno, illus.
Sara, Louis Lee Floethe
Richard Floethe, illus.

VISION BOOKS

Florence Nightingale's Nuns, Emmeline Garnett
Anne Marie Jauss, illus.
Pope Pius XII: The World's Shepherd, Louis de Wohl
Harry Barton, illus.

FALL 1961

Mirror, Mirror on the Wall: Invitation to Beauty, Gayelord Hauser
Cripple Mah and the New Order, C. Y. Lee
The Custard Boys, John Rae
George Washington September, SIR!, Ronald Harwood
On the Contrary, Mary McCarthy
The Poor Old Liberal Arts, Robert I. Gannon, S.J.
Selected Tales, Nikolai Leskov
A Memoir of Mary Ann: By the Nuns Who Took Care of Her, Flannery O'Connor, ed.
Night Song, John A. Williams
The Spinoza of Market Street, Isaac Bashevis Singer
The Function of the Orgasm, Wilhelm Reich
The Church: A Pictorial History, Edward Rice
The Frontenacs, François Mauriac
A History of India, Michael Edwardes
A Racing Car Driver's World, Rudolph Caracciola
Imitations, Robert Lowell
The Ground I Walked On, George Shuster
The Empty Canvas, Alberto Moravia
Wilson's Night Thoughts, Edmund Wilson
The Murderers: The Story of the Narcotic Gangs, Harry J. Anslinger and Will Oursler
Leaves from a Journal, Queen Victoria
Break of Day, Colette
Before I Sleep: The Last Days of Dr. Tom Dooley, James Monahan, ed.
Alone with God, Dom Jean LeClercq, O.S.B.
Barbarian's Country, Jean Hougron
A New Life, Bernard Malamud
Toward Modern Science, Robert M. Palter, ed.
40th Art Directors Annual, Art Directors Club of New York
Mystery and Manners, Flannery O'Connor
Sally and Robert Fitzgerald, eds.

ARIEL CHILDREN'S BOOKS

Rich Boy, Poor Boy, Theodora DuBois
Drinkers of the Wind, Carl R. Raswan
Hotshot, John F. Carson
The Secret of the One-Eyed Moose, Milton Lomask
W. T. Mars, illus.

COVENANT BOOKS

The Scholar-Fighter: The Story of Saadia Gaon, Libby M. Klaperman
Charles Walker, illus.

VISION BOOKS

The Way We Worship, Milton Lomask and Ray Neville

St. Jerome and the Bible, George Sanderlin
Harry Barton, illus.

Saints of the Byzantine World, Blanche Jennings Thompson
Donald Bolognese, illus.

SPRING 1962

A Holiday by the Sea, Gerald Brenan

The New Man, Thomas Merton

Selected Works of Djuna Barnes, Djuna Barnes

Think, Sister: Thoughts in a Convent Garden, John E. Moffatt, S.J.

Four Days, John Buell

Agency House, Malaya, Susan Yorke

The Jews: A Christian View, Friedrich Wilhelm Foerster

A Reader's Guide to Herman Melville, James E. Miller, Jr.

A Reader's Guide to Marcel Proust, Milton Hindus

A Reader's Guide to Dylan Thomas, William York Tindall

The Contemporary English Novel, Frederick R. Karl

Embattled Critic: Views on Modern Art, John Canaday

Phenomenology and Science in Contemporary European Thought, Anna-Teresa Tymieniecka

The Favourite, Françoise Mallet-Joris

"Some of My Best Friends . . . ," Benjamin R. Epstein and Arnold Forster

Psychoanalysis and Religion, Gregory Zilboorg, M.D.
Margaret Stone Zilboorg, ed.

A Girl like Scranton, John F. Leeming

The Revolt of Zengo Takakuwa, Richard M. Baker, Jr.

Robert Lowell: The First Twenty Years, Hugh B. Staples

God Made Little Apples, John D. Sheridan

The Slave, Isaac Bashevis Singer

Close to Home, Erskine Caldwell

ARIEL CHILDREN'S BOOKS

A Wrinkle in Time, Madeleine L'Engle

The Violet Tree, Doris Troutman Plenn
Johannes Troyer, illus.

Treegate's Raiders, Leonard Wibberley

Andy Johnson: The Tailor Who Became President, Milton Lomask

A Girl Called Chris, Marg Nelson

Dr. Tom Dooley, My Story, Thomas A. Dooley, M.D.

BELL BOOKS

Paco's Miracle, Ann Nolan Clark
Agnes Tait, illus.

Keeper of the Wild Bulls, Heinz Sponsel
Helmar Becker-Berke, illus.

COVENANT BOOKS

Sound of Bow Bells, Robert D. Abrahams

VISION BOOKS

Chaplains in Action, Rosemarian Staudacher
H. Lawrence Hoffman, illus.

St. Catherine Labouré and the Miraculous Medal, Alma Power-Waters
James Fox, illus.

FALL 1962

Diamond, Brian Glanville

A View of My Own, Elizabeth Hardwick

Mountain Standard Time, Paul Horgan

Wise Blood, Flannery O'Connor

Big Sur, Jack Kerouac

Mrs. Seton: Foundress of the American Sisters of Charity, Joseph I. Dirvin, C.M.

The Violent Man, A. E. van Vogt

Life with Mother Superior, Jane Trahey

The Monkeys, G. K. Wilkinson

God's Little Acre, Erskine Caldwell

The Novels of A. C. Swinburne: Love's Cross Currents, Lesbia Brandon, A. C. Swinburne

52 West, Ann Pinchot

The Sitzkrieg of Private Stefan, Erich Kuby

Everyone Is Someone, Fifi Monteux

41st Art Directors Annual, Art Directors Club of New York

The Seven Sisters, Frederic Prokosch

Mirgorod, Nikolai Gogol

Madame Castel's Lodger, Frances Parkinson Keyes

Promises to Keep, Agnes W. Dooley

ARIEL CHILDREN'S BOOKS

Elephi: The Cat with the High I.Q., Jean Stafford
Erik Blegvad, illus.

The Library Mice, Ann Sanders
Eugene Fern, illus.

Bride of Glory, Margaret Leighton

John Marshall: The Great Chief Justice, Caroline Tucker

I See What I See!, George Selden
Robert Galster, illus.

BELL BOOKS

The Giving Gift, Alma Power-Waters
Velma Ilsley, illus.

Angel in the Tower, Elizabeth Dralle

The Winged Watchman, Hilda van Stockum

COVENANT BOOKS

Fighter from Whitechapel: The Story of Daniel Mendoza, Harold U. Ribalow
Simon Jeruchim, illus.

VISION BOOKS

Mother Barat's Vineyard, Margaret Ann Hubbard
Frank Nicholas, illus.

Charles de Foucauld, Adventurer of the Desert, Emmeline Garnett
Leo Summers, illus.

SPRING 1963

Sissie, John A. Williams
Conquistadors, Paul Horgan
Dr. Barnes of Merion, Henry Hart
The Great Deception: The Inside Story of How the Kremlin Took Over Cuba, James Monahan and Kenneth O. Gilmore
Vision of Peace, Wilfrid Tunink, O.S.B.
The Greater Darkness, David Rubin
A Crown of Wild Myrtle, H. E. Bates
Room 3603, H. Montgomery Hyde
Gayelord Hauser's Treasury of Secrets, Gayelord Hauser
Young Man in Chains, François Mauriac
Italian Women Confess, Gabriella Parca, ed.
The Trial of Marie Besnard, Marie Besnard
A Life of One's Own, Gerald Brenan
Memoirs of Hadrian, revised, Marguerite Yourcenar
In Search of a Yogi, Dom Denys Rutledge
Undertow, Helen Parkhurst
You Are Not the Target, Laura Huxley
The Messenger, Charles Wright
The Need to Be Loved, Theodor Reik
Letters from Vatican City, Xavier Rynne
A Cool Million & The Dream Life of Balso Snell, Nathanael West
William Shakespeare: A Reader's Guide, Alfred Harbage

ARIEL CHILDREN'S BOOKS

Easter Pony, Susie Blair
Photographs by Tommy T. Kohara
Toby and the Nighttime, Paul Horgan
Lawrence Beall Smith, illus.
Mystery at Little Squaw River, Marg Nelson
The Moon by Night, Madeleine L'Engle
Pitcher and I, Stephen Cole

BELL BOOKS

Medicine Man's Daughter, Ann Nolan Clark

VISION BOOKS

Martin de Porres, Saint of the New World, Ellen Tarry
James Fox, illus.
Marguerite Bourgeoys, Pioneer Teacher, Sister Mary Genevieve, C.N.D.
Harry Barton, illus.
A Young People's Pictorial History of the Church, Vols. 1 and 2, Edward Rice

FALL 1963

Miss Bannister's Girls, Louise Tanner
The Chinese Garden, Rosemary Manning
Visions of Gerard, Jack Kerouac
The Stone Face, William Gardner Smith
The Benefactor, Susan Sontag
The Last Night of Summer, Erskine Caldwell
American Poster 1963, Jack Amon, ed.
The Early Years of Alec Waugh, Alec Waugh
What I Believe, François Mauriac
Idiots First, Bernard Malamud
The Blue Lantern, Colette
This High Man: The Life of Robert H. Goddard, Milton Lehman
Florine Stettheimer: A Life in Art, Parker Tyler
The Strategy of Deception: A Study of Worldwide Communist Tactics, Jeane J. Kirkpatrick, ed.
Oscar Wilde: The Aftermath, H. Montgomery Hyde
The Great Collectors, Pierre Cabanne
Apollinaire, Francis Steegmuller
The Cold War and the Income Tax: A Protest, Edmund Wilson

ARIEL CHILDREN'S BOOKS

The American Indian Story, May NcNeer
Lynd Ward, illus.
Dolls, Bettina
Plunkety-Plunk, Peter Lippman
The Mystery of the Missing Monkey, John F. Carson
John Bartram, illus.
Court Clown, John F. Carson
Young Man from the Piedmont: The Youth of Thomas Jefferson, Leonard Wibberley

BELL BOOKS

The Skies of Crete, James Forman
Nacar, the White Deer, Elizabeth Borton de Treviño
Enrico Arno, illus.

VISION BOOKS

Father Kino, Priest to the Pimas, Ann Nolan Clark
H. Lawrence Hoffman, illus.
Children Welcome, Rosemarian V. Staudacher
A Young People's Pictorial History of the Church, Vols. 3 and 4, Edward Rice

SPRING 1964

The Lyndon Johnson Story, revised, Booth Mooney
Creative Fidelity, Gabriel Marcel
At War as Children, Kit Reed
Oh! To Be in England, H. E. Bates
After the Cossacks Burned Down the "Y," Eddy Gilmore
The Dark Dancer, Frederic Prokosch
Knowledge and Experience in the Philosophy of F. H. Bradley, T. S. Eliot
Pagan Rites in Judaism, Theodor Reik
Doings and Undoings: The Fifties and After in American Writing, Norman Podhoretz
The John F. Kennedys: A Family Album, Mark Shaw
A Love Affair, Dino Buzzati
Comrade Don Camillo, Giovanni Guareschi
Seed Money: The Guggenheim Story, Milton Lomask
Royal Flush, William Dryden
The Mortal Wound, Raffaele La Capria
The Singing Forest, H. Mortimer Batten
The Protectors, Harry J. Anslinger, with J. Dennis Gregory
77 Dream Songs, John Berryman
Okee: The Story of an Otter in the House, Dorothy Wisbeski

More Roman Tales, Alberto Moravia
The Second Session, Letters from Vatican Council II: The Debates at St. Peter's, Xavier Rynne
A Letter to Myself, Françoise Mallet-Joris
The Death of Artemio Cruz, Carlos Fuentes
Saint Angela: The Life of Angela Merici, Foundress of the Ursulines, Philip Caraman, S.J.
Selected Poems, Derek Walcott
All in Favor Say No, Robin White

ARIEL CHILDREN'S BOOKS
Arripay, Rosemary Manning
Victor Ambrus, illus.
The Mystery of the Tarnished Trophy, John F. Carson
Word of Honor, Ruth Adams Knight and Claud W. Garner
Tiger Burning Bright, Theodora DuBois
Flip, Jane Belk Moncure
Photographs by Morris H. Jaffe

VISION BOOKS
St. Gregory the Great, Consul of God, George Sanderlin
Christopher Curtis, illus.
Peter and Paul: The Rock and the Sword, Blanche Jennings Thompson
Harry Barton, illus.

FALL 1964
The Pilgrim, Michael Serafian
Sargent Shriver: A Candid Portrait, Robert A. Liston
The Lonely Years: 1925–1939, Isaac Babel
The Arts and Crafts of India and Ceylon, Ananda K. Coomaraswamy
A Reader's Guide to William Faulkner, Edmond L. Volpe
Things As They Are, Paul Horgan
A Moment in Time, H. E. Bates
Ready for the Tiger, Sam Ross
The Exact and Very Strange Truth, Ben Piazza
For the Union Dead, Robert Lowell
Speak Not Evil, Edwin Lanham
A Reader's Guide to Geoffrey Chaucer, Muriel Bowden
Bad Characters, Jean Stafford
Cabot Wright Begins, James Purdy
Rasputin and the Fall of the Romanovs, Colin Wilson
Short Friday, Isaac Bashevis Singer
After More Black Coffee, Robert I. Gannon, S.J.
Through Europe with a Jug of Wine, Morrison Wood
Voices from the Inaudible, Theodor Reik
Around About America, Erskine Caldwell

ARIEL CHILDREN'S BOOKS
Castaway Christmas, Margaret J. Baker
Richard Kennedy, illus.
Mystery on a Minus Tide, Marg Nelson
Soldier and Statesman: General George C. Marshall, Harold Faber
The Star and the Flame, Rosemary Weir
William Stobbs, illus.
Bittersweet Summer, Louise Lee Floethe
A Dawn in the Trees: Thomas Jefferson, the Years 1776–1789, Leonard Wibberley
Papillot, Clignot et Dodo, Francis Steegmuller and Norbert Guterman
Barbara Cooney, illus.
The Twenty-four Days Before Christmas, Madeleine L'Engle
Inga, illus.
Writing!, Murray McCain
John Alcorn, illus.

VISION BOOKS
Irish Saints, Robert T. Reilly
Harry Barton, illus.
Dear Philippine: The Mission of Mother Duchesne, Margaret Ann Hubbard
John Lawn, illus.

SPRING 1965
Listen, Little Man!, Wilhelm Reich
William Steig, illus.
The Ability to Love, Allan Fromme
A History of Pornography, H. Montgomery Hyde
An Age of Fiction: The Nineteenth Century British Novel, Frederick R. Karl
The White Father, Julian Mitchell
Lord Haw-Haw—and William Joyce: The Full Story, J. A. Cole
Sometimes I Wonder, Hoagy Carmichael, with Stephen Longstreet
The Game of Dostoevsky, Samuel Astrachan
Henry Garnet and the Gunpowder Plot, Philip Caraman, S.J.
The Mechanical Pianos, Henri-François Rey
In Search of Bisco, Erskine Caldwell
The Fly, Richard Chopping
White Marble Lady, Roi Ottley
The Prince's Person, Roger Peyrefitte
Songs After Lincoln, Paul Horgan
O Canada, Edmund Wilson
The Escape Artists, David Wagoner
Ladies of the Rachmaninoff Eyes, Henry Van Dyke
The Fetish and Other Stories, Alberto Moravia
Everything That Rises Must Converge, Flannery O'Connor
The Third Session: The Debates and Decrees of Vatican Council II at St. Peter's, Xavier Rynne
The King of the Cats and Other Remarks on Writers and Writing, F. W. Dupee
The Kandy-Kolored Tangerine-Flake Streamline Baby, Tom Wolfe
Seeds of Destruction, Thomas Merton

ARIEL CHILDREN'S BOOKS
Emeralds on Her Hand, Nancy Paschal
The Arm of the Starfish, Madeleine L'Engle
Voyage to Coromandel, Margaret Leighton
Here Is England, Elizabeth Burton
Ready, Wrestle!, Sam G. Barnes

BELL BOOKS

Ring the Judas Bell, James Forman
Promise of the Rainbow, Rosalie K. Fry
Robin Jacques, illus.

VISION BOOKS

Peter Claver, Saint Among Slaves, Ann Roos
H. Lawrence Hoffman, illus.
John Neumann, the Children's Bishop, Elizabeth Odell Sheehan
Harry Barton, illus.

FALL 1965

The Flight from Woman, Karl Stern
A Mouse Is Miracle Enough, Myna Lockwood
40,000 Years of Music, Jacques Chailley
Square's Progress, Wilfrid Sheed
Deities and Dolphins: The Story of the Nabataeans, Nelson Glueck
Cordelia and Other Stories, Françoise Mallet-Joris
Yes I Can: The Story of Sammy Davis, Jr., Sammy Davis, Jr., Jane and Burt Boyer
Cassio and the Life Divine, David Rubin
It's All in the Music: The Life and Work of Pierre Monteux, Doris Monteux
A Sense of Where You Are: A Profile of Bill Bradley at Princeton, John McPhee
The MacArthur Controversy and American Foreign Policy, Richard H. Rovere and Arthur Schlesinger, Jr.
The Myth and the Powerhouse, Philip Rahv
Give Joy to My Youth: A Memoir of Dr. Tom Dooley, Teresa Gallagher
Questions of Travel, Elizabeth Bishop
The Irish Republic, Dorothy Macardle
The Great Bridge, Lili Réthi, F.R.S.A., and Edward M. Young
La Bâtarde, Violette Leduc
Cynthia, H. Montgomery Hyde
The Mule on the Minaret, Alec Waugh
The Old Glory, Robert Lowell
The New York Times Book of Interior Design and Decoration, George O'Brien, ed.
The Bit Between My Teeth: A Literary Chronicle of 1950–1965, Edmund Wilson
Aura, Carlos Fuentes
Seasons of Celebration, Thomas Merton
To Criticize the Critic and Other Writings, T. S. Eliot
Reconstruction in the South, 1865–1877, Harvey Wish, ed.
Curiosities of the Self, Theodor Reik

ARIEL CHILDREN'S BOOKS

The Shoe Shop Bears, Margaret J. Baker
C. Walter Hodges, illus.
The Voice of Apollo, Mary Ray
Enrico Arno, illus.
The High King's Daughter, Theodora DuBois
John Hardy, illus.
Katrina of the Lonely Isles, Margaret Ruthin
The Gales of Spring: Thomas Jefferson, the Years 1789–1801, Leonard Wibberley
The Show Ring, Susie Blair
John Quincy Adams, Milton Lomask
Mystery of the Missing Dowry, Marg Nelson

BELL BOOKS

I, Juan de Pareja, Elizabeth Borton de Treviño
The Sea Wall, Eilís Dillon
W. T. Mars, illus.

VISION BOOKS

St. Francis de Sales, Blanche Jennings Thompson
Charles Walker, illus.
Sarah Peter, Alma Power-Waters
John Lawn, illus.

SPRING 1966

Against Interpretation, Susan Sontag
Man as an End, Alberto Moravia
Corporal Glass's Island: The Story of Tristan da Cunha, Nancy Hosegood
The Wig: A Mirror Image, Charles Wright
Biological Treatment of Mental Illness, Max Rinkel, M.D., ed.
A Mother in History, Jean Stafford
The Knowledge Explosion, Francis Sweeney, S.J., ed.
The Uncompromising Heart, Françoise Mallet-Joris
The Panic in Needle Park, James Mills
Hogan's Goat, William Alfred
The Mystic in the Theatre: Eleonora Duse, Eva Le Gallienne
In My Father's Court, Isaac Bashevis Singer
The Delights of Growing Old, Maurice Goudeket
The Crystal World, J. G. Ballard
Memories of the Future, Paul Horgan
Earthly Paradise: An Autobiography of Colette, Robert Phelps, ed.
The Wreck of the Cassandra, Frederic Prokosch
A Season in the Life of Emmanuel, Marie-Claire Blais
The Last Gentleman, Walker Percy
The Lie, Alberto Moravia
Modern Occasions, Philip Rahv, ed.
The Insecurity of Freedom, Abraham Joshua Heschel

ARIEL CHILDREN'S BOOKS

The King Who Was Too Busy, Eugene Fern
Small Creatures in My Garden, Christopher Reynolds
The Growing Season, Stephen Cole
The Man Who Cared: A Life of Harry S Truman, Victor Wolfson
The Lion of Judah: A Life of Haile Selassie I, Charles Gorham
"I Do Solemnly Swear . . .": The Story of the Presidential Inauguration, Milton Lomask
Tormented Angel: A Life of John Henry Newman, Emmeline Garnett

BELL BOOKS
The Shield of Achilles, James Forman
Seasons: A Cycle of Verse, Emmeline Garnett, ed.
The White Goddess, revised, Robert Graves

VISION BOOKS
Good Pope John, Elizabeth Odell Sheehan
Harry Barton, illus.

FALL 1966

The Fourth Session, Xavier Rynne
Career Planning for the Blind, Fred L. Crawford, Ph.D.
Philadephia, Here I Come!, Brian Friel
The Magic of Shirley Jackson, Stanley Edgar Hyman, ed.
The Children of the South, Margaret Anderson
Europe Without Baedeker, Edmund Wilson
The Fixer, Bernard Malamud
Office Politics, Wilfrid Sheed
The Headmaster, John McPhee
The Many Faces of Sex, Theodor Reik
Diary of an Art Dealer, René Gimpel
The Love Letters, Madeleine L'Engle
The Woman with the Little Fox, Violette Leduc
Beatrice Cenci, Alberto Moravia
My Home, Sweet Home, Giovanni Guareschi
The Collected Works of Jane Bowles, Jane Bowles

ARIEL CHILDREN'S BOOKS
Sleepy People, M. B. Goffstein
Hannibal and the Bears, Margaret J. Baker
C. Walter Hodges, illus.
The Canyon Castaways, Margaret Leighton
The Cloud Forest, Joan North
Mystery of the Missing Cannon, Marg Nelson
The Eastern Beacon, Mary Ray
Enrico Arno, illus.
This Slender Reed: A Life of James K. Polk, Milton Lomask
Time of the Harvest: Thomas Jefferson, the Years 1801–1826, Leonard Wibberley

BELL BOOKS
Yeshu, Called Jesus, Claire Huchet Bishop
Donald Bolognese, illus.

SPRING 1967

Near the Ocean, Robert Lowell
Sidney Nolan, illus.
Oranges, John McPhee
Mystics and Zen Masters, Thomas Merton
The Better Part, Kit Reed
Berryman's Sonnets, John Berryman
The Day Is Dark and *Three Travelers*, Marie-Claire Blais
The Sea Wall, Marguerite Duras
The Loves of Cass McGuire, Brian Friel
The Paste-Pot Man, Edwin Lanham
The Pope's Back Yard, Curtis G. Pepper
The Peach Stone: Stories from Four Decades, Paul Horgan
The Heights of Macchu Picchu, Pablo Neruda
The Family Tree, Dorothy Yates
The Singing Lizard, John Knowler
Eustace Chisholm and the Works, James Purdy
Six Metaphysical Poets: A Reader's Guide, George Williamson
The Flagellants, Carlene Hatcher Polite
The Dhammapada, P. Lal, trans.
A Prelude: Landscapes, Characters and Conversations from the Earlier Years of My Life, Edmund Wilson
I Thought of Daisy and *Galahad*, Edmund Wilson
Memoirs, Clara Malraux

ARIEL CHILDREN'S BOOKS
The King of the Hermits and Other Stories, Jack Sendak
Margot Zemach, illus.
The Golden Key, George MacDonald
Maurice Sendak, illus.
Birthday Presents, Eugene Fern
Anna of the Bears, Bjorn Rongen
Jane Paton, illus.
Dick Foote and the Shark, Natalie Babbitt
The House of Cats and Other Stories, John Hampden
Enrico Arno, illus.
Katia, E. M. Almedingen
Victor Ambrus, illus.
Encounter Near Venus, Leonard Wibberley
Alice Wadowski-Bak, illus.
Madame Prime Minister: The Story of Indira Gandhi, Emmeline Garnett
From Sea to Sea: The Growth of the United States, Harold Faber

BELL BOOKS
Horses of Anger, James Forman
Casilda of the Rising Moon, Elizabeth Borton de Treviño

VISION BOOKS
Brother André of Montreal, Ann Nolan Clark
Harold Lang, illus.
Edel Quinn: Beneath the Southern Cross, Evelyn M. Brown
Harry Barton, illus.

FALL 1967

The Chinese Looking Glass, Dennis Bloodworth
Thérèse and Isabelle, Violette Leduc
Signs and Wonders, Françoise Mallet-Joris
Hunger, Knut Hamsun
Death Kit, Susan Sontag
The Uncommitted Man, R. E. Pickering
Poems Written in Early Youth, T. S. Eliot
Scutari, Mladin Zarubica
Randall Jarrell, 1914–1965, Robert Lowell, Peter Taylor, and Robert Penn Warren, eds.
The Stories of the Greeks, Rex Warner
The Revolutionary, Hans Koningsberger

The Pure and the Impure, Colette
The Manor, Isaac Bashevis Singer
A Husband in Boarding School, Giovanni Guareschi
O the Chimneys, Nelly Sachs
A Malamud Reader, Bernard Malamud
Ooty Preserved: A Victorian Hill Station in India, Mollie Panter-Downes
My Brother Evelyn and Other Portraits, Alec Waugh
Delano: The Story of the California Grape Strike, John Gregory Dunne
Reich Speaks of Freud, Mary Higgins and Chester M. Raphael, M.D., eds.
The Young Stalin, Edward Ellis Smith
Our Troubled Selves, Alan Fromme
Short Poems, John Berryman
Vatican Council II, Xavier Rynne
A Change of Skin, Carlos Fuentes
Shalom: Peace, the Sacrament of Reconciliation, Bernard Häring, C.Ss.R.
The Missolonghi Manuscript, Frederic Prokosch

ARIEL CHILDREN'S BOOKS

Brookie and Her Lamb, M. B. Goffstein
Mazel and Shlimazel, or The Milk of a Lioness, Isaac Bashevis Singer
Margot Zemach, illus.
A Thousand and One Buddhas, Louise Lee Floethe
Richard Floethe, illus.
Bears Back in Business, Margaret J. Baker
Daphne Rowles, illus.
The Hatching of Joshua Cobb, Margaret Hodges
W. T. Mars, illus.
The Last Dodo, Richard Boyde
High Courage, Rosemary Weir
Ian Ribbons, illus.
The True Story of Okee the Otter, Dorothy Wisbeski
The Black Coast: The Story of the PT Boat, Basil Heatter
Mystery Rides the Charter Boat, Marg Nelson
The Whirling Shapes, Joan North
The Journey with Jonah, Madeleine L'Engle
Leonard Everett Fisher, illus.

BELL BOOKS

Two against the Tide, Bruce Clements

SPRING 1968

Lord Reading, H. Montgomery Hyde
A Garland of Weights, Frank J. Manheim
Melba: A Biography, John Hetherington
The Impossible Proof, Hans Erich Nossack
The Committee, Walter Goodman
Russian Themes, Mihajlo Mihajlov
The Selected Works of Cesare Pavese, R. W. Flint, ed.
The Pine Barrens, John McPhee
Melinda, Gaia Servadio
Babel to Byzantium: Poets and Poetry Now, James Dickey
Twiggy and Justin, Thomas Whiteside
Slouching Towards Bethlehem, Joan Didion
Lovers, Brian Friel
Narcissus and Goldmund, Hermann Hesse
The American Literary Anthology I, Various
Unspeakable Practices, Unnatural Acts, Donald Barthelme
The Serpent, Luigi Malerba
The World We Imagine: Selected Essays, Mark Schorer
Gazapo, Gustavo Sainz
This Timeless Moment, Laura Archera Huxley
The Horsemen, Joseph Kessel
The Creep, Jeffrey Frank
A Change of Skin, Carlos Fuentes

BOOKS FOR YOUNG READERS

Martze, Jack Sendak
Mitchell Miller, illus.
Phoebe's Revolt, Natalie Babbitt
Summer Is for Growing, Ann Nolan Clark
Agnes Tait, illus.
Elli of the Northland, Margaret Ruthin
A Hole in the Hedge, Margaret Leighton
Young Mark, E. M. Almedingen
Victor Ambrus, illus.
The Sea Dreamers, Basil Heatter
Attar of the Ice Valley, Leonard Wibberley
The Young Unicorns, Madeleine L'Engle
Corcoran's the Name, Olaf Ruhen
Constellation: A Shakespeare Anthology, Margaret Hodges
The Ballad of the Burglar of Babylon, Elizabeth Bishop
Ann Grifalconi, illus.

FALL 1968

Beowulf, Kevin Crossley-Holland, trans.
This Timeless Moment, Laura Archera Huxley
Acting on the Word, Bernard Häring, C.Ss.R.
Baby, Come On Inside, David Wagoner
A Mauriac Reader, François Mauriac
The Pump House Gang, Tom Wolfe
The Electric Kool-Aid Acid Test, Tom Wolfe
The Blue Estuaries, Poems: 1923–1968, Louise Bogan
Everything to Live For, Paul Horgan
Along the Roads of the New Russia, Hans Koningsberger
The Séance, Isaac Bashevis Singer
The Red Book and the Great Wall, Alberto Moravia
Beneath the Wheel, Hermann Hesse
The Blacking Factory and *Pennsylvania Gothic*, Wilfrid Sheed
Duncan & Clotilda, Giovanni Guareschi
The Literary Life: A Scrapbook Almanac of the Anglo-American Literary Scene from 1900 to 1950, Robert Phelps and Peter Deane, eds.
His Toy, His Dream, His Rest, John Berryman
Homage to Mistress Bradstreet and Other Poems, John Berryman
Z, Vassilis Vassilikos

Tell Me That You Love Me, Junie Moon, Marjorie Kellogg
The Old Glory, revised, Robert Lowell
The Voyage and Other Versions of Poems by Baudelaire, Robert Lowell
The Boys in the Band, Mart Crowley

BOOKS FOR YOUNG READERS
Mystery of the Starboard List, Marg Nelson
Venture for a Crown, Constance Fecher
The House of the Nightmare and Other Eerie Tales, Kathleen Lines, ed.
New Worlds Ahead, John Hampden, ed.
C. Walter Hodges, illus.
The Gingerbread Boy, William Curtis Holdsworth
Lorenzo and Angelina, Eugene Fern
Sing Out, Charley!, Margaret Hodges
Velma Ilsley, illus.
Man of Liberty: A Life of Thomas Jefferson, Leonard Wibberley
Whistler in the Mist, Rosalie K. Fry
Robin Jacques, illus.
The Land Seekers, Alan Boucher
The Traitors, James Forman
Turi's Poppa, Elizabeth Borton de Treviño
Enrico Arno, illus.
When Shlemiel Went to Warsaw and Other Stories, Isaac Bashevis Singer
Margot Zemach, illus.
Across the Sea, M. B. Goffstein
The Fool of the World and the Flying Ship, Arthur Ransome
Uri Shulevitz, illus.

SPRING 1969
The London Novels of Colin MacInnes, Colin MacInnes
Queen Christina: A Biography, Georgina Masson
The Complete Poems, Randall Jarrell
Blood of Strawberries, Henry Van Dyke
Styles of Radical Will, Susan Sontag
Trip to Hanoi, Susan Sontag
A Roomful of Hovings and Other Profiles, John McPhee
The Duke of Palermo and Other Plays, Edmund Wilson
The Collected Stories, Jean Stafford
A Reader's Guide to Finnegans Wake, William York Tindall
Cancer Ward, Aleksandr Solzhenitsyn
The Studio, John Gregory Dunne
Going Places, Leonard Michaels
Rafferty & Co., Betty Wahl
The Complete Poems, Elizabeth Bishop
What I'm Going to Do, I Think, Larry Woiwode
The Bouviers: Portrait of an American Family, John H. Davis
Prometheus Bound, Robert Lowell
Pictures of Fidelman, Bernard Malamud
Israel: An Echo of Eternity, Abraham Joshua Heschel
Gertrude, Hermann Hesse
Speech, for Instance, Sidney Goldfarb
Salomé: Notes for a New Novel / Don Giovanni: Notes for a Revised Opera, Gaia Servadio
Notebook 1967–1968, Robert Lowell

BOOKS FOR YOUNG READERS
Mystery in Hawaii, Marg Nelson
Floating Market, Louise Lee Floethe
Richard Floethe, illus.
A Candle at Dusk, E. M. Almedingen
Home from the Hill, Margaret J. Baker
W. T. Mars, illus.
Odd Destiny: A Life of Alexander Hamilton, Milton Lomask
Dance in the Desert, Madeleine L'Engle
Symeon Shimin, illus.
The Search for Delicious, Natalie Babbitt
Tucker's Countryside, George Selden
Garth Williams, illus.
Lady Queen Anne, Margaret Hodges
Here Is France, Claire Huchet Bishop
Eighty Days to Hong Kong, Basil Heatter
Black Bondage: The Life of Slaves in the South, Walter Goodman

FALL 1969
Voyager: A Life of Hart Crane, John Unterecker
A Family Romance, Richard Wollheim
Command, and I Will Obey You, Alberto Moravia
You Must Know Everything, Isaac Babel
Culture Gulch, John Canaday
Three Novellas, Ivan Turgenev
What Is This Buzzing, Do You Hear It Too?, Luigi Malerba
Fat City, Leonard Gardner
Peter Camenzind, Hermann Hesse
The Prosecutor, James Mills
Ceremonies in Dark Old Men, Lonne Elder III
Corky's Brother, Jay Neugeboren
Beeton's Book of Household Management, Isabella Beeton
The Witches, Françoise Mallet-Joris
Levels of the Game, John McPhee
Pilgrims, Jean Valentine
The Collected Stories, Peter Taylor
Henry James at Home, H. Montgomery Hyde
The Third Book of Criticism, Randall Jarrell
The Estate, Isaac Bashevis Singer
A Degree of Difference, George Barry Ford
The Dream Songs, John Berryman
Don Camillo Meets the Flower Children, Giovanni Guareschi
Westward to Laughter, Colin MacInnes

BOOKS FOR YOUNG READERS
The Little Red Hen, William Curtis Holdsworth
Hi-Jinks Joins the Bears, Margaret J. Baker
Leslie Wood, illus.
The Ghosts, Antonia Barber
Heir to Pendarrow, Constance Fecher

Overhead the Sun, Walt Whitman
Antonio Frasconi, illus.
Rain Rain Rivers, Uri Shulevitz
Goldie the Dollmaker, M. B. Goffstein
Riverboat Family, Elizabeth Wilton
The Face of Abraham Candle, Bruce Clements
Wordhoard, Kevin Crossley-Holland and Jill Paton Walsh
Cleopatra: Sister of the Moon, Margaret Leighton
Lines Scribbled on an Envelope, and Other Poems, Madeleine L'Engle
The Light Princess, George MacDonald
Maurice Sendak, illus.
The Judge: An Untrue Tale, Harve Zemach
Margot Zemach, illus.
How the Children Stopped the Wars, Jan Wahl
Mitchell Miller, illus.
A Monkey's Uncle, Wilhelm Hauff
Mitchell Miller, illus.
"Wreck Ashore!," Basil Heatter
The Haunted Journey, Robert Murphy
The Cow Neck Rebels, James Forman
African Heroes, Naomi Mitchison
William Stobbs, illus.
A Day of Pleasure: Stories of a Boy Growing Up in Warsaw, Isaac Bashevis Singer

SPRING 1970

The Life and Loves of Mr. Jiveass Nigger, Cecil Brown
A Reader's Guide to W. H. Auden, John Fuller
Kaspar and Other Plays, Peter Handke
The Encounter, Malachi Martin
The Love-Girl and the Innocent, Aleksandr Solzhenitsyn
Rosshalde, Hermann Hesse
A Reader's Guide to Walt Whitman, Gay Wilson Allen
Nathanael West: The Art of His Life, Jay Martin
A Spy in the Family: An Erotic Comedy, Alec Waugh
Dionysus in 69, The Performance Group
Two Plays: Crystal and Fox and *The Mundy Scheme*, Brian Friel
Tomi Ungerer's Compromises, Tomi Ungerer
Poems, Hermann Hesse
Portrait of India, Ved Mehta
City Life, Donald Barthelme
A Theology of Protest, Bernard Häring, C.Ss.R.
The Gulf, Derek Walcott
Powerful Long Ladder, Owen Dodson
Max Jamison, Wilfrid Sheed
Exiles, Michael J. Arlen
The Crofter and the Laird, John McPhee
The Manuscripts of Pauline Archange, Marie-Claire Blais
Maltaverne, François Mauriac

BOOKS FOR YOUNG READERS

Elephant Boy, William Kotzwinkle
Joe Servello, illus.
Journey to Untor, Leonard Wibberley
Fireweed, Jill Paton Walsh
Mystery on a Full Moon, Marg Nelson
Two Piano Tuners, M. B. Goffstein
Tell Me a Mitzi, Lore Segal
Harriet Pincus, illus.
The House on the Common, Alison Prince
W. T. Mars, illus.
Fanny, E. M. Almedingen
Ian Ribbons, illus.
Up on the Rim, Dale Eunson
Here Is Mexico, Elizabeth Borton de Treviño
Sir Tristan of All Time, Sabra Holbrook
Circle of Seasons, Ann Nolan Clark
W. T. Mars, illus.
Kneeknock Rise, Natalie Babbitt
Leader at Large: The Long and Fighting Life of Norman Thomas, Charles Gorham

FALL 1970

Play It As It Lays, Joan Didion
The Movies As Medium, Lewis Jacobs, ed.
D. W. Griffith: The Years at Biograph, Robert M. Henderson
Louise de Marillac, Joseph I. Dirvin, C.M.
Duet for Cannibals, Susan Sontag
David Holzman's Diary, L. M. Kit Carson and Jim McBride
Little Fauss and Big Halsy, Charles Eastman
Dream on Monkey Mountain and Other Plays, Derek Walcott
An Eye for the Dragon, Dennis Bloodworth
Maximum Security Ward, Ramon Guthrie
Professional Secrets: The Autobiography of Jean Cocteau, Robert Phelps, ed.
Jean Cocteau, illus.
Love & Fame, John Berryman
Whitewater, Paul Horgan
The Family Guareschi, Giovanni Guareschi
A Friend of Kafka and Other Stories, Isaac Bashevis Singer
Where Is My Wandering Boy Tonight?, David Wagoner
Klingsor's Last Summer, Hermann Hesse
Honor to the Bride, Jane Kramer
Notebook, revised, Robert Lowell
Three Years to Play, Colin MacInnes
Maurice Baring Restored, Paul Horgan, ed.
Lights and Shadows of New York Life, James D. McCabe, Jr.
The Seeker and Other Poems, Nelly Sachs
All Men Are Mad, Philippe Thoby-Marcelin and Pierre Marcelin
The Quest for Christa T., Christa Wolf
The Mass Psychology of Fascism, Wilhelm Reich
Babi Yar, A. Anatoli (Kuznetsov)
Radical Chic and Mau-Mauing the Flak Catchers, Tom Wolfe

BOOKS FOR YOUNG READERS

Joseph and Koza, Isaac Bashevis Singer
Symeon Shimin, illus.

Snowed Up, Rosalie K. Fry
Robin Jacques, illus.
Storm and Other Old English Riddles, Kevin Crossley-Holland
Miles Thistlethwaite, illus.
The Something, Natalie Babbitt
Against Odds, Basil Heatter
So Ends This Day, James Forman
The Day They Gave Babies Away, Dale Eunson
Douglas Gorsline, illus.
The Family at Ditlabeng, Naomi Mitchison
Joanna Stubbs, illus.
The Lion and the Rose, Rosemary Weir
Richard Cuffari, illus.
Ellen, E. M. Almedingen
Bright Star: A Portrait of Ellen Terry, Constance Fecher
Awake and Dreaming, Harve Zemach
Margot Zemach, illus.
Elijah the Slave, Isaac Bashevis Singer
Antonio Frasconi, illus.

FEBRUARY TO AUGUST 1971

The New Novel: From Queneau to Pinget, Vivian Mercier
A Percentage of the Take, Walter Goodman
The Heartland, Stuart Legg
The Other Side of the Sun, Madeleine L'Engle
If the War Goes On . . ., Hermann Hesse
The Brother, F. D. Reeve
Messages, Sidney Goldfarb
The Stream, Robert Murphy
The Isaac Bashevis Singer Reader, Isaac Bashevis Singer
The Weekend Man, Richard Wright
The Paper House, Françoise Mallet-Joris
Miss Thistlebottom's Hobgoblins, Theodore M. Bernstein
Ready for the Defense, Martin Garbus
John Is Easy to Please, Ved Mehta
Delano, revised, John Gregory Dunne
Knulp, Hermann Hesse
Morality Is for Persons, Bernard Häring, C.Ss.R.
Love in the Ruins, Walker Percy
Stories and Prose Poems, Aleksandr Solzhenitsyn
One Day in the Life of Ivan Denisovich, Aleksandr Solzhenitsyn
Carnal Knowledge, Jules Feiffer

BOOKS FOR YOUNG READERS

Bugaboo Bill, Palmer Cox
William Curtis Holdsworth, illus.
The Making of Joshua Cobb, Margaret Hodges
W. T. Mars, illus.
The Link Boys, Constance Fecher
Richard Cuffari, illus.
One Summer in Alaska, Marg Nelson
The Beast of Monsieur Racine, Tomi Ungerer
Reggie and Nilma, Louise Tanner
In the Trail of the Wind, John Bierhorst
Goody Hall, Natalie Babbitt
Song of Jubilee, James Forman
The Glass Room, Mary Towne
The Singing Turtle and Other Tales from Haiti, Philippe Thoby-Marcelin and Pierre Marcelin
George Ford, illus.
Leopard's Prey, Leonard Wibberley
Beyond the Gates of Hercules, Elizabeth Borton de Treviño
American Painter in Paris: A Life of Mary Cassatt, Ellen Wilson

FALL AND WINTER 1971–72

Encounters with the Archdruid, John McPhee
The Collected Poems of H. Phelps Putnam, Charles R. Walker, ed.
Von Stroheim, Thomas Quinn Curtiss
Mysteries, Knut Hamsun
Upstate, Edmund Wilson
The Morning After, Wilfrid Sheed
Dead Piano, Henry Van Dyke
The Tenants, Bernard Malamud
Mad in Pursuit, Violette Leduc
The Invasion of Compulsory Sex-Morality, Wilhelm Reich
The d'Arthez Case, Hans Erich Nossack
Male/Female, William Steig
The Complete Stories, Flannery O'Connor
London War Notes: 1939–1945, Mollie Panter-Downes
Skate, Jon Appleby
A Reader's Guide to the Contemporary English Novel, revised, Frederick R. Karl
Stalin, H. Montgomery Hyde
Wandering, Hermann Hesse
On the Slain Collegians, Herman Melville
Antonio Frasconi, ed. and illus.

BOOKS FOR YOUNG READERS

One Misty Moisty Morning: Rhymes from Mother Goose, Mitchell Miller
Return of Crazy Horse, William Kotzwinkle
Joe Servello, illus.
Amos and Boris, William Steig
Alone in the Wild Forest, Isaac Bashevis Singer
Margot Zemach, illus.
The Dragon Horde, Tanith Lee
Graham Oakley, illus.
The Slightly Irregular Fire Engine or the Hithering Thithering Djinn, Donald Barthelme
Little John, Theodor Storm
Anita Lobel, illus.
Learn to Say Goodbye, Dolores Warwick
A Penny a Look, Harve Zemach
Margot Zemach, illus.
The Man Who Built a City: A Life of Christopher Wren, Rosemary Weir
The Other Island, Margaret Leighton
The Light Maze, Joan North
The Black Wolf of River Bend, Helene Widell
The Rights of the People, Elaine and Walter Goodman

SPRING AND SUMMER 1972

A Siberian Encounter, Gaia Servadio
A Circle of Quiet, Madeleine L'Engle
T. S. Eliot's Social Criticism, Roger Kojecky
Two: A Phallic Novel, Alberto Moravia
In the Reign of Peace, Hugh Nissenson
Three Popes and the Cardinal, Malachi Martin
Autobiographical Writings, Hermann Hesse
Theodore Ziolkowski, ed.
A Reader's Guide to Ernest Hemingway, Arthur Waldhorn
Faster!, Jackie Stewart and Peter Manso
America, My Wilderness, Frederic Prokosch
Daddyji, Ved Mehta
Delusions, Etc., John Berryman
The Goalie's Anxiety at the Penalty Kick, Peter Handke
Strange News from Another Star, Hermann Hesse
Conventional Wisdom, John Bart Gerald
To the Finland Station, Edmund Wilson
A Window on Russia, Edmund Wilson
Enemies, a Love Story, Isaac Bashevis Singer
Report to the Commissioner, James Mills
Encounters with Stravinsky, Paul Horgan
The Taxi, Violette Leduc
The Poems of Trumbull Stickney, Amberys R. Whittle, ed.

BOOKS FOR YOUNG READERS

The Repair of Uncle Toe, Kay Chorao
Soldier and Tsar in the Forest, Richard Lourie, trans.
Uri Shulevitz, illus.
Dominic, William Steig
Minna and Pippin, Harriet Pincus
The Path to Snowbird Mountain: Cherokee Tales, Traveller Bird
Mungo, Rosalie K. Fry
Velma Ilsley, illus.
The Wicked City, Isaac Bashevis Singer
Leonard Everett Fisher, illus.
The Underside of the Leaf, M. B. Goffstein
Penengro, Hilda van Stockum
A King in Haiti: The Story of Henri Christophe, Basil Heatter
Toni Evins, illus.
Anna, E. M. Almedingen
The Last Elizabethan: A Portrait of Sir Walter Ralegh, Constance Fecher
From Ice Set Free: The Story of Otto Kiep, Bruce Clements
Flint's Island, Leonard Wibberley
People of the Dream, James Forman
A Stranger in My Land: A Life of François Villon, Sabra Holbrook
Francis in All His Glory, Burke Wilkinson
Billy Bartram and His Green World, Marjory Bartlett Sanger

FALL AND WINTER 1972–73

The Shrewsdale Exit, John Buell
August 1914, Aleksandr Solzhenitsyn
The Blue Cat, F. D. Reeve
The Benevolent Bean, Margaret and Ancel Keys
Splendor and Death of Joaquín Murieta, Pablo Neruda
Making Fine Wines and Liqueurs at Home, Leigh P. Beadle
Like the Lion's Tooth, Marjorie Kellogg
Sadness, Donald Barthelme
Stories of Five Decades, Hermann Hesse
Theodore Ziolkowski, ed.
Sunday Driver, Brock Yates
The All-American Boy, Charles Eastman
Any Number Can Play, Dennis Bloodworth
The Manipulated Man, Esther Vilar
Black Studies, Charles Wright
Greek Art, R. M. Cook

BOOKS FOR YOUNG READERS

Animal Castle, Tanith Lee
Helen Craig, illus.
Land of Muscovy, E. M. Almedingen
Michael Charlton, illus.
Small Poems, Valerie Worth
Natalie Babbitt, illus.
Hunted Like a Wolf, Milton Meltzer
Goldengrove, Jill Paton Walsh
Snow-White and the Seven Dwarfs, Brothers Grimm
Randall Jarrell, trans.
Nancy Ekholm Burkert, illus.
The Serpent and the Sun, Cal Roy
Enough!, Doris Faber
Hopkins of the Mayflower, Margaret Hodges

SPRING AND SUMMER 1973

Nobel Lecture, Aleksandr Solzhenitsyn
Marinetti: Selected Writings, R. W. Flint, ed.
American Mischief, Alan Lelchuk
Another Life, Derek Walcott
Absolutely Nothing to Get Alarmed About, Charles Wright
A Reader's Guide to Charles Dickens, Philip Hobsbaum
Recovery, John Berryman
Moly and *My Sad Captains*, Thom Gunn
People Will Always Be Kind, Wilfrid Sheed
Bought and Sold, Alberto Moravia
The Devils and Canon Barham, Edmund Wilson
The American Cider Book, Vrest Orton
Folklore and Odysseys of Food and Medicinal Plants, Ernst and Johanna Lehner
Billy Bitzer: His Story, G. W. Bitzer
Rembrandt's Hat, Bernard Malamud
The Deltoid Pumpkin Seed, John McPhee
City Police, Jonathan Rubinstein
Ether, God and Devil and *Cosmic Superimposition*, Wilhelm Reich
After Claude, Iris Owens
Selected Writings, Wilhelm Reich
History, Robert Lowell
For Harriet and Lizzie, Robert Lowell
The Dolphin, Robert Lowell

Ninety-Two in the Shade, Thomas McGuane
The Cancer Biopathy, Wilhelm Reich
A Reader's Guide to Samuel Beckett, Hugh Kenner
Heirs Apparent: What Happens When Mao Dies?, Dennis and Ching Ping Bloodworth
The Fatal Gift, Alec Waugh
Approaches to Writing, Paul Horgan
Adventures with D. W. Griffith, Karl Brown
Kevin Brownlow, ed.
The Quintessence of Hesse, Hermann Hesse
Volker Michels, ed.

BOOKS FOR YOUNG READERS

The Woman Who Lived in Holland, Mildred Howells
William Curtis Holdsworth, illus.
The Genie of Sutton Place, George Selden
Sunrise Tomorrow: A Story of Botswana, Naomi Mitchison
Blood Royal, Rosemary Weir
Richard Cuffari, illus.
Princess Hynchatti & Some Other Surprises, Tanith Lee
Velma Ilsley, illus.
The Leopard Dagger, Constance Fecher
The Other World: Myths of the Celts, Margaret Hodges
They Named Me Gertrude Stein, Ellen Wilson
A Wind in the Door, Madeleine L'Engle
Duffy and the Devil, Harve Zemach
Margot Zemach, illus.
King Grisly-Beard, Edgar Taylor, trans.
Maurice Sendak, illus.
The Real Thief, William Steig
The Supreme, Superb, Exalted and Delightful One and Only Magic Building, William Kotzwinkle
Joe Servello, illus.

FALL AND WINTER 1973–74

The Truth about Kent State, Peter Davies
Two Citizens, James Wright
A Passion for Truth, Abraham Joshua Heschel
In the Middle of a Life, Richard B. Wright
My Belief: Essays on Life and Art, Hermann Hesse
Theodore Ziolkowski, ed.
Crash, J. G. Ballard
The Age of the Avant-Garde, Hilton Kramer
The Diary of Samuel Sewall Vol. I (1674–1708) and Vol. II (1709–1729), M. Halsey Thomas, ed.
A Crown of Feathers and Other Stories, Isaac Bashevis Singer
The Hundred Glories of French Cooking, Robert Courtine
The Man-Eating Machine, John Sack
White Colors, F. D. Reeve
Xingu: The Indians, Their Myths, Orlando Villas Boas and Claudio Villas Boas

BOOKS FOR YOUNG READERS

Red Pawns, Leonard Wibberley
Shelley's Mary: A Life of Mary Godwin Shelley, Margaret Leighton
The Fools of Chelm and Their History, Isaac Bashevis Singer
Uri Shulevitz, illus.
Joy in Stone, Sabra Holbrook
Herbert Danska, illus.
All the Way Home, Lore Segal
James Marshall, illus.
The Spring on the Mountain, Judy Allen
The Knee-Baby, Mary Jarrell
Symeon Shimin, illus.
The Life and Death of Yellow Bird, James Forman
The Juniper Tree and Other Tales from Grimm, Brothers Grimm
Lore Segal and Randall Jarrell, trans.
Maurice Sendak, illus.

SPRING AND SUMMER 1974

Enormous Changes at the Last Minute, Grace Paley
Cults of Unreason, Christopher Evans
The Family as Patient, Horst E. Richter
The Road to Many a Wonder, David Wagoner
The Priest of Love, revised, Harry T. Moore
Paradiso, José Lezama Lima
Reflections, Hermann Hesse
Volker Michels, ed.
Number One with a Bullet, Elaine Jesmer
The Making of Modern Drama, Richard Gilman
The Life and Death of Yukio Mishima, Henry Scott-Stokes
Against Rape, Andra Medea and Kathleen Thompson
Cooking with Rice, Paul Eve
Four Masterworks of American Indian Literature, John Bierhorst, ed.
Memoirs of a Scam Man, Patsy Anthony Lepera and Walter Goodman
The Curve of Binding Energy, John McPhee
The Sexual Revolution, revised, Wilhelm Reich
The Best, Peter Passell and Leonard Ross
Each Man in His Time, Raoul Walsh
Carrying the Fire, Michael Collins
The Last Season of Weeb Ewbank, Paul Zimmerman

BOOKS FOR YOUNG READERS

Why Noah Chose the Dove, Isaac Bashevis Singer
Eric Carle, illus.
Ralph and the Queen's Bathtub, Kay Chorao
The Devil's Storybook, Natalie Babbitt
Nobody's Family Is Going to Change, Louise Fitzhugh
Songs of the Chippewa, John Bierhorst, ed.
Joe Servello, illus.
The Emperor's Winding Sheet, Jill Paton Walsh
The First American Revolution, Milton Lomask
I Tell a Lie Every So Often, Bruce Clements
Brothers by Choice, Elfreida Read
The Perfect Life, Doris Faber
The Painter of Miracles, Cal Roy

FALL AND WINTER 1974–75

Solzhenitsyn: A Pictorial Autobiography, Aleksandr Solzhenitsyn

Extravagaria, Pablo Neruda
Brother Carl, Susan Sontag
Short Letter, Long Farewell, Peter Handke
Toward the Splendid City: Nobel Lecture, Pablo Neruda
Guilty Pleasures, Donald Barthelme
The Hermann Hesse 1975 Calendar, Milton Glaser, illus.
Miriam at Thirty-four, Alan Lelchuk
Ordinary Things, Jean Valentine
A Breeze from the Gulf, Mart Crowley
St. Lawrence Blues, Marie-Claire Blais
To the Unknown Hero, Hans Erich Nossack
High Windows, Philip Larkin
Which Tribe Do You Belong To?, Alberto Moravia
Report on Torture, Amnesty International
The House by the Medlar Tree, Giovanni Verga
Concrete Island, J. G. Ballard
The Adversary Literature: The Eighteenth-Century English Novel, Frederick R. Karl
The Sporting Club, Thomas McGuane
The Mullendore Murder Case, Jonathan Kwitny
Gayelord Hauser's New *Treasury of Secrets*, Gayelord Hauser
The Goodbye People, Herb Gardner
In Defense of Homo Sapiens, Joan Marble Cook
The Summer of the Great-grandmother, Madeleine L'Engle
Waltz across Texas, Max Crawford
The Life of Emily Dickinson, Richard B. Sewall

BOOKS FOR YOUNG READERS

Harry Cat's Pet Puppy, George Selden
Garth Williams, illus.
Juárez, Man of Law, Elizabeth Borton de Treviño
World of Our Fathers, Milton Meltzer
Guarneri, Leonard Wibberley
Joi Bangla!: The Children of Bangladesh, Jason Lauré, with Ettagale Lauré
Photographs by Jason Lauré
Six Days to Saturday, Jack Newcombe
Me and My Captain, M. B. Goffstein
Farmer Palmer's Wagon Ride, William Steig
Dawn, Uri Shulevitz
The Freewheeling of Joshua Cobb, Margaret Hodges
Richard Cuffari, illus.

SPRING AND SUMMER 1975

Mawrdew Czgowchwz, James McCourt
A Sorrow Beyond Dreams, Peter Handke
The Straw Man, Barbara Goldsmith
Reading Myself and Others, Philip Roth
American Made, Shylah Boyd
Literary Terms: A Dictionary, revised, Karl Beckson and Arthur Ganz
Fully Empowered, Pablo Neruda
The Wanderer, Knut Hamsun
I Would Have Saved Them If I Could, Leonard Michaels
The Message in the Bottle, Walker Percy
The Great Victorian Collection, Brian Moore
Early Writings Vol. I, 1920–1925, Wilhelm Reich
Love and Success, Karl Stern
Country Music, C. W. Smith
Crisis, Hermann Hesse
The Haunted and the Haunters, Kathleen Lines, ed.
How to, Peter Passell
Dead in the Water, Brock Yates
Hermann Hesse: A Pictorial Biography, Volker Michels, ed.
Pieces of the Frame, John McPhee
Pottery on the Wheel, Elsbeth S. Woody
Lamy of Santa Fe, Paul Horgan
Selected Poems, Osip Mandelstam
The Twenties: From Notebooks and Diaries of the Period, Edmund Wilson
Leon Edel, ed.

BOOKS FOR YOUNG READERS

The Family, Elaine and Walter Goodman
Backwater War, Peggy Woodford
The Princess and Froggie, Harve and Kaethe Zemach
Margot Zemach, illus.
Tuck Everlasting, Natalie Babbitt
The Trouble with Alaric, Jane Williamson
Introducing Shirley Braverman, Hilma Wolitzer
The Ides of April, Mary Ray
On a Tree of Trouble, Beth Roy
Sunil Jana, illus.
Follow the River, James Forman
The Borrowed House, Hilda van Stockum

FALL AND WINTER 1975–76

The Painted Word, Tom Wolfe
The Ascent of Mount Fuji, Chingiz Aitmatov and Kaltai Mukhamedzhanov
Krishnamurti: The Years of Awakening, Mary Lutyens
Sister X and the Victims of Foul Play, Carlene Hatcher Polite
The Wisdom of Heschel, Abraham Joshua Heschel
Ruth Marcus Goodhill, ed.
Passage to Ararat, Michael J. Arlen
Beyond the Bedroom Wall, Larry Woiwode
Persons and Masks of the Law, John T. Noonan, Jr.
The Dead Father, Donald Barthelme
The Clewiston Test, Kate Wilhelm
The Survival of the Bark Canoe, John McPhee
The Peyote Dance, Antonin Artaud
Cornelia Vanderbilt Whitney's Dollhouse, Marylou Vanderbilt Whitney
Scandinavian Design, Eileene Harrison Beer
Lawyering, Helene E. Schwartz
Selected Prose of T. S. Eliot, Frank Kermode, ed.
Passions, Isaac Bashevis Singer
Tales of Student Life, Hermann Hesse
Theodore Ziolkowski, ed.
Brew It Yourself, revised, Leigh P. Beadle
Between Heaven and Earth, Laura Archera Huxley
Oscar Wilde, H. Montgomery Hyde
The Verdict, Hildegard Knef

BOOKS FOR YOUNG READERS

The Young Person's Guide to Love, Morton Hunt
The Huffler, Jill Paton Walsh
Juliette Palmer, illus.
Mommy, Buy Me a China Doll, Harve Zemach
Margot Zemach, illus.
The Legend and the Storm, Cal Roy
Coming Home to a Place You've Never Been Before, Hanna and Bruce Clements
Start with the Sun, Ben Simpson

SPRING AND SUMMER 1976

Playground, John Buell
The Shackle, Colette
The Red Swan: Myths and Tales of the American Indians, John Bierhorst, trans. and ed.
Selected Poems, Robert Lowell
The Freedom of the Poet, John Berryman
The Abyss, Marguerite Yourcenar
My Own Ground, Hugh Nissenson
The Chinese Machiavelli: 3,000 Years of Chinese Statecraft, Dennis and Ching Ping Bloodworth
Sea Grapes, Derek Walcott
God in Search of Man, Abraham Joshua Heschel
Lover, Lawrence Edwards
A Voice from the Chorus, Abram Tertz
People in Trouble, Wilhelm Reich
The Franchiser, Stanley Elkin
The Ride Across Lake Constance, Peter Handke
Lucinella, Lore Segal
Antonin Artaud: Selected Writings, Susan Sontag, ed.
Lenin in Zurich, Aleksandr Solzhenitsyn

BOOKS FOR YOUNG READERS

Abel's Island, William Steig
A Tale of Three Wishes, Isaac Bashevis Singer
Irene Lieblich, illus.
The Last Battle, Leonard Wibberley
The Survivor, James Forman
Black Rainbow: Legends of the Incas and Myths of Ancient Peru, John Bierhorst, trans. and ed.
More Small Poems, Valerie Worth
Natalie Babbitt, illus.
Some Swell Pup, or Are You Sure You Want a Dog?, Maurice Sendak and Matthew Margolis
Maurice Sendak, illus.
Dragons in the Waters, Madeleine L'Engle
Unleaving, Jill Paton Walsh
Escoffier, Marjory Bartlett Sanger

FALL AND WINTER 1976–77

The View from Highway 1, Michael J. Arlen
The Doctor's Wife, Brian Moore
Warning to the West, Aleksandr Solzhenitsyn
The Balloonist, MacDonald Harris
Yes, My Darling Daughters, Ralph Schoenstein
The Complete Claudine, Colette
Mitsou and *Music-Hall Sidelights*, Colette
The John McPhee Reader, William L. Howarth, ed.
Christopher and His Kind, Christopher Isherwood
Geography III, Elizabeth Bishop
Mauve Gloves & Madmen, Clutter & Vine, Tom Wolfe
The Book of the Body, Frank Bidart
Terra Nostra, Carlos Fuentes
Memoirs, Pablo Neruda
Jack Straw's Castle and Other Poems, Thom Gunn
The Acts of King Arthur and His Noble Knights, John Steinbeck
Amateurs, Donald Barthelme
The Life and Extraordinary Adventures of Private Ivan Chonkin, Vladimir Voinovich
Torch Song, Anne Roiphe
Goethe's Faust, Part I, Randall Jarrell, trans.
Nixon vs. Nixon, David Abrahamsen, M.D.
Portraits, Richard Avedon
Carnival Strippers, Susan Meiselas
When Two or More Are Gathered Together, Neal Slavin

BOOKS FOR YOUNG READERS

Fly by Night, Randall Jarrell
Maurice Sendak, illus.
Clever Bill, William Nicholson
Naftali the Storyteller and His Horse, Sus, Isaac Bashevis Singer
Margot Zemach, illus.
The Amazing Bone, William Steig
Out of Love, Hilma Wolitzer
Flying to the Moon and Other Strange Places, Michael Collins
Taking Root: Jewish Immigrants in America, Milton Meltzer
Knight Prisoner, Margaret Hodges
Vegetables in Patches and Pots, Lorelie Miller Mintz
The White Crow, James Forman

SPRING AND SUMMER 1977

Lancelot, Walker Percy
Old Wives' Lore for Gardeners, Maureen and Bridget Boland
Prussian Nights, Aleksandr Solzhenitsyn
Property of, Alice Hoffman
When to Sell, Justin Mamis and Robert Mamis
Reunion, Frederick Uhlman
The Other One, Colette
Close Quarters, Larry Heinemann
Sita, Kate Millett
The Best, Encore, Peter Passell
Fat and Thin, Anne Scott Beller
Letters on Literature and Politics: 1912–1972, Edmund Wilson
Elena Wilson, ed.
A Moment of True Feeling, Peter Handke
The Ivankiad, Vladimir Voinovich
The Thin Mountain Air, Paul Horgan
The Game They Played, Stanley Cohen
Henry's Fate and Other Poems 1967–1972, John Berryman
French Cooking in Ten Minutes, Edouard de Pomiane

BOOKS FOR YOUNG READERS
Summer on Cleo's Island, Natalie G. Sylvester
It Could Always Be Worse, Margot Zemach
Salt, Harve Zemach
Margot Zemach, illus.
Margaret Fuller, Ellen Wilson
My Village, Sturbridge, Gary Bowen
Gary Bowen and Randy Miller, illus.
Gay: What You Should Know About Homosexuality, Morton Hunt
The Fox at Drummers' Darkness, Joyce Stranger
William Geldart, illus.
Jovem Portugal: After the Revolution, Jason and Ettagale Lauré
Photographs by Jason Lauré
To Hilda for Helping, Margot Zemach

FALL AND WINTER 1977–78
Yukiko, MacDonald Harris
Stuttering, Gerald Jonas
Day by Day, Robert Lowell
You're Not Too Old to Have a Baby, Jane Price
Pieces of Life, Mark Schorer
In Such Dark Places, Joseph Caldwell
On Photography, Susan Sontag
The Professor of Desire, Philip Roth
Belles Saisons: A Colette Scrapbook, Colette
Robert Phelps, ed.
Coming into the Country, John McPhee
Delmore Schwartz, James Atlas
Dominus, Natalie Gittelson
Even Tide, Larry Woiwode
The Ideal Cheese Book, Helen McCully and Edward Edelman
Gardener's Magic, Bridget and Maureen Boland
To a Blossoming Pear Tree, James Wright
Collected Poems 1919–1976, Allen Tate
The Joker of Seville and *O Babylon!: Two Plays*, Derek Walcott
Jackson's Way, Gérard Herzog

BOOKS FOR YOUNG READERS
Sid and Sol, Arthur Yorinks
Richard Egielski, illus.
Prison Window, Jerusalem Blue, Bruce Clements
Caleb and Kate, William Steig
The Eyes of the Amaryllis, Natalie Babbitt
Tell Me a Trudy, Lore Segal
Rosemary Wells, illus.

SPRING AND SUMMER 1978
Ibsen: The Complete Major Prose Plays, Henrik Ibsen
Love and Sex: A Modern Jewish Perspective, Robert Gordis
Selected Poems, Witter Bynner
Richard Wilbur, ed.
Light Verse and Satires, Witter Bynner
William Jay Smith, ed.
The Chinese Translations, Witter Bynner
James Kraft, gen. ed.
The Innocent Libertine, Colette
My Apprenticeships, Colette
Easy Money, Donald Goddard
Music of Three Seasons 1974–1977, Andrew Porter
The Family, David Plante
Mara, Tova Reich
Cinder, Rick Demarinis
Sakuran, Edward Tolosko
The Left-Handed Woman, Peter Handke
Set in Motion, Valerie Martin
The Women at the Pump, Knut Hamsun
Defective Medicine, Louise Lander
Neglected Lives, Stephen Alter
Dorothea Lange: A Photographer's Life, Milton Meltzer
Illness as Metaphor, Susan Sontag
Miss Rhode Island, Norman Kotker

BOOKS FOR YOUNG READERS
Idle Jack, Antony Maitland
Family Scrapbook, M. B. Goffstein
Toby Lived Here, Hilma Wolitzer
Carrot Nose, Jan Wahl
James Marshall, illus.
Bella, Anne and Edward Syfret
The Stars in the Sky, Joseph Jacobs
Airdrie Amtmann, illus.
Children of the Fox, Jill Paton Walsh
Robin Eaton, illus.
Timothy's Dream Book, Pierre Le-Tan
Perilous Gold, Leonard Wibberley
A Swiftly Tilting Planet, Madeleine L'Engle
The Lightning Time, Gregory Maguire

FALL AND WINTER 1978–79
Shosha, Isaac Bashevis Singer
Avedon Photographs: 1947–1977, Richard Avedon
The Oresteia of Aeschylus, Robert Lowell, trans.
Panama, Thomas McGuane
Wrinkles, Charles Simmons
Citizen Paul, Ralph Schoenstein
The Hydra Head, Carlos Fuentes
Dialogue with Photography, Paul Hill and Thomas Cooper
The Star-Apple Kingdom, Derek Walcott
Handbuilding Ceramic Forms, Elsbeth S. Woody
I, etcetera, Susan Sontag
Joseph Conrad, Frederick R. Karl
Prose Pieces, Witter Bynner
James Kraft, ed.
Great Days, Donald Barthelme
Enquire Within, Anonymous

BOOKS FOR YOUNG READERS
Tiffky Doofky, William Steig
It Can't Be Helped, Benjamin Lee
A Fine, Soft Day, James Forman
The Treasure, Uri Shulevitz
A Special Gift for Mother, Gary Bowen
Gary Bowen and Randy Miller, illus.
Still More Small Poems, Valerie Worth
Natalie Babbitt, illus.

What Is a Man? What Is a Woman?, Morton Hunt
A Chance Child, Jill Paton Walsh

SPRING AND SUMMER 1979
Dubin's Lives, Bernard Malamud
The Habit of Being: Letters, Flannery O'Connor
Sally Fitzgerald, ed.
Hours in the Garden, Hermann Hesse
The Cajuns: From Acadia to Louisiana, William Faulkner Rushton
The Possible She, Susan Jacoby
Decadence, Richard Gilman
The Four Gospels and *The Revelation*, Richmond Lattimore, trans.
Big and Little, Botho Strauss
Devotion, Botho Strauss
The Messenger, Jean Valentine
Alexandra, Valerie Martin
The Flight to Lucifer, Harold Bloom
Love and Living, Thomas Merton
When Memory Comes, Saul Friedländer
Aaron Burr: The Years from Princeton to Vice President 1756–1805, Milton Lomask
Onward and Upward in the Garden, Katharine S. White
I Love: The Story of Vladimir Mayakovsky and Lili Brik, Ann and Samuel Charters
In Plain Russian, Vladimir Voinovich
Giving Good Weight, John McPhee

BOOKS FOR YOUNG READERS
The Bear and the Kingbird, Brothers Grimm
Retold by Lore Segal
Chris Conover, illus.
Will You Count the Stars Without Me?, Jane Breskin Zalben
Natural History, M. B. Goffstein
Some of Us Survived, Kerop Bedoukian
The Human Rights Book, Milton Meltzer
James Marshall's Mother Goose, James Marshall, illus.

FALL AND WINTER 1979–80
The Right Stuff, Tom Wolfe
Nobel Lecture, Isaac Bashevis Singer
The Ghost Writer, Philip Roth
Josiah Gregg and His Vision of the Early West, Paul Horgan
The Mangan Inheritance, Brian Moore
Venice for Pleasure, J. G. Links
Selected Poems 1950–1975, Thom Gunn
William Steig: Drawings, William Steig
Selected Letters of Gustav Mahler, Knud Martner, ed.
The Obstacle Race, Germaine Greer
Field Work, Seamus Heaney
Chinese Encounters, Inge Morath and Arthur Miller
Old Love, Isaac Bashevis Singer
The Morning of the Poem, James Schuyler
Rounds, Frederick Busch
Darkness Visible, William Golding
The Beirut Pipeline, Ray Alan
My Guru and His Disciple, Christopher Isherwood
The Unity of Nature, Carl Friedrich von Weizsäcker
The Forbidden Experiment, Roger Shattuck
Winterreise, Gerhard Roth
Genitality, Wilhelm Reich
Institute of Fools, Victor Nekipelov

BOOKS FOR YOUNG READERS
The Fisherman and His Wife, Brothers Grimm
Randall Jarrell, trans.
Margot Zemach, illus.
An Address Book with Riddles, Rhymes, Tales and Tongue-Twisters, Monika Beisner
My Diary, Engravings by Edmund Evans
Curlicues: The Fortunes of Two Pug Dogs, Valerie Worth
Natalie Babbitt, illus.
A Ballad for Hogskin Hill, James Forman
The Stray, Betsy James Wyeth
Jamie Wyeth, illus.
A Season In-Between, Jan Greenberg
The Daughter of the Moon, Gregory Maguire
South Africa: Coming of Age under Apartheid, Jason and Ettagale Lauré
Photographs by Jason Lauré

SPRING AND SUMMER 1980
Thirty Seconds, Michael J. Arlen
Kipling, Auden & Co., Randall Jarrell
Wayfarers, Knut Hamsun
Early Disorder, Rebecca Josephs
A Part of Speech, Joseph Brodsky
The Chinese Looking Glass, revised, Dennis Bloodworth
Silk and Steel, Stephen Alter
Summer Light, Herbert Mason
A Giacometti Portrait, James Lord
Burnt Water, Carlos Fuentes
A Book about My Mother, Toby Talbot
Time of Desecration, Alberto Moravia
Under the Sign of Saturn, Susan Sontag
The Second Coming, Walker Percy
Of Kennedys and Kings, Harris Wofford
The Thirties: From Notebooks and Diaries of the Period, Edmund Wilson
Leon Edel, ed.
The Nonviolent Alternative, Thomas Merton
Remembrance and *Pantomime*, Derek Walcott
A Model Childhood, Christa Wolf
City Police, Jonathan Rubinstein
Pilgrimage of Peace, Pope John Paul II

BOOKS FOR YOUNG READERS
Louis the Fish, Arthur Yorinks
Richard Egielski, illus.
Oliver and Alison's Week, Jane Breskin Zalben
Emily Arnold McCully, illus.
A Ring of Endless Light, Madeleine L'Engle
Anywhere Else But Here, Bruce Clements
The Heavenly Zoo, Alison Lurie
Monika Beisner, illus.

The Crime of Martin Coverly, Leonard Wibberley
The Dark Lord of Pengersick, Richard Carlyon
Pauline Ellison, illus.
Rineheart Lifts, R. R. Knudson
The Spirit of 1787, Milton Lomask
A Place Apart, Paula Fox

FALL AND WINTER 1980–81
The Chief Field Marshal Lord Wavell, Ronald Lewin
Lord of Misrule, Gareth Jones
A Philip Roth Reader, Philip Roth
The New Brew It Yourself, Leigh P. Beadle
Delirium, Barbara Alberti
In Our Time, Tom Wolfe
Hearts, Hilma Wolitzer
Rites of Passage, William Golding
Cleaning House, Nancy Hayfield
Twelve Years: An American Boyhood in East Germany, Joel Agee
Preoccupations: Selected Prose 1968–1978, Seamus Heaney
Poems: 1965–1975, Seamus Heaney
The Expanding Circle, Peter Singer
An Outside Chance, Thomas McGuane
Reaches of Heaven, Isaac Bashevis Singer
Ira Moskowitz, illus.
Letters from Colette, Robert Phelps, ed.
Baryshnikov: From Russia to the West, Gennady Smakov
Housekeeping, Marilynne Robinson
The Camera Age: Essays on Television, Michael J. Arlen
Sue Your Boss, E. Richard Larson

BOOKS FOR YOUNG READERS
The Little Humpbacked Horse, Margaret Hodges
Chris Conover, illus.
The Old Man of Lochnagar, H.R.H. The Prince of Wales
Sir Hugh Casson, illus.
Laughing Latkes, M. B. Goffstein
The Power of Light, Isaac Bashevis Singer
Irene Lieblich, illus.
How Brown Mouse Kept Christmas, Clyde Watson
Wendy Watson, illus.
The Iceberg and Its Shadow, Jan Greenberg
Fours Crossing, Nancy Garden
Lights on the Lake, Gregory Maguire
The Pumpkin Shell, James Forman
Gorky Rises, William Steig

SPRING AND SUMMER 1981
The Issa Valley, Czeslaw Milosz
Record of a Friendship: The Correspondence of Wilhelm Reich and A. S. Neill, Beverley R. Placzek, ed.
Basin and Range, John McPhee
Philadelphia: Patricians and Philistines, 1900–1950, John Lukacs
The Men's Club, Leonard Michaels
Thomas Merton's Dark Path, William H. Shannon
The Temptation of Eileen Hughes, Brian Moore
The Collected Stories of Caroline Gordon, Caroline Gordon
The Book for Normal Neurotics, Allan Fromme
Dale Loves Sophie to Death, Robb Forman Dew
Fires, Marguerite Yourcenar
Isla Negra: A Notebook, Pablo Neruda
What Is Sexuality?, Wilhelm Reich
The World of Don Camillo, Giovanni Guareschi
Zuckerman Unbound, Philip Roth
Love and Responsibility, Pope John Paul II
Pretender to the Throne, Vladimir Voinovich
Selected Letters, Witter Bynner
James Kraft, ed.
Schubert, Hans J. Frohlich

BOOKS FOR YOUNG READERS
Chester Cricket's Pigeon Ride, George Selden
Garth Williams, illus.
Oh, Simple!, Jane Breskin Zalben
Pennies for the Piper, Susan McLean
No Scarlet Ribbons, Susan Terris

FALL AND WINTER 1981–82
From Bauhaus to Our House, Tom Wolfe
The Polish Complex, Tadeusz Konwicki
The Care of Time, Eric Ambler
Distant Relations, Carlos Fuentes
Take This Man, Frederick Busch
Pills That Don't Work, Sidney M. Wolfe, M.D., Chrisopher M. Coley, and The Public Citizen Health Research Group
Easy Travel to Other Planets, Ted Mooney
Legacies: Selected Poems, Heberto Padilla
The Fortunate Traveller, Derek Walcott
Mind, Mood, and Medicine, Paul H. Wender, M.D., and Donald F. Klein, M.D.
Poppa John, Larry Woiwode
Fading Feast, Raymond Sokolov
Mexico Bay, Paul Horgan
Nobel Lecture, Czeslaw Milosz
The American Magic, Ronald Lewin
This Was Harlem: A Cultural Portrait 1900–1950, Jervis Anderson
Pictor's Metamorphoses and Other Fantasies, Hermann Hesse
Theodore Ziolkowski, ed.

BOOKS FOR YOUNG READERS
The Gathering Room, Colby Rodowsky
Upon the Head of the Goat: A Childhood in Hungary 1939–1944, Aranka Siegal
Lives of the Artists, M. B. Goffstein
Fabulous Beasts, Alison Lurie
Monika Beisner, illus.
The Cat's Elbow, Alvin Schwartz, ed.
Margot Zemach, illus.
The Green Book, Jill Paton Walsh
Lloyd Bloom, illus.
A Folding Alphabet Book, Monika Beisner
The Kolokol Papers, Larry Bograd

First Affair, Peter Burchard
Jake and Honeybunch Go to Heaven, Margot Zemach

SPRING AND SUMMER 1982

The Collected Stories of Isaac Bashevis Singer, Isaac Bashevis Singer
Maimonides, Abraham Joshua Heschel
Thoreau in the Mountains, Henry David Thoreau
William Howarth, ed.
China Companion, Evelyne Garside
Sexism: The Male Monopoly on History and Thought, Marielouise Janssen-Jurreit
Aaron Burr: The Conspiracy and Years of Exile 1805–1836, Milton Lomask
The Gardener's Diary, The Metropolitan Museum of Art
Hitler: A Film from Germany, Hans-Jürgen Syberberg
So Reason Can Rule, Scott Buchanan
The Seizure of Power, Czeslaw Milosz
Visions from San Francisco Bay, Czeslaw Milosz
The Frog Who Dared to Croak, Richard Sennett
Water, Fred Powledge
A Coin in Nine Hands, Marguerite Yourcenar
Me Again: Uncollected Writings of Stevie Smith, Stevie Smith
How to Buy, Justin Mamis
A Susan Sontag Reader, Susan Sontag
A Moving Target, William Golding
The Killing Ground, Mary Lee Settle
The Questionnaire, or Prayer for a Town and a Friend, Jiří Gruša
Aunt Julia and the Scriptwriter, Mario Vargas Llosa
The Passages of Joy, Thom Gunn
No Place on Earth, Christa Wolf

BOOKS FOR YOUNG READERS

The Violin-Maker's Gift, Donn Kushner
Doug Panton, illus.
Doctor De Soto, William Steig
Annie on My Mind, Nancy Garden
The Pig-Out Blues, Jan Greenberg
Terpin, Tor Seidler
Wings and Roots, Susan Terris
Maybe It Will Rain Tomorrow, Jane Breskin Zalben

FALL AND WINTER 1982–83

God's Grace, Bernard Malamud
The Torch in My Ear, Elias Canetti
The Purple Decades, Tom Wolfe
Acts and Letters of the Apostles, Richmond Lattimore, trans.
My Wife Maria Callas, G. B. Meneghini
Selected Stories, Robert Walser
Mozart, Wolfgang Hildesheimer
Stieglitz: A Memoir/Biography, Sue Davidson Lowe
Nostradamus: The Man Who Saw Through Time, Lee McCann
Vital Signs: A Young Doctor's Struggle with Cancer, Fitzhugh Mullan, M.D.
A Severed Wasp, Madeleine L'Engle
The X-Ray Information Book, Priscilla Laws, Ph.D., and the Public Citizen Health Research Group
In Suspect Terrain, John McPhee
New Islands, María Luisa Bombal
Passions and Impressions, Pablo Neruda
Days without Weather, Cecil Brown

BOOKS FOR YOUNG READERS

The Birthday Book of Beasts, Sue Porter
Applebet, Clyde Watson
Wendy Watson, illus.
Bad Apple, Larry Bograd
The BFG, Roald Dahl
Quentin Blake, illus.
The Golem, Isaac Bashevis Singer
Uri Shulevitz, illus.
Herbert Rowbarge, Natalie Babbitt
H, My Name Is Henley, Colby Rodowsky
Hallucination Orbit: Psychology in Science Fiction, Isaac Asimov, Martin Greenberg, and Charles Waugh, eds.
Caught in the Organ Draft: Biology in Science Fiction, Isaac Asimov, Martin Greenberg, and Charles Waugh, eds.
Just Another Love Story, R. R. Knudson

SPRING AND SUMMER 1983

Power and Principle, Zbigniew Brzezinski
Kleist: A Biography, Joachim Maass
For Your Own Good: Hidden Cruelty in Child-Rearing and the Roots of Violence, Alice Miller
1934, Alberto Moravia
Eichmann Interrogated: Transcripts from the Archives of the Israeli Police, Jochen von Lang, ed.
Representing Yourself, Kenneth Lasson and the Public Citizen Litigation Group
The Natural Man, Ed McClanahan
Krishnamurti: The Years of Fulfillment, Mary Lutyens
The Forties: From Notebooks and Diaries of the Period, Edmund Wilson
Leon Edel, ed.
The Ladies' Oracle, Cornelius Agrippa
In the Palomar Arms, Hilma Wolitzer
Voices, Frederic Prokosch
Lost in the Cosmos: The Last Self-Help Book, Walker Percy
Children of the Future: On the Prevention of Sexual Pathology, Wilhelm Reich
The Lizard's Tail, Luisa Valenzuela

BOOKS FOR YOUNG READERS

The Favershams, Roy Gerrard
Molly Whuppie, Walter de la Mare
Errol Le Cain, illus.
Chester Cricket's New Home, George Selden
Garth Williams, illus.
The Granny Project, Anne Fine
It Happened in Pinsk, Arthur Yorinks
Richard Egielski, illus.
Octopus Pie, Susan Terris
Watersmeet, Nancy Garden

Amen, Moses Gardenia, Jean Ferris
Pack, Band, and Colony, Judith and Herbert Kohl

FALL AND WINTER 1983–84
A Vanished World, Roman Vishniac
The Stories of Bernard Malamud, Bernard Malamud
Midsummer, Derek Walcott
The Collected Stories of Colette, Robert Phelps, ed.
Roald Dahl's Book of Ghost Stories, Roald Dahl, ed.
The Penitent, Isaac Bashevis Singer
Corydon, new trans., André Gide
The Anatomy Lesson, Philip Roth
60+: Planning It, Living It, Loving It, Allan Fromme
At the Bottom of the River, Jamaica Kincaid
Yentl the Yeshiva Boy, Isaac Bashevis Singer
Antonio Frasconi, illus.
The Complete Poems 1927–1979, Elizabeth Bishop
The Collected Prose, Elizabeth Bishop
Robert Giroux, ed.
The Princess of Siberia: The Story of Maria Volkonsky and the Decembrist Exiles, Christine Sutherland
A Minor Apocalypse, Tadeusz Konwicki

BOOKS FOR YOUNG READERS
The Witches, Roald Dahl
Quentin Blake, illus.
The Little Red Hen, Margot Zemach
Los Alamos Light, Larry Bograd
Gypsy Gold, Valerie Worth
It's Not Fair, Susie Morgenstern
Kathie Abrams, illus.
Keeping Time, Colby Rodowsky
Matilda Jane, Jean Gerrard
Roy Gerrard, illus.
Monika Beisner's Book of Riddles, Monika Beisner
A Parcel of Patterns, Jill Paton Walsh
No Dragons to Slay, Jan Greenberg
Sea Change, Peter Burchard
Me, the Beef, and the Bum, Charles Hammer

SPRING AND SUMMER 1984
The Assault on Truth: Freud's Suppression of the Seduction Theory, Jeffrey Moussaieff Masson
Austin and Mabel: The Amherst Love Affair and the Letters of Austin Dickinson and Mabel Loomis Todd, Polly Longsworth
The Nightmare of Reason: A Life of Franz Kafka, Ernst Pawel
Of America East and West, Paul Horgan
La Place de la Concorde Suisse, John McPhee
The Weight of the World, Peter Handke
The Paper Men, William Golding
Edisto, Padgett Powell
Heroes Are Grazing in My Garden, Heberto Padilla
A Man with a Camera, Nestor Almendros
Home Ground: A Gardener's Miscellany, Allen Lacy
Sweeney Astray, Seamus Heaney
Thou Shalt Not Be Aware: Society's Betrayal of the Child, Alice Miller
Cassandra: A Novel and Four Essays, Christa Wolf
The Land of Ulro, Czeslow Milosz
Required Writing: Miscellaneous Pieces 1955–1982, Philip Larkin
Montefiore: The Hospital as Social Instrument, 1884–1984, Dorothy Levenson
Mouroir: Mirrornotes of a Novel, Breyten Breytenbach
Alexis, Marguerite Yourcenar

BOOKS FOR YOUNG READERS
Dirty Beasts, Roald Dahl
Rosemary Fawcett, illus.
Yellow and Pink, William Steig
Zan Hagen's Marathon, R. R. Knudson
The Long Night Watch, Ivan Southall
Here's Looking at You, Kid, Jane Breskin Zalben
Fat Man in a Fur Coat and Other Bear Stories, Alvin Schwartz, ed.
David Christiana, illus.
Coming About, Bruce Clements

FALL AND WINTER 1984–85
Say Goodbye to Sam, Michael J. Arlen
The War of the End of the World, Mario Vargas Llosa
The Innocent Eye, Roger Shattuck
A Fanatic Heart: Selected Stories of Edna O'Brien, Edna O'Brien
The Dark Brain of Piranesi, Marguerite Yourcenar
Station Island, Seamus Heaney
August Strindberg, Olof Lagercrantz
The True Confessions of an Albino Terrorist, Breyten Breytenbach
An Axe, a Spade and Ten Acres, George Courtauld
Ruminations, William Steig
The Love for Three Oranges, Frank Corsaro
Maurice Sendak, illus.

BOOKS FOR YOUNG READERS
Wish You Were Here, Hilma Wolitzer
The Winter Wren, Brock Cole
A House Like a Lotus, Madeleine L'Engle
Summer of the Zeppelin, Elsie McCutcheon
Sir Cedric, Roy Gerrard
Stories for Children, Isaac Bashevis Singer
Prisoner of Vampires, Nancy Garden
Boy: Tales of Childhood, Roald Dahl
Baby-Snatcher, Susan Terris
Gaffer Samson's Luck, Jill Paton Walsh
Brock Cole, illus.
Hiawatha's Childhood, Henry Wadsworth Longfellow
Errol Le Cain, illus.
C D C!, William Steig

SPRING AND SUMMER 1985
Annie John, Jamaica Kincaid
Later the Same Day, Grace Paley
The Tragedy of Zionism, Bernard Avishai
The Lamplit Answer, Gjertrud Schnackenberg
Slow Homecoming, Peter Handke
The Image and Other Stories, Isaac Bashevis Singer
Dogwood Afternoons, Kim Chapin
My Editor, M. B. Goffstein

The Hidden Ground of Love: Letters on Religious Experience and Social Concerns, Thomas Merton
William H. Shannon, ed.
Giacometti: A Biography, James Lord
Oriental Tales, Marguerite Yourcenar
Zuckerman Bound, Philip Roth
All What Jazz: A Record Diary, Philip Larkin
Linda Mason's Sun Sign Makeovers, Linda Mason
Tremor: Selected Poems, Adam Zagajewski

BOOKS FOR YOUNG READERS

Tog the Ribber: Or Granny's Tale, Paul Coltman
Gillian McClure, illus.
Small Poems Again, Valerie Worth
Natalie Babbitt, illus.
The Little Father, Gelett Burgess
Richard Egielski, illus.
Taildraggers' High, Larry Sutton
Gentleman Bear, William Pène du Bois
What's Inside?: The Alphabet Book, Satoshi Kitamura
Julie's Daughter, Colby Rodowsky
The Secret of Thut-Mouse III, or Basil Beaudesert's Revenge, Mansfield Kirby
Mance Post, illus.
The Winged Watchman, Hilda van Stockum
Bye, Bye, Miss American Pie, Jan Greenberg
The Bombers' Moon, Betty Vander Els

FALL AND WINTER 1985–86

Table of Contents, John McPhee
My Father, His Daughter, Yaël Dayan
The Cunning Little Vixen, Rudolf Tesnohlidek
Maurice Sendak, illus.
Victory Celebrations, Prisoners, and *The Love-Girl and the Innocent*, Aleksandr Solzhenitsyn
The Real Life of Alejandro Mayta, Mario Vargas Llosa
Earwitness: Fifty Characters, Elias Canetti
Famous People I Have Known, Ed McClanahan
The Old Gringo, Carlos Fuentes
Collected Poems 1948–1984, Derek Walcott
Grenville Clark: Public Citizen, Gerald T. Dunne
Erotic Tales, Alberto Moravia
Dating Your Mom, Ian Frazier
The Emerald Forest Diary, John Boorman

BOOKS FOR YOUNG READERS

Solomon the Rusty Nail, William Steig
The Giraffe & the Pelly & Me, Roald Dahl
Quentin Blake, illus.
Ludlow Laughs, John Agee
Grace in the Wilderness: After the Liberation, 1945–1948, Aranka Siegal
Fox Hill, Valerie Worth
Peace, O River, Nancy Garden
Tales of Trickery from the Land of Spoof, Alvin Schwartz
David Christiana, illus.
Golden Girl, Nancy Tilly
The Latchkey Kids, Susan Terris
King Matt the First, Janusz Korczak

SPRING AND SUMMER 1986

Less Than One: Selected Essays, Joseph Brodsky
Perfection Salad: Women and Cooking at the Turn of the Century, Laura Shapiro
Kangaroo, Yuz Aleshkovsky
Flowers and Fruit, Colette
Robert Phelps, ed.
Three Plays: The Last Carnival; Beef, No Chicken; A Branch of the Blue Nile, Derek Walcott
The Play of the Eyes, Elias Canetti
The Cambridge Apostles, Richard Deacon
Pictures of a Childhood: Sixty-six Watercolors and an Essay, Alice Miller
Terrorism: How the West Can Win, Benjamin Netanyahu, ed.
Essays in Honor of Elias Canetti, Various
A State of Independence, Caryl Phillips
The Country Girls Trilogy and Epilogue, Edna O'Brien
Farther Afield: A Gardener's Excursions, Allen Lacy
Spring Jaunts: Some Walks, Excursions, and Personal Explorations of City, Country, and Seashore, Anthony Bailey
Blood Libels, Clive Sinclair
Portrait of Delmore: Journals and Notes of Delmore Schwartz: 1939–1959, Elizabeth Pollet, ed.
Mishima: A Vision of the Void, Marguerite Yourcenar
Endpapers: Political Essays, Breyten Breytenbach
Break It Down, Lydia Davis
Here Lies, Eric Ambler
The Fifties: From Notebooks and Diaries of the Period, Edmund Wilson
Leon Edel, ed.

BOOKS FOR YOUNG READERS

The Giant's Toe, Brock Cole
The Stainless Steel Rule, Jean Ferris
Froggie Went A-Courting, Chris Conover
Visiting Miss Pierce, Pat Derby
Secret Spells and Curious Charms, Monika Beisner
A Rat's Tale, Tor Seidler
Fred Marcellino, illus.
Run for Your Sweet Life, Rex Benedict
David Christiana, illus.
Exercises of the Heart, Jan Greenberg
The Rat War, Elsie McCutcheon

SEPTEMBER 1986 TO FEBRUARY 1987

Zorina, Vera Zorina
Quiet Rage: Bernie Goetz in a Time of Madness, Lillian B. Rubin, Ph.D.
Assignments in Africa: Reflections, Descriptions, Guesses, Per Wästberg
Celebration, Mary Lee Settle
Nunca Más: The Report of the Argentine National Commission on the Disappeared
The Mystery of the Sardine, Stefan Themerson
The Spell, Hermann Broch
Rising from the Plains, John McPhee
The Perpetual Orgy, Mario Vargas Llosa
Going Solo, Roald Dahl

Paco's Story, Larry Heinemann
A Dark Science: Women, Sexuality, and Psychiatry in the Nineteenth Century, Jeffrey Moussaieff Masson
The Counterlife, Philip Roth
Two Lives and a Dream, Marguerite Yourcenar

BOOKS FOR YOUNG READERS
Many Waters, Madeleine L'Engle
When Sheep Cannot Sleep: The Counting Book, Satoshi Kitamura
The Three Wishes, Margot Zemach
Rachel, Ivan Southall
Brave Irene, William Steig
Hey, Al, Arthur Yorinks
Richard Egielski, illus.
Sir Cedric Rides Again, Roy Gerrard
Small Poems Again, Valerie Worth
Natalie Babbitt, illus.
The Strange and Exciting Adventures of Jeremiah Hush, Uri Shulevitz
Flame-Colored Taffeta, Rosemary Sutcliff
Harry Kitten and Tucker Mouse, George Selden
Garth Williams, illus.
The Marzipan Pig, Russell Hoban
Quentin Blake, illus.
Rinehart Shouts, R. R. Knudson
Invincible Summer, Jean Ferris
Water from the Moon, Jane Breskin Zalben

MARCH TO AUGUST 1987
Conspiracy of Silence: The Secret Life of Anthony Blunt, Barrie Penrose and Simon Freeman
The Thanatos Syndrome, Walker Percy
The Voyeur, Alberto Moravia
Two Fables, Roald Dahl
Graham Deane, illus.
I'm Not Doing It Myself, Home Renovation Associates
The Irrational Season, Madeleine L'Engle
The Female of the Species, Lionel Shriver
William Golding: The Man and His Books—A Tribute on His 75th Birthday, John Carey, ed.
The Lamberts: George, Constant & Kit, Andrew Motion
Collected Prose, Robert Lowell
Robert Giroux, ed.
That Night, Alice McDermott
The Casualty, Heinrich Böll
Major André, Anthony Bailey
Fierce Attachments, Vivian Gornick
War Music: An Account of Books 16–19 of Homer's Iliad, Christopher Logue
A Woman Named Drown, Padgett Powell
The European Tribe, Caryl Phillips
Nobody Better, Better Than Nobody, Ian Frazier
Flesh and Blood, C. K. Williams
The Forbidden Zone, Michael Lesy
Last Letters: Prisons and Prisoners of the French Revolution, 1793–1794, Olivier Blanc
Enigma: The Life of Knut Hamsun, Robert Ferguson
Mother Love, Candace Flynt
Close Quarters, William Golding
The Hottentot Room, Christopher Hope
Who Killed Palomino Molero?, Mario Vargas Llosa
Abraham Joshua Heschel and Elie Wiesel: You Are My Witnesses, Maurice Friedman
Presumed Innocent, Scott Turow
Moonrise, Moonset, Tadeusz Konwicki
The Arkansas Testament, Derek Walcott

BOOKS FOR YOUNG READERS
The Devil's Other Storybook, Natalie Babbitt
Paper John, David Small
Bury the Dead, Peter Carter
The Goats, Brock Cole
Quack-Quack, Frédéric Stehr
Fitchett's Folly, Colby Rodowsky
The Treasure of Plunderell Manor, Bruce Clements
The Tar Pit, Tor Seidler
The Ghost Drum: A Cat's Tale, Susan Price
Storm Bird, Elsie McCutcheon
The Door Between, Nancy Garden
Wrong-Way Ragsdale, Charles Hammer
One Friend to Another, Elizabeth Feuer

SEPTEMBER 1987 TO FEBRUARY 1988
The Bonfire of the Vanities, Tom Wolfe
The Haw Lantern, Seamus Heaney
Ivan: Living with Parkinson's Disease, Ivan Vaughan
Pushkin House, Andrei Bitov
The Day of Judgment, Salvatore Satta
Poet in New York, Federico García Lorca
Christopher Maurer, ed.
Hard to Be Good, Bill Barich
A House of Trees: Memoirs of an Australian Childhood, Joan Colebrook
Captivity Captive, Rodney Hall
Zeno Was Here, Jan Mark
Born Brothers, Larry Woiwode
Zone Journals, Charles Wright

BOOKS FOR YOUNG READERS
Crows: An Old Rhyme, Heidi Holder
Simple Simon, Chris Conover
The Zabajaba Jungle, William Steig
Nell's Quilt, Susan Terris
Growltiger's Last Stand and Other Poems, T. S. Eliot
Errol Le Cain, illus.
Hello Mr. Scarecrow, Rob Lewis
The Old Meadow, George Selden
Garth Williams, illus.
Mystery of the Night Raiders, Nancy Garden
Maxie's Ghost, James VanOosting
Leaving Point, Betty Vander Els
Gay: What You Should Know about Homosexuality, revised, Morton Hunt

MARCH TO AUGUST 1988
To Urania, Joseph Brodsky
An Age Ago: A Selection of Nineteenth-Century Russian Poetry, Joseph Brodsky and Alan Myers, eds.

Myself with Others: Selected Essays, Carlos Fuentes
The Days of Creation, J. G. Ballard
The Standard Life of a Temporary Pantyhose Salesman, Aldo Busi
The King of Children: A Biography of Janusz Korczak, Betty Jean Lifton
Labrador, Kathryn Davis
On Bended Knee: The Press and the Reagan Presidency, Mark Hertsgaard
The Death of Methuselah and Other Stories, Isaac Bashevis Singer
A Small Place, Jamaica Kincaid
Repetition, Peter Handke
The Yellow Wind, David Grossman
The American Gardener: A Sampler, Allen Lacy, ed.
Tallien: A Brief Romance, Frederic Tuten
Loonglow, Helen Eisenbach
Selected Poems, James Schuyler
White Boy Running, Christopher Hope
Checker and the Derailleurs, Lionel Shriver
The Lantern-Bearers and Other Essays, Robert Louis Stevenson
Jeremy Treglown, ed.
Passion of Youth: An Autobiography, 1897–1922, Wilhelm Reich
Mary Boyd Higgins and Chester M. Raphael, M.D., eds.
A Vow of Conversation, Thomas Merton
Naomi Burton Stone, ed.
Fishing with John, Edith Iglauer
Subject to Change, Lois Gould
Silver, Hilma Wolitzer
The Government of the Tongue: Selected Prose, 1978–1987, Seamus Heaney
Seven Thousand Days in Siberia, Karlo Štajner

BOOKS FOR YOUNG READERS

Friska, the Sheep That Was Too Small, Rob Lewis
Topsy Turvy, Monika Beisner
Whose Side Are You On?, Emily Moore
The Secret in the Matchbox, Val Willis
John Shelley, illus.
Torch, Jill Paton Walsh
Sir Francis Drake: His Daring Deeds, Roy Gerrard
Gulliver, Frédéric Stehr
Consider the Lemming, Jeanne Steig
William Steig, illus.
A Long Long Song, Etienne Delessert
Sweet Creek Holler, Ruth White

SEPTEMBER 1988 TO FEBRUARY 1989

The Facts: A Novelist's Autobiography, Philip Roth
The Twenty-Seventh City, Jonathan Franzen
Poems 1963–1983, C. K. Williams
Eliot's New Life, Lyndall Gordon
Caldecott & Co.: Notes on Books and Pictures, Maurice Sendak
Giving Birth: How It Really Feels, revised, Sheila Kitzinger
One L, Scott Turow
Adventures on the Wine Route, Kermit Lynch
The King of the Fields, Isaac Bashevis Singer
Europeans, Jane Kramer
The Meat and Potatoes Cookbook, Maria Luisa Scott and Jack Denton Scott
Judas Eye and *Self-Portrait / Deathwatch*, Breyten Breytenbach
AIDS and Its Metaphors, Susan Sontag
The High Road, Edna O'Brien
Skin Deep, Guy Garcia
Two-Part Invention, Madeleine L'Engle
Kisses of the Enemy, Rodney Hall
Tocqueville: A Biography, André Jardin
Families of the World, Vol. I, Hélène Tremblay
Born Brothers, Larry Woiwode
Krishnamurti: The Open Door, Mary Lutyens
The Encyclopedia of the Dead, Danilo Kiš
Fire Down Below, William Golding
See Under: Love, David Grossman
Mother Country, Marilynne Robinson

BOOKS FOR YOUNG READERS

Dear Mili, Wilhelm Grimm
Ralph Manheim, trans.
Maurice Sendak, illus.
The Incredible Painting of Felix Clousseau, Jon Agee
Bravo, Minski, Arthur Yorinks
Richard Egielski, illus.
The White Bicycle, Rob Lewis
Spinky Sulks, William Steig
Just the Two of Us, Jan Greenberg
The Three Little Pigs: An Old Story, Margot Zemach
Mystery of the Midnight Menace, Nancy Garden
My Underrated Year, Randy Powell
The Enchanter's Daughter, Antonia Barber
Errol Le Cain, illus.
Rain Forest, Helen Cowcher
Super Dooper Jezebel, Tony Ross
Don't Call Me Little Bunny, Grégoire Solotareff
Tales for a Winter's Eve, Wendy Watson
Little Sophie and Lanky Flop, Els Pelgrom
The Tjong Khing, illus.
Gold and Silver, Silver and Gold, Alvin Schwartz
David Christiana, illus.
Blackbird, Ivan Southall
Children of the Maker, Lucy Cullyford Babbitt
Looking for Home, Jean Ferris

MARCH TO AUGUST 1989

Marbles: A Play in Three Acts, Joseph Brodsky
Great Plains, Ian Frazier
Collected Poems, Philip Larkin
Anthony Thwaite, ed.
Winter Losses, Mark Probst
Who Whispered Near Me, Killarney Clary
How Old Is This House? A Skeleton Key to Dating and Identifying Three Centuries of American Houses, Howard Hugh for Home Renovation Associates
Being Homosexual: Gay Men and Their Development, Richard A. Isay, M.D.
Accident: A Day's News, Christa Wolf
The Outer Banks, Anthony Bailey

The Evening Wolves, Joan Chase
A Disaffection, James Kelman
God's Dust: A Modern Asian Journey, Ian Buruma
Life with a Star, Jiří Weil
A Late Summer Passion of a Woman of Mind, Rebecca Goldstein
A Link with the River, Desmond Hogan
From Beirut to Jerusalem, Thomas L. Friedman
Collected Poems, 1937–1971, John Berryman
Charles Thornbury, ed.
Becoming a Poet, David Kalstone
Robert Hemenway, ed.
The Control of Nature, John McPhee
Seminar on Youth, Aldo Busi
Memory of Snow and of Dust, Breyten Breytenbach
August 1914: The Red Wheel / I, revised and new trans., Aleksandr Solzhenitsyn
The Afternoon of a Writer, Peter Handke
The Secret Heart of the Clock, Elias Canetti
Christopher Unborn, Carlos Fuentes
The Mambo Kings Play Songs of Love, Oscar Hijuelos
The Road to Joy: Letters to New and Old Friends, Thomas Merton
Robert E. Daggy, ed.

BOOKS FOR YOUNG READERS

I Want a Cat, Tony Ross
Who Killed Cockatoo?, W. A. Cawthorne
Rodney McRae, illus.
An Occasional Cow, Polly Horvath
Gioia Fiammenghi, illus.
Eleanor, Elizabeth, Libby Gleeson
El Güero, Elizabeth Borton de Treviño
Leslie W. Bowman, illus.
Ned and the Joybaloo, Hiawyn Oram
Satoshi Kitamura, illus.
Mystery of the Secret Marks, Nancy Garden
Sydney, Herself, Colby Rodowsky
Goodbye Emily, Hello, Pat Derby

SEPTEMBER 1989 TO FEBRUARY 1990

Charley Bland, Mary Lee Settle
W. B. Yeats: A New Biography, A. Norman Jeffares
A Summer World, Stefan Kanfer
Elizabeth Cole, Susan Cheever
The Chase, Alejo Carpentier
Danube, Claudio Magris
Rondo, Kazimierz Brandys
Chuck Amuck: The Life and Times of an Animated Cartoonist, Chuck Jones
Where Joy Resides: A Christopher Isherwood Reader, Don Bachardy and James P. White, eds.
The Labyrinth of Exile: A Life of Theodor Herzl, Ernst Pawel
Ackerley: The Life of J. R. Ackerley, Peter Parker
The Storyteller, Mario Vargas Llosa
Running Wild, J. G. Ballard
Selected Poems, Randall Jarrell
William H. Pritchard, ed.
Randall Jarrell: A Literary Life, William H. Pritchard
Fall from Grace: The Failed Crusade of the Christian Right, Michael D'Antonio
The Iron Lady: A Biography of Margaret Thatcher, Hugo Young
V. and Other Poems, Tony Harrison
The Neumiller Stories, Larry Woiwode
The Hand: Or, the Confession of an Executioner, Yuz Aleshkovsky
Correspondence, 1945–1984, François Truffaut
Gilles Jacob and Claude de Givray, eds.
The Bacchae of Euripides, C. K. Williams
The People and Other Uncollected Fiction, Bernard Malamud
Robert Giroux, ed.
To the Birdhouse, Cathleen Schine
Self-Portrait of the Other: A Memoir, Heberto Padilla
Rootie Kazootie, Lawrence Naumoff
Constancia and Other Stories for Virgins, Carlos Fuentes
Absence, Peter Handke

BOOKS FOR YOUNG READERS

Valentine & Orson, Nancy Ekholm Burkert
Rosie and the Rustlers, Roy Gerrard
Oh, Brother, Arthur Yorinks
Richard Egielski, illus.
The Clock Shop, Simon Henwood
An Acceptable Time, Madeleine L'Engle
We'll Ride Elephants Through Brooklyn, Susan L. Roth
Nellie: A Cat on Her Own, Natalie Babbitt
The Companions, Lygia Bojunga-Nunes
Larry Wilkes, illus.
Finn Family Moomintroll, Tove Jansson
Carl Goes Shopping, Alexandra Day
Witch Watch, Paul Coltman
Gillian McClure, illus.
UFO Diary, Satoshi Kitamura
The Abduction, Mette Newth
The Meal a Mile Long, Frieda Hughes
Earth to Andrew O. Blechman, Jane Breskin Zalben
Noël's Christmas Secret, Grégoire Solotareff
Frog in Love, Max Velthuijs
An ABC Bestiary, Deborah Blackwell
The Witch's Hand, Peter Utton
Celine, Brock Cole
The Sandman, Rob Shepperson
Birdy and the Ghosties, Jill Paton Walsh
Alan Marks, illus.
Miko, Little Hunter of the North, Bruce Donehower
Tom Pohrt, illus.
Wendell, Eric Jon Nones
Mother Goose and the Sly Fox, Chris Conover

MARCH TO AUGUST 1990

In the Western Night: Collected Poems 1965–90, Frank Bidart
The Desire of My Eyes: The Life and Work of John Ruskin, Wolfgang Kemp
In a Father's Place, Christopher Tilghman

A Shout in the Street, Peter Jukes
Photographs by Theresa Watkins
Selected Poems 1966–1987, Seamus Heaney
Bohin Manor, Tadeusz Konwicki
Blood, Class, and Nostalgia, Christopher Hitchens
Encounters and Reflections, Arthur C. Danto
Even Now, Michelle Latiolais
Above the River: The Complete Poems, James Wright
My Life as a Dog, Reidar Jonsson
Hourglass, Danilo Kiš
The Burden of Proof, Scott Turow
An Open Adoption, Lincoln Caplan
Lantern Slides, Edna O'Brien
Majoring in the Rest of Your Life, Carol Carter
Your Breasts: A Complete Guide for the Informed Woman, Jerome F. Levy, M.D., with Diana Odell Potter
A Lot to Make Up For, John Buell
Jump Start: Japan Comes to the Heartland, David Gelsanliter
Another Present Era, Elaine Perry
Black in Selma: The Uncommon Life of J. L. Chestnut, Jr., J. L. Chestnut, Jr., and Julia Cass
Erotic Wars: What Happened to the Sexual Revolution?, Lillian B. Rubin, Ph.D.
Monica: Heroine of the Danish Resistance, Christine Sutherland
Omeros, Derek Walcott
Shuffle, Leonard Michaels
Take a Good Look, Tor Seidler

BOOKS FOR YOUNG READERS
A Piece of Luck, Simon Henwood
Antarctica, Helen Cowcher
The Mysterious World of Marcus Leadbeater, Ivan Southall
The Treasure of Cozy Cove, Tony Ross
Quest for a Maid, Frances Mary Hendry
Drawer in a Drawer, David Christiana
Author! Author!, Susan Terris
The Wonder Shoes, Eva Bernat
Fiona Moodie, illus.
Tom Loves Anna Loves Tom, Bruce Clements
Balloons and Other Poems, Deborah Chandra
Leslie W. Bowman, illus.
No More Cornflakes, Polly Horvath
Paper Doll, Elizabeth Feuer
The Shining Company, Rosemary Sutcliff
Electing J.J., James VanOosting
Borderlands, Peter Carter

SEPTEMBER 1990 TO FEBRUARY 1991

Looking for a Ship, John McPhee
Wolfwatching, Ted Hughes
In Praise of the Stepmother, Mario Vargas Llosa
The Bleeding Heart, Lionel Shriver
The World of the Ten Thousand Things: Poems 1980–1990, Charles Wright
Love and Its Place in Nature: A Philosophical Interpretation of Freudian Psychoanalysis, Jonathan Lear
My Son's Story, Nadine Gordimer
Road Show, Roger Simon
Lucy, Jamaica Kincaid
The School of Charity, Thomas Merton
Brother Patrick Hart, ed.
A Home at the End of the World, Michael Cunningham
Road Song: A Memoir, Natalie Kusz
The Polk Conspiracy: Murder and Cover-up in the Case of CBS News Correspondent George Polk, Kati Marton
Apollo in the Snow: Selected Poems 1962–1988, Aleksandr Kushner
The Smile of the Lamb, David Grossman
Continual Lessons: The Journals of Glenway Wescott, 1937–1955, Robert Phelps, ed., with Jerry Rosco
The Old Testament Made Easy, Jeanne Steig
William Steig, illus.
Resuscitation of a Hanged Man, Denis Johnson
New World Avenue and Vicinity, Tadeusz Konwicki
Germany: The Empire Within, Amity Shlaes
Rescues: The Lives of Heroes, Michael Lesy
The Smart Parents' Guide to Summer Camps, Sheldon Silver, with Jeremy Solomon

BOOKS FOR YOUNG READERS
Hilary and the Lions, Frank DeSaix
Debbi Durland DeSaix, illus.
Shrek!, William Steig
Elephant and Crocodile, Max Velthuijs
Ugh, Arthur Yorinks
Richard Egielski, illus.
Happy Blanket, Tony Ross
Tales of the Early World, Ted Hughes
David Frampton, illus.
Puss in Boots, Charles Perrault
Malcolm Arthur, trans.
Fred Marcellino, illus.
The Surprise in the Wardrobe, Val Willis
John Shelley, illus.
Rattlesnake Stew, Lynn Rowe Reed
Henrietta's First Winter, Rob Lewis
One Gorilla, Atsuko Morozumi
The Bouncing Dinosaur, Emma Chichester Clark
Carl's Christmas, Alexandra Day
The Busy Day of Jack Rabbit, Anne-Marie Dalmais
Graham Percy, illus.
The Busy Day of Mama Pizza, Anne-Marie Dalmais
Graham Percy, illus.
Toddlecreek Post Office, Uri Shulevitz
The Marvelous Journey Through the Night, Helme Heine
Catch That Cat!, Monika Beisner
It Ain't Always Easy, Kathleen Karr
Laughing Time: Collected Nonsense, revised, William Jay Smith
Fernando Krahn, illus.
Daddy Has a Pair of Striped Shorts, Mimi Otey
Across the Grain, Jean Ferris
Comet in Moominland, Tove Jansson
Mik's Mammoth, Roy Gerrard

Black Beauty, Anna Sewall
Charles Keeping, illus.
Dog Days, Colby Rodowsky
Kathleen Collins Howell, illus.

MARCH TO AUGUST 1991

Siro, David Ignatius
Madoc: A Mystery, Paul Muldoon
Music Sounded Out, Alfred Brendel
Author and Agent: Eudora Welty and Diarmuid Russell, Michael Kreyling
Scum, Isaac Bashevis Singer
The Fever, Wallace Shawn
The Death of Artemio Cruz, new trans., Carlos Fuentes
Which Side Are You On? Trying to Be for Labor When It's Flat on Its Back, Thomas Geoghegan
Mendelssohn Is on the Roof, Jiří Weil
War Fever, J. G. Ballard
The Cure at Troy: A Version of Sophocles' Philoctetes, Seamus Heaney
Games for Learning, Peggy Kaye
Perdido, Chase Twichell
Typical: Short Stories, Padgett Powell
Playing the Game, Ian Buruma
The Preservationist's Progress: Architectural Adventures in Conserving Yesterday's Houses, Hugh Howard
Last Lovers, William Wharton
This Is the Life, Joseph O'Neill
Signposts in a Strange Land, Walker Percy
Patrick Samway, S.J., ed.
The Way We Live Now, Susan Sontag
Howard Hodgkin, illus.
By With To & From: A Lincoln Kirstein Reader, Nicholas Jenkins, ed.
The Jameses: A Family Narrative, R.W.B. Lewis
Bonneville Blue, Joan Chase
Soul of the Age: The Selected Letters of Hermann Hesse, 1891–1962, Theodore Ziolkowski, ed.
Collected Poems, Frederico García Lorca
Christopher Maurer, ed.

BOOKS FOR YOUNG READERS

Old Mother Hubbard and Her Wonderful Dog, James Marshall
A Boy Wants a Dinosaur, Hiawyn Oram
Satoshi Kitamura, illus.
Frog and the Birdsong, Max Velthuijs
Don't Wake the Baby, Jonathan Franklin
Moominsummer Madness, Tove Jansson
Mr. Mistoffelees with Mungojerrie and Rumpelteazer, T. S. Eliot
Errol Le Cain, illus.
You Call That a Farm?, Sam and Beryl Epstein
The Great Eggspectations of Lila Fenwick, Kate McMullan
Diane de Groat, illus.
Mouse Around, Pat Schories
Strandia, Susan Lynn Reynolds
Lark in the Morning, Nancy Garden
The Canary Prince, Eric Jon Nones
Echoes of War, Robert Westall
Shadows, Dennis Haseley
Leslie Bowman, illus.
The Weather Sky, Bruce McMillan

SEPTEMBER 1991 TO FEBRUARY 1992

In the Eye of the Storm: The Life of General H. Norman Schwarzkopf, Roger Cohen and Claudio Gatti
From Beirut to Jerusalem, revised, Thomas L. Friedman
Jump and Other Stories, Nadine Gordimer
The Four of Us, Elizabeth Swados
Low Life, Luc Sante
Seeing Things, Seamus Heaney
Kings: An Account of Books 1 and 2 of Homer's Iliad, Christopher Logue
The Second Bridegroom, Rodney Hall
Rebuilding Russia, Aleksandr Solzhenitsyn
The Kindness of Women, J. G. Ballard
The Boys Who Stole the Funeral, Les Murray
The Campaign, Carlos Fuentes
One Day in the Life of Ivan Denisovich, new trans., Aleksandr Solzhenitsyn
The German Comedy, Peter Schneider
Tombstones: A Lawyer's Tales from the Takeover Decades, Lawrence Lederman
Father Must, Rick Rofihe
The Runaway Soul, Harold Brodkey
The Tango Player, Christoph Hein
Russia: A Portrait, Lev Poliakov
A Fountain, a House of Stone, Heberto Padilla
The Secret Alliance: The Extraordinary Story of the Rescue of the Jews Since World War II, Tad Szulc
The Fifth Corner of the Room, Israel Metter
Dear Departed, Marguerite Yourcenar
Canvas, Adam Zagajewski
Only Man Is Vile: The Tragedy of Sri Lanka, William McGowan
Strong Motion, Jonathan Franzen
Beginning with My Streets: Essays and Recollections, Czeslaw Milosz
Wise Children, Angela Carter
Under the 82nd Airborne, Deborah Eisenberg
High Cotton, Darryl Pinckney
The Rabbiter's Bounty, Les Murray
Elisabeth Bing's Guide to Moving Through Pregnancy, Elisabeth Bing
"Get Out of My Life, but First Could You Drive Me and Cheryl to the Mall?," Anthony E. Wolf, Ph.D.

BOOKS FOR YOUNG READERS

Nature by Design, Bruce Brooks
Predator!, Bruce Brooks
Silent Lotus, Jeanne M. Lee
Alpha and the Dirty Baby, Brock Cole
Carl's Afternoon in the Park, Alexandra Day
The Girl Who Danced with Dolphins, Frank DeSaix
Debbi Durland DeSaix, illus.
The House on the Hill, Christin Couture
Camilla's New Hairdo, Tricia Tusa

The Shiniest Rock of All, Nancy Ruth Patterson
Karen A. Jerome, illus.
The Money Tree, Sarah Stewart
David Small, illus.
The Troubled Village, Simon Henwood
The Howling Dog, Tracey Campbell Pearson
Uncle Harold and the Green Hat, Judy Hindley
Peter Utton, illus.
Mollywoop, Helme Heine
Tigress, Helen Cowcher
Hildegard Sings, Thomas Wharton
A Pocket Full of Posies, Roy Gerrard
The Mystery in the Bottle, Val Willis
John Shelley, illus.
The Clay Marble, Minfong Ho
The Gold of Dreams, José María Merino
Family Dinner, Jane Cutler
Philip Caswell, illus.
Gypsy Bird Song, Susan L. Roth
The Kingdom by the Sea, Robert Westall

MARCH TO AUGUST 1992

Way Past Cool, Jess Mowry
At Weddings and Wakes, Alice McDermott
The Man with Night Sweats, Thom Gunn
Primitive People, Francine Prose
The Last Shot, Hugo Hamilton
Marine Life, Linda Svendsen
The Wreck of the Barque Stefano *off the North West Cape of Australia in 1875*, Gustave Rathe
Rings: On the Life and Family of a Southern Boxer, Randolph Bates
The Springs of Contemplation: A Retreat at the Abbey of Gethsemani, Thomas Merton
Jane Marie Richardson, ed.
Cooler by the Lake, Larry Heinemann
That Mighty Sculptor, Time, Marguerite Yourcenar
Three Evenings, James Lasdun
Time and Tide, Edna O'Brien
Watermark, Joseph Brodsky
Money of the Mind, James Grant
A Dream of Mind, C. K. Williams
Antiquity Street, Sonia Rami
A Captive of the Caucasus, Andrei Bitov
Gilgamesh, David Ferry, trans.
Le Petit Garçon, Philippe Labro
The Journey, Ida Fink
An Afghanistan Picture Show: Or, How I Saved the World, William T. Vollmann
The Night of Wishes, Michael Ende
Regina Kehr, illus.
Easy Keeper, Mary Tannen
The Volcano Lover: A Romance, Susan Sontag
Beyond the Brillo Box, Arthur C. Danto
Virgin Time, Patricia Hampl
Grand Illusion: Critics and Champions of the American Century, John Judis

BOOKS FOR YOUNG READERS

Go Hang a Salami! I'm a Lasagna Hog! and Other Palindromes, Jon Agee
Losing Things at Mr. Mudd's, Carolyn Coman
Lance Hidy, illus.
White Nineteens, David Christiana
Grace, Jill Paton Walsh
Crocodile's Masterpiece, Max Velthuijs
Grandpa Putter and Granny Hoe, Kimberly Olson Fakih
Tracey Campbell Pearson, illus.
Lucy Peale, Colby Rodowsky
Beaver Ball at the Bug Club, Mike Craver
Joan Kaghan, illus.
Oh, Those Harper Girls!, Kathleen Karr
Angelita's Magic Yarn, Doris Lecher
Weeping Willow, Ruth White
From Acorn to Zoo and Everything in Between in Alphabetical Order, Satoshi Kitamura
Is Kissing a Girl Who Smokes Like Licking an Ashtray?, Randy Powell
Under the Mummy's Spell, Kate McMullan

SEPTEMBER 1992 TO FEBRUARY 1993

Before and After, Rosellen Brown
Shakespeare and the Goddess of Complete Being, Ted Hughes
Forgotten Fatherland: The Search for Elisabeth Nietzsche, Ben Macintyre
Dame Edna Everage and the Rise of Western Civilisation, John Lahr
The Death of Napoleon, Simon Leys
The Murder of Albert Einstein, Todd Gitlin
Sweeney's Flight, Seamus Heaney
Photographs by Rachel Giese
Upland Passage: A Field Dog's Education, Robert F. Jones
Photographs by Bill Eppridge
Certain Women, Madeleine L'Engle
In My Place, Charlayne Hunter-Gault
The Fourteen Sisters of Emilio Montez O'Brien, Oscar Hijuclos
Truck Stop Rainbows, Iva Pekárková
Evidence, Luc Sante
The Certificate, Isaac Bashevis Singer
A Separate Cinema: Fifty Years of Black-Cast Posters, John Kisch and Edward Mapp
Outlaw Cook, John Thorne, with Matt Lewis Thorne
A Gilded Lapse of Time, Gjertrud Schnackenberg
Ulverton, Adam Thorpe
Sleeping on a Wire: Conversations with Palestinians in Israel, David Grossman
Jesus' Son, Denis Johnson
The Sixties: The Last Journal, 1960–1972, Edmund Wilson
Lewis M. Dabney, ed.
Assembling California, John McPhee
Dog Fox Field, Les Murray
What Remains and Other Stories, Christa Wolf
The Author's Dimension: Selected Essays, Christa Wolf
Alexander Stephan, ed.
Martin and John, Dale Peck
Getting What You Came For: The Smart Student's

Guide to Earning a Master's or a Ph.D., Robert L. Peters, Ph.D.
Graduating into the Nineties, Carol Carter and Gary June

BOOKS FOR YOUNG READERS

The Return of Freddy LeGrand, Jon Agee
Rainy Day Dream, Michael Chesworth
Carmine the Crow, Heidi Holder
Sam Panda and Thunder Dragon, Chris Conover
Stormsearch, Robert Westall
Ishi's Tale of Lizard, Leanne Hinton, trans.
Susan L. Roth, illus.
Carl's Masquerade, Alexandra Day
A Walk in the Woods, Christin Couture
Ghost Song, Susan Price
Tinker Jim, Paul Coltman
Gillian McClure, illus.
The Hidden Jungle, Simon Henwood
The Butterfly Night of Old Brown Bear, Nicholas van Pallandt
Jocasta Carr, Movie Star, Roy Gerrard
For the Life of Laetitia, Merle Hodge
The Sea and I, Harutaka Nakawatari
An Illustrated History of the World, Gillian Clements
Dr. Gravity, Dennis Haseley
Rich Lizard and Other Poems, Deborah Chandra
Leslie Bowman, illus.
Moominland Midwinter, Tove Jansson
Jake: A Labrador Puppy at Work and Play, Robert F. Jones
Photographs by Bill Eppridge
Dragon Sword and Wind Child, Noriko Ogiwara
No Dogs Allowed, Jane Cutler
Tracey Campbell Pearson, illus.

MARCH TO AUGUST 1993

The Antilles: Fragments of Epic Memory (The Nobel Lecture), Derek Walcott
Pleading Guilty, Scott Turow
The Man Who Wasn't Maigret: A Portrait of Georges Simenon, Patrick Marnham
Picasso and Dora: A Personal Memoir, James Lord
The Virgin Suicides, Jeffrey Eugenides
A Dancer to God: Tributes to T. S. Eliot, Ted Hughes
A Philosophical Investigation, Philip Kerr
Remembering Denny, Calvin Trillin
The Odyssey: A Stage Version, Derek Walcott
The Supreme Court Confronts Abortion, Leon Friedman, ed.
Vindication, Frances Sherwood
The Courage for Truth: Letters to Writers, Thomas Merton
Christine M. Bochen, ed.
Kipper's Game, Barbara Ehrenreich
My Tokyo, Frederick Seidel
Safe Conduct, Elizabeth Benedict
The Last Empire: De Beers, Diamonds, and the World, Stefan Kanfer
Compulsory Happiness, Norman Manea
Lenin's Brain, Tilman Spengler
Ottoline Morrell: Life on the Grand Scale, Miranda Seymour
Alice in Bed, Susan Sontag
The Evening Star: Venus Observed, Henry S.F. Cooper, Jr.
Collected Poems, James Schuyler
Before Our Eyes, Lawrence Joseph
Tsvetaeva, Viktoria Schweitzer
A Very Long Engagement, Sébastien Japrisot
Sade: A Biography, Maurice Lever
School Savvy, Diane Harrington and Laurette Young

BOOKS FOR YOUNG READERS

Matthew and the Sea Singer, Jill Paton Walsh
Alan Marks, illus.
Moonfall, Susan Whitcher
Barbara Lehman, illus.
Back to Bataan, Jerome Charyn
The Princess in the Kitchen Garden, Annemie and Margriet Heymans
The Stones of Muncaster Cathedral, Robert Westall
Gideon and the Mummy Professor, Kathleen Karr
The Boy and the Giants, Fiona Moodie
Caleb's Friend, Eric Jon Nones
Deep Dream of the Rain Forest, Malcolm Bosse
Blue Moon Soup Spoon, Mimi Otey
In the Back Seat, Deborah Durland DeSaix
Super-Duper Jokes, Frederica Young
Chris Murphy, illus.
The Dream of the Stone, Christina Askounis
Claire and the Friendly Snakes, Lindsey Tate
Jonathan Franklin, illus.
The Apprentice, Pilar Molina Llorente
Juan Ramón Alonso, illus.
Relative Strangers, Jean Ferris
The Chronicles of Little Nicholas, Sempé and Goscinny

SEPTEMBER 1993 TO FEBRUARY 1994

Smilla's Sense of Snow, Peter Høeg
Tracings: A Book of Partial Portraits, Paul Horgan
Man Kills Woman, D. L. Flusfeder
Sappho: A Garland—The Poems and Fragments of Sappho, Jim Powell, trans.
The Peaceable Kingdom, Francine Prose
Elizabeth Gaskell: A Habit of Stories, Jenny Uglow
The Grisly Wife, Rodney Hall
Echoes of Eden: Being a Commonplace Book about Animals, Lovers, Eating, Eccentrics, Artists, and Me, Jean-Isabel McNutt
Value Judgments, Ellen Goodman
A Village in the Vineyards, Thomas Matthews
Photographs by Sara Matthews
Six Out Seven, Jess Mowry
The Table Beckons: Thoughts and Recipes from the Kitchen of Alain Senderens, Alain Senderens
Izhar Cohen, illus.
Mark Morris, Joan Acocella
Damascus Nights, Rafik Schami
Sex with Strangers, Geoffrey Rees
Why Should You Doubt Me Now?, Mary Breasted

Minding Mr. Market, James Grant
Splendours and Miseries: A Life of Sir Sacheverell Sitwell, Sarah Bradford
Selected Letters of Philip Larkin 1940–1985, Anthony Thwaite, ed.
Philip Larkin: A Writer's Life, Andrew Motion
The Silence of the Body, Guido Ceronetti
Skadden: Power, Money, and the Rise of a Legal Empire, Lincoln Caplan
I Am Snowing: The Confessions of a Woman of Prague, Pavel Kohout
Make Me Work, Ralph Lombreglia
Going Native, Stephen Wright
In Touch: The Letters of Paul Bowles, Jeffrey Miller, ed.
Anonymity, Susan Bergman
Kay Boyle: Author of Herself, Joan Mellen
The Final Station: Umschlagplatz, Jaroslaw M. Rymkiewicz
Profane Friendship, Harold Brodkey
Translations from the Natural World, Les Murray
Under the Bone, Anne-christine d'Adesky
The Akhmatova Journals: Volume I, 1938–1941, Lydia Chukovskaya
And the Stars Were Shining, John Ashbery
The Multicultural Student's Guide to Colleges, Robert Mitchell

BOOKS FOR YOUNG READERS

The Secret Room, Uri Shulevitz
The Billy Goat Show, Joan Kaghan
He's Your Dog!, Pat Schories
The Butterfly Boy, Laurence Yep
Jeanne M. Lee, illus.
Subway Sparrow, Leyla Torres
The Family Reunion, Tricia Tusa
Carl Goes to Daycare, Alexandra Day
The Christmas Donkey, Gillian McClure
A Creepy Crawly Song Book, Lyrics by Hiawyn Oram
Music by Carl Davis
Satoshi Kitamura, illus.
Peboan and Seegwun, Charles Larry
MicroAliens: Dazzling Journeys with an Electron Microscope, Howard Tomb and Dennis Kunkel
Tracy Dockray, illus.
Moominpappa at Sea, Tove Jansson
Making Sense, Bruce Brooks
Grams, Her Boyfriend, My Family, and Me, Pat Derby
Demons and Shadows, Robert Westall
Real Mummies Don't Bleed, Susan Whitcher
Andrew Glass, illus.
Tell Me Everything, Carolyn Coman

MARCH TO AUGUST 1994

One Art: Letters, Elizabeth Bishop
Robert Giroux, ed.
Ancient Land, Sacred Whale: The Inuit Hunt and Its Rituals, Tom Lowenstein
The Orange Tree, Carlos Fuentes
Deadline Poet: Or, My Life as a Doggerelist, Calvin Trillin
Collected Poems, Thom Gunn
The Collected Stories, Grace Paley
Six Exceptional Women: Further Memoirs, James Lord
Meshugah, Isaac Bashevis Singer
Roald Dahl, Jeremy Treglown
Blood and Belonging: Journeys into the New Nationalism, Michael Ignatieff
The Magus of the North: J. G. Hamann and the Origins of Modern Irrationalism, Isaiah Berlin
The Wages of Guilt: Memories of War in Germany and Japan, Ian Buruma
Mosaic: Memoirs, Lincoln Kirstein
A Fish in the Water: A Memoir, Mario Vargas Llosa
Embodied Meanings, Arthur C. Danto
The Weekend, Peter Cameron
The Agony of Flies: Notes and Notations, Elias Canetti
White Man's Grave, Richard Dooling
House of Splendid Isolation, Edna O'Brien
Rattlebone, Maxine Clair
Out of Danger, James Fenton
The Marks of Birth, Pablo Medina
The Bird Artist, Howard Norman
The Jukebox and Other Essays on Storytelling, Peter Handke
The Father: A Life of Henry James, Sr., Alfred Habegger
The World Is Round, Iva Pekárková
The Black Book, Orhan Pamuk
The Book of Intimate Grammar, David Grossman
Mallarmé: A Throw of the Dice, Gordon Millan
The State within a State: The KGB and Its Hold on Russia—Past, Present, and Future, Yevgenia Albats
A Year of the Hunter, Czeslaw Milosz
Face of an Angel, Denise Chávez
The Inferno of Dante: A New Verse Translation, Robert Pinsky
Michael Mazur, illus.

BOOKS FOR YOUNG READERS

A Tooth Fairy's Tale, David Christiana
Wildflowers, Anne Velghe
Archibald Frisby, Michael Chesworth
The Thief's Daughter, Alan Marks
Heads or Tails: Stories from the Sixth Grade, Jack Gantos
High on the Hog, Kimberly Olson Fakih
Shades of Darkness, Robert Westall
The Road to Wembley, Kim Chapin
Come Go with Me: Old-timer Stories from the Southern Mountains, Roy Edwin Thomas, ed.
Laszlo Kubinyi, illus.
The Way Home, Leigh Sauerwein
Miles Hyman, illus.
Hannah In Between, Colby Rodowsky
Beyond the Ancient Cities, José María Merino

Leona: A Love Story, Elizabeth Borton de Treviño
The Hunted, Peter Carter

SEPTEMBER 1994 TO FEBRUARY 1995

None to Accompany Me, Nadine Gordimer
Mrs. Thatcher's Minister: The Private Diaries of Alan Clark, Alan Clark
Scar Tissue, Michael Ignatieff
Sophie's World, Jostein Gaarder
Raising Children Toxic Free, Herbert L. Needleman, M.D., and Philip J. Landrigan, M.D.
Ghosts of Manila, James Hamilton-Paterson
Goldberg's Angel, Dan Hofstadter
Witness to Freedom: The Letters of Thomas Merton in Times of Crisis, William H. Shannon, ed.
Aristocrats: Caroline, Emily, Louisa, and Sarah Lennox, 1740–1832, Stella Tillyard
Family, Ian Frazier
The Annals of Chile, Paul Muldoon
Cora Fry's Pillow Book, Rosellen Brown
The Ransom of Russian Art, John McPhee
Selected Poems, C. K. Williams
A Nation Under Lawyers, Mary Ann Glendon
The Coming Plague, Laurie Garrett
Oedipus at Stalingrad, Gregor von Rezzori
Borderliners, Peter Høeg
Mea Cuba, Guillermo Cabrera Infante
To the Center of the Earth, Michael Fried
Making Modernism: Picasso and the Creation of the Market for Twentieth-Century Art, Michael C. FitzGerald
Beyond Psychology: Letters and Journals 1934–1939, Wilhelm Reich
Mary Boyd Higgins, ed.
Cock-a-doodle-do, Philip Weiss
Terrible Honesty: Mongrel Manhattan in the 1920s, Ann Douglas
Out of Egypt, André Aciman
Konfidenz, Ariel Dorfman
The Monkey Link, Andrei Bitov
The City of Florence, R.W.B. Lewis
After Ovid: New Metamorphoses, Michael Hoffman and James Lasdun, eds.
The End of the Story, Lydia Davis
Two Cities: On Exile, History, and the Imagination, Adam Zagajewski
Revolution of the Mind: The Life of André Breton, Mark Polizzotti
The Tummy Trilogy, Calvin Trillin
My Five Cambridge Friends, Yuri Modin
The Quotable Paul Johnson, Paul Johnson
George J. Marlin, Richard P. Rabatin, and Heather Richardson Higgins, eds.

BOOKS FOR YOUNG READERS

Hey Diddle Diddle, James Marshall
Sleep Well, Little Bear, Quint Buchholz
George Washington's Cows, David Small
Croco'nile, Roy Gerrard
Carl Makes a Scrapbook, Alexandra Day
My Puppy's Record Book, Alexandra Day
The Princess and the Painter, Jane Johnson
Catcher, Mia Wolff
Troll's Search for Summer, Nicolas van Pallandt
So Many Dynamos! and Other Palindromes, Jon Agee
All the Small Poems and Fourteen More, Valerie Worth
Natalie Babbitt, illus.
Bibles and Bestiaries, Elizabeth B. Wilson
Troubling a Star, Madeleine L'Engle
The Ch'i-lin Purse, Linda Fang
Jeanne M. Lee, illus.
Christmas Spirit, Robert Westall
John Lawrence, illus.
Moominpappa's Memoirs, Tove Jansson
The Happy Yellow Car, Polly Horvath
My Wartime Summers, Jane Cutler
The Cave, Kathleen Karr
Ghost Dance, Susan Price
Getting Him, Dennis Haseley
The Examination, Malcolm Bosse
The Frozen Waterfall, Gaye Hiçyılmaz
92 Queens Road, Dianne Case

MARCH TO AUGUST 1995

Flesh and Blood, Michael Cunningham
Red Sauce, Whiskey and Snow, August Kleinzahler
Drinking the Rain, Alix Kates Shulman
The Snarling Citizen, Barbara Ehrenreich
Lytton Strachey: The New Biography, Michael Holroyd
"It's Not Fair, Jeremy Spencer's Parents Let Him Stay Up All Night!": A Guide to the Tougher Parts of Parenting, Anthony E. Wolf, Ph.D.
Chickamauga, Charles Wright
In Good Hands, Charles Fish
Jackie Under My Skin, Wayne Koestenbaum
The Black Diaspora, Ronald Segal
Woodholme: A Black Man's Story of Growing Up Alone, DeWayne Wickham
Hunters and Gatherers, Francine Prose
Zola: A Life, Frederick Brown
Giant Bluefin, Douglas Whynott
Too Soon to Tell, Calvin Trillin
Looking through Glass, Mukul Kesavan
Galatea 2.2, Richard Powers
Breaking Free, Susan Eisenhower
The Black Envelope, Norman Manea
"The Russian Question" at the End of the Twentieth Century, Aleksandr Solzhenitsyn
The Golden Plough, James Buchan
How Many Years, Marguerite Yourcenar
A Little Too Much Is Enough, Kathleen Tyau
The Poet Dying: Heinrich Heine's Last Years in Paris, Ernst Pawel
The Chess Garden, or The Twilight Letters of Gustav Uyterhoeven, Brooks Hansen
Green, Frances Sherwood
Edwin Hubble: Mariner of the Nebulae, Gale E. Christianson
The French Secret Service, Douglas Porch

Homo Poeticus: Essays and Interviews, Danilo Kiš
Susan Sontag, ed.
Games for Writing, Peggy Kaye
The Illustrated Who's Who of Hollywood Directors, Vol. I: The Sound Era, Michael Barson
The Yandilli Trilogy, Rodney Hall
Majoring in High School, Carol Carter

BOOKS FOR YOUNG READERS

Dear Elijah, Miriam Bat-Ami
The Painter Who Loved Chickens, Olivier Dunrea
Paper Dinosaurs, Satoshi Kitamura
Signs of Life, Jean Ferris
Lost Summer, Elizabeth Feuer
Dean Duffy, Randy Powell
Sidney, Invincible, Colby Rodowsky
The Library, Sarah Stewart
David Small, illus.
Saturday Sancocho, Leyla Torres
The King's Shadow, Elizabeth Alder
Working River, Fred Powledge
Brainstorm! The Stories of Twenty American Kid Inventors, Tom Tucker
Richard Loehle, illus.
Falling into Glory, Robert Westall

SEPTEMBER 1995 TO FEBRUARY 1996

The Autobiography of My Mother, Jamaica Kincaid
Panama, Eric Zencey
Griefwork, James Hamilton-Paterson
The Poetical Cat: An Anthology, Felicity Bast, ed.
Robert Clyde Anderson, illus.
The Husbands: An Account of Books 3 and 4 of Homer's Iliad, Christopher Logue
From the Beast to the Blonde: On Fairy Tales and Their Tellers, Marina Warner
Laments, Jan Kochanowski
The Double Tongue, William Golding
Prairie Reunion, Barbara J. Scot
The Redress of Poetry, Seamus Heaney
Signals of Distress, Jim Crace
The House on the Lagoon, Rosario Ferré
Diana: The Goddess Who Hunts Alone, Carlos Fuentes
The Death of Satan: How Americans Have Lost the Sense of Evil, Andrew Delbanco
The History of Danish Dreams, Peter Høeg
Luck: The Brilliant Randomness of Everyday Life, Nicholas Rescher
Battlefields and Playgrounds, János Nyiri
Can You Hear, Bird, John Ashbery
Not Entitled, Frank Kermode
Wild Meat and the Bully Burgers, Lois-Ann Yamanaka
The Law of Enclosures, Dale Peck
No Downlink: A Dramatic Narrative about the Challenger *Accident and Our Time*, Claus Jensen
Sweet Mystery, Judith Hillman Paterson
Anecdotage, Gregor von Rezzori
The Love Affair as a Work of Art, Dan Hofstadter
Death in the Andes, Mario Vargas Llosa
Fighting Terrorism, Benjamin Netanyahu

On Grief and Reason: Essays, Joseph Brodsky
The Second John McPhee Reader, John McPhee
Majoring in Law, Stefan Underhill
Majoring in Engineering, John Garcia

BOOKS FOR YOUNG READERS

Jack's New Power: Stories from a Caribbean Year, Jack Gantos
Junebug, Alice Mead
Dinah Forever, Claudia Mills
Angela's Wings, Eric Jon Nones
The Night Is Like an Animal, Candace Whitman
Carl's Birthday, Alexandra Day
Returning Nicholas, Deborah Durland DeSaix
Marrying Malcolm Murgatroyd, Mame Farrell
Dove and Sword, Nancy Garden
In the Kaiser's Clutch, Kathleen Karr
Television: What's Behind What You See, W. Carter Merbreier, with Linda Capus Riley
Michael Chesworth, illus.
Coyote Goes Walking, Tom Pohrt
The Golden Goose, Uri Shulevitz
Something for Everyone, Susan Whitcher
Barbara Lehman, illus.
Tales from Moominvalley, Tove Jansson
Outcast, Rosemary Sutcliff

MARCH TO AUGUST 1996

A Single Shot, Matthew F. Jones
Piano Pieces, Russell Sherman
The Figured Wheel: New and Collected Poems 1966–1996, Robert Pinsky
Elizabeth: A Biography of Britain's Queen, Sarah Bradford
Legacies, Starling Lawrence
A New Time for Mexico, Carlos Fuentes
Dance Real Slow, Michael Grant Jaffe
Omon Ra, Victor Pelevin
A Live Coal in the Sea, Madeleine L'Engle
Catherwood, Marly Youmans
Smokestack Lightning, Lolis Eric Elie
Photographs by Frank Stewart
Independent Spirit, Hubert Butler
Lush Life: A Biography of Billy Strayhorn, David Hajdu
Coyote v. Acme, Ian Frazier
The Frequency of Souls, Mary Kay Zuravleff
Messages from My Father, Calvin Trillin
The Book of Mercy, Kathleen Cambor
Baker's Dozen, Michael M. Thomas
The Spirit Level, Seamus Heaney
Crediting Poetry (The Nobel Lecture), Seamus Heaney
Tie My Bones to Her Back, Robert F. Jones
Becoming Modern: The Life of Mina Loy, Carolyn Burke
The Lost Lunar Baedeker: Poems of Mina Loy, Roger L. Conover, ed.
Life of a Poet: Rainer Maria Rilke, Ralph Freedman
Moral Grandeur and Spiritual Audacity: Essays, Abraham Joshua Heschel
Susannah Heschel, ed.
Tinisima, Elena Poniatowska
Psalm at Journey's End, Erik Fosnes Hansen

My Favorite War, Christopher John Farley
The Solitaire Mystery, Jostein Gaarder
The Slam and Scream, Carole S. Fungaroli
Adopt International, O. Robin Sweet and Patty Bryan
Taking Time Off, Colin Hall and Ron Lieber

BOOKS FOR YOUNG READERS

The China Garden, Liz Berry
This Is Me, Laughing, Lynea Bowdish
Walter Gaffney-Kessell, illus.
Casey in the Bath, Cynthia DeFelice
Chris L. Demarest, illus.
All That Glitters, Jean Ferris
William Tell, Leonard Everett Fisher
Wagons West!, Roy Gerrard
Sheep in Wolves' Clothing, Satoshi Kitamura
This and That, Julie Sykes
Tanya Linch, illus.
Belle Prater's Boy, Ruth White
Rats!, Jane Cutler
Tracey Campbell Pearson, illus.
Carl's Baby Journal, Alexandra Day
First, Second, Daniil Kharms
Marc Rosenthal, illus.
Remembering Mog, Colby Rodowsky
Over Under In the Garden, Pat Schories
The Topsy-Turvy Emperor of China, Isaac Bashevis Singer
Julian Jusim, illus.

SEPTEMBER 1996 TO FEBRUARY 1997

The Laws of Our Fathers, Scott Turow
So Forth, Joseph Brodsky
Some Remarkable Men, James Lord
Homage to Robert Frost, Joseph Brodsky, Seamus Heaney, and Derek Walcott
Couplings, Peter Schneider
Swimming the Channel, Sally Friedman
Augustus John, revised, Michael Holroyd
High Latitudes, James Buchan
Jewish Days: A Book of Jewish Life and Culture Around the Year, Francine Klagsbrun
Mark Podwal, illus.
The Family Markowitz, Allegra Goodman
Starry Messenger: Galileo Galilei, Peter Sís
In a Pig's Ear, Paul Bryers
Wonder Tales: Six French Stories of Enchantment, Marina Warner, ed.
The Christmas Mystery, Jostein Gaarder
Exchanging Hats: Paintings, Elizabeth Bishop
William Benton, ed.
The Bounty, Derek Walcott
The Book and the Sword, David Weiss Halivni
The Women, Hilton Als
The Woman and the Ape, Peter Høeg
The Fate of a Gesture: Jackson Pollock and Postwar American Art, Carter Ratcliff
Mrs. Ike, Susan Eisenhower
Rubber Bullets: Power and Conscience in Modern Israel, Yaron Ezrahi
The Vigil, C. K. Williams
Striving Towards Being: The Letters of Thomas Merton and Czeslaw Milosz, Robert Faggen, ed.
The Designated Mourner, Wallace Shawn
The Enchantress: Marthe Bibesco and Her World, Christine Sutherland
Andorra, Peter Cameron
Never Eat Your Heart Out, Judith Moore
Blue Mondays, Arnon Grunberg
Utopia Parkway: The Life and Work of Joseph Cornell, Deborah Solomon
Zero Tolerance, Thomas Richards
The New Life, Orhan Pamuk
Lives of the Monster Dogs, Kirsten Bakis
Walker Percy: A Life, Patrick Samway, S.J.
Becoming Mae West, Emily Wortis Leider
The Stories (So Far) of Deborah Eisenberg, Deborah Eisenberg

BOOKS FOR YOUNG READERS

Cat and Mouse, Tomek Bogacki
Cat Is Sleepy, Satoshi Kitamura
Dog Is Thirsty, Satoshi Kitamura
Duck Is Dirty, Satoshi Kitamura
Squirrel Is Hungry, Satoshi Kitamura
Mr. Chips, Laura Kvasnosky
The Apprenticeship of Lucas Whitaker, Cynthia DeFelice
The Tale of Hilda Louise, Olivier Dunrea
The Whistling Toilets, Randy Powell
Fenwick's Suit, David Small
Dangerous Skies, Suzanne Fisher Staples
Gift of the Sun, Dianne Stewart
Jude Daly, illus.
Brother Wolf, Harriet Peck Taylor
The War Between the Vowels and the Consonants, Priscilla Turner
Whitney Turner, illus.
Spider Spider, Kate Banks
Georg Hallensleben, illus.
Good Moon Rising, Nancy Garden
When the Circus Came to Town, Polly Horvath
Yoshiko and the Foreigner, Mimi Otey Little
Adem's Cross, Alice Mead
The Ugly Menorah, Marissa Moss
Becoming Felix, Nancy Hope Wilson
The Friends, Kazumi Yumoto

ACKNOWLEDGMENTS

With grateful acknowledgment to:

Roger Straus and Robert Giroux, Founders of the Feast over fifty and forty years ago respectively, and gracious instigators of the volume at hand.

Ethan Nosowsky, assistant editor, who for the final six months of compilation has been sword, shield, and buckler to deponent.

The editorial staff for their devoted guidance and resonance: Robert Giroux, Jonathan Galassi, Elisabeth Sifton, John Glusman, Margaret Ferguson, Elisabeth Dyssegaard, Paul Elie, Aoibheann Sweeney, Becky Gallagher, Robbie Mayes, and intrepid managing editor Elisheva Urbas.

Cynthia Krupat, whose magic powers of design have made this mosaic of a book an organic whole; Tom Consiglio and Harvey Hoffman in the production department, who, from cast-offs on, have brought the book into being; copy editors Lynn Warshow, Elaine Chubb, and Karla Reganold; Erika Seidman, ever-resourceful contracts director; and Karla Eoff for her assiduous help on the chronology.

A succession of interns provided cheerful, tireless, and invaluable assistance: Ashley Anderson, Manuela Fremy, Alexandra Marolachakis, and Carey Goldstein. Special mention and thanks go to Gunnar Cynybulk, student from Germany, whose profound knowledge of modern literature and unfailing good spirits made the last three chaotic months of assemblage not only survivable but pleasurable.

Finally, along with gratitude to everyone whose gracious path I crossed, special thanks to those whose aid made me feel so at home at Farrar, Straus and Giroux: Peggy Miller, assistant to Roger Straus; Ellen Faran, chief financial officer; Joy Isenberg, director of operations; Stephen Brown, office manager; Jeff Seroy, publicity director; Sam Owens and Terrence Smith in the mailroom; and Toleda Bennett, unfailingly warm Greeter at the Gate.—A.D.W.